BY RICHARD COHEN

How to Write Like Tolstoy:
A Journey into the Minds of Our Greatest Writers

Chasing the Sun:
The Epic Story of the Star That Gives Us Life

By the Sword:
A History of Gladiators, Musketeers, Samurai,
Swashbucklers, and Olympic Champions

MAKING HISTORY

THE STORYTELLERS
WHO SHAPED THE PAST

RICHARD COHEN

Simon & Schuster

NEW YORK LONDON TORONTO
SYDNEY NEW DELHI

Simon & Schuster
1230 Avenue of the Americas
New York, NY 10020

First Simon & Schuster hardcover edition March 2022

SIMON & SCHUSTER and colophon are registered
trademarks of Simon & Schuster, Inc.

For information about special discounts for bulk purchases,
please contact Simon & Schuster Special Sales at 1-866-506-1949
or business@simonandschuster.com.

The Simon & Schuster Speakers Bureau can bring authors to your live event. For
more information or to book an event, contact the Simon & Schuster Speakers
Bureau at 1-866-248-3049 or visit our website at www.simonspeakers.com.

Manufactured in the United States of America

1 3 5 7 9 10 8 6 4 2

Library of Congress Cataloging-in-Publication Data is available.

ISBN 978-1-9821-9578-6
ISBN 978-1-9821-9580-9 (ebook)

For Kathy

And in memory of Dom Aelred Watkin, O.S.B.,
who inspired my love of history and
who wrote of one of my essays,
"What is this farrago of nonsense?"

Before you study the history, study the historian.

E. H. CARR, *What Is History?* (1961)

Beneath every history, there is another history—
there is, at least, the life of the historian.

HILARY MANTEL, THE REITH LECTURES (2017)

CONTENTS

———

LIST OF ILLUSTRATIONS
AND PHOTOGRAPHIC CREDITS

COLOR ILLUSTRATIONS
Between pages 202 and 203

ILLUSTRATIONS IN THE TEXT

CARTOONS IN THE NOTES

MAKING HISTORY

PREFACE

———

A man sets out to draw the world. As the years go by,
he peoples a space with images of provinces, kingdoms,
mountains, bays, ships, islands, fishes, rooms, instruments,
stars, horses, and individuals. A short time before he dies,
he discovers that the patient labyrinth of
lines traces the lineaments of his own face.

—JORGE LUIS BORGES, 1960

FIRST, SOME PERSONAL HISTORY. IN SEPTEMBER 1960 I ENROLLED AT
Downside School, set in the heart of the English countryside, about
half an hour's journey from the ancient city of Bath. This all-boys
Roman Catholic academy was under the direct control of Downside
Abbey, an offshoot of a Benedictine community founded in the
Habsburg Netherlands four centuries before and driven to England by
the French Revolution.

I was put into a group of twelve boys, aged thirteen (as I was) to
fifteen, to study medieval history. Our special subject was Henry VIII's
dissolution of the monasteries and its leading authority was one David
Knowles, then professor of medieval history at Cambridge. His view
of the worldly monks was forthright: "They had it coming." It was
only toward the end of my time at Downside that I learned that
Knowles himself had once been a monk there and had left some twenty
years earlier under something of a cloud. It passed into my unformed
mind that his judgments must surely have been colored by his time in
orders.

After my schooldays, I began to wonder about other writers who
have framed the way we conceive the past. How did their lives shape
what they wrote? I read John Lukacs, who noted that "history" has a

double meaning, as "history" is the past but also a *description* of that past, so every author of a work of history is an interpreter, a filter, with his or her own personal input.

The list of books, even in English, about the nature of history and those who practice it is a long one, with plenty of room for going one's own way. Closest to what I am trying to do is *A History of Histories* (2009) by the late John Burrow, who, true to his name, closeted himself away in his Oxford study with thirty-seven chosen texts to produce his own magisterial tome. As he notes, "Almost all historians except the very dullest have some characteristic weakness: some complicity, idealization, identification; some impulse to indignation, to right wrongs, to deliver a message. It is often the source of their most interesting writing." He goes on to examine how the depiction of past events has changed over the years under different political, religious, cultural, and patriotic forces. But he concentrates on ancient and medieval history and is mainly interested in historiography—the study of historical writing—and less so in the historians themselves. This is where our perspectives diverge.

Edward Gibbon, whose account of the fall of the Roman Empire is one of the best known of all historical works, also wrote six substantially differing volumes of autobiography and was well aware how accounts of the past are necessarily the children of the shaping intellect. In an unpublished manuscript, the "Mémoire sur la monarchie des Mèdes," he reflected:

> Every man of genius who writes history infuses into it, perhaps unconsciously, the character of his own spirit. His characters, despite their extensive variety of passion and situation, seem to have only one manner of thinking and feeling, and that is the manner of the author.

Men of genius, the people who write history, the manner of the author— these phrases need unpacking. The present book attempts to do so, taking in the rivalries of scholars, the demands of patronage, the need to make a living, physical disabilities, changing fashions, cultural pressures, religious beliefs, patriotic sensibilities, love affairs, the longing for fame. It seeks also to narrate the changing ideas of what a historian is, while explaining why the great practitioners came to set down their versions as they did. Martin Heidegger is said to have begun a seminar by saying, "Aristotle was born, he worked, and he died. Now let's move on to his thought." For me, such a division makes little sense.

I have selected writers whose work has weathered the test of time—Herodotus and Thucydides, Livy and Tacitus, on through Froissart, Gibbon, the great nineteenth-century historians, and up to the present day. But I have also included Winston Churchill, never a great historian but crucially a *participant* recorder, both highly persuasive and widely read, and historians such as Simon Schama and Mary Beard, whose fame and influence grew to a different order once they appeared on television.

It may be presumptuous to use my chosen title, as "History" might more accurately appear in parenthesis, since it has—well, a complicated past. My criteria are more based on that issue of "influence" than a reflection of some agreed-upon pantheon, for it is remarkable how many people who have profoundly given us our history would not have called themselves historians. As the Black academician W. J. Moses wrote nearly a quarter of a century ago, "Historical consciousness is neither the independent creation nor the exclusive possession of professional scholars." I have included the composers of the Bible, several novelists, one dramatist—William Shakespeare, judging him to have formed more people's ideas of the past than any writer of history *or* of literature—and a diarist, Samuel Pepys. Some may argue that Pepys's private musings are primary sources rather than works of history, but they are both, showing preeminently what middle-class life in England was like during the second half of the seventeenth century. Diaries are also a form of secret history, consciously kept out of sight, whispers that challenge the public assertions of the powerful. In the Second World War, the best diarists were women—in Italy, Iris Origo; in Holland, Anne Frank; in Germany, Ursula von Kardorff—while in certain countries (Australia, for instance) keeping a diary could be a court-martial offense. In 1941, at the start of the siege of Leningrad, diary writing was encouraged as a form of witness; later on, such records were censored, as they might undermine the collective narrative of daily heroism.

It is obviously impossible to give an account of all historians throughout time and geography, and although I have done my best according to what interests me—and my lived experiences—I am one more example of how anyone writing about the past is subjective, bounded by circumstances, experiences, and time. However, the fight over the narratives of who we are and who gets to write history shows itself in all cultures, and what we understand of our history affects what we do and what we believe. As James Baldwin wrote:

> History does not refer merely, or even principally, to the past. On the contrary, the great force of history comes from the fact that we carry it within us, are unconsciously controlled by it in many ways, and history is literally *present* in all that we do. It could scarcely be otherwise, since it is to history that we owe our frames of reference, our identities, and our aspiration.

Some years ago, as I was setting out on this book, I gave a talk about it to a group of history professors at Amherst College in Massachusetts. Afterward, a professor of Latin American history came up and, after a few kind words about the lecture, told me: "You take a horizontal approach to your subject. We here take a vertical one. You'd never get tenure at Amherst." I do not find this geometry convincing, but historians in our universities may be unhappy even at such a broad church as I am attempting.

When I was at Cambridge in the mid-1960s the doyen of the history faculty was the German-born Tudor specialist G. R. Elton. In 1967 he published *The Practice of History,* in which he argued that only "the professional" writes real history, while "the hallmark of the amateur is a failure of instinctive understanding. . . . The amateur shows a tendency to find the past, or parts of it, quaint; the professional is totally incapable of this." In the final analysis, he went on, it is "imagination, controlled by learning and scholarship, learning and scholarship rendered meaningful by imagination" that comprise the tools of the professional. I know from conversations I have had with Sir Richard Evans, a brilliant interpreter of twentieth-century Germany and until recently Regius Professor of Modern History at Cambridge, that Elton's views still hold sway. For Evans, no biographer, no memoirist, nor anyone approaching his or her subject with an agenda can be a legitimate historian. Welsh chapels can be lonely places.

Objectivity is a fine concept, but when in 2011 I asked the ninety-two-year-old Eric Hobsbawm whether it was possible to be objective as a historian, he laughed. "Of course not," he replied. "But I try to obey the rules." Most modern writers make some attempt to come clean about their prejudices. As Arnold Toynbee observed, "Every nation, every people has an agenda, either conscious or unconscious. Those who do not become the victim of other people's agendas." One should remember that objectivity is an agenda too.

It is impossible to eradicate every bias, and I have not eradicated mine. But that is my point. Sometimes I have chosen stories because they interest me, but in the main I have selected historians who have preeminently formed our ideas about what the past was like. I recognize that my chosen group may annoy, perhaps even outrage, the "professional" historian. Unmentioned, or given the smallest walk-on parts, are such eminent practitioners as Cassius Dio, the Earl of Clarendon, Baron de Montesquieu, Jules Michelet, Giambattista Vico (who invented the philosophy of history), Francesco Guicciardini (Machiavelli's friend and neighbor), Giorgio Vasari (the founder of art-historical writing), Theodor Mommsen (the only professor of history to receive a Nobel Prize in literature), Jacob Burckhardt (rated by Lukacs as perhaps the greatest historian of the last two centuries), Francis Parkman, Thomas Carlyle (whose history of the French Revolution, for its "sheer volcanic literary eruptions," was in Simon Schama's list of top ten historical works), Henry Adams, F. W. Maitland, Johan Huizinga, Pieter Geyl, Eduardo Galeano (the great historian of Latin America); the outstanding chronicler of Mao's early years, Gao Hua (d. 2011) and his mentor Chen Yinke; the oral historians Studs Terkel (whom I once edited) and Oscar Lewis, the Australian omnivore Robert Hughes, and Ron Chernow, whose biography of Alexander Hamilton led to the most influential musical of the century. I also believe we are in the midst of a golden period, and I have a list of more than thirty contemporary historians who have published important works. They are not included here (with the exception of some who have won widespread acclaim through TV), as it is too soon to judge how they will fare in the long term.

My approach is generally chronological, but not rigidly so. I offer several main themes, which I hope evolve over the course of the book: how our accounts of the past come to be created and what happens to them after they have been set down; how the use of sources—from archives to contemporary witnesses and the development of "dumb" evidence (buildings, gravesites, objects)—has changed through the centuries; the nature of bias, its failings and, counterintuitively, surprising strengths, as passionate subjectivity in a historian, when combined with talent, can be a blessing; the relationship of historians to governments and the demands of patriotism; the role of storytelling and the relationship between narrative and truth.

When Herodotus composed his great work, people named it *The Histories,* but scholars have pointed out that the word means more accurately "inquiries" or "researches." Calling it *The Histories* dilutes its originality. I want to make a larger claim about those who have shaped the way we view our past—actually, who have *given* us our past. I believe that that wandering Greek's investigations brought into play, 2,500 years ago, a special kind of inquiry—one that encompasses geography, ethnography, philology, genealogy, sociology, biography, anthropology, psychology, imaginative re-creation (as in the arts), and many other kinds of knowledge too. The person who exhibits this wide-ranging curiosity should rejoice in the title: historian.

OVERTURE

The Monk Outside the Monastery

However evolved our methods, we are never in the
presence of unmediated history, but of history recounted,
presented, history as it appeared to someone, as he or she
believes it to have been. This has been the nature of the
enterprise always, and the folly may be to believe
one can resist it.

—RYSZARD KAPUŚCIŃSKI, 2007

IN THE SUMMER OF 1963, THE FRIENDS, PUPILS, AND COLLEAGUES OF
David Knowles (1896–1974) presented him with a collection of his essays on the occasion of his retirement as Cambridge's Regius Professor
of Modern History, one of the most prestigious posts open to a historian. During the second half of the twentieth century Knowles, an
ordained priest, was regarded as the foremost recorder of England's
religious past and the most formidable scholar since the great legal analyst Frederic William Maitland (d. 1906). He wrote about an astonishingly long period, from around A.D. 800 to the end of the fifteenth
century; published twenty-nine books; and enjoyed an awesome reputation both in Britain and abroad—"a poet among historians," "one of
the great oaks of the forest, a poet in prose," "unsurpassed . . . unequalled."

The Festschrift opens with a summary of his career; how he was
born Michael Clive Knowles before being given the monastic name
David. Following school at Downside, he immediately entered the
monastic community. From 1923 he taught in the school and began his
career as a writer. In 1928, at the age of thirty-two, he was appointed
Novice Master, giving him responsibility over those training to be

monks. In 1933 he moved to Ealing Priory, an outpost of Downside, where he devoted himself to his major work, *The Monastic Order in England*.

The rest of the biography details an unbroken outflow of books, articles, lectures, teaching assignments, and academic honors. In 1944 he was made a fellow of Peterhouse, Cambridge, and in 1954 Winston Churchill appointed him Regius Professor, making Knowles the first Roman Catholic to be given the post since Lord Acton in 1895 and the first (also the last, one suspects) priest and monk since the Reformation. "It became clear to a wider public that here was a medieval historian of the first rank," continues the summary, written by his Oxford friend and co-medievalist William Abel Pantin.

Dom David Knowles in 1965. In his 1956 novel Anglo-Saxon Attitudes, *Angus Wilson describes the character based on Knowles as having "a distinguished ascetic face which was yet strangely goat-like."*

You may sense a "but" coming—although it is a complicated conjunction. The curriculum vitae makes no mention of the dramatic rebellion Knowles fomented at Downside, nor the most important relationship of his last thirty-five years, with a woman. Rather, the Festschrift memorializes the sanitized version of the life that the abbey had for years been at pains to promote. Yet his years of crisis are at the heart of what made him so redoubtable a historian, and they also illustrate some of the main themes of this book. I appreciate that, to a modern audience, mid-twentieth-century monasticism may seem an arcane subject, and while Knowles was much honored in his own time he is largely forgotten in ours. Bear with me, though; his story is not only exceptionally dramatic, it also tells how one human being shaped his understanding of the past through the prism of his own beliefs and prejudices, and it will be our compass as we follow historians through the centuries.

* * *

I HAVE MENTIONED HOW I was introduced to Knowles's writing and was struck by his antagonism toward the religious orders of England in the years before their dissolution, given that he himself was a monk. In March 2010, I wrote to Downside's then abbot, Dom Aidan Bellenger, who had studied medieval history at Cambridge. Had he known Knowles? He emailed that indeed he had: "There's a *lot* I can tell you." Some weeks later Dom Aidan ushered me into his tiny office in the abbey. "I've been thinking about David Knowles over the past two days," he began. "You see, we have his unpublished autobiography here." My unvoiced question hung in the air. "Yes, of course you can read it," he added with a chuckle, and so, secure in the monastery library at a special scholar's desk, read it I did.

Knowles began his autobiography in 1961, when he was sixty-five. Most of the memoir was completed between 1963 and 1967, then frequently revised, so that there are now three versions (the longest is 228 pages), although he was still making changes in 1974, the year he died. Some sections have different drafts, while others have paragraphs scored out, as if too intimate for others' eyes. The three vary in tone and degree of revelation, but together they show the strengths of his published works: a strong sense of place, fine analysis of character, frequent literary allusions, and an unbending religious code.

He was born into a family of nonconformists and ardent Liberals who lived in the largest house in a village near Stratford-upon-Avon, in Warwickshire, where his paternal grandfather employed fully half the population. He was an only child and addressed his father as "Sir." Despite this formal note, their relationship was a close one; Harry Knowles introduced his son to a love of the countryside, old buildings, and cricket as well as his literary enthusiasms. Knowles wrote that his father "had the deepest influence on my mind and character, had been my nearest and dearest friend from nursery days."

Knowles Senior (a prosperous timber merchant who also manufactured the needles for "His Master's Voice" turntables) was much taken by the ideas of Cardinal (later Saint) John Henry Newman, the leading British literary Catholic of the late nineteenth century; in 1897, when his son was a year old, Knowles and his wife converted to Catholicism. He decided that his one offspring should not attend formal school until he was ten. David Knowles grew up isolated in a large house with an overprotective mother, herself in frail health. Once he began to read, it was Scott and Twain, Stevenson's *Black Arrow,* Blackmore's *Lorna Doone;* surprisingly, no Dickens. He knew the Gilbert and Sullivan operettas by heart and also came to love trains, so intimate with their timetables that he delighted in finding a misprint in the schedule for a train to the Isle of Man. He was lonely, intense, and precociously bright. Already there was one certainty:

> I cannot remember when first I knew that I would be a priest. I say "know" because at no time did I ever consider or decide, nor did my father ever express a wish in the matter, but I must have felt certain before my first Communion, for I remember very clearly that I wondered, as I lay in bed that evening, when and where my last Communion would be, and thinking of myself as a priest receiving it.

In 1906 he was sent to West House, a Catholic preparatory school on the outskirts of Birmingham. Four years later he won a scholarship to Downside.

* * *

THE COMMUNITY (AS A gathering of monks is known) descended from a group of English and Welsh monks who in 1606 came together in Douai, then in the Spanish Netherlands, to form the monastery of St. Gregory the Great. In 1795, after a period of imprisonment, they were expelled and settled in England, initially in Shropshire and then in 1814 at Mount Pleasant, set in a countryside of quarries, green fields, and nuggety stone villages, midway between the abbeys of Bath and Glastonbury.

By the 1840s, Downside had become host to more than sixty children, aged nine to nineteen, mainly from upper-middle-class families. In 1909 Michael Clive Knowles arrived at the age of thirteen to join a school that by then had swelled to two hundred. Amid his peers, with, in his words, "their mixture of devilry, conservatism, sensuality, cruelty and emotional idealism," he lived "like a piece of driftwood in a river," susceptible to the influences and temptations of male boarding-school life. In his third year he befriended Gervase de Bless, son of a barrister father and a mother who came from a well-established Catholic family. Gervase was two years younger, well read and well traveled. "Suddenly, unexpectedly," Knowles recorded, "without any experience or forewarning, I found myself caught and entangled in a deep emotion."

In their dormitory, after lights out, they would talk in low voices of everything under the moon:

> Above all, and raising the whole of life to a new power for me, was the rich and delightful contact with Gervase's mind and character. I had never before had such an experience, and I felt at the time that it was worth losing all for this, and yet that by allowing it to absorb all my thoughts I was somehow running upon darkness and danger . . . the vision of something that would remain forever desirable and yet unattainable.

This friendship continued to delight and torment him, for, as Knowles's memoir attests, de Bless distrusted intimacy and made sure to have other friends. Unwilling to tolerate limits on what they had together, Knowles, behaving like a possessive suitor unsure how best to consummate his longings, ended the friendship. The headmaster took him to one side: "You are behaving like a jealous woman, hurting someone who has done you no harm." In his autobiography, Knowles chastises himself, quoting from A. E. Housman: "Give crowns and pounds and guineas/But not your heart away."

By September 1914 his anguish was extreme: "I had lost my heart to Downside as well as to Gervase; in both cases I had failed to find what I desired." That year was his eighteenth, and his school days were at an end. They had not been unsuccessful. He was an exceptional student, while in his final term he made the first cricket team, playing "with enthusiasm, if without great skill." He also edited the school magazine and began writing a novel.

Within a few months the First World War erupted. Knowles was old enough for active service, but he had already asked to become a

Downside Abbey and School from the air, taken in the early 1920s.
By then, the monks were set on building a major private academy,
expected to educate more than five hundred boys.

novice and so was exempt. He was now required to observe the Benedictine Rule for a year, after which he would profess "simple vows,"
then remain in the monastery for a further three years before taking his
final oaths. He soon realized that novices were almost completely segregated; under the Rule, he was not allowed to read newspapers, nor
any light or secular literature. (This did not stop him from learning
Macbeth by heart.) The austere regime began at 4:30 A.M. and ended
around 11:00 P.M. following Compline and Night Prayers, after which
came the Great Silence, when it was forbidden to speak or make unnecessary noise.

Gervase had enlisted as a midshipman. At the end of March 1916 he
died aboard the battlecruiser *Revenge,* reportedly from a diabetic seizure brought on by flu. Knowles was devastated (for the next fifty
years he would carry in his breviary blue petals from de Bless's grave-
yard) and was also racked by renewed self-recrimination, made worse
by his friend's mother treating him virtually as a second son. Norman
Cantor, a Canadian-American medievalist who has written on
Knowles's life, notes: "This failure to serve in the war, in which many

of his friends died in the mud and slaughter of the Western Front, placed a pressure of guilt upon him and with it the conviction that his service to God as a monk and priest had to be of a very special and burdensome kind to justify his survival."

What should that "very special" service be? For Knowles, being sent out to parishes or to teach in the school was not what he sought:

> I was beginning to be aware of a tension that was to endure, two questions that demanded an answer. The first was, could the life of a monk, the journey to God, be combined with sharing in all the interests of the world in literature, art, travel, games and the rest? The other, peculiar to Downside at that time, [was] could parish work outside the monastery be compatible with a purely monastic vocation?

This paragraph appears in the first draft of his autobiography; in the final version it is crossed out, with some force, in heavy red ink.

* * *

IN 1917, ALLOWED A brief furlough from the abbey, Knowles visited a group of Carmelite nuns in north Cornwall and was impressed by their self-denying existence, severed from all human ties. On his return that August, he asked to see Downside's abbot, Cuthbert Butler, a formidable presence who had already influenced his young charge through his own writings on mysticism and spirituality. Knowles revealed that he found the abbey "too easy and too human" and that he "still felt strongly the call to a stricter monastic life." Should he instead join the Carthusians, an order of monks founded in 1084 whose members were devoted to solitary work and prayer? Butler counseled against a hasty decision, and the two men agreed that Knowles should put off any move for five years. In October 1918, aged twenty-two, Dom David took his solemn vows.

Butler suggested to Knowles that he read up on Cluny, the great French abbey of the Middle Ages and the embodiment of the mainland European monastic tradition. Billeted on the top floor of the abbey at Downside, in a room so deprived of heat that he worked with a dressing gown over his habit, Knowles began to research the history of the Benedictines, but rather than being inspired, his questioning increased:

It was argued that the monastic vocation differed from the apostolic; that St. Benedict demanded of his monks that they should remain in their monastery till death. The parish life, it was said, differed scarcely at all from that of the secular priesthood; this was contrasted with the community life and rich liturgical service at Downside.

The abbey had originally been a priory of fifteen to twenty men, and over the next few decades it remained roughly the same. But "gradually and silently . . . a great change was impending." By the early 1920s the monks were set on building a major private school, with a projected enrollment of more than five hundred boys. To Knowles's dismay, the enterprise demanded more and more of the abbey's resources and seemed a contradiction of St. Benedict's original intentions.

For a while, any personal crisis was put off by another move away from the monastery. From the time of Cuthbert Butler, brighter novices had been sent to Cambridge, most often to Christ's College, with whom the abbey had an understanding, and Knowles was soon a full-time student, taking a normal three-year course. He was determined to get a top degree, and duly did,* but almost immediately after it was awarded, "the first moment of delight was followed by the realization that this was not the goal at which my real self was aiming with such hesitation." The battle between following his intellectual interests and surrendering them to a life of prayer was intensified by his doubts about whether Downside was the right place for him. In 1922 he returned to the abbey a troubled spirit.

His fellow monks saw little of this inner questioning. His life seemed to be progressing smoothly as he grew in maturity and confidence. While his own reading of the spiritual classics remained heavy, he was teaching twenty-eight classes a week and supervising rugby and

---

* That is to say, he received a First. The classification system used throughout Britain since 1918 has first-class honors awarded typically for 70 percent or higher; second-class honors divided between an upper division (known as 2:1) of 60 to 69 percent and a lower division (2:2) of 50 to 59 percent; and third-class honors (3rd) of 40 to 49 percent. At Cambridge, if a student is awarded first-class honors in two different parts of his or her degree course, this is judged a "double First." Some courses are awarded a "starred First," for examination scripts that "consistently exhibit the qualities of first class answers to an exceptional degree." Knowles was given a First in both philosophy and classics.

cricket in the afternoons. He also filled in at one of the local Mass centers. These were full years, and he was even spoken of as a future abbot.

At last, as a full monk allowed to use the monastery library, he set about working his way through the major English poets and most of the great historians—Macaulay and Gibbon but also the Ancient Greeks and Romans. Four years later, out of the blue, Oxford University Press asked him to write a short life of Robert E. Lee, the American Confederate general, and this totally unexpected commission grew into his first book—a sketch, some two hundred pages, of the entire Civil War. In it, he gives a romantic vision of the industrialized North trampling over the chivalric Old South (he had never visited America), which he invests with the high ideals and gracious ways of life he missed in his community (he credits Lincoln with many of the qualities he sought in an ideal abbot). As with his achievements at Cambridge, he could not accept the book's success and recorded his accomplishment as "a rival to the recollection of a life of prayer . . . a negation of the deep and true movement towards God."

Working on the commission had given Knowles an excuse to be away from the abbey, researching in Oxford. His next project was *The Benedictine Centuries* (1927), which would be his blueprint for an ideal monastic community, a gathering of the dedicated who would also be an intellectual elite. It was not hard to see the work as an indirect attack on "the past history and present predicament of Downside," as he put it. Butler had stepped down as abbot shortly after Knowles's ordination, to be replaced by the headmaster, Leander Ramsay, whom Knowles found sympathetic. By the summer of 1928, Downside was planning a new monastery wing and library extension: Knowles opposed both, and the debate spluttered into the following year, when Ramsay unexpectedly died. Knowles felt his time at the abbey was running out.

He set his sights on a return to Cambridge, to head up Bene't (a contraction of "Benedict") House, a hostel for "black monks," as Benedictines were known, that had been reopened in 1919. But that summer a car he was in crashed into a Nestlé milk truck, and he was nearly killed—flung against the windscreen, suffering a throat hemorrhage and a serious concussion. Two operations followed, and it was feared he might lose the sight of one eye. Although that tragedy was averted, his health was never the same: "My youth has ended," he recorded in his autobiography. Further, according to a memoir by a colleague, the accident upset his whole psyche, and thereafter he exhibited instead "a certain authoritative intransigence."

The convalescent Knowles, now thirty-two, was told that he would spend the next twelve months as temporary Novice Master. When that role had run its course, the new abbot, Dom John Chapman, rather than sending him back to Cambridge, made him Junior Master, in charge of any post-novice not yet a priest. He also became editor of *The Downside Review,* in short order turning it into the leading Catholic journal of serious opinion in England. But he was furious at Chapman for refusing him the chance of university life, and he characterized his spiritual superior as both indecisive and intolerant, a man who "hardened towards critics and never forgot what they had said or done."

* * *

THE OUTSIDE WORLD OF the 1920s, at least among the well-to-do, was one of pleasure, featuring the new sound of jazz as a release from the years of carnage. Perhaps partly in reaction, Knowles's lifestyle became progressively more austere, his range of sympathies contracting. By 1930 he had given up reading fiction or listening to music, or playing tennis or squash, although he was physically able (even after his accident, he had a sinewy, athletic body and walked quickly, with vigor). Over the rest of his life he would see just six films, all from the silent era; plays not at all. The radio he listened to once a year, when carols were broadcast on Christmas Eve. Television he watched on two occasions, a cricket match and an interview with the breakaway Rhodesian leader Ian Smith. Letters, which he used to round off "Yours affectionately," he now ended "Yours to Him."

Knowles had always possessed a thin face, almost creaseless, with small eyes, thin lips, sunken cheeks, and a piercing gaze, but these features, framed by steel-gray, close-cropped curly hair, now seemed exaggerated.* His manner suggested a confident determination but also the withdrawn chill of an ascetic.

Abbot Chapman meanwhile was full of new enterprises, most of which Knowles argued strenuously against, on the grounds that they

---

* He would be satirized as "the great Benedictine scholar" Father Lavenham in Angus Wilson's 1956 novel *Anglo-Saxon Attitudes,* "a small clerical figure" with "a distinguished ascetic face which was yet strangely goat-like." Knowles never read the novel; just as well.

gave priority to the school rather than to the nurturing of monastic life: "monastery," he pointedly recalled, came from the Greek, μόνος, *monos,* "alone." The early part of 1930 he describes as "the most searching six months of my life," and he was soon to find others who agreed that Downside had lost its way. A handful of monks, "the quieter and more studious brethren," mainly novices or juniors who held Knowles in awe, asked if he would lead in pushing for a different form of monastic commitment.

Then that June a project arose that captured Knowles's imagination and seemed to provide a solution. Some years before, Downside had received a generous gift from an Australian who wanted to establish a Benedictine community in his home country. Knowles proposed that, together with his disciples (by this time nine strong), he be put in charge of such an outpost. They set about persuading other monks to join them, but again Knowles had his hopes thwarted by Chapman, and angry letters crossed between the two. For his abbot, Knowles was becoming unreasonable, compulsive, bizarre—a pain under the collar.

Chapman was unwilling to engage in person, writing to Knowles at one point: "I am not suggesting you are not good people—but that you lack the monastic vocation." This was hard to take, since the nub of the rebels' case was that they believed the original aims of St. Benedict had been discarded. The plotting continued, and the group even gave itself a name—the *usque* movement, from the Latin phrase *usquequaque perfectionem,* meaning "towards perfection." By August 1933 Chapman charged Knowles with causing disturbances and disobedience and characterized his Junior Master as "a storm-centre . . . an unreliable and disobedient subject, who has led younger monks astray . . . a rival who must be put down."

The would-be radicals were all younger than Knowles by some years; three were still in simple or temporary vows. When they could not get meaningful support from the rest of the community, they had no stomach for further battle and surrendered to their abbot's wishes. Knowles was told he would be sent away to a daughter house governed by Downside, a priory in Ealing, a lower-middle-class suburb of West London. And so to this new home—in Knowles's view "a fourth-rate, unobservant house" of some fourteen monks—this turbulent priest would go.

Still he would not be silenced, filing appeals that he had been treated unjustly. In November, Abbot Chapman died, to be succeeded by Bruno Hicks, whom Knowles, master of the character sketch, described as "cold, neither inviting nor inspiring confidence, fluid as water and fundamentally unreliable." Even so, Hicks suggested Knowles take his case to Rome, to that part of the Vatican supervising religious orders. He did, but in June 1934 his petition was rejected, Pius XI himself sending—in Knowles's words—"a somewhat jejune reply." He was furious: "The Primate has shown himself as a willow, not as an oak." From then on, he largely forsook life at the priory, taking on minimal church duties and a few classes in the school, at mealtimes not speaking unless spoken to, and avoiding visitors. He spent most of his six years there in the British Museum or the London Library, buried in research. Then, one night in 1939, at the age of forty-three, he bundled up a minimum of clothes, a Greek Testament, and the autumn quarter of his breviary—and disappeared.

★ ★ ★

IT TOOK THE ABBEY several weeks to learn what had happened. Some four years before, the prior at Ealing, Benedict Kuypers, had asked Knowles to interview a medical student who had asked for spiritual direction. As Knowles tells it, one evening "I was told that someone in the parlor was waiting to see me. As I entered I saw a lady of thirty or so, in a short fur coat, black skirt and hat, with hair that appeared to be bobbed, but was in fact set closely to her head. She spoke quietly and in perfect English though with a slightly unusual pronunciation."

The student, Elizabeth Kornerup, turned out to be a Scandinavian psychiatrist in training (she would later work at the prestigious Tavistock Clinic) and a Lutheran convert to Catholicism. Born on Christmas Day 1901 to Danish parents, she had unruly fair hair, wore glasses, had a stammer, and was far from alluring. Despite that, in Denmark, she had received several proposals of marriage and would continue to do so in London. Knowles wrote of her:

> Elizabeth was not at first sight striking in appearance. No one passing her, even when I first knew her in her early thirties, would have thought her remarkably beautiful, still less "pretty." Her facial appearance could vary to an unusual extent, especially in later years. She was always pale, and when tired or ill

she could look her age in years, and at times her face, seen in repose, had a lifeless, sallow appearance.

This was the woman with whom he almost immediately became obsessed, seeing her as "a perfect soul and a saint." Above all, she was deeply religious, had taken a vow of chastity, and had originally hoped to be a missionary nun in India. She would spend long hours in prayer, most often at night, while early in her twenties she had taken to carrying, without permission, a consecrated host (the wafer used in Communion). For several months she had attempted to live without food or drink, an endeavor that obviously failed (although some late medieval holy women, the virtuosos of abstinence, allegedly lived for weeks on the Eucharist alone) and had left her a semi-invalid. She would go to confession every day, an extreme practice so frowned upon by the Church that she had to find different confessors for each day of the week—Jesuits, Redemptorists, Passionists, parish priests, whoever. Would Dom David become her confessor? When that same evening he did hear her confession, she announced that . . . she had nothing to confess! Knowles asked himself whether his visitor was in fact a "bogus, self-seeking neurotic" but concluded, "I accepted her . . . in the forty years that have passed since that day I have never regretted my decision or doubted its truth."

When they first met, Kornerup was living in a small flat in Pimlico, just south of Victoria Station. She had built up a flourishing private practice while also working as an assistant pathologist at two London hospitals. Knowles took to writing to her daily, telephoning her sometimes twice a day, and paying frequent visits, which would be spent together in silent prayer. His colleagues in Ealing knew nothing of this, imagining Dom David away at a library:

> I was well aware of the difficult position I should find myself in
> if I were challenged. I realize fully what it was for a priest to go
> almost daily for hours to the room, and later the house, of one
> who an unmarried woman, and then young. But I knew
> also that it was my spiritual, priestly duty to do so.

By 1937, Kornerup had moved into a larger flat in Gloucester Street, also part of Pimlico, and singlemindedly set about ousting the middle-aged woman who lived in the apartment below. On August 28, 1939, she asked Knowles to move in. "I will come," he told her. "Shakespeare's line passed through my mind: 'There is a tide in the affairs of men,' and I felt a deep joy that I had taken it at the flood." He and "Sister Bridget," as he dubbed her, would be inseparable for the rest of his life; she would die a year after he.[*] Knowles came to believe that his primary duty as a priest was to protect her; she in turn held that her mission was to assist him in all his endeavors. "Her life," he wrote, "gave my life its purpose." She was "an exhibit, a marvel, who showed all the textbook signs of holiness" and even "resembled Our Lord."

Following Kornerup's advice, Knowles severed all external contacts, including any communication with Downside. By 1938, Bruno Hicks had resigned as abbot, possibly suffering a mental breakdown (he was an active homosexual at a time when to be so was a criminal offense). He was succeeded by the long-serving headmaster, Dom Sigebert Trafford, who, despite all the ructions within the community, had always regarded Knowles sympathetically and even as a possible successor. Urged on by a Rome anxious to avoid scandal, Trafford made several journeys to London to meet Knowles, only to be turned away at the door.

For the two years after his flight, any message to Knowles had to go through Kornerup, who said he was suffering from mild schizophrenia and had to be handled with the utmost care. "Elizabeth had decided that our best policy now was to create the impression that I had had a breakdown," he wrote. This way, he might remain where he was without losing his position as a monk. There is no firm evidence either way on whether he was ever mentally ill. Adrian Morey believed that he "would have ended in a mental home had she not taken him in." On one occasion when Trafford arrived in Gloucester Street, bringing with him a longtime Downside physician named Dr. Bradley, Kornerup threatened to call the police. Knowles eventually agreed to be examined by two psychiatrists. One asked questions "suggesting that Elizabeth had won my confidence by minor sexual gratifications." The

---

[*] In a letter to Dom Adrian Morey of January 29, 1977, Christopher Brooke, Knowles's close friend and literary executor, states that people in Cambridge did not even know of her existence until 1963; she appeared in public with Knowles only in his very last years. "After his death . . . she was pathetic and lost. . . . As I knew her, she was evidently a very able, sharp-witted, intelligent, yet also sweet and romantic person. . . . She was certainly the serpent and the dove," he wrote, his last phrase repeating Knowles's own description of his lifetime companion.

other recommended electric-shock treatment. "There was an element of the ridiculous," Knowles acknowledged, "that I think we both appreciated." And more than an element of dissembling, for as early as 1939, the two made inquiries about a civil marriage in case Kornerup was to be deported as an alien; many years later, when she entered the hospital for a serious operation, Knowles stayed overnight in her room posing as her husband, and indeed during the years that they lived in south London they were known locally as Mr. and Mrs. Knowles.* Nobody knows for sure the nature of their partnership. There are letters at Downside from Knowles to the authorities in Rome stating that he was physically incapable of a full sexual relationship.

At the monastery under Trafford, there was great compassion for its former brilliant member—all this amid the outbreak of the Second World War. Yet Knowles posed a problem; by canon law, his conduct meant automatic suspension as both monk and priest and ipso facto excommunication from the Church, which included no longer being allowed to celebrate Mass. He refused outright to accept these penalties, continuing to hold that he had been treated unjustly. When in a spirit of compromise Abbot Trafford wrote asking if he wished exclaustration (whereby a monk may live for a limited time away from his abbey, usually with a view to deciding whether to depart definitively) or remain a member of the community with permission to live outside the monastery, he received the reply: "Downside does not observe the Rule either in the letter or the spirit, still less the Gospel teaching upon which the Rule depends. . . . I cannot in conscience ask for absolution from faults which I am not conscious of having committed." Eventually, around 1944, he was given permission again to celebrate Mass, but this was made contingent on his making a brief annual visit to Downside. He refused, while also turning down any other solution.

There was a further dimension to the problem. During all this time, despite the upheavals and the enormous tension he was under, Knowles had been extraordinarily productive. In June 1940 *The Monastic Order*

---

* Knowles's decision to live with Kornerup caused a temporary rupture with his father. His mother had died in 1930, and the widower had moved first into a small house in the village of Chilcompton, just two miles from Downside, then into a home some hundred yards from the abbey, so that he could be close to his son. Before long he had become an alcoholic. But he eventually came to accept his son's new partner and gave Kornerup a £200 annuity, which for some time was the couple's main source of income. The elder Knowles died in 1944.

in England: A History of Its Development from the Times of St. Dunstan to the Fourth Lateran Council, 940–1216 was published. At around six hundred pages (even then Knowles had had to cut a hundred pages from his initial draft, as there was a wartime paper shortage), the book was expensive to set, and he accepted a profit-sharing arrangement in lieu of royalties. Cambridge University Press seemed to have little expectation of success, printing only five hundred copies (at the then-high price of forty-five shillings, even though Knowles's father paid £200— in modern currency, about $6,000—toward the cost of production) and immediately broke up the type, preventing any easy reprint.*

Despite such a modest beginning, the book was hailed as a masterwork. Downside was stymied. How could the abbey admit that this "great Catholic medievalist," who with a single publication had resurrected the history of monastic life in England, was a monk on the run, a renegade priest? Either way, the career of David Knowles, celebrated medieval historian, was born.

* * *

THE MONASTIC ORDER IN ENGLAND was to be the first of four books on his chosen subject. It tells how monastic life in England developed from the Norman Conquest to the thirteenth century in prose at once beautifully clear, full of literary allusion, and possessed of a narrative power that recalls two of Knowles's heroes, Macaulay and Trevelyan. The depth and breadth of his scholarship still inspire, while the sheer readability of his prose, over the decades, has had commentators reaching for superlatives. "Had Cicero written on monasticism he could hardly have written with greater elegance" is a typical example. Others praise his "novelist's skill" and "quiet humor."

The criticisms would come. In the century of Marxism, Knowles shows little interest in economics; for all the book's length, not until

---

* In the Benedictine Order, all theological books had to be submitted for censorship, but works of history didn't, so although written by a priest, the book appeared without the usual "Nihil Obstat" ecclesiastical imprimatur to certify that nothing in it was offensive to faith or morals, nor did his later works carry this stamp. Even so, Knowles's dispute with the Church rumbled on for years. In October 1952, the Roman Congregation of Religious officially exclaustrated him but did not excommunicate him or deny him "spiritual privileges." Unbowed, he replied that the whole order was invalid but nevertheless delayed saying Mass again until January 1, 1957, in the hope that his abbot would somehow relent and also because he didn't want people to feel that his position had been "regularized"—that he might have admitted any original fault. To the end of his life he regarded himself as a monk.

page 105 is there mention of a price expressed in actual monetary units (his 1952 work, *Monastic Sites from the Air,* on the other hand, shows considerable understanding of economics). Knowles could also be naïve, several times relying on medieval texts that scholars have since determined to be forgeries. He has the casual anti-Semitism of his class and time; hardly mentions female religious, seeing no trace of "any saintly or commanding figure of a woman" worthy of study; and exhibits a prejudice against smaller monastic or preaching associations. That last led to a distortion: Cistercians, Augustinians, and friars such as Franciscans and Dominicans are largely ignored. Knowles was an elitist with a sometimes self-conscious literary style, aping Thucydides one moment and quoting in European languages the next.

His writing was in part a counterblast against a pioneering contemporary, G. G. Coulton, three of the four volumes of whose *Five Centuries of Religion* were already in print. Coulton was an Anglican deacon who had lost his faith and become a preparatory schoolmaster before returning to Cambridge. Until Knowles appeared he was viewed as the world's leading authority on English medieval monks, but Knowles believed that Coulton "knew little of Catholic spirituality" and belittled him by giving him a single footnote—yet it was his rival's remark, in a 1929 volume, that the history of monasticism in England had yet to be written that inspired him to fill that gap.

Much that has been published on medieval religious practice is predicated upon the foundations laid by Knowles. Throughout the 1930s, readers had been served only by Coulton's viciously antiCatholic interpretation. The only different discourse on monasticism was to be found in the work of European scholars, which was slowly becoming available in translation. Knowles seemed daring—and new. If historians resented the insertion into history of Christian presupposition, it was that very insertion that made his project unique. His Peterhouse colleague Maurice Cowling sums up that achievement: "He came nearer than any 20th-century English historian had come to finding a language through which to insert into the structure of a major work of scholarship conceptions of the reality of God, religion and eternal life. . . . That makes his historical writing one of the most compelling Christian productions to have been published in England in [the twentieth] century."

This was not a small canvas. The monasteries held a central place in medieval life, with by the late 1530s nearly nine hundred religious houses in England and some twelve thousand men and women in orders. Yet by 1540 every monastery had been swept away during Henry VIII's concerted attack on them. Until the 1880s, the Church showed scant interest in the period, and no adequate account of British monasticism existed. But Knowles was far from done. The first volume of his survey, *The Religious Orders in England,* appeared in 1948 (covering the period 1216–1340), the second in 1955 (1340 to about 1500), and the third in 1959, the final, magisterial volume being subtitled "The Tudor Age" and extending from 1485 until 1620 with the reestablishment of the English Benedictine congregation. The whole work runs to more than two thousand pages. It is a huge undertaking, covering more than six hundred years not just of religion but of British cultural history. Further, at a time when the historical profession was being transformed in the pursuit of "scientific" research, Knowles reminded his colleagues of the appeal of—and the need for—a clear and unequivocally argued narrative case. Kenneth Clark, narrator of the BBC's *Civilisation* series, writing in 1977, called *The Religious Orders* "one of the historical masterpieces of this century."

Knowles shows how even great writers can ignore "objective" history, selecting what suits the agenda they have chosen to pursue; in the battle between any duty he had as a historian and the demands of his chosen creed, he told the truth as he saw it, because it was *his* truth. He came to historical research as a reader himself, and like any reader he selected from it according to his tastes. Writing of *The Monastic Order* and the first volume of *The Religious Orders,* Norman Cantor states bluntly:

> These two books were written out of despair, anger, yearning for revenge, internal resourcefulness, a sense of personal calling that make them, chapter after chapter and especially in their discussions of religious leaders and the overall cultural and ecclesiastical ambience, works of forceful passion and imaginative power that have very rarely been equaled in writing about the Middle Ages or the history of the Catholic Church.

Knowles's dissatisfaction with the Benedictines of his time infects not only *The Monastic Order* (of which whole sections can be described as individual or group biography—with each abbot or religious figure getting a trenchant end-of-term report) but all his histories. He deals harshly with any abbot who in his view fails to serve as a true spiritual father to his monks or whose tyranny attains such proportions that he must be disobeyed. Whereas his longtime nemesis, Abbot Chapman, had argued that sanctity could never be an obligation but only a goal, for Knowles, on the page as in his life, the monastic vocation included the clear duty to strive toward such a state. He quotes Aquinas's belief that the zeal for souls most acceptable to God is that through which a man "devotes his own soul or that of another" to "contemplation" rather than to "action." Then again, in his epilogue to the final volume, he returns to his theme of the nemesis of sanctity:

> When once a religious house or a religious order ceases to direct its sons to the abandonment of all that is not God, and ceases to show them the rigours of the narrow way that leads to the imitation of Christ in His Love, it sinks to the level of a purely human institution, and whatever its works may be, they are the work of time and not of eternity. The true monk, in whatever century he is found, looks not to the changing ways around him or to his own mean condition, but to the unchanging everlasting God, and his trust is in the everlasting arms that hold him.

The irony is that, had his abbots not opposed his wishes to start a new community, be it in Australia, India, Kenya, or the north of England (all were mooted at one time or another), he would never have written the books he did. His issues with Downside gave his judgments focus and conviction. It is the further great irony of writing about the past that any author is the prisoner of their character and circumstances yet often they are the making of him. So it was with Michael Clive Knowles.

After leaving for the priory at Ealing, he returned to Downside only once, for the funeral of Cuthbert Butler in 1934. Yet, at his death, Knowles was reconciled with the abbey and given the prayers and dues of a deceased monk. He was buried, like any true Benedictine, in his cowl.

CHAPTER I

THE DAWNING OF HISTORY
Herodotus or Thucydides?

———

The conversion of legend-writing into the science
of history was not native to the Greek mind, it was
a fifth-century invention, and Herodotus was
the man who invented it.

—R. G. COLLINGWOOD

Exiled Thucydides knew
All that a speech can say
About Democracy,
And what dictators do,
The elderly rubbish they talk
To an apathetic grave;
Analysed all in his book.

—W. H. AUDEN, "SEPTEMBER I, 1939"

NO ONE KNOWS FOR SURE THE DATES OF HERODOTUS'S OWN STORY. HE
was probably born c. 485 B.C. and lived into the 420s, since he refers
to events early in the Peloponnesian War of 431–404. He was part of
an intellectual world that included early medical investigations and
creative speculation of all kinds. Among his contemporaries or near-
contemporaries were Aeschylus (525–456 B.C.), Aristophanes (c. 448–
c. 380 B.C.), Euripides (c. 484–c. 408 B.C.), Pindar (522–c. 443 B.C.), Plato
(c. 429–347 B.C.), and Sophocles (496–406 B.C.), who composed a poem
in his honor.

Most records before Herodotus are dry chronicles, even those that evince a rudimentary attempt at narrative. There is no evidence of "history" as a concept, although the Hebrew words *toledot* (genealogies) and *divre hayyamin* (the matter of those days) suggest at least some interest in tracking the past. Homer, best treated as a plural noun, a group effort that produced *The Iliad* and *The Odyssey,* provided a way station on the road to writing history. As Adam Nicolson puts it in *Why Homer Matters:* "Epic, which was invented after memory and before history, occupies a third space in the human desire to connect the present to the past: it is the attempt to extend the qualities of memory over the reach of time embraced by history." He dates the oral creation of both poems to c. 1800 B.C., their being written down to around 700 B.C.

The Greeks knew something of their past from these oral traditions, often versified, but anything that occurred more than three generations distant would be only loosely remembered if not forgotten altogether. Oral customs tend to avoid stories that an audience doesn't want to hear. In 492, when Phrynikhos, one of Aeschylus's rivals, presented his play *The Fall of Miletus* on that city's destruction by the Persians, "the audience burst into tears, fined him 1,000 drachmas for reminding them of their own evils, and ordered that no one should ever perform this play again." Herodotus would have known that poets from a previous age were primarily there to please those who had come to hear them and so often made things up, even if they protested that they never did such things.

Of those previous poets, Hesiod (active c. 700 B.C.) had introduced the idea of a succession of declining ages. Hecataeus of Miletus (550–476 B.C.), whose *Journey Round the World* was built on his travels around the Mediterranean, is otherwise the most significant predecessor. Among other notable writers, Hellanicus of Lesbos (c. 490–405 B.C.) wrote long parallel chronologies, listing not just a single line of rulers, and Philistus, Theopompus, and Xenophon, all of whom flourished in the fourth century B.C., wrote accounts of real value.

This line of historians encompassed a revolution. Between 2000 and 1200 B.C., the unnamed people whom we retrospectively call Indo-Hittites burst over Europe and South Asia, and one of these invading tribes raised a group of small settlements around the Mediterranean and the Black Sea. When this hyper-dynamic culture came into con-

*An 1814 imagining of Homer and his audience. In the sixth century B.C.,
a popular poem had spoken of "the sweetest of all singers," identifying
him as "a blind man and he makes his home in rocky Chios."
This "evidence" was enough for Thucydides to declare,
a century on, that Homer was the author alluded to.*

tact with another of a similar nature, a new consciousness began to grow. These years saw substantial advances in abstract reasoning, and people began to connect with the past in a new way. (It is worth bearing in mind that the Inca, that most ordered of preliterate cultures, had four versions of history, ranging from secret to popular, all propagated under the empire's strict control.)

Some historians argue that the victory at Marathon in 490 B.C. during the first Persian invasion of Greece marked East and West as different cultural entities and so was a turning point. The Greek golden age possibly coincided with a surge of abundance, akin to that which preceded the Industrial Revolution in Britain, with higher rates of food production, capital investment, and a leap in population. But the resultant cultural explosion was matched only once in history, by the Renaissance in Europe, and although "history" was not at any one point in time a *necessary* development, certain discoveries are requisite if a civilization is to evolve, and a sense of the past is one of them.

Although writing had begun in Sumeria (southern Iraq) by the

third millennium B.C., it was Herodotus who authored the oldest surviving book-length work of prose on any subject. He wrote the first
account in the Western tradition that is recognizably a work of history
as we might now define it, covering the recent human past and not
concentrating on myth and legend (although not by any means passing
over them, either; he would likely have agreed with Plato's declaration
in the *Republic* that myth is "the noble lie" or pious fiction that binds
society together). He is also the first to provide a sustained record of
past occurrences along with self-conscious discussions about how to
obtain knowledge of days gone by and the first to ponder why particular events happened in the first place. Above all, he asks questions. He
is the world's first travel writer, investigative reporter, and foreign correspondent. He covers ethnography (which existed as a literary genre
prior to history, so its incorporation into *The Histories* is not surprising), military and local history, biography, poetry, philology, genealogy, mythography, anthropology, geology, botany, zoology, and
architecture, while at the same time he is, to use Ryszard Kapuściński's
description in his *Travels with Herodotus,* "a typical wanderer . . . a pil-
grim . . . the first to discover the world's multicultural nature. The
first to argue that each culture requires acceptance and understanding,
and that to understand it, one must first come to know it."

The immediate impression on reading even a few of his pages is that
he finds everything of interest. Sometimes he offers a judgment, at
others just reports; his approach characterized by *opsis* ("seeing"), from
which we get a word more associated with crime novels—*autopsy,*
"seeing for oneself." Much of his knowledge comes from the voyages
that Greeks, Egyptians, and Phoenicians had been making both around
the Mediterranean and outside it, but it is likely he traveled extensively, not only throughout the Greek states but to Egypt, Phoenicia
(roughly, modern Lebanon and Syria), Babylon (Iraq), Arabia, Thrace
(Bulgaria and the European section of Turkey), and up through modern Romania, Ukraine, southern Russia, and Georgia.

Most of these journeys were formidable undertakings. To get to
what is modern Odessa, for instance, he would have had to voyage
along the western and northern shores of the Aegean; then through
the Dardanelles, the Sea of Marmara, and the Bosporus; and last, along
the western shore of the Black Sea, past the mouth of the Danube to
that of the Dnieper: with fair winds and no mishaps, a voyage likely to

have taken three months—and that was just one of many trips. The two most powerful Greek cities of the time were Athens—its citizen population just 100,000—and Sparta, to the south. (The latter's citizens were called *Spartiatai,* but an alternative form was *Lakon,* from which comes "laconic": Spartans were known for their terse speech, hence when in c. 338 B.C. Philip of Macedon told them, "If I invade your territory, I will destroy you," they sent back a one-word reply: "If.")

Herodotus's home city of Anatolian Halicarnassus was on the edge of what was then the vast cultural space of the ancient Near East, a Greek colony that in about 545 B.C. had been absorbed into the Persian Empire along with Lydia (covering much of what is now western Turkey). Caught between two worlds, the city had a non-Greek native population—known as Carians—and drifted away from its close relations with its Dorian neighbors to help pioneer Greek trade with Egypt, which was becoming an internationally-minded port.

Because of an uncle's fondness for political intrigue, Herodotus found his family put under a cloud and himself, at the age of around thirty, sent away from Halicarnassus (today's Bodrum, a small city on the southwest coast of Turkey). For much of the next five years he traveled, landing in Athens in c. 447 B.C., already armed with a rich store of notes about the eastern Mediterranean. He originally began his history of the area with the Persian attack on the city in 490 B.C., then expanded it to cover Persia's invasion of the whole peninsula ten years later—the defining event of his boyhood. One story, likely a myth, has Herodotus as a child standing on the quay at Halicarnassus as the defeated ships returned from the Battle of Salamis and asking, "Mother, what did they fight each other for?"

In 499 B.C. the Carians had joined with the Greek coastal towns in revolting against Persia; by the time Herodotus left on his travels, his family, one of the noblest (and most politically involved) of the city, would likely have had connections in other parts of the Persian kingdom that would have made his researches easier. *Xenía,* the Greek word for the concept of courtesy shown to those far from home, is generally translated as "guest-friendship" because the ways in which hospitality was exercised created a reciprocal relationship between guest and host. In addition, Herodotus, although he spoke only Greek comfortably, would have enjoyed the institution of the *proxenos,* "the guest's friend," a type of consul who voluntarily or for a fee cared for visitors from his native city. Finally, no one could be sure of new arrivals whether they were merely human or gods in human form: best to be hospitable.

Possibly Herodotus began as a sea captain and merchant. His knowledge of geography is well ahead of that of his known predecessors, and he takes for granted climate, topography, and access to resources. Before him, there is scant evidence that anyone was interested in preserving knowledge of the causes of recent events; Greek states had no state archives or even lists of magistrates to help construct a chronology. Athens, remarkable for its concern for commemoration, lacked a central archive until the end of the fifth century.

Herodotus planned both to instill a sense of the past and to leave a record, but he also gave his curiosity full rein. His book contains, to borrow one recent biographer's list, "illicit eroticism, sex, love, violence, crime, strange customs of foreign peoples, imagined scenes in royal bedrooms, flashbacks, dream sequences, political theory, philosophical debate, encounters with oracles, geographical speculation, natural history, short stories and Greek myths." Herodotus notes, with typical fascination, that Egyptians eat in the street and relieve themselves indoors; their men urinate sitting down, their women standing up (2.35, 2–3), whereas in the Greek world the reverse applied. Ethiopians, he observes blithely, speak a language unlike any other, squeaking like bats (4.183) or twittering like birds (2.57). He loves to report strange deeds of all kinds, to "seek out side issues" (4.30). Aristophanes satirized his opening line of inquiry as "look at the women" or, as we might joshingly put it, *Cherchez la femme,* for he is evidently fascinated by sexual conventions. Thus, of Libyan customs: "When a Nasamonian man marries for the first time, it is customary for his bride to have intercourse with all the guests at the feast in succession, and for each of these guests to then present a gift he has brought." Among another Libyan tribe, the Gindanes, the women "wear many leather ankle bracelets. It is said that they put on one of these for every man with whom they have had intercourse, and the woman who wears the most is considered to be the best, since she has won affection from the most men" (4.172, 4.176). His handling of the telling detail can take one's breath away: when in 479 B.C. the Athenians held a prolonged siege of Sestos, on the Hellespont, "within the city wall, the people by now were reduced to utter misery, even to the point of boiling the leather straps of their beds and eating them" (9.118). One wonders how Herodotus knew this.

At one point in his account of Xerxes's campaigns, the ruthless, all-mighty ruler of the vast Persian empire, the largest realm the world had ever seen, is surveying the great host of men he has called up to overwhelm the Greeks:

> As Xerxes looked over the whole Hellespont, whose water was completely hidden by all his ships, and at all the shores and the plains of Abydos, now so full of people, he congratulated himself for being so blessed. But then he suddenly burst into tears. . . .

When one of his officers asks what has caused such sorrow, Xerxes replies: "I was overcome by pity as I considered the brevity of human life, since not one of all these people here will be alive one hundred years from now" (7.46). The Persian monarch is not always so compassionate. Herodotus, who tends to invest Persians with the characteristics that the Greeks most despised, notes that just a few weeks later, Xerxes was forced to beat a hasty retreat back home. A storm threatened his ship:

> The King fell into a panic and shouted to the helmsman, asking if there was any way they could be saved. The helmsman replied, "My Lord, there is none, unless we rid ourselves of these many men on board." Upon hearing this, Xerxes said, "Men of Persia, it is now the time for you to prove your care for your king. For in you, it seems, lies my safety." After he had said this, his men prostrated themselves, leapt out into the sea, and the now lightened ship sailed safely to Asia. As soon as Xerxes stepped safely onto shore, he gave the helmsman a gift of a golden crown in return for saving his life, but then, because he had been responsible for the death of so many Persians, he had his head cut off. (8.118)

Herodotus several times writes that he does not believe this or other stories he tells but feels he must repeat them because they are too good to leave out. Talking of livestock in Scythia, he suddenly says, "a remarkable fact occurs to me (I need not apologize for the digression—it has been my plan throughout this work)." After the powerful anecdote

*The world as Herodotus saw it. In 499–498 B.C., Aristagoras,
tyrant of Miletus, made a tour of mainland Greece, taking with him
what Herodotus calls "a bronze tablet with an engraving of a map of
the whole world, with all its rivers and seas."*

of the boatswain, he adds that readers should not regard it as a historical fact (8.118–19); the tale is included because it embodies how a tyrant
exercises "justice," and its ideological significance outweighs, for him,
its likely historical falsehood. Furnishing evidence for his wilder claims
doesn't interest him.

He relates, without qualification, that the semen of Ethiopians and
Indians is "as black as their skin" and tells of winged snakes, phoenixes,
and headless men with eyes in their chests (although he rejects stories of
a race of one-eyed men, and of Indians with feet so large that they use
them as sunshades). We read of the giant "gold-digging ants" of India
and learn that because Egyptians venerate cows above all animals and
Greeks eat cows, Egyptians will never kiss a Greek man on the mouth
(2.41) and find out that "there are fewer bald men in Egypt than anywhere else, which is a fact that anyone can see for themselves" (3.12).

Libyans cure children in convulsions by sprinkling them with goat's
urine: "I am simply reporting here what the Libyans themselves say"
(1.175, 4.187). He knew that what might appear irregular, peculiar, or
paradoxical (even if accepted by the indigenous culture) would appeal to
his audience. And he is often funny; repeating a Persian axiom, he tells
us: "If you take a decision when drunk, review it when you are sober;
but if you take a decision when sober, review it again when you are
drunk" (1.133). (Centuries on, Ernest Hemingway would offer the same
advice about writing fiction. The two men would have gotten along.)

Herodotus also has a gift for aphorism: "In war, fathers bury their sons; in peace, sons their fathers" (1.87.4; this despite never having seen military service). Or: "A man who has great wealth but is unhappy outdoes the fortunate man in only two ways, while the fortunate man outdoes him in many ways" (1.32). Again: "The most painful anguish that mortals suffer is to understand a great deal but to have no power at all" (9.16).

John Gould ends his excellent study of Herodotus:

> The most lasting of all impressions that one takes away from a reading of his narrative is exhilaration. It comes from the sense one has of Herodotus' inexhaustible curiosity and vitality. He responds with ever-present delight and admiration to the "astonishing" variety of human achievement and invention in a world which he acknowledges as tragic; he makes you laugh, not by presenting experience as comic, but by showing it as constantly surprising and stimulating; he makes you glad to have read him by showing men responding to suffering and disaster with energy and ingenuity, resilient and undefeated.

I concur. While working on this chapter, I would take *The Histories* to the supper table and read passages to my wife, two or three paragraphs at a time. This continued until I had exhausted my sum of Herodotus anecdotes. My wife was bereft. Thucydides, Tacitus, Livy—no one quite matched up.

The entire *Histories,* in its English translation some six hundred pages (twice as long as *The Iliad*), has been divided into nine sections, not by its author but by later Alexandrian scholars. In the first four "books," the main theme is the expansion of the Persian kingdom from the accession of Cyrus in 550 B.C. to about 500 B.C., but there are digressions on various aspects of Persian culture and, at considerable length, on Egypt's customs and early history. Herodotus then gives us an account of Athens from 560 B.C. on. Books V and VI cover the Ionian Revolt of 499–494 B.C. and the Persian expedition that was defeated by the Athenians at Marathon in 490 B.C., but the narrative is never simple, and Herodotus regularly veers off and tells us about contemporary events in the Greek states. The last three books are an account of the expedition that Xerxes, Persia's fifth "King of Kings," took to add Greece to his empire—and his unexpected defeat.

That event and all that led to it gave Herodotus the impetus he needed for his researches to be worth the telling. And he had a strong image of what it meant to be Greek. As he declares in his opening paragraph:

What follows is a performance [literally, a display] of the enquiries of Herodotus of Halicarnassus, so that human events do not fade with time. May the great and wonderful deeds—some brought forth by the Hellenes,* others by the barbarians—not go unsung; as well as the causes that made them make war on each other. (1.1)

Herodotus's reference to "performance" in the very first line emphasizes that his text was to be read aloud in public. In Greek, "to read" carries the meanings both "to hear" and "to recognize again." Previously, poets had been the interpreters of human experience, and Homer makes but a single obscure reference to writing in all his works; by Herodotus's time, however, composing in prose was no longer a second-class activity, and rhetoricians busied themselves establishing principles for how best to express thoughts in the new medium. Although it might be easier to commit a thousand lines of poetry to memory than a hundred of prose, once it was possible to carry around rolls of writing the ability to create long narrative passages was an obvious advantage, while the old techniques were no longer up to holding in one's mind the more complex thoughts that people were now entertaining.†

Herodotus himself was no stranger to prose exposition, having

---

* "Hellas" was, from the time of the mythical Trojan War (twelfth century B.C.) on, the word Greeks used to refer to their territory, as most city-states—there were nearly a thousand—were small, ranging from the Crimea to northern Spain: thus "Hellenes," after their legendary founder, Helen. That its people were ever called "Greeks" is something of an insult, an attempt to diminish an invaded population. The Greek people of Thessaly, called the Graikoi, provided the Romans with their name for Hellenes—rather as if the United States had been invaded from the south and the entire population was subsequently named "Floridians."

† Will Durant, author of a multi-volume world history, perceptively comments on this: "Poetry seems natural to a nation's adolescence, when imagination is greater than knowledge. . . . Prose is the voice of knowledge freeing itself from imagination and faith; it is the language of secular, mundane, 'prosaic' affairs; it is the emblem of a nation's maturity, and the epitaph of its youth." See Will Durant, *The Life of Greece: The Story of Civilization,* vol. 2 (New York: Simon & Schuster, 1939), p. 139.

grown up enjoying intellectual connections with the nearby cultural hothouse of Miletus. As for the noun *history,* the term had a skeptical connotation in Ionia, where Herodotus grew up. He himself preferred "to inquire or investigate" to describe what he was writing, and one effect is that the original meanings have been swallowed up. Possibly because, in Homer, a *histor* is "a good judge," who gives his opinion based on the facts resulting from an investigation, *historie* became an all-encompassing term, indeed one that Herodotus employs twenty-three times.

His general approach had its downside. He not only passed on doubtful information; he also invented material, even how he obtained it. Cicero (106–43 B.C.), who wanted to define history as a branch of rhetoric, while acclaiming Herodotus as the "father of history," bracketed him with Theopompus (d. 320 B.C.), author of a twelve-volume history of Greece but a notorious liar, and refers slightingly to his "innumerable tales." Aristotle weighed in by noting Herodotus's "string-along style" and mentions his being a storyteller in a pejorative sense. Other ancients were similarly dismissive, and soon Cicero's sobriquet was joined to Plutarch's famous putdown, "father of lies." As it was, Herodotus was charged with consciously creating an illusion of accuracy by mentioning specific details around stories that he well knew were made up. "Herodotus seems to be dancing away the truth, and saying, 'I could hardly care less,'" commented Plutarch (c. A.D. 46–120) in an unbridled attack openly titled "On the Malice of Herodotus."

Investigate and select as Herodotus might—and there are 1,086 examples of his self-recorded presence as eyewitness or investigator—he still found room for most local beliefs, legends, and folktales, only occasionally making comment. When Arion of Methymna is described as being carried on the back of a dolphin, Herodotus concludes: "I have my own opinion about these claims" (2.56)—but nothing more, a prime example of his paralipsis—a useful word meaning the pretense of leaving things to one side. In telling Egypt's history, he compresses ten thousand years (and three hundred kings) into a single paragraph. Generally he employs a broad brush for dates and times—"at this time," "after this," "up to my day," "still now" are typical—but then he probably lacked access to more precise information. "Very few things happen at the right time, and the rest do not happen at all," he says. He is conscientious about readability, not accuracy.

His inexactness is particularly evident in the way he exaggerates the size, equipment, tactical acumen, and leadership of the Persian forces in order to show the Greeks triumphing against overwhelming odds. He describes an army so enormous that it bankrupted cities that attempted to feed it for even a single day. We are told that all previous military expeditions added together paled against the size of Xerxes's forces. But were his suspiciously precise figure of 5,283,220 men true, a column marching in file would have stretched two thousand miles, with its head reaching Thermopylae in eastern central Greece at the same time as its tail was leaving western Iran. In those days, it took some four weeks for an army to cover three hundred or so kilometers. The Persian march would have lasted months.

Herodotus's dimensions may frequently be incorrect, as are his measurements generally, but in his time no universal standards for units of distance, currency, or capacity existed. It was an age that was inexact about dates, distances, and times, so his reports may well have been above the usual standards of accuracy. As the great Italian historian Arnaldo Momigliano has written, "If we had to give an *a priori* estimate of the chances of success in writing history by Herodotus' method, we should probably shake our heads in sheer despondency."

In the end, Herodotus's failings pale beside his achievements. Early in Michael Ondaatje's novel *The English Patient,* Hana, who is nursing a mysterious burn victim in a grand, empty house, "picks up the notebook that lies on the small table beside his bed. It is the book he brought with him through the fire—a copy of *The Histories* by Herodotus that he has added to, cutting and gluing in pages from other books or writing in his own observations—so they all are cradled within the text of Herodotus," one solitary book forming the matrix for a new way of seeing.

* * *

BUT OF COURSE THERE were to be other ways. Thucydides (c. 460–c. 395 B.C.) wrote a generation after Herodotus and in contrast approached writing about the past through the lens of a high-ranking citizen-soldier—as he himself was—someone who had endured plagues (particularly the typhoid epidemic that struck Athens in 430 B.C., killing two-thirds of its residents) and witnessed shocking military defeats.

He was born in Halimous, a southwestern suburb of Athens, his father a rich landowner and his mother a Thracian aristocrat. In 424 B.C., aged about thirty-six, he was elected general, one of ten men who served as the foremost military and political leaders in Athens, then chosen to be the second of two admiral-cum-generals (a naval commander would also lead his men on land) in charge of seven warships dispatched to protect a vital stronghold in Thrace. When he lost to the dynamic Spartan Brasidas in the first decade of the Peloponnesian War, he suffered the full brunt of popular indignation—he was removed from his post and exiled for a minimum twenty years. He spent this time traveling—especially in the Peloponnesus, the mountain peninsula of southern Greece—interviewing, researching records, and collecting eyewitness accounts: "I had leisure to observe affairs more closely," he tells us curtly. He probably died in his late sixties, leaving his account in mid-sentence.

His great work *The History of the Peloponnesian Wars* records the fifth-century-B.C. struggle between Sparta and Athens, each supported by a number of smaller states, and is the first surviving example of political as well as military history. Taking up 552 pages in its 1996 English translation (edited by Robert B. Strassler and published by the Free Press), it is divided into eight books. Part I frames the first ten years of the war, from 431 to 421 B.C., and Part II, following a brief phony peace, the next decade, which saw the political weakening of democratic Athens. Seven years are left unrecorded, the work breaking off amid the disorder of the events of the twenty-first year.

In reading him, one has to get used to his impersonal high style, often involved and overwrought—"in almost impossibly difficult Greek," complains the classicist Mary Beard. "His dry parts," noted Thomas Babington Macaulay, "are dreadfully dry." Yet he can be tensely vivid. He considers causes, developments, and results, often speaking as an eyewitness, his technique in essence like a modern journalist's. For stylistic reasons, ancient historians did not commonly include these elements in their texts, but in several instances Thucydides does. A stickler for accuracy, he admits the dangers to which a historian is regularly exposed—moral bias and failures of memory, but also heedlessness and insufficient observation. The ethicist and philosopher Thomas Hobbes (1588–1679), the first to translate the *History* into English directly from the Greek, commented that while Herodotus might "delight more the ear with fabulous narrations,"

> Thucydides is one, who, though he never digress to read a lecture, moral or political, upon his own text, nor enter into men's hearts further than the acts themselves evidently guide him: is yet accounted the most politic historiographer that ever writ.

The great and the good have added to this praise. Rousseau, Jefferson, and Nietzsche were admirers, Nietzsche judging him "the grand summation, the last manifestation of that strong, stern, hard matter-of-factness instinctive to the older Hellenes." Simon Schama, in a 2010 essay, writes how Thucydides was "analytically concentrated, critically sharp; unapologetic about history as the origins of the contemporary; unsurpassed as a narrative craftsman and rhetorician." The famed Athenian orator Demosthenes (384–322 B.C.) copied out the entire *History* eight times, so that he might emulate its prose.

Thucydides seems to have developed the art of war reporting almost overnight. The first four books, covering the period before his exile, are particularly powerful and contain almost two-thirds of some forty speeches by important participants (all of them made up by Thucydides but sticking, he contends, as closely as possible to what was actually said).* These orations account for approximately a quarter of the *History*'s contents and are vital to his purpose, although there is actually more hard information in any daily edition of *The New York Times* (reckoned to contain 150,000 words, excluding advertisements) than in the entire 153,260 words that he set down.

His approach also owes something to medical treatises of the time—it is likely that he knew the principal work of Hippocrates of Kos (c. 460–c. 370 B.C.), *The Complicated Body,* remarkable for its precise observation of symptoms. Thucydides would be equally detailed, as in

---

* Something of their dramatic quality can be seen from a 1991 film, *The War That Never Ends,* a reconstruction by John Barton of Thucydides (with some interpolations from Plato), breaking off after the destruction of the Sicilian expedition. Directed by Jack Gold, the film has an exceptional cast, including Alec McCowen as Thucydides and Ben Kingsley as Pericles, as well as David Calder, Michael Kitchen, Nathaniel Parker, Bob Peck, Ronald Pickup, Sara Kestelman, Don Henderson, and Norman Rodway. It makes compelling drama.

his account of the plagues of 430 and 427 B.C., which carried off Pericles and fully a third of his fellow Athenians:

> Externally the body was not very hot to the touch, nor pale in its appearance, but reddish, livid, and breaking out into small pustules and ulcers. But internally it burned so that the patient could not bear to have on him clothing or linen even of the very lightest description; or indeed to be otherwise than stark naked. What they would have liked best would have been to throw themselves into cold water; as indeed was done by some of the neglected sick, who plunged into the rain tanks in their agonies of unquenchable thirst; though it made no difference whether they drank little or much. . . . All the birds and beasts that prey upon human bodies either abstained from touching them (though there were many lying unburied), or died after tasting them.* (2.49–50)

Thucydides's military life ended in such disappointment that we can only imagine what he suffered in terms of pain and disillusion; several commentators have speculated that he died of a broken heart (possibly like his great admirer Lord Macaulay). He saw himself as uniquely positioned to record the main events of his time and was writing in part from "that experience which is learnt in the school of danger" (1.18.27), showing the perspective of an able young company commander who cannot quite come to terms with what has happened to his beloved city. The greatness of Athens, he argued, depended on her being a democracy led by Pericles, but sound habits can be weakened through popular pressure and the constraints of war. Thucydides passed from being a democrat in his youth to a conservative in his maturity, distraught at the loss of so uniquely enlightened a ruler (2.60.5).

For all his emphasis on accuracy, however, he lets his hero worship of Pericles shape his judgment. The great leader is made out to act always in the public interest, so that, in the famous funeral speech for his fallen warriors, delivered at the end of the first year of the Peloponnesian War, we read:

---

* Daniel Defoe read Thucydides's account before embarking on his novel *A Journal of the Plague Year,* based on the outbreak in London in 1664–65. A century later, Gibbon also borrowed material for his version of the twenty-one-year plague that afflicted the Romans from A.D. 165 on.

Our constitution does not copy the laws of neighboring states; we are rather a pattern to others than imitators ourselves. Its administration favors the many instead of the few; this is why it is called a democracy. If we look to the laws, they afford equal justice to all in their private differences; if to social standing, advancement in public life falls to reputation for capacity, class considerations not being allowed to interfere with merit; nor again does poverty bar the way, if a man is able to serve the state, he is not hindered by the obscurity of his condition. The freedom which we enjoy in our government extends also to our ordinary life. There, far from exercising a jealous surveillance over each other, we do not feel called upon to be angry with our neighbor for doing what he likes, or even to indulge in those injurious looks which cannot fail to be offensive, although they inflict no real harm. But all this ease in our private relations does not make us lawless as citizens. (2.37)

While this may be wishful thinking, the quality of the writing, as with the other speeches that Thucydides created, is extraordinary; modern speechwriters should be bottle green with envy. In making up his many orations, Thucydides did not bother to make one speaker sound different from others; but then, until the last two hundred years, speeches were generally reported inaccurately, and people assumed as much. His own view was: "It proved difficult for me to report the exact substance of what was said, whether I heard the speeches myself or learned of them from others. I have therefore made the speakers express primarily what in my own opinion was called for under the successive circumstances, at the same time keeping as close as possible to the general import of what was actually said" (1.22.1).*

Seemingly, if his versions could not have the merit of exact reportage, they would at least clarify what had taken place. His priority may have been verisimilitude, but he gives himself a good deal of rope. He

---

* From 1740 on, Samuel Johnson reported speeches in the House of Commons for the influential *Gentleman's Magazine*. He simply made them up, not even bothering to go to the House. Some speeches, at least as he wrote them, were marvels of scholarly diction, and the resultant printed versions surprised even the members themselves. His custom was "to fix upon a speaker's name, then to make an argument for him, and conjure up an answer." He did this so well that Voltaire, reading the debates, exclaimed: "The eloquence of Greece and Rome is revived in the British Senate." See John Pendleton, *Newspaper Reporting* (London: Elliot Stock, 1890), p. 38.

was also confident that the events he was describing would never be paralleled. "The Peloponnesian War went on for a very long time," he writes, "and there occurred during it disasters of a kind and number that no other similar period of time could match" (1.23). But *why* had Athens failed to win these wars, conflicts from which it should have emerged victorious? Was the war truly inevitable, or might it have been avoided by better diplomacy? The city he loved came so close to primacy of the Greek world, and Thucydides seems to be saying: We reached for it, and failed, and we will never be able to attain it again. He was like a physician writing up his notes after a patient has died, admitting, "We could not save him." Sparta got between Athens and the Sun.

* * *

I HAVE GIVEN THIS chapter an adversarial title because Herodotus and Thucydides display such different characters and contrasting approaches. For both men, history was about conscious actions, consciously recorded. But Herodotus drew from other writers; Thucydides depended solely on his own research: It is impossible to imagine the Greeks not seeing a radical contrast between the two. In Schama's view, Thucydides (whom he calls "a rebarbative critic of Herodotus's playing fast and loose with the sources") gained as a historian from himself having fought in the war. "He wanted to know how it happened. Herodotus was more of a rambling wanderer, a gossip, someone who sees both myth and the importance of the minute and the incidental." Herodotus may have helped create a concept of what the activity of writing about the past could be, but Thucydides solidified (while also narrowing) the new form. He actually considers history as a discipline although pointedly does not refer to his own work as a *historia*. He detested what he saw as Herodotus's lackadaisical ways. While he never mentions his predecessor by name, he aims a well-directed blow at "the prose chroniclers, who are less interested in telling the truth than in catching the attention of their public, whose authorities cannot be checked, and whose subject-matter . . . is mostly lost in the unreliable streams of mythology" (1.21). But then a literary convention existed among ancient historians that each should pose as in some way superior to his predecessors. Maybe it still does.

Thucydides may well have been the first Western author to address

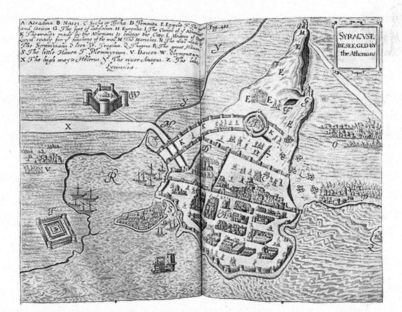

*Syracuse as besieged by Athens in 414–13 B.C., which led to the
total defeat of the Athenian army. During the siege there was a spate of
counterwalling, the Athenians trying to wall the Syracusans in
and the Syracusans building counterwalls.*

himself to posterity—unlike Herodotus, he is aware of a readership
extending beyond his own time. He is also the first to proclaim that
history should be *useful;* he wants present and future politicians to learn
from what he recorded. Perhaps in reaction to Herodotus, he mentions
virtually no informants, no divergent views. His mind stands aloof and
distant, telling us nothing of life in the cities, or of social institutions,
or women, or any work of art. There are no private motivations or il-
lustrative digressions. "The absence of romance in my history," he
writes, "will, I fear, detract somewhat from its interest" (1.22.4).[*]

In recent years, classical historians have reviewed his writing anew
and concluded that, far from being a cool and distanced historian, he
had a clear agenda, shaping his material so that readers would fall in
with his version of events. Among his most formidable commentators

---

[*] "Romance" seems a suspiciously modern label, although all current translators employ it.
Paul Cartledge, professor emeritus of Greek culture at Cambridge University, told me that the
original Greek more accurately means "the telling of stories for entertainment purposes,"
which Thucydides would have viewed with a jaundiced eye.

is the Yale classicist Donald Kagan, who in a 2009 study argued that Thucydides goes out of his way to deny that Periclean Athens was a democracy—against widespread contemporary opinion—and deliberately stacks the evidence against Cleon, the Athenian general who came to power after Pericles's death, whom he paints as a reckless and lucky madman rather than the shrewd and daring leader that events suggest he was. He claims to know what is in the minds of others (particularly the entire Athenian populace) and commonly omits such important facts as the position of leading figures in significant debates. In his handling of Nicias (c. 470–413 B.C.), the elderly general finally responsible for the disastrous Sicilian campaign, he unconvincingly paints as a hero a man whom the Athenians regarded as a cowardly ditherer.

Thucydides believed in democracy, but only when well managed, as it was when it had Pericles at the helm, a dictator in all but name. He backed the ultimate supremacy of Athens but wanted it to fight a more limited war. Once the city had embarked on its fateful clash with Syracuse, he felt that the ruling group in Athens had made fateful decisions and that Nicias was the wrong leader. He was a passionate man trying to write soberly, torn between what he wanted to believe and what he knew had taken place; yet his respect for the evidence means that one can see where his judgments go astray, by using the very accounts that he himself provides. He cannot stop himself being the accurate reporter, even when events prove him mistaken. It is a strangely conflicted performance, one that R. G. Collingwood in *The Idea of History* (1946) attributes to a bad conscience.

One consequence of Thucydides's convoluted single-mindedness is that there is a temptation to see him as a literary Octavian to Herodotus's Antony, responsible manager to risk-taking adventurer. In fact, the two historians had much in common. Both were outsiders, Herodotus's hometown being a Greek settlement that had been overrun, and Thucydides being an ex-army officer who had had to come to terms with life outside his beloved Athens. Whereas Herodotus, a born cosmopolitan, never felt that he had adequate room in an occupied city, Thucydides found himself driven into exile by his own people. Each had private means—Herodotus from his merchant father, Thucydides from family-owned gold mines in Thrace. Not only did each spend years in exile; as recorders of the recent past they faced common problems.

How, for instance, did they take in such a multitude of facts and experiences or write them down—with what, on what—lacking the help of aids they could not even name—pens, notepaper, encyclopedias, a universal calendar, almanacs? Finally, how did they garner any kind of reputation for their work?

We can answer at least some of these questions. In the West, as for the world generally, for thousands of years simply writing anything down was far from easy. The Greeks worshipped memory—literally. They had a goddess of remembering, Mnemosyne, said to have been the mother of the (usually) nine muses who inspired epic poetry, love poetry, hymns, dance, comedy, tragedy, music, astronomy—and, pertinently, history. The ordering and retention of knowledge was a vital instrument; thus learning to memorize was a way of strengthening a person's character. The Athenian statesman Themistocles supposedly learned by heart the names of twenty thousand of his fellow citizens; a contemporary of Socrates boasted of having memorized the entire *Iliad* and *Odyssey,* nearly forty thousand lines; and prisoners in Syracuse incarcerated following the Athenian expedition were allegedly rewarded with their freedom if they could sing any passage from a chorus of Euripides (one of the first writers known to have condemned slavery). Several are said to have done so, then made their way back to Athens to thank the playwright for saving their lives.

We can only guess, but Herodotus (more than Thucydides, who did not find note-taking a problem) would have been affected by these traditions, causing him to develop a memory far better than we possess today. Possibly he carried—or had an accompanying slave carry—rolls of papyrus, clay tablets, brushes, ink, although we do not know. But when he mentions by name more than 940 individuals or provides in precise detail aspects of Egypt's cultural life or the many different groups, styles of dress, and weapons of war that made up Xerxes's army, his powers of recall seem formidable.*

---

* Joshua Foer gives a good idea of what ancient memorizers might have been capable of. Some "ultra-Orthodox Jews who had memorized all 5,422 pages of the Babylonian Talmud so thoroughly that when a pin is struck through any of the Talmud's sixty-three tractates, or books, they could tell you which words it passed through on every page." See Joshua Foer, *Moonwalking with Einstein: The Art and Science of Remembering Everything* (New York: Penguin, 2011). In our own time, truck drivers struck in traffic play "air chess," while London cabbies-in-waiting must spend up to four years memorizing "The Knowledge," encompassing the locations of all twenty-five thousand streets in their city. Studies of London taxi drivers found that the navigation parts of their brains were larger than normal and contain more gray matter in the region of

Herodotus settled in Thurii, in modern-day Calabria (southern Italy), Thucydides on his Thracian estate, where he "had great influence" among the leading men of the region (4.105.1), paying soldiers from Sparta and Athens out of his own deep pockets to give him details about the war. Once either man started to draft his work, areas were set aside in which the person dictating (not necessarily the author) would read aloud to a number of scribes—certain manuscripts have repetitions in the text suggesting that the lector stammered. Thucydides wanted his words to be copied as often as possible, to gain the widest readership—although it was scholars of a much later period who decided that it would be the histories of Thucydides and Herodotus they would keep on copying. One should also remember that around 480 B.C. only at most 5 percent of Greeks could read.*

The Greek alphabet had a democratizing element in that, unlike many other scripts, no special scribe was needed to compose or read it. Dramatic works were almost impossible without it (the earliest surviving Greek tragedy, *The Persians,* by Aeschylus, composed in 472 B.C., is also the sole drama of that period based on a historical event). Greek theater flourished only when literacy was firmly established. Writing allowed prose to happen.

Then there were the implements of authorship. The Egyptians moved from prehistory to history by creating a written language and by developing a medium other than stone, brass, copper, or leaves to transcribe upon. Homer's works had been inscribed on serpent intestines; Thucydides wrote on clay fragments of wine jars. The Egyptians realized they could find a new use for the stem of the papyrus plant, a triangular reed that grew almost exclusively around the Nile delta. Its deployment goes back at least as far as the First Dynasty (3150 B.C. to

---

the hippocampus responsible for complex special representation than the brains of London bus drivers. Brain-scan results from retired drivers suggest that the volume of gray matter decreases when this ability is no longer required.

* The development of script had other advantages, although in the West, at least, in some cases it took centuries for them to show themselves. Dante, pitching it high, says in his time (1265–1321) a thousand forms of Italian existed in Italy; while William Caxton (1422–91) commented on how difficult it was to buy eggs in England, as there were so many different words for the product. Printed script stabilized language—but only to an extent. The Homilies of Aelred had to be rewritten twice in a hundred years, as so few people were literate that the "freezing" effects of written language did not operate. Of all scripts, Chinese changed least. Whether one speaks Cantonese or Mandarin, one has to write them the same even while speaking them differently. Only about 6 percent of the thousands of languages spoken in human history has ever been written down.

2890 B.C.), but from the fifth century B.C. on it served throughout the Mediterranean for building furniture as well as for baskets, boxes, rope, sandals, and boats. Now it became the prime surface for writing down what one wanted to say.

Papyrus originally meant "that which belongs to the house," its varieties and sizes often named in honor of emperors or officials. The Greeks called the plant *biblos,* from Byblos, the Phoenician seaport through which papyrus mainly passed, and which in time led to the English word *book*. Herodotus is said to have given public readings at Olympia, maybe during one of the city's festivals, but he first made a reputation in Athens, giving a series of public readings there for ten talents (the equivalent of 570 pounds of silver), probably in the agora, the gathering place that was the civic center of any Greek polis. Notices of performances were posted in public places, and the readings themselves required skill. They were recited in roofless spaces, so one had to project considerably.

It is recorded that Thucydides decided to write history after listening to Herodotus declaim (in his distinctive Ionic dialect) and when his own time came delighted in performing the speeches of his major characters; Plato's approval of these readings helped Thucydides gain posthumous celebrity, while later writers such as Quintilian and Dionysius all remarked on the dramatic power of his prose. Cicero had little time for his rhetoric, as "these famous speeches contain so many obscure and impenetrable sentences as to be scarcely intelligible, which is a cardinal sin in a public oration," but he still praised him as someone who "surpasses everyone else in dexterity of composition."*

Herodotus the traveler, who cannot resist gilding the lily, interested in everything; Thucydides the didact, who restricts his remit to a case study in war and high politics: the transformation of history tacks

---

* Thucydides's Greek was famously difficult to digest, even in his own time. So it has been down the ages. In one Sherlock Holmes story, Arthur Conan Doyle has an Oxford scholarship paper consist of a half-chapter of Thucydides, and it takes the presiding examiner fully an hour and a half just to proofread the printed sheet. See Arthur Conan Doyle, "The Three Students," *The Return of Sherlock Holmes* (London: Geoffrey Newnes, 1905), p. 227. And in Evelyn Waugh's post–World War II novella, *Scott-King's Modern Europe,* Scott-King, the graying classical master at Grantchester School, is trying to interest his charges in the Peloponnesian Wars. "After Latin gerunds they stumbled through half a page of Thucydides. He said: 'These last episodes of the siege have been described as tolling like a great bell,' at which a chorus rose from the back bench—'The bell? Did you say it was the bell, sir?' and books were noisily shut. 'There are another twenty minutes to go. I said the book tolled like a bell.'" Too late, too late. See Evelyn Waugh, *Scott-King's Modern Europe* (Boston: Little, Brown, 1949), pp. 11–12.

sometimes in the direction of one, sometimes the other. "It was once common to contrast Herodotus as a poetic tale-teller with Thucydides as scientific historian," writes the classical scholar Andrew Ford. "The difference between the mind of Herodotus and that of Thucydides is almost the difference between adolescence and maturity," is Will Durant's harsher view. But as has been well said, no college student is likely to ask his or her tutor, "Sir, if Herodotus was such a fool, why do we read him?"

Both men were part of a transformation of consciousness that we still stretch to understand. One might assume that earlier cultures thought about the past in a way that was continuous, but historical consciousness is not like that. Previous ages lacked such concentrated inquiry. The writers of the old sagas were not competing with the historical record. And while for many centuries there had been great archives—at Tel-el-Amarna, in Upper Egypt (founded by Akhenaten c. 1350–1330 B.C.), or the cuneiform (from the Latin, *cuneus,* a wedge) archive of c. 1400 B.C. at Boghazköy, some 150 miles from Ankara— they passed not into historical work but into high-level bureaucratic files and never reached the public. The first private library was probably Aristotle's, built up around 340 B.C.

Should the historian's task, as exemplified by Thucydides, be restricted to certain disciplines, in search of objective truths? Or is the true historian one engaged in pursuing an open-ended investigation, ignoring boundaries of definition? For over 2,500 years we have benefited from the tension between such questions. We should appreciate the degree of sophistication that the two men offer and the explosion of writing that followed them. But what is sometimes called "the Greek Enlightenment" happened in just a few cities of Asia Minor. Even so, during little more than two generations, Greece became *the* great creative force in mathematics, astronomy, geometry, physics, drama, rhetoric, logic, philosophy—and history (all names that derive from Greek words), starting an adventure that continued for nearly a thousand years.

CHAPTER 2

THE GLORY THAT WAS ROME

From Polybius to Suetonius

———

> One may think him bold in his relations; as where he
> [Tacitus] tells us, that a soldier carrying a burden of wood,
> his hands were so frozen and so stuck to the load that they
> there remained closed and dead, being severed from
> his arms. I always in such things bow to the authority
> of so great witnesses.
>
> —MICHEL DE MONTAIGNE, 1588

THUCYDIDES HAD NO REAL SUCCESSOR, AND WOULD NOT TILL THE DAYS of Polybius some two centuries later. Why such a gap? Perhaps recording the past seemed an exercise in humiliation: after the disasters of the Peloponnesian War, the Greeks had a sense of catastrophic unfulfilled promise. They had no wish for reminders.

Aristotle would never have called himself a historian and is explicit that, because history is empirically unverifiable, it has no proper place among the most rigorous branches of knowledge. Yet in the *Poetics* he states that writing about the past must adhere to certain aesthetic principles and carefully separates history from poetry:

> The distinction . . . is not in the one writing prose and the other
> verse—you might put the work of Herodotus into verse, and it
> would still be a species of history; it consists really in this, that
> the one describes the thing that has been, and the other a kind of
> thing that might be. Hence poetry is something more philosophic and of graver import than history, since its statements are

of the nature rather of universals, whereas those of history are singulars.

It is possible that this downgrading had its effects. A young reporter from *Newsweek* not long ago asked a Columbia University professor, "When did historians stop relating facts and start all this revising of interpretations of the past?" Around the time of Thucydides, he told her. Maybe; yet after Thucydides, while there were those who wrote about the past, the work that has survived is by lightweights. It is estimated that fewer than 20 percent of the major Greek classical writings have come down to us.

The ancient Romans fared no better. The work of Virgil's friend Gaius Asinius Pollio (d. A.D. 4) has disappeared entirely; of Sallust we have just his minor works; while what survives of both Livy and Tacitus is a fraction. The pages bearing the 116 poems of Catullus (84–54 B.C.) were saved (in part) because they had been compressed to make a plug for a wine barrel that was found in Verona during the fourteenth century. *De Architectura,* the one surviving major work on the subject, written by Vitruvius (c. 75–15 B.C.), and the only source we have for certain key battles and sieges of the period, was found on the shelf of a Swiss monastery in 1414. We know about as much of the ancient world as we might gain, say, from a badly bombed record office (this effective if unusual simile comes from the classicist A. R. Burn, writing shortly after the end of the Second World War).

There is one exception to this roster of also-rans: Xenophon (c. 430–c. 354 B.C.).* He wrote several minor works, including *Hellenica,* a history of Greece that begins at the point where Thucydides breaks off, in 411 B.C. (after Thucydides's death a rash of "continuations" and imitations broke out, a little like the Star Wars franchise), but it is dis-

---

* In her novel *Last of the Wine,* in which Xenophon is a major character, Mary Renault has fun with his love of horses, but she also provides a reading that seems uncannily accurate, judged from the personality that emerges from his writing. He is introduced to us when young as "a handsome boy, big for his age, with dark red hair and grey eyes." In adulthood, he was "every inch the old-style Athenian knight; soldierly, well-bred, the sort of cavalryman who breeds his own horse, schools and doctors it; who prides himself on being quick in war, and in talk at the supper-table, but says he has no time for politics, meaning that his politics are set and that's the end of it. . . . He was always a practical man, honourable, religious, with a set of fixed ethics, not wrong but circumscribed. Point out to such a man a clear and simple good, and he will follow it over the roughest country you like to show him. . . . He was a soldier and no fool." See Renault, *The Last of the Wine* (New York: Pantheon, 1956), pp. 16, 253–54, 373.

appointingly partisan and unreliable. His one masterpiece is *Anabasis* (the term refers to any expedition from a coastline into the interior, thus the alternative title *The March Upcountry,* or, in some translations, *The Persian Expedition*). Born into the Athenian gentry, Xenophon as a young man took part in the two-year (401–399 B.C.) campaign of the Persian prince Cyrus the Younger against his brother, Artaxerxes II. *Anabasis* recounts his time as a soldier.

The whole venture failed catastrophically when Cyrus was killed. His ten-thousand-strong army was stranded in enemy territory (modern Turkey and Iraq) and had to fight its way back to the sea. John Burrow, in his chronicle of historical writing, is rhapsodic over the adventure, describing it as "a military man's vindication of his own conduct and that of the force to which he belonged. It is an enthrallingly detailed, first-hand account. . . . Xenophon is his own hero." The moment when the troops reach the Black Sea coast at Trebizond (in northeast Turkey) is justly famous:

> When the men in front reached the summit and caught sight of the sea there was great shouting. Xenophon and the rearguard heard it and thought there were some more enemies attacking the front, since there were natives of the country they had ravaged following them up behind, and the rearguard had killed some of them and made prisoners of others in an ambush, and had captured about twenty raw ox-hide shields, with the hair on. However, when the shouting got louder and drew nearer, and those who were constantly going forward started running towards the men in front who kept on shouting, and the more there were of them the more shouting there was, it looked then as though this was something of considerable importance. So Xenophon mounted his horse and, taking Lycus and the cavalry with him, rode forward to give support, and, quite soon, they heard soldiers shouting out *Thálatta! Thálatta!* [The sea! The sea!] . . . and when they had all got to the top, the soldiers, with tears in their eyes, embraced each other and their generals and captains.

However, fine writing though this is, much of the account is special pleading. Xenophon was writing in response to two similar criticisms: that of his fellow adventurers, who questioned his motives and, after his return home, that of his peers, who charged that he had enlisted as a mercenary rather than for the rightness of the cause. Aristocrats did not fight for money; so Xenophon emphasizes his incorruptibility by distinguishing between hospitality presents—a legitimate part of *xenía*—and *dôra* (bribes). To his principal patron, Seuthes, he writes: "I have neither received anything from you that was intended for the soldiers, nor have ever asked what was theirs for my private use, nor demanded from you what you had promised me; and I swear to you that even if you had offered to pay what was due to me, I should not have accepted it unless the soldiers also were at the same time to recover what was due to them." One of the great adventure stories of the ancient world was set down as an impassioned attempt at self-justification.*

★ ★ ★

LEGEND HAS IT THAT Rome was settled in 753 B.C., when the infant twins Romulus and Remus were rescued by a she-wolf. Romulus went on to erect the first walls of the so-called Roma Quadrata, or "four-square Rome" (a transliteration of the Greek word for "strength"). Just possibly something like this may have happened, but tales of exposed infants who go on to great deeds are common in ancient mythology. *Lupa* means "she-wolf" but is also slang for "prostitute"; anyway, once they were adults the brothers quarreled, and (according to Livy) Romulus struck Remus dead, went on to found his city (-*ulus* was the Etruscan suffix denoting a founder), became increasingly autocratic, and abruptly exited history during the thirty-seventh year of his reign, swept up by a storm cloud and simply disappearing.

The Romulus and Remus myth has its parallel in the story of the wandering hero Aeneas, son of a mortal father and the goddess Venus, who was said to have founded Rome around 1184 B.C. "In order to fill the long time gap," writes the classical expert Anthony Everitt, "a catalog of totally imaginary kings . . . was cooked up to link the two legends. . . . Rome's historians . . . did not regard themselves as professional scholars but . . . tended to be unemployed members of the

---

* Other celebrated soldier leaders did make some attempt at recording their deeds. From 334 B.C. until his death in 323 B.C., Alexander the Great conquered three empires: the Egyptian, the Persian, and the Indian. His invasions were variously recorded, but no eyewitness account has survived—the history by his chosen recorder, Callisthenes, the nephew of Aristotle, was cut short when Alexander had him executed for conspiracy. And while Hannibal kept two Greek writers in his retinue to set down his triumphs, their works are lost.

ruling class." They wanted to be true to the essential truths of their history, but when "handicapped by a lack of facts they accepted legends and were not beyond filling gaps with what they felt must, even should, have happened." As the Italian saying has it, *Se non è vero, è ben trovato*—maybe it's not true, it's still a good story.

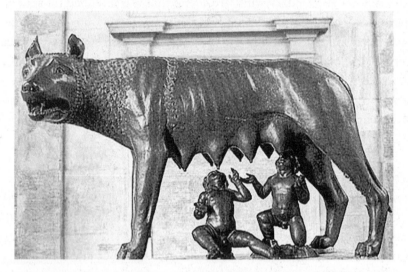

Romulus, Remus, and the wolf. The wolf is eleventh or twelfth century, while the baby twins are fifteenth-century additions, meant to promote the founding myth. Copies have spread worldwide, mainly due to Mussolini distributing them as a propaganda tool.

At the height of Romulus's power, Rome, situated at the lowest practical crossing point on the Tiber and lodged on a chain of volcanic crests in a floodplain, housed some three thousand people. It would be centuries before it produced any historian of note, for although records may have existed from earlier times, Latin literature did not get under way until the third century B.C. After Romulus, Rome's rulers were Etruscans—from Etruria, north and east of the city (modern Tuscany). Around 500 B.C. the Romans revolted and after a prolonged struggle claimed their independence, forming a republic. Its mark of authority was *Senatus Populusque Romanus,* denoting the elders and the people of Rome; the abbreviation "SPQR" still appears on manhole covers and rubbish bins.

The Gauls sacked the city in 387 B.C. It would be vandalized a further six times but continued to grow, so that by 323 B.C. it stretched almost four thousand square miles (about three times the size of Rhode Island or a bit less than the English county of Yorkshire). But Rome—unlike Greece—was a society that for half a millennium could have been taken off the map at any time. Not until its war with Pyrrhus of Epirus (280–275 B.C.) was the city to dominate the central Mediterranean. Even then it took several generations before it began to consider its role as a great naval power: Livy, writing of the days before a navy existed, tells of citizen soldiers learning to row in the sand. Nevertheless, by Trajan's reign (A.D. 98–117), "the forest of buildings that is Rome," in Ovid's phrase, hosted 1.4 million people, the largest concentration of humanity in the world, of whom one in three was a slave, one in ten a soldier. It consumed twenty-five million liters of wine and five million of olive oil every year.

At its height, Rome's spread was prodigious. In Africa, it commanded the provinces of Numidia, Mauretania, Cyrenaica, and Africa Vetus, "Old Africa." It ruled all of (fabulously wealthy) Egypt as well as the Iberian peninsula, Gaul (France), and Britain (there are Roman ruins in Scotland). It reached the frontier provinces of Germany, the lands along the natural frontier of the Danube, and not only the Greek peninsula but also much of Asia Minor. Its farthest eastern provinces included Judaea, Syria, and Mesopotamia. This colossal empire numbered 50–60 million people, all overseen by the personal relations of about a hundred men and their retinues. From shortly after its annexation, Greece became the key eastern province, and the influence of all things Hellenic was considerable, with many Greek intellectuals making the journey to Rome to pursue their careers. Rome's own elite regarded Greek as the true language of civilization, and from as early as 250 B.C. well-off parents would employ Greek-speaking teachers for their children and often spoke Greek themselves. As Horace wrote: "Once made captive, Greece captivated her captor."*

---

* Ancient Romans wrote in Latin, a formal and basically written language, but on the streets they spoke a patois, "Romanicus." There was no such thing as "popular literature" in the Roman Empire, but by the Middle Ages people wanted to read stirring stories in an idiom they could easily understand, *romanice scribere,* written in Romanic (the *-us* had been dropped by this stage). By the late thirteenth century, Dante was suggesting that this "vulgar tongue" was even more noble than Latin, for as it was that first spoken by Adam in Eden it was natural, while Latin was "artificial," and few knew how to speak it. Voltaire says that another name for the language was "Ruftica" and that it lasted till the time of Frederick II (Voltaire, *Essay on the Manners and Spirit of Nations,* vol. 1, p. 94). Not all versions of Romanic were the same, but its prevalence in Rome, France, Spain, and Romania led to it becoming the catchall term for stories about brave,

These Hellenic influences cover at least three hundred years, from 148 B.C. to A.D. 150. The first works of Latin literature appear about 240 B.C., the recording of past events some time later. The figures who turned to the writing of history were all practical men—administrators, soldiers, and politicians—who yet had time on their hands. By Nero's day, Rome had 159 public holidays a year—three a week—effectively one holiday for every day of work, itself only six hours long. No doubt for the vast majority of Roman citizens daily life was still a battle for survival and holidays were often working days, but for the privileged few there were leisure hours that gave plenty of time for writing.

Rome's historians were nearly all high achievers. To list just the eight generally taken to be the leading among them: Polybius (c. 208–c. 116 B.C.) was the son of a Greek politician and became a cavalry general. Sallust (c. 86–35 B.C.) was a tribune, provincial governor, and senator. Julius Caesar (102/100–44 B.C.) claimed descent from one of the oldest families in Rome. Livy (59 B.C.–A.D. 17) was friendly with the Julio-Claudian clan and in later life was as famous as a rock star, becoming so celebrated that one enthusiast traveled all the way from Cadiz to Rome just to see him. Josephus (37–100) was a friend of Vespasian's son Titus, while Tacitus (c. 56–c. 117) was a senator. Plutarch (46–120) became mayor of his hometown and enjoyed the rank of a former consul. Suetonius (69/75–c. 130) was favored both by Trajan, under whom he was director of the imperial archives, and Hadrian, serving as his secretary. None had to sing for their supper.

* * *

POLYBIUS IS THE FIRST on this literary map. In *The Histories,* or, as it is often titled, *The Rise of the Roman Empire,* he charted Rome's ascent over 120 years from 264 B.C., when Romans first crossed the sea, to Sicily, where they came into conflict with the Carthaginians, to the destruction of Carthage in 146 B.C.* However, the period to 241 B.C. is little

---

handsome knights and damsels in distress, and by degrees the word was changed to *romances,* and attempts to reproduce the atmosphere of such stories were soon described as *romantic.* See Mark Forsyth, *The Etymologicon: A Circular Stroll Through the Hidden Connections of the English Language* (London: Icon Books, 2011).

* "Carthage" or "Qart Hadasht" was founded by Phoenician traders, originally from Lebanon; the name means "New Town." The Romans called its inhabitants "Poeni" (a nod to the Phoenicians), from which the adjective *Punic* is derived. *Punicus* eventually came to mean "treacherous."

more than a preamble. His real subject is the half century from the outbreak of the Second Punic War (218–202 B.C.), and one of his principal
motives was to educate his fellow Greeks in the new world order, the
decline of his homeland, and Rome's rise to power. He knew there were
lands beyond the western Mediterranean, but as John Burrow says, "for
him Asia had been, as we should say, 'done.' Rome, and Rome's expansion south and east, was where world history was now in the making."

Polybius had reason to know. He was among a thousand Greek
gentry taken to Rome after the Battle of Pydna in 168 B.C. as hostages
and kept there without trial for sixteen years (167–150 B.C.). Finding a
common interest in books, he struck up a friendship with Publius
Scipio, the son of the commander of the Roman forces at Pydna, and
unlike his fellow detainees was allowed to stay on in the capital. Still
exiled from the country of his birth (as were Thucydides, Xenophon,
and, later, the Jewish historian Josephus), he was yet popular in Greece
for mediating between his countrymen and their new masters, and
when he died statues were erected in his honor in at least six cities. He
perished from a fall from his horse at the age of eighty-two. Of his
many works, which included a biography of a Greek statesman, a work
on military tactics, and a short history of his time serving under Scipio
Africanus in the twenty-year war in Spain, all that survive are from
The Histories, his forty-volume account of the Roman Republic from
264 to 146 B.C. They include the first five books, much of Book VI, and
fragments of the remaining thirty-four—but still, in translation, a
healthy five hundred pages. The original work must have been four to
five times longer than Herodotus's—history had grown. But that so
little has survived is not surprising when every copy had to be labori-
ously made by hand and writing materials were expensive.

As a recorder of the past, Polybius was a stickler for what he conceived of as the rules of his craft. "It is not a historian's business to
startle his readers with sensational descriptions," he insisted. "Nor
should he try as the tragic poets do, to represent speeches which might
have been delivered [Take that, Thucydides!]. . . . It is his task first and
foremost to record with fidelity what actually happened." Works of
history should be useful and not entertaining; Polybius rebukes previous chroniclers for exaggeration, indecent language, picaresque em-
bellishments, "gossipy chatter," playing to the reader's prejudices
(Theopompus, in describing the dissolute court of Macedon), bias (Fa-

bius and Philinus, toward Rome and Carthage, respectively), or limiting the narrative to a single theme; and since world history now had a
central subject, the rise of Rome in roughly fifty-three years (220–167
B.C.), any work unrelated to that topic was petty and parochial. Not by
accident, Thucydides is mentioned once, Herodotus not at all. "What
difference is there between us and the worst kind of scribbler?" Polybius asks. "Readers should be very attentive to and critical of historians
and constantly on their guard."

He does not start with the foundation of Rome, taking its earliest
years for granted, and centers on just the last century, and here unwit-
tingly sets himself up as the chief rival of Livy, who came more than
fifty years later and wrote about much the same time span. For Polybius, history goes in predictable cycles of power, a view he inherited
from the Hellenic theorists, and he argues that there are three types of
polity: monarchy (which is not the same as kingship, although closely
allied), aristocracy, and democracy. These in time will decay into, respectively, tyranny, oligarchy, and mob rule—a reading that was to
inform Machiavelli, Montesquieu, Gibbon, and even the Whig interpreters of history, all of whom believed in historical cycles. The most
stable constitution is one that mixes all three in healthy balance, but
that balance will always be subject to change.

Polybius shares his cyclical view of history with a number of leading commentators, including the Islamic historian Ibn Khaldūn, the
early-twentieth-century German philosopher Oswald Spengler, and
several Confucian thinkers. He is preoccupied with what causes events
(he is particularly good on weaponry and its influence on military
outcomes).* To these he adds the lessons of experience and the influence of fortune (in the form of the Greek goddess Tyche, or "Luck,"
who governed the destiny of cities), which he groups together under
the heading "Pragmatic History." Thus the historian should teach lessons and also honor "the dignity of history."

Luckily for us, this austere vision of his calling does not prevent
Polybius from including dramatic episodes; thus when Hannibal's

---

* To provide perspective: In 216 B.C., at Cannae, Hannibal's army slaughtered 50,000 Roman
troops out of some 80,000 men. In 1916, on the first day of the Somme, there were 57,000 British
casualties, most of whom survived. Unlike at Cannae, there was little killing of prisoners; fewer
than 20,000 perished outright, and the weapons they faced were German machine guns, not
Punic spears and swords.

army crosses the Alps we read about avalanches, pack animals falling over precipices, mules and horses stuck in snowdrifts, and the way-wardness of elephants. At one point, he describes Hannibal blasting away a wall of solid rock by heating it with fires and then dashing onto it gallons of raw wine. He can be ambivalent toward Rome, and in re-cording events he gives a full account of his own achievements and the great deeds of his friend and patron, Publius Scipio. His style derives from the courts of the Greek states and can be ploddingly correct. He may also at points be carping, repetitive, or numbingly sententious, but at his best he is a thrilling narrative historian.

Polybius insists that, while documentary sources have their place, to write the history of recent events one needs the testimony of "those who have played some part in affairs themselves." Telling the truth is all-important, even if it may be tempered by patriotism: "I would admit that authors should show partiality towards their own country, but they should not make statements about it that are false." The con-scientious historian should be familiar with cities, districts, rivers, har-bors, and geographical features generally (the beginning of a vital tradition in the writing of history); have experience of political life (which includes warfare); and must generally be a seasoned traveler. He himself ventured widely, "through Africa, Spain and Gaul, and voy-ages on the sea which adjoins these countries on their western side." Invited to join Scipio in North Africa, on his way back to Rome he made a detour through the Alps "to obtain first-hand information and evidence" about Hannibal's crossing seventy years before.

Although in the historian's armory he rates such practical experi-ence above the study of documents, it is clear that he had access to memoirs and records besides archives and inscriptions, through which we know he diligently combed. In the years when he was writing, there were libraries in more than a hundred cities throughout Italy. No one can say for certain when they originated, although archives—collections of records, rather than of written works per se—existed in both Egypt and Babylon before 3000 B.C. and institutions that we would call libraries before 2000 B.C. As Mary Beard notes, such places

> are not simply the storehouses of books. They are the means of organizing knowledge and . . . of controlling that knowledge and restricting access to it. They are symbols of intellectual and

political power, and the far from innocent focus of conflict and opposition. It is hardly for reasons of security that so many of our great libraries are built on the model of fortresses.

What is taken into libraries and what gets kept there are political even more than literary decisions. By Polybius's time, Rome had a considerable literature; its first public library was created in 39 B.C. Augustus built two more, while controlling their contents—he removed the works of Julius Caesar and Ovid. Later, Caligula banned Virgil and Livy from all public book collections, simply because he didn't like them. By the fourth century Rome had eleven public baths, twenty-eight libraries—and forty-six brothels.

Because literary texts could be copied without penalty (the first copyright law in any country was the British Statute of Anne in 1710), corrupted texts often circulated more readily than originals. All this was important for historians, since writing tends to canonize knowledge. Even allowing that in the ancient world a "book" roughly corresponded to a chapter in a modern volume, for centuries no private citizen had more than a small library.* Dancing through the centuries, we know that Chaucer (1343–1400) owned just forty books and Leonardo da Vinci (1452–1519) thirty-seven, although Ben Jonson (1572–1637) had some two hundred. In Rome, one went to the large public collections or one borrowed. In short, Polybius might have had to cast around, but most of what he wanted to read was available to him.

* * *

Why would the historian who is following faithfully every least detail of the account that was given to him be guilty? Is it his fault if the characters, seduced by passions which he does not share, unfortunately for him, lapse into profoundly immoral actions?

This is not Sallust but Stendhal, in *The Charterhouse of Parma*. The sentiments of the two men are identical, and Sallust could well have

---

* It was possible to write two thousand "books" in one lifetime. Marcus Terentius Varro (116–27 B.C.), who supported Pompey against Caesar and was put to work as a librarian after his troops deserted him, wrote some 490 chapters, and his vast *Nine Books of Disciplines* became a model for encyclopedists. After the fall of the Roman Empire, the move from Egyptian papyrus to locally prepared animal skins changed the shape of books from square to rectangular, for the simplest reason: Most mammals are oblong.

written them. Caius Sallustius Crispus—Sallust—is the first known Roman whose works about the past survive: two extended essays on near-contemporary history, *The Conspiracy of Catiline* (about the attempted overthrow of the government by the demagogic ruined aristocrat in 63 B.C.) and *The Jugurthine War* (covering the corrupt late Republic's war against Numidia—roughly modern-day northern Algeria—from 112 to 106 B.C.), and the larger *Histories* (of which little survives), Rome's history from 78 to 67 B.C. Tacitus admired him, while Quintilian preferred him as a historian to Livy, even putting him on a par with Thucydides—a remarkable reputation to rest on two short monographs about events that were dramatic but not really significant, and a history of Rome of which we have but five hundred fragments—a congregation of just seventy-five paragraphs.

Sallust was born about sixty miles northeast of Rome, and after a wild youth embarked on a political career. He led some of Caesar's forces during the war against Pompey and aided in the defeat of Caesar's opponents in Africa. For this, Caesar helped restore him to the Senate, where he became praetor in 47 B.C., and made him governor of Numidia, which is where he encountered the stories of Jugurtha's rebellion against Rome. Although accused of extortion during his governorship, Sallust always sidestepped trial and remained fabulously wealthy. After Caesar's assassination, he retreated from public life, devoting himself to writing. He may have been bitter at his removal from political power, but he had the satisfaction of marrying Cicero's ex-wife, Terentia, who had been given a large dowry, including two tenement blocks in Rome as well as a forest and a large farm on its outskirts.

Colin Wells wittily describes Sallust as "an Ian Fleming trying to pass as a Graham Greene," pretending to a strict code of ethics but being fundamentally frivolous. That is hardly just. In his first book, he was writing only twenty years after Catiline's attempted coup, and his depiction of the conspirators shows him appalled at the moral decline of his city. But while he castigates his protagonist's actions (fair enough: Catiline was said to have killed his own son just to curry favor with his mistress), Sallust allows him several noble qualities too.

The Jugurthine War goes back to an earlier time, 111–105 B.C., but one still in living memory; the book concerns an African king of the province Sallust himself had governed. Jugurtha, a client ruler who had set himself against Rome, faced a succession of consuls and commanders sent to quell him, but he simply bribed them all into repeated truces. At last he was summoned to present himself in the Forum but was protected from the fury of the people by one of the tribunes, whom he had also bought off. Ordered to leave Rome by the Senate, he turned to look back at the urban landscape and famously said, "Yonder is a city put up for sale, and its days are numbered if it finds a buyer." However, by this time Gaius Marius, a general of real probity, had been put in command against him, and Jugurtha was taken captive, paraded through the capital as part of Marius's triumph, then strangled.

Sallust employs this unedifying story as further evidence of the erosion of standards but does so in a style very different from that of his contemporaries. His model is Thucydides, whom he imitates, sometimes becoming willfully obscure, although overall his narrative is lucid and dramatic and his denunciations of corruption impressive. However, he was not so dedicated a chronicler or didactic a critic as the next historian to chart Rome's history, the author known to us as Livy.

* * *

"LATIN IS A RATHER chunky language," says the polymath Daniel Mendelsohn. A page of it "can look like a wall of bricks." When I was at school, Titus Livius Patavinus was my regular homework, the author of thickets of impenetrable paragraphs, the constructor of ablative absolutes, of datives and vocatives and accusatives everlasting. It is odd to read him now as one of the great historians. He was born in 59 B.C., the year of Caesar's first consulate, and died in A.D. 17, at Patavium (Padua), the second-wealthiest city in the Italian peninsula, well known for its conservative values. He expresses deep affection for his hometown, although he mostly lived in Rome. Despite holding republican sympathies, he was a familiar of Augustus and a good friend to Emperor Claudius, whom he tutored and encouraged to write history.*

---

* Claudius (10 B.C.–A.D. 54) was a prolific author. Besides a history of Augustus's reign (forty-one volumes), his works included an Etruscan history (twenty volumes), a Carthaginian history (eight volumes), an Etruscan dictionary, a book on dice-playing, a defense of Cicero, and an autobiography (another eight volumes). He proposed adding three new letters to the Latin alphabet, two of which served the function of the modern w and y. He also tried to put dots between successive words, since classical Latin was written without spacing. According to Suetonius, he even issued an edict promoting unrestrained farting at table as a health measure. Unfortunately, none of his writings survives, even in part.

Livy seems to have devoted his life to writing, and his *Ab Urbe Condita* ("From the Founding of the City") covered nearly eight centuries and consisted of an amazing 142 books. These were known as "decades": ten of them could fit into an early manuscript book (a rough calculation suggests that the entire work would have filled some two dozen crown-octavo volumes of three hundred pages each). Of the completed works thirty-five remain, plus synopses of the rest. What survives, less than a quarter, ends in 167 B.C., over a hundred years before Livy's birth. The missing volumes would have covered the first Punic War, the troubled times of the Gracchi, the days of Cato and the third Punic War, as well as the wars of Pompey, Caesar, Anthony, and Augustus—major subjects, so a major loss.*

However, what remains confirms how far the writing of history had evolved: It was now a narrative of the past, remote or recent, and increasingly with a focus on the political and military. Unlike Sallust or Cicero, Livy was writing at the climax of Rome's transformation from republic to center of an empire, and he believed implicitly in its own greatness. Unusually for a Roman historian, he was not active in politics. He viewed one-man rule as a necessary evil and was capable of criticizing Augustus ("the one to be revered"), although he withheld publication of the books that dealt with the civil wars and Augustus's rise to power until after the emperor's death, a wise move.

A crucial goal was to contrast the greatness of early Rome with the moral decline he saw about him—not so different from others who chronicled the city's past. Livy drew on a wide range of sources without being particularly concerned about their accuracy, just as he concentrated on key speeches of his main protagonists, often making up the words he gave them (although, unlike Thucydides, he tried to ensure that the orations reflected the character of the speaker). He relied

---

* During the early Middle Ages Livy was not much read, but he was to become a central figure of the Renaissance, during which it was learned that his manuscripts were no longer complete and collectors exchanged large sums of money to acquire them. The poet Antonio Beccadelli (1394–1471), for example, sold his country home to purchase a single composition. Both Petrarch (1304–74) and Pope Nicholas V (1397–1455) initiated searches for the missing books, and myths grew up about where they might be. Only clever forgeries were ever detected; as recently as 1924, a reputed Livy scholar announced that he had located a complete copy of *Ab Urbe Condita,* including the ten lost books, in the cranny of an ancient monastery. Alas, it was one more hoax. See *The Daily Princetonian,* vol. 45, no. 98, October 6, 1924. *Punch* at once published an article by the humorist A. P. Herbert that protested, on behalf of the Amalgamated Society of Schoolboys, Past, Present and Future, against the finding of any more Livy tomes.

entirely on the work of other historians, confident that he could write his story better and to greater purpose. He composed the definitive history of Rome in a way that no one before him had quite managed while also supplying a repertoire of folklore, from the she-wolf's suckling of Romulus and Remus on to the Rape of the Sabine Women and Horatius at the Bridge, almost as rich a line of legends as Greek mythology or the Bible.

We get nearly all our human-interest stories of Rome's early days from Livy: legendary tales of Roman patriotic heroism and self-sacrifice. Accounts of prodigies and supernatural occurrences appear repeatedly; he takes note of (even as he withholds belief in) weeping statues; downpours of blood, stones, or meat; monstrous births; and a talking cow. Livy is part tabloid journalist, and an unrepentant one: "So much license we concede to antiquity by mingling human agency with divine to render the foundation stories of cities more venerable."

Exceptional events aside, he was essentially a literary artist applying himself to history, not a formal scholar—the Spanish rhetorician Quintilian (A.D. 35–100) would characterize his prose as exhibiting *lacteal ubertas*—"milky richness"—so for instance in describing the war with Hannibal, while leaning heavily on Polybius, he writes up what took place in just that picturesque way his predecessor hated. Sometimes he puts down events, one feels, just because they are there in the record book, as if he were only an annalist, but it is rarely long before we are in the midst of some action-filled story. Here are Hannibal's men, making their way on the Apennines, facing the elements:

> Heavy rain and a violent wind right in their faces made progress impossible; they could not hold their weapons, and, if they tried to struggle on, the wind spun them round and flung them off their feet. The strength of it made it impossible to breathe, so all they could do was to turn their backs to it, crouching on the ground. Then the sky seemed to burst in a roar of sound, and between the horrific thunderclaps lightning flashed. They were blinded and deafened and benumbed with terror. (12.58)

In his preface Livy says he wants, even more than historical accuracy, to instruct his readers about the conduct and men they should imitate. The symptoms of decay he inveighs against range from foreign luxuries to the lack of respect shown to parents but also take in bedspreads and sideboards and female lute players, while "the cook, who had been to the ancient Romans the least valuable of slaves, and had been priced and treated accordingly, began to be highly valued, and what had been a mere service came to be regarded as an art" (39.6). He makes it clear that his purpose is not only to set down Rome's history:

> Here are the questions to which I should have every reader give his close attention: what life and morals were like; through what men and by which policies, in peace and in war, the empire was established and enlarged. Then let him note how, with the gradual relaxation of discipline, morals first subsided, as it were, then sank lower and lower, and finally began the downward plunge which has brought us to our present time, when we can endure neither our vices nor their cure.

This is typically pessimistic, but then Livy saw the past as morally and intellectually superior to his own time. Yet one should not think of him as rueful. Most of the time, he was anything but—as in his description of the flute players of Rome, who in 311 went on strike. They had been forbidden to hold their annual banquet, a privilege they had enjoyed for decades, since Rome was in the middle of a war. Highly indignant, they set off in a body for Tibur, a town some twenty miles east-northeast of Rome, leaving no one to play at a number of important religious ceremonies there. The Senate was desperate and called on the people of Tibur to help. Since it was a feast day, the local citizens invited the musicians to their houses, where they plied them with food and wine—especially wine, "of which players as a class are extremely fond." Soon the flautists were drunkenly asleep. Seizing their chance, the townsfolk loaded them onto improvised carts and drove them back to Rome, dumping them in a heap in the Forum. When the next morning the musicians awoke, feeling considerably the worse for wear, they found themselves surrounded by a large crowd, which urged them to play. And so they did—being rewarded by the Senate with the privilege of parading through the city on three days every year, dressed in fancy clothes and free from restraint. Everybody won.

* * *

IF HISTORY WAS NOW firmly a branch of literature, the story of Josephus would seem to belong to the realm of fiction. In A.D. 66, well into the period of recorded history, the Palestinian Jews revolted against their Roman masters. Josephus, then called Yosef Ben Matityahu, was a Jewish scholar, a priest, and a Pharisee, a cautious moderate who had little sympathy with the rebellion, but when the Jews drove the Romans out of Jerusalem, he accepted command of the northern region of Galilee. Emperor Nero called upon Vespasian, who had been a successful officer in the conquest of Britain, to suppress the uprising.

A large Roman force, some sixty thousand men, invaded the territory, and after the second bloodiest battle of the revolt Josephus and his troops were forced to withdraw to the fortress at Yodfat, in lower Galilee, where for the next forty-seven days they were besieged. Hiding with forty of his men, Josephus was discovered by Vespasian's soldiers. A young man of twenty-nine, he wanted to surrender, but his men said a more honorable course was a suicide pact. Josephus argued that suicide was a detestable act and suggested instead that they draw lots to kill each other. And so it was agreed.

As their commander, Josephus supervised the ballot, seeing to it that he was one of the last remaining. In his own words in the history he wrote of the rebellion, "he counted the numbers cunningly and so managed to deceive all the others." One by one the men dispatched each other, until—"shall we put it down to divine providence or just to luck?"—only a single other soldier was left. Josephus persuaded him that a life in captivity was not the worst option, and they gave themselves up. After being taken prisoner by the Romans, Josephus claimed to have experienced a vision and prophesied that Vespasian would become emperor. Viewed as a possible diviner, he was kept alive, as a hostage and slave. Two years later, in A.D. 69, when Vespasian became ruler of all Rome, he recalled Josephus's forecast and granted him his freedom. Josephus, for his part, took on the emperor's family name, outlived three (Jewish) wives, and became a counselor and translator to Vespasian's son Titus.

Flavius Josephus, as he now was known, proceeded to write the history of the uprising, *The Jewish War* (both Vespasian and Titus are said to have vetted the text), and then *Jewish Antiquities,* a long précis of the

Hebrew Bible, with multiple additions and omissions. Together the books make up the first authoritative Jewish secular history covering over two centuries, from the Maccabees who had led an earlier revolt against Rome to the *sicarii* or "dagger men" who assassinated collaborators and the razing of Jerusalem under Titus, all created for the benefit of a non-Jewish, Greek-speaking audience. "No destruction ever wrought by God or man," he wrote, "approached the wholesale carnage of this war," and the details he gives of the atrocities of these years rival the horrors depicted by other historians of earlier savagery among the ancients.

Part of Josephus's motivation was to refute the charge that he was a collaborator and to explain that he had simply made the best of his chances. He portrays himself as a fearless and effective general whose capture by the Romans was generally regarded as a national disaster. But he is also keen to explain his people's laws and customs to the Greek-speaking part of the Roman Empire (*The Jewish War* was first written in Aramaic, his own language, and only later translated into Greek). Josephus says little about Jesus or the early Christians (so little,

Flavius Josephus, originally the Jewish rebel leader Yosef ben Matityahu, kneeling before the Emperor Vespasian, who is about to grant him his freedom. Had he not made one of history's luckiest guesses, providing the future Roman emperor a patina of legitimacy, he would have been shipped off to Nero, and almost certain death.

in fact, that Christian scribes later inserted passages to supply details they thought should be included), but he does provide a valuable supplementary history to the events of the New Testament.

When in the summer of 2013 I visited Jerusalem for the first time, the writings of Josephus were everywhere—on museum captions and stone signs, in local handouts and in all the history books. I toured the fortress of Masada, site of another of the great legends of twentieth-century Zionism, and listened as our guide quoted Josephus's account of his earlier escape from what seemed certain death. The guide ended: "Who wouldn't have chosen survival, given the chance? And who wouldn't want to be thought a hero?" We all nodded, imagining ourselves besieged, desperately living out what we believed to be our final moments. But little wonder Mary Beard dubs Josephus "the luckiest traitor ever."

* * *

HE HAS BEEN CALLED Rome's greatest historian, the most acute analyst of the autocratic rule of its emperors. His actual last name means "silent," yet Publius Cornelius Tacitus was a formidable and highly articulate orator and an outspoken author of several books. Born around A.D. 56 somewhere in the northern provinces, he was a boy in the time of Nero and spent his early career in public affairs. His father was probably an equestrian official and chief financial officer of Belgic Gaul, thus near the top of Roman society, although not an aristocrat. The equestrian order was like a club, entry to which was tied to personal wealth. Its members had many special privileges, although these were not quite as extensive as those of the senatorial class.

Tacitus himself was a praetor by the time he was thirty, was promoted to the Senate, then, after four years away from Rome with his new wife, the daughter of a consul, became consul. He was thus one of the two leading magistrates in the city, commanding the army and presiding over the Senate. He achieved particular celebrity in A.D. 100, when, working alongside his friend Pliny the Younger he successfully prosecuted a proconsul under Nero for bribery and extortion. Tacitus might have risen even higher, but he ended his public life as governor of what is now modern Turkey. "Over the course of a glittering career," writes Tom Holland, he had "demonstrated a canny, if inglorious, instinct for survival." As emperors did terrible things, he "opted to keep his head down, his gaze averted." But he was to make up for that conservatism once he took to writing history.

The year after his consulship, Tacitus published two short books: *Agricola,* a biography-cum-eulogy of his late father-in-law, governor of Britain (the earliest reference to London by name is by Tacitus), and the *Germania,* a treatise of some thirty pages on the Germanic peoples that catered to the tastes of educated Romans, who at the time were keenly interested in the independent tribes of Germany and their army's campaigns against them. For Tacitus the books were good first subjects on which to hone his writing skills. Agricola himself never comes entirely to life, there is little anecdotal material, and the military campaigns are roughly drawn—Tacitus, who probably never visited Germany, has often been described as an unmilitary historian. But the incisive judgment that distinguishes his later work is there already; after outlining Agricola's measures to promote the Romanization of Britain, Tacitus comments: "Our style of dress was admired and the toga became fashionable. Little by little they lapsed into those allurements to vice, the public lounge, the bath, the eloquent banquet. In their ignorance they called it culture, when it was part of their enslavement." With his father-in-law in mind he gives us this epigram: "Even under bad rulers there can be great men." And the words put into the mouth of a British chieftain about his Roman occupiers famously read: "They rob, kill and plunder all under the deceiving name of Roman Rule. They make a desert and call it peace."

Tacitus went on to write much more polished works: a treatise on rhetoric, *Dialogus de Oratoribus; The Histories,* from the fall of Nero in A.D. 68 and the accession of Tiberius through the "Year of the Four Emperors" (A.D. 68–69: Galba, Otho, Vitellius, and Vespasian), ending with the death of Domitian in A.D. 96; and, more than a decade later, a history that has been known since the sixteenth century as *The Annals,* from the death of Augustus to Claudius, breaking off mid-sentence in A.D. 66. Overall, more than half *The Annals* has been lost, including the middle section that deals with the mad emperor Caligula.

As with Livy, Tacitus is keen to provide moral lessons:

It is no part of my purpose to set forth every motion that was made in the Senate, but only such as were either honorable or especially disgraceful in their character. For I deem it to be the chief function of history to rescue merit from oblivion, and to hold up before evil words and evil deeds the terror of the reprobation of posterity.

He seems uninterested in the long rhetorical flourishes of oral recitation and is more concerned with reaching the private reader. He has few settled ideas in philosophy or religion and his writing has inconsistencies, although his continuing fondness for epigrams rivals Herodotus: "Once killing starts, it is difficult to draw the line"; "The desire for glory clings even to the best men longer than any other passion"; "The more numerous the laws, the more corrupt the government"; "Benefits are acceptable, so long as it seems possible to repay them; when they exceed that point, hatred takes the place of gratitude." The balanced rhythm of this final aphorism has something of Samuel Johnson in it.

In his later books, Tacitus was writing about the civil wars of his own time, and his descriptions of human suffering combine fascination, disgust, and an almost cinematic sweep. In A.D. 9, three Roman legions had been lured into Teutoburg Forest (now Lower Saxony), where they were ambushed by the young German hero Arminius. Five years later, another Roman army, this time under Germanicus, visited the site:

> The scene lived up to its horrible associations. . . . A half-ruined breastwork and shallow ditch showed where the last pathetic remnant had gathered. On the open ground were whitening bones, scattered where men had fled, heaped up where they had stood and fought back. Fragments of spears and of horses' limbs lay there: also human heads, fastened to tree trunks. In groves nearby were the outlandish altars at which the Germans had massacred the Roman officers.

Despite such passages, Tacitus is not really interested in the Roman Empire at large ("my chronicle is quite a different matter from histories of early Rome") and focuses on the private lives of the emperors, on the court and its intrigues, and on the governing class to which he belonged. At the beginning of *The Annals,* he declares that he plans to write "unmoved, as I have no reason to be moved, by either hatred or partiality." The truth is different, and in *The Histories* his distaste for

Domitian, to whom he admits he owed in part his own advancement, is obvious; one of the emperor's enthusiasms, he tells us, was stabbing flies with a sharpened stylus. Tacitus's portraits of Tiberius (of whose

A modern image of Tacitus, who records Emperor Tiberius as saying: "Marble monuments, if the verdict of posterity is unfriendly, are mere neglected sepulchers." Literally, monuments means reminders. In A.D. 109, Pliny the Younger wrote: "A monument is money wasted. My memory will live on if my life has deserved it."

final years he has scarcely a good word), Claudius, and Nero are close to caricature, so strong are his feelings. After the death of Tiberius he sums up:

> His character passed through like changes to his fortunes. Admirable in conduct, and in high esteem, while in a private station, or filling commands under Augustus; dark and artful in affecting virtue, so long as Germanicus and Drusus lived, he presented the same mixture of good and evil until his mother died. Then came a period of fiendish cruelty, but masked libertinism, during the days when he loved and feared Sejanus: until at last, freed from all fears, lost to all shame, he broke out in wickedness and wantonness alike, and showed himself in no character but his own.

Rousing stuff, only contradicted by other accounts that attest to Tiberius being conscientious to the last and hold that the frenzied orgies and reign of terror that Tacitus later describes never took place. But his is the source one remembers, with its lurid detailing of Tiberius having his testicles licked by young boys or having the children of Rome's great families "perform multiple couplings in front of him." In many of his pen portraits, he is a skillful psychologist, and yet he conceived of character as static and unchangeable, so the view that Tiberius ended his reign a dictator obliges him to assume the emperor was vicious from the first. At other times he can see that moral decay is a process, often taking years; it was the emperors he could not forgive. They fail to cope with their scheming, murderous wives; their junior ministers wheedle and connive; and the blood-crazed mob that makes up the imperial army disposes of emperors and laws alike with impunity. By A.D. 68, not a single descendant of Augustus was still alive.

Tacitus had great descriptive powers, especially when writing of war. He was an unceasing moralist, even if it was easy to make a stand against a court characterized by "unprecedented agitation and terror . . . cruel orders, unremitting accusations, treacherous friendships, envy, sloth, corruption, bloodlust, flattery, stupidity, malevolence, and sexual excess." Overall he exhibits a zeal for truthful presentation and a sifting of evidence; yet success did not arrive overnight. Pliny the Younger may have been so certain that Tacitus's histories would last through the centuries that he pleaded with him to be mentioned in them, but historians of the later imperial years hardly mention him, and he was little read before the fourteenth century, in part because of the Christian antipathy toward a writer regarded as pagan. *The Annals* and *The Histories* survived the Middle Ages each in but a single manuscript, *The Annals* in an incomplete and badly damaged copy.

However, the accolades were about to pour in. Gibbon acclaimed Tacitus as the model "philosophical historian." Machiavelli states in *The Prince* that reading *The Annals* and *The Histories* opened his eyes to the amorality of power. Stendhal refers over fifty times to Tacitus in his novels and read him on his deathbed. Jefferson loved him above all other ancient historians, writing to his granddaughter, "Tacitus I consider the first writer in the world without a single exception." Simon Schama even for a time used "Tacitus99" as part of his email address.

Yet he was and remains controversial, much being made of his claim that the German tribes were racially unmixed, "a people of their own, pure and like no other." *Germania,* which so praised their simple virtues, became a literary source for the German Protestants' revolt against Catholicism in the sixteenth century and, far less sympathetically, for

German nationalism in the nineteenth and twentieth. Critics have charged that Tacitus was anti-Semitic, and in our own time his books have been banned in eastern Europe. The Stanford classics professor Christopher Krebs, in *A Most Dangerous Book,* describes how the Nazis would extol *Germania* as "a bible," a "golden booklet," signal proof of Germany's glorious antiquity. Heinrich Himmler, exulting in the portrayal of ancient Germans as free-spirited warriors, wrote the foreword to a 1943 edition of the book. The Third Reich was infamous, however, in distorting the messages of writers to suit their propaganda. It is enough to conclude that for nearly two thousand years Tacitus has exerted a profound influence.

* * *

ROME IS ALMOST CERTAINLY the most written-about city in human history, but two other historians during this period are worth mentioning—Plutarch (A.D. 46–120), who professed himself "not really interested in history," yet was Shakespeare's main source for his Roman plays (the famous description of Cleopatra in her barge is taken almost word for word from Plutarch); and Suetonius (A.D. 69–c. 130), whose racy accounts were possibly the origin for Robert Graves's *I, Claudius.*

Plutarch came from a town in Boeotia in central Greece, a provincial backwater, and his command of Latin was variable—he felt unable, he wrote, to appreciate "the beauty of the Roman style and its quickness, and the figures of speech and the rhythms." His output was vast, at least 227 titles, including essays whose subjects ranged from "The Face in the Moon" to "On Praising Oneself Inoffensively." His aim was to have his cake and eat it—to entertain and to instruct. He believed that history is shaped by the deeds of great men alone, and his *Lives of the Noble Graecians and Romans,* commonly shortened to *Parallel Lives* or *Plutarch's Lives,* consists of twenty-three biographical pairings of famous men (as well as four unpaired individual lives and an additional set of four) and spreads itself over the whole of antiquity from Aeneas down to Augustus, although nearly a third is devoted to men who flourished in the middle decades of the first century B.C., all of whom knew one another well: Pompey, Crassus, Cato, Caesar, Brutus, Antony, and Cicero (who gets paired with Demosthenes). Plutarch's object was to bring out the moral character of his subjects, and

*The third volume of a 1727 edition of Plutarch's biographies of
famous Greeks and Romans. Two "lives" are lost to us, and the
surviving forty-six are in pairs, one Greek and one Roman.*

he often looked to the writing or speaking style of his chosen figures
for clues about their personalities. As he explained his method:

> For it is not histories we are writing, but Lives. Nor is it always
> the most famous actions that reveal a person's good or bad qual-
> ities; a clearer insight into character is often given by a small
> thing or a word or a jest than by engagements where thousands
> die, or the biggest of pitched battles, or the sieges of cities.

The great Dutch humanist Erasmus was to liken the results to "a
most exquisite mosaic work." But although the portraits can sometimes be psychologically complex, Plutarch had little interest in accurate research or keeping faith with his sources—surprisingly, in that he
was a dedicated hunter of old manuscripts. Nonetheless, his biographies are highly readable, and his ideas about Roman republican virtue
were taken up enthusiastically in late-eighteenth-century France:
Charlotte Corday spent the morning before she stabbed Marat reading

the bloodiest sections of the *Lives*. Plutarch can also be wittily playful, as in his *Quaestiones Romanae*:

Question 49: Why did those canvassing for office do so in togas without the tunic?

Question 55: Why do flute-players walk about the city on the Ides of January dressed as women?

Question 87: Why do they part the hair of brides with the point of a spear?

Question 93: Why, in augury, do they use vultures more than any other bird?

Plutarch's contemporary Suetonius, like Tacitus's father, belonged to the equestrian order, so was of a reasonably high social standing. His most influential surviving work is a set of biographies of twelve Roman rulers from Julius Caesar to Domitian, entitled *De Vita Caesarum,* or *The Twelve Caesars*. Each of the twelve accounts receives the same treatment: what the ruler looked like, omens, his family history, quotations from or about him, then the narrative of his life. Reading him is fun (an obsessive characterizer, he describes Vespasian as habitually wearing the expression of "someone straining on the lavatory"),* but one believes everything he writes at one's peril. Since his span was roughly the same as Tacitus's, the two were often compared, and in the years

---

* Suetonius is full of such anecdotes—a word that comes from the controversial Greek historian Procopius (500–565), meaning "the unpublished," since in his—much later—time, under the rule of Justinian, it was not possible to publish some material, certainly not the savage, dubious memoirs that he penned about his emperor and his circle. He would attribute natural disasters, such as earthquakes, to Justinian's private conduct, while the Empress Theodora was, in his account, sex-obsessed, a harlot (which she had indeed been in her early years), and guilty of murder as well as infanticide. Theodora "had an attractive face and a good figure, but was short and pallid . . . to her bodily needs she devoted quite unnecessary attention, though never enough to satisfy herself. She was in a great hurry to get into her bath and very unwilling to get out again. . . ." Procopius wrote two other genuinely important works, *History of the Wars* and *The Buildings,* but the *Secret History* (*Anekdota*), discovered in the Vatican Library in 1623, accorded him far greater fame. He remains the only ancient historian whose work we possess to have published an account of a living emperor's reign, and which charts the transition from the ancient to the medieval world. See Averil Cameron, *Procopius and the Sixth Century* (Berkeley: University of California Press, 1985), p. 8.

after their deaths Suetonius was the more popular (he is our main source for the lives of Caligula and Claudius, and among other details was the first to record Julius Caesar's epilepsy).

While it is true that Suetonius set out to use the imperial archives to uncover eyewitness accounts, shortly after he began his research he was refused access and had to rely on other evidence, mainly gossip and fellow historians. A number of his lost or incomplete works concern culture and society—the Roman Year, the names of seas, or *On Famous Courtesans*—but we know about them only through others' writings. Given the years he covers, it is interesting that there is a reference—just one—to a figure Suetonius names "Chrestus," while in his biography of Nero he mentions a sect known as Christians.

* * *

IN *A GLOBAL HISTORY OF HISTORY*, Daniel Woolf argues that, under the Romans, history became moral teaching by examples; but it was surely so under the Greeks as well, who like their Roman successors had little to say about social matters, the status of women, or economic development and instead concentrated on political and military affairs. Nevertheless, writing about the past did develop in these years. The approach of the Romans raises important new questions: How does one distinguish between a sense of the past and history? When did the former develop into organized history, not just memory and tradition? And when does history become a matter of a conscious interrogative spirit? Such questions are more pertinent as the writing of past events became more purposeful: history as testament. It is time to consider the historians of the Bible.

CHAPTER 3

HISTORY AND MYTH

Creating the Bible

———

Remember the days of old; consider the generations
long past. Ask your father and he will tell you, your elders,
and they will explain to you.

—DEUTERONOMY 32:7

Bibles laid open, millions of surprises. . . .

—GEORGE HERBERT, 1633

THE BIBLE IS NOT ONLY THE BESTSELLING BOOK OF ALL TIME, IT IS THE
bestseller of the year, every year—in John Updike's words, "the world's
bestseller." In a typical twelve months, North Americans alone purchase some twenty-five million Bibles—twice as many as the most successful Harry Potter adventure. Ninety-one percent of U.S. households
own at least one copy; the average home owns four. There are more
than five hundred translations of the Bible—itself a translation—just
in English, with special editions for members of the LGBTQ+ community, for surfers and skateboarders, for recovering addicts and even
a superheroes version for children.

Bible comes from the Greek *biblia*, possibly derived from the Leba-
nese coastal town of Byblos, from which Egyptian papyrus was exported to Greece. It means "little books," for this most daunting of
texts is an anthology, written by more than forty authors, in three different languages, on three different continents over twelve hundred
years, like the formation of geological strata. It is generally understood

to comprise sixty-six books, although that is a simplification, as the Hebrew Bible, the Tanakh, has twenty-four; the Protestant churches include thirty-nine books in the Old Testament, but Roman Catholics accept forty-six; the Eastern Orthodox have forty-eight to fifty, depending on the tradition or church; and although the New Testament is usually fixed at twenty-seven books, well over a hundred further gospel accounts have varying claims to be included. As the Bible customarily appears, it contains poetry, an anthology of often disjointed inspirational stories, law, prophecy, wildly beautiful flights of imagination, and history—*The Song of Deborah,* for instance, which predates both *The Iliad* and *The Odyssey,* was an actual war chant rooted in real events.

The Bible refers to many different peoples who mixed on the lands it describes: Canaanites, Hittites, Amorites, Perizzites, Hivites, Girgashites, Jebusites, as well as Philistines, the Phoenicians to the north, Syrians along the eastern borders, then Ammon, Moab, and Edom to the south. From the twelfth century B.C. on, the most numerous were the Israelites, while the land (the size of Wales or Maine) was a trade route between Africa and Asia. The Old Testament was put together, mainly in Hebrew, largely between the eighth and fourth centuries B.C.; the Books of Wisdom and the Maccabees were both composed in the second century B.C., while the first book of the New Testament was probably 1 Thessalonians, written around A.D. 50. The last book is Revelation, said to be the work of St. John of Patmos, produced during the reign of Domitian (A.D. 81–96).

To our modern eyes, the Old Testament alone provides a host of contradictions and impossible events. As a headline in the satirical newspaper *The Onion* had it, "Slight Inconsistency Found in Bible." It also plagiarizes from the Code of Hammurabi, the 282 laws of ancient Iraq (among whose scaled punishments is "an eye for an eye, a tooth for a tooth"), and lifts large sections of the Noah flood story from the Epic of Gilgamesh, the Mesopotamian epic poem of the eighteenth century B.C. Even the Ten Commandments were derived in part from treaties enacted by the Hittites, who established an empire in north-central Anatolia around 1600 B.C. One wonders why the Bible was ever taken literally; the Hebrews always understood the early parts of Genesis to be fables. The modern insistence on literalism is largely due to the influence of southern U.S. Protestants around 1910.

This extraordinary publication may more accurately be called a creation myth. Its first five books are Genesis (in Hebrew, *bereshith,* "In the beginning"), Exodus, Leviticus, Numbers, and Deuteronomy ("The Words"), together known as the Pentateuch (from the Greek, Πεντετεύχως, meaning "five scrolls") or the Torah (Hebrew for "instruction").* They are also called the Five Books of Moses, and down to the end of the seventeenth century that great prophet was taken to be their sole author.

Back in the eleventh century, a Jewish physician in Muslim Spain, Isaac ibn Yashush, listed various historical inconsistencies in the five books and argued that parts of the Pentateuch had to have been written after Moses. Yashush's reward was to be nicknamed "Isaac the Blunderer," but by the fifteenth century others were sharing his worries, pointing out that, among other considerations, Moses could hardly have recorded his own death, described in Deuteronomy 34:5 (unless it was a fine example of hyperthymesia—a rare medical condition defined as "unusual autobiographical remembering"). Even so, the belief that Moses was the only begetter persisted, and those who argued otherwise (among them the Jewish Dutch philosopher Baruch Spinoza and the English political philosopher Thomas Hobbes) found their work placed on the Catholic Index of prohibited books. Within six years of Spinoza making his case he was excommunicated, had at least thirty-six edicts issued against him, and an attempt was made on his life. No wonder, since he was arguing that the Bible contained no privileged information about historical events or the nature of divinity so should be studied like any other book, and that it followed that one should consider its authors' motives. But even though Spinoza's critics branded him an atheist, the doubters wouldn't go away, and by the end of the nineteenth century the Pentateuch was accepted as the work of several hands writing from 1000 B.C. (the time of David) to 500 B.C. (the time of Ezra), reaching its present form between 538 and 332 B.C.

* By the thirteenth century advances in bookmaking technology meant that the Bible could be produced in a single volume, yet each copy still had to be written out by hand and weighed more than ten pounds. Punctuation, spelling, and capitalization were frequently erratic, with 1,500 misprints over the first few years of printed versions. Most notable was the omission of "not" from the commandment about adultery, which edition became known as "the Wicked Bible." (The printers were fined.) The "Vinegar Bible" has "vinegar" instead of "vineyard," while the "Murderer's Bible" has "Let the children first be killed," instead of "filled." "Hating life" becomes "hating wife"—though here no one was penalized. The printer who published, in Psalm 14, "The fool hath said in his heart, 'There is a god,' " rather than " 'There is no God,' " found himself ruined. See Melvyn Bragg, *The Book of Books* (London: Hodder, 2011), p. 50.

One of the characteristics of the Old Testament is its "doublets"—the same story told twice. There are two Creation accounts, two stories of the covenant between God and the Patriarch Abraham, two stories of the naming of Abraham's son Isaac, and many other instances. The idea took shape that the first five books were the result of several older sources being combined or conflated. Starting around 1780, scholars began to give the original documents alphabetical symbols, beginning with "J," standing for Yahwist (*Jahwist* in German), and "E," the Elohist, so named because of the documents' pervasive use of the word *Elohim* (which means both "god" and "gods" in Hebrew). By examining the language of the Book of Genesis, it was possible to identify two or possibly three authors, even sometimes writing their versions of events on the same page. Soon the number was expanded to include "D," a source found only in Deuteronomy, and later still the Elohist source was split into Elohist and Priestly ("P"), increasing the number of accounts to four.

But in what order, and why four versions? Further, "Who were the artists? If we think of [the Bible] as a source to be examined in the study of history, then whose reports are we examining?" These are the words of Richard Elliott Friedman (b. 1946), an American scholar who in 1987 published *Who Wrote the Bible?* It offers the most convincing answers I have found.

There were clues as to how to answer all these questions, he says; the texts reflected different stages of the ancient Israelite religion, so could be variously dated, while the J and E documents were apparently unaware of matters that were treated in the other two, so must have been written earlier. P was the latest of the four because it referred to events unknown to the others; it had also evidently been written to contain the latest developments of Israelite religion, based on priests, sacrifices, ritual, and law.

These first five books had an extraordinary manner of composition. "Imagine assigning four different people to write a book on the same subject," writes Friedman, "then taking their four different versions and cutting them up and combining them into one long, continuous account, then claiming that the account was all by one person. Then imagine giving the book to detectives and leaving them to figure out (1) that the book was not by one person, (2) that it was by four, (3) who the four were, and (4) who combined them." For there was evidence of an extremely skilled collator, a person who had organized the separate elements into a single endeavor sufficiently cohesive to be read as a continuous narrative. But was there just one redactor or several?

By the late nineteenth century, scholars had analyzed the J and E authors, and by focusing on the names used for God, *Yahweh* and *Elohim,* as employed in each of the two versions of the same stories, it was possible to tell that the author of J, "the Yahwist," was of King David's immediate family, used Israel's own name for God, came from Judah, and wrote between 848 and 722 B.C. Many of the most beloved biblical stories come from J—Adam and Eve, the Tower of Babel, Moses, Exodus, the burning bush, to name a few. The author of E was from Israel and wrote between 922 and 722 B.C. The author of J was more sophisticated, neither making his or her heroes perfect (both Friedman and Harold Bloom have written that the author was a woman, although the evidence is scant), nor his or her villains caricatures.*

In 622 B.C., a priest named Hilkiah claimed that he had fortuitously unearthed a scroll in the Temple of Yahweh in Jerusalem. This was proclaimed to be the fifth book of Moses, Deuteronomy. But the finding was exposed as a hoax, with the scroll written not long before its "discovery," explicitly to provide grounds for the religious reforms of Josiah, then king of Judah.

Who was the forger? In 1943, a German biblical scholar, Martin Noth, showed that Deuteronomy had much in common with six other books of the Bible (Joshua, Judges, and the two books each of Samuel and Kings), with similarities of language that went far beyond coincidence. Taken together, the seven accounts told a continuous story of the history of the people of Israel, extending from Moses (his dates given with suspicious exactitude as 1391–1271 B.C.) to the destruction of the kingdom of Judah by the Babylonians in 587 B.C. While more than a single author had evidently composed this story, the finished product was by a lone scribe working both as writer and editor. As Friedman sums up, "He had arranged the texts but had also shortened and added to them, had inserted occasional comments of his own, and had written introductory sections."

---

* When the author Andrew Solomon was the subject of a "By the Book" interview in *The New York Times Book Review,* he was asked which author, dead or alive, he would like to meet, and what he would want to know. His reply was the J writer. "I'd want to ask him [*sic*] what he intended to be literal and what he intended to be figurative. And I'd point out that confusion around this question has had a toxic effect on the rest of history." Many would agree. See *The New York Times Book Review,* September 26, 2013, p. 8.

By further analysis, it was determined that the legal code described in Deuteronomy originated with the sacred caste of Levitical priests in Shiloh (a city situated in the hill country of Mount Ephraim, northwest of the Dead Sea, and the capital of Israel in the days before King David). The priests of Shiloh had a revered literary tradition. "They wrote and preserved texts over centuries: laws, stories, historical reports, and poetry," writes Friedman. In the days of King Josiah (traditionally 648–609 B.C.), the compiler of Deuteronomy took the texts about his people's arrival in Israel—the accounts of Joshua, Jericho, and the conquest of Canaan—adding lines at the beginning and end to give the story context, and this became the Book of Joshua. This redactor then did the same for Judges, Samuel, and Kings. There had previously been no single history of the two kingdoms of Israel and Judah; the author of Deuteronomy took one history of the kings of Israel and one of the kings of Judah, sliced them up, and spliced them in between each other, fashioning an account of his people, inserting special references to the Davidic covenant—that King David's family had a special right to rule, even when members of that family did serious wrong. As Friedman says, "His task was both to record history and to interpret history in the light of tradition."

After the death of Josiah, however, that history was rudely upset. In 603 B.C. the Babylonians invaded Judah, and the so-called eternal kingdom was suddenly no more. The Judahites put up a fight, but their rebellion was short-lived. In 586 B.C., the invaders recaptured Jerusalem, destroyed the city, and took the population captive. The House that would "never be cut off from the throne" was forced into exile. The organizing editor of Deuteronomy, faced with putting together a second edition of biblical history after proclaiming that David's family had a divine right to rule, was now faced with having to explain why this dream had failed.

His solution was not to add some statement at the end of the book about the Babylonian invasion but in various places to mention the possibility of exile, so that conquest and banishment were seen as constant threats (as they must have been in real life), almost a theme running through the entire narrative. He was not just producing a record but *interpreting* it, so that the well-being of David's people depended not on a promise to a king in Jerusalem but on the people's fidelity to their covenant with God. Even if the throne of David was at that moment unoccupied, it was eternally available, and a descendant of David, a messiah, might always return to claim it. In Friedman's view, the implications for Judaism and Christianity were huge. Remarkably, the exiled author of Deuteronomy "had given a new shape and direction to the story without, apparently, deleting a word of the original. . . . He designed his account not only to tell the past but to give hope for the future."

It seems likely that the original manuscript, which had to have been written before Josiah was killed in 609 B.C., and the revised version, which must have been composed after the Babylonian destruction in 587 B.C., were the work of the same person, writing twenty-two years apart. Who was he?

The one figure who was in the right place at the right time is the prophet Jeremiah, one of the priests of Shiloh, who was in Jerusalem in the days of Josiah and in Egypt after the Babylonians invaded. And the Book of Jeremiah is filled with exactly the language and phrases found in both versions of Deuteronomy. That is not to say that he was the author, however. We know that Jeremiah associated with a particular scribe, one Baruch, son of Neriyah, who is mentioned on several occasions in the Book of Jeremiah. Our best guess is that Jeremiah was the prophet and inspiration and Baruch the amanuensis who interpreted history through Jeremiah's eyes.

We know little of the events following the disasters of 586 B.C., and instead the Old Testament jumps forward fifty years, to Ezra and Nehemiah. But what is clear, as Friedman points out, is that "theology and history were now on a collision course. How God was understood determined how the exiled people appreciated their situation." In 538 B.C., the Persians conquered the Babylonians, creating a huge and powerful empire under the rule of Cyrus the Great. Cyrus allowed the Jews to return to Judah and rebuild their temple, which was completed in 515 B.C. The Bible seemed more important than ever—"a link with the past, a connection that meant that, for the returned exiles, this was a rebuilding, not just a new start."

As scholars started seeking to identify the author of P, they deduced that he was an Aaronid priest (the Aaronids were the priests in authority at the central altar of the Temple) or at least someone representing the priesthood's interests, almost certainly from Jerusalem. Friedman reckons that P's author was writing before that city's fall—thus after 722 B.C. and before 609, probably during the reign of King Hezekiah (715–

687 B.C.), but this is an issue on which Jewish and Christian scholars tend to differ, with Jewish ones such as Friedman—generally regarded as taking a conservative view—preferring an earlier dating, Christians a later one. What is clear is that the author had to deal with challenges from other priests and rival religious centers, so his motives were theological, political, and economic. He produced his work as a deliberate alternative to J and E—only for a later hand to combine them.

The single largest source of the Old Testament was written by P, which is the length of the other three Old Testament narratives put together and turns out to be responsible for the creation story in the first chapter in the Bible, the cosmic version of the two flood stories, the accounts of Abraham and Jacob, the journey through the wilderness, about thirty chapters of Exodus and Numbers, and all of Leviticus. This final redactor was not simply cutting and combining J and E as parallel accounts; at their end he set Deuteronomy, cast as the valedictory of Moses, and merged these four different, often conflicting sources so artfully that it would take millennia to sort them out.

And the author for all this? Ezra.

In the entire Bible, only two men are cast as lawgivers, Moses and Ezra, the latter also a priest and a scribe. He had the backing of the Persian emperor, and, although not a high priest, wielded enormous authority, with access to documents. He could not preserve J, E, D, and P side by side (like the gospels of the New Testament), for by Ezra's time all four sources had come to be attributed to Moses, even though on numerous occasions they contradict one another. Instead, Ezra set about combining the versions. Here his work differed importantly from that of the producers of P. The Jeremiah/Baruch partnership fashioned a work that was an alternative to J and E; Ezra was intent on *reconciling* them. The P texts struggled with the earlier accounts; Ezra's embraced them. Friedman notes:

> All of the texts pictured events in the order in which they were understood to have occurred in historical sequence. . . . We may argue about whether it is good history-writing or bad . . . but the fact remains that it is the *first* history writing.[*]

---

[*] Since I am writing about the Bible as a whole—which includes the New Testament—I chose as my first chapters the ancient Greek and Roman historians, whose work generally predates the gospel writers. Friedman is otherwise correct.

Thus we have a continuous story ranging across eleven books: Genesis, Exodus, Leviticus, Numbers, Deuteronomy, Joshua, Judges, 1 and 2 Samuel, and 1 and 2 Kings—what has been referred to as "the First Bible." It formed the launching pad for all the rest (thus including the Book of Ruth, the supposed great-grandmother of David), telling the stories that—as Friedman rounds off his persuasive reading—"set the stage for everything that was to happen later: the creation, the birth of the people, the settlement in the land, the establishment of the messianic line." Within it were the four major covenants (Noah, Abraham, Sinai, David). The Old Testament can thus be seen as "a synthesis of history and literature, sometimes in harmony and sometimes in tension, but inseparable."

* * *

WHAT OF THE NEW TESTAMENT?* For a start, "New Covenant" is a better translation of the original Greek, since Paul's word, *diatheke,* means a pact. Either way, this New section of the Bible is a different kind of history than the Old, fashioned with the primary motives of inspiring and expanding allegiance to Christ and serving as a means of remembering him. It consists of twenty-seven books: the gospels (the English term for the Greek word ευαγγέλιον, or "good message") of Matthew (in Hebrew, "Mattith-yahu"), Mark ("Ioannes-Markos"), Luke (in Greek, "Loukás") and John ("Ioannes"); the Acts of the Apostles; and fourteen epistles attributed to St. Paul.

Of those eight epistles definitely written by others than Paul, the first is James (traditionally attributed to James the Just, but more likely of composite authorship); then 1 Peter (probably composed during St. Peter's time as Bishop of Rome); 2 Peter; 1 John (probably written by John the Evangelist, most likely in Ephesus between

---

* The notion of "old" and "new" testaments dates from the end of the 2nd century A.D. Melito, bishop of Sardis (d. 180), writes in a letter that he "learnt accurately the books of the Old Testament," especially "how many they are in number, and what is their order." Even if the term *New Testament* is not explicitly used, it is implied by the designation "Old Testament," which is introduced without explanation—understandably, as the New Testament refers to itself as such at least eight times. See David Trobisch, *The First Edition of the New Testament* (New York: Oxford University Press, 2000). Otherwise, the first use of the term is found in the writings of the theologian Tertullian (c. A.D. 155–220). As Frank Kermode comments in *The Genesis of Secrecy* (Cambridge: Harvard University Press, 1980), only once in the history of culture has a book had its entire meaning altered by renaming it—specifically, as the "Old" Testament. Since "old" can be construed as pejorative, recent academic writing has used the expressions "the Hebrew Bible" or "the Hebrew Scriptures" instead.

A.D. 95 and 110), 2 John, and 3 John; and Jude (at twenty-five verses, one of the shortest books in the Bible; Jude was the brother of James the Just).

The final book is the Apocalypse, or Revelation. By turns epistolary and prophetic, it is in *koiné* Greek—that is, the colloquial tongue of the Mediterranean, that vernacular in which Polybius and Plutarch wrote, although ironically a language that Jesus and his apostles didn't speak and couldn't write—and derives its title from its opening word, *apokalypsis,* meaning "unveiling" or "revelation." Its author identifies himself simply as "John" and says that he is from the Greek Aegean island of Patmos, making it likely that he is a local man, certainly not John the Evangelist.

The various epistles were never intended to be works of history, although they have historical value. The gospels, however, even if their main purpose was to proselytize, were attempts to record the life of Jesus and as such have had an enormous effect as recorded history. They were not written immediately after Jesus's death because there was no apparent need. Initially the gospel spread by word of mouth and brief written notes; those in the Jerusalem region had either encountered Jesus directly or were well aware of his preaching, and so it remained until the gospel spread. (Remarkably, Christian believers number from about a thousand in A.D. 60 to forty thousand in 150, to 2.5 million in 300, and by 1400 some 60 million— evolving, as in Ernest Hemingway's theory of bankruptcy, gradually, then suddenly.)

Mark's gospel, we are told, was probably composed some years before the destruction of the main temple in Jerusalem in the first Jewish rebellion of A.D. 70, and Matthew's, the teaching gospel, recounting many of Christianity's most familiar sermons, between 75 and 85, maybe a little later. The erudite Luke wrote his account most likely between 80 and 95, although there is evidence it was still being revised as late as 110. John—the theologian, the prophet—is typically fourth, composing his version around 95–100, but in the earliest surviving collation, Papyrus 45 of the third century, it appears second after Matthew, an order also found in other early New Testament manuscripts.

The current order of Matthew, Mark, Luke, and John holds sway because St. Augustine (354–430) believed that this reflected their composition, although most experts now disagree. The first three gospels are usually referred to as the "synoptics" ("giving an account from the same point of view"), either because they look at the same events in a similar way or for their similarities of style. St. Irenaeus, a late-second-century bishop of Lyon in Roman Gaul and an aggressive enemy of texts he considered (with good reason) to be heretical, was the first to assert that Mark, Matthew, Luke, and John should be the only gospels that Christians read. (Nietzsche was to lament: "Sadly, there was no Dostoyevsky in the vicinity of this interesting decadent.") For Irenaeus, the number four struck him as appropriate: there were four winds, four directions, and the four elements (earth, air, fire, and water). Four gospel accounts rounded things off nicely.

By then, the books of the New Testament were already being collated, and at some point in the middle of the fourth century the many other accounts that existed were put aside. In his Easter letter of 367, the formidable Athanasius, bishop of Alexandria, named the works that would become accepted by the Church and used the phrase "being placed in the canon" about them. In 382, the Council of Rome under Pope Damasus I issued an identical formula, and Damasus's decision to commission an authoritative Latin edition of the Bible (known from the thirteenth century on as the "Vulgate," or *versio vulgata*—the "commonly used translation") that same year effectively fixed the doctrine in the West. The four gospels were then approved at the Council of Hippo in A.D. 393 and at the Council of Carthage in A.D. 397. These texts were further revised as other councils met and deliberated, "bawling and scratching one another," in the poet Andrew Marvell's memorable phrase, and some sections—those the Church saw as diminishing its authority—were excluded. Theological niceties mattered.

Controversy, of course, did not die away. In 1945, the discovery of other gospel accounts, more than fifty among a cache of codices (books as opposed to scrolls) uncovered in Egypt near the village of Nag Hammadi, set off a firestorm. Many claim that these further gospels, several written in the second and third centuries, should have found a place in the canon. Luke remarks that even in his time many accounts had been written about Christ and his earliest disciples—perhaps as many as two hundred—yet all but the favored four were cast aside by the Church as heresies.*

* * *

JESUS EXISTED. FLAVIUS JOSEPHUS (A.D. 38–100), as already described, wrote about him in his *Jewish Antiquities,* saying that he was "a wise man who did surprising feats, taught many, won over followers from among Jews and Greeks, was believed to be the Messiah, was accused by the Jewish leaders, was condemned to be crucified by Pilate, and was considered to be resurrected." Suetonius, Thallus, and Pliny the Younger also wrote about early Christian history consistent with New Testament accounts. Even the Talmud concurs about the major events of Jesus's life. Our knowledge of the four evangelists is scant, however, and their gospels are a mix of mythmaking and history.

Matthew was a Galilean born in the first century A.D. who under the Roman occupation collected taxes from Jews living in the mountainous part of northern Israel for Herod Antipas, the local ruler (according to St. Luke, Jesus referred to Herod as "that fox"). Hebrews who became rich from such duties were generally looked down on as collaborators, and perhaps for that reason Matthew's gospel was originally anonymous. However, his job would have involved his being literate in both Aramaic and Greek, the language used in the marketplace.

The earliest quotation from Matthew's account is found in Ignatius, who died around A.D. 115, so his gospel must have been in circulation well before Ignatius's time. As attested in the New Testament, Matthew was one of the witnesses of both the Resurrection and the Ascension, and is mentioned among the twelve apostles. He composed his gospel for Hebrew Christians, and it was then translated into Greek, but those versions have perished. Lately, the priority of his version has come under suspicion, and Mark's is now accepted as the first written.

---

* Archaeologists have recovered about 5,500 manuscripts, either fragments or complete books. Nobody knows how many gospels there were originally, and some may still be discovered. Of those completely preserved, we know of Thomas; the Gospel of Truth; the Coptic Gospel of the Egyptians; that of Nicodemus (also known as the "Acts of Pilate") and of Barnabas; and the Gospel of Gamaliel. A whole genre was created specifically dealing with Jesus's childhood, appropriately called the Infancy Gospels. One of the most famous is that of James (although it was not written by him). There are also the Gospel of the Nativity of Mary; the Gospel of Pseudo-Matthew; the Infancy Gospel of Thomas; the Arabic Infancy Gospel; and the Syriac Gospel of the Boyhood of Jesus.

Matthew would seem to have used Mark's account as a guide, adding and clarifying certain events as he and others remembered them.

Harold Bloom, in his highly personal book about the gospels, calls Mark "weird . . . reminds me of Edgar Allan Poe." Certainly Mark's account is odd, his Jesus showing a "gloomy ferocity" as well as a short temper and an ironic wit. According to the Coptic Church, Mark was one of the seventy disciples sent to spread the gospel throughout Judea and was a disciple of Peter, who is said to have guided him in putting his testament together. Modern scholars, though, reject the Mark mentioned in Acts as the gospel's author, arguing that his promotion by the Church is an attempt to link the gospel to an authoritative figure close to Jesus's life. Rather, they see Mark's account as the work of an unknown author, writing in Greek for a gentile audience and working with collections of miracle stories, parables, and a passion narrative—but not as the testimony of an actual associate of Jesus. It is not certain that "according to Mark" is even intended to refer to the John Mark of Acts. The gospel, whoever its true author, is nevertheless still seen as the most reliable of the four in terms of its overall description of Jesus's life story. It's just that it comes down to us as a compilation, not a direct testament.

* * *

THIRD IN THE CHURCH'S canon of gospel writers is Luke, a native of Antioch, in Syria. The early Church fathers declared that Luke was the author of both the gospel that bears his name and the Acts of the Apostles, the two originally forming a single work, usually called "Luke-Acts." Together they account for 27.5 percent of the New Testament, the largest contribution by any one author. While Luke was not an eyewitness to the life of Christ, he had ample opportunity to interview contemporaries. Since he so often agrees with the other evangelists and there is no contradictory information coming from any disciples, his account is considered particularly reliable.

At the beginning of his gospel, he tells us: "Many have undertaken to draw up an account of the things that have been fulfilled among us, just as they were handed down to us by those who from the first were eyewitnesses and servants of the word. With this in mind, since I myself have carefully investigated everything from the beginning, I too decided to write an orderly account for you, most excellent Theophilus [literally, "friend of God," so most likely an honorary form of address], so that you may know the certainty of the things you have been taught." A sixth-century legend has it that Luke was a painter and did portraits of the Virgin Mary and of Saints Peter and Paul, so he is the patron saint of artists. A winged ox represents him because he begins his gospel with an account of a priest sacrificing that animal. This may be why Luke is also the patron saint of butchers (and surgeons).

While he makes it clear that he was never a direct witness to Jesus's ministry, Luke repeatedly uses the word *we* in describing the Pauline missions, indicating that he participated in that spreading of the word. The composition of the writings as well as the range of vocabulary used show he was well educated (he is referred to as a doctor in the Pauline epistle to the Colossians), so is accepted both as a physician and one of Paul's disciples.

Based on Luke's accurate description of towns, cities, and islands, as well as correctly naming various official titles, the noted amateur biblical scholar Sir William Ramsay (1852–1916) reckoned that "Luke is a historian of the first rank; not merely are his statements of fact trustworthy . . . [he] should be placed along with the very greatest of historians." The noted champion of old-school Bible scholarship E. M. Blaiklock (1903–83) concurred: "For accuracy of detail, and for evocation of atmosphere, Luke stands, in fact, with Thucydides. The Acts of the Apostles is not the shoddy product of pious imagining, but a trustworthy record."

A miniature portrait of St. Luke from a sixteenth-century book of hours. Luke appears at his desk, with his winged ox beside him, and again at the bottom right, working at an easel painting the Virgin Mary.

Yet these admiring estimates are of their time, and Luke's accuracy has been questioned. His work, scholars say, contains chronological difficulties and statistical improbabilities such as the size of the crowd addressed by Peter in Acts 4:4 (although estimating crowd numbers is always tricky). Further, a narrative that relates fantastic things such as angels and demons is problematic. The Nativity account, in which a Roman census forces Joseph and Mary to return to Bethlehem, is an obvious invention, since there was no such census at that time, and it would have been deeply impractical to order people back to be counted in cities that their families had vacated hundreds of years before. Simply, Luke drew upon the story to put Jesus in David's city. He wanted to record history but also to proclaim and persuade.

* * *

AT LAST WE COME, by his own gospel's account, to "the disciple whom Jesus loved," John the Apostle, one of the Twelve. The truth, however, is that there was no one author of John's gospel but rather a "Johannine community" that oversaw the writing in three distinct phases, reaching its final form between A.D. 90 and 100, thus forty to forty-five years from any original drafting. That there was more than one author was a theory launched in 1941 by the German Lutheran theologian Rudolf Bultmann (1884–1976), a conclusion that so outraged his contemporaries that even in the mid-twentieth century heresy proceedings were instituted against him. But there is general agreement now about the three stages of authorship that went into John's gospel:

1. An original version based on firsthand experience of Jesus (the writer of John's gospel seems to have been an eyewitness of Christ's life, and speaks of having been present at many of the events of Jesus's ministry);
2. A structured literary creation, possibly by John himself, but that draws upon several other sources;
3. The final gospel, as polished by others, which becomes available c. A.D. 85–90.

One possible reading, based on the internal evidence, is that John wrote an account of Jesus's life but died unexpectedly, so that a new version had to be improvised. Though the three synoptic gospels overlap considerably, over 90 percent of John's gospel appears in his version alone. Mark, Matthew, and Luke cover the final three years of Jesus's life; John adds his last ten weeks. The synoptic gospels describe much more of the Messiah's time on earth, as well as his miracles, parables, and exorcisms. However, as the literary critic Terry Eagleton notes, "The New Testament represents Jesus as a character of sorts, but it has no interest in delving into his mind. Such psychologizing would be irrelevant to its purposes. The work is not intended to be a biography. It does not even tell us what its central character looked like. If they were taking a creative writing course today, the Gospel writers might well find themselves handed a shamefully low grade."

In his Jerusalem utterances, John's Jesus makes derogatory comments about the Jews, and overall his gospel is the primary source of "the Jews" acting collectively as the enemy of the Son of God. Such references may constitute retaliation on the part of the author against Jewish criticism of the early Church. In 2013, Diarmaid MacCulloch, reviewing an account of Jesus's life, *Zealot,* by Reza Aslan, says he believes that all four Gospel writers, "terrified of being tarred with the same revolutionary brush, did their narrative best to shift the blame for Jesus' death away from the Romans to an artificial caricature of the Jewish people, both leadership and bloodthirsty mob." Yet the Gospel of John collectively describes the enemies of Jesus as "the Jews," and in none of the other gospels do "the Jews" come together to demand the death of Jesus; instead, the plot to have him put to death is described as coming from a particular small group of priests, the Sadducees (who, along with the Essenes and the Pharisees, were one of the three main Hebrew political and religious groups at that time).

John's account should be treated with caution. Critical scholarship in the nineteenth century, distinguishing between the "biographical" approach of the Synoptics and John's "theological" method, began to disregard the fourth gospel as a historical source (in our own day, critics have even referred to "John the novelist"). But scholars also agree that John's gospel has considerable historical value. A distinctive feature is that it provides an alternative timeline for Jesus's earlier life, giving no account of Christ's nativity, for instance, unlike Matthew and Luke. Major speeches found in the three other gospels are absent, including the Sermon on the Mount. But then John—the original

John or the later redactors—had a different aim than his co-evangelists. He wanted to underline the allegorical and the spiritual.

In his essay "John Come Lately," the biblical scholar Donald Foster underlines how "John everywhere is at pains to tell the *true* history of Jesus' life, as opposed to the stories and rumors circulated by his forebears." He writes:

> Where Matthew, Mark, and Luke contradict him, they are simply wrong; and if we need proof, we need only look at how clearly the deeds of Jesus' life, as related by John, figure forth doctrinal truths in a way that the synoptic accounts can never hope to match. The implicit allegory is the *guarantee* of his narrative's historical accuracy.

So while showing a casual disregard for getting the facts right, John claims to be *more* historical. As with many writers in ages to come, his gospel was aiming at a "larger truth." The great literary critic Frank Kermode (1919–2010) has argued that narrative itself begins as interpretation, then begets new narrative as commentary on itself. All storylines, he says, are full of interpretive fictions; every one, whether history, fiction, or gospel, must censor, select, interpret, fill in gaps, forge connections. This form of narrative is integral to the Bible, and we should recognize it as a revolutionary means of writing about the past.

* * *

EVEN SO, THE RELATIONSHIP between the Bible narratives and history is complex. "The Old Testament is the literature of a nation, written over some centuries, and having a certain official character," writes the distinguished theologian John Barton. "The New Testament is the literature of a small sect, distributed all over the eastern Mediterranean world, and in its origins unofficial, even experimental writing." We may accept that Jesus was a real person and that some of what both the Old and the New Testament writers say actually happened (it can be left as a matter of individual faith whether we believe in the Virgin birth, the parting of the Red Sea, the Resurrection, and much else), but how much counts as history? Here we must look at the Old Testament again, but from a different perspective.

Until the last century, there was little help to be had from scholars (in the main, they were Christian apologists who accepted the Bible as the word of God). The tendency has been to describe the history and culture of the land of the Bible with idealistic and romantic metaphors, employing a rhetoric that supports the assumption that the Bible is historically accurate. Before the end of the Second World War there was little specialization in ancient Near Eastern studies. Everyone did everything; yet since 1918 there has been a vast and increasing number of texts and archaeological material pouring in from excavations (there are now more than thirty thousand archaeological sites in Israel alone), all providing evidence of a very different history, but theologians and conservative scholars have pushed back against anything that questions the Bible's authority, prisoners of what one modern scholar calls a "watershed" mentality, exhibiting little more than "emotions captured in ink":

> We are perfectly ready to accept that the Bible's "earliest" periods were not historical, and as evidence has accumulated we have reluctantly accepted that ever more recent periods were similarly unhistorical. The period before the flood was the very first to become unhistorical. Then came the patriarchs, the Mosaic period, the conquest and the period of the Judges. However, we have been loath to make such judgments. Period after period has been tenaciously retained as valid history until proven entirely impossible. As soon as we find anything at all that can be linked with historical evidence, we stop being critical. We have insisted that the biblical narrative be historical.

The man who wrote this is Thomas Larkin Thompson, now in his mid-eighties. Raised as a Catholic in Pennsylvania, he completed his PhD dissertation on the historicity of the Patriarchal Narratives in late 1971. One of his examiners was Joseph Ratzinger, later Pope Emeritus Benedict XVI, who declared the doctorate unfitting for a Catholic theologian and failed it. The study was then rejected by various Catholic university presses until it was finally published in 1974 in Germany, but the controversy it provoked prevented Thompson from obtaining an academic position, and he worked in various pickup jobs, including janitor and housepainter, until in 1984 he became a guest professor at the École Biblique in Jerusalem, a French research center run by Dominicans specializing in archaeology and biblical exegesis—where he came under fire, only this time from the Jewish community, for the doubts he had expressed about the historical accuracy of the Jewish origin narratives.

In 1993, after several other adventures, Thompson joined the theology faculty at Copenhagen University as a professor in Old Testament exegesis.* He went on to publish eighteen books, but his most influential study came in 1999. In *The Bible in History: How Writers Create a Past* he argued that the Old Testament was created almost entirely between the fifth and second centuries B.C. Again his detractors came out in force; the book was called unscholarly ("rollicking, silly nonsense," "palpably false"), anti-Semitic, a diatribe, an offense to Christianity, even "a danger to Western civilization." It's certainly far from perfect: It has no index and an idiosyncratic bibliography, the writing is sometimes turgid, and Thompson, intent on getting his case across, constantly repeats himself—maybe because he feels he has to make his points several times as he has so often been misinterpreted. But his overall thesis is convincing. It is also deeply appreciative of the Bible as a work of huge cultural importance.

Thompson's argument is that we misunderstand the Bible if we read it as history, which he considers a modern concept incompatible with the worldview of antiquity. Not until about the 1960s was the biblically oriented history of Israel deconstructed step by step, as historians used more critical methods. We are still largely ignorant of most of the centuries covered by the Bible, he contends, and must distinguish between what is reliable and what is not.

As recently as the 1970s, scholars described kings in biblical times facilely as "despotic" or "oppressive," with cities drawn in the image of Sodom and Gomorrah, even though such notions have little to do with evidence from archaeology or ancient texts. The historical sections of the Old Testament cover the inhabitants of the central and northern Palestinian highlands during parts of the Iron Age (roughly,

* He is closely associated with the movement known as the "Copenhagen School" or, to its critics, the group that espoused "biblical minimalism." Its major figures hold that current archaeological evidence not only fails to support the Bible's version of history but threatens its authority as a credible version of past events. More recently, *The Quest for the Historical Israel: Debating Archaeology and the History of Early Israel,* edited by Israel Finkelstein, Amihai Mazar, and Brian B. Schmidt (San Diego: SBL Press, 2007), argues that modern archaeology enables us to recognize a middle ground between the two more extreme points of view, both of which should be rejected.

1250–600 B.C.). Some parts of the Bible are likely to have been written close to the events they describe and suggest that their authors did not have a heavy ideological bias. However, the majority of the authors lived many centuries after the events, real or imagined, about which they wrote, and they constructed their histories without regard to sources. In the manner of Scheherazade's and Grimm's tales, they populated their world with as many kings and princes as possible, even creating dynastic lists to link independent stories about religious heroes and antiheroes such as Joseph and Moses, Elijah and Elisha, Hezekiah and Josiah.

In one sense ancient Israel held the past in great awe—but it is not historical accuracy that the Bible means to emphasize. (To take one typical instance, many of the cities Joshua is said to have sacked in the late thirteenth century B.C. had ceased to exist by that time.) Its authors concentrated instead on what might be learned from the supposed "events." Such an approach has its origins in long-fictionalized "memories" of a real historical conquest by semi-nomads and comes from a time when most people were farmers. Thus Adam is himself made up from a piece of ground ('adamah in Hebrew) as the "earthly" source of our humanity ('adam, thus an effective pun), while Eve is further wordplay—the "mother of all living" (hevah). The longing for the Bible to be historically true has only confused the discussion about how its books relate to the past. It doesn't deal with what happened but what was thought, written, and transmitted within a particular tradition formed centuries later.

According to the Bible, Saul (c. 1082–1007 B.C.) was the first king of the united kingdom of Israel and Judah. His successor was his son-in-law David (c. 1040–970 B.C.), and David's son Solomon reigned from his father's death till 931 B.C. But we do not have external evidence that kings called Saul, David, or Solomon ever existed—no traces that archaeologists can examine, no mentions in the records of other nations in the region. How many Davids might there be, given that, in early Hebrew, the name is rendered dwd, meaning simply "the beloved"? They may have once lived, but we do not know. Nadav Na'aman, an authority on Jewish history, describes the story of a King David as an "extraordinary fiction."

Throughout the Bronze Age, armies as such did not exist in Palestine, either for conquest or defense. Words like city-states and kings mislead, since in Hebrew city can refer to a hamlet, a town, or even a few scattered tents servicing a dozen or more people, and *king* can be an autonomous village headsman. Only in the first century B.C. did Jerusalem establish itself as the religious and political center for nearly all of Palestine. Yet the notion of a vast united monarchy has served as a historical watershed within the biblical account. What came before has generally been accepted as prehistory and folklore, while events from the time of Saul forward are held to be closer to historical realities, and scholars have felt comfortable paraphrasing the Bible's account. There is no archaeological, historical, or cultural evidence for an exodus from Egypt; nor, as David Plotz has noted, any "proof that the Israelites ever invaded, much less conquered, Canaan; no indication that Jericho was ever sacked." If there was an exodus, it may have been only a small affair, with a few families.

Biblical Israel is a theological and literary creation, built up out of traditions, stories, and legendary lore. Exodus, exile, and the so-called return to the land are metaphors that point to an apostate past and a pious future. As Thompson notes, "The language of political propaganda helped change and determine the language of religious metaphor." Most of the stories in the Bible are neither whole nor original compositions but a collection of fragmented traditions that have survived the past, which are then interpreted, and nearly always it is the interpretation that matters most to the writer. It is not that the Bible, taken as a whole, can be dismissed as without historical value; its authors are surprisingly realistic and truthful. As Thompson says,

> They are talking about a real world, and they write about it in ways we can often understand quite well. They write however with ideas, thoughts and images, metaphors and motifs, perspectives and goals, that are quite at a tangent to those of the present day. . . . The conflict surrounding the Bible and history . . . is essentially a false controversy. It has occurred only because our commitment to myths of origin as part of an historically based modern world has caused us to interpret the biblical perspective as historical, until faced with definitive proof to the contrary. We should not be trying to salvage our origin myths as history.

How reliable is Thompson? More recently, the biblical historian Philip Davies has buttressed his conclusions, asserting that the writers of the Old Testament are "quite incoherent and self-contradictory," that "most of the 'biblical period' consists not only of unhistorical persons and events, but even of tracts of time *that do not belong in history at all*" (emphasis in original), and that overall "religious commitments should not really parade as scholarly methods." John Barton writes that "there is probably not a single episode in the history of Israel as told by the Old Testament on which modern scholars are in agreement," but he takes Thompson seriously, "although he likes twisting biblical scholars' noses a bit too much and ends in slightly excessive skepticism." Tellingly, in a 1988 study the great biblical commentator Giovanni Garbini concluded:

> There is *no evidence* to provide a basis for the usual datings . . . ; they are only chronological hypotheses, when they are not merely wishful thinking. . . . In the Old Testament it is difficult, I would say impossible, to draw a dividing line between what is "history" and what is "religion," because its "religion" is not our "religion" and its "history" is not our "history."

It is not that most of the Bible's historical books are invalid as history; rather, it is that we need to extract historical information even from nonhistorical material by "torturing it," in the sense that we can take nonhistorical material and find that in places it contains genuine recollection. Debunking is not enough; the Bible is not mere myth. As Simon Schama has noted, "the 'minimalist' view of the Bible as wholly fictitious, and unhooked from historical reality, may be as much of a mistake as the biblical literalism it sought to supersede."

Even if trying to establish specific biblical events is largely a futile enterprise, one of whose principal temptations is to think that the Bible's authors wrote like modern historians, the historical presence in the Bible is plentiful and various, however imperfectly rendered. We can take from it political history, narrative history (the chronology of events), intellectual history, cultural history, and natural history (how humans discover and adapt to their environment). The Bible is not only a work of myth and propaganda; it is also a historical document. It creates a library for the wisdom of the past, and it genuinely counts as a form of history, only of a highly fictionalized and mediated kind.

CHAPTER 4

CLOSING DOWN THE PAST

The Muslim View of History

———

I did not get my picture of the world by satisfying myself
of its correctness. . . . No: it is the inherited background
against which I distinguish between true and false.

—LUDWIG WITTGENSTEIN, *ON CERTAINTY*

Edward Gibbon, despite early well-intentioned attempts,
never learned Arabic; but from his mid-teens on he had a lifelong fascination with "Mohammedanism," as he called Islam. In *The Decline and
Fall of the Roman Empire*, he argues that Muhammad, the founder of
Islam, "asserted the liberty of conscience, and disclaimed the use of
religious violence." However, even among peaceful Muslims, there is
an intransigence where the writing of history is concerned, its scholars
and clerics arguing that the Qur'an and its commentaries are all that is
needed to comprehend the past. "Islam cancels all that was before it"
runs their maxim—"cancels" in the sense that the Qur'an makes all
previous history irrelevant. Muslim historians thus face a specific problem: how much leeway, if any, do they have to use their own judgment? Their religion is not anti-intellectual; but it does set forbidding
limits. As the Islamic scholar Israr Ahmad Khan has written, "Despite
the lapse of fifteen hundred years since the revelation of the Qur'an,
the dispute over abrogation [or *naskh*, sometimes translated as "cancel"]
in the Qur'an is as fresh today as it might have been at its early stage."

Islam is the fastest growing religion in the world. About 1.6 billion
Muslims, a quarter of humankind, are alive today. Some 44 million are
based in western Europe, with 3.45 million in the U.S., where they are

the country's third largest religious grouping after Christians and Jews. Muslims can come from different cultural backgrounds, speak different languages, and even hold different beliefs—depending on their interpretation of the Qur'an, for example, or which *hadith* (sayings of Muhammad) they hold to be true.[*]

Arabic is the language of Islam, yet today less than 20 percent of Muslims are Arab, and since A.D. 900, Islam has been distinct unto itself. An Arab is simply a member of a people that speaks the same language, predominantly Arabic. The root letters of the word "Arab" are common to "desert" (in Hebrew the words *'arav* and *'aravah* translate as "desert" or "steppe"), "merchant," and even "raven" (a bird known for crisscrossing land, as Arabs do). Some forms of the word evolved from the Arabic for "moving around," hence the further meanings of "passerby" and "nomad."

Arabs first appear in the historical record in an Assyrian inscription of 853 B.C. Originally they inhabited parts of the Middle East, the marshes of the great empires of the ancient world, but by the early eighth century A.D. they had conquered the centers of ancient Near Eastern civilization, spreading from the Pyrenees to the Himalayas; from Morocco to Spain, Sicily and southern Italy, Syria, Iraq, Iran, Anatolia, Armenia, Azerbaijan, much of Central Asia, the Fertile Crescent (the region that curves, like a quarter-moon shape, from the Persian Gulf through modern-day southern Iraq, Syria, Lebanon, Jordan, Israel, and northern Egypt), and all those countries east of the Red Sea. They created empires based upon a single faith, while at the same time transforming Arabic from a desert dialect into a world language that, for hundreds of years, supplanted Mandarin, Latin, and Greek as the main repository of human knowledge.

It was not just a question of territory or numbers. From the second half of the eighth century to the beginning of the twelfth, Arabic was the principal scientific language of mankind and Arab scientists were the most advanced (Ptolemy, for instance, survived only through Arab sources). They were also to the fore in jurisprudence, poetry, theology, and much else. Only in one area of knowledge did they fall short; from the ninth century, books of history were produced in great quantity,

---

[*] Although I have consulted Arabic and Islamic authorities, as cited in the book's endnotes, the majority of comments in this chapter are from Western Europeans. This is not a sign that I take Western civilization as the only or even an ideal yardstick.

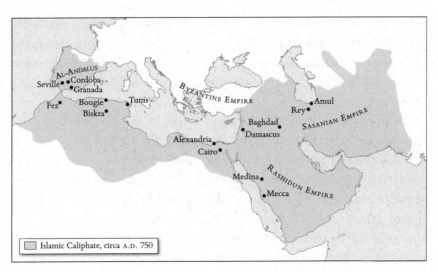

Islamic Caliphate, circa A.D. 750

but they did not occupy as prestigious a place in the world of Islamic learning as other disciplines. (Better at least than Mongol society, where historians were placed at the bottom of the social scale, lower than prostitutes.) This chapter surveys (it can do no more than that) more than eight hundred years of Islamic culture, describing the strict parameters that have controlled the ways in which historians were expected to write.

Throughout its history, the Islamic world has been a highly diverse one: the Abbasid period (750–1258) is distinct from the Umayyad era (661–750), which in turn is distinct from the Mamluk years (1250–1517), and then from the Ottoman period (1299–1922), each having its own historical tradition. During this long stretch of years there were few historians of outstanding individual importance, although among them were Abū al-Ḥasan (893–956), known as the "Herodotus of the Arabs" and author of a celebrated history combining science, biography, geography, and social commentary, *The Meadows of Gold and Mines of Gems*; and Abū Rayḥān al-Bīrūnī (973–after 1050), an Iranian scholar who wrote the treatise on eleventh-century Indian culture *Tārīkh al-Hind* (History of India) that earned him the title *al-Ustadh* ("the Master"). However, I have selected two other Arab historians who have exerted an even greater influence, the Iranian Jarīr al-Ṭabarī (839–923) and the Tunisian Ibn Khaldūn (1332–1406). I have also risked some generalizations—such that, for instance, through the centuries, the at-

titude that most Muslims took toward their history appears markedly
different from that of any other cultural or religious group, from the
early days of oral recollection through the Islam-dominated approach
post-Muhammad. Theirs is the most telling example of the channeling
of history-writing for theological ends.

Among pre-Islamic Arabs, people spoke of the past; they did not
write about it. Families, clans, tribes, and confederations of tribes were
held together by kinship, and written descriptions had no practical use.
With oral communication, content could be adapted to the changing
requirements of tribal societies, where people's identities were determined principally by whom they knew and to whom they were related. Those favored were integrated into a shared past ("we migrated
together," "we fought together"), while others were excluded. A
tribe's genealogy could thus change over time; oral history can be as
flexible as a society wants it to be. The past is plastic. Whereas written

*A Maqam miniature
showing a storyteller
and his audience. The
Maqāmat, short rhymed
prose with illustrations,
were invented by Badī'
al-Zamān al-Hamadhānī
(d. 1007 A.D.). Later,
Al-Harīrī (1054–1122)
elaborated on the genre.*

history *can* be made to conform to the imperatives of the present, oral
history *always* does; it is more a barometer of social change, especially
over how people come to terms with the present by the way they re-

view the past.* The ancient Greeks (not the only comparison available but here the most appropriate) may have scorned the written word and valued more what was committed to memory, but for them it was intellectual laziness to rely on what was written down—as Socrates had it, once people recorded an event on scrolls they wouldn't feel the need "to remember it from the inside, completely on their own." One thinks of the two basic classifications of Hindu texts: *Shruti*—what is heard—and the less authoritative *Smriti*—what is remembered. For both pre- and post-Islamic societies oral history played the more vital role. It was more reliable, allowing ideas to change in real time, the way they do in the mind during oral exchange.

When a people has no tradition of writing history, its past becomes the stuff of legend, myth, and reasonable guesses. Arabs have always put a high value on poetry, especially odes, which over the centuries before Muhammad (born in the late sixth century A.D.) became the tribal method of recording past events, with ballads commemorating victories and defeats and tales of special valor. Many such poems were autobiographical. Heroic fighters went into battle reciting verses they themselves had composed, and their surviving comrades would remember the lines, preserve them, and transmit them. The tasks of circulating news, predicting the future, representing the opinion of one's group, and providing entertainment were discharged by diviners, soothsayers, and tribal spokesmen. At fairs or festivals or in private commissions, indeed wherever there was an audience to entertain, professional storytellers strutted their stuff, performing nightlong recitations, sometimes continuing for seven or eight hours with only a short break. *Qusas* (storytellers) would form circles and recite tales, usually about well-known figures or escapades that showed members of the tribe to advantage, but they could also be about the merits of a horse or camel, hunting adventures, love complaints, and sometimes encounters with foreign powers. Often, they would just make up stories, and this was generally tolerated, even expected. (One thinks of Saki's

---

* This emphasis features in many cultures. The language of Tahitians was not written down until 1805. Indian literacy too was late in comparison with other great civilizations. In the third century B.C. the great Indian scholar Pāṇini wrote a Sanskrit linguistic analysis-cum-grammar in verse as the only way it could be remembered—there was no other system of writing. Writing preserves the thought only of the literate.

carefree line: "A little inaccuracy sometimes saves tons of explanation."*)
Ballads in particular were deeply unreliable and partisan. If later historians relied on such accounts, it was because they had no other source. The vagueness of the records was in part due to migration. People moved on; new neighbors moved in.

Yet it is important to note that oral history is not necessarily less reliable than written accounts, nor are oral cultures more prone to changing stories of their past and believing in myths and legends. They are no more likely to make up stories than written cultures and are surprisingly robust: precisely because knowledge is not written down, there is a stronger ability to retain information and transmit it accurately. Even though it may seem that written sources are less malleable, the reality is that they are often limited (since so few people in the past were literate) and do not typically mention their sources. In short, oral history is no more prone to making things up or changing the past to suit the present than is written history.

Even in cultures where oral history was dominant, books of history were composed, and indeed Mesopotamia (roughly, modern Iraq) was the first state to have written records. Any city dweller lived in a world filled with reminders of the past, from pyramids and tombs, Greek and Roman theaters and baths, Sasanian palaces and Byzantine churches to tonsured monks and curious religious figures perched on pillars fifty feet in the air. As the larger cities grew to between ten and fifteen thousand strong, their citizens were keen to know how their towns were founded and how their chief buildings had been erected; thus, writing about the past came to be. The word for "history"—*ta'rikh*—may be translated as "dating" or "assigning the month." *Ta'rikh 'ala al-sinin* was "history organized by annual entries," *khabar* (plural: *akhbar*) a sense of story, an anecdote, but also an account that had primarily historical rather than legal significance; and an *akhbari* was one who wrote, collected, or transmitted *akhbar*—hence, a historian.

---

* Saki (otherwise the British writer H. H. Munro) penned this aphorism in his story "Clovis on the Alleged Romance of Business"—hardly the obvious place to discuss the Arab character, but in context it fits well: "It was the unledgered wanderer, the careless-hearted seafarer, the aimless outcast, who opened up new trade routes, tapped new markets, brought home samples or cargoes of new edibles and unknown condiments. It was they who brought the glamour and romance to the threshold of business life, where it was promptly reduced to pounds, shillings, and pence; invoiced, double-entried, quoted, written-off, and so forth; most of those terms are probably wrong, but a little inaccuracy sometimes saves tons of explanation."

These early writings were often expressly forged for political ends, while a romantic literature sprang up alongside the historical one. Barring catastrophe—one volume was lost forever because its Cordovan author passed it for safekeeping to his servant, who promptly fell into a nearby river—once a work was finished, multiple reproduction was relatively straightforward. Authors could copy out their own work or employ scribes. Writing was tiring, and copyists would often nap after making rough drafts, all too aware that handwriting worsened with fatigue.

Midway through the second century A.D. it became a fashion among the rich to accumulate libraries. Abū 'Ayyūb al-'Aṭā had his house piled up to the ceiling with books—a remarkable enthusiasm when one considers that he died in 154, when prose literature had only just begun. Before his death he burned every volume he owned, a practice several professional writers imitated, anxious that they should remain the ultimate authority on a subject and that future rivals should not have the benefit of their research materials. This "precaution" continued through the centuries, and there are several examples of aged scholars who set fire to their books, putting forward as a justification that they feared the mistakes they contained might lead others astray.

* * *

WE COME TO THE founder of Islam, Muḥammad ibn Abdallāh, born into considerable poverty around A.D. 570 in the western Arabian city of Mecca, orphaned by the age of six, and brought up by his paternal grandfather and later by an uncle in the Quraysh tribe, which had become rich by trading in the surrounding countries. Muhammad first helped shepherd the flock of his wet nurse, we are told, then for some years worked as a merchant for a rich merchant's widow, whom he eventually married, to the great annoyance of her family, when he was twenty-five and she forty, and together they had several children. By the time he too was forty, he had a vision of being visited by the archangel Gabriel and began proclaiming that he was a messenger of God, sent to complete the teaching of all past prophets, not just Jesus and Abraham.

In 622, to escape persecution from local polytheists, he migrated from Mecca together with some seventy families to what is now Medina (also in western Arabia), the leading town in the area; before long he had a loyal following that accepted him as a de facto military leader and prophet. After eight years of intermittent fighting with Meccan tribes, he assembled an army of ten thousand men, with which he returned to Mecca and took it over. In the decade before his death in 632, most of the Arab peninsula came under Islamic rule. Up till then, the Arabs had had no great prophet of their own and no scripture in their language. For the first time, an empire was created based entirely upon a single religion, bound by its laws and devoted to its dissemination. "A spreading inkpot," scholars have called it.

Over a career of twenty-three years, Muhammad is said to have continued to receive revelations, and it is these that form the verses of the Qur'an, the "recitation" or "reading aloud" (to give its literal meanings) around which Islam is based. Some 77,430 words divided into 114 chapters and 6,236 verses (as conventionally reckoned; there are many ways of counting). These lines of often rhyming prose were initially passed on by word of mouth, but within a generation of Muhammad's death they began to be written down too, on a variety of surfaces, including pottery shards, pieces of leather, and animal bones.

Do we really know who Muhammad was? There is more than enough material, exceeding that which exists for Jesus Christ or the Buddha, yet it is hardly reliable. (Tom Holland, who describes the lack of contemporary evidence as "devastating," quips, "the further in time from the Prophet a biographer, the more extensive his biography was likely to be.") Allusions to Muhammad's life within "the Noble Qur'an," as Muslims call it, are so opaque as to be almost impenetrable, the Prophet being mentioned by name just four times. We should not doubt his existence (there are disinterested references to him within a decade of his death), but it is reasonable to ask how such a dense, elliptical, and allusive recitation should have come from the lips of an illiterate man living in a pagan city in the middle of a desert, someone so little commented on in his lifetime. Of course, similar skepticism has been voiced over Jesus Christ and William Shakespeare, but even so, Islamic records are disappointing. It was not until the late seventh century that a caliph first inscribed Muhammad's name on a public monument, and only in the middle of the eighth century did the first biographies appear, with the earliest surviving example coming from the ninth. Others quickly followed, all aiming to serve as models of piety. But how true are the *hadith*, the sayings that accompanied his vision? The respected Muslim scholar Muḥammad al-Bukhārī (810–70) amassed six hundred thousand supposed precepts of the Prophet—then dismissed all but 7,225.

Doubts about the truth of Muhammad's claims made little difference to the spread of the new faith. By the early ninth century, the Qur'an (for all Muslims, revelations received directly from God) and its accompanying sayings (known as *sunnah*: the Prophet's "way," as expressed in *hadith*) were together accepted as fundamental to Islamic thought. The "science of traditions," which meant compiling, editing, and commenting on the *sunnah*, was soon the prestige activity of Islamic scholarship, with the constant temptation to let faith dictate interpretation (to question the Qur'an is not to be a Muslim); what the *sunnah* expressed were not historical facts but elucidations about the way the Prophet lived his life, thus what the community should hold to be the right way to live.* If some fact did not seem to mesh with the words of the Qur'an, one should not assume that the problem was with the information itself, but that one had not understood the Qur'an correctly. Arabic is a flexible enough language that a word can be interpreted in more than one way, and scholars should realize that sometimes their interpretation would be wrong.

The notion that, a fresh era having commenced, previous epochs should be consigned to oblivion has occurred at other times, for instance during the French Revolution. Like that far-reaching upheaval, the recording of time was now altered. Year 1 in the Islamic calendar begins on the date that Muhammad fled his hometown for Medina, July 16, A.D. 622 (under the Julian calendar); thus 846, when an Arab army raided Rome, in Islamic reckoning is the year 224. Islam also held that the Qur'an was a flawless book that required no change, revision, or editing.

At best, you might write something as an aid to memory, but once you knew it by heart (the Qur'an, long though it be, is designed for memorizing), you should destroy all your notes. The very word *Qur'an* is derived from an Arabic verb for speaking from memory. When the Umayyad caliph 'Abd al-Malik ibn Marwān (646–705) discovered that

---

* This topic is a minefield for the general reader. In the 1960s the British-German scholar Joseph Schacht (1902–69) wrote how after A.D. 720 many of Muhammad's supposed sayings were self-serving fabrications—as demonstrated in his study *The Origins of Muhammadan Jurisprudence* (Oxford: Oxford University Press, 1950). More recently, Columbia University's Wael Hallaq has criticized this view, and in such books as *Authority, Continuity, and Change in Islamic Law* (Cambridge: Cambridge University Press, 2001) and *Origins and Evolution of Islamic Law* (Cambridge: Cambridge University Press, 2005) has argued that Islamic law is capable of profound change. Enter who dare.

one of his sons owned an account of Muhammad's companions in book form he ordered it burned; his progeny should read the Qur'an and learn the traditions, but he would permit no other form of study. It was to Muslims what the Bible was for Christians: an "axial text . . . an end and a beginning." As the historian James Westfall Thompson has it, "It is as if historiography began with a clean slate."

One reason for such traditionalism was that it kept Muslims moored to their Arabian origins. It was a way of ordering society (just as caste is intrinsic to Hinduism). The Qur'an came to be regarded as the prime example of *al-'arabiyyatu*, the language of the Arabs, and its words were not considered convertible to any other tongue. Thomas Carlyle, having worked his way through an English translation, considered the book "as toilsome reading as I ever undertook. A wearisome confused jumble, crude, incondite; endless iterations, long-windedness, entanglement. . . ." To Islamists such an attack was deeply ignorant and highly offensive (one can hardly dispute that it is, although I too, reading the sacred text in English, found it hard going); besides, many Muslims feel that the text must be read in Arabic, not in translation, and is best chanted, not read.

Loyalty to the Qur'an has even affected mapmaking, which became, in effect, as in western Europe, a branch of theology. Judeo-Christian tradition orients maps as well as places of worship toward the east, which it regards as the location of earthly paradise. In contrast, the west is associated with mortality, the direction Christ faced on the cross, and the north with satanic influence, the direction the heads of the unbaptized and the excommunicated face when they are buried. Islamic cartographers have inherited the same reverence for the east but, given the Qur'anic injunction for believers to pray in the sacred direction of Mecca and that early on most Islamic converts lived directly north of that sacred city, their maps have generally been oriented with south at the top. Even that has not been enough, and when maps were introduced into Ottoman schools in the 1860s conservative Muslims were so outraged that they ripped them off the walls of classrooms and threw them down the latrines. A celebrated *hadith* runs, "Bestowing knowledge on the wrong people is like putting necklaces of pearls, gold, and jewels on pigs."

Those who wrote about the past were expected not so much to explain human actions as to illustrate what were regarded as known truths by providing examples. Continuity was essential, and given the tribal preoccupation with genealogy, historical works remained largely kinship lists. Factual accuracy was less important than adhering to a life vision. As a matter of course, dialogue was made up rather than accurately recorded, to be placed in the mouths of caliphs and governors as appropriate. Few dared to stray from such a prescription, even if skeptical. One such, the tenth-century senior bureaucrat Abū Isḥāq Ibrāhīm ibn Yaḥyā al-Naqqāsh al-Zarqālī, composing an official history of the Buyid dynasty, was asked what he was doing. "Compiling packs of lies," he replied. When his employer the vizier ʿAḍud al-Daulah (949–83) heard this, it was with difficulty that he was restrained from ordering Ibrahim's execution.

Much of what is attributed to early Muslim authors never actually issued from their pens. The fame of scholars was judged by the number of inkwells used per lecture (which could total up to a thousand); their students would take down their words, then with or without their permission put them into book form. Oral communication was still of prime importance, and historians came to rely on *isnad*—the chain of authorities whereby a narrative could be traced back to an original eyewitness, then transmitted to the final narrator through a list of intermediaries. There is a lot, a lot, a lot of repetition.

Even as writing became a more general skill, it was frequently disparaged. Some viziers held the view that their rulers should not be left to read works of history precisely because they might learn something. Recording the past compared badly to those disciplines that lay at the heart of the Islamic sciences—particularly language and grammar, which served as a means of understanding scripture, but also geometry and astronomy, both of which were used to determine the directions and timings of daily prayer.

From around 610 till about 730, the prevalence of oral storytelling continued, but thereafter a new culture emerged; events began to be dated, even if documentary material was not yet archived. Chroniclers compiled lists of who fought whom and where, with the most comprehensive accounts considered the best. Early on, Caliph ʿUthmān ibn ʿAffān (576–656), for instance—one of Muhammad's original companions and twice his son-in-law—ordered the codification of the Qurʾan. This stimulated Arabian calligraphy, which was to become the quintessential form of artistic expression in the Islamic world.

During a second period, from 730 until around 830, a way of writing history evolved. Chase Robinson, a leading historian of Islam, talks of an "explosive growth of historiography" during these years, when Baghdad would produce more narrative history in a week than all of France or Germany could produce in a year. The great ninth-century essayist Abū ʿUthmān ʿAmr ibn Baḥr al-Jāḥiẓ (meaning "goggle-eyed"), paralytic in his old age, is reported to have been crushed to death by his books, while one tenth-century courtier declined a posting as it meant having to move his library, which he reckoned would have taken up four hundred camel loads—these for just the theology titles.

The Qurʾan may not be a history book, but, as Tarif Khalidi has noted, it is obsessed with the past. And the political struggles of the early community of Muslims acted as a powerful stimulus for historical writing, "since many of Islam's earliest sects tried to justify their views by appealing to historical precedent." The foundation of Baghdad (the first brick was laid on July 30, 762) marked the symbolic moment in Arabic history when books began to be composed for reading as well as reciting, and within two hundred years the eastern half of the city could boast a hundred bookshops. History was now not only a record of events; it was also a register of religious learning—what men needed to remember of the past. Already in the ninth century, the art of biography had become limited to the selective enumeration of "glorious exploits," "excellences," and "virtues," the point for their authors being not to understand their subjects (usually military heroes, caliphs, or jurists) but to present them as archetypal holy warriors. The phrase for "memoirs," *kitab al-Iʿtibar*, translates as "a book of teaching by example."

* * *

THE WRITING OF HISTORY was thus closely related to the rise of Islam. In two long generations, the political and religious landscape of the Mediterranean was being redrawn, with men of humble Arab origins finding themselves ruling the richest provinces of Persia or Byzantium (the old eastern Roman Empire), and, since it had become the prestige language of scholarship, Arabic also became the tongue of historiography. Progress varied; in Spain, for instance, this new form of writing emerged about a century later than it did in the Fertile Crescent. Also, whereas ancient Greek and Roman historians put the highest value on oral testimony for contemporary history, early Muslim historians relied on word-of-mouth evidence for noncontemporary accounts. Writing about the present day was considered hubristic and irrelevant.

Maybe they were making a virtue of necessity; only a handful of manuscripts of any sort—paper, parchment, or animal skin—remains from the ninth century. Besides natural decay in the humid atmosphere of many parts of the Middle East (where paper may have been cheaper and easier to handle than parchment or papyrus but was less durable), in the early years of Islam, when institutions were still forming, manuscripts were often misplaced, stolen, or deliberately or accidentally destroyed; in one case, in eleventh-century Cairo, the city's libraries were systematically plundered by soldiers furious at not having been paid.

Postcard of an Arab storyteller, circa 1925.

Whatever the rates of progress from country to country, the Islamic worldview was dominant. As the Arabic scholar D. S. Margoliouth described it, "The different paths are like separate strands all going to strengthen the rope." God's will was seen as the ultimate cause of all events, and the tools He preferred were the actions of elite individuals. As a reflection of that, until well into the fifteenth century, recorders of the past were mainly drawn from privileged families, overlapping with members of the religious elite, the legal profession, the court, and other kinds of state servants. Muslim historians say little about non-elites in general and rural non-elites in particular. Even that great collection of fictional stories, *The One Thousand and One Nights*, in its Iranian and Iraqi renderings, transforms its main characters into honorary Baghdadis.*

The celebrated German Arabist Heinrich Ferdinand Wüstenfeld (1808–99) once made as full a list as he could of Arab historians from the first millennium of Islam, reaching the figure of 590, but many must have escaped him. Of these, during the eighth and ninth centuries, at least a dozen were of some influence. 'Aḥmad ibn Yaḥyā al-Balādhurī, author of the *Book of the Conquest of Lands*, who died in 892 and who got his name because of his addiction to a memory-enhancing nut, the balādhur, which he consumed in such quantities that his wits supposedly deserted him, is particularly notable. But still, one rose above all others: Abū Ja'far Muḥammad ibn Jarīr al-Ṭabarī.

This remarkable scholar was the ultimate polymath; he composed all his works in Arabic, covering religion, poetry, mathematics, ethics, medicine, grammar, and lexicography. By report he was an imposing, lean figure with large eyes and a brown complexion, and although he used no dye both his beard and head hair were said to have remained black till his death at eighty-five. He possessed a beautiful reciting voice and was probably unmarried. Witty and urbane, he was health-conscious, avoiding red meat, fats, and other foods, and whenever he was ill, he medicated himself—to the surprised approval of his little-involved physicians.

He was born during the winter of 838–39 in Amul, a city in Tabaristan, in northern Iran. Almost as soon as he could read, Ṭabarī was introduced to pre-Islamic and early Islamic history, and by the time he was seven is said to have known the Qur'an by heart. Two years later, his father dreamed that he had seen him in front of Muhammad, throwing stones at the Prophet from a satchel, which he strangely

---

* Often known as *Arabian Nights* (the first English-language edition was in 1706), this landmark of Arabian literature is a series of tales collected over several centuries across western, central, and southern Asia and North Africa. At some time, probably in the early eighth century, the tales were translated into Arabic under the title *Alf Layla*, or "The Thousand Nights," and formed the basis of *The Thousand and One Nights*. The original core of stories was quite small, but from the ninth century on, further tales were added to reach the full 1,001 nights of story-telling.

The tales cover histories, love affairs, tragedies, comedies, poems, burlesques, and erotica and have had an immense influence, affecting writers from Fielding and Thackeray through Dickens and Tolstoy to Borges and Orhan Pamuk. One would have expected the tales to have influenced Arabian historical writing, but apparently not. Fiction was held in low regard by medieval Arabs, and the tales were generally derided as *khurafa* (improbable conceits fit only for diverting women and children), and even today have a poor reputation in the Arab world.

interpreted as meaning that Ṭabarī would become a champion of the Qurʾan, from then on encouraging his son to become a scholar.

Shortly before his twelfth birthday, Ṭabarī left home, and for the next two decades he traveled widely, first to Rey (now a suburb of Tehran), where he remained for five years, studying Muslim jurisprudence. He finally settled in Baghdad, where he remained until his death. Legend has it that he wrote forty pages daily for forty years. Yet several Muslim authors completed works as long as Ṭabarī's. Even so, he must have been amazingly industrious. It may have helped that he had a private income from his father from rents in his hometown and later received an inheritance. Not once in his life did he take a government or judicial position.

By 875 Ṭabarī was well versed in Islamic jurisprudence in all its diversity, and by the age of forty he was considered an expert in tradition, law, the Qurʾan, and history. He was a famous if controversial personality. Although he set greatest store by his legal works, among the many books he wrote, two of them, neither about the law, are outstanding. The first, *Tafsīr al-Ṭabarī*, is a lengthy commentary on the Qurʾan, which quickly became the cornerstone of Islamic exegesis. The second is *Taʾrikh al-Rusul wa al-Mulūk* ("History of the Prophets and Kings" or "The Annals"), that combines the history of creation and prophecy with a chronicle of various ancient nations, especially the Persians. It is said that each work was originally thirty thousand leaves but that his pupils, expected to take notes from his dictation, found they could not keep up, so he condensed the books to a tenth of their size, complaining, "God help us! Ambition is extinct."*

Ṭabarī was well into his seventies when his *History* was finally published. His words in printed form fill just under 7,500 leaves, one and a half printed pages roughly corresponding to a single leaf of manu-

---

* It was almost de rigueur for those who wrote about the past to include long lists of names of writers who had gone before—sometimes as many as twelve thousand, as in the "Great History" of al-Bukhārī (d. 870). The original *History of Damascus* by Ibn Asakīr (d. 1176), recently published in seventy volumes, was when it first appeared far larger, perhaps sixteen thousand folios. Part of this was showing off: the longer the lists, the greater one's presumed industry and knowledge. The Baghdadi traditionist Ibn al-Jawzī by his own reckoning wrote two thousand volumes; an objective observer totaled it at one thousand. A fellow historian recorded: "It is related that the parings of the reed pens with which he wrote *The Traditions* were gathered up and formed a large heap; these, in pursuance of his last orders, were employed to heat the water for washing his corpse [a standard Hanifi Muslim practice], and there was more than enough for the purpose."

script. It is an inferior work to the *Commentary*, maybe due to the author's advanced age, the inequality of his sources, or perhaps the relatively hasty condensation of the original draft. This did not restrict its popularity; there were reportedly twenty copies (one of them in Ṭabarī's own hand) in the library of the Fāṭimid caliph Abū Manṣūr Nizār al-Azīz Billāh (955–96), and by the time Saladin became lord of Egypt in 1169, the royal library is said to have contained an astonishing 1,200 copies of the original, so admired was its author.

To a modern eye the book is unsatisfactory. Even though Ṭabarī had an enormous amount of material at his disposal, no more than 10 percent is concerned with contemporary history; when he does write of events from his own time, he omits important details, and major figures are left in shadow. He never cites another work about the past, recording that such books were discouraged or forbidden. He was well aware of what he could do and what he had to avoid, setting out his stall early in a careful and legalistic style:

> Let him who examines this book of mine know that I have relied, as regards everything that I mention therein which I stipulate to be described by me, solely upon what has been transmitted to me by way of reports which I cite therein and traditions which I ascribe to their narrators, to the exclusion of what may be apprehended by rational argument or deduced by the human mind, except in very few cases. This is because knowledge of the reports of men of the past and of contemporaneous news of men of the present do not reach the one who has not witnessed them nor lived in their times except through the accounts of reporters and the transmission of transmitters, to the exclusion of rational deduction and mental inference. Hence, if I mention in this book a report about some men of the past which the reader or listener finds objectionable or worthy of censure because he can see no aspect of truth nor any factual substance therein, let him know that this is not to be attributed to us but to those who transmitted it to us and we have merely passed this on as it had been passed on to us.

As the Arab scholar Tarif Khalidi has noted, for Ṭabarī, knowledge of the past cannot be deduced or inferred, only transmitted. He courted controversy when he stuck his neck out by assessing which of his sources were accurate, but this does not mean he saw himself as innovative. For that reason, he is more a jurist and a collector of traditions than a historian. (Although, on one occasion, needing to explain an allusion in the Qur'an, he mentions that King Solomon devised a depilatory paste to cure the Queen of Sheba's hairy legs.) Crucially, he was writing at a time when he felt he had to reshape accounts so that they would conform to both the form and the substance of the Qur'an. As the aphorism had it, the wise man is like a jeweler who skillfully arranges precious stones in necklaces but is not himself their discoverer.

To a modern reader, this can be hard going. Tabari's preference, at least where historical records were concerned, was to "rely upon the traditions and reports on the authority of our Prophet and that of the righteous early Muslims before us, and we do not use reason and thinking." Like the Assistant Commissioner in Conrad's *The Secret Agent*, his "thought seemed to rest poised on a word before passing to another, as though words had been the stepping-stones for his intellect picking its way across the waters of error." He might rock the boat, but he would never suggest that another vessel might be just as seaworthy.

Throughout all these years, he kept in touch with his hometown. He returned at least twice, the second time in 903, when his blunt way of talking led to his quick departure after a friend warned him that the governor of the province had ordered his arrest; his companion, however, was less fortunate, being seized by the authorities and scourged. On another occasion, back in Baghdad, Tabari criticized the sect leader Ibn Hanbal, claiming that Hanbalism was not a legitimate school, as its founder was not a proper jurist. His final years were marked by conflicts with Hanbal's followers ranging from inkstands being thrown at him during lectures to more serious attacks. The harassment reached the point where Abbasid authorities had to quell Hanbal's followers by force. The Baghdad chief of police suggested a debate between the two sides to settle their differences. Tabari accepted, but the Hanbalites refused, and instead came to bombard his house with stones, "which rose in a great heap." Tabari lived out the rest of his life fearing the Hanbalites would attack him again.

He died in Baghdad on February 17, 923, the Abbasid authorities burying him surreptitiously, at night, to avoid setting off yet more demonstrations. In his final moments he granted forgiveness to all his enemies, with one exception—those who had charged him with "introducing new ideas into religion," for him the unpardonable offense, as he had lived all his life loyal to the traditions he had inherited.

* * *

FOR SEVERAL CENTURIES, ISLAMIC writing of all kinds was at odds with the freedom of thought at least partially responsible for the dominance of the modern West. Works that count in Europe as models of historical writing were unknown to their Arab fellow practitioners. As for the preservation of texts, Arabs would religiously pick up scraps of paper in the street, then kiss them, in case the word of God was written on them and His teachings might otherwise be defiled.

In almost every culture, historians generally have focused on an attractive style, and their work has been judged for its artistry as much as for truthfulness. Muslim historians were primarily concerned with compiling self-contained stories that they could attribute to earlier authorities. By the end of the ninth century, collections of narrative history were the norm: long accounts of conquests, civil wars, and the overthrow of the Ummayad Caliphate, a revolution that marked the beginning of a multiethnic state in the Middle East. After Ṭabarī, his immediate great successor was al- Mas'ūdī, who refined history into a more sophisticated discipline, grouping events around dynasties, kings, and peoples in his ambitious thirty-volume history of the entire world.

Written work, often triggered by caliphal patronage—frequently extended biographies of Muhammad but also of influential governors and rebels—was more than a new enthusiasm; it had a role to play. Annals, after all, do not analyze; as they were produced by a culture that valued record-keeping, keeping records became a political activity, and the concept of Muhammad the lawgiver began to eclipse that of Muhammad the charismatic leader. Early Muslims thought historically, and although that did not make them historians, ideas about years gone by began to crystallize in literary form. Muslims began to show an interest both in their own past and that of the peoples they had subjugated.

As H. G. Wells described it, "under the stimulus of the national and racial successes [the Arab mind] presently blazed out with a brilliance second only to that of the Greeks during their best period." This was particularly true of the region known as Al-Andalus, the Muslim part of Iberia, at its greatest geographical extent covering much of Spain and Portugal and a part of present-day southern France. Governed by Muslims (known under the generic name of Moors), it became a center of learning, especially during the Caliphate of Córdoba (929–1031). The city of Córdoba, the largest in Europe at the time, became one of the leading cultural and economic centers throughout the Mediterranean basin, Europe, and the Islamic world.

The spectacular success of Islam created a market of readers hungry for stories that offered lessons for rulers and their courts and urban elites. A huge number of biographies appeared—of poets, physicians, and jurists. After the thirteenth century a more self-confident and dynamic tradition emerged, so that historical writing attracted ambitious authors who recognized that narrative could function on several levels at once. At first, students of history and tradition were identical, but gradually the two subjects diverged, and writing about the past became a distinct discipline. Despite this development, even the most daring went on seeking the same, relatively modest goal of previous Islamic scholars—at best, to be "incrementally innovative," either to write within a recognizable genre or within the confines of popular conventions. Independent thought was a danger to the established order, so the schools were filled with *taqlīd*, or emulation.

Revelation, not reason, was the surest guide to living. Thus many new books remained reproductions or abbreviations of classic texts or else were marked by literary artifices. But although Muslim interest in how history should be written still concentrated on prophetic poetry about their founder, and although having to shape everything to an Islamic worldview was restrictive, liveliness of detail, emphasis on characterization, and pleasure in wordplay can be found in many works of this time, be they sacred history, tribal records, histories of countries and cities, or world surveys. The spread of Arabic in the Middle East produced a volume and variety of literature that rivals that of any other linguistic tradition.

Also, during the eleventh and twelfth centuries many historians were employed initially as bureaucrats, so bringing to their historical work the linguistic virtuosity that their patrons now demanded. One al-Sakhāwī (d. 1497) was bold enough to write a polemical work, *The Public Denunciation of Those Who Criticize History*. Anecdotal writing remained popular—one tome was titled *The Notorious Liars of Quraish*, another *The Great Commanders Who Were One-Eyed*, while Shihāb al-Dīn al-Nuwayrī, an early-fourteenth-century bureaucrat from an elite family, produced *The Ultimate Ambition in the Arts of Erudition: A Compendium of Knowledge from the Classical Islamic World*, a sprawling two million words spread over thirty-three volumes, much of it history but also inclusion of the various Arabic words for dust ("the dust that swirls round the hooves of horses . . . dust stirred up by the wind . . . the dust of a battle . . . the dust of feet"); the uses of radishes in defending against scorpions; recipes for homemade aphrodisiacs; the contents of a sultan's buttery; and a gruesome summary of a plague in Cairo. Another admired writer, al-Ṣafadi (d. 1363), wrote a dictionary devoted entirely to blind scholars. By his time, nearly all the Islamic states offered at least some patronage to historians, each ruler seeing the opportunity to have his own realm's history represented—or misrepresented.

This more confident period welcomed in the *Muqaddimah* ("Introduction to History"), the most sophisticated program of thought produced by any premodern historian of any culture, a work written in 1377 and still relevant after more than six hundred years. Its author, Ibn Khaldūn, was confident of his originality: "It should be known that the discussion of this topic is something new, extraordinary, and highly useful. . . . In fact, I have not come across a discussion along these lines by anyone." The prolegomena (as its title translates) is a lengthy theoretical examination of the laws of history while also serving as a general survey of Islamic societies and their arts and sciences. It is divided into six sections: chapter 1 deals with society in general; chapter 2, nomadic society; chapter 3, states, caliphs, and kings; chapter 4, civilized society and towns; chapter 5, trade and ways of earning a livelihood; and chapter 6, science and the arts.

Ibn Khaldūn became the first historian to factor systematic social analysis into his narrative. "It deals with such conditions affecting the nature of civilization as, for instance, savagery and sociability, group feelings, and the different ways by which one group of human beings achieves superiority over another," he wrote. He does not seem to have regarded history as a separate discipline. At the heart of his thinking was the need for ʿasabiyya (the word appears over five hundred times in the *Muqaddimah*), a special kind of group solidarity, the sense of being bound together and the unanimity of a tribe. Too often he notes its absence, and ever a pessimist he did not expect human beings to get any better: "The entire world is trifling and futile. It leads to death and annihilation." But that view was common to other leading Arab historians of the fourteenth and fifteenth centuries.

Political scientists have ranked Ibn Khaldūn's book with Aristotle's *Poetics*, and indeed, he drew heavily on a compendium entitled "Secret of Secrets," believed to be a letter composed by Aristotle for the guidance of Alexander the Great. He was to win similar plaudits. "What Thucydides was to Greece, Tacitus to Rome, Otto of Freising to the Middle Ages, that Ibn Khaldūn was to Mohammedan historiography— its greatest historian," eulogized the historian Westfall Thompson, while Arnold Toynbee, not one to mince words if he could cook himself into a grand stew, called the *Muqaddimah* "undoubtedly the greatest work of its kind that has ever yet been created by any mind in any time or place." Ibn Khaldūn's contemporary 'Ali al-Maqrizi commended his style more poetically as "more brilliant than a well-arranged pearl and finer than water fanned by a zephyr." The book's ideas are taken up in Bruce Chatwin's novel-cum-travelogue *The Songlines*, underpin Frank Herbert's *Dune* cycle, shape Isaac Asimov's science fiction Foundation trilogy, and cumulatively outline an entirely new science—a disquisition on the past's "inner meaning," pioneering what would become known as the philosophy of history.

Gibbon divided Arab historians into dry chroniclers and flowery orators; Khaldūn was the exception. What was original in his writing was that he challenged the majority view of theologians—a group that had questioned the truthfulness of history—on many controversial issues. (He also, blissfully, tried to minimize repetition.) Even more important, he was determined to understand the causes of social change. "The past resembles the future more than one drop of water another," he wrote. Universal laws governed the fortunes of society, but deciphering long-gone happenings was deceptively complex:

> For on the surface history is no more than information about political events, dynasties, and occurrences of the remote past, elegantly presented and spiced with proverbs. . . . The inner meaning of history, on the other hand, involves speculation and an attempt to get at the truth, subtle explanation of the causes and origins of existing things, and deep knowledge of the how and why of events.

He wanted to understand history as it unfolded over generations. This was a new approach among Muslim writers—one that looks ahead to the theories of G. W. F. Hegel (1770–1831), who argued that the historian's prime purpose was not to write about the past per se but to find an overarching theoretical frame on which the facts could be hung, or even to the long-term approach to history promulgated by Fernand Braudel in the twentieth century. Ibn Khaldūn was writing at the time of the Mamluk Dynasty that ruled over Egypt, the Levant, Iraq, and India for nearly three centuries, from 1250 to 1517, and while he accepted that power was just a commodity, in itself neither good nor bad, the exercise of that power required a special kind of skill. He propounded the earliest general theory of the nature of civilization and how it might progress, for which he considered the enduring collisions between the unrefined lives of Arab tribesmen and highly developed urban society a central constituent. But he also found room to discuss such subjects as secretarial skills, dreams, mystical experiences, and the principles of pedagogy as well as his favorite Arabic poetry.* "These things are not strictly relevant to the understanding of historical processes," writes Robert Irwin, in his authoritative 2018 biography. "They were perhaps an advertisement for himself." Irwin adds that Ibn Khaldūn also wrote (as did Machiavelli) to understand why in his own wanderings in the corridors of power he was a political failure.

A major, complex, and conflicted figure, then. Let us join him as he sways in midair, his life hanging by a few interwoven threads . . .

★ ★ ★

ONE JANUARY MORNING IN 1401, Ibn Khaldūn found himself, nearly seventy years old, dangling high off the ground (like St. Paul thirteen centuries before) as he was lowered at the end of a rope. The Tunis-born Ibn Khaldūn (this is his foreshortened family name; the full version, in Arab fashion, runs two Muhammads longer than one's arm) had been

---

* He also had a fondness for poetic images. Chapter 3 of the *Muqaddimah* tells the following fable: King Bahrām ibn Bahrām, who ruled the Sassanian Empire from A.D. 271 to 274, on hearing an owl screech asked his most senior religious adviser what it meant. The priest replied that when a male owl wanted to marry a female, she insisted on twenty ruined villages, so that she could hoot in them to her heart's content. The male replied that he could arrange this easily so long as King Bahrām continued to rule in his current fashion, since the owl would be able to give her a thousand such villages. Hearing this, the admonished king resolved to reform himself. See Ibn Khaldūn, *The Muqaddimah*, vol. 2, pp. 104–5.

trapped within the besieged city of Damascus, and it was from its walls that he was suspended. He was seeking to meet the city's besieger, Tamerlane the Great, leader of the Chagatai Turks and ruler of an empire that included much of Central Asia, Iran, and Iraq, not least to question him as part of his research into a history of the Tartars and Mongols. And indeed they did meet, Ibn Khaldūn walking unannounced into the chieftain's camp. According to a later Egyptian chronicler, Tamerlane was at once struck by Ibn Khaldūn's charismatic demeanor, and over a macaroni soup called *rishtah* he formed a friendship with his visitor. The siege continued unabated for another thirty-five days, which Ibn Khaldūn spent discussing the nature of history with his inquisitive host (himself an author of a memoir and a treatise on the art of war), concentrating on the political conditions in Egypt and northwest Africa.* Tamurlane was also keen to buy Ibn Khaldūn's exceptionally fine gray mule (which presumably did not have to be lowered from the city's wall on a rope and was allowed through the gates). In the circumstances, Ibn Khaldūn offered it to him as a gift, saying, "One like me does not sell to one like you, but I would offer it to you in homage."

And so they parted. As ruthless as ever, Tamburlane, or Tamerlane (in Turkish, Timurlenk, lame from an arrow wound in his right thigh, hence "Timur-lame"), was to break the terms of surrender and pillage Damascus, but he granted Ibn Khaldūn and his close friends safe passage to Egypt. Nonetheless Ibn Khaldūn did not emerge unscathed as he was attacked by thieves on his way home and lost all his belongings.

We know much of this from Ibn Khaldūn's autobiography, one of the most detailed in medieval Islamic literature, if hardly a personal document. His parents, of southern Arabian origin, settled in Seville after the Muslim conquest of Spain and played a leading part in the intellectual life of the city. Shortly before the Christian reconquest, they left for Tunis, where Ibn Khaldūn was born on May 27, 1332. But the Black Death was raging throughout North Africa, taking both his parents while he was still a teenager. After studying the traditional religious sciences, he was trained for a career in government, and by the

---

* Ibn Khaldūn believed that the word *Africa* or *Ifriqiya* derives from Ifriqos bin Qais bin Saifi, a Yemeni king, but there are other readings, one of which is that it comes from the Arabic word for "clear," because in Africa there are said to be no clouds. The Spanish geographer and diplomat Leo Africanus (c. 1494–c. 1554) posits that "Ifriqiya" is based on the Arabic *Farawa*, "to divide," since the Mediterranean detaches Africa from Europe while the Nile acts as a barrier between it and Asia. The issue is clouded.

time he was twenty had won a minor position in the chancery; he soon joined his mentor, the philosopher and mathematician al-Abilī of Tlemcen, who had moved to Fez, one of the two largest cities in Morocco and at the heart of the cutthroat political world of North Africa and Islamic Spain. But he also acquired practical experience beyond the cities (what Moroccans used to call the "lands of insolence"). Frequently commissioned to negotiate with Berber tribesmen, on one occasion he was obliged to eat his own horse.

Over his whole long life, Ibn Khaldūn was to suffer a pinball existence, bouncing from academic research to court appointments and political intrigues, from one city or country to another, enjoying times of considerable affluence then suffering years of austerity and self-sacrifice. During his eight years in Fez, he kept up his studies but was also involved in politics. Suspected of plotting against the sultan, in 1357 he was sentenced to a prison term of twenty-one months. Under a later governor, he again held high positions but became discouraged by court politics—even as he took part in them. More than once, he seemed on the verge of becoming the power behind a throne, but he often fared badly in his intrigues, in one instance failing to prevent the murder of his brother, Yahya, a vizier and respected historian and poet.

Precluded by the Marinid court—in the fourteenth century the Marinids briefly controlled all the Maghreb—from moving to the rival court at Tlemcen, in northeast Algeria, he turned instead to Granada, where he was welcomed by the young ruler Muhammad V and his vizier, Ibn al-Khaṭīb, a much-respected local scholar whose friendship Ibn Khaldūn had gained during his time in Fez. Before long, his intimacy with Muhammad made the vizier jealous, and Ibn Khaldūn was advised to set out on his travels once again, in 1365. Ibn al-Khaṭīb was the wise one on this occasion, as soon after, Muhammad revealed himself to be a bloodthirsty tyrant.

An invitation now came from Ibrahim II, the Hafsid ruler of the Mediterranean port of Bougie (today Béjaïa, in Algeria), to become his minister. When a year later Ibrahim was killed by his cousin, Abū al-Baqā' Khālid, Ibn Khaldūn went to work for Khalid instead but soon left as a result of yet more court plotting. The next nine years were turbulent. As the historian Patricia Crone has written, "most high-ranking governors and generals died violent deaths; and torture, assassination, and extortion were matters of routine." Thoroughly disappointed with his experiences of power (by his mid-thirties, he wrote, he had been "cured of the temptation of office"), Ibn Khaldūn spent his time in research and teaching in Biskra and Fez. However, local rulers continually asked him to take on political assignments on their behalf, and he did not always say no.

It was too much. Ibn Khaldūn retreated to the remote castle of Qalʿat Banū Salāma in western Algeria, perched atop a cliff, where he spent more than three years in complete seclusion, pondering why the Muslim world had degenerated into division. "I was inspired by that retreat," he wrote, "with words and ideas pouring into my head like cream into a churn." A further four years later, he completed the *Muqaddimah*, two fat volumes in its English translation, yet still only the prologue to seven large books. The first question he poses is, Why do historians make mistakes? He gives three reasons: partisanship, gullibility, and ignorance of what is intrinsically possible.

He could be gullible himself. In one of his essays he reports without comment that an ancestor lived for twelve hundred years and fathered four thousand males and one thousand females. In another, he writes that the Sun is neither hot nor cold, just an uncomposed substance that gives light. He was obsessed with the occult, magic ("no intelligent person doubts the reality of sorcery"), and predicting the future. He would quote Muhammad's saying that a good dream was "the 46th part of prophecy." He claimed to have a firsthand understanding of the supernatural and wrote of "rippers" in North Africa "who could tear apart the stomach of an animal or a garment just by pointing at it." He also imbibed and built upon the unchallenged racism of his time. "The Negro nations are, as a rule, submissive to slavery," he contended, because Black people were "less than human." But not irretrievably; should physically inferior African people be placed in a proper cold environment, they would find their skin became white and their hair straighten. In today's climate, such words are especially hard to read.

By 1379 Ibn Khaldūn was back in Tunis, for the city's archives beckoned. He soon found himself yet again enmeshed in court intrigues and in 1382 made a hurried departure for Egypt under the pretense that he was making a pilgrimage to Mecca. His personal life involved at least one major tragedy beyond the assassination of his brother. In 1383, in his early fifties, having moved to Cairo he arranged for his wife and five daughters to join him, but their ship was wrecked off the port of Alexandria and everyone on board lost their lives (and Ibn Khaldūn his entire library). At least his two sons arrived separately later, and he also eventually remarried. During the last twenty years of his life, he enjoyed the patronage of two local sultans, was granted professorships in a number of colleges, and on half a dozen occasions, austere and incorruptible, was appointed a chief judge, though only for short stretches, as he was criticized for being too strict, liable to fly into rages, his neck reddening with anger. His critics said that he had little real knowledge of jurisprudence and that he was saved by his eloquence, which "could make lies seem like truth." An unabashed elitist, he was seen as aloof and arrogant, an outsider who refused to wear the official garb of an Egyptian *qadi* (a judge in a shari'a court) and instead dressed in a Moroccan burnouse.*

Most of his time he still devoted to his studies, but besides lecturing and writing, he began to look after other people's money for safekeeping, a profitable sideline. Late in life he settled in a house by the Nile where, his enemies alleged, he delighted in the company of singing girls and young men. Otherwise he made one further pilgrimage to Mecca and two trips to Damascus, the second leading to his chats with Tamerlane. He died, still in office, on March 17, 1406.

* * *

IN HIS WAKE, HISTORIANS have made various attempts to analyze how Arab historians wrote about the past by category: biography (the lives of exemplary or otherwise distinctive individuals); prosopography (the history of groups and their common characteristics); or chronography (annals, the detailing of events as they occur, or history organized by a timeline of caliphs). There are also the four separate yet overlapping ways of writing: *hadith* (more tied to theology than history, yet conveying the past by way of reports, anecdotes, and stories, and incorporating *isnad*, as already defined); *adab*, a special form of educated writing, what we might term "belles-lettres"; *hikmat*, meaning "sound judgement" or "wisdom," the historian's proper subject matter, taking in the natural and philosophical sciences; and *siyasa*, which best describes Ibn Khaldūn's approach, often concerning itself with acts of government that lay outside the scope of shari'a.

---

* Along with other teachers, he observed the custom of sitting on a chair while his students sat at his feet. Hence the word *chair* came to signify a university professorship.

All these categories are helpful but do not explain why, for hundreds of years, Muslim civilization became suffocatingly parochial. Between the eleventh and thirteenth centuries it endured the terrifying onslaughts of Crusaders and the Seljuk Turks. The Mongols' destruction of Baghdad in 1258, as well as many other places where there were important libraries, also took a severe toll, but after Ibn Khaldūn there was no lack of Arab historians, Egypt being especially rich in chronicles, biographies, and comprehensive histories. However, although the *Muqaddimah* was widely read in Persia throughout the Middle Ages, Arabs ignored it. Not until 1850, when a French translation appeared, was Ibn Khaldūn discovered by the West. Yet he is the ultimate one-off. As the historian Colin Wells summarizes his achievement, "He stands out with irremediable starkness, a jutting spike on the flat-lining graph of Islamic historiography. Just as he lacked any real predecessors, so too did he lack any real successors."

Even during Ibn Khaldūn's life and accelerating after his death, many parts of Islam began a long cultural decline, during which philosophers and scientists were accused by various religious authorities of pursuing an alien agenda. One finds that ownership of a printing press, across many parts of the Middle East and North Africa, could be a capital offense. A small class of Muslim scholars known as "learned men" (*ʿulama*) rejected such technology on the grounds that "making the Qur'an accessible would only enable the ignorant to misinterpret it." By the time Napoleon invaded Egypt in 1798, only 3 percent of Muslims could read (as against 68 percent of English men and women in the same period).

Gibbon's harsh judgement on Islamic civilization was that it lacked "the spirit of enquiry and toleration." This is not to say it was opposed to scholarship, for in many areas Islam produced formidable scholars, but rather that religious fundamentalists exerted an undue influence. There was one brief period of hope: in the early eighteenth century, led by monks in Lebanon whose monasteries became centers of learning, Arabic literature enjoyed a renaissance, and among clergy and laity alike there developed an interest in secular history. Historians and scholars scarcely known to the West such as the cleric Rifaa al-Tahtawi (1801–73), Khayr al-Din (d. 1890), Jamāl al-Dīn al-Afghānī (d. 1897), and, some decades on, Taha Husayn (1889–1973) and Malek Bennabi (1905–73) worked to integrate traditional concepts of Islam into the dominant ideas of Europe: al-Tahtawi in particular embarked on what amounted to an intellectual revolution by translating some two thousand European and Turkish works, including Voltaire's biography of Peter the Great. This Muslim Enlightenment, however, was short-lived, and the suffocating effects of Islamic fundamentalism, notably in Iraq, Iran, and the formerly Iranian part of Central Asia, cut short attempts at reform.

An example of blighted freethinking comes in the twentieth-century figure of Ehsan Yarshater (1920–2018), an Iranian historian who founded an encyclopedia of his country's history and culture that today has some 7,300 entries by 1,600 authors and ranges from ancient Persian philosophy to the nature of cabbages. In the 1950s he established a translation and publishing institute, a reflection of his belief that embracing what the West had to offer would not cause Iran to lose its authenticity, as fundamentalists feared. (He was also the editor of a forty-volume translation of al-Ṭabarī.) The encyclopedia was his main concern, but it was interrupted by the 1979 revolution while he was still at work on the letter "A," the new Islamist regime forcing him to suspend the project. He moved to North America and restarted at Columbia University, never to visit Iran again. "The encyclopedia's impartiality does not please the current Persian government," he drily noted in 2011.

Even Ibn Khaldūn believed that Christians and Jews had just three options. They could convert to Islam, or submit to Islamic rule and pay a special tax, the *jizya*, or they could be killed. He did not question the Qur'an. Intellect, he believed, should not be employed on divine matters. In the centuries since his death, the study of history throughout the Middle East has remained in thrall to the same orthodoxy. I do not mean to be anti-Islam or uncaringly critical of Muslim culture, but certain tendencies are hard to ignore. By the end of the twentieth century a daunting proportion of the Muslim world had been swept up in religious fanaticism, intellectual intolerance, and dogmatic nationalism, in a movement tellingly referred to as both the "Counter-Enlightenment" and "Islamism." A Prophetic *hadith* runs, "Whoever imitates a people becomes one of them," a saying that became the keynote expression of the Sunni doctrine to distinguish Muslims from those not of the faith, reflecting anxieties about loss of identity and the dangers of taking in ideas from other cultures. Once more, historians today are regarded with suspicion, if not contempt. The past has become a foreign country.

CHAPTER 5

THE MEDIEVAL CHRONICLERS

Creating a Nation's Story

———

All that is really *known* of the ancient state of Britain is contained in a few pages. We *can* know no more than what the old writers have told us; yet what large books have we upon it, the whole of which . . . is all a dream.

—SAMUEL JOHNSON

The best portraits are perhaps those in which there is a slight mixture of caricature; and we are not certain that the best histories are not those in which a little of the exaggeration of fictitious narrative is judiciously employed. Something is lost in accuracy; but much is gained in effect.

—THOMAS BABINGTON MACAULAY

"EVEN WHEN IT COMES TO NOTABLE EVENTS," WROTE TACITUS, "WE are in the dark." Today, however, academic historians do not react favorably should one refer to "the Dark Ages," but that was how I first learned to describe the extended period in western Europe that runs from the ending of the Western Roman Empire, fixed precisely as September 4, 476, when the Scythian rebel Odoacer deposed Emperor Romulus Augustulus, until the Carolingian Renaissance of the early ninth century. Some historians have stretched the years of darkness yet further, to the first shoots of the Italian Renaissance in the mid-fourteenth century—nearly a millennium of perceived stagnation and decay.

The sobriquet "Dark Ages" was coined in the 1330s by the Italian poet-diplomat Francesco Petracco (1304–74), anglicized as Petrarch, who used the phrase *saeculum obscurum* to criticize the literature that followed classical antiquity. It was then extended to describe the Early Middle Ages, say to about 1000. Later historians expanded the term to refer to the period between Roman times and the High Middle Ages (from around the eleventh to the thirteenth century), years blighted by population decrease, limited new architecture, little historical writing, and a notable lack of cultural achievements. The Black Death, beginning in 1347, wiped out about two hundred million people, almost 60 percent of the global population. By the seventeenth century, "Dark Ages" was being widely used in various languages throughout western Europe. Phases beget phrases. I find "the Dark Ages" helpful.

History writing itself suffered during this long period. Petrarch's great friend Giovanni Boccaccio (1313–75), one of the few in the Late Middle Ages who tried to recover ancient manuscripts, often came upon them in monastery storerooms that had never been locked, with pages torn out by the fistful and what remained covered in garbage, mutilated, faded, riddled with scribal errors, or well on the way to dust. In 1363, he visited the great abbey of Monte Cassino, perched on a towering height midway between Rome and Naples, and the home of St. Benedict (480–543), the founder of Western monasticism. When he saw how much had been destroyed, he burst into tears.

* * *

THROUGHOUT WESTERN EUROPE, well up to the eleventh century, confidence in written records was neither immediate nor automatic. When information about the past was needed, people would not consult books or scrolls but would listen to what their elders could tell them. If there is any theme to arise from studying the historians over this long stretch of time, it is that these writers were either concerned to use the past to pursue a religious agenda or to create an origin tale that, like the works of the Roman historians, presented their respective countries with accounts of noble and courageous acts in which their respective people could take pride. And, of course, some of the most readable historians just wanted to tell a good tale, less for money than for renown. But as the distinguished Oxford historian Chris Wickham writes, every narrative for the late Roman and early medieval period "has recently been . . . analysed as a piece of free-standing rhetoric . . . and presented as useless for understanding anything except the mind and the education of the author." I think that is an overly pessimistic view, but it still serves as a timely warning.

From 476, although there are some notable early historians of the period—for instance, Gregory of Tours (538–594), or "Trollope with bloodshed," in John Burrow's nice phrase, and the Venerable Bede (673–735)—theirs is predominantly a religious record, credulous about miracles, heavily hagiographical and designed mainly as an aid to faith. Saints' lives replace secular biographies, which as a category disappear for centuries. Between 550 and 750, the copying of valuable texts nearly ceased, while reading and writing was sustained almost wholly in religious enclaves.

Most historians in western Europe were male, usually clerics, and largely wrote for fellow religious. Without exception, each was relatively prosperous, either having been born into the landholding class or composing for that audience. No medieval English work where the authorship is known was by a female. In other parts of Europe, women did occasionally write about the past, for instance the romantic poet Marie de France (fl. 1160–1215), but mainly they focused on hagiography or mystical works.

A central reason for this male dominance is that, from the conversion of Constantine on, western Europe was under the growing influence of the Church. The life choice of monasticism became popular in the first quarter of the fourth century, and by the early Middle Ages— from the fifth to tenth centuries*—monks, along with priests and other secular clergy, were almost the only educated people, and most of what we read was either copied out by monastic scribes (transcribing

---

* The term "Middle Ages" has had as troubled a history as "Dark Ages." It is generally defined as running from the conversion of the Emperor Constantine in 312 to the fall of Constantinople in 1453, although some historians extend it to the mid-eighteenth century. Repudiating Petrarch, Roman Catholics depicted the High Middle Ages as a period of social and religious consensus, and certainly not "dark." In his *Annales Ecclesiastici,* covering the first twelve centuries of Christianity up to 1198, Cardinal Caesar Baronius assigned "dark age" just for the period between the end of the Carolingian Empire in 888 and the first inklings of the Gregorian Reform in 1046. The label struck historians as something they could use. Thus Edward Gibbon expressed contempt for the "rubbish of the Dark Ages." In spite of this, "Middle Ages" did not become current until William Camden introduced the phrase in his study *Britannia* (1695). The earliest recorded use of the English word *medieval* wasn't until 1827. And, as A.J.P. Taylor observed, "The men of the Middle Ages . . . were unaware that they were living in the middle of anything." See A.J.P. Taylor, *From Napoleon to the Second International* (London: Faber, 1950), p. 27.

at least six hours a day, their hands going numb in unheated scriptoria) or written by these groups of interacting male clerisies. As time went on, the Church established universities to foster the preservation of knowledge: Oxford, Cambridge, Paris (by 1250 the mendicant teaching orders of the Dominicans and Franciscans had assumed control of the intellectual life of the French), Bologna (established in 1088, the first university to be defined as such, and which became known for law), Toledo, Orleans, and nearly every leading academy in Europe. Men of privilege ruled, in the writing of history as in the organizing of life.

By the latter part of the sixth century, the decline of learning was serious, but works of history continued to be written. The most lasting historian before the eighth century was an aristocratic Frenchman from central Gaul, a bishop who tried to be viewed as a serious scholar but failed utterly—he was simply too readable, his anecdotes too vivid, his love of a good story making him more like a Gallic Herodotus.

Gregory of Tours (538–94) was born in Clermont, the modern Clermont-Ferrand, in central Gaul. His father was a Gallo-Roman aristocrat, his family tree filled with senators and bishops. By his thirty-fifth birthday he too had been consecrated bishop—all but five of his predecessors were blood relatives. At Tours, he met everybody of influence, since the city was sited on the watery highway of the Loire and on the main thoroughfare between the Frankish north and southwest France, on into Spain. As the center for the popular cult of St. Martin (famed for having cut his cloak in two, so that he might give half to a beggar clad only in rags), Tours was also a pilgrimage site and political haven.

As a leader Gregory was zealous and conscientious, navigating his way through a politically turbulent time. At one point in his career, he was accused by a parishioner of slandering the queen of Gaul, Fredegund, and had to assert his innocence under oath. At the trial "his bearing was so full of dignity and uprightness that he astonished his enemies," and he was unanimously acquitted.

From the time of his election as bishop he began to write. He summarized his works as "ten books of *historia,* seven of miracles, one on the lives of the Fathers, a commentary in one book on the psalter, and one book on ecclesiastical liturgy." His first work, four volumes recounting the miracles of St. Martin, was written between 575 and 587, although the final volume was never completed. In 587, he also began a "Book of the Glories of the Martyrs," dealing with the miracles wrought in Gaul by martyrs of the Roman persecutions. Other publications followed, with *Liber vitae Patrum* being the most interesting, providing out-of-the-way stories about the upper classes of the period. (He wrote in Latin: French first developed as a written language not in France but in England in the hundred years or so after the Norman Conquest.)

Gregory's fame rests on *History of the Franks,* a ten-volume account of his own times. Book I summarizes world history from Adam forward, along with a general history of the Church, moving quickly to Gregory's own birthplace, Clermont, and the conquest of Gaul by the Franks, ending with the death of St. Martin in 397. Book II describes Clovis, the political and religious founder of the Frankish empire, and his conversion to Christianity, then continues to 591, still mixing ecclesiastical and secular events. From Book V Gregory plays a prominent part himself, concentrating on events in and around his diocese. His style is conversational, often humorous, but one takes away a lopsided impression—his focus gets easily diverted: crimes, miracles, wars, excesses of every kind, especially the homicidal feuds that followed Clovis's death. Gregory hero-worships Clovis but can still tell us that the Frankish king would on a whim split a local citizen in two with his axe. He can be credulous, but his narrative is rarely less than gripping:

> When King Clovis was dwelling at Paris he sent secretly to the son of Sigibert saying: "Behold your father has become an old man and limps in his weak foot. If he should die," said he, "of due right his kingdom would be yours together with our friendship." Led on by greed the son plotted to kill his father. And when his father went out from the city of Cologne and crossed the Rhine and was intending to journey through the wood Buchaw, as he slept at midday in his tent his son sent assassins in against him, and killed him there, in the idea that he would get his kingdom. But by God's judgment he walked into the pit that he had cruelly dug for his father. He sent messengers to King Clovis to tell about his father's death, and to say: "My father is dead, and I have his treasures in my possession, and also his kingdom. Send men to me, and I shall gladly transmit to you from

his treasures whatever pleases you." And Clovis replied: "I thank you for your good will, and I ask that you show the treasures to my men who come, and after that you shall possess all yourself." When they came, he showed his father's treasures. And when they were looking at the different things he said: "It was in this little chest that my father used to put his gold coins." "Thrust in your hand," said they, "to the bottom, and uncover the whole." When he did so, and was much bent over, one of them lifted his hand and dashed his battleax against his head, and so in a shameful manner he incurred the death which he had brought on his father.

Although he conveys political and other messages, Gregory's principal aim is to highlight the pretensions of secular life, which he contrasts with the exemplary conduct of the saints. He seems to have had an acute sense of himself as author and even pleaded that his successors could rewrite his account in verse if they so wished (no one to date has taken up the offer). But the good bishop is such a born storyteller that what we remember best are his tales of domestic slaves, artisans, contumacious nuns, impostors (a particular worry), drunks—including several bishops—as well as fornicating priests and ferocious Frankish nobles like Roccolen. Gregory conjures up not only the ghost of Herodotus; we are looking at a sixth-century Boccaccio.

* * *

JUST AS GREGORY PRESERVED Frankish history, were it not for Bede (673–735) and his *Historia Ecclesiastica Gentis Anglorum* (The Ecclesiastical History of the English People), completed in a Northumberland monastery in 731, we would know almost nothing of eighth-century England, Wales, and Ireland. Sir Frank Stenton (1880–1967), a highly respected historian on the period, regarded Bede's history as one of the "small class of books which transcend all but the most fundamental conditions of time and place," its quality resting on Bede's "astonishing power of coordinating the fragments of information which came to him through tradition, the relation of friends, or documentary evidence." Compared to Gregory of Tours, "Bede was a scholar who labored in the quiet of a rich library. . . . Gregory's work is racy [*sic*] of the soil. Bede's work is redolent of a burning candle." That metaphor summons up the comment by the Roman historian Seneca, made shortly before his death in A.D. 65: "Nothing could be fainter than those torches which allow us, not to pierce the darkness, but to glimpse it." Glimpses can be valuable, though, as Bede shows.

He was born in Monkton, Durham, but little is known of his background. His name comes from the Anglo-Saxon for "to bid, command." At the age of seven he was entrusted to the monastery of St. Peter at Wearmouth, on England's northeast coast. Two years later, after its abbot had founded a sister establishment at nearby Jarrow, he was moved there. Four years on, in 687, plague broke out. The *Life of Ceolfrith,* an anonymous work written in about 710, records that only two surviving monks were able to sing the full offices, one a boy of fourteen, almost certainly Bede. Before the age of thirty he was a full priest.

By about 701, he had written his first works, the *De Arte Metrica* and *De Schematibus et Tropis,* both intended for use in the classroom. He eventually completed over sixty books, nearly all of which survive. We know these as Bede's because he was working in a culture that more or less shared our understanding of authorship and put in place institutions to ensure that books, once written, remained inviolably the property of their authors. His scholarship covered a wide range of subjects; for instance, he was the first to use the A.D. system of dating, an immense improvement. When an event took place was not the problem— the Battle of Kos in 261 B.C., for instance, had been a common dateline among historians ever since Thucydides—but the method used was ungainly. Bede's method of tagging what had happened either from the time of Christ's birth—i.e., A.D., "in the year of our Lord," or B.C., "before Christ"—came into general use through the popularity of the *Historia Ecclesiastica* and his two works on chronology. The new system effectively synchronized timekeeping in the West, even if it took many years to become the norm.

Although Bede is now mainly read as a historian, during his life his treatises on the Bible and on grammar and chronology were considered just as important. His writings fall into distinct categories: poetry, grammatical and "scientific" works, scriptural commentary (hagiography, martyrology, and hymnology), and historical and biographical studies. It was for his theological writings that he was made a saint, and he is still the only Englishman ever named a Doctor of the Church. By the ninth century he had become known as "Venerable," but this was not because he was thought of as a future saint. One account has it that the monk tasked with composing a suitable inscription on his tomb got as far as the couplet *Hac sunt in fossa/Bedeae* _____ *ossa* ("This grave contains the _____ Bede's remains") but was then stumped. Divine guidance came in the night, and the next day he was able to fill in the blank: *Venerabilis.* It is a nice story, and by the eleventh century Bede's honorific had become commonplace.

The opening page of Bede's ecclesiastical history of England. It was probably produced within a few decades of his death in 735.

His great work, the *Historia Ecclesiastica,* is divided into five books, the first of which begins with some geographical context, deliberately painting Britain in rosy hues to recall the description of the Garden of Eden in Genesis (so that its peoples can later be "redeemed" by the coming of Christianity), then sketching the history of England from Caesar's invasion of 55 B.C. A brief description of Christianity in Roman Britain is followed by the recounting of how the Saxon, Angle, and Jutish invaders in the fifth century established themselves and the tale of Augustine's mission to England in 597, which brought Christianity to the Anglo-Saxons. The second book begins with the death of Pope Gregory the Great in 604 and follows the progress of Christianity in the south of England and the first attempts to evangelize in the north. The third recounts the growth of Christianity in Northumbria, climaxing in a long account of the Council at Whitby, at which the unity of the Church in Britain was secured. The fourth tells of the efforts to extend Christianity to all parts of Britain and "obstinate" Ireland; the fifth takes the chronicle up to Bede's own time.

His primary intention was to show the growth of a united Church throughout the country; by the books' end the English and their Church are dominant. His descriptions are designed to promote his reform agenda, so he paints a highly optimistic picture, as opposed to the pessimism of his private letters. He focuses on heresies and the efforts to root them out; secular history is brought in only where it helps him make a moral point—although he did also want to entertain his readers with tidbits of interesting information. For instance, he claims that the stakes driven into the bed of the Thames as part of the Britons' defense against the invading Romans are still to be seen, seven hundred years later, and he describes them. We know little about him as a person. At one point he mentions that he enjoys music, and he was said to have been an accomplished reciter of poetry.*

One paradox, considering Bede's respect for evidence, is that the books are overloaded with miracles, miracles, miracles—along with holy deaths, visions of heaven and hell, potent relics, uncorrupted and fragrant corpses, and even a divine intervention involving a distressed horse—about 40 of the 140 chapters are devoted to such stories. So maybe the venerable monk and Gregory of Tours are not that different after all. Bede must have believed what he wrote was true, because the work is evidently that of a scholar scrupulous in assessing the accuracy of his sources and to record only "what I was able to learn myself from the trustworthy testimony of reliable witnesses."

---

* For centuries, authors wrote history expressly to be read out loud in public. It might seem odd that reading silently was ever seen as a special gift, yet it is mentioned as early as 405 B.C., in Aristophanes's *Frogs* (52–53), and Plutarch records how, in the fourth century B.C., Alexander the Great silently read a letter from his mother while his troops, watching, stood amazed. In 63 B.C., Servilia, Cato the Younger's half-sister and Julius Caesar's mistress, wrote a sexually explicit letter to her lover that was handed to him during a Senate debate. Cato, suspecting that the letter referred to a political conspiracy, demanded that Caesar read it aloud. Caesar's lips were then seen moving, as he first read the missive to himself. Cato then read it out, to his considerable embarrassment—just what Caesar was hoping for. In the first account of someone reading silently without moving their lips, in St. Augustine's *Confessions,* written between A.D. 397 and 400, he sees his tutor, Ambrose, the bishop of Milan, reading in this way and speculates about the advantages—and about reading's individualistic appeal, one that would become universal only during the Middle Ages.

Bede acknowledges that he had help from the abbot of St. Augustine's Abbey in Canterbury, an indication of how communication from one end of England to the other was not an insurmountable problem. The monastery at Wearmouth-Jarrow was also a renowned center of learning, with an excellent library of some two hundred books. It was a vibrant and sophisticated place, by 710 the home of more than six hundred monks. Even so, there was no one in Northumbria with whom Bede could profitably argue his case. In the centuries after his death the *Historia Ecclesiastica* was copied often, and about 160 manuscripts survive, many outside Britain. His overriding authority may well have deterred others from writing and even have led to the disappearance of other, older works. Certainly his achievement, revered on the Continent as well as in England, had no comparable successor until the mid-twelfth century, close to four hundred years later.

* * *

"WHAT MAKES A NATION is the past," declared the great historian Eric Hobsbawm, "what justifies one nation against others is the past, and historians are the people who produce it." However, some great works of history have not necessarily been graced by any one author or organizing member. So we reach the *Anglo-Saxon Chronicle,* a remarkable enterprise unique in Europe, at least up to the beginning of the thirteenth century. The *Chronicle,* each entry a single short paragraph, tells us the word on the street—what has leaked through, what its contributors heard. It was composed in the vernacular, so was free of the flowery rhetoric and insistent moralizing that disfigure similar Continental works in Latin, and much of the information is not recorded elsewhere, since archives were still virtually nonexistent. This collation of different accounts evolved from what were known as Easter Tables, calendars that helped the clergy determine the future dates of church festivals. A page consisted of a series of horizontal lines followed by astronomical information, with room for short notes distinguishing one year from another. Monks began to enter jottings of all kinds in the margins, and over time this individualized commentary grew. Sometimes the lineages of royal houses and even smatterings of popular songs and items from local legends and customs were written in. (Across the Channel, Charlemagne, quickly grasping the value of the practice, ordered every monastery in his kingdom to keep similar annals.)*

Most English religious houses, and even those in Wales and Ireland, maintained chronicles of some sort, as did many parish churches. Histories of this period aspired to be little more than that. Between the seventh and ninth centuries, however, various abbots and men of religion wrote accounts of the deeds of prominent men, "and thereof they made great books, and called them chronicles." When in 871 Alfred (849–99) took over as king of Britain, he aimed to make such information more available and had an early version of the *Chronicle* (composed in Winchester but expanded between 855 and 892 by incorporating other local annals) "fastened . . . to a pillar, so that no-one could remove it or take it away, so that every man could see it and look at it, for in it are the lives of all the kings that ever were in England."

The *Chronicle* was subsequently copied and distributed to a range of religious houses. As the enterprise developed, it was less a series of lists, and the notes became longer, growing into historical records, as calendars mutated into annals, annals into chronicles, and chronicles into works of history. Many later entries are marked by a homeliness and vigor in the language that makes the *Chronicle* the supreme example of Old English prose.

At least nine chronicles of the original *Anglo-Saxon Chronicle* still exist; the earliest, though compiled in the ninth century, is dated 60 B.C.

---

* The chronicles belong to what one might call the "collective historians." The seventeenth-century *Gallia Christiana,* for instance, of which there have been several versions, is a documentary catalogue of all the Catholic dioceses and abbeys of France and their occupants. The Bollandists, named after Jean Bolland (1596–1665), are a Benedictine community that set the pace in hagiography: an association of paleographers and historians (originally all Jesuits, but now including people outside the order) who since the early seventeenth century have studied the lives of Christian saints. Their most important publication is the *Acta Sanctorum* (Deeds of the Holy). It begins with all the saints of January, and after four hundred years its authors had reached December 1, at which point they gave up.

Turning to Germany, the *Allgemeine Encyclopädie der Wissenschaften und Künste* (Universal Encyclopedia of Sciences and Arts) was a nineteenth-century encyclopedia published by Johann Samuel Ersch and Johann Gottfried Gruber, generally known as the "Ersch-Gruber." One of the most ambitious encyclopedia projects ever, it remains uncompleted. Begun in 1813, it was briefly stopped by the Napoleonic Wars, and the first volume did not appear till 1818. By 1889, when the project was abandoned, it had reached 167 separate books, the article about Greece alone covering 3,668 pages.

In China, the Song dynasty commissioned *The Four Great Books of Song,* a massive omnibus which took a hundred years to complete, and the Ming dynasty oversaw the 11,095 volumes of the *Yongle Encyclopedia*—until the digital age, the largest encyclopedia ever attempted.

(the annals' date for Caesar's invasions of Britain), and includes material up to the year in which a particular chronicle was written. In one case, the *Chronicle* was still being actively updated in 1154. Some of the entries are obviously biased, showing the contributor's point of view, and important events can be omitted or glossed over. Taken as a whole, however, it is the single most important account we have of English history between the departure of the Romans and the decades following the Norman Conquest.

* * *

ANNALS HAVE NOTHING TO say about causes, significance, implications, or consequences; by design, they leave interpretation aside. Yet "history as a genre," as John Burrow writes, "characteristically involves extended narrative, relevant circumstantial detail, and thematic coherence; the recording of facts is dictated by thematic, dramatic and explanatory considerations, rather than just chronological juxtaposition and convention." He was thinking of written accounts, yet one of the most effective works of the eleventh century is a woven artwork—the Bayeux Tapestry. It is still the best record of its time, pictorial or otherwise, even as it is criticized as French propaganda, "a tapestry of lies," giving a false account of the most important event of the eleventh century, the Norman invasion of Britain.

Whatever its truthfulness, the tapestry is a unique record of Anglo-Saxon life, of medieval weaponry, clothing, and other equipment beyond anything else that still exists from this period. Measuring 224.3 feet long and eighteen inches high, it is also a text, since a verbal narrative in Latin runs its entire length (the word *text,* after all, comes from the Latin *texere,* to weave). The main figures are complemented by narrow horizontal bands, top and bottom, that show scenes from ordinary life. Men feast on spitted birds, hit each other with shovels during an argument, wade through shallow water to load heavy provisions onto a waiting ship, carry a pig on their shoulders, sow, or go to church. There is even the occasional erotic incident clearly portrayed. (Scott Fitzgerald, writing in 1931, tells of a "judge from some New York district who had taken his daughter to see the Bayeux Tapestries and made a scene in the papers advocating their segregation because one scene was immoral.")

Depicted are 626 human figures (just 15 of them named), 202 horses, 55 dogs, 505 other animals, 49 trees, 37 buildings, and 41 ships. Only five women are featured (including Harold's mistress, the intriguingly named Edith Swan-Neck). It is a man's tale, if stitched together by women. The end of the tapestry has long been lost, and the final caption, *Et fuga verterunt Angli* ("and the English left fleeing") was added by French weavers shortly before 1814 during the Napoleanic Wars. When first created, the hanging was significantly longer, with maybe two extra panels, probably one of which included William's coronation.

The tapestry, or *La telle du conquest,* depicts what happened leading up to the most decisive year in English history, culminating in the Battle of Hastings of October 14, 1066. It consists of some seventy-five scenes with Latin inscriptions, embroidered with woolen yarn in eight interlaced sections on linen cloth (rather than woven, so strictly speaking it is not a tapestry, although always referred to as such; in an embroidery the stitching often rises above the ground fabric). It was probably commissioned by William's greedy and ambitious half-brother, Odo, bishop of the cathedral city of Bayeux, and made in England—not Bayeux—in the 1070s. Odo became earl of Kent after the Conquest and, when William was absent in Normandy, also served as regent of England. It was designed to hang in the hall of his palace, then eventually in the cathedral he built. Few venues were large enough to display such a decoration in full; like some enormous strip of film, it is longer than Nelson's Column by more than a third of its height.[*]

The tapestry begins with the English king, Edward the Confessor, then about sixty and with no clear successor, sending his brother-in-law, the Earl Harold Godwinson, earl of Essex, to Normandy, possibly to promise Duke William that he will succeed Edward as king. After various adventures including shipwreck and imprisonment (from the last of which William obligingly rescues him), Harold leaves for home and in another panel comes up before Edward, who appears to be telling him off, even wagging his index finger at his visibly cringing brother-in-law.

When Edward dies, Harold takes the crown for himself. The news of his act of treachery reaches Normandy, and according to the tapestry William orders a fleet to be assembled, although it is Odo who is shown

---

[*] In my school and college years and for years afterward, I spent much time in a close friend's family home in Gloucestershire, where the living room had a sofa and armchairs covered in a Bayeux Tapestry print. I loved this furniture, and when the family eventually moved was bequeathed it. Sadly, the covering has fared less well than the original, and all I have now is a much-loved cushion, with its famous frieze. *The New Yorker,* shortly after D-Day, devoted its cover (July 15, 1944) to an imitation of the original.

directing the craftsmen. The invaders cross the Channel and land on a beach near the village of Pevensey. Messengers are sent between the English (actually, Anglo-Danish) and Norman armies, and William, an impressive five foot ten, tall for his day, makes a speech to prepare his men for battle. Next we see troops being butchered, and mutilated corpses litter the ground. King Harold is shown at the moment of his death, but not as customarily understood. The tapestry shows an English figure with a golden arrow piercing his eye, but this is not Harold, who was almost certainly trampled by a charger, then hacked to pieces by four Norman knights who had broken through the Anglo-Saxon lines. According to the historian Ben Macintyre, the arrow-in-the-eye story was cooked up afterward to lend political and religious legitimacy to the precarious new dynasty, becoming embedded in legend by the twelfth century, then stitched into the tapestry when it was restored early in the nineteenth century. A single, fateful missile hurtling out of the sky to strike down the king was thus presented as an act of God, divine punishment for Harold's breaking his oath to support William.

Given that Anglo-Saxon needlework was acclaimed across Europe, the likely makers of the tapestry were needlewomen attached to St. Augustine's Abbey in Canterbury and the designer probably its abbot, who had an international reputation for such work and who would have had no choice but to follow instructions from his new masters. Since the narrative links Harold's activities in Normandy with the invasion two years later, the tapestry is generally seen as an apologia for the Conquest. In fact, though, it is a fascinating mix of Norman propaganda and Anglo-Saxon counterpropaganda, and while the main story might appear a celebration of the invaders' victory, the tapestry is encoded with covert messages intended to undermine Norman claims. For instance, Harold is presented as brave (he saves two soldiers from a river while in France), and his men are not belittled, while we see the invaders torching a building with a woman and child inside. *What a tangled web we weave. . . .*

The Bayeux Tapestry's durability over nine centuries is extraordinary. It has influenced our understanding of history possibly more than any other pictorial artifact. Only the fresco cycle by Piero della Francesca, painted between 1452 and 1456 in the basilica of San Francesco in Arezzo, is both a greater work and gives us an overwhelmingly powerful historical narrative.

* * *

"YOU SEE!" EXCLAIMS THE professor in Tom Stoppard's play *Arcadia*. "They wrote—they scribbled—they put it on paper. It was their employment. Their diversion. Paper is what they had. And there'll be more. There is always more. . . ." Indeed, the 1120s and 1130s marked a high tide in British history writing, and three of its most prominent authors, Geoffrey of Monmouth, Henry of Huntingdon, and William of Malmesbury, are well worth reading nine centuries later.

Whether composing for courtly entertainment or out of serious scholarly interest, most medieval historians tried to be truthful, if with a particular slant and conditioned by what they could discover. Geoffrey (c. 1100–c. 1155) was not of their number. He is the best known of the trio, yet even in his own day was castigated for being a master of make-believe. He may not have been from Monmouth or even from Wales. After taking holy orders and settling in Oxford, he started to write *Historia Regum Britanniae* (History of the Kings of Britain), which was immediately popular and remained so well into the sixteenth century; 215 medieval manuscripts survive. Composed in Latin, still regarded as the language of "serious" history (the nobility spoke Anglo-Norman, much closer to French* than to English, the common people a mixture of tongues, including Welsh, Cumbric, Cornish, Breton, and English), it relates the supposed history of Britain from the twelfth century B.C. and its settlement by Brutus of Troy, after whom the country was named, to the death of Cadwallader, the last in a long line of British kings, in the seventh. More than a hundred sovereigns are named as having ruled during these years, including Lear ("Leir"), Cymbeline, Old King Coel, and Vortigern, the man Geoffrey claims was responsible for inviting the Angles and Saxons across from Germany in the fifth century. Most famously, Arthur is by some margin the overall hero of Geoffrey's tale, valiant and purposeful, conquering thirty kingdoms and founding the most glamorous court in history.

Geoffrey created and peopled whole worlds for which there was

---

* By 1086, when William commissioned his controlling Domesday Book, fully half of England was held by just eleven of his closest followers; around 10 percent of England's population were slaves. Of the two hundred or so aristocrats and adventurers who held another quarter of the country, just four were English. Only in 1362 did French cease to be the language of Parliament, and not till the fifteenth century did English emerge as the nation's common vernacular.

hardly a shred of evidence (not least, there are scores of place-names for which he gives entirely fictitious etymological explanations). William of Newburgh (c. 1136–c. 1198), himself a successful historian, protested: "only a person ignorant of ancient history would have any doubt about how shamelessly and impudently he lies. . . . It is quite clear that everything this man wrote about Arthur and his successors, or indeed about his predecessors from Vortigern onwards, was made up." Yet Geoffrey goes to some lengths to present himself as a serious historian. In his preface he explains that a document was placed in his hands that "set forth the doings of them all in due succession and order . . . all told in stories of exceeding beauty." This document was a "certain most ancient book in the British [i.e., Welsh] tongue," supplied to him by the archdeacon of Oxford. Cue: flying pigs. No other contemporary chronicler seems to have had access to the volume, and subsequent research has not unearthed it. Rather, much of what Geoffrey wrote is based on Bede's books, while the legend of King Arthur makes its earliest appearance in *Historia Brittonum,* a Welsh-Latin work by an obscure ninth-century Welshman named Nennius (b. 769) that conjures up a dozen battles that Arthur is supposed to have fought but without dating them and in one of which his hero singlehandedly slays 960 men. "I heaped together [*coacervavi*] all I could find," says Nennius. Geoffrey took the heap and made good use of such compost.

I recently came across a new word: *nefelibata*—one who lives in the clouds of his own imagination or dreams. It fits Geoffrey well. Even so, what did he think he was doing? Filling a void, for a start. Next to nothing was known of Britain during those early centuries, and he provided a captivating account with as much imagination—and cunning—as he could muster. His reshaping of the Merlin and Arthur myths ensured their vast popularity and encouraged others to join in. In 1191, the reputed remains of Arthur and his queen, Guinevere, were "discovered" by the monks of Glastonbury; before long, Gawaine and the Holy Grail, Kay, Bedevere, Lancelot, and the ideals of courtly love were added. Later writers, including a host of poets, were haunted by Geoffrey's fables, repeating and embellishing his stories as if they were historical fact. Geoffrey saw that Arthur was a British prince who could rival true-life legends such as Alexander or Charlemagne. Why shouldn't Britain have its own heroes? *Historia Regum Britanniae* provided the British with an origin myth. "Fact" did not acquire its current meaning of "true thing" for several more centuries. And legend may not *be* history, but it can profoundly affect our sense of the past.[*]

A long line of chroniclers accepted all this in good faith. By 1152 Geoffrey's storytelling had won him official favor, for he was consecrated bishop of St. Asaph, in Denbighshire, North Wales. Meanwhile, the *History* was being widely disseminated across western Europe, and two hundred years after his death his repute was such that Chaucer gave him a high place in his *Hous of Fame*. William Caxton (1422–91) chose the *History* as one of the first books for his new printing press, while Milton planned an epic based on Arthur; only later did he settle for Satan instead.

★ ★ ★

THE MOST IMPORTANT ANGLO-NORMAN historian to emerge from the secular clergy (as opposed to the monastery) is Henry of Huntingdon (c. 1088–c. 1157). A vicar's son, he was the author of *Historia Anglorum* (The History of the English), first published around 1129, an account of England from its beginnings to his own day. He distinguished himself in his youth by writing eight books of epigrams, eight books on love, and eight books on herbs, spices, and gems united by a medical theme. In 1110 he succeeded his father as archdeacon of Lincoln, a substantial inheritance for a man not yet thirty. No personal correspondence survives, and no one considered him important enough to have written his biography. We know that he was part of the extended family of Robert Bloet, bishop of Lincoln, and grew up amid England's richest episcopal court. It was Bloet's successor, Alexander, who suggested he write his *Historia*.

Henry went on to publish new editions, the fifth and final version reaching 1154, supposedly to conclude with the death of Stephen, his whole account grouped into eight books (no one knows why he had this obsession with eight). There is some evidence that Henry intended

---

[*] A.J.P. Taylor notes, "In most European languages, 'story' and 'history' are the same word: *histoire* in French, *Geschichte* in German. *Quelle histoire* or *Was für eine Geschichte* does not mean 'What admirable history' . . . but 'What a far-fetched yarn.' It would save much trouble if we had the same coincidence of words in English. Then perhaps we should not be ashamed to admit that history is at bottom simply a form of story-telling." A.J.P. Taylor, *From Napoleon to the Second International: Essays on Nineteenth-Century Europe* (London: Hamish Hamilton, 1993), p. 36. It seems appropriate to add that in Arabic the modern term for "politics" is *siyasa,* a word that began as a medieval term for the "management or training of horses and camels."

another book that would cover the first five years of Henry II's reign, but its author must have been at least seventy by the time Henry was crowned, and died shortly thereafter.

Huntington's sources inevitably included Bede as well as a now-lost version of the *Anglo-Saxon Chronicle* that contained detailed accounts of several battles of the Saxon invasions preserved only in his history. At one point a fellow antiquarian gave him a copy of Geoffrey's *Historia,* which he used uncritically, so that some of its fictions became even further embedded in popular beliefs. Henry added some touches of his own: King Canute's showing his obsequious court that he could not stem the incoming tide by royal command, for instance, and Henry I's death from overindulging in lampreys (a jawless fish, similar to an eel, widely eaten by the upper classes). Such imaginative leaps made his work extremely popular, and although he is not reliable he offers a valuable insight into the mindset of historians of his day.

So too does his contemporary William of Malmesbury (1095–1143), generally considered the foremost English historian of the twelfth century, even if he ceded popularity and influence to Geoffrey of Monmouth. The American medievalist C. Warren Hollister ranks him among the most talented since Bede: "a gifted historical scholar and an omnivorous reader . . . Indeed, William may well have been the most learned man in twelfth-century Western Europe." William himself would probably have agreed with the assessment, since he lamented that, from Bede's death in 735 until the succession of Edgar the Peaceful in 959, there were "two hundred and twenty-three years . . . and in that interval history limps along with no support from literature." So much for Geoffrey and Henry of Huntingdon.

William's father was Norman but his mother English, and he spent his adult years as a monk at Malmesbury Abbey in Wiltshire. Its library boasted at least four hundred works by two hundred–odd authors. William put together a miscellany of medieval histories, which led him to write a popular account closely modeled on Bede's, the *Gesta Regum Anglorum* (Deeds of the English Kings), completed in 1125 and spanning 449 to 1120. He later expanded it up to 1127, releasing a much-improved edition that disclosed "in his second thoughts, the mellowing of age." This was followed in 1125 by the *Gesta Pontificum Anglorum* (Deeds of the English Bishops), a vivid descriptive history of the country's abbeys and bishoprics. Beginning about 1140, William then set about producing his *Historia Novella* (Modern History), a three-book chronicle that stretches from 1128 to Stephen's reign (1135–54). It breaks off in 1142; presumably William died then.

He is still well worth reading for his strong documentation and clear, engaging voice. A Latin stylist, he shows literary instincts that are, for his time, remarkably astute. Some scholars call his arrangement of material careless, but he remains celebrated for good reason. In particular, he was keenly interested in personality, which he illustrated through anecdote, direct speech, physical depiction, and a sprinkling of his own opinions. There are myriad examples, none better than his portrayal of William II (1056–1100):

> He respected God too little, and man not at all. . . . Abroad and in the gatherings of men his aspect was haughty and unbending; he would fix the man before him with a threatening gaze, and with assumed severity and harsh voice overbear those with whom he spoke. . . . At home and in the chamber with his private friends, he was all mildness and complaisance, and relied much on jest to carry a point, being in particular a merry critic of his own mistakes, so as to reduce the unpopularity they caused and dissolve it in laughter. . . . The cost of his clothes he liked to be immensely inflated, and spurned them if anyone reduced it. For instance, one morning when he was putting on some new shoes, he asked his valet what they had cost. "Three shillings," the man replied, at which the king flew into a rage. "You son of a bitch!" he cried; "since when has a king worn such trumpery shoes? Go and get me some that cost a mark of silver."

It makes one wonder whether people of that period were really so different from us or, as Voltaire was to put it, just like we are now—only with bad teeth.

* * *

IN ITS CHAPTERS ON the Middle Ages, *A Global History of History* makes room for several lesser-known western European figures, such as the German Widukind of Corvey (925–80), the Frenchman Hugh of St. Victor (c. 1096–1141), and John of Salisbury (c. 1120–80). It also covers a range of writing that I have not even mentioned—Chinese authors from the end of the Eastern Han Dynasty in 220 to the invention of a historical encyclopedia at the end of the eighth century, Japanese chroniclers from the sixth century on, and historians from Russia, Mongolia, the Islamic world, Korea, and Denmark. But nowhere does it find room to discuss one of the most-read writers of his time, the thirteenth-century monk of St. Albans Abbey in Hertfordshire, Matthew Paris.

Writing with a goose quill on parchment in a crabbed, angular gothic script, Matthew (c. 1200–1259) completed several works, mostly historical, which he illustrated himself, to the extent that his pictures, "lively and demotic and sometimes macabre," are part of his appeal. John Burrow, whose words those are, also calls him "populist, scathing, cynical, violently partisan, prejudiced and funny," not dissimilar to Gregory of Tours. Burrow grants that Paris was more a chronicler than a historian, his *Chronica Majora* a vivid and highly personal view of the world, full of snorts of indignation and disgust. If Paris disapproved of someone there was no holding back, as over a lawsuit involving the St. Albans church:

> There was in this church among the brothers a certain person who was indeed cowled, though by no means a monk, but rather like Lucifer among the angels or Jude among the apostles, a worthless hypocrite among monks, himself not a monk but rather a living demon.

We even get a name, one William Pigun. He does not come off well.

In spite of his surname, Paris was English, although early on he may have studied in the French capital. He may also have become a monk only after enjoying a career in the secular world, since he was clearly at ease with the gentry and even the royal court, suggesting that he came from a well-connected family. The first we know of him (from his own writings) is that he was admitted as a monk in 1217 and in 1236 succeeded Roger of Wendover, the abbey's official recorder, furnishing new material to include events of his own time.

Apart from a couple of bookish missions to Norway, from 1217 till his death he kept to the abbey and to writing history, a pursuit for which St. Albans is celebrated, its chronicle eventually covering more than two hundred years; it was the effective center of historical writing in late medieval England. Paris completed several books besides *Chronica Majora,* among them *Historia Anglorum* (written about 1253), *Deeds of the Abbots of the Monastery of St. Albans,* and biographies of St. Alban, Edward the Confessor, and Thomas Becket. *Chronica Majora* remains an important measure for understanding the period, even if Paris's prejudices make him an unreliable guide. He denigrated the pope whenever he could, for example, and glorified Frederick II (1194–1250)—yet paradoxically, in *Historia Anglorum,* the holy Roman emperor is a "tyrant" who "committed disgraceful crimes."

Matthew Paris's sketch of the town band of Cremona perched on an elephant. His pictures, "lively and demotic and sometimes macabre," are part of his appeal.

Much of his information Paris derived from people at court and from conversations with eyewitnesses. Among his sources was Henry III, who was well aware that Paris was recording events and wanted him to be well informed. In 1257, during a week's visit to St. Albans, he kept the chronicler beside him; the king "guided my pen," says Paris. Given this, it is curious that the *Chronica* provides so critical an account of Henry's reign, but possibly Paris never intended his work to be read in the form it has come down to us. Many passages have written next to them, in red, *vacat, offendiculum,* or *impertinens,* suggesting that they should be omitted. Unexpurgated copies were made in his lifetime, however, and his own outspoken manuscript copy has survived. While he tried to erase some more egregious indiscretions, bowdlerizing his own work was, to quote Burrow again, "like trying to de-vein Gorgonzola." Had he been more successful in his edits, we wouldn't be reading him still.

* * *

DURING THE MIDDLE AGES (the extended version), there were at least three periods future ages dubbed "renaissances" (a word that did not appear in English until the 1830s). That initiated by Charlemagne (768–814) was first, followed by the rule of Otto I (936–973), whose assumption of imperial power brought him into close contact with the ablest men in his kingdom, which in turn led to significant reforms. The third renaissance, that of the twelfth century, has been identified as the most thorough, as it included social, political, and economic transformations and a revitalizing of both the arts and sciences—all of which paved the way for the artistic movements of the fifteenth century, the Renaissance renaissance.

The death of Roland, in a manuscript illustration by Jean Fouquet, circa 1455–60, of The Song of Roland, *an epic poem of some four thousand lines that is the oldest surviving major work of French literature. Composed between 1040 and 1115, it is based on the Battle of Roncevaux Pass in 778, in which the rearguard of Charlemagne's forces was ambushed by a Muslim army in the mountains between France and Spain.*

Charlemagne ruled over practically all western Christendom, an area roughly equivalent to France, Germany, the Low Countries, Austria, Switzerland, Italy, and Slovenia, excepting only southern Italy, the Asturias in Spain, and the British Isles—four hundred thousand square miles of territory—but his attempts at cultural renewal were largely limited to a group of court scribes and painters. Those scribes crucially copied classical texts, both Christian and pagan, the first six books of Tacitus's *Annals* surviving thanks to monks at Fulda in central Germany and Caesar's *Gallic War* to Fleury, a Benedictine abbey on the Loire. In addition, Charlemagne's highly educated younger sister, Gisela, an abbess of a convent near Paris, commissioned a set of annals centered on her and her brother's ancestors. Charlemagne also decreed that all churches within his kingdom should have schools for children of both sexes, a small revolution, but as a whole his Renaissance was a false dawn, in that outside the court it was confined almost exclusively to the clergy; within a couple of generations its gains had largely melted away from the heat of civil war and the depredations of ravaging Vikings, Saracens, and Magyars. It did produce some formidable historians, however, none more so than a scholar named Einhard (c. 775–840), whose main work is a life of Charlemagne, written shortly after the emperor's death in 814. It is the best known of medieval biographies.

Like the Venerable Bede, Einhard was given over as a young boy to a local monastery, and, perhaps due to his small stature, he concentrated on scholarship. Around 791, he joined Charlemagne's court, where he became a favorite of the emperor and carried out several missions of state for him. In particular, he was interested in architecture, and Charlemagne put him in charge of completing several palace complexes, earning him the nickname "Bezaleel," an affectionate reference to Exodus 31:2–5.*

His study of Charlemagne, largely complimentary, was modeled in tone and structure on Suetonius's biography of Augustus in *The Lives of the Caesars,* and although he lamented that he knew little of his subject's childhood, with the use of state documents and archives he was able to bring "Carolus Magnus" to convincing life—Charlemagne the

---

* "See, I have called by name Bezaleel. . . . And I have filled him with the spirit of God, in wisdom, and in understanding, and in knowledge, and in all manner of workmanship, to devise cunning works, to work in gold, and in silver, and in brass. And in cutting of stones, to set *them,* and in carving of timber, to work in all manner of workmanship." Not a bad nickname.

six-foot-three conquering warrior, hard but not unfeeling, the eager conversationalist welcoming foreigners and intellectuals to his court, the enthusiastic hunter and swimmer, a man with a quick temper and a crude sense of humor, an emperor who could not sign his name but appreciated poetry and theology and longed to educate himself:

> He also tried to write, and used to keep tablets and blanks in bed under his pillow, that at leisure hours he might accustom his hand to form the letters; however, as he did not begin his efforts in due season, but late in life, they met with ill success.

Einhard took care to exculpate Charlemagne in some matters and to gloss over others, such as the behavior of his libidinous daughters; by contrast, certain issues are openly discussed, like the emperor's many mistresses (he also had five wives and nineteen children). He certainly helped the art of biography to become increasingly popular. A biography was even written of Charlemagne's prized elephant, Abul-Abbaz, first mentioned by Einhard. In sum, he produced not only the first life of a secular figure written in the West for centuries but also a clear-eyed portrait of the founder of Europe.

France under Charlemagne, as in England, provided a centralizing monarchy that encouraged the writing of chronicles and created an opening for a national history. The quality and range of these chronicles was not as great as their English rivals, but they continued through the decades, and in the thirteenth century the monks of Saint-Denis, who had become the official historians to the royal court, began writing the *Grandes Chroniques de France,* tracing the history of French kings from their origins in Troy to the death of Philip II in 1223. These chronicles continued on to the end of the fifteenth century. By that date a chronicler had arisen who became one of the most formidable historians of his day. Let him introduce himself:

> Since, at some point in the future, someone might want to know who wrote this history, and who made it, I would like to name myself: I am called, by those who wish to honour me, Sir Jean Froissart, born in the county of Hainault, in the good and bountiful town of Valenciennes [then Flanders, now northern France].

For most of his life Froissart (c. 1337–c. 1405) was a court historian and, aside from composing a long Arthurian romance and a large body of poetry, the author of *Chroniques de France, d'Angleterre, d'Ecosse, de Bretagne, de Gascogne, de Flandre et lieux circumvoisins*. For centuries, what became known as "Froissart's Chronicles" were a main source for the first half of the Hundred Years' War and also the chief expression of the notions of chivalry that had been evolving since the twelfth century and reached their height in the fourteenth-century Kingdom of England and France (as it was called)—that romanticized code of knightly behavior which arose from the idealization of cavalrymen (*chivalry* derives from the Old French term *chevalerie*, "horse soldiery"), in large part the unruly child of Geoffrey of Monmouth's extravagant tales of King Arthur.

Jean Froissart was a court historian, as his plush surroundings suggest. His Chronicles *are our main source for the first half of the Hundred Years' War, which began in 1337.*

Froissart's main purpose in writing was to educate the French in values that he felt they had forgotten. On one occasion he braved midnight storms for six winter weeks to read his Arthurian romance *Méliador* to an insomniac Count de Blois. "Again I entered my smithy to work and forge something from the noble material of time past," he famously wrote. That familiar smithy was not a French but an English one. Around the age of twenty-four, in 1361 or 1362, Froissart entered the service of Philippa, queen consort of Edward III of England. This did not entail an official position and was probably a grace-and-favor arrangement. After the queen's death in 1369, he enjoyed the patronage of other court members (he met both Richard II and his father, the Black Prince) and absorbed their values. When the birth of Richard II was announced at the French court, the marshal of Aquitaine turned to the young chronicler and whispered, "Froissart, write that down and make it memorable." Some years later, having taken orders, he became canon of Chimay, near Liège in the Belgian province of Hanault, giving him money enough to finance further travels and research. In 1395, he returned to England but was disappointed by changes he saw as portending the end of chivalry.

His *Chroniques de France* range from 1327 (the accession in England of Edward III) to 1400, after the deposition of Richard II, and marks the emergence of the chronicle as a reaction against the great classical histories. Like Herodotus or Gregory of Tours, to name but two, he will often include a story just because he likes it. While slapdash with details (he was more interested in qualitative description), he is highly readable. He loves the flourish and display of chivalry, the silken pavilions, elaborate tableaux, royal entrances, festivities, knighting and marriage ceremonies, and even suggests that being in love was a combat advantage; above all he is the chronicler of war as the theater for "great marvels and wonderful feats of arms." He writes in the vernacular, clearly for a lay audience. Will Durant's judgment strikes the right note: "He did not inquire into motives; he relied too trustfully on embellished or prejudiced accounts; he made no pretense of adding philosophy to narrative. He was only a chronicler, but of all chroniclers the best."

The great medievalist Johan Huizinga sees Froissart's main shortcoming in that he shortcuts real thought, and his characterizations can be clichéd. This may be true, but each generation has its own sense of the past. In one respect, we simply see what is before us. Thus a man in the fourteenth century might think that the Romans did things that his own times were incapable of matching, and the best of such behavior was worth celebrating. As to those supposedly dark ages, they bequeathed us—to give just one list—castles, cathedrals, Italian and Flemish and Byzantine art, printing, plainsong, and parliaments, as well as universities. By the end of the fourteenth century, writers about the past had grown up. Annals say nothing about causes, significance, implications, or consequences; they do not interpret. Chroniclers, on the other hand, were no longer content to be mere annalists; they were becoming more self-confident and thus more willing to indulge in digression, refinement, and amplification. Few probably thought of themselves as "historians," yet that thousand years or more produced some of the most influential works of history ever set to paper (or vellum, or canvas). Writing of these times, Petrarch concluded: "Amidst the errors there shone forth men of genius; no less keen were their eyes, although they were surrounded by darkness and dense gloom."

CHAPTER 6

THE ACCIDENTAL HISTORIAN
Niccolò Machiavelli

———

Princes should have more to fear from historians
than have ugly women from great painters.

—ANTONIO PÉREZ, SECRETARY TO
KING PHILIP II OF SPAIN, C. 1585

A man of mediocre status needs very little history;
those who play some part in public affairs need a great deal
more; and a Prince cannot have too much.

—CARDINAL FLEURY, ADVISER TO
KING LOUIS XV OF FRANCE, C. 1720

Niccolò Machiavelli (1469–1527) lies buried within the imposing Franciscan basilica of Santa Croce, in the southeastern section of Florence, the city of his birth. The inscription at the foot of his tomb reads: *Tanto nomini nullum par elogium*—"For so great a name, no words will suffice." In the nearby Uffizi Gallery, a statue shows him thoughtfully stroking his chin, while his other hand holds a thick volume, evidently not *The Prince,* which is barely eighty pages, but some other tome of considerable thickness.

I like to imagine that the book in Machiavelli's hand is his one true work of history, *Istore fiorentine,* commissioned by Pope Leo X in 1520. Its full title, as chosen by later editors, is: *The History of Florence and of the Affairs of Italy from the Earliest Times to the Death of Lorenzo the Magnificent.* It was the first modern analytical study, and it marked a turning away from a God-centered universe toward a man-centered one, in which the heavenly returns of virtuous behavior were no longer seen as a safe bet. In denying the Christian tenet that political states, as well as citizens, are bound by a single moral code, Machiavelli was a stormy petrel in how history was to be recorded; the way he wrote helped usher in a revolution.

Ever since the early fifteenth century, Italy's rulers had commissioned writers to record their histories, and in 1516 the Venetian government had paid another writer to tell their city's story. Possibly the traditional rivalry between the two republics provoked the Florentine project. The work was printed posthumously, in eight volumes, in 1532. It joined not only *The Prince* but also *The Art of War* (the only book of Machiavelli's to be published in his lifetime); *Discourses on the First Ten Books of Titus Livy;* two sex farces, *La Mandragola* (which dramatizes several key themes of *The Prince*) and *Clizia;* and lesser works such as *The First and Second Decennale* and *The Life of Castruccio Castracani.* By 1559, *The Art of War* had gone through thirteen editions, the *Discourses* twenty-six, *The Prince* seventeen, and *Florentine Histories* fifteen. Within two decades of his death Machiavelli was one of the biggest-selling authors in Europe. At the same time, by that very year, 1559, he was among the first to be placed on the Papal Index of Prohibited Books (some six hundred publications won this disfavor). A particularly ineffective excoriation, the Index carried weight only in Italy and Spain, and a majority of the 158 editions of Machiavelli's writings in the century after his death were published following the ban. But the Vatican stubbornly kept the Index going until 1966.

Machiavelli became a professional writer almost by chance—so that he could sign off a letter to his great friend Francesco Guicciardini, "History writer, Comic writer and Tragic writer" as a joke between them.*
He was not always the best judge of his work. Although *Florentine Histories* has also been taken by some commentators as an amplification of the

---

* Guicciardini (1483–1540), who lived just a few houses down from Machiavelli, was a papal administrator who wrote several books about his native city and the Italian Wars. He was able to draw on his time as Florentine orator in Spain from 1512 and governor of Modena and Reggio from 1516, commissary general of the papal army (1521), president of the Romagna (1524), and lieutenant general (1526). All his works were published posthumously, but his reputation is now so secure that his name is often linked with Machiavelli's. Some commentators see him as the greatest historian between Tacitus and Voltaire and compare him with his Roman predecessor in terms of objectivity, characterization, use of language, and the structure of the speeches he gives his principal actors. Importantly, he and Machiavelli pushed each other forward.

rules expounded in *The Prince*—evidence that he was essentially an accidental historian—others see it as a landmark in the way history could be written, less utopian and more concrete than his other writings. (Karl Marx was to call the *Florentine Histories* a masterpiece.) What is indisputable is that for Machiavelli "true history" was humanist history, not the lives of saints and religious figures but the political and military world. He wrested accounts of past times from their traditional ethical framework and in so doing not only showed that history was a storehouse of examples and analogies that could help the wise to direct the future—he also radically enlarged its scope and ambitions.

It helped that Machiavelli lived at a time of continual unrest. "Italy" was no more than a geographical term, not a unified nation but a battleground for warring territorial states containing a number of cities, chief among them the Duchy of Milan and the republics of Florence (a republic in name only and, in the words of Machiavelli's latest biographer, one "gradually settling into oligarchy"), Venice, Siena, Lucca, and Genoa. And the pope in Rome was as much a temporal potentate as any city or national ruler.* The kings of France and Spain were for most of Machiavelli's adult life looking to use Italian lands as a battlefield, with diplomatic relations so riven by factions that alliances might be made and broken before a treaty's ink had dried.

Power tended to be concentrated in the hands of a few families or even a single one: in Milan, the Visconti and then the Sforza; in Ferrara, the Este; in Mantua, the Gonzaga; in Perugia and Urbino, both papal states, the Baglioni and the Montefeltro; and in Florence (for the most part) the Medici. In each city, to be on the wrong side was to court imprisonment, torture, and violent death. It mattered whom you knew and with whom you sided. Machiavelli's family background was not particularly prosperous. His father, an impractical intellectual who on more than one occasion had to sell his clothes to make ends meet, owned a tumbledown palazzo in Florence and a smallholding in

---

* The pope's secular rule extended over the province of Lazio (6,657 square miles); Umbria (3,265 square miles); the Marches (some 3,700 hilly square miles to the east of Tuscany); and Emilia-Romagna (northeast Italy, with Bologna its capital, more than 8,600 square miles). This totaled a huge area—a broad belt stretching across central Italy from sea to sea and containing twenty-six cities. Further, Sicily and the Kingdom of Naples were papal fiefs, while from 1107 on the pope claimed sovereignty over nearly all Tuscany, including Florence, Lucca, Pistoia, Pisa, Siena, and Arezzo.

a Tuscan village just ten miles south of the city, in the wine-making region of Chianti. The author of *The Prince* began as small fry.

Even as a young man Machiavelli was interested in politics, but his entry into that world took time. In September 1494, Charles VIII of France invaded Italy and threatened to march on Florence. The charismatic, theatrical Dominican friar Girolamo Savonarola (1452–98), who had been stirring up the local people with apocalyptic sermons and demands that the Church be cleared of corruption—"O Italy! O Princes! O prelates of the Church! The wrath of God is upon ye!"—took it upon himself to act as an unlikely peacemaker, the Florentines expelling the ruling Medici. The following year, when the city, traditionally an ally of France, refused to join Pope Alexander VI's coalition against the French, Savonarola defied the pontiff by preaching under a ban and was excommunicated. The standoff between preacher and pope continued for almost another three years, and Machiavelli was already twenty-eight, having not settled to any particular job, when in 1498 he was commissioned by the Florentine ambassador to the Holy See to spy on the unruly preacher, who that same year landed in prison, "confessed" that he had invented his visions (he was "put seven times to the torture," wrote Voltaire, not normally a reliable source but here probably well informed), then was hanged from a gibbet in the main square in Florence before being burned at the stake.

Machiavelli's report on all this impressed his employers, and although he was an obscure young man with no experience in government, he was asked to join the Florentine bureaucracy as second chancellor of the republic. He had evidently lobbied for the job, and his politics made him acceptable, but it was still a slice of luck. The work involved handling state correspondence, but he also plunged into domestic and foreign affairs and soon was given the additional title of secretary to the Ten of War, a decad of elders that oversaw the republic's diplomatic relations.

In the months following Savonarola's death, various groups jockeyed for power, giving Machiavelli his first lesson in politics: that it was a world of unceasing battle affected by class, patronage, and personal rivalries. The reverberations of the French invasion four years before still shaped the structures of all the leading cities, and much of his work dealt with military matters. In March 1499, he was sent to talk with mercenaries employed by the city who were threatening to desert their posts unless they were better paid. He managed to persuade their general to adhere to the original conditions of hire, but the experience soured him against reliance on professional soldiers, and he spent the rest of his career arguing for a citizens' militia.

Another mission took him to Forlì, a city in the Papal States some fifty miles northeast of Florence, ruled by Caterina Sforza (1463–1509), a woman both courageous and strikingly beautiful. Her father had ruled Milan until he was assassinated, and his long-suffering subjects had also killed off her cruel and violent husband (whom she had married at fourteen). When rebel leaders took her two young children hostage and threatened to murder them unless she surrendered, she leapt onto the parapet of her castle, pulled up her skirts, pointed to her genitals, and declared, "Do it, if you want to: even hang them in front of me. . . . Here I have what's needed to make others!" The rebellion collapsed. After her second husband met the same fate as her first, she tortured and executed forty suspected conspirators in the public square, including their wives and mistresses and even their children, several in early infancy. She evidently took no prisoners.

Engraved portrait of Machiavelli, from the Peace Palace Library's Il Principe, *published in 1769. An earlier painting was discovered in 2019 that may be of Machiavelli by his contemporary Leonardo da Vinci. It awaits authentication.*

Machiavelli arrived to find, as he wrote in his subsequent report, Caterina's court "crowded with Florentines," so he had hopes that they would support his cause. Present also were agents from the Duke of Milan, Caterina's uncle, but after days of negotiating Machiavelli put together an agreement that he believed Caterina had accepted. The next day he was summoned before the countess, who told him she had changed her mind, on the grounds that Florentine words "had always satisfied her, whereas their deeds had always much displeased her." She was settling with the Milanese instead. Machiavelli was treated as a person of little consequence (in letters home he christened himself "Sir Nihil"), a mid-level bureaucrat when Caterina expected at least a full ambassador to treat with her. He returned to his colleagues shamed but wiser.*

Throughout Machiavelli's years of public service, his beloved Florence stuttered between opposing forces, unsure which would grant her protection and a measure of prosperity and which might destroy her. But all the time he was learning. Pope Alexander VI, otherwise the Spanish-born Rodrigo Borgia, had an infamous daughter (this was a time when popes were not only power-hungry but had multiple affairs, siring children whom they then assigned to high office), the thrice-married and often-loved Lucrezia (1480–1519), three sons by his principal mistress, Donna Vannozza, including the elder Cesare and the paternal favorite Juan (Giovanni), Duke of Gandia, as well as several children by other women. One night Cesare and Juan went to dine with their mother. Riding home that night, the brothers parted company in Rome's Jewish quarter. Cesare made it to his house; Juan did not. When the next day Juan's corpse, stabbed nine times, was found washed up on the banks of the Tiber, possibly murdered on Cesare's orders, Alexander was at first inconsolable but within weeks simply switched his affections, determining that it was now Cesare who should be his favored child.

Cesare had been made a bishop at sixteen and a cardinal two years

---

* Caterina's own fortunes continued to fluctuate. She soon found her city besieged by the notorious Cesare Borgia. When he came near the fortress to talk to her, she tried to capture him, but the attempt failed. Instead he stormed her citadel and cast her into prison. Ever resourceful, she captured Cesare's eye and the two became lovers. Machiavelli believed that, in an attempt to further her career, at one point she attempted to poison the pope. In her later years, she entered a nunnery, confiding to a monk: "If I had the skill to write it all down, I would shock the world."

later, but he now renounced holy orders for a military career. Before his twenty-second birthday, in 1496, he was in charge of the papal army. King Louis of France saw the advantages of an alliance with the pope and invited Cesare to visit him, bestowing on him the Duchy of Valentinois and promising him a prominent role in the army. Delighted, Cesare was soon at the head of the French troops. First Milan fell, then Forlì, Pesaro, and Rimini. In the space of a few months, he won a reputation not only for his military prowess but for his guile and ruthlessness; he was also immensely strong (it was said he could twist a horseshoe with his bare hands) and was considered the handsomest man in Italy. He had the "air of one who felt that he inherited the world" but could play the fox as well as the lion (conjoined in the adage, "Since a prince is required to play the beast, he must learn from both the fox and the lion, because a lion cannot defend himself against snares, nor the fox against wolves"), able to say one thing convincingly while intent on its opposite. Among his other activities, he was running a Mafia-like protection racket, with a predeliction for slicing bodies in half and leaving them in public squares.

On July 18, 1500, Machiavelli set out for France as part of a two-man mission to convince Louis how dangerous and unpredictable Cesare was. It was his first opportunity to view at close range the inner workings of one of the great powers of the day, following the court from chateau to chateau. His biographer Miles Unger well describes what this was to mean for the future writer:

> These were not places for the faint of heart or the easily deceived. Latin orations modeled on Cicero delivered by ambassadors dressed in cloth of gold and sparkling with pearls, the culture of flattery and obfuscation—Machiavelli saw through it all. Beneath the glittering surface something far more savage was taking place.

His stay lasted nearly six months. The following spring, Cesare's army advanced on Florence, and alarming reports, including tales of atrocities by Cesare's troops, were landing on the second chancellor's desk almost daily. The city, too weak to confront its enemy, was forced to play for time, offering a contract to acquire three hundred men at arms in return for the hefty fee of thirty-six thousand ducats. When the Duchy of Urbino fell, Cesare asked Florence to send a delegation to parley with him, and Machiavelli became the mission's second in command.

Savonarola had not dazzled him; Cesare (or Valentino, as he was now also called) did. No one believed that Cesare was a good man, but in contrast to Florence's relative weakness he appeared able to seize the initiative in battle and to employ a gift for theatrical display in negotiation that intimidated his rivals. "This Lord is of such splendid and magnificent bearing," an enamored Machiavelli reported from Urbino,

> and in war so decisive that there is no thing so daunting that it does not seem to him a small matter; and for the sake of glory and in order to secure his state he never rests, nor does he know weariness or fear. He arrives at one place before one hears he has left the other; he treats his soldiers well; he has acquired the best men in Italy: all of which, in addition to his eternal good fortune, makes him formidable and victorious.

This may have been the awe that the deskbound scribe feels for the man of action. Not only action. For about a year, under Cesare's instruction, Machiavelli took on Leonardo da Vinci as his military architect and engineer.* But Cesare's insatiable desire for new conquests made his chief lieutenants fear for their safety, and the plotting against him began. The momentum shifted, shifted again. Then, on August 5, 1503, Pope Alexander and his son Cesare, returning together from a dinner, both caught a high fever, possibly malaria. As a cure, the doctors sank Cesare into a huge jar of iced water; somehow, he survived. His seventy-two-year-old father lingered on for almost two weeks but then succumbed, and with his death Cesare's fortunes turned. Without the legitimacy conferred by the Holy Father, his whole world came under threat. Territories strained to break free; friends became hard to

---

* In 1502 they worked together on an outlandish scheme to defeat rival Pisa by diverting the Arno (the vital artery for both cities), thus starving them of supplies and commerce, but the project collapsed due to uncooperative laborers, unenthusiastic supervisors, and constant harassment from Pisan troops. Machiavelli also knew Michelangelo, Botticelli, and a number of other leading figures of the Renaissance.

find. The new pope, Pius III, supported Cesare but died after twenty-six days in office.

Machiavelli found himself dispatched to Rome—to witness the next conclave and to call on Cesare in order to assess his position. The great warrior's deadly enemy, Giuliano della Rovere, was unanimously elected pope, taking the name Julius II, having tricked Cesare into supporting him by offering money and continued papal backing, promises he disregarded upon taking office. Realizing his mistake, Cesare tried to garner new allies, but Julius made sure he failed at every turn. Machiavelli, watching the man he had once considered the perfect leader become a pathetic, ranting husk of his previous self, took his leave as quickly as he could. In his official report he concluded: "Little by little this Duke is slipping into his grave."*

* * *

THE SHIFT IN THE Italian balance of power was immediate. For Machiavelli it meant not only a prolonged period of further politicking but also the responsibility of raising a citizens' militia against his city's longtime thorn, Pisa. Thanks in large part to his organizing abilities, Florence triumphed. But while Spain and France remained the two most powerful military powers on the peninsula, Julius II—who soon acquired the nicknames "The Warrior Pope" and "Il Papa Terribile" for his ferocity—was determined to wrest back territories for the Church. Soon the Holy See was warring with France, while the Spanish aligned themselves with the Medici in the search for new conquests. Florence, along with Naples, Milan, and Venice, looked first one way then the other. It is a complicated story, one that culminates in September 1512 with the pope's forces driving the French out of Italy and the Spanish leader, Giuliano de' Medici (1479–1516), marching into Machiavelli's hometown.

---

* Machiavelli was getting ahead of himself. Not until March 1507 did Cesare meet his actual end. He fled to Spain, fought for the king of Navarre (his brother-in-law), and laid siege to a rebel stronghold. Its commander, Luis de Beaumont, was able to get a caravan of mules carrying provisions into the castle under cover of a sudden storm. Cesare, alerted, led seventy horsemen out to attack de Beaumont and his escort. In his eagerness he far outdistanced his men and was ambushed. Badly outnumbered, he was yanked from his horse, had his armor pulled away, and his bloody, naked body punctured by twenty-five sword thrusts. His attackers did not even know who he was. He was thirty-one. See Richard Cavendish, "Death of Cesare Borgia," *History Today*, vol. 57, March 3, 2000.

Machiavelli was at first optimistic that he might survive any new administration, as in his youth he had been friendly with several of the Medici circle, but within two months he was thrown out of office, "dismissed, deprived, and totally removed," as the official decree pronounced. He was forced to post a thousand-lira bond to guarantee he would not travel out of the region and banished from government buildings for a year. He retired to his country home, angry and deflated, but feeling that the worst was probably over. Then in February 1513 an informant told the authorities that he knew of twenty conspirators who planned to assassinate Giuliano de' Medici and stage a coup. The names were on a list that had fallen from the pocket of a young rabble-rouser. Machiavelli, who had no knowledge of the conspiracy and had always written trenchantly about the foolishness of such initiatives—"though many conspiracies have been attempted, very few have attained the desired end"—was one of those named, possibly as someone who might be approached at a later stage in the uprising. He was arrested and taken to Le Stinche, a fetid jail close to the offices where he had worked for so many years.

For the next twenty-two days he lay hunched in a vermin-infested cell from which he was taken to a room where he endured the "strappado," in which a prisoner has his wrists tied behind his back, then is hoisted into the air before being suddenly dropped to the floor. As the rope hoisting the prisoner aloft is attached to his wrists, the procedure usually dislocates the shoulders, tears the muscles, and renders one or both arms useless. The torture is repeated as often as necessary to extort a confession. As Machiavelli had nothing to confess (besides a lifelong enthusiasm for prostitutes), he remained silent: four times at least was he hoisted aloft, possibly six. Remarkably, once his jailers had had their way with him, he was returned to his cell, where he asked for a pen and paper and composed a pair of sonnets addressed to the "Magnificent Giuliano," in an attempt to win his sympathy. "I have on my legs . . . a pair of shackles," he wrote, before going on to describe the stench and the lice, as big as butterflies, on the broken walls while the noise of key and padlock boomed around him like thunderbolts from the gods, before rounding off, in an attempt at gallows wit: "Thus the way poets are treated!"

There is no evidence that the poems were ever sent to Giuliano, and indeed one wonders what he would have made of this mixture of honesty, self-pity, and grim humor, but they mark both the collapse of Machiavelli's political career and the beginnings of another, that of writer. Even so, he might have continued to languish in his "dainty hospice" had it not been for some good fortune. On February 20, 1513, Pope Julius fell ill from malaria, dying a few days later. In his place the cardinals elected Giovanni de' Medici, Giuliano's thirty-eight-year-old brother, who thus became the first Florentine to sit on the papal throne, taking the name of Leo X. Giuliano seized the opportunity to show his magnanimity, releasing a mass of prisoners, including the former second chancellor. Machiavelli was free to go.

Home was more than just a small country estate. Back in August 1501, the thirty-two-year-old Machiavelli had taken to wife Marietta Corsini, a young woman from a distinguished local family, and over the years she bore him six children. She also bore a succession of indignities, as Machiavelli, not unusual in a man of his background, regularly visited whorehouses and male brothels and into his fifties kept up a number of liaisons, as we know from his ribald and salacious letters to *la brigata* ("the gang"), his circle of male friends. A "connoisseur of depravity," as one historian has dubbed him, he consorted with people even he called "lice." Yet he and Marietta were obviously fond of each other (the one letter she sent him that survives is endearing), and her main complaint seems to have been his frequent absences on government business. Now all such trips were at an end.

He had little to live on and time on his hands. He would chat to the woodcutters on his farm or play cards in the local inn. For those without power in Florence, "there isn't even a dog who will bark in your face," as he wrote in his play *The Mandrake*. Feeling redundant and forgotten, he cast around for some project to occupy him. Might he work his way back into government service? His first act was to pen another sonnet to Giuliano de' Medici, which this time he did send off, together with a brace of game birds: hardly presents enough to grease any wheels. He decided on a new venture: to dedicate to de' Medici a book of advice written by him, a tract bringing together all he had learned from his years of service, an entirely honest, even impudent primer on how power should be won and exercised. It was not so much a work of history but one that made use of history and as such gave its author immediate comfort:

Come evening, I return to my house and enter my study; on the threshold I take off my ordinary clothes, covered with mud and dirt, and wrap myself in robes meant for a court or palace. Dressed appropriately, I enter the ancient courts filled with ancient men where, affectionately received, I nourish myself on that food that alone is mine and for which I was born; where I am unashamed to converse and ask them to explain their actions, and where they, kindly, answer me. And for four hours at a time I feel no boredom, I forget all my troubles, I have no fear of poverty, or even of death.

* * *

MACHIAVELLIANISM EXISTED, AS A way of thinking and acting, long before Machiavelli. "Politics, these days, is no occupation for an educated man, a man of character. Ignorance and total lousiness are better. . . . A demagogue must be neither an educated nor an honest man; he has to be an ignoramus and a rogue." These cynical views belong to Aristophanes, as voiced in *The Knights*. His fourth play, it was first produced in 424 B.C. In the fifth book of Thucydides's *History of the Peloponnesian War* there is a similar dialogue between the Athenians and the Melians, and in Euripides's *Phoenician Maidens* (ll. 524–25) we hear: "If wrong may e'er be right, for a throne's sake were wrong most right." The fourth century B.C. Indian classic the *Arthashastra,* a treatise on scruple-free statecraft, is said to make *The Prince* seem harmless. Over the centuries, many other writers have professed a similarly cynical view of power politics, but after contemplating Cesare's "well-used" cruelties for several years, Machiavelli it was who became the supreme analyst of how to acquire and retain power without regard to scruple.

While the statement that the end justifies the means never appears in the actual text, the phrase is taken as its author's rule of thumb, not only in politics but in society generally: winning, no matter how, is all. There are chapters on how to deal with flatterers and how to treat government ministers. The text concludes with Machiavelli encouraging a leader to use the lessons of the book and to step forward to rid Italian soil of barbarians. But those are not the sections that people remember best:

A man who strives for goodness in all his acts is sure to come to ruin. . . .

A wise prince cannot keep his word when the situation alters to his disadvantage. . . .

It is necessary to be a great pretender and dissembler. . . .

Since love and fear can hardly exist together, if we must choose between them, it is far safer to be feared than loved. . . .

Everything considered, he will discover things which, though seeming virtuous, will cause his ruin, and others which, though seeming wicked, will make him secure and promote his well-being.

No wonder the Catholic Church raised its hands in horror. It didn't help that Machiavelli's model for the ideal prince was that figure of darkness, Cesare Borgia, soon dubbed "Machiavelli's Muse" (and the subject of an entire chapter). Tellingly, Napoleon is said to have written extensive annotations to his copy of the book and Stalin to have kept a translation on his nightstand. I can well recall my time at Cambridge University, when studying in my final year an eccentric "module" within the English tripos called "The Moralists," which involved reading everyone from Samuel Johnson to Friedrich Nietzsche, George Eliot to D. H. Lawrence, and the time came to read Machiavelli. At a tutorial with my professor and one other student, I was so incensed (priggish and callow as I was) that we were being asked to consider *The Prince* outside any ethical framework that I actually stormed out of the room. All that can be said in my defense is that for centuries the world has viewed Machiavelli as a cynical ne'er-do-well, a moral barbarian, even an enemy to good government. While the word *Machiavellisme* was first coined in France in 1581 and its English form in 1589, it was left to Frederick II, the king of Prussia, to write an entire book, *Anti-Machiavel* (published by Voltaire!), fulminating against a work that "is in point of Morality, what Spinoza's Work is with regard to Faith: Spinoza sapped the Foundations of Faith, and aimed at nothing less than overturning the whole Fabrick of Religion; Machiavel corrupted Politicks, and undertook to destroy the Precepts of sound Morality."

*Alleged portrait
of Cesare Borgia
(1475–1507),
known as Valentino,
an illegitimate son of
Pope Alexander VI who
became an inspiration
for Machiavelli in*
The Prince. *Groomed
for the Church,
he abandoned it to
become a soldier
of fortune.*

But Machiavelli was in many respects an intensely moral man and was only putting down his observations of how politics actually worked. It took another century before Francis Bacon (1561–1626) could declare that "we are much beholden to Machiavelli and others, that write what men do, and not what they ought to do."* In later years, Benito Mussolini and Silvio Berlusconi would both write introductions to editions of the work.

In highly readable prose, honed in his native Tuscan-inflected Italian rather than in scholarly Latin and shorn of hypocrisy or wishful thinking, Machiavelli described how affairs were decided in the turbulent Italian republics of his day. "One cannot call it virtue to murder one's fellow citizens, to betray one's friends, to be without faith, without mercy, without religion," he freely acknowledged, but he lived in

---

* During the late fifteenth century a great variety of writings appeared on the subject of the role of princes, even developing into a literary form, in which each author held up a mirror to the nature of princeship. *The Prince* in this context is not unusual, and in a sense belongs alongside works by Erasmus, Thomas More, Dante, and Aquinas, all of whom wrote treatises on the nature of leadership or its equivalent; but Machiavelli's work was in total contrast to these. As for Frederick the Great's lambast against *The Prince*, Voltaire's acerbic comment ran: "If Machiavelli had had a prince as his disciple, the first thing he would have recommended would have been to write a book against Machiavellianism." See *Memoirs of the Life of Monsieur de Voltaire Written by Himself* (London: Hesperus, 2007), p. 16.

a world where such conduct brought dividends. Cesare was his hero, just as Bismarck would later be to Nietzsche. Why should such a leader be honest, above all things? "A prince is successful when he fits his mode of proceeding to the times, and is unsuccessful when his mode of proceeding is no longer in tune with them." This may be taken as moral relativism—or plain common sense. Machiavelli was hardly an innocent and took obvious pleasure in scandalizing his readers, yet he observed conventions as strict as any he abandoned. Indeed, a recent biographer, the political philosopher Erica Benner, goes so far as to argue that Machiavelli was writing ironically, his whole book a send-up:

> The *Prince* claimed to put hard political facts ahead of moral ideals. But as a handbook on how to secure power, its advice was flagrantly unrealistic. Machiavelli's self-proclaimed realism, his book's main selling point, was a fraud.

It is a deeply implausible reading, not least because for centuries Machiavelli's advice to rulers has been taken at face value, and if one wants a clue as to Machiavelli's intentions it is relevant that he was so impressed that not once did he censure Cesare for any ruthlessness. He divorced public from private morals and argued that a prince may commit crimes if they are in the service of the state, a view, as Garry Wills has noted, that makes Machiavelli "a sponsor of the Higher Cheneyism." And, as Simon Schama says, "For Machiavelli political theory and history were inseparable."

At first his doctrines had little following, and his little book turned out to be the most ill-advised job application in history. Giuliano de' Medici never even lived to receive it, dying in 1516. Its anxious author duly changed both the title from *De principatibus* to the more individualized *Il principe* and the dedication, making it to Giuliano's despotic nephew Lorenzo (1492–1519), the Duke of Urbino, to whom Giuliano had handed over the reins of his power in 1513. If Lorenzo ever read the treatise, it made no impression, and the story is told that when Machiavelli presented his script to Lorenzo, he ignored him in favor of a client offering a pair of hunting dogs. Machiavelli (who throughout his life was not particularly Machiavellian and had a sad history of backing the losing side in nearly all his endeavors) was left to trudge back to his writing desk.

Each of the four canonical gospel writers is indicated by an evangelical symbol—Matthew (a man), Mark (a lion), Luke (an ox), and John (an eagle)—in this illuminated ninth-century manuscript. All four evangelists appear to be Caucasian; this was almost certainly not true.

This statue of Herodotus of Halicarnassus, sited in Bodrun, on the west coast of Turkey, is really just a man with a beard—no one knows what Herodotus actually looked like.

A detail from the Bayeux Tapestry, woven in the 1070s, most likely by English craftswomen. It has influenced our understanding of history possibly more than any other pictorial artifact. "A shaft pierces Harold [left] with deadly doom," wrote a Norman propagandist of the time, only it doesn't; later legend insisted he was shot in the eye, but more likely he is the one being hacked down (he is carrying a Dane axe). The arrow was a later addition; medieval iconography regularly depicted perjurers with a sharp weapon driven through the eye.

Execution of the French rebel Étienne Marcel in 1358, who rebelled against England's King John and was assassinated by royalist guards at the gates of Paris. Froissart's chronicles contain 110 miniatures like this, painted by some of the best Brugeois artists of the day.

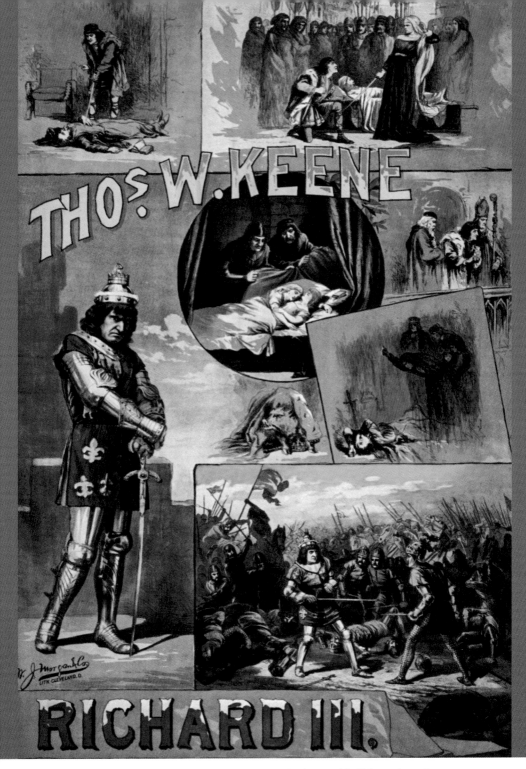

By the time Shakespeare died, Richard III *had outsold all his other plays.
This 1884 poster advertising an American production manages to fit in many
of its key scenes.*

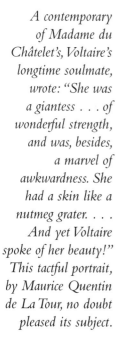

"They share the same disdain for human religions or superstitions, but their literary conduct differs greatly," wrote Jorge Luis Borges of Voltaire and Gibbon. This pastel of Voltaire was made by Maurice Quentin de La Tour in 1735, when Voltaire was thirty-nine.

A contemporary of Madame du Châtelet's, Voltaire's longtime soulmate, wrote: "She was a giantess . . . of wonderful strength, and was, besides, a marvel of awkwardness. She had a skin like a nutmeg grater. . . . And yet Voltaire spoke of her beauty!" This tactful portrait, by Maurice Quentin de La Tour, no doubt pleased its subject.

Edward Gibbon, oil portrait by Sir Joshua Reynolds, circa 1779. He was about four feet eight inches tall, with bright ginger hair. Virginia Woolf is merciless: "The body in Gibbon's case was ridiculous—prodigiously fat, enormously top-heavy, precariously balanced upon little feet upon which he spun round with astonishing alacrity."

Sir Walter Scott, by Sir Francis Grant. He wanted, he said, to "contribute somewhat to the history of my native country." He shaped the way historical fiction was written for the next hundred years.

To fight off boredom, he read Petrarch. Even before embarking on *The Prince,* he had been working at *Discorsi sopra la prima deca di Tito Livio* (The Discourses on the First Ten Books by Titus Livius), a far longer and more discursive volume, in which he takes Livy's account of the history of Rome from its founding through to 293 B.C. and posits what can be learned from these years. He chose Livy as his chief analogue, as his father, an impoverished intellectual (he held a law degree but, unlike most of the lawyers and notaries in Florence, earned little from his profession), had spent nine months compiling an index of place-names for a new multivolume edition, and in exchange for his labors was allowed to keep the original books. So Machiavelli knew Rome's early years well and regarded them as the high point of civilization; he even apologizes when referring to contemporary events to further his argument.

As he proceeded with the *Discourses,* he realized that they would be too long to serve as a practical gift to the Medici, which is why he broke off to write what he intended should be a summary of his conclusions. The *Discourses* was completed only in 1519 and at far greater length considers the nature of government and how states have been formed, this time in reference to republics rather than principalities. Political greatness comes and goes, Machiavelli argues, but then history works in cycles, constantly repeating itself. He considers the different claims of monarchy, aristocracy, and democracy and also that same trio in debased form: tyranny, oligarchy, and anarchy. Good government will come from selfish people pursuing selfish ends, where base human nature is exploited to increase the well-being of all. Wisdom and justice are best achieved in the give-and-take of competing interests. Here, he concludes, quoting Livy (it was Machiavelli who ensured that the Roman historians would chiefly inspire the writing of history right down to the eighteenth century), history was "the best medicine for the sick mind," since it records the mistakes of the past. Since human nature is the same everywhere, at all times, we are condemned to repeat the errors of those who have gone before us, and the immutability of that human nature can be extended to families, institutions, even countries. However, while no perfect form of government is possible, history teaches us how man can slow Fortune's wheel. Temporary improvement is possible, but that is the best we can hope for.

It is a theme he returns to in *Florentine Histories,* declaring in a paraphrase of Sallust: "Thus [states] are always descending from good to bad and rising from bad to good. For valor leads to tranquility, tranquility to ease, ease to disorder, and disorder to ruin. And similarly, from ruin, order is born; from order, virtue; and from virtue, glory and good fortune." All three books, *The Prince,* the *Discourses,* and *Florentine Histories,* are of a piece, building on each other in advancing the same arguments. While none was published during their author's lifetime, manuscripts, surreptitiously copied, were eagerly passed around, so that although Machiavelli never breached the Medici inner circle, his ideas became well known.

They were not his only literary efforts. For years he had been a keen versifier, mainly working on classical themes; now, of all things, he turned to comedy. If he couldn't be a well-regarded political theorist or senior bureaucrat, he could make fun of his reduced circumstances. He took on nicknames, some kinder than others: the public called him "Old Nick," the most apposite of Nick-names, and a softer version of "Satan"; friends dubbed him *il Macchia* (the Blot), suggesting his witty, irreverent nature but also his tactlessness, sharp tongue, and prickly personality. He penned a novella, *The Fable of Belfagor,* a satire on marriage in which a demon is sent to Earth by Pluto to see if it is true that wives are the source of all men's ills, and two plays, *La Mandragola* (The Mandrake, 1518) and *Clizia* (1525), sex farces that ridiculed Machiavelli's own character and lustful propensities but were also informed by the same worldview as his serious writings. Both plays were initially performed as private productions but took on a life of their own, so much so that Pope Leo, his interest piqued by word-of-mouth recommendation, asked for a performance of *La Mandragola* at the papal court, and the comedy was soon playing to sold-out houses during carnival season. And so in 1520, the same year Leo excommunicated Martin Luther, Machiavelli won as a comic writer the recognition he had so craved as a consigliere.

That March, on the back of the pope's approval, he visited another Medici, Cardinal Giulio de' Medici, who had become one of the main political powers in Florence. The meeting must have gone well, for shortly after Old Nick was commissioned to write a history of the city. Although this was not the employment he had hoped for, he accepted it as a route back to favor, with further commissions to follow. The wage was not princely: fifty-seven florins per year—in today's currency, some $8,000, later raised to $14,000—while the composition of Florence's checkered past presented a problem. What was expected, if not a glorification of the Medici, was a treatise without polemics, a showcase of style and form. Machiavelli, disregarding factual accuracy and plagiarizing from previous historians, produced a smooth-flowing, compelling narrative about the conflicting families, classes, and interests that had been and still were Florentine politics. He divided his account into "books" with nonhistorical introductions, his eyes firmly on his own time, and invented speeches that he presented as if they were actual reconstructions—even reports of passionate factional struggles and the city's increasing military incompetence.

In 1525, the finished work was presented to Giulio de' Medici, installed two years previously as Clement VII. Machiavelli himself read some passages to His Holiness, which the pope seemed to enjoy, and he expressed his appreciation by giving the author 120 ducats from his private purse. At the same time, Machiavelli submitted a plan to arm the people of Rome—it was his old project of a Florentine militia adjusted to the needs of the Papacy. Clement was inclined to take the project further, but events dictated otherwise. The pope had given his support to the French in an attempt to free the Papacy from dependency on the holy Roman emperor, but he ran out of funds to pay his thirty-four thousand troops, who mutinied and forced their commander to march on Rome, which they easily overran, pillaging and destroying at will. The fall of the Medici in Florence soon followed.

Machiavelli, never blind to opportunity, immediately lobbied for his old job back, but his recent employment by Clement was against him, as was his reputation as author of *The Prince*. Niccolò, now almost sixty, had become a saddened, disappointed man. Worn out by years of stress and overwork, he fell ill, suffering violent stomach spasms, to pass away on June 22, 1527, in his beloved home city. He died without confessing his sins and said that he looked forward to going to hell, where he could chat with pagans like Plato and Seneca. As he had written in *La Mandragola*, "How many worthy men there are there!" But he also went against the convictions of a lifetime and accepted the Church's last rites. Always better to hedge one's bets.

CHAPTER 7

WILLIAM SHAKESPEARE
The Drama of History

———

Think ye see
The very persons of our noble story
As they were living. . . .

—WILLIAM SHAKESPEARE, *HENRY VIII*

Iₙ ITS PROGRAM FOR 2000–2001, THE ROYAL SHAKESPEARE COMPANY staged Shakespeare's history plays as a cycle called "This England," stating that the eight dramas formed "a collage of one man's insight into English history." Yet Shakespeare is rarely praised as a historian, even though no other writer, of any time or place, gives us a more lasting impression of what most of the fourteen Plantagenet kings were like. As the commentator Peter Saccio says, "It is he who has etched upon the common memory the graceful fecklessness of Richard II, the exuberant heroism of Henry V, the dazzling villainy of Richard III." The same is true for the Roman plays—for Cleopatra and Mark Antony, Brutus and Coriolanus. Heinrich Heine described Shakespeare as "not only a poet but a historian . . . he is like the earliest writers of history, who also knew no difference between poetry and history, and so . . . enlightened truth with song."

If that has a grandiose ring to it, it is worth recalling that Aristotle attributed the unadorned statement of fact to the historian and the search for something's true nature to the poet, reasoning that historians deal in relative truths, based on hearsay and tied to random facts, whereas poetry has access to a higher form of truth. This overlap of history with literature made it a natural subject for the Elizabethan stage. And certainly Shakespeare's kings seem more real than those of academic description, his characterizations more memorable, his villains more engaging. As the literary critic Jonathan Bate summarizes those times:

> In the absence of newspapers and television, there were just two places where the public gathered together to be informed, cajoled, and provoked to thought on great issues of religion and politics: the church and the playhouse. Public sermons . . . were a major spectator sport. But the message from the pulpit was invariably orthodox. Homilies on obedience to king and law were regularly delivered in every parish in the land. . . . Political dissent was a pact with the devil. The message from the stage was different.

Between the middle of the sixteenth century and the English Civil War of 1642, we know that at least seventy historical dramas were written, probably far more, but so many were either lost or never published, the majority performed in the final decade and a half of Elizabeth I's reign. Simon Schama enjoys himself by calling Elizabeth "the ultimate drama-Queen." He adds "the startling fact that in the 16th century only the English had custom-built, site-specific commercial theatre. In Italy the peripatetic *commedia dell'arte* performed on the street; in Spain and the Netherlands plays were acted on decorated carts and wagons." By 1595 English was being spoken as the national tongue, and historical texts, chronicles, and chapbooks (short, inexpensive booklets) were widely read—the literate middle class believing that, next to the Bible and the classics, history best instructed one how to live a moral life.*

In the cities, people got their sense of the past from dramas not only by Shakespeare but also by Marlowe, Heywood, Jonson, Massinger, Fletcher, and Ford. In the period of Shakespeare's lifetime, *history* could

---

* According to a recent study, in Elizabethan England "poesy and the arts" were equal second with "history" ("religion" finished first) in the six main categories of book sales, well ahead of "science and maths," "schoolbooks," and "society and conduct." See Andy Kesson and Emma Smith, *The Elizabethan Top Ten, Defining Print Popularity in Early Modern England* (London: Routledge, 2016).

refer to a range of writings—plays, poems, memoirs, biographies, current affair narratives, annals, chronicles, surveys, and antiquarian records. The chorus in *Henry V* asks his audience to "admit [him] chorus to this history," suggesting that a literary work dealing with matters of historical record can be regarded as "history." The quarto edition of *King Lear* claims to offer a "true chronicle history," and even in *The Taming of the Shrew* the playlet staged before Sly is described as "a kind of history," implying that an imaginary work may still carry that authority.

The first time that the name of Shakespeare appears in print is in the adulterated 1598 published version of *Henry IV*. By 1623, Shakespeare's great friends and fellow actors, John Heminge and Henry Condell, had put together the first collected edition of the thirty-eight surviving plays of one firmly named as William Shakespeare (no longer Shakespear, or Shakespere, Shazpere, Shaxberd, or Schaftspere).* This edition, known as the First Folio—second, third, and fourth folios were issued in 1632, 1663, and 1685—divides the plays into Comedies (fourteen in all), then plays about English kings as Histories (ten: *King John, Richard II, Henry IV* parts 1 and 2, *Henry V, Henry VI* parts 1, 2, and 3, *Richard III*, and *Henry VIII*), and plays about Rome under the rubric of Tragedies (eleven: *Coriolanus, Julius Caesar, Antony and Cleopatra,* and *Cymbeline,* then also *Titus Andronicus, Romeo and Juliet, Timon of Athens, Macbeth*—set in Scotland—*Hamlet, King Lear,* and *Othello*). They could have intended no generic distinction, although there is possibly a nationalistic impulse in elevating the English plays into a category all their own.

Finally, *Troilus and Cressida* inhabits a no-man's-land between histories and tragedies. The editors of the First Folio originally planned for it to be in the section containing the tragedies. Due to a conflict with the printer, however, it appears after the rest of the tragedies, placed just in front of the histories. There are other anomalies: *Henry VI* is a fixed part of the canon, although co-written with Christopher Mar-

---

* Just nineteen of Shakespeare's plays got printed during his lifetime, possibly because he didn't think of longevity or building a canon. Indeed, none of his manuscripts—or copies made by scribes—has survived. The "Quartos" (so called because of their format: large sheets folded into four) contained single plays and were sold at sixpence each, compared with the pound charged for the First Folio. At least eight plays in the First Folio included work from collaborators—in the case of *Henry VI, Part I,* maybe 80 percent. The histories and tragedies especially were printed in full, whereas in performance they were often cut to save time.

lowe (among others), but *Pericles* is not included, as Shakespeare wrote only the second half; nor *The Two Noble Kinsmen,* like *Henry VIII* co-written with John Fletcher (who succeeded him as house playwright for the King's Men company), nor the drama *Edward III,* published anonymously in 1596 but now said to be Shakespeare's. Significantly, the histories appear not in the order in which they were written but in order of reigns, as if they are part of some grand authorial scheme, but if there ever was such a plan it emerged only in retrospect. Yet the editors of the First Folio ended up, whether by accident or design, creating a new genre: the history play. Significantly, after the death of the childless Elizabeth, James I takes the throne, has three children, and questions of succession recede; the writing of history plays stops almost immediately.

To the modern eye, such divisions seem eccentric. "Tragedy" anyway entered English usage as a theatrical qualifier only in 1559, with the translation of Seneca's ten plays. The quartos of *Richard II* (1597) and *Richard III* (1597) both offered "Tragedy" on their title pages. The First Folio describes *King John* as a tragedy, and a later quarto lists *King Lear* and *The Merchant of Venice* as histories. Further categorizations have included Romances, Late Romances, Problem Plays, and the Roman Plays (*Antony and Cleopatra, Julius Caesar, Coriolanus,* and *Titus Andronicus*). These last four, the first three written in rapid succession, are obviously at some level histories, as they deal with real-life figures. The same is true of the two Greek dramas, *Timon of Athens* and *Pericles.* Both sets of plays are based on Plutarch's *Parallel Lives* (the great advantage for Shakespeare was that Plutarch wrote history through biography). *Cymbeline* is better considered one of the Roman plays too, as it is set in Britain at the time of Augustus Caesar, Romans take part, and by the end Rome wins the day. *Troilus and Cressida* remains in limbo. History or myth? Shakespeare didn't conjure up his story but used sources, in particular Chaucer's *Troilus and Criseyde* and George Chapman's translation of Homer.

"There is as much history in *Macbeth* as in *Richard [II],*" reckoned Coleridge, the Scottish play being based on Raphael Holinshed's *Chronicles,* an account of England, Scotland, and Ireland published in 1587 (although all Shakespeare found there about Lady Macbeth was: "But specially his wife lay sore upon him to attempt the thing, as she that was very ambitious, brenning [burning] in unquenchable desire to beare the name of a queene"). The story of King Lear appears in Geoffrey of Monmouth's *Historia Regum Britannia* and is repeated in Holinshed (where Cordelia and Lear both survive). Hamlet may have been only a character that Shakespeare took from a twelfth-century Danish legend, but both Rosencrantz and Gyldenstierne were real courtiers. *Othello* was inspired by a 1565 story, "Un Capitano Moro," by Giovanni Cinthio, which in turn may have been based on an incident in Venice around 1508. In short, more than half of Shakespeare's plays are rooted in history—as is his long poem *The Rape of Lucrece* (1593–94), depicting the expulsion of the Tarquins from Rome in 496 B.C. and the start of the Republic.*

Certainly, Shakespeare has his own take on the real-life people of his plays (did a maddened Titus Andronicus really try to kill a fly with a knife?), but recent research indicates that his characterizations are far more accurate than previously thought. Henry VII, so drab a figure as Richmond, may be presented in sympathetic terms, and Cleopatra may be more beautiful than her real-life model—in her biography, Stacy Schiff charges that accepting Shakespeare's portrait is "a little like taking George C. Scott's words for Patton's." Later she notes that "Shakespeare may be as much to blame for our having lost sight of Cleopatra VII as the Alexandrian humidity, Roman propaganda, and Elizabeth Taylor's limpid lilac eyes." Again, Mark Antony is not the drunken boor described in the records, but generally the characterizations in the plays fit what has come down to us. Otherwise Shakespeare changes Holinshed or Plutarch at will, altering people's ages, lineages, family details, and relations, plundering his sources for the plots he wanted. Hotspur is presented as a young man, when at the time given in the play he was well into middle age, while in *Richard II* Queen Isabel is a woman of mature years, whereas in life she was just eleven.

The great example of this is Richard III, who in Shakespeare's vi-

---

* "This is not to say that rights to the term 'history' were not hotly contested in Elizabethan England," says Richard Helgerson. "They were"—just not by playwrights. See Richard Helgerson, "Shakespeare and Contemporary Dramatists of History," *A Companion to Shakespeare's Works: The Histories* (Oxford: Blackwell, 2006), p. 27. As for Raphael Holinshed (c. 1529–80), he was less a lone author than director of a team of writers commissioned to provide a history of Britain, reserving that of England for himself. He used a variety of sources, both contemporary chronicles and Renaissance narratives, and included material he knew was dubious, so that readers could get a variety of perspectives. He died shortly after the volume's first publication in 1577. The 1587 revised version, the one used by Shakespeare, brought up to the year 1553, while still known as Holinshed's, was largely the work of others.

sion is physically misshapen ("Deformed, unfinish'd . . . scarce half made up"), a tyrannical all-around figure of evil, likened to a hound, a boar, a toad, a spider, and finally to a monstrous cockatrice and foul lump of matter. Despite its huge cast, the play has no subplots; it is all about the great usurper. On stage, and on a killing spree, Richard not only murders Henry VI, Edward of Lancaster, William, Lord Hastings, and, most famously, Hastings's two child nephews, but also contrives the death of his own brother and to round things off poisons his wife so he might marry his niece. Shakespeare paints him in an even darker light than Holinshed or his other sources, including Polydore Vergil's *Anglica Historia* (1534, which largely exonerates Richard), and makes the king directly responsible for the princes' deaths.

For more than 350 years his version of events has held the public imagination (as did his portrayal of the Wars of the Roses, lasting from 1399 till 1487, as an unceasing period of bloody confrontation, which it wasn't). Other writers hastened to take up Shakespeare's portrayal of a murderous usurper—thus in *The Pickwick Papers* the cockney wordsmith Sam Weller, the character that made Dickens famous, roundly declares, "Business first, pleasure afterwards, as King Richard the Third said ven he stabbed the t'other king in the Tower, afore he smothered the babbies." No matter that in Shakespeare's play Richard kills the Duke of Somerset, while in fact Richard was only three years old at the time; and woe betide any production that strays from the evil hunchback version. (During the Second World War, a period when the Nazi horror haunted all Europe, the English actor-manager Donald Wolfit inserted imitations of Hitler into his performances as Richard.)

Then in 1951 the Scottish mystery writer Josephine Tey published *The Daughter of Time,* in which her detective hero, Inspector Alan Grant, becomes intrigued by a portrait of Richard that suggests a benign and considerate man. How strong is the centuries-old case that he murdered his nephews? Grant (acting as Tey's mouthpiece) discovers that there never was a bill of attainder, coroner's inquest, or any other legal measure that implicated Richard in any foul play. The princes' mother, Elizabeth Woodville, remained on good terms with him until his death. Further, there was no political advantage for Richard in killing the children. He was the legitimate king. The princes were more of a threat to his successor, Henry VII. There is no evidence that the princes were missing from the Tower when Henry took over. (In the summer of 2016, newly discovered dental records suggested that Richard and the princes did not share the same DNA, so there was even less reason to kill them.) Grant concludes that Richard's guilt is a Shakespearian fabrication—as is the portrayal of him as a hunchback, often with a withered arm. Thus are myths constructed, he concludes (as, to be fair, Horace Walpole did too, back in 1768; Richard has had many defenders). In this case the Tudors saw to it that their narrative of the murderous Plantagenet ruler prevailed.

The historian Alison Weir has pointed out several flaws in this reasoning, drawing attention to the fact that Tey was not acquainted with some then-unpublished source material; the murder of Hastings, for instance, has now been proved beyond any legal doubt. Still, there are several areas where Richard's portrayal has been shown to be false; while the 2011 discovery of the dead king's skeletal remains, in a coffin of golden English oak with an incised white rose representing the House of York, buried beneath a council parking lot in Leicester, twenty miles from the battle that killed him, provides sure evidence that he was indeed deformed, but by severe spinal scoliosis suffered in adolescence. Shakespeare twisted the facts to make his villain a freak show,* emphasizing Richard's physical deformities as a reflection of his inner deviousness. Yet Richard's heroic end and the sketchy characterization of Henry, Earl of Richmond, allow playgoers to leave the theater still a bit on the hunchback's side. "Something in us," confesses Stephen Greenblatt, "enjoys every minute of his horrible ascent to power." By the time Shakespeare died, *Richard III* had outsold all his other plays.

* * *

EVEN SO, WHY DID Shakespeare write Richard's story the way he did? At one obvious level, he was concerned with spinning a good yarn—this is shown by his failure even to mention such dominating events as the Peasants' Revolt of 1381 in *Richard II* or the signing of Magna Carta in *King John*. To build on Jonathan Bate's point, in a world without newspapers, radio, TV, film, or internet, the theater had a special place,

---

* An article by Max Fisher in *The Washington Post* on February 4, 2013, got this online reply by "Crocheron" on May 24, 2014: "I have scoliosis. One shoulder is higher than the other. My scoliosis curves to the right and I have a hump on the right side of my upper back. My surgery was in 1973. They call it a rib hump and it can now be corrected during the fusion surgery." Thus the twisted spine of scoliosis and the "hunchback" of kyphosis may be separate conditions, but they look the same.

Laurence Olivier in Richard III, *1955.*
According to the British Film Institute, the film
"may have done more to popularise Shakespeare
than any other single work."

offering a wondrous mix of imagination and chronicle. As James Shapiro says, it was "the one place where rich and poor could congregate and see enacted, through old or made-up stories, the refracted image of their own desires and anxieties." Even if they knew nothing about the history when they went in, they would emerge with a powerful sense of the shape of the past—albeit the playwright's shape.

Shakespeare began his career during the increasingly tense years of Elizabeth's decline, in a country racked by malnutrition, unemployment, poor harvests, and food riots. By 1597 the average wage was less than a third, in real terms, of what it had been a century before. It is a wonder that any working person could afford the theater, not least because most plays were performed in early afternoon, usually starting at 2 P.M. and lasting two to three hours. Yet throughout these years, playhouses—or play sites—continued to be wildly popular with the laboring classes. And his audiences were practiced listeners anyway, since they had to go to church and had become accustomed to following long sermons (and sermons were even more widely attended than plays).

Part of the reason for theater's popularity was that Shakespeare and his fellow playwrights were riding a tide of patriotic fervor following the naval success of 1588. Philip II sent Spanish fleets to invade England five times in all, but the Armada of late May suffered eight thousand casualties in a single day. Over three weeks Spain lost seventeen thousand men; England forfeited not a single ship. All this induced a spike in patriotism, of which Shakespeare took full advantage. It is no surprise that, just a few years later, *King John* was produced, pandering to those same feelings.

Although Elizabeth's reign saw several thousand titles published, few of her citizens could read (she could, of course, indulging herself in a diet of trashy Italian novellas). The only way to reach ordinary people in numbers was through a new kind of spectacle. Public playing had been banned during the radical Protestantism of Edward VI (1547–53), but for much of Elizabeth's reign, licensed companies could travel the country, playing in tavern courtyards. Shortly after the sinking of the Armada came the idea that, instead of taking drama to the punters, why not have the punters come to the drama? And where better than in London, in the slums that teemed on the edge of the city, alongside other attractions such as bull- and bear-baiting, cock-fighting, and public executions? And the capital was exploding—fifty thousand inhabitants in 1500, by 1600 London numbered two hundred thousand; only Paris and Naples were larger. Life expectancy ranged between twenty-five and thirty-five, so the city was overwhelmingly a youthful place, and its suburbs (where the creative Huguenots settled) a hive of entrepreneurial activity, offering everything from weaving to soap-making. The South Bank had its disreputable side (the brothels and gaming-houses that led to the area south and east of the Thames were soon dubbed "the suburbs of sin"), but it was far more than that.

In the years both before and particularly following the Armada victory, London playhouses sprang up almost overnight. In 1576, three theaters opened in Shoreditch alone. Most companies performed at least five different plays a week, and while they would round out their repertory with tried and popular works, they still needed to acquire some twenty new plays a year; playwrights were hard-pressed to keep up with the demand. By the 1590s, some fifteen to twenty thousand Londoners were seeing a play every week. Between 1567 and 1642, records show the extraordinary figure of fifty million paying customers—two thousand spectators a day—about 1 percent of the city's population, this even though none of Shakespeare's plays is set in London, nor any in his own time. Prices ranged from 4 pence for gentlemen to 1 penny for the rest of the audience.* These figures were achieved despite regular closings of theaters due to bouts of the plague, and as soon as James I became king he shut down theaters on Sundays.

Standards of acting varied widely, and by the end of the sixteenth century most theatergoers accepted that there were just two acting companies of note, the Admiral's Men and the Lord Chamberlain's Men. The latter was Shakespeare's troupe, formed in 1594 as a joint-stock company, with profits shared among the actors. In May 1603, less than two weeks after James VI of Scotland arrived in London to take up office in succession to Elizabeth I, the troupe became "the King's Men," the playwright and his fellow shareholders paying six shillings and eight pence—the equivalent of £1,000 today—for the title. Shakespeare probably made between £150 and £200 a year from his shareholding, between $40,000 and $100,000 in today's terms. Theaters great and small were buzzing with new work, often coarse, boisterous, and violent, showplaces "of all beastly and filthy matters," making the playhouses, in George Bernard Shaw's phrase, "pestiferous with plays." Unlike today, where a single play aims to be kept for long runs, as Garry Wills tells us,

> in the month of January, 1596 . . . the Admiral's Men played on every day except Sundays and presented fourteen plays. Six were given only one performance in the month, and no play was presented more than four times. The shortest interval between the repetition of any single play was three days, and the next shortest five. Although all except one were old plays, this record represents an achievement that would almost certainly be beyond the capacities of actors in the modern theatre.

* In a period overlapping with Shakespeare's writing life, 1558–1603, prices rose considerably and currency values fluctuated, but a quart of small beer cost a penny and a quart of good ale four pence, 180 pages of prose romance a shilling or less, and for three pence one had one's choice of a pipeload of tobacco, a ride in a light rowboat on the Thames, or a cheap meal. A trip to the Globe was good value. See Leonard Ashley, *Elizabethan Popular Culture* (Bowling Green, Ohio: Bowling Green State University, 1988), p. 24.

The memories of the actors must indeed have been exceptional. And not only was Shakespeare one of those actors (unlike his greatest theatrical contemporary, Christopher Marlowe, who married play-writing to spying for the government, not to appearing on the boards himself); he was composing narrative poems and sonnets, managing the company, writing new plays, and often (we may presume) was de facto director too, there being no formal position of "director" in his day. Scripts were bought by playing companies for between £5 and £11 each; if a play was later printed, the playwright could expect to receive as little as £2 extra; writing plays did not make for a lavish life-style.

Companies were usually composed of nine to twelve adults, with maybe two boy actors. Although in Spain, France, and Italy women could appear onstage, and in England too in court masques, on the London stage boys performed their parts until the 1660s and the Resto-ration. This tied Shakespeare's hands. Boy actors were not easy to find or to train in the short period before their voices broke, and women's parts make up only 13 percent of the lines in his plays. When a talented boy actor came through, the situation changed, so for instance Cleopa-tra has 678 lines, and there are substantial parts for Lady Macbeth, Ophelia, Juliet, Desdemona, Beatrice, and Kate in *The Taming of the Shrew;* Rosalind has a quarter of all the lines in *As You Like It*—686, still a lot to learn. (The actor who plays Hamlet has 1,476.) And young actors had to be carefully husbanded: Lady Macbeth has just one brief appearance (20 lines) in the last two acts of the play, as the leading boy actor of the company, a lad named John Rice, was needed to double as Lady MacDuff (45 lines) in Act III. The same restriction applies in *King Lear,* where the same actor was used for both Cordelia and the Fool. Shakespeare was as much juggler as word-conjuror.* Bob Dylan's

---

* Word-conjuror he certainly was. Between 1500 and 1650, some twelve thousand new words entered the English language, and half are still in use today. At least eight hundred—a phenom-enal percentage—are Shakespeare's personal coinage: *good riddance, fob off, puke, queasy, excellent, critical, foul-mouthed* are just a few, let alone phrases such as *better days, strange bedfellows,* or *sorry sight.* But other percentages show how kind history has been to us. Of the 230 play texts that exist from this time, an amazing 15 percent are by Shakespeare, and of the twenty-nine plays of three thousand lines or more that survive from 1590 to 1616, twenty-two are by Ben Jonson or Shakespeare. The latter's survival is all the more surprising in that, in the century after their deaths, Ben Jonson's name appeared in print three times as often as his rival's. Based on his plays, Shakespeare had a vocabulary of more than thirty thousand words, as compared to Milton, say, who employs only eight thousand. The first biography of Shakespeare did not appear until 1709; it contained eleven pieces of information, eight of them false. And the first lecture about him at

words after being awarded the 2016 Nobel Prize for Literature suggest a fellow artist's mindset:

> When he was writing *Hamlet,* I'm sure he was thinking about a lot of different things: "Who're the right actors for these roles?" "How should this be staged?" "Do I really want to set this in Denmark?" His creative vision and ambitions were no doubt at the forefront of his mind, but there were also more mundane matters to consider and deal with. "Is the financing in place?" "Are there enough good seats for my patrons?" "Where am I going to get a human skull?"

* * *

IN HIS TWO TELEVISION documentaries about Shakespeare, Simon Schama makes the point that, in the years since the Reformation, the "Great Rebuilding" (in which stone and brick replaced most wooden houses, so that the look of most English towns fundamentally changed), Francis Drake sailing round the world, and then the Armada victory, the English needed to know just who they were, what made them unique, at a time when declining feudalism and nascent capitalism were on a collision course. The Globe Theatre was a mass-education facility, seating just under three thousand people a day, six days a week (Blackfriars, in contrast, was much smaller and had an audience capacity of barely six hundred). And Shakespeare saw that the best way to grapple with the present was to engage with the past.

It is in his histories, says Schama, especially in his masterpieces *Henry IV Parts 1 and 2,* that Shakespeare presents us with "England unedited, the complete thing, the cream and the scum . . . that's what we want . . . the dirt and the devilry." *Henry IV* accordingly is not really about kings but a groundbreaking, authentic portrait of England, warts and all (no matter that the tavern environment of Eastcheap belongs more to the late sixteenth century than to the early fifteenth), with Falstaff the living embodiment of a small country that suddenly has an outsize sense of itself. Audiences could see England on the stage

---

a British university was not until 1751, at Oxford, by one William Hawkins—in Latin. Today four thousand new works on Shakespeare are published every year. This is not the outcome of post-four-hundredth-anniversary enthusiasm. In 1997, for instance, 4,780 books or articles on Shakespeare were published, 342 on *Hamlet* alone.

almost before it existed in reality. The old culture was being wiped out, but Shakespeare's England could be born only when a much older theater, Catholic theater, had been killed off. And no longer was the divinity of kings a topic reserved only for princes to consider in private. As Schama puts it, history was becoming the country's new theology. In presenting England's recent past in the way he did, setting one plot against another, the urban center against the court, putting side by side different strata of society, Shakespeare was not just recording the nation; he was helping create it, staking his claim to be the voice of the new Britain. As James Shapiro has noted, in every one of the histories "there is always one speech about what England is—'this sceptr'd isle,' in *Richard II*—where Shakespeare stops and tells you what this nation is about."

At one level, he was acting as a propagandist for the Tudor cause and its claim that Britain was a unified society. (*Henry VIII* even ends with an extravagant honoring of the birth of Elizabeth; that play, together with *Henry V,* are the only times Shakespeare portrayed an admirable ruler of England.) At the same time, the country was being ripped apart by religious conflict. Pope Pius V had excommunicated Elizabeth in 1570, and in 1588 Sixtus V issued a papal bull excusing England's Catholics from obeying her laws, effectively a fatwah on the English queen that led to all Catholics being suspected of treason. Plays were meant to show the folly of rebellion. How to end such interminable civil strife?

When in 1558 Elizabeth I was crowned queen, Protestants saw her as the proper successor, Catholics as the excommunicated Henry VIII's bastard daughter who had usurped the throne from the legitimate inheritor, Mary, Queen of Scots. *Henry VI, Part I* has an obvious Yorkist slant: Henry VI is anemic, indecisive, and sanctimonious; neither Yorkists nor Queen Margaret think him a suitable king. The Yorkist case is put so clearly that Henry admits, in an aside, that his claim is weak—"the first time," notes Henry Kelly, a Tudor historian, "that a Lancastrian admission of this sort has been conjectured in the historical treatment of this period." However, as Kelly argues, Shakespeare's celebration of Tudor rule is less important than his presentation of the spectacular collapse of the medieval order. His great success with the *Henry VI* trilogy was partly fueled by patriotic feeling (which had also contributed to the appeal of the more traditional chronicle plays), while toward the close of Elizabeth's reign unease over the succession meant that dramas based on earlier dynastic struggles from the reign of Richard II, which focuses on the last two years of the king's twenty-two-year reign, 1398–99, to the Wars of the Roses were especially topical. While patriotism and love of country are themes in all the history plays, a quarter of them are built around the question of succession.

Another Shakespeare scholar, John F. Danby, in *Shakespeare's Doctrine of Nature* (1949), examines a thorny question: "When is it right to rebel?" His conclusion is that Shakespeare's thought ran through three stages. First, in the plays that cover the Wars of the Roses (1455–85), *Henry VI* to *Richard III*, he implies that rebellion against a legitimate and pious king is wrong and that only an evident villain such as Richard of Gloucester would have attempted it. Second, in *King John* and the *Richard II* to *Henry V* cycle, he adopts the official Tudor line, by which rebellion, even against a usurper, can never be condoned. Finally, from *Julius Caesar* on, he justifies tyrannicide, but to do so disguises his motives by writing of Roman, Danish, Scottish, or ancient British events. (There is a tendency to think of Shakespeare as an Elizabethan, but as a playwright he was at least as much a Stuart; whereas under Elizabeth he concentrated on English history, under James I he focused on British. Of his 143 uses of the adjective "English," 126 occur in his Elizabethan plays, only 17 in his Jacobean.)

Shakespeare's plays are full of small inaccuracies and anachronisms (in *Coriolanus,* Cato is mentioned—three centuries before he actually lived; in *Julius Caesar,* a character asks "What's o'clock?" centuries before clocks were invented; *King Lear,* set in prehistorical Britain, has a reference to Bedlam, an insane asylum in Elizabethan London; the real-life Banquo was a co-conspirator with Macbeth, not his victim). But as Coleridge noted in Shakespeare's defense:

> In order that a drama may be properly historical, it is necessary that it should be the history of the people to whom it is addressed. In the composition, care must be taken that there appear no dramatic improbability, as the reality is taken for granted. . . . The events themselves are immaterial, otherwise than as the clothing and manifestation of the spirit that is working within.

Ron Rosenbaum, author of *The Shakespeare Wars*, builds on this argument: "The greater the artist, the more the distortions of history become interesting for what they reveal about the artist. Only a fool would take a novel's view of history as what actually happened. The quality of the artist affects my judgment on how interesting the departure from the facts are—aspects of his mind, his world view." As the wise clown Touchstone says in *As You Like It*, "The truest poetry is the most feigning."

One of the reasons for the popularity of the history plays was that they provided a cover for talking safely about the present through the prism of the past—so long as one did not try to get away with too much. (This is also true of Victorian fiction, which can be read as historical novels about the present; but then their authors were never in danger of summary execution.) There is scant evidence about which historical parallels were picked up by Elizabethans or what the impact of these observations might have been, but the governments of both Elizabeth and James I viewed English historical materials as subject to their control. Sir Walter Raleigh advised any would-be historian not to follow truth too near the heels if he did not want his teeth struck out, and the Privy Council ruled that no book on English history could be published without express authorization. (Even the 1587 edition of Holinshed's history fell afoul of the council, several passages being removed from the book, to be separately published in 1723.)

Shakespeare was well aware of the game he was playing; in *Hamlet*, Claudius asks if there is any offense in the argument of *The Murder of Gonzago*, only to receive the caustic reply that there is none. And he was ever alert to the ironies of history. In *Henry V*, Harry boasts that "We few, we happy few, we band of brothers" will be remembered on the feast day of St. Crispin "from this day to the ending of the world." However, as a result of the Elizabethan Protestant reform of the liturgical calendar, St. Crispin's Day was not celebrated in Shakespeare's time. His dramas may have functioned as a rationale for royal legitimacy (the King's Men were required to give more command performances at court than any other theater company), but they also opened up the possibility of challenging a reigning monarch. For example, the first part of *Henry IV* dramatizes that king's troubled stewardship following his usurpation as he confronts rebellious nobles and a wayward son. In *Henry V*, Shakespeare courted royal disapproval by including the first public mention of how, immediately after the Battle of Agincourt, English troops were commanded to massacre their French prisoners—Henry orders that "Every soldier kill his prisoner" (Act IV, scene vi, l. 37). The execution of French POWs was even then a war crime, and for Shakespeare to pen such details during a Tudor monarchy was daring, coming the same year, 1599, that the government decreed that all plays had to be licensed directly by the Privy Council.

Two years later, rebels under the Earl of Essex commissioned a performance of *Richard II*—"the play of the deposing and killing of King Richard"—paying the company 20 percent more than their normal fee: 40 shillings on top of their "ordinary" rate for a command performance of £10. The very next day, the botched uprising began. Early in the play, Gaunt accuses Richard, "Landlord of England art thou and not king" (Act II, scene i, ll. 13–14). Elizabeth I is said to have yelled to a courtier: "I am Richard II. Know ye not that?" The script had been published in quarto format in 1597 and twice reprinted, each time excluding a 160-line sequence in which Richard formally hands over his throne. This deposition scene was never published in Elizabeth's lifetime, being printed as a "new addition" in a 1608 quarto edition and in the 1623 folio version; while in February 1601, the day the Earl of Essex, "with rebellion broached on his sword," was executed, Shakespeare's company was back performing before the queen and her court; he had escaped retribution.

The "Essex affair," what the queen's protector Lord Cecil called "this dangerous accident," was the playwright's one serious brush with political disaster. But government surveillance and paranoia ran through the sixteenth century into the seventeenth. A 1599 law ruled that scripts had to be presented to a government functionary known as "the Master of the Revels" for state censorship. If, despite such screening, the play was considered seditious or libelous in the way it was performed, the actors were responsible—along with the author—and could be fined, suspended, jailed, or even mutilated, usually by branding or ear- or nose-cropping; alternately their theater could be shut down. Shakespeare knew how to toe the line. Indeed, when in the early 1590s Henry Chettle's play *Sir Thomas More* was objected to by officialdom, Shakespeare was brought in to rewrite the offending scene.

Some of his contemporaries were not so politic. In the summer of 1597 Ben Jonson was arrested for co-authoring a "lewd, seditious and slanderous" satire, *The Isle of Dogs* (a play that so enraged the authorities that the order went out for all theaters to be torn down, only to be rescinded because the royal court needed the players). In 1605 Jonson was arrested again for an anti-Scottish comedy called *Eastward Ho*— earning him a two-month stay in jail. And Marlowe's revelations about the St. Bartholomew's Day massacre of 1572 in his *Massacre at Paris* (1593) may even have got him killed, stabbed to death by a twelvepenny dagger inserted just above the eye. (At least Ben Jonson survived into his mid-sixties, having the good fortune, at twenty-six, to kill his fellow duelist rather than being killed by him.) This was the kind of personal danger that Shakespeare faced, although in his case the authorities may have underestimated the power of his plays to influence public opinion, or his propagandizing for the Tudor cause may have been an effective smokescreen. He was also adept at rarely making an argument for just one point of view.

Paola Pugliatti, a new recruit to the crowded ship of Shakespeare studies, is good here:

> To go fishing for subjects in the established corpus of facts and political issues relating to national history was certainly a more demanding and more risky undertaking than simply ransacking the repertories of Italian novellas or even Plutarch's *Lives*. The risks involved were both theatrical and political. In the first place, the dramatist could not make indiscriminate alterations to the events narrated in the chronicles, since these were to a certain extent common knowledge, and therefore the audience expected to see them more or less accurately reproduced on the stage; and in the second place, the treatment of national political issues was more likely to attract the attention of the censor.

Toleration and *liberal democracy* were hardly words in the Elizabethan or Stuart lexicon, yet in play after play Shakespeare took up major themes of how England or Britain should be governed, each time providing his own spin. *Richard III,* for example, shows an English court hopelessly compromised by amoral opportunism. In the victory of Henry VII over Richard III and the consolidation of society after the Wars of the Roses, England was in a perfect position to make important advances in the arts and sciences. These developments were in large part derived from the ideas of statecraft of France's Louis XI, in whose court Henry VII was raised, and also from the Italian Renaissance. Shakespeare was steeped in that culture through his friendship with John Florio, the Anglo-Italian who was tutor to the playwright's early patron, the Earl of Southampton, and who in 1603 published a translation of Montaigne's *Essays*.

Such influences are possibly why Shakespeare chose to write about ancient Rome rather than, say, ancient Greece or the England of King Alfred or of Arthurian legend: Rome was seen as a model for the England of his time, and his audiences would have recognized that. After finishing his cycles of English history plays, he shelved his Holinshed for a number of years. He did write about ancient England twice, on the first occasion in one of his greatest plays. In 1606 he was forty-two, an old man for his day, and in need of a major hit after what for him had been a relatively quiet period, one that coincided with a miserable time for playgoers. Theaters were closed from May 1603 to April 1604, then from May to September 1604, October to December 1605, and for at least half of 1606, each time because of plague. But it was in 1606— the year the Union Jack, another symbol of nationhood, was first flown—that he once again turned to the question of royal succession, in the story of an old king who surrenders his power.

Shakespeare generally started his plays in the middle of a narrative, and sure enough *King Lear,* set in 800 B.C., opens with the question of a divided kingdom—Kent's first words are "I thought the King had more affected the Duke of Albany than Cornwall": Jacobean playgoers knew that King James I's elder son, Henry, was the current Duke of Albany and his younger son, Charlie, the Duke of Cornwall. Since both James and his father had been Dukes of Albany, such a reference was to speak of Scotland. So who should rule England now? Further, Shakespeare would have known that James I had advised his son and heir, Prince Henry, not to divide his kingdom in *Basilikon Doron,* a bestselling book of paternal advice that the king wrote (in Greek) and that had been published in London in 1603. *King Lear* thus offers a lesson in dramatic form on the theme of James's words to his son. Only in *Lear* it is not just a question of who should succeed or by what rights; it is the issue of what has happened to the nature of government itself.

Lear makes a series of errors, and his kingdom is soon threatened by courtiers willing to govern without ethical considerations; only at the play's end is the country saved by a revival of proper stewardship.

Even "good" characters like Hamlet and Laertes perceive the political world as working to different ethical rules from that of the personal, and they worry about the consequences. The good must be on their guard, because the lords of misrule have become ever more cunning. Reenter, at this point, our Florentine companion from the previous chapter. Machiavelli, his surname anglicized to the sinister-sounding "Machevil," was well known to Shakespeare through John Florio's 1603 translation of *The Prince*, while Marlowe's play *The Jew of Malta* (c. 1589) opens with a speech delivered by a character called Machiavel ("Admired I am of those that hate me most"), a ghost based on Machiavelli; the Italian courtier-diplomat's writings became crucial works of reference for Shakespeare (and of course the book's appearance on the Vatican Index was no constraint on Rome-hating English Protestants). He acknowledged the Machiavellian aspects of his concept of kingship in *Henry VI, Part 3* in the words he put into the mouth of the future Richard III, at this point still a young Duke of Gloucester:

> *Why, I can smile, and murder while I smile;*
> *And cry, Content, to that which grieves my heart;*
> *And wet my cheeks with artificial tears,*
> *And frame my face to all occasions.*
> *I'll drown more sailors than the mermaid shall;*
> *I'll slay more gazers than the basilisk;*
> *I'll play the orator as well as Nestor;*
> *Deceive more slyly than Ulysses could;*
> *And, like a Sinon, take another Troy:*
> *I can add colors to the chameleon;*
> *Change shapes with Proteus for advantages;*
> *And set the murderous Machiavel to school.*
> *Can I do this, and cannot get a crown?*
> *Tut, were it further off, I'll pluck it down!*

By the time Shakespeare composed *Lear*, opportunists like Cornwall, Goneril, and Regan, or even more the sinister Edmund, had become staples. The man or woman who is governed only by ambition—the political machiavel, the "politique" courtier—is a dangerous citizen but a key subject. The Bastard in *King John*, Gloucester in *Richard III*, Aaron the Moor in *Titus Andronicus*, Iago ("I am not what I am") in *Othello*, Antonio in *The Tempest*, even young Hal, setting himself up to be visibly flawless, are "machiavels," characterized by their pursuit of "Commodity," variously interpreted as advantage, profit, and expedience, and by their persuasive way with words and their powers of self-transformation. Terry Eagleton has noted that we are seeing "the emergence in the seventeenth century of the doctrine of possessive individualism." If the leaders of the nation, or any nation, fail to act as they should, the Machiavel will triumph. And when history is presented it is to interrogate it, its players, and its means of representation. As Machiavelli observed, political power is secured by theatrical illusion—a people can be controlled best by dissimulation, image-making, role-play. Kingship, once seen as sacramental, a gift of the gods, amounts to no more than good acting.

Contemporary audiences may have loved lively battle scenes, but they were becoming increasingly interested in the notion of character as a driver of events. In nearly all Shakespeare's histories there is a significant subtext devoted to middle-class and working-class figures, whom Shakespeare uses to suggest the possibilities of alternative voices and conflicting views of what has been taking place—the incompetent legal officers from Justice Shallow through Master Fang and Master Snare in *Henry IV, Part 2*, the murderer and scrivener in *Richard III*, the miserable and starving Apothecary from whom Romeo buys his poison, the vagrant Simcox in *Henry VI, Part 2*, the fisherman in *Pericles*, or the three English soldiers in *Henry V*—"Shakespeare's marginals," as they have been called. Those soldiers are given names—John Bates, Alexander Court, and Michael Williams—and an individual life, as shown in their conversation with the stranger who has joined them, the disguised King Harry, about loyalty in a just cause:

BATES

> . . . *We know*
> *enough, if we know we are the king's subjects: if*
> *his cause be wrong, our obedience to the king wipes*
> *the crime of it out of us.*

WILLIAMS

> *But if the cause be not good, the king himself hath*
> *a heavy reckoning to make, when all those legs and*
> *arms and heads, chopped off in battle, shall join*
> *together at the latter day and cry all "We died at*
> *such a place"; some swearing, some crying for a*
> *surgeon, some upon their wives left poor behind*
> *them, some upon the debts they owe, some upon their*
> *children rawly left. I am afeard there are few die*
> *well that die in a battle; for how can they*
> *charitably dispose of any thing, when blood is their*
> *argument? Now, if these men do not die well, it*
> *will be a black matter for the king that led them to*
> *it; whom to disobey were against all proportion of*
> *subjection.*

Shakespeare shows that it is possible to review the past from different perspectives and provides both the major and minor figures of history a psychological depth they had not received before in English drama. (Schama reckons the encounter between the king and Michael Williams the most important in the play.) Also, by simplifying his sources he gave his subplots a series of contrasts, adding a texture to everything he covered. Source manipulation and sheer invention of an order far beyond the creations of Geoffrey of Monmouth or Henry of Huntingdon—both now become part of the historian's armory. Pandora's box had been opened, and writing about the past would never be the same.

CHAPTER 8

ZOZO AND THE MARIONETTE INFIDEL

M. Voltaire and Mr. Gibbon

———

The arch-scoundrel . . . has finally kicked the bucket.

—MOZART, ON HEARING OF VOLTAIRE'S DEATH

"He is a disagreeable dog, this Gibbon," Mrs. Thrale said.
"He squeaks like Punch. I imagine he'll squeak indeed before he dies, as he had a religious education." "Yes," said I
ludicrously. "He is an infidel puppet: *le marionette infidel.*"

—JAMES BOSWELL, MARCH 28, 1781

Two MEN, THE FRENCHMAN VOLTAIRE AND THE ENGLISHMAN EDWARD
Gibbon, in their opposition to organized Christianity, also changed
the way history was written, not as Shakespeare did, but by freeing it
(for a while, at least) from mythmaking and the prism of Church doctrines, casting off the shackles that hindered earlier historians. Jorge
Luis Borges concludes his essay on the author of *The Decline and Fall of
the Roman Empire* as follows:

To think of Gibbon is to think of Voltaire. . . . They share the
same disdain for human religions or superstitions, but their literary conduct differs greatly. Voltaire employed his extraordinary style to show or suggest that the facts of history are
contemptible; Gibbon has no better opinion of humanity, but
man's actions attract him as a spectacle, and he uses that attraction to entertain and fascinate the reader.

In 1767 Voltaire had cynically claimed that history was "nothing more than a tableau of crimes and misfortunes," although, contrary as ever, he also said that it was the form of literature that has the most readers. Gibbon agreed. "History is the most popular species of writing," he echoed, and together these two spearheaded a new way of thinking about how to write about the past. No longer was that past—like the future—part of a divine plan, a working out by man of God's will. It was there to be recorded as each individual chose.

The two men overlapped, but Voltaire (1694–1778) was by forty-one years the elder. In a writing life that stretched over half a century, he completed fifty plays, dozens of treatises on science, politics, and philosophy, the celebrated novella *Candide* and seven works of history. Along the way, he managed a mountain of verse and an entire range of correspondence, some twenty thousand letters (published in thirteen volumes, each of more than 1,200 pages), far exceeding the word count of the Bible.* He supposedly kept up his prodigious output by spending up to eighteen hours a day writing or dictating to secretaries, often from bed. He was also fueled by daunting amounts of caffeine—fifty cups between waking and sleep, Frederick the Great reported, usually at the Café Procope, in Paris's fashionable sixth arrondissement.

According to Victor Hugo, "To name Voltaire is to characterize the entire eighteenth century." Goethe judged him the greatest literary figure of his day. So much depends on one's point of view. No wonder that Mozart, ever the ardent Christian, thought Voltaire a scoundrel. Voltaire was undeniably an unabashed self-promoter, reckless and restless, inconsistent, a vacillator, irascible, altruistic, vain, capable of malice and outrageous hypocrisy, materialist to the core (his shopping lists at his country homes would make Martha Stewart blush), and uneasy with spirituality. In the words of Lytton Strachey, he was also "a fighter, without tenderness, without scruples, and without remorse. . . . He seems to resemble some great buzzing fly, shooting suddenly into a room through an open window and dashing franti-

---

* Voltaire's only rival is Goethe (1749–1832), whose collected works run to 143 volumes (including three of the most influential novels in European literature), as well as twenty thousand letters, all of which he accomplished while working as a senior civil servant in the duchy of Weimar. The Voltaire Foundation in Oxford is publishing a complete chronological series of Voltaire's writing, some two hundred volumes, due for completion by 2023. Only five to go.

cally from side to side; when all at once, as suddenly, he swoops away and out through another window which opens in quite a different direction, towards wide and flowery fields; so that perhaps the reckless creature knew where he was going after all." Such contradictions worried Voltaire not a whit: "The character of every man is a chaos," he explained.

Thomas Carlyle, in a perceptive essay (through the centuries, hardly any writer of note can leave the Frenchman alone), notes that Voltaire fails above all to understand the social importance of religion. As for history, he reads it "not with the eye of a devout seer, or even of a critic; but through a pair of mere anti-catholic spectacles." But he adds, in a wonderful phrase, Voltaire "is found always at the top, less by power in swimming, than by lightness in floating."

Voltaire—otherwise, François-Marie Arouet—never explained his pen name. The most popular theory maintains it is an anagram of a Latinized spelling of "Arouet" plus the first letters of *Le Jeune* ("The Younger"), but others have claimed it a nod to *le petit voluntaire* ("the volunteer"), a nickname the young Voltaire was given as a sarcastic reference to his innate bloody-mindedness. But he had more than one sobriquet, including the delightful "Zozo," connoting a clumsy and silly boy. Either way, "Arouet" was not for him. He had a strained relationship with his father, a society lawyer, who, viewing a writer's life as "an open sesame to destitution," tried to force his son into a legal career; in 1718, possibly to show his rejection of paternal values, François-Marie not only claimed that his real father was a long-forgotten poet named Rochebrune, a musketeer and officer, but dropped his family name when his first play, *Oedipe,* a reworking of Sophocles's tragedy, was performed at the Comédie-Française, and so "Voltaire" entered the world.

The youngest of five children, he was born a sickly creature who was not expected to live. Surviving was his first triumph. He was schooled by Jesuits, for seven years learning little, he protested, but "Latin and a lot of nonsense," although he became adept in that dead language, and in later years fluent in Italian, Spanish, and English. In 1713, after two years of enforced legal studies, he was sent to be secretary to the French ambassador (the brother of Voltaire's godfather) at The Hague, where he fell for a penniless beauty, Olympe Dunoyer. The ambassador discovered their affair and Voltaire was ordered home.

His father disinherited him and even threatened to have him shipped off to the West Indies, a decision rescinded only after Voltaire promised to devote himself to the law. Instead he spent his days composing satirical verses for the high-living social set in which he immersed himself. By the time he was twenty-one he was describing himself as "thin, long, and fleshless, without buttocks," and by most accounts was not strongly sexed; but what he may have lacked in testosterone he more than made up for in hyperactivity. He was looking for controversy as well as celebrity, and found them.

He first got into trouble in May 1716, when he was briefly exiled from Paris for composing poems mocking the daughter of the regent (the man who governed France while Louis XV was a minor). By the following May he was in hot water again for further impious verses, which for once he had not authored, but such was his notoriety that no one believed his denials. He was sentenced to eleven months in the Bastille Saint-Antoine, the medieval fortress on the eastern edge of Paris used as a prison for upper-class members of society who incurred royal displeasure.

Despite its reputation the Bastille was no vermin-infested hellhole: Voltaire was allowed books, furniture, linen, a nightcap, even perfume; he often dined with the governor and played billiards and bowls with the guards (the only time he is said to have enjoyed any sport). He later boasted that his windowless cell, with its ten-foot-thick walls, provided useful time for reflection (it was here that he set upon his new name), and although he was not allowed writing paper—in his hands a dangerous weapon—he started an epic poem about the bold and lecherous Henry IV of France (1553–1610), inscribing the verses between the lines of a printed book. *La Henriade* was his first significant work of history and his opening joust against the evils of religious fanaticism. The epic approved Henry's conversion to Catholicism and glorified his attempts to end the Catholic-Protestant massacres but criticized the Vatican as a power "inflexible to the conquered, complaisant to conquerors, ready, as interest dictates, either to absolve or to condemn." The poem was banned, though a pirated edition sold out.

Oedipe opened in mid-November 1718, seven months after his release from jail. The ecstatic reception from both critics and public immediately made him a celebrity. The wunderkind's plays and verses continued to arouse animosity and admiration in equal measure, and he could not stop himself from picking arguments with enemies in high places. Before long he was back in the Bastille, serving eleven months for planning to duel a powerful young nobleman who had had him beaten up. Worried that the courts might extend his jail time, Voltaire suggested that as an alternative punishment he exile himself, to which the French authorities agreed. He packed his bags for England, where he remained for nearly three years, drinking coffee with Pope, Swift, and Congreve and accepting invitations to soirees from luminaries such as Lady Mary Wortley Montagu and the Duchess of Marlborough. A few decades on, Dr. Johnson was to note, "No authors ever had so much fame in their own lifetime as Pope and Voltaire." Voltaire would record, "How I love the English boldness!" From whatever motive, he was also responsible for promoting the legend that Newton had hit upon his theory of gravity by watching an apple fall.

He was already comfortably off. Besides what funds he managed to extract from his father, he started lending money at handsome rates to various French dukes and European crowned heads, bringing him not only profit but diplomatic influence. His plays ran for satisfyingly long runs, and he was well remunerated, even securing an early pension from the government. Voltaire was adept at creating money as easily as verses or adversaries. In 1729, following a chance conversation at a dinner party with an enterprising mathematician, Charles Marie de la Condamine, he borrowed funds from his banker friends to exploit a French national lottery in which the government had mistakenly created cash prizes much greater than the collective cost of the tickets. Voltaire's syndicate cornered the market and made massive winnings. The comptroller general refused to pay, so Voltaire took his case to court and got his money. The scheme left him with a windfall of nearly half a million francs ($1,485,000 in today's rates), setting him up for life.

* * *

DENIED A LICENSE TO make his books available, in August 1722 he left the country once again, keen to find a publisher outside France. (A new mistress accompanied him, Marie-Marguerite de Rupelmonde, a thirty-five-year-old widow "with hair like golden flame.") He continued to write in nearly every form available and on almost any subject—from the real-life character on whom Don Quixote was based to the teachings of the prophet Muhammad or the qualities that make a good duelist.

By the 1720s Voltaire was the leading controversialist in France.* Many of his prose works, usually composed as pamphlets (of which he completed nearly two thousand), were written as polemics. "Why do people insist in trying to see a humorist in a man who is really a fanatic?" wrote Flaubert. "His whole intelligence was an instrument of war." Voltaire agreed, writing to a friend, "To hold a pen is to be at war." But it had to be guerrilla brawling. Since he denigrated everything from organized religion (his particular bête noire; the Holy Roman Empire, he once said, was neither holy nor Roman nor an empire) to the justice system, running up against the censors was a constant hazard. While in England he had written *Essay upon Poetry* and *Essay upon the Civil Wars in France* as well as starting a biography of Charles XII of Sweden, in which he suggested that human beings controlled their own destiny and were not reliant on divine intervention—a provocative, even dangerous argument. (Then as now, it was reckoned that a successful work of history should use a topic or a restricted period as a peg on which to hang philosophical reflections or as the focus of a general sociological survey.) In 1734, his *Letters Concerning the English Nation* declared the British system of government far superior to that of the French. This too caused a predictable outcry, although it has since been accepted as Voltaire's first contribution to the Enlightenment, the radical intellectual movement, also known as "the Age of Reason," that emphasized individualism rather than tradition.

Like other leading Enlightenment figures, Voltaire accepted the idea of a supreme being, albeit one that did not interfere directly in the world. But in the mid-1730s it was the traditionalists who held sway. His publisher was consigned to the Bastille while the book, denounced as "scandalously contrary to religion, morals and society," was publicly burned by the state's public hangman in the courtyard of the Pal-

---

* One of his foremost opponents throughout his adult life was Jean-Jacques Rousseau (1712–78). Since the Swiss author of *The Social Contract* excoriated urban intellectuals, Voltaire exposed him, in one of his unsigned pamphlets, as a sanctimonious advocate of family values who yet had turned over his five young children to a foundling hospital. He then suggested that the first half of Rousseau's novel *Julie* had been written in a brothel and the second half in an asylum, while he dismissed Rousseau's treatise on education, *Emile*, as "a hodgepodge of a silly wet nurse in four volumes," adding that it was "regrettable that they should have been written by . . . such a knave." The two men died within a few weeks of one another, and in 1794 Rousseau's remains were moved to the Panthéon, close to those of Voltaire.

ais de Justice. A police officer appeared at Voltaire's house with a warrant; tipped off, the errant author had fled five days before. Once again he was forced to escape Paris, this time for a new patron and a new home, the Château de Cirey-sur-Blaise, a dilapidated thirteenth-century pile on the borders of northeastern France.

Voltaire technically remained a bachelor all his life, but he had a series of mistresses, enjoying a famous affair with the brilliant scientist and author Madame du Châtelet. Born Gabrielle Émilie Le Tonnelier de Breteuil, the marquise was twenty-six to his thirty-eight when they met, already married and with two children (a third died at birth or shortly after). In May 1733 the two fell in love, and at her invitation he joined her at Cirey; their *amour,* one of bigamous devotion, lasted nearly sixteen years and ended only with her death, aged forty-two, in 1749. Her husband in what had been an arranged marriage not only knew of their affair but even tolerated it and would often stay at Cirey, discreetly keeping to his own apartment and observing separate meal-times.

By 1744 the physical side of Voltaire and Émilie's relationship had run its course, and their time together was stormy and punctuated by frequent arguments (each kept a suite of rooms, located at opposite ends of the château). Even so, they shared many interests and together amassed some twenty-one thousand books that they discussed at length, as well as performing scientific experiments together in their homemade laboratory: Voltaire, while the junior scientist of the two, came close to discovering oxygen. Émilie for her part translated from the Latin, with a learned commentary, Newton's *Principia Mathematica.* She even invented a verb, "to Newtonize," to characterize her and Voltaire's thinking.

She was above all a first-rate mathematician and physicist, but with Voltaire by her side she also studied history and philosophy, teaching herself German so that she could read Leibniz in the original. It was she who, by her contempt for the subject, inspired him to write history, to prove to her that it was a worthy pursuit.[*] The marquise inhabited no

---

[*] She wrote: "I have never yet been able to finish any long history of our modern nations. I can see scarcely anything in them but confusion: a host of minute events without connection or sequence, a thousand battles which settled nothing. I renounced a study which overwhelms the mind without illuminating it." See Will and Ariel Durant, *The Age of Voltaire* (1965; repr. New York: Simon & Schuster, 2011), p. 483.

ivory tower; she liked to dance, was a passable performer on harpsi-chord and spinet, sang opera (the doting Voltaire said she had a *"voix divine"*), and was a keen amateur actress. As a teenager, short of money for books, she had devised strategies for gambling, an enthusiasm she never gave up; in 1747, in one evening alone, she frittered away eighty-four thousand francs.

Their years together passed quickly, with Émilie making regular trips to Paris, often in attempts to save her lover from prosecution, while when it was safe Voltaire too traveled there, either to see about the production of one of his plays or to drink coffee (inevitably) with friends. Émilie would tell Voltaire's agent, "I cannot be away from him for two hours without pain." However, with Voltaire jealous yet ac-quiescent, she took on a lover, a captain of the guards at the French court, and soon to her consternation fell pregnant. On the night of September 4, 1749, she gave birth to a baby girl but passed away six days later from a pulmonary embolism. (The daughter was to die before her second birthday.) Voltaire staggered from Émilie's deathbed and in his distraction fell downstairs, cracking his skull. His memoirs record: "I was overwhelmed by a sense of utter devastation."

* * *

HE WAS SAVED BY the oddest of friendships, one that had been evolving for a long time. On August 8, 1736, when he was forty-two, he had received a letter from the young crown prince of Prussia, the future Frederick the Great (1712–86). Voltaire was flattered, replied respect-fully, and soon the prince was sending him verses he had written to polish (Frederick disliked the German language and wrote his literary efforts in workmanlike French). A highly charged exchange of letters followed, in which Frederick repeatedly tried to get the great writer to visit. Craving the company of men, he never included du Châtelet in his invitations, earning her unswerving hatred; one short visit aside, only after her death did Voltaire journey to meet the monarch. The Frenchman was ever candid. On being sent a long poem the king had composed, he records: "Several lines are pillaged from the Abbé de Chaulieu and myself. The ideas are often incoherent, and the verses in general unmusical; but there are some good; and it was a great thing for a king to write two hundred bad verses in the state he then was." For all that, after one particularly damning letter from Voltaire and a temporary cooling, the two men resumed their correspondence, aired mutual recriminations, and took up as friends once more.

In 1750, just a few months after du Châtelet's death, Voltaire accepted a permanent position in Frederick's court, for which he was remunerated with a grand apartment in the king's favorite home, the palace at Sanssouci, in Potsdam, fifteen miles southwest of Berlin, with the king's servants at his disposal and an annual salary of twenty thousand francs. "I have found a port after thirty years of storms," he wrote. At mealtimes he would sit at the king's side, and the two would talk together animatedly. But he was ever difficult to live with, often quarreling with his host's friends and alarming the king by his avarice, his indiscretions (he had even taken to sending letters back to France as a paid spy, revealing details about Prussian foreign policy), one act of outright forgery, and of course his provocative writings. For his part, Frederick had his own agenda. "I need him another year at most," he reportedly told a courtier, on being asked how much longer he would put up with the Frenchman's vagaries. "When one has sucked the orange, one throws away the skin." The remark was passed on to the orange himself, but it did not chasten him. Finally, after Voltaire had made a particularly pithy attack on one of the king's inner circle, Frederick burned his guest's pamphlet publicly and put him under house arrest ("Four soldiers dragged us through the midst of the dirt . . ."), an incarceration lasting thirty-five days, after which the distinguished visitor had had enough, and in March 1753 he left Prussia for good. The two men never saw each other again.

Back home, Voltaire began writing his *Mémoires*. On its completion the manuscript was stolen and a pirate copy published in Amsterdam as *The Private Life of the King of Prussia*. In it, Voltaire wrote without constraint of Frederick's homosexuality and the dissipated character of his court. Frederick certainly spent much of his time in an exclusively male circle, and his palace gardens included a "Temple of Friendship," which celebrated the homoerotic attachments of the ancient Greeks. Even so, the book is an extraordinary memoir for one friend to write about another.

Its revelations could be brutally funny. Their friendship had begun as a flirtation, Voltaire confiding, "I soon felt myself attached to him, for he had wit, an agreeable manner, and was moreover, a King; which is a circumstance of seduction hardly to be vanquished by human weakness." Frederick's father, Frederick William I ("the most intolerant of all kings"), was appalled that his son had taken not to militaristic pursuits or religious observance but to music and literature, then, at sixteen, formed an attachment to the king's thirteen-year-old pageboy. Frederick Junior made plans to elope, aided by his teenage sister, the Princess Wilhelmine. In a rage, the king seized not his son but his daughter and attempted to kick her out of the castle window, the girl being saved by the Queen Mother, who grabbed hold of her daughter's petticoats as she tottered on the window ledge.

Voltaire in the balance by Pablo Morales de los Ríos, 2004.

* * *

SINCE SO MUCH OF his writing was suppressed, Voltaire either had his work printed abroad or published under a range of pseudonyms, and during his lifetime used at least 178 noms de plume. His most celebrated work, *Candide, or Optimism* (1759), just seventy-five pages in its English translation, he originally attributed to a "Dr. Ralph, with additions found in the pocket of the Doctor when he died." He actively tried to distance himself from it after both the civil authorities and the Church condemned it: "People must have lost their senses to attribute to me that pack of nonsense. I have, thank God, better occupation." Few believed him.

In English, the words *candid* and *candor* have almost completely lost their meaning; in Voltaire's time, they, like their French counterparts, referred not to the telling of perhaps painful truths but to doing one's very best to think well of others—as Candide ever does. A "philosophical romance" that attacks un-thought-out religious and philosophical optimism (a little-disguised attack on Leibniz's view that everything was for the best in the best of all possible worlds), the story has Candide, a young man who, combining "an honest mind with great simplicity of heart," experience a bizarre sequence of adventures, being preyed upon by a gallery of rogues, forced into the Bulgarian army, flogged, shipwrecked, betrayed, and robbed, all the while trying to reconcile his experiences with the philosophy taught by "the most profound metaphysician in Germany," Doctor Pangloss (which means "all-tongues"). He ends with the realization that the best way of living is to stay within one's own environs—"to cultivate one's garden."

The world Candide is exposed to may be an evil place, but it can be great fun to read about. Even the disembowelings and rapes that he witnesses, or the cutting-off of one buttock of every available woman, are described with breezy matter-of-factness. At one point, Candide learns that in Britain it is considered wise to kill an admiral every now and then, *"pour encourager les autres."* When Candide attends a dinner after a visit to the theater, "The supper was like most Parisian suppers, first of all silence followed by an indistinguishable noise of words, then some witticisms, most of which were insipid, some scandal, some false reasoning, a little politics and a good deal of slander." This was pretty broad fare, but the darts found their mark.

* * *

AT COURT BACK IN his home country, Voltaire had become the confidant of a Madame d'Étoilles, and when she found herself promoted to become the king's mistress, assuming the title of Madame de Pompadour, she repaid her old friend by seeing that he would be made a member of the Académie Française and appointed historiographer of France. "It is better to say a few words to a king's mistress than write a hundred tomes," he observed. But the tomes were nonetheless being written. Adam Gopnik, in a *New Yorker* article, calls Voltaire's books "potted, vivid histories," but that is belittling. Voltaire himself would often discount the writing of history himself: "Historians are gossips who tease the dead," he would say. Or, "History is nothing more than a tableau of crimes and misfortunes." But he didn't really believe such aphorisms; not for long, anyway. He contradicted himself endlessly.

Whatever his misgivings, many of his plays are about historical figures—including *La Henriade, Mariamne* (set in ancient Jerusalem), *Mahomet* (about Islam's founder), *Zaire* (seventh-century Jerusalem), *Adelaide du Guesclin* (fifteenth-century France), *La Mort de César, Alzire* (sixteenth-century Peru), and *Socrates*—and then there are the formal prose works, beginning with his *History of Charles XII, King of Sweden* (1731), which critics judged a revelation in writing history—of structure, color, form, and style. It became an international bestseller.

His next excavations into the past took twenty years of primary-source research. (He might have completed the first book earlier, but du Châtelet hid the manuscript and insisted that he concentrate on scientific experiments.) Eventually the volumes came in a rush: *The Age of Louis XIV* (1751), *The Age of Louis XV* (1746–52), a cultural history of France under Louis XIV (1751), a volume on the War of 1741 (1755), one on Russia under Peter the Great (1760), a history of the Parliament of Paris (1769), and in the midst of all these the highly ambitious *Essay on the Manners and Spirit of Nations* (1756). This last, an overarching summary of civilization (the word *moeurs* in the French title, *Essai sur les moeurs,* assumes not only manners and morals but customs, ideas, beliefs, and laws) was made up of 174 chapters discussing Europe from Charlemagne until the age of Louis XIV, France's colonial history, India, China, and the Islamic world. Voltaire elected to begin with Charlemagne, he explained, out of respect for Jacques-Bénigne Bossuet (1627–1704), the late bishop of Meaux, whose biblically inspired *Discourse on the Universal History* of 1682 (every major event in history being, in his view, part of the divine plan) had ended with Charlemagne and was still widely read (Gibbon was to attribute his conversion to Catholicism to it). In fact Voltaire had little time for Bossuet's approach and writes at some length on events preceding 800, but it was good public relations to revere the great preacher.

These books together had an enormous effect on the way the writing of history evolved. As early as 1738, Voltaire staked out his position: "One must write history as a philosopher." Fifteen years later, in the article on "History" that he submitted for Denis Diderot's *Encyclopédie,* he wrote: "One demands of modern historians more details, better ascertained facts, precise dates, more attention to customs, laws, mores, commerce, finance, agriculture, population." In this he was enunciating a new doctrine, breaking away from the tradition of narrating diplomatic and military events to emphasize, probably for the first time in a book about the past, the growth of technology as a vital area of investigation. Historical writing was most effective when it connected "to the knowledge of the invention and the progress of the arts the description of their mechanism." It was as if Madame du Châtelet were standing at his shoulder. In all this he succeeded in freeing the writing of history both from antiquarianism and from an overemphasis on Europe (which he treated as a whole, not just a collection of nations). He was not content to concentrate on kings and queens but when he did write of them his insights were acute. Of Elizabeth I of England he noted, with subtle observation:

> Elizabeth, during her confinement, and the state of persecution under her sister Mary, made the best use of her misfortunes, by improving herself in the languages, and in various branches of literature. But of all the arts in which she excelled, that of carrying herself well with her sister, with Catholics as well as Protestants, of dissembling and learning to reign, was her proper characteristic.

Voltaire's approach has obvious shortcomings. He could be cavalier about facts (a French scholar published a two-volume *Erreurs de Voltaire*), calling details "the vermin that destroy great works," and he freely uses the writings of others without acknowledgment. His world history lacks narrative drive. He repeatedly warns against bias on the part of the historian, yet throughout ridicules the Catholic Church. Émilie du Châtelet had criticized previous works of history because so often they were dull lists of facts. Voltaire made sure that was not the case with him (once he'd wrested his manuscript back from her). As Virginia Woolf was to write of Gibbon, "Without haste or effort he swings his lantern where he chooses."

* * *

THEN THERE WAS THE swinging of his bodily lantern. On a visit to Paris in 1744, while still living with Émilie, he had found a new love—Marie

Louise Mignot (the daughter of his sister, Catherine), eighteen years his junior. At first, he was quite smitten by his paramour, and although such an infatuation seems ludicrous (she was far from being a beauty), in 1957 a cache of letters he wrote to his niece was discovered. The following, written on July 27, 1748, is representative: "I shall be coming [to Paris] only for you, and if my miserable condition permits, I will throw myself at your knees and kiss all your beauties. In the meantime I press a thousand kisses on your round breasts, on your ravishing bottom, on all your person, which has so often given me erections and plunged me in a flood of delight."

Following the death of her widowed father in 1737, Voltaire had provided Marie Louise with a dowry and, after her husband's premature death, she became her uncle's housekeeper, hostess, and companion. A female friend of Voltaire's described her as "a fat little woman, as round as a ball. . . . She has no intellect. . . . Voltaire laughs at her and worships her." Mignot, having no wish to follow her lover to Frederick's court, joined up with him again only after Voltaire, having fled Potsdam and finding himself unable to return safely to France following another controversial publication, bought—for eighty-seven thousand francs—a country house, Les Delices ("The Delights"), on the shores of Lake Geneva.

He fitted out his new home in great style, installing a private theater (he loved to perform his own plays), six horses, four carriages, a coachman, a postilion, two footmen, a valet, a French cook, a secretary, and a monkey. He also acquired several nearby properties in different jurisdictions, giving him a bolthole or three (Geneva was an inward-looking, suspicious Calvinist city-state, so such precautions were necessary).

At the end of 1758 he acquired an even more sweeping estate, at Ferney, a few miles from Geneva, (just) on French soil. There he entertained a stream of visitors, giving himself the ironic title *maître d'hôtel de l'Europe* and appearing in a flower-patterned dressing gown, an immense wig topped with black velvet, red breeches, gray stockings, and shoes of white cloth. Cosmetics, perfumes, and pomades completed the ensemble. Describing himself as "ridiculous for not being dead," he began to regret his lack of children, and in 1760 adopted a destitute young woman named Marie-Françoise Corneille, a great-cousin of the tragedian. He paid the dowry for her marriage and often referred to

Mignot and himself as her parents. He and his niece never married but lived together for over two decades.

On some matters one does not give Voltaire a pass. Some of his views were detestable. In the 1740s and again in 1751 he invested in the slave trade (through the French East India Company), writing in *Les Lettres d'Amabed* (1769) that Africans were "animals," each with a "flat black nose with little or no intelligence." He was also an unapologetic anti-Semite, in a 1772 essay declaring Jews were the most barbarous of all nations: "You deserve to be punished, for this is your destiny." So much for the author of *A Treatise on Tolerance* (1763).

Yet in these later years, he also began a series of human rights campaigns—alongside a stream of subversive writings, including the *Dictionnaire philosophique* (1764), a devastating commentary on every conceivable subject connected with religion, morality, and current beliefs. His work on behalf of the oppressed and the unjustly accused won him a new reputation: "a philanthropist masquerading as a cynic." As Tom Holland sums him up, he was "the prototype of the Christian-hating progressive who was saturated with Christian ethics."

Voltaire's writing, especially his private letters, frequently contains the word *l'infâme* and the expression *écrasez l'infâme,* or "crush the loathsome thing." The phrase, first coined in 1759, refers to the alliance of religious fanaticism and the instruments of the state, the cruelties committed in the name of the Catholic Church, and also the superstition and intolerance that the clergy bred within people. In his last two decades, his hatred of organized religion intensified to the point of obsession. But none of his crusades was all-consuming. While living in Ferney, he started up two industries, one the weaving of stockings, for which his garden's mulberry trees provided silk, and the other a watch-making business, begun when he took up a group of displaced Swiss horologists. At one point he had eight hundred employees, and during his time the village attached to his estate grew from four hundred peasants to a town of 1,200, Catholics and Protestants living there happily together. With Voltaire acting as manager, financier, and brilliant salesman, the clock- and watch-making endeavor grew into an industry (he built a hundred houses for his workers), making as much as £600,000 a year, and Ferney timepieces came to rival the best in Europe. Among the customers were Catherine the Great of Russia and King Louis XV of France; Catherine, with whom Voltaire shared a lively correspondence for more than fifteen years, later bought up his library of 6,814 books and transported them to the Hermitage Museum in St. Petersburg, where they reside still.

Voltaire died on May 30, 1778, a few months after returning to Paris for the first time in twenty-eight years to oversee the production of his play *Irène*. Over the last few days of his life, Catholic clergy repeatedly visited him in the hope of a deathbed confession. His refusal meant that he was denied a Christian burial, but his nephew smuggled the corpse out of Paris and arranged a secret interment. On July 10, 1791, he was enshrined in the Panthéon, after his remains had been brought back to Paris. It is said that a million people attended the exequies—a magnification of which Voltaire himself would have been proud.

* * *

OVER THE DECADES, FIRST at Les Delices and then at Ferney, the great and the hopeful would come to pay court: Giacomo Casanova, James Boswell, and Adam Smith, among others. In 1757 Voltaire's guest was the twenty-year-old Edward Gibbon. It would not be his only visit.

The lives of Voltaire (1694–1778) and Gibbon (1737–94) overlapped by more than four decades, but when they first met Voltaire received his guest with indifference, and anyway the younger man was in disgrace. Gibbon's paternal grandfather, Edward Gibbon I, had been a prosperous businessman, then as a director of the South Sea Company had lost all but £10,000 of his fortune ("and as much more as he had been able to conceal") when in 1720 the company famously crashed. However, he quickly rebuilt his fortune and handed over to his son, Edward Gibbon II, not only a large country house in Hampshire but also a safe seat in Parliament. Gibbon II—the historian's father—was "a vague impulsive person" with no head for business. His wife, Judith, gave birth to seven children, all but Edward dying in infancy. She too succumbed early, in 1747, with Edward in his tenth year, leaving her spinster sister as a substitute mother. Catherine Porten—addressed by Gibbon in letters as "My dear Kitty"—provided the attention his mother never gave him. Kitty introduced him to the world of books, and they would sit discussing Alexander Pope, or Aesop's fables, or the characters in Homer. Through her, he developed an early "invincible love of reading." That did not stop Gibbon from one day informing his aunt that he proposed to kill her. "You see," he explained, "you are perfectly good now, so if you die you will go to heaven. If you live you may become wicked and go to hell." When Catherine asked where he expected to go if he killed her, he went on: "That, my godfather will answer for. I have not been confirmed." The adult Gibbon never denied or confirmed the story.

The call of history came to him first at fourteen, when he discovered in a library in Wiltshire a volume of Laurence Echard's history of Rome: "I was immersed in the passage of the Goths over the Danube, when the summons of the dinner bell reluctantly dragged me from my intellectual feast." He was blessed with an optimistic temperament, and this helped him survive a miserable time at Westminster School before being sent to Magdalen College, Oxford, a month short of his fifteenth birthday. He arrived "with a stock of erudition that might have puzzled a doctor and a degree of ignorance of which a schoolboy would have been ashamed."

The teaching there he found even worse than at Westminster, and for the most part he was left without supervision. He took to dressing in black; he was usually late for college dinner, although he was, and remained throughout his life, an early riser. He was already interested in religious controversy and soon discovered the writings of Bishop Bossuet as well as those of the Elizabethan Jesuit Robert Parsons (1546–1610), announcing to a friend "with the pomp, the dignity and the self-satisfaction of a martyr" that he would forthwith convert to Roman Catholicism. A local bookseller introduced him to a priest, who received him on June 8, 1753. He was just sixteen.

To go over to Rome, especially when a gentleman commoner at an Oxford college, was technically high treason; the law might be little observed, but still people talked, and it became a choice item of London gossip. Clearly Gibbon could not continue at university. A cousin suggested to his incensed father—who was threatening to disinherit his son—that Lausanne would be a good place to send the young renegade, and so in 1753 began the unrepentant Gibbon's long association with the Swiss city on the southern shores of Lake Geneva.

* * *

GIBBON'S FATHER MAY HAVE been negligent over his own finances, but he tried to keep a careful watch on his son. He commissioned a Calvinist pastor, a M. Pavilliard, to take the teenager in hand, and over the next eighteen months Edward was turned from his new faith back to the religion of his family, finally concluding, with some animus, that Roman Catholicism was contradicted by reason. "I am now a good Protestant," he wrote to Aunt Kitty, "and extremely glad of it." Other enthusiasms varied. He never learned much Greek and wrote so often in Latin and French (reading ten to twelve hours each day) that he lost his ear for English idiom; by the time he was eighteen he could hardly write in his native tongue at all.

It was not all work. On one occasion Gibbon escaped the supervision of his handler and lost forty guineas gambling with friends, then lost seventy more trying to rescue his initial outlay. Panicking, he borrowed a horse and set off for London, where he hoped to raise the money, getting as far as Geneva before Pavilliard caught up with him: Gibbon's father was eventually prevailed upon to pay the debt.

Despite this episode, Lausanne was an idyll. And in the summer of 1757, in his twenty-first year, he fell in love. The object of his affections was an eighteen-year-old Swiss, Suzanne Curchod, a pastor's daughter from Cressy, four miles from Lausanne. She was pretty, clever, lively, and since not from a rich family was open to the attentions of a well-off, appreciative Englishman. "Carried away by love," Gibbon wrote to her, "I swore an attachment beyond the assaults of time. You did not withdraw your eyes and in them I thought I read your tenderness and my happiness." He compares her to an angel, but she is quick to point out that she is far from being one. She also reminds him that love is about action—not words. But if he was in love with the idea of being in love, he was genuinely smitten, writing to say, "I don't want to die until I can assure you that I would die your slave more now than ever." He keeps obsessive note of how long they are apart—21 hours, 18 minutes, and 33 seconds—and counts how many times he's read her letters: "fifteen times because it comes from a person I love, nine times because the writing is beautiful, and ten times because I'm your servant." He was said to have stopped strangers in the lanes around Lausanne and used a dagger to force them to acknowledge Suzanne's beauty. That November he proposed; she accepted. But England beckoned, and in the spring of 1758 he returned to the family mansion in Hampshire, to find his father remarried (to Dorothea Paton, on May 8, 1755) while his grandfather had died, leaving the bulk of his fortune to his daughters.

On learning that his son intended to marry a poor clergyman's off-spring, Gibbon's father became incensed, and after two hours' painful argument the younger Gibbon gave way, later recording, "Without his consent I was myself destitute and helpless. . . . I sighed as a lover, I obeyed as a son." Gibbon wrote to Suzanne, who suggested as a compromise that he spend three months every year in Switzerland until his father died, but the new Mrs. Gibbon intercepted her letters and wrote to her telling her, not without kindness, that the situation was hopeless. Biographers have since concluded that Gibbon was relieved, realizing that such a marriage would have been a mistake, but some months after his father's initial outburst he renewed his plea, suggesting that indeed it was more than a holiday romance. His father, though, remained firm: "Even if you could afford to marry, Suzanne is a foreigner. You are too fond of foreign ways already—you cannot even speak English properly. She would be uncomfortable in England and she would always be trying to get you back to Switzerland. I could not blame her, but for me it would be a misery, for you a crime."

Gibbon gave up Suzanne as a wife but not as a friend. He continued to visit her throughout his life, even after she had made an advantageous marriage to Jacques Necker (1732–1804), a Swiss banker who went on to become finance minister to Louis XVI. Necker and Suzanne had one child, Anne-Louise Germaine (1766–1817), who on one of Gibbon's visits to their home suggested that she and Gibbon marry; she was eleven at the time. We now know her as Madame de Staël, one of the leading figures of early-nineteenth-century France, Napoleon's archenemy. Imagine had Gibbon waited a few years and then taken her up on her offer!

It seems amazing that he should have found female companions at all. For Gibbon was formidably ugly. A certain grand social evening in Paris fleshes out this fact. A celebrated society hostess, Madame du Deffand (1697–1780), whose salon was among the most famous in Europe, had lost her sight at the age of fifty-seven and would thereafter as a matter of course pass her hands over her guests' faces. Voltaire's, she said, was "all stretched skin and bone." One evening she chose to feel Gibbon's cheeks and, missing his button nose, she started back, under the impression that the historian, with his small "o" of a mouth and great puffy cheeks—"those Brobdingnatious cheeks," as Fanny Burney called them—was proffering not his head but his bare buttocks.

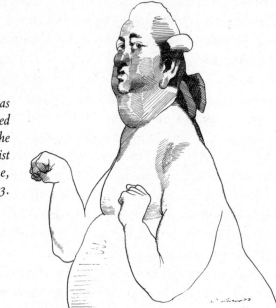

Gibbon as uncovered by the caricaturist David Levine, 1973.

His face was not the end of it. He was about four feet eight inches tall, with bright ginger hair curled at the side and tied at the back. Virginia Woolf is merciless: "The body in Gibbon's case was ridiculous— prodigiously fat, enormously top-heavy, precariously balanced upon little feet upon which he spun round with astonishing alacrity." Forced to leave school because of ill health, the young Gibbon endured fevers and lethargies, a fistula in one of his eyes, a tendency to consumption, contraction of the nerves, and a variety of other nameless disorders, even a bite from a rabid dog. Early in adult life, he developed gout, "the unwalkable disease," as Hippocrates had termed it. In an epoch when close-fitting clothes were the fashion for men, during his time in the militia Gibbon developed a "hydrocele," a swelling in his left testicle, and for the rest of his life suffered from a distended scrotum, causing him embarrassment and pain (it once turned septic) and requiring constant lancing to remove excess fluid, sometimes as much as four quarts. His proposal of marriage late in life to one Lady Elizabeth Foster was not only met with her helpless laughter, but when she begged him to rise he was unable to do so, and two stout Swiss helpers had to pull him to his feet. Thereafter, Suzanne Curchod reprimanded him on the dangers of a late marriage: "An imperfect association resembles the statue in Horace where a beautiful head is joined to the body of a stupid fish." How can Gibbon's physical shortcomings *not* have affected the way he viewed the world, and so the way he wrote? He was self-conscious enough about his appearance that he "met emotion by bleeding it dry with irony." Yet he could also observe, "Beauty is an outward gift which is seldom despised, except by those to whom it has been refused."

* * *

AFTER HE GAVE UP Suzanne, he had to decide on a career, and although he was immersed in the country life of his father and stepmother (who once made him tramp nearly five miles after rabbits), he was determined to become a historian. In Lausanne he had already started his first book (composing in French, and inspired by Voltaire's *Age of Louis XIV*), *Essai sur l'Étude de la Littérature,* and in 1761 it was published, "the loss of my literary maidenhead." Philosophy, he wrote, is the search for first principles; history, for the principle of movement. The historian, like the naturalist, must collect everything and put his system together as the meaning of the evidence becomes clear. He dedicated the work to Suzanne; he did not formally break off their engagement till August 1762.

Gibbon might have returned to Lausanne, but the Seven Years' War was raging, and his father signed both of them up to the local militia, never expecting to be commissioned, but by June 1760 the two men (as Captain Gibbon the Younger and Major Gibbon the Elder) were defending the nation against invasion, and the next two years the nascent historian spent tramping across the South Hampshire downs (taking a portable library with him on maneuvers). It brought him closer to his father, whom he grew to like, and to the peasants under his care. The militia, he wrote, "made me an Englishman and a soldier." To his surprise he found himself good at soldiering. By the time war with France was over, he had turned down a chance to become a member of Parliament, having been offered the safe East Hampshire seat of Petersfield in the days when the house of government, in the immortal words of television's Blackadder, was a place for "fat Tory landowners who get made MPs when they reach a certain weight."

Instead he seized the new opportunity to travel and, winning his father's permission to spend money that had been earmarked to get him into Parliament, embarked on a full-blown European tour, starting in Paris and, inevitably, taking in Lausanne. According to G. M. Young's biography, Suzanne Curchod was by this time a governess in nearby Geneva, "in the prime of her short-lived beauty and brilliant colour, blue-eyed and golden-haired, the admiration of all men and the envy of all women." In September of 1763, the two storm-tossed lovers met by accident at Voltaire's theater, and over the next six months saw each other regularly (they even went to Voltaire's *Zaïre* together). But Gibbon was adamant—they could be friends but nothing more. M. Necker, far from being jealous, often left the two of them alone and went to bed or to work. The whole affair recalls Henry Fielding's comment in *Tom Jones:* "It has been observed by wise men or women, I forget which, that all persons are doomed to be in love once in their lives."

Gibbon wrote home regularly, signing off his letters to his father with "I am Dear Sir with the greatest respect and sincerity your most obedient and most dutiful son." Meanwhile his tour continued— across the Alps to Milan, on to Genoa and Florence, until, at last, he reached the eternal city:

> It was at Rome, on the 15th of October 1764, as I sat musing amidst the ruins of the Capitol, while the barefooted friars were singing Vespers in the Temple of Jupiter, that the idea of writing the decline and fall of the City first started to my mind.[*]

By the time he returned to England he was twenty-eight; time was passing, and he was still undecided on his future, or at least the subject he should write about next. He remained an officer in the militia— indeed, a lieutenant colonel—but now it bored him, and he resigned his commission. He considered and rejected half a dozen subjects—a history of Florence under the Medici, perhaps? A life of Sir Walter Raleigh? Over the next three years he even completed, in French, the first (remarkably dull) *History of the Liberty of the Swiss* and two collec-

---

[*] Except that the Ara Celi, where they were singing vespers, is on the site of the Temple of Juno, not the Temple of Jupiter. Not surprisingly, he corrected himself in the third version of his autobiography. It is not wrong to correct a faulty memory, except this event was such a life-changing one. Gibbon further claimed that his journal dated the event as October 15, when in fact the journal, which still exists, gives no date.

tions of book reviews. The sum copies sold appear to have been twelve in the United Kingdom, twenty-five abroad. Hume wrote to him begging him to write in English, predicting that their mother tongue would soon surpass French in spread and influence. Gibbon complied, although no less an authority than Borges says that French remained the language of his innermost thoughts, and Cardinal Newman, who based his own style on Gibbon, still reckoned him, intellectually, "half a Frenchman."

In 1770 his father died, leaving the family's financial affairs in disarray. Gibbon had to sell off half the estate, and it took until he was thirty-five for the family monies to be stabilized. He left Hampshire for London in 1772, moving to 7 Bentinck Street, off Portman Square, accompanied by six servants (most notably his valet, Caplin), a pet parrot, and a Pomeranian dog called Bath (or possibly Muff), all the time reading, reading, stocking his mind with information that he would raid in the years to come. He eagerly consumed two great histories of the period, Hume's account of England's past (published between 1754 and 1761) and William Robertson's of Scotland (1759), while making his war with Voltaire as a historian, calling him "the dupe of his own cunning." He no longer dressed in black but purchased the latest men's fashions, the gaudier the better, and dined out every night. He took to London society, frequenting the theater, becoming a Freemason, consuming vast amounts of snuff, and joining no fewer than four gentlemen's clubs: the Cocoa Tree, White's, Brooks's, and finally Samuel Johnson's select gathering, usually known simply as "the Club."*

Reversing an earlier inclination, in November 1774 Gibbon entered the House of Commons as MP for Liskeard, Cornwall, a "pocket borough" controlled by a relative, becoming the archetypal backbencher,

---

* Johnson and the portraitist Joshua Reynolds founded the Club in 1764, quite early in their careers. For the first eight years, its twelve members (which included Oliver Goldsmith and Edmund Burke) met once a week at 7 P.M. at the Turk's Head Tavern on Gerrard Street in Soho for evenings of coffee, clay pipes, and gallons of port. Elections were made by unanimous vote. By 1780, the club included Garrick, Boswell, Sheridan, and Adam Smith; by 1784 membership had swollen to thirty-five. The main purpose was to display one's wit, and Johnson in particular had no scruples on whom that wit was bestowed, soon nicknaming Gibbon, voted a member in 1774 after initially being blackballed, "Monsieur Pomme de Terre." Boswell was even more critical: "He is an ugly, affected, disgusting fellow, and poisons our literary Club." See *Letters of James Boswell, Addressed to the Rev. W. J. Temple,* 1857. In reply, Gibbon pointedly omitted Boswell's name from his autobiography. Others dubbed the new member "Pudding-faced Gibbon," noting "his chubby cheeks . . . and his weakness for puce-colored velvet suits and orange zig-zag dimity waistcoats."

never making a speech (shyness, he said) and invariably, snuff box in hand, voting for the Tory faction. Even before he entered Parliament he had made a momentous decision; he would write a history of the Roman Empire. The project was to take nearly twenty years and fill seventy-one chapters in which not only Roman emperors such as Julian and Constantine are brought to life but such figures as Alaric and Attila, Genghis Khan and Tamerlane, Boethius and Muhammad (like Voltaire, Gibbon was both fascinated and repelled by the founder of Islam).

Was his main impulse to write pure history—if such a phrase even has meaning? Hardly. Gibbon knew that all accounts of the past have a contemporary relevance, and in his case he wrote explicitly to teach the lessons of the Roman Empire's strengths and weaknesses, to train the then-current British imperial leaders to avoid the mistakes made by the Romans (in fact, his writing set in train an epidemic of fear that Britain's empire was about to crumble in a similar way: the first volume coincided with the American War of Independence). His books were far from ordinary academic treatises, but what generations have taken away from them is far less his imperial message than the pleasures of his engrossing narrative drive, his mastery of subjects large and small, his pithy sayings ("All that is human must retrograde if it do not advance"; "Every physician is prone to exaggerate the inveterate nature of the disease which he has cured"; "History is indeed little more than the register of the crimes, follies, and misfortunes of mankind"),* and his commentaries, sardonic and ironic by turns, alongside the main text. Who else but Gibbon could write, of the trial of the antipope John XXIII in 1414, "the most scandalous charges were suppressed; the

* One might compare Gibbon's comment with Voltaire's "History is but the record of crimes and misfortunes" (*L'Ingénu*, ch. 10). Again, *Decline and Fall* has: "Winds and waves are always on the side of the ablest navigators" (vol. 1, ch. 68), while Voltaire, in a letter to M. le Riche dated 1770, eight years before Gibbon's coinage, wrote: "I have always noticed that God is on the side of the heaviest battalions." Coincidence, great minds composing alike, or stolen wisdom? Voltaire, the Durants reckon, was Gibbon's "unacknowledged teacher." *Rousseau and Revolution*, op. cit., p. 804. Yet Gibbon dismissed his sometime mentor as a superficial historian who did no more than cast "a keen and lively glance over the surface of history" and "follows some compilation, varnishes it over with the magic of his style, and produces a most agreeable, superficial, inaccurate performance." But Evelyn Waugh had it right: "We remember the false judgments of Voltaire and Gibbon . . . long after they have been corrected, because of their sharp, polished form and because of the sensual pleasure of dwelling on them." *Waugh Without End: New Trends in Evelyn Waugh Studies,* ed. Carlos Villar and Robert Murray Davis (New York: Peter Lang, 2005), p. 89.

Vicar of Christ was only accused of piracy, murder, rape, sodomy, and incest"?

Volume One of *The History of the Decline and Fall of the Roman Empire* (finished during Gibbon's first session in Parliament) took him seven years and appeared early in 1776, the same year Adam Smith published his *Inquiry into the Nature and Causes of the Wealth of Nations*. Gibbon starts with the death of Marcus Aurelius in A.D. 180 and ends with the fall of Constantinople in 1453, taking in not only the Roman Empire but also the founding of Islam and the story of Byzantium. The book accelerated through three printings, the first thousand copies, priced at a guinea (in today's terms, roughly $75), taking six weeks to go, the second edition of 1,500 copies selling out in three days.

Gibbon's publisher boasted that the book "sold like a threepenny pamphlet on current affairs." By March, 3,500 copies had been sold (not counting the sales lost to two Irish pirated editions). Here indeed was "literature" (a newly minted French word). David Hume, in the year of his death, sent Gibbon a letter of undiluted praise, its delighted recipient declaring that such approval "overpaid the labor of ten years." At that point, Gibbon was thirty-nine.

Later generations were just as admiring. Gladstone (1809–98) reckoned Gibbon to be one of the three greatest historians of all time, comparable to Shakespeare in drama and Milton in poetry. When in June 1786 Voltaire's great patron, Frederick the Great, fell mortally ill, his doctor prescribed Gibbon's work to calm him; and when in the early 1830s John Percival, son of the assassinated British prime minister Spencer Percival, was detained in an asylum, the one book he requested was *Decline and Fall*. England's great novelists took note. In *The Mill on the Floss,* first published in 1860, George Eliot has the young Maggie Tulliver make out the back of a book her elders clearly hold in esteem: Gibbon's masterpiece. In *Our Mutual Friend,* which Charles Dickens wrote over 1864–65, Noddy Boffin, the "golden dustman" who accidentally inherits a fortune and wants to be seen as an educated man, hires Silas Wegg the ballad seller to read him an archetypal Great Book—Gibbon again.

And so it was through the decades. In 1896, the young Winston Churchill, holed up in Bangalore, three thousand feet above sea level, sets about a course of self-education: "In history I decided to begin with Gibbon. Someone had told me that my father [Lord Randolph

Churchill, briefly chancellor of the exchequer] had read Gibbon with delight; that he knew whole pages of it by heart, and that it had greatly affected his style of speech and writing." Without more ado the gauche army lieutenant set about the eight volumes his mother had posted out to him.* "I was immediately dominated both by the story and the style. All through the long glistening middle hours of the Indian day, from when we quitted stables till the evening shadows proclaimed the hour of Polo, I devoured Gibbon. I rode triumphantly through it from end to end and enjoyed it all."

Ah, that Gibbon style! The set pieces in *Decline and Fall* are marvels of clear narration, while he seems to have studied every aspect of his chosen period, including roads, coins (which he likened to fossils), weights, measures, distances, inscriptions, architecture, the details of ancient geography, the "order of time and place." He appeared so preoccupied with time that he earned himself a new nickname: "Mr. Clockwork."

Volumes Two and Three appeared together on March 1, 1781, before long rising "to a level with the previous volume in general esteem." Volume Four was finished in June 1784; the final two by 1787, Gibbon laying down his pen on June 27. Readers responded to his tone of voice, his favorite adjectives, his selection of anecdotes, his epigrams ("The public favour . . . seldom accompanies old age," vol. 1, p. 224), and even putting up with his increasing use of italics. (His control of narrative was one thing, his caustic footnotes another.) He had lost his seat in Parliament in 1780, but the following year, thanks to the patronage of Lord North, the prime minister, was returned in a by-election, this time

---

* The Oxford edition consists of eight volumes, each of four or five hundred pages, the whole totaling 3,860. As one nineteenth-century reader wearily acknowledged, "The fondest admirers of Gibbon cannot say that it is light reading. Evening after evening goes by, and, if the reader is conscientious, and does not skip, it is a long time before the work is read. Indeed, in these degenerate days I doubt whether there are many persons in the world who can say that they have read their Gibbon right through." See Sir Arthur Phelps, *Brevia: Short Essays and Aphorisms* (Boston: Roberts Brothers, 1871), pp. 116–17. One day in Parliament, Richard Sheridan, a Whig MP as well as a playwright and poet, complimented Gibbon on his "luminous pages." Gibbon beamed—although Sheridan had probably said "voluminous." In a famous put-down, variously attributed to King George III or to his brother, Prince William Henry, upon receiving the second (or third, or possibly both) volumes of Gibbon from the author, the royal person quipped: "Another damned thick square book! Scribble, scribble, scribble, eh, Mr. Gibbon?" See Sir Leslie Stephen, *Dictionary of National Biography*, 1921, vol. 21, p. 1133. I also have sympathy for Clive James's likening Gibbon's book to a beached whale: "a hulking forecast of St. Pancras Station . . . [it] is a Grand National with a fence every ten yards, each to be jumped backwards as well as forwards; and you have to carry your horse." See Clive James, *Cultural Amnesia: Necessary Memories from History and the Arts* (New York: Norton, 2007), pp. 263, 267.

for Lymington, a port town in the New Forest district of Hampshire. The wits said that George III had bought "The Gib" so that the author could not record the decline and fall of the British Empire.

He had planned for the long haul, and the conclusion of the third volume had been in draft before the first was written, while a hand-written chronological table of the centuries he intended to cover, composed between the ages of fourteen and sixteen, has recently been discovered. Originally the project was to have ended with the fall of the Roman Empire in the West in 476, but with the publication of Volume Three he grew restless and decided to interpret "Roman Empire" to encompass the Eastern as well as the Western, to continue on to the destruction of Byzantine rule through the conquest of Constantinople by the Turks in 1453: another thousand years to research and record. That way he remained true to what he called, a little puzzlingly, "my other wife."

His great friend Lord Sheffield, who as his literary executor was in 1796 to put together a single volume of Gibbon's autobiography, a patchwork drawn from six partly overlapping drafts left at his death,[*] wrote: "It is very true, that before he sat down to write a note or letter, he completely arranged in his mind what he meant to express." Gibbon himself boasted: "It has always been my practice to cast a long paragraph in a single mould, to try it by my ear, to deposit it in my memory, but to suspend the action of the pen till I had given the last polish to my work." He would make notes on playing cards as he read; compose a paragraph at a time, walking up and down his room; then commit it to paper, adding the references.

Above all, he loved antitheses: "Revenge is profitable, gratitude is expensive." Of living under a dictatorship: "To resist was fatal, and it was impossible to fly." Or: "Where error is irretrievable, repentance is useless." As Virginia Woolf remarks somewhat caustically, it becomes inevitable after a while that "destroyed the confidence" should be fol-

---

[*] We may have wished for a wiser editor. Lord Sheffield's amalgam gives a life story "purged of self-doubt, inconsistency, bad taste, and contradiction . . . more resolutely and triumphantly 'Gibbonian' than Gibbon ever managed to be." See Charlotte Roberts, *Edward Gibbon and the Shape of History* (London: Oxford University Press, 2014), p. 4. Thus Gibbon's "I was too young and bashful to enjoy, like a manly Oxonian, the taverns and bagnios of Covent Garden" becomes, in the edited version, ". . . the pleasures of London" See J. B. Bury, introduction to *Autobiography of Edward Gibbon* (Oxford: Oxford University Press, World's Classics edition, undated), p. v.

lowed by "and excited the resentment." Many people have written pastiches of the Hemingway style, and indeed when he writes badly that style is easy to parody; but only Hemingway could write a *good* Hemingway sentence. Perhaps this is true for Gibbon too.

Gibbon's fluency and ease of composing, however, are only partly true. The first volume was hard labor: "Many experiments were made before I could hit the middle tone between a dull chronicle and a rhetorical declamation. Three times did I compose the first chapter, and twice the second and third, before I was tolerably satisfied with their effect." Gibbon rewrote many other passages. In particular, he heavily revised chapters 15 and 16, the troublesome chapters, as he knew they would be; the chapters that would, for all the praise, engulf him in controversy.

* * *

EARLY ON, GIBBON ASSERTS that, from the death of Augustus Caesar to the Antonines (whom Machiavelli dubbed the "five good emperors," Nerva, Trajan, Hadrian, Antoninus Pius, and Marcus Aurelius), a period spanning A.D. 96 to 180, Rome was secure and well governed, exerting a beneficial impact over the known Western world. As he wrote, even slavery during these years was ameliorated by the possibility of any slave becoming a freedman and that the courts, not the slave owners, oversaw punishment of their charges. Then came the new religion.

Empires crumble, according to the orthodox view, because they meet the Five Horsemen of the Apocalypse: climate change, migration, famine, epidemic, and state failure; for Gibbon, it was the advent of Christianity that was responsible for bringing down the Roman Empire, and in chapters 15 and 16 he sets out his case. First, superstition (as he had it) prepared minds for tyranny and provided scope for fanaticism. More widely, the ability of the empire to rule over many cultures and gods was ruined by "the inflexible and, if we may use the expression, the intolerant zeal of the Christians." Believers "boldly excommunicated the rest of mankind." Rome was further weakened by the Christians' questioning of Roman authority while their evangelizing made them profoundly revolutionary, "an independent and increasing state in the heart of the Roman Empire" that openly predicted the fall of "Babylon"—that is, Rome. Gibbon had hit upon a certain truth: that, as Catholic Orthodox Christianity came to dominate Rome, intolerance followed in its wake, and the city's military culture was undermined. The consequence was catastrophic. The resultant decline brought on an almost thousand-year dark age, which ended with the population of the Mediterranean region collapsing from 47 million to about 29 million, some 40 percent. The final sentence of *Decline and Fall* declares: "I have described the triumph of barbarism and religion."

Gibbon, from his reconversion to Protestantism on, would go to church regularly, and an English Bible was always at his bedside (in an age when religion in England was in retreat; on Easter Day 1800, for instance, just six people took communion in St. Paul's Cathedral). He even partnered the wife of the Archbishop of Canterbury at cards. Belief in an all-powerful god was not a problem for him, and generally he avoided any direct expression of hostility to Christianity, but a combination of his own experience and what he felt to be his duties as a historian produced an animus against the destructive role of religion, especially religious fanaticism. He did not view Protestantism as intrinsically more liberal or tolerant than Catholicism; both were equally pernicious. (Witches were still being burned in his lifetime.) But his pronounced, almost malicious skepticism showed he was all too willing to believe in the wickedness of priests and the lasciviousness of emperors. Thus his conclusion: "The propagation of the gospel and triumph of the Church are inseparably connected with the decline of the Roman Monarchy."

Such an argument, surely consciously positioned at the end of his book, unleashed a barrage of criticism. In Lord Macaulay's view, Gibbon wrote of Christianity "like a man who had received a personal injury." Witness the edge to his voice when he writes that certain prophecies must be taken as "sorry evidence of the political craft of the powerful, the gullibility of the populace, the adulation of historians and the fraud of priests" or describes the homilies of monks (an especial bugbear of his) as "an absurd medley of declamation and scripture."

Gibbon's condemnation of Catholicism led to his work being banned in several countries. Academics from leading universities and several senior clerics assailed his objectivity, his scholarship, and his moral character. Cambridge's leading classicist, Richard Porson, foreshadowed Macaulay's judgment, stating: "Such is his eagerness in the cause that he stoops to the most despicable pun or to the most awkward perversion of language for the purpose of turning the Scripture into ribaldry, or of calling Jesus an imposter." Finally, in 1779, Gibbon, incensed, wrote *A Vindication of Some Passages in the Fifteenth and Sixteenth Chapters of the History of the Decline and Fall of the Roman Empire:*

> When I delivered to the world the First Volume of an important History, in which I had been obliged to connect the progress of Christianity with the civil state and revolutions of the Roman Empire, I could not be ignorant that the result of my enquiries might offend the interest of some and the opinions of others.

His rebuttal, aimed at showing his good faith as a historian, showed that not once had he misquoted and that his evidence was genuine and his motives sincere. His vigorous defense was written with the force of a man-o'-war in full sail bearing down on a tugboat. But at least Gibbon's critics were silenced (if not wholly answered), and he could move on. Nevertheless, in revised editions, he tried to remove suggestions that philosophy was antithetical to Christianity and while the second edition was at the printers thought of cutting chapters 15 and 16 altogether, until persuaded otherwise.

* * *

ANOTHER PROBLEM IS GIBBON'S tone. Outside his personal letters, he is forever detached, sardonic, writing one thing and leaving it to his reader to appreciate what meaning is between the lines. When it works, as it so often does, "Gibbon's Table-Talk," as his comments became known, could be devastating and often very funny. For instance, of Gordian II (c. 192–238), Roman emperor for just a single month before his death in battle: "Twenty-two acknowledged concubines, and a library of sixty-two thousand volumes, attested the variety of his inclinations; and from the productions which he left behind him, it appears that the former as well as the latter were designed for use rather than for ostentation." Or again: "When he was master of Normandy, the chapter of Seez presumed, without his consent, to proceed to the election of a bishop 'upon which he ordered all of them, with the bishop elect, to be castrated, and made all their testicles be brought him in a platter.' Of the pain and danger they might justly complain; yet since they had vowed chastity he deprived them of a superfluous treasure" (vol. 6, ch. 68). A final example, from Volume Four: "The more stubborn Barbarians sacrificed a she-goat, or perhaps a captive, to the gods of their fathers. . . . Gregory the Roman supposes that they likewise adored this she-goat. I know but of one religion in which the god and the victim are the same"—the crucified Christ.

Over the course of his history, these comments take on an element of malice, an overweening display of moral and cultural superiority. Byron, otherwise a great supporter, wrote of "his weapon with an edge severe,/Sapping a solemn creed with solemn sneer,/The lord of irony." Boswell too had written of Gibbon's "usual sneer," presumably at meetings of the Club. Virginia Woolf, in her 1942 essay, is unforgiving of Gibbon's complacency and self-satisfaction: "What he could not understand, he mocked." Gibbon himself admitted that he could be crude. G. M. Young, not normally Francophobic, rounds out the criticism:

> Both [Edmund] Burke and [Samuel] Johnson, though in their way fanatics, have a reserve of ease and tolerance which is lacking in the detachment of Gibbon. There is something alien in his composition, a certain knowingness, quite unlike the dogmatism of Macaulay, equally unlike the searching judgment of Tacitus, but very like that self-centered malice which to an Englishman is often the most conspicuous, and always the least agreeable, element in French literature, French manners and French diplomacy.

Did the unloved child, the ugly adult, the lonely bachelor, take to castigating the declining Romans with unseemly glee? If so, he was more in tune with Voltaire than he ever acknowledged. But he, like his French counterpart, had achieved fame, influence, and financial security. Beyond his income from writing, an investment in a Cornish copper mine netted him £750 a year. In 1781 he confided to Suzanne that he would retire to Lausanne, and in 1787, shortly after completing the final volume of *Decline and Fall,* despite his relatively young age, he left "the tumult" of London, "its smoke and wealth and noise," to share a mansion home with a close friend, Georges Deyverdun. He took with him his formidable library of six to seven thousand tomes—his "Seraglio," as he suggestively termed it, after the women's apartments in an

Ottoman palace. "I can part with land," he wrote to Lord Sheffield. "I cannot part with books."

He had always had good male friends, yet he pined for a female companion. He started to court Lady Elizabeth Foster ("Eliza"), a young widow of twenty-six, whom he pronounced "irresistible"— she might entice the Lord Chancellor from off his woolsack, he told one companion. The very day he finished his history, he read some chapters to Eliza, after which they lunched alone, and as they walked together around his garden he suddenly dropped to his knee and proposed. But it was not to be, and she met his profession of love with astonished laughter. And yet any deflation he felt did not last long. In 1784 he wrote to Lady Sheffield:

> Should you be very surprised to hear of my being married? Amazing as it may seem, I do assure you that the event is less improbable than it would have appeared to myself a twelvemonth ago. Deyverdun and I have often agreed, in jest and in earnest, that a house like ours would be regulated, and graced, and enlivened, by an agreeable female Companion. . . . Not that I am in love with any particular person. I have discovered about half a dozen *Wives* who would please me in different ways, and by various merits: one as a mistress . . . ; a second, a lively entertaining acquaintance; a third, a sincere good-natured friend; a fourth, who would represent with grace and dignity at the head of my table and family; a fifth, an excellent economist and housekeeper; and a sixth, a very useful nurse. Could I find all these qualities united in a single person, I should dare to make my addresses.

Not quite in earnest, nor yet quite in jest.*

So much of Gibbon's life was the experience of loss. In his last years, "old, rich and lazy," as he joked of himself, he grew increasingly iso-

---

* For the archetypal bachelor-scholar, Gibbon spent a surprising amount of time during his later years reflecting on his suitability for marriage. His dalliance with Lady Elizabeth was all of a piece with his internal debate. "Sometimes in a solitary mood," he confessed to Lord Sheffield, "I have supposed myself married to one or other of those whose society and conversation are the most pleasing to me, but when I have painted in my fancy all the probable consequences of such an union, I have started from my dream, rejoyced in my escape, and ejaculated a thanksgiving that I was still in possession of my natural freedom." See *The Letters of Edward Gibbon,* vol. 3, p. 196, letter to Lord Sheffield, August 7, 1790.

lated, and spent more and more time with a local Swiss family, the de Séverys. In 1786 his beloved Aunt Kitty died; three summers on, Deyverdun too passed away, and Gibbon, restless and lonely, attempted to adopt the Séverys' son, Wilhelm—an odd symmetry with Voltaire's taking in Marie-Françoise Corneille. He was so afflicted with "my old Enemy, the gout" that he took to a special wheelchair or used two sticks to "crawl about the house." He was also alarmed by the revolutionary events taking place in Paris ("Poor France! the state is dissolved, the nation is mad!"), fearing that another Anglo-French war would drive him from his home.

For a while he thought of writing an entirely new book, on "the lives or rather the characters of the most eminent persons in arts and arms, in Church and State who have flourished in Britain from the reign of Henry the Eighth to the present age"; but the idea died, and he settled back instead on the account of his life. Why did his own story take so many drafts? They were not just refinements and polishings, but different, overlapping versions of the truth. He worried about how history would judge him, so, just as he had shaped Roman imperial history, he continued molding his own story to the end, dying at fifty-six. In his will he wrote, "Dare I say it, that a monument would be superfluous?"

CHAPTER 9

ANNOUNCING A DISCIPLINE

From Macaulay to von Ranke

———

Why should history be the discipline that
dare not speak its name?

—SIMON SCHAMA, 2009

E VERY GREAT WAY OF THINKING, FROM PHILOSOPHY TO ATOMIC THEORY,
has its revolutions; in the nineteenth century it was history's turn. For
at least three hundred years, debate had raged over what history was
and how it should be written. The *Oxford English Dictionary* marks the
first appearance of the word *history* ("a formal record") in 1482, and of
historian about half a century on—both strangely late. Machiavelli and
his Florentine contemporary Francesco Guicciardini (1483–1540) had
introduced the secular writing of history, not so much in terms of
scholarship as interpretation. In the late sixteenth and early seventeenth centuries, a deluge of national and religious partisanship had
overwhelmed their approach, and that partisanship continued well
into the eighteenth; but other forces were making themselves felt.

The emergence of a historical consciousness may have been even
more important than the evolution of scientific principles. Information about the past rarely produced *history,* in the sense of a systematic
analysis of evidence. There was little statistical information anywhere
in the world before the end of the eighteenth century. That was now
set to change. Here Thomas Babington Macaulay (1800–59) paved the
way by becoming not only a critically acclaimed writer but also a
highly celebrated one—Peter Gay even calls him "the most popular
historian ever to write in the English language" and "one of the cul-

tural arbiters of his time." He made books about the past bestsellers, and that led to his contemporary and the leading German historian of his day, Leopold von Ranke, establishing the study of history, not just the recording of it, as an accepted occupation at universities.

The time had come. Dr. Johnson may have condemned one leading historian's work—"It is not history, it is imagination"—and denigrated the activity itself as "mere mechanical compilation," but historical plays, even Johnson's own *Irene,* filled the London theaters, while commercial art galleries throughout western Europe celebrated the heroes of bygone times.* Hundreds of books about the past poured off the presses. In addition, over the next two centuries religious disputes led to a vast output of polemical history, all in the service of arguments about the status of the Bible.

The rapid development in research techniques was directly connected with the struggle over belief; but the various branches of Christianity were not the only ones sprouting new leaves. In Germany, an initiative named "Monumenta Germaniae Historica," founded in Hanover in 1819, published thousands of documents about its national story. In France, a group of French priests known as the "Erudites" or "Antiquaries" for the first time applied critical methods to the examination of medieval texts and questionable legends and sources. The French Revolution had attempted to abolish the notion that the past was the property of a single class, succeeding in at least one aspect; as Alberto Manguel has written, from being solely an aristocratic entertainment, the collecting of ancient objects became a bourgeois hobby, first under Napoleon, with his love of the trappings of ancient Rome, and later in the republic. By the turn of the nineteenth century the displaying of frowsty bric-a-brac, old masters' paintings, and antiquarian books had become a fashionable middle-class pastime. In 1792 the Louvre Palace was turned into a public gallery. A few years later, the Museum of French Monuments was established, to preserve the statuary and masonry of the mansions and monasteries, palaces and churches that the revolution had plundered.

---

* London's National Portrait Gallery was opened in 1859. Gladstone, then chancellor of the exchequer, wrote to thank Lord Ellesmere for initiating the collection. Ellesmere replied that the trustees were concerned that the gallery make "history, and not art, the governing principle." Not three centuries before, Titian (1488–1576) and others had painted biblical scenes and people in sixteenth-century clothes, with sixteenth-century Italian houses in the background.

The nineteenth century has been called the golden age of reading, and statistics bear this out. As the result of lending libraries and the spread of compulsory education, by midcentury about half Europe could read, though with notable differences between north and south, Protestant and Catholic. The literacy rate for Sweden was about 90 percent, for Scotland and Prussia, 80; for England and Wales, between 65 and 75; for France, 60; Italy, 20. In Russia, where the serfs were not freed until 1861, only 5–10 percent of the population was literate. (Tolstoy had a larger readership in western Europe than in his own country.)

By the 1840s, those interested in the past not only took up a new belief in its importance but also came to realize that it was in the minute details of everyday life that pertinent history resides, and human inquiry spread at a rush into the smallest provinces, expanding history's domain by taking in categories not previously considered. Had others in previous centuries not realized this? Of course; but never in such quantity or over so many subjects. Even in Gibbon's day, for instance, it was important to have a working knowledge of numismatics, as coins provided vital evidence to date dead emperors. The history of the 8th and 9th Ptolemys was written by two Frenchmen based entirely on marked pieces of coin, their only means of access. Important truths in history could be found in unusual objects. Even British nursery rhymes were seen to derive from specific historical events.

Monographs appeared on salt, sewage, the history of oaths, metals, fossils. J. E. Neale's 1841 study of church pews—an obsession in the nineteenth century—revealed new truths about the nature of worship, with most churches in Washington, D.C., for instance, still renting out their pews as late as 1854. Even cold stone unearthed its secrets; there was a Dark Age for Greece between 1100 and 800 B.C. when the historical record falls silent. One aspect of this is the poor quality of grave goods—virtually nothing of any worth is buried with the dead.

An important essay explaining the evolution of fighting methods was on the evolution of the stirrup. If you are controlling your horse with your knees, you can't charge a whole line of soldiers armed with spears. Another historian investigated the dates on which Japan's mountain lakes first melted, from which it was possible to work out the climatic history of medieval Japan and to correlate that to the food supply, to illuminate a society living on the edge of subsistence. Again, in the fourteenth century the cost of corn rose steeply (due to famine); historians realized its changing price could be matched to the peaks in the crime rate, as starving people began to steal. None of these truths had historians previously thought to mention, far less to research. Other newcomers included heraldry, folk etymology, and toponymy (the science of place-names); the English village of Kirby Overblow was the only evidence that Anglo-Saxons had a special word for "furnace." Everywhere people looked, details from everyday life could be turned to historical gold.

Suddenly world history was seen as vastly more than an account of generals, kings, and cardinals. But the "great man" approach had always been in part the result of lack of sources—and resources. Evidence of the lives of kings and emperors was just easier to find. Now, as more historians set to work, they discovered that government could not be taken for granted. In Richard II's day, for instance, Parliament carefully taxed the presumed (guessed at) forty thousand parishes of England, then discovered there were fewer than nine thousand. The whole notion of a common impersonal history was a late development. It took a long time for people to realize that great works of the past rest on masses of printed documents, tiny monographs, the records of civil servants, and endless lesser historians—a quadruple distillation. Stefan Zweig, writing after the First World War, captures this truth in his novel *Beware of Pity*:

> The so-called "chancery double," a folded sheet of paper of prescribed dimensions and format, was perhaps the most indispensable requisite of the Austrian civil and military administration. Every request, every memorandum, every report, had to be sent in on this neatly trimmed form, which, owing to the uniqueness of its format, enabled official documents to be distinguished at a glance from private correspondence. From the millions and millions of such forms piled up in government offices it may one day be possible to glean the only reliable account of the history and misfortunes of the Hapsburg monarchy.

Throughout the second half of the nineteenth century, in Britain alone, people founded bodies like the Camden Society, an amateur organization devoted to historical study, mainly medieval, as well as reputable publications of great antiquarian value, full of every class of person quietly beavering away to get material into the public sphere. Outside London, the Surtees Society, based in Durham, began in 1835; the Chetham Society, based in Manchester, in 1844; there were many others. The encyclopedia became fashionable.* In the late seventeenth century a researcher named Thomas Rymer (1643–1713) was commissioned to edit British government archives. Fifty volumes were eventually published, all garnered from massive piles of paper in Whitehall. They were taken out of the oven a little too early, but his range of reference was considerable, and his work was feasted on by later historians. Thousands of people published material in obscure journals—the researches of persons with a patience that eluded established historians.

History, the new generations realized, usually goes on without people noticing. Some fifty years ago, an 1851 translation of Thucydides turned up in the Signet Society Library at Harvard, a poorly produced edition evidently used as a student aid. It has written on a flyleaf—its cover at an angle, so the presiding professor could not see it—in very small script (paper was scarce): "They say in town that Lee has surrendered"—a great event (the news of Lee's surrender didn't reach deep into the North until the following day) reduced to a student's scribble, evidently pushed over to a mate in class. We can precisely date this newsflash to 8–10 A.M. on Monday, April 10, 1865—a little meteor trace through history. The century was full of such small stones flying through the heavens.

* * *

THE TIMES WERE RIGHT for Thomas Babington Macaulay. He was a senior politician, a barrister, a popular poet, and the first "literary" figure to be raised to the House of Lords. But principally he wrote four volumes (published under the collective title *The History of England from the Accession of James the Second*) that were the most read of his time throughout the English-speaking world, reaching an audience of Dickensian

---

* Ironically, the best training in research was not at the ancient universities but in the offices of a commercial publisher. In 1882, a London businessman, George Smith, managing director of a shipping agency specializing in trade with India, commissioned a new dictionary of universal biography. He had also founded the *Cornhill Magazine,* and when he consulted its editor, Leslie Stephen, he was advised to limit it to British history. Thus was born the *Dictionary of National Biography,* which, with sixty thousand biographies, 72 million words, and eleven thousand portraits, is now an indispensable tool for historical research.

proportions both in the U.K. and in America. Two young girls, it is told, were visiting London Zoo, opened to the public only in 1847. "Look, Emily," says one, "there's a hippopotamus." "Never mind that," replies Emily, staring rapt in the opposite direction. "There's Mr. Macaulay!"

His father, Zachary, was the son and grandson of firm-minded Scottish Presbyterian ministers, but by his mid-teens had become a heavy drinker and general dissolute—only with a difference. According to the memoir Zachary wrote at the age of twenty-nine, in 1789 he underwent a spiritual conversion, becoming a member of the reformist Anglican Clapham Sect (the family had moved to High Street, Clapham, where many like-minded Evangelicals lived), and an ardent abolitionist. After spells as a colonial governor in Jamaica and Sierra Leone, he married and in 1800 Tom (as he was called) was born. Noted as a prodigy, as a three-year-old he peeked out of the window at the chimneys of a local factory and asked whether the smoke was being pumped from the fires of hell. Tom was joined by five sisters and two brothers: Jane, Fanny, Selina, Henry, John, and the youngest, Margaret and Hannah, ever his favorites. Of the two, Margaret was "the more warm-hearted and affectionate," writes his biographer John Clive, Hannah "the more querulous and high-strung."

The household was strict—no theater, and the eight children's behavior constantly monitored by their demanding father—but lively. There were costume parties; Tom once dressed up as Napoleon. He wrote hymns before he had reached double figures. Sent to boarding school, he took part in earnest debates by the time he was eight, having already outlined a history of the world, penned compositions imitating Virgil in Latin, and written a tract for the proselytizing of heathen savages. His mother would regularly send two guineas to help him get by, money he spent acquiring copies of Hume or Tobias Smollett or preferably French literature, so long as his father approved the purchase as ethically acceptable. He ended his schooldays as head boy, his father noting, "So far all is well."

That may have been so academically, but there was much room for improvement. Tom had grown fat and ungainly following a teenage fever. His father feared his own faults—pride, disdain for society, and an excessively vivid imagination—had been inherited by his son, who furthermore was, in Zachary's eyes, loud-mouthed, lacking in good manners, and careless over his dress and deportment. He told his son so, regularly.

In 1819, Tom went up to Trinity College, Cambridge: where Dryden had studied, Newton made his breakthroughs, and Byron kept a bear, which he would walk around the college on a chain, having successfully argued that there was nothing in Trinity's statutes against it. Macaulay loved the place, earning himself the nicknames "The Novel-Reader" (he was a devotee of Scott's novels) and, for his unkempt appearance, "The Beast." For two years, he won the Chancellor's Gold Medal for poetry, wrote for student publications, and also busied himself at the Cambridge Union, where he rose to secretary. In the time when Macaulay was to the fore, his side of the debates won fourteen out of the seventeen held. A contemporary wrote of him, not unkindly:

> *A presence with gigantic power instinct,*
> *Though outwardly, in truth, but little graced*
> *With aught of manly beauty—short, obese,*
> *Rough-featured, coarse-complexioned, with lank hair,*
> *And small grey eyes,—in face (so many said)*
> *Not much unlike myself,—his voice abrupt,*
> *Unmusical;—yet, when he spake, the ear*
> *Was charmed into attention, and the eye*
> *Forgot the visible and outward frame*
> *Of the rich mind within.*

Macaulay's tutors (bar those for mathematics, a sore subject in the Macaulay household) were equally impressed. His relations with his father remained strained, however, the more so as at Cambridge he left Evangelicalism behind him. "My father," Tom confided to Hannah (whom he nicknamed "Nancy"), "holds smoking, eating underdone meat, liking high fame, lying late in a morning, and all things which give pleasure to others and none to himself to be absolute sins." But domestic life was still vital to him, and following his matriculation, although he began to study for the bar, he continued to live at home, now a large house in Great Ormond Street, in the center of London.

The abolition of slavery was the great issue of the day, and on June 25, 1824, at a meeting of the Society for the Mitigation and Abolition of Slavery (a group founded by Zachary the previous year) held in London at Freemason's Hall, then the largest public assembly rooms in England, Tom was invited to make one of the principal speeches. His eloquence caused a sensation, while in the gallery were many influential figures, including a representative of the royal family, William Wilberforce himself, and Zachary, listening to his son orate on his favorite cause. He must have been moved, yet characteristically, on their walk home afterward, he remarked, "By the way, Tom, you should be aware that when you speak in the presence of royalty, you should not fold your arms."

The next breakthrough was in journalism. The *Edinburgh Review,* founded in 1802, had become Britain's preeminent journal as well as one of the principal organs of the reformist Whig Party. In January 1825, Macaulay wrote an article against slavery, and it was well received, enough for the journal's editor to commission another, more literary piece, a forty-two-page discussion of a long-lost essay by Milton. Like all articles in the magazine, it was anonymous, but its impact was such that its authorship became an open secret, bringing Macaulay renown on the same scale that had met Scott when *Waverley* was published. Partly it was the Macaulay style, full of similes, epigrams, invective, and memorable illustrations, but he also used the review to analyze the political struggles of seventeenth-century England and their relevance to contemporary politics.

In 1826 Macaulay was called to the bar, joining the northern circuit, but he had a hard time getting briefs. He anyway far preferred sitting in the Strangers' Gallery of the Commons, listening to debates, while he also took an active part in politics, helping an abolitionist campaign for a seat at Leicester. And he continued writing for the *Edinburgh Review,* as he would for the next twenty years. He was becoming famous, "a bumptious youth on the warpath." Friends might describe him as ardent and romantic; but he could be vindictive and grudge-bearing. After he had written a particularly sharp piece attacking Utilitarianism, John Stuart Mill (1806–73) was overheard saying, "Macaulay—I will smash him to atoms." Macaulay in reply composed a series of articles attacking Mill's character. Then, having taken his revenge, he relaxed: "I have quite forgiven Mill for what he said."

In early 1830, Lord Lansdowne, one of the Whig Party's moderate leaders, impressed with Macaulay's articles, offered him the vacant parliamentary seat of Calne, in Wiltshire, a borough under his control. Macaulay was unanimously elected (in those days only twenty people in the borough had the right to vote) and on February 18 of that year entered the House of Commons, eager for the fray.

Macaulay in his early twenties and in his final years—as a contemporary wrote, "A presence with gigantic power instinct, / Though outwardly, in truth, but little graced / With aught of manly beauty . . ." The younger portrait is a generous one.

The immediate issue was the very one that had seen him so easily elected, for the voting system was conspicuously unfair, as only those men who paid certain taxes or had property were allowed the franchise. Powerful landowners could nominate whomever they liked, as Lansdowne had done, and votes were openly bought and sold. Nothing might have changed, but the French Revolution of the previous July had concentrated minds, and the Whig Party set about introducing a reform bill that would not only right many injustices but would, they hoped, sweep them into power. In the autumn of 1830, violent protests broke out throughout the south (parts of Bristol were set on fire), then spread west and north, while strikes erupted in some northern industrial towns, the beginnings of what was dubbed the "British Revolution." The government, under the premiership of the Duke of Wellington, duly fell, and the Whigs returned to power. Reform proposals were soon presented to the House, with sixty boroughs (including Macaulay's) to lose their representatives. But the passing of the bill became a prolonged struggle, and the new young MP found himself in the thick of it. His reputation as an orator was the result of the perorations he made in these debates.

He delivered his maiden speech almost a year before those motions began, in favor of Jews being allowed to sit in Parliament. It was a great success, although when his sister Margaret asked afterward how he felt he told her, "Oh, desperate, you know! Quite desperate!" In many ways he was not a natural declaimer. He spoke so quickly that reporters were unable to write down all he said. One critic compared his "inconceivable velocity" with an express train that did not stop, even at the main stations. Nor was his voice ideal, being monotonous and high-pitched; moreover, his delivery featured both a lisp and a burr. Prodigiously uncoordinated, he was clumsy, so much so that one rival wrote a lampoon that talked of "his arms and his metaphors crossed." Yet by the time he made his first speech on the Reform Bill, the day after its introduction into the House, to the three hundred MPs present, he was used to the place's attitudes and atmosphere and gave an address that confirmed his reputation. He became so exhausted by the passion he put into parts of his speech that one MP felt the need to offer him oranges to refresh him, but taken as a whole the effect on listeners was overpowering. He may have been "a dumpling of a fellow,"* as the Tory periodical *Blackwood's* called him—pudgy, splayfooted, barely able to tie his own shoelaces and certainly all at sea knotting his kerchief—but he quickly became a national figure. He was an overwhelming presence in the Commons up to 1857. The most blasé members would run to hear him on even the most unappealing topics.

He had no ear for music, no interest in art, and despite paying occasional lip service eschewed anything spiritual, religious or otherwise. But he had a prodigious memory, was capable of reading an entire Shakespeare play in the course of an evening, and is said to have amused himself on a night packet-boat trip to Ireland by reciting the whole of *Paradise Lost*. This story seems apocryphal—the poem is over ten thou-

---

* During his time as a government official in India, Macaulay was to make a four-thousand-mile journey across the south of the country, traveling "on men's shoulders." The bearers kept up a chant, which the eminent statesman presumed to be "extemporaneous eulogies" but which he later learned was very different—roughly translated, what the bearers were singing was: "There is a fat hog, a great fat hog / How heavy he is, hum-hum / Shake him, shake him well." See Raleigh Trevelyan, *The Golden Oriole* (London: Secker & Warburg, 1987).

sand lines—but it shows people's estimations of his powers. And in our own time the literary critic Harold Bloom could perform the same feat.

Meanwhile, the speeches continued, with Macaulay displaying all his capacities as a historian, an actor, and an epigram-maker ("Revolutions produced by violence are often followed by reactions; the victories of reason once gained, are gained for eternity"). He was regularly compared with parliamentary orators of the past—Edmund Burke, Charles James Fox, George Canning—while he was already a familiar figure in London society. In the summer of 1832 came a new appointment, as one of the commissioners of the Board of Control for India, and later in the year, after the Great Reform Act was finally passed,* he fought a tough election for a new constituency, Leeds, one of the freshly enfranchised industrial boroughs, triumphing over his Tory challenger by 1,984 votes to 1,596.

His two jobs were demanding, yet by 1833 his total wealth (presuming his debtors paid up) was a paltry £709, with which he had to support both his father and his sisters. But a vacancy occurred on the Supreme Council that governed India, with a salary of £10,000 a year. Macaulay reckoned that if he stayed in the post for four years and could save half his income, the money from the capital would set him up for life. Eager to accelerate "the reconstruction of a decomposed society," he angled for the position and caught his fish (generously, Mill put in a good word for him). On February 15, 1834, he and his sister Hannah, whom he had persuaded (by way of more than seventy manipulative letters to her) to accompany him as housekeeper, sailed for Calcutta. Hannah took three hundred oranges for nourishment, her brother a library "not large, but excellently chosen," including the complete works of Gibbon, Voltaire, Samuel Richardson, Horace, and Homer. Their sister Fanny described the effect on their family as "something like what would ensue upon the sun's deserting the earth."

* * *

AT THE TIME OF their arrival, India was home to forty thousand Europeans, mostly British, thirty-seven thousand of them soldiers. Macaulay and Hannah were to stay for six years. During that period his beloved

---

* It was hardly a great reform, increasing voter numbers only from 366,000 to 650,000, some 18 percent of the adult men of England and Wales. But it gave cities such as Liverpool and Manchester their first MPs.

Margaret died from scarlet fever and Hannah found a husband—within six months of arrival. The day after the marriage, Macaulay committed to paper perhaps his most honest attempt at self-analysis:

> I am a changed man. My sense and my humanity will preserve me from misanthropy. My spirits will not easily be subdued by melancholy. But I feel that an alteration is taking place. My affections are shutting themselves up and withering. I feel a growing tendency to cynicism and suspicion. My intellect remains and is likely, I sometimes think, to absorb the whole man. I still retain not only undiminished, but strengthened by the very events which have deprived me of everything else. . . . I know this state of mind will not last. . . . Ambition will again spring up in my mind. I may again enjoy the commerce of society and the pleasures of friendship. But a love like that which I bore to my two youngest sisters, and which, since I lost my Margaret, I felt with concentrated strength for Nancy, I shall never feel again.

Macaulay may have considered his time on the subcontinent a period of exile, but it was productive. He sailed out nearly penniless, but in less than fifty months he was rich. His newfound wealth was deserved. Such was his disdain for India and its people that Indians to whom he spoke "became almost invisible to him," yet he was largely responsible for shaping the country's education for the next hundred years, while the penal code he created is essentially still in force today. For most of his adult life, he kept a detailed daily journal, and was an indefatigable letter writer. While in India,* he read every ancient Greek and Roman text he could lay his hands on. He also taught himself German, Dutch, and Spanish but never bothered to learn the local languages. And he started to write books, not only his major poetic work, *Lays of Ancient Rome,* but also his *History of England,* a project he had

---

* It is a mystery why India has no tradition of historical record and analysis (although today the subcontinent has historians of high quality). There are religious texts such as the Hindu *Vedas* (Knowledge) and the radically different versions of the 24,000-verse *Rāmāyaṇa,* as well as novels such as *Dasakumaracharita* (The Tale of the Ten Princes) and poems like "Subhasaratnakosha" ("The Treasury of Well-Made Verse") or the epic of the Bharata Dynasty, the *Mahābhārata,* almost 100,000 couplets, which is regarded as a kind of history (*itihasa*—literally, "that's what happened"); but not history writing as such.

been nursing since the late 1820s, while he found an eager publisher for his *Critical and Historical Essays*. By the end of 1835 he was writing to a friend that he was inclined to leave politics altogether, to "undertake some great historical work which may be at once the business and the amusement of my life."

The *Lays,* a series of poems about heroic episodes in Roman history, were composed in his spare moments, of which, despite his many duties, he had plenty. His intention was to write a surrogate national epic resembling what might have been sung in ancient times. He had a talent for light verse, and the *Lays,* with their "rocking-horse rhythms," despite a small initial print run of 750 copies, proved immensely popular, by the summer of 1875 selling more than a hundred thousand copies; often reprinted, they became standard reading in British public schools for more than a century. Macaulay's sister Hannah thought the verses "poor stuff," but they had been well researched, and critics saw them as a work of history, not just entertainment. Winston Churchill memorized them while at Harrow and later used the *Horatius* poem to exhort his cabinet to stand firm during the worst moments of the Second World War.

"Real" history was to prove more difficult. Macaulay's plan was not to write a complete account of Britain's past[*] but a record from "the Revolution which brought the Crown into harmony with the Parliament" (1688) to "the Revolution which brought the Parliament into harmony with the nation" (1832). He returned home on June 1, 1838, the project firmly fixed in his mind. His journal the following spring reads: "*March 9, 1839.* Began my history—sketch of early revolutions of England—pretty well, but a little too stately and oratorical."

He still found time to complete two long review articles for the *Edinburgh Review,* one on Sir Francis Bacon and the other principally on Sir John Temple, author of a sensational 1645 bestseller on the Irish

---

[*] Such a version had appeared recently. In 1819 the Rev. Dr. John Lingard (1771–1851), an English Catholic priest, published an eight-volume history of England, *From the First Invasion by the Romans to the Accession of Henry III*. Although his purpose was to emphasize the disastrous effects of the Reformation, he aimed to write an impartial history (there is no indication he was a priest on the title page), using primary sources. Early on, he argues that one of his chief duties was "to weigh with care the value of the authorities on which I rely, and to watch with jealousy the secret workings of my own personal feelings and prepossessions. Such vigilance is a matter of necessity to every writer of history." See John Lingard, *The History of England,* vol. 1 (London: Charles Dolman, 1854), p. 6. The historian David Starkey rates Lingard one of the first great English writers of history, and a biography of him is pointedly titled "The English Ranke."

Rebellion of 1641. The Temple essay used Irish history as a peg on which to hang his views on how empires should be built; controversially, it advocated imperial slaughter as an acceptable instrument of policy. In the name of English progress, the review approved of the lethal calculus of "extirpation" and "eradication" so long as it served British long-term needs. Both the "aboriginal" Irish and the "uncivilized" Indians might be killed en masse for a greater good. What is surprising about this embrace of genocide (the actual term not being coined till the closing stages of the Second World War)* was that other leading figures of Macaulay's day shared his views, so although the advocacy of mass slaughter appears horrendous to modern eyes, he escaped serious challenge.

Nor did the article harm Macaulay's fortunes. In 1839, as he continued to plot his next book, he accepted the offer from the prime minister, Lord Melbourne, of becoming secretary of war, with a seat in the cabinet. Work on the *History* was slow, but Melbourne's government fell in 1841 and Macaulay had more time to write, although he returned to office as paymaster-general in 1846. In the election of 1847 he lost his new seat, in Edinburgh, but five years later the voters offered to reelect him. He accepted, on the condition that he would not have to campaign or promise to uphold any political position. The voters were unexpectedly compliant, and he was soon representing his third constituency.

★ ★ ★

IN HIS BOOK *The History Men,* a survey of British historians from the seventeenth to the late twentieth century, John Kenyon describes Macaulay at this time as having "to an abundant degree all the less pleasing Victorian attributes, of complacency, self-satisfaction, personal *pudeur* and condescension." The reception of his historical work could only have exacerbated those shortcomings. On November 7, 1848, he pub-

---

* In 1941, Winston Churchill, describing the German invasion of the Soviet Union, was to speak of "a crime without a name." The term *genocide* was used first by Raphael Lemkin, a lawyer of Polish-Jewish descent, in his book *Axis Rule in Occupied Europe,* published in 1944. Lemkin reportedly learned about the concept of mass atrocities while, as a teenager, reading Henryk Sienkiewicz's novel *Quo Vadis,* notably where Nero threw scores of Christians to the lions. Not until Lemkin devised the term and perpetrators of the Holocaust were prosecuted at the Nuremberg trials did the United Nations establish the crime of genocide under international law.

lished the first two volumes of *The History of England from the Accession of James the Second*. The morning of publication, Ludgate Hill was jammed with booksellers' carriages trying to get to his publishers' offices in nearby Paternoster Row. Macaulay was keen to exploit the same readership that Gibbon had courted; he aimed "at interesting and pleasing readers whom ordinary histories repel." He would avoid the heights and depths of human experience and instead provide "something which shall for a few days supersede the last fashionable novel on the tables of young ladies."

The books covered a period of less than sixteen years, but they were a showcase for Macaulay's narrative skills (especially his set-piece battle scenes), his strong sense of the dramatic, and his evocation of place. His character portraits could be damning: James I was "one of those kings whom God seems to send for the express purpose of hastening revolutions." By year's end, a fourth printing was exhausted. On New Year's Day he predicted, "I shall be a rich man if this mine bears working." In the years 1848–57, the first volume sold more than 30,000 copies; by 1875, the figure had reached just under 150,000. Summoned to Buckingham Palace by Prince Albert, he was offered the Regius Chair of Modern History at Cambridge and turned it down. Meanwhile, by 1850 the *History* had also sold more than one hundred thousand copies in the United States. He may well have been the world's first literary millionaire. Remarkably, the book has never been out of print. Macaulay exulted, triumphing all the more when he spotted a copy of David Hume's history of England in a bookseller's window, reduced to two guineas, with a notice saying: "highly valuable as an introduction to Macaulay." "I laughed so convulsively," he confessed, "that the other people who were staring at the books took me for a poor demented gentleman."

The third and fourth volumes, ending in 1697 with the Peace of Ryswick (which ended the Nine Years' War against France), appeared in 1855 with a first printing of twenty-five thousand copies, but Macaulay, becoming bored intellectually with his grand enterprise and already prey to bouts of migraine, suffered two heart attacks in as many years, and by the end of January 1856 had resigned his Commons seat. In 1857 he was raised to the Lords but seldom attended. He was still working on the fifth volume, bringing the *History* down to William

III's death in 1702—far from his original plan to end with George III's death in 1820—when on December 28, 1859, he suffered a third heart attack and passed away, aged fifty-nine.

Macaulay died from a malfunctioning heart, not a broken one, yet for some time it seemed he would be brought down by personal sorrows. When Margaret died he was inconsolable, and he grieved again when Hannah married and moved away; by his life's end he was a chronic depressive. He had like Gibbon one serious involvement, in his twenties, with a woman named Maria Kinnaird, a wealthy ward, but it never came to anything. Also like Gibbon he was self-conscious to the point of obsession with what he thought his ugliness and corpulence. He conjured a nickname for himself, "Poor Presto," Swift's mocking name for himself in *Journal to Stella,* and decided fairly early that he would not only remain a lifelong bachelor but also a celibate one. Instead he developed an almost operatic possessiveness toward Hannah and Margaret, setting up house with the two of them.

In the summer of 1832, he would write to Hannah (the clever one) and Margaret (hardly unclever—she wrote a good book of reminiscences—but she was the more openly affectionate), "How dearly I love and how much I miss you. I am glad I have business to transact, for I would find it in my heart to whimper as I used to do when I went to school at twelve years old." Or again, to Hannah: "My dear girl, my sister, my darling—my own sweet friend—you cannot tell how, amidst these tempests of faction and amidst the most splendid circles of our nobles, I pine for your society, for your voice, for your caresses. I write this with all the weakness of a woman in my heart and in my eyes."

The day Hannah wed, he plunged into such despondency that it took several weeks to recover. Simon Schama notes: "It is quite impossible for a modern reader to take in the elemental passion of many of [Macaulay's] letters and not find them, at many points, implicitly incestuous." Even his contemporaries sensed something odd, even inappropriate. Hannah and her husband eventually moved back to England and had several children (one of whose own offspring became the famous historian G. M. Trevelyan). To these young things Macaulay was "the irrepressibly high-spirited uncle, regaling them with poems and stories and outings and treats." As Hannah grew older, he formed a close attachment to her daughter Margaret, whom he called "Baba." He would attribute his ability to make history exciting to the fact that he spent so much time talking to children.

Whatever the wellsprings of his appeal, each volume of his *History* found a ready audience, his sonorous prose style buttressing his confident emphasis on how Britain was in a constant state of improvement. "The history of England is emphatically the history of progress," he wrote in an 1835 essay. "It is the history of a constant movement of the public mind." The citizens of Britain had never had it so good. His seemingly boundless optimism about Britain's role made him yet more popular, but he had his detractors. By the end of the nineteenth century, concerted attacks were building up against "the Whig interpretation of history," with Macaulay its leading target. Defining the differences between a Whig and a Tory is tricky. *Whig* (said to be derived from the cry "Whiggam!" used to spur on their horses) is a mid-seventeenth-century coinage that originally described a participant in the Whiggamore Raid, a march against the new king in Edinburgh in 1648. In the following two centuries *Whig* came to mean anyone who opposed the Tories; in real terms it was what became the conservative core of the Liberal Party.

Across the Atlantic, allegiances were very different. A Whig supported the War of American Independence and most likely was a member of the political grouping of propertied and professional interests that opposed the Democratic Party. How much of all this truly defined Macaulay's position is doubtful; like most political labels, *Whig* covered a wide range of craniums.

Even so, Macaulay has been identified with the Whig cause and his historical works with its values. The crucial attack on his reputation came long after his death, in a book published in 1931, *The Whig Interpretation of History,* written by Cambridge's Regius Professor of History Herbert Butterfield (1900–79). His argument was that in Britain in the nineteenth century historians had been mainly Protestant, progressive, and Whig and that they saw events from previous centuries as always related to the here and now, as if the past existed only for the sake of the present. Butterfield's book effectively scuttled both Poor Presto's reputation and, with it, the Whig style of historical writing.[*] Even in

---

[*] Besides his high writing style, he was a vigorous if random researcher (like Gibbon, he never asked others to do his work for him) and unusually for his time would travel widely for material, even tracking transient ballads and other elements of popular culture. Maybe Butterfield was

Macaulay's day the approach had become outdated. Fresh ideas were arising about the province of the historian and the new pastures on which he might graze.

★ ★ ★

EVERY GREAT SOCIAL SCIENCE passes through a period during which its high practitioners are not just experts but sages. Gibbon and Macaulay were seen as pioneers of purpose, unveiling great mysteries, but their social position (outside their standing as MPs) was a different matter. How reputable, or financially rewarding, was it to be a full-time historian? Was it even possible? The Victorian man of letters needed to be a generalist, not least because it was usually impossible to earn a living from a single specialism. Writing about the past as a career option needed to become respectable. Here the Germans took the lead, especially in the universities of Berlin and Göttingen, recasting history as a *discipline,* a word significantly denoting that its practitioners needed to behave in a controlled way and observe accepted standards. The increasing achievements of the natural sciences meant that science was perceived as the road to the future, Auguste Comte (1798–1857), the founder of positivism, teaching that all true knowledge was scientific. What better manifesto for the study of history than to proclaim it as a science (in the sense of *Wissenschaft,* "scholarship" or "organized knowledge," not natural science narrowly conceived), governed by the same rules of gathering evidence, primary research, and impersonal analysis?

The acknowledged master of this approach was Leopold von Ranke (1795–1886), the German scholar whose long life spanned most of the nineteenth century and whose works run to fifty-four volumes. "Ranke is the representative of the age which instituted the modern study of History," wrote Lord Acton. Edward Muir, a specialist on Ranke's career, is equally admiring: "Ranke is to historians what Darwin is to biologists and Freud to psychologists, the revered author of the discipline's methods and the presiding personality from an age when science promised so much for the betterment of humanity."

---

overstating his case; some of his contemporaries certainly thought so. Sir Lewis Namier (1888–1960), A.J.P. Taylor's great mentor, was caustic as only a fellow academic could be. "Poor old Herbert," he said in mock kindness, "he swallows a nail and shits a screw"—that is, he always complicated matters.

This transformative figure, the eldest of nine children, was born on December 21, 1795, in Wiehe, a small town in central Germany, in a valley called the Goldene Aue, the "golden pasture," an area bordered by mountains and forests, close to where Martin Luther grew up, but which was largely under the control of revolutionary France, where boys copied out Napoleon's bulletins as lessons on their slates. In 1815 it all became part of Prussia. Many of Ranke's family were Lutheran pastors, and he was expected to follow in their footsteps. However, although deeply religious, he was drawn to philology, which he studied at Leipzig University, where he was taught that without a thorough knowledge of linguistics one could not understand other civilizations. This was a convincing argument, for widely variant readings in surviving manuscripts of ancient texts—mistakes by scribes, interpolations by later writers, gaps that may or may not have been filled by speculation—often made it difficult to know what the author had originally written. Intimate understanding of the linguistic context was a powerful tool for reconstructing the original text.

At first Ranke knew only that he wanted to be a scholar, not necessarily a historian. He read voraciously, immersing himself in philosophy and in the leading writers of the German Romantic movement. When eventually he turned to studying the past, he would saturate himself in archival material, then search for the "hand of God" behind the assembled facts. First he had to have the historical truth; then he would divine the wishes of God amid the crucial moments of history.

From Leipzig he moved to Frankfurt an der Oder, to teach classical languages to well-heeled secondary school students. There he began his first book, published in 1824, the *History of the Latin and Teutonic Peoples from 1494 to 1514*. It won immediate recognition, not least because it was written without access to the nation's great public libraries, although he made frequent trips to Berlin to use the book collections at the prestigious university there. The Prussian minister of education read Ranke's work and noted its freedom from dangerous political opinions; soon the young academic was invited to join the new university (founded in 1810 by the diplomat Wilhelm von Humboldt, brother of Alexander) as an assistant professor in history. He was to stay almost fifty years. Among his colleagues were the theologian Friedrich Schleiermacher, the philosopher Georg W. F. Hegel (whose views Ranke came to criticize, despite or perhaps because of Hegel's moving the writing of history into a branch of philosophy), and Barthold Georg Niebuhr, whose *History of Rome* (1811) had been one of Ranke's earliest treasured possessions. The shy Saxon found himself welcomed by both liberal and conservative circles and, exhibiting a lifetime fondness for the powerful, fell under the spell of the leading government figures he met. In short, he grew into a Prussian conservative, part of a university founded to be "a weapon of war as well as a nursery of learning."

In a contentious appendix to his first book Ranke takes to task his predecessor in the field, Francesco Guicciardini, whose *History of Italy* had covered much the same ground, attacking him for using secondary sources, misrepresenting evidence, altering facts, even inventing details. He then adds an axiom that was to become his calling card: "You have reckoned that history ought to judge the past and to instruct the contemporary world as to the future. The present attempt does not yield to that high office. It will merely tell how it really was" (*wie es eigentlich gewesen,* sometimes translated as "to show the actual past," "to tell how it actually happened," or "to show what actually took place," each with its own shades of meaning). However, this phrase was only his starting point. From the evidence he would proceed to "historical truth," just as the focused philologist would advance from a study of grammar and text to an understanding of the life and thought of the ancients. He would avoid contemporary histories, so often riddled with error or bias, and concentrate instead on government decrees, bureaucratic files, and diplomatic reports (especially Italian *relazioni*— "relations"—whose authors had a European-wide reputation). With these documents, historians could write "scientific" histories, for the older a text, the more likely its authenticity, and he personally relished the liveliness of such sources, their gossip and anecdote (such as Swiss mercenaries being "brave against iron but cowards against gold").

Even before he departed for Berlin, Ranke had published a second book, *The Ottoman and Spanish Empires,* and in 1825, still only thirty, he traveled to Venice on a research trip. As Ranke's main biographer, Edward Muir, relates, the city had been harshly treated by Napoleon in 1797, then in the peace congress in Vienna further diminished by becoming a subject province of the Austrian Empire. Without an independent government to protect its interests, its archives were made available without restriction at a time when virtually no other European state permitted full access. The city's patrician families were desperately short of cash, and were forced to sell off paintings, books, and private papers that in many cases included copies of *relazioni* that distant ancestors had sent to a now nonfunctioning Senate. It was a historian's Aladdin's cave, forty-seven folios of reports, "a world of dark and secret romance," in Mark Twain's admiring phrase.

Never mind that Ranke's view of this hoard was an illusion, since the *relazioni* were not the result of objective truthtelling, but rather the constructions of a self-interested ruling elite. At any rate, he was the first scholar to make use of such material.* He felt, he wrote, "like a new Columbus." Here was "mankind as it is, explicable or inexplicable," material that in time he might mold into something much more ambitious—a history of the growth of modern Europe. His easy reproduction of the reports was one reason he was able to write so many books so quickly. The immediate result was a long essay, "The Conspiracy Against Venice."

From there Ranke (he had yet to earn the honorific "von") moved on to Rome, where he believed the papacy was in the sunset of its authority, and so a dispassionate evaluation of its history was at last possible. As a Protestant he was barred from using the Vatican archives, but there were other sources, and he immersed himself among "books, or rather among often somewhat rotting papers." Down to the eighteenth century, history had been customarily written from secondary material: Guicciardini was hardly unusual in his methods. It took two hundred years after the invention of the printing press for primary sources just to start to be published. For Ranke, documents explained themselves, and needed only to be verified and arranged in the proper order. Much of the material he encountered in Rome was not edited or easily accessible, and he spent months sifting, selecting, and copying before he ever set about composing a version of his own. Yet in the letters he sent home there is never a trace of boredom or fatigue. In one, dated November 1829, he admitted to his brother Heinrich:

---

* Winston Churchill jibed: "Diplomats tell the truth to their governments. Of course, I except the Italians." When informed that Italy was joining in the Second World War on the side of the Germans, he replied, "That seems only fair. We had them last time." Italy seems to have been the punching bag of choice for witty Englishmen in his era. Early in his book *The Struggle for Mastery in Europe: 1848–1918,* A.J.P. Taylor adds the footnote: "It becomes wearisome to add 'except the Italians' to every generalization. Henceforth it may be assumed." On the other hand, from the seventeenth century on up to 1917 all western European ambassadors wrote to their own foreign offices in French—except for the British.

I have been here in Rome for a long time. All summer long, I indefatigably kept it up. There is something invigorating and refreshing in this searching and finding, in the uninterrupted pursuit of a greater universal purpose, although my universe is only a library.* . . . I was called to this, for this I was born, for this I exist: in this I find my joys and sorrows.

After his return to Berlin in 1831, he wrote his most famous work, *The History of the Popes: Their Church and State in the Sixteenth and Seventeenth Centuries.* It took three volumes, and despite the Vatican placing the books on the Index, Ranke tried to be as objective as possible—coining the term "Counter-Reformation" in the process and taking on the role of that movement's first authoritative interpreter. As a result, many Protestants denounced his work as not anti-Catholic enough. In keeping with his principles of how historians should proceed, Ranke used a wide variety of sources, including memoirs, diaries, personal and formal missives, diplomatic dispatches, and firsthand accounts of eyewitnesses but always stressing the spiritual essences at play and the intuition needed to understand them.

Religious rivalries were one thing, politics another. His doctorate in 1817 had been on the political ideas of Thucydides, while he had made his reputation largely on his use of the highly detailed reports of Venetian ambassadors. In addition, Ranke was personable, deferential, and popular with both crowned heads and leading statesmen. A political-historical phase to his life was about to begin, one that he welcomed.

Germany was divided into some three hundred principalities, its hopes of unification dashed by the Congress of Vienna of 1814–15, although the settlement had at least reduced the number of states to about three dozen. Prussia was regarded as halfway between revolution and reaction. Frederick William IV, then in the middle of his thirty-

* Ranke, able to purchase much of what he read, assembled an extensive book collection. After his death, bureaucratic red tape and political infighting kept the Prussian government from purchasing his books, and on April 22, 1887, Ranke's son sold the entire collection to Syracuse University (in the heart of New York State)—some seventeen thousand volumes, four thousand pamphlets, and 430 manuscripts. There are still a number of books in his library that contain his notes and underlinings. Sometimes one finds a row of numbers at the bottom of a page where Ranke tried to add up troop sizes to see if they tallied. See Andreas D. Boldt, "Leopold von Ranke on Irish History and the Irish Nation," published online April 17, 2017.

year reign, was generally popular—on his accession a Berlin tailor had caught the country's mood with his much-quoted rhyme *Unter deinen Flügeln/kann ich ruhig bügeln* ("Under your wings/I can quietly do my ironing")—but the king was getting old, and as he weakened the conservative elements in his court gained ascendancy. In 1832, prompted by the government, Ranke founded and edited a political quarterly, the first historical journal in the world, the *Historische-Politische Zeitschrift,* and was soon using the magazine to attack liberal thought. "Not again will I so easily find such a good opportunity to become acquainted with the affairs, the situation, and the interests of the present world," he wrote to his brother.

In two central articles in which he attempted to apply his philosophy of history to politics, "The Great Powers" (1833) and "Dialogue on Politics" (1836), he claimed that every state receives a special moral nature from God, developing along lines determined by that essential character, and that individuals should strive to fulfill the "idea" of their particular community. This idealized abstraction was his way of urging readers to reject the precepts of the French Revolution, which he claimed were meant for France only; a nation should not imitate others but be true to itself. Any German problem required a German solution.

Like Plato, with whom he liked to compare himself, Ranke aimed at a recognizable style, one that would inspire his readers; and he had yet a further agenda, one he was happy to declare—always behind the record of man's history was "the hand of God." Whatever happened represented the divine will, and it was the job of the historian, "with humble tenderness," to ascertain God's intention, the "overruling compulsion of the innate life-germ." This he termed, rather unhelpfully to non-German-speakers, *Einfühlungsvermögen,* the capacity for adapting the spirit of the age whose history one is writing and of entering into the very being of historical personages, no matter how remote.

Lord Acton, writing about Ranke, spoke of his "heroic study of records," but these had to be solid, not speculations or rationalizations. Each source had to be placed in its historical context and individually analyzed for its trustworthiness. This was the core of Ranke's "scientific" approach. One wonders how much of his work is read now, given its religious overtones and philosophical ambitions, but his method, the way he set about evaluating evidence, has lasted through the centuries. In homage to the sciences, Ranke also ushered in a fashion among historians not to issue moral judgments on the past, an approach later echoed by Einstein's comment that great science is always impersonal. So he beavered on, busying himself with articles on domestic policy and foreign affairs. But the magazine—ponderous, scholarly, high-minded, with most of its articles written by its hardworking editor—failed to garner enough readers, and after a year he resigned; by 1836 the quarterly was no more. On reflection, back in his study, he reassessed the part he might play in national life and decided it was the politician's job to take up where the historian left off. The historian, through analysis and contemplation of past events, furnished the essential sense of direction to the man of affairs. The latter then led his people into the future on the road mapped out for him.

Leopold von Ranke, from the 1850s (left) and from 1875. Ranke pioneered the use of a wide range of sources, including "memoirs, diaries, personal and formal missives, government documents, diplomatic dispatches, and first-hand accounts of eye-witnesses."

An unexpected extension of this argument was that, in the interaction between states, Ranke viewed war as the supreme moment in which a nation found itself. "It is infinitely false," he wrote, "to see in the wars of historical powers only the play of brutal force. . . . In power itself lies a spiritual genius, with a life of its own." Grand armies were formed to carry out great ideas, and while God was not necessarily on the side of the big battalions, He was there looking down benignly on those who emerged victorious. Thus the foremost historian of his age set out a philosophical template by which, eighty years on, the leaders of a united Germany marched to war.

Ranke himself never experienced armed conflict. His contribution to the world of politics was to write history, and his output continued with a new volume every two years. Betraying his Romantic sympathies, after he was knighted in 1859 he put on his coat of arms the motto *Labor ipse voluptas*, "Work is pleasure." Erotic terminology evidently did not frighten him. For most of his adult life he pursued a chaste and solitary existence, yet he did eventually marry, at the age of forty-eight, choosing the daughter of a Dublin barrister, Clarissa Helena Graves, a woman thirteen years his junior. They met in Paris in 1843 (the same year Ranke met Macaulay, whom he viewed as a deluded rival)* and would have three children. The poet and novelist Robert Graves was his great-nephew.

All this while he was also teaching, mainly in Berlin. He was an appalling public speaker (one pupil complained in 1857, "That was no lecture, but a mumbled, whispered, groaned monologue"), and one of his habits was to get tired of a sentence midway through and simply stop short, leaving his audience in the air, but he attracted gifted students. He in turn took an avuncular interest in his undergraduates, who eventually occupied almost every chair of history in Germany. Henry Adams (1838–1918), grandson of the American president John Quincy Adams and great-grandson of the president and Founding Father John Adams, thought it imperative to go to Germany to discover how to be a historian—just as hundreds of young Americans made their way to Paris, then the medical capital of the world, which would transform American health practice. Ranke's followers developed the school known as *Historismus*. Its influence long outlasted their mentor's own career.

---

* A breakfast meeting was arranged between them when Ranke was visiting England. It was recorded by the diarist Charles Greville, who was present: "There never was a greater failure. The professor, a vivacious little man, not distinguished in appearance, could talk no English, and his French, though spoken fluently, was quite unintelligible. On the other hand, Macaulay could not speak German, and he spoke French without any facility and with a very vile accent." Soon the Scot, growing impatient, "broke into English, pouring forth his stores to the utterly unconscious and uncomprehending professor." The breakfast was quickly wrapped up, with Ranke characteristically fleeing to the archives.

One of Ranke's charges, Wilhelm von Giesebrecht (1814–89), penned a revealing description from these years:

> If you saw him on the street, you would at once notice his hasty gesticulations, his hopping gait, still more the disproportion between the upper and lower parts of his body. His small stature was out of proportion with his mighty head with its sharply drawn features framed by flowing dark hair. His face acquired a peculiar radiance from the penetrating glance of his large blue eyes.

Besides his lectures, Ranke implemented the seminar teaching method, "the weekly crucifixion," as one student called it, in which groups of young professors-in-training met to present papers, which were then critiqued under the guidance of an older professor, in Ranke's case a demanding if compassionate referee; it was considered a special honor when he himself assumed the central role. Many American historians of Europe, especially Continental Europe, can trace their intellectual genealogy directly back to such forums. That is especially true of specialists in German and Italian. Both the University of Chicago and Johns Hopkins adopted the Ranke seminar model in the late nineteenth century and led the professionalization of history in the United States. California at Berkeley, Michigan, Wisconsin, and Iowa did the same slightly later. The Ivy League schools, except for Columbia, long lagged in following the Ranke example. The doctorate of philosophy, a German degree adopted in the United States in the 1880s, became the historian's indispensable badge of competence, an idea taken directly from medieval German guilds, where admittance required that one had trained under a master craftsman and had also produced an original piece of work, hence the word "masterpiece." The history doctorate spread from Germany to Spain, thence to Russia and beyond; the first American doctorate was at Johns Hopkins in 1881.

The historian Theodore Von Laue may not be overstating it when he says that Ranke "achieved a peculiar sainthood," not in a specifically religious or ethical sense "but in the field of historical scholarship and writing." His life proceeded peacefully through the decades, with teaching in Berlin and occasional trips abroad. He was "as contented as a man can possibly be." Eventually failing eyesight and hearing forced him to resign his tutorial duties, yet he still accomplished a work he had long wanted to complete, eight volumes of ancient and medieval history, his *Weltgeschichte,* dictated with the help of two secretaries. By the 1880s he had grown into a national treasure, the symbol of how history should be written; his ninetieth birthday was declared a holiday throughout Germany. He died in May 1886, a year later, his final great project having reached only the twelfth century, but from student notes it was completed down to 1453. The career that had started at the Frankfurt *Gymnasium* with a study of the Renaissance had arrived almost full circle.

* * *

FOR ALL RANKE'S INFLUENCE, history as a reputable university discipline took time to establish itself. The first chair at Oxford may have been endowed as early as 1622, but the Regius chairs of modern history founded in 1724 by George I at both Oxford and Cambridge were simply sinecures (worth a distinctly handy £400 a year, more than $75,000 now), and history—apart from the study of the ancients—formed no part of the curriculum. (Even in 1762 a fellow of Trinity College applied for the Cambridge chair with the appeal: "Unsuccessful in my profession, and infirm and lame, I am impelled to solicit for some addition to my present income." He was not successful.) The teaching duties of Oxford professors were restricted to the training of young diplomats. The first degree for history was offered by Göttingen in 1776. The first active professor at Cambridge was appointed in 1807, while the subject was a subsidiary section of the moral sciences examination in 1851, then part of the examination in law and history (in imitation of Oxford), and not introduced as a separate entity until 1856, with doctorates available from 1920 on. In the United States, doctorates were established at Yale in 1861 (to be delivered in Latin). Thereafter, the institution of the PhD had a decisive effect on research.

Academics didn't actually write books about the nonclassical past until the 1850s, but by then the wisdom was that graduates of the leading universities went into the civil services, not, as previously, into holy orders, so the history of all manner of things acquired a new vitality. Specialist disciplines sprang up—the history of warfare, or medicine, or industrial development, or exploration. Likewise, the kind of person who became a historian altered. (At Cambridge, a statute allowing college fellows to marry was passed only in 1868.) Studying the past became an acceptable subject for statesmen. It helped that from mid-century on archives increased prodigiously both in quantity and in number and became a crucial source (if one could only get into them). As just one example, Leo XII (1760–1829) was the first pope to admit scholars to the Vatican archives—Catholic scholars, anyway, as Ranke could testify.

This new respect spread into allied pursuits. As Chase Robinson describes it: "The common understanding of history today, as a variety of non-fiction that is distinguished from 'literature,' even an autonomous branch of learning, is relatively new. . . . Because we regard history as a useful and important thing, in some measure because we have rooted our national identities in it, we give it a variety of institutional forms, such as museums, local historical societies, dedicated sections in bookshops and libraries, and university departments."

The writing of history may have been distinguished from literature (English literature as an academic discipline was another late-nineteenth-century invention), but it still owed imaginative writing an immense debt. In an 1828 essay, Macaulay acknowledged as much, but he also drew up battle lines. "By judicious selection, rejection, and arrangement," he wrote, the ideal historian reclaims for nonfiction narrative the "attractions" that novelists have "usurped." He was aware that to a remarkable degree the father of nineteenth-century history was not himself or Ranke but the great historical novelist Sir Walter Scott, who showed that history was indeed an imaginative profession.

At almost the same instant that Macaulay was penning that essay, Ranke determined to become a historian. He had read several of Scott's novels "with lively interest," he was to write, "but I was also offended by them." For him, to go deliberately against known facts was unforgivable. Scott had not only included many "unhistorical" details; he seemed to have done so deliberately. "I felt unable to pardon him," Ranke concluded. Thus was his new career set. Even so, Scott had heralded a new way of bringing the past to life.

CHAPTER 10

ONCE UPON A TIME
Novelists as Past Masters

———

Historian: an unsuccessful novelist.
—H. L. MENCKEN

If we write novels so, how shall we write History?
—HENRY JAMES, REVIEWING *MIDDLEMARCH*, 1870

J ANE AUSTEN MAY NOT DISCUSS THE CAUSES OF THE NAPOLEONIC WARS head-on, but she gives us a profound sense of what it was like to live in her times, and that provides the first clue about what fictions can add to history; they fill in the gaps that formal accounts cannot cover, when what historians might call "hard evidence" does not exist.

Austen always had an interest in what was happening beyond her immediate world. Even at the age of seven she would talk of parliamentary reports that she'd read in the newspapers. At sixteen, while pouring out a stream of wickedly funny and often violent childhood stories, she composed a parody of Oliver Goldsmith's *History of England,* keeping his title but adding: "By a partial, prejudiced, & ignorant historian. . . . There will be very few Dates in this History." In adulthood, she made her views known obliquely; thus the "Mansfield" of *Mansfield Park* is her homage to William Murray, first Earl of Mansfield (1705–93), an MP and later Lord Chief Justice, who fought against slavery, while the obnoxious, status-seeking Mrs. Norris received her name from Mansfield's leading opponent. But Austen's main contribution to history was to show what it felt like to live in her day.

From the earliest fictions, writers have sought to augment our understanding of the past either by setting made-up stories within a historical framework (Homer again, but *The Golden Ass* too) or giving an alternative account of what happened, inventing characters and events as required. Austen operated on a domestic level; a sea change in the settings for historical fiction came in 1814, with the publication of Walter Scott's *Waverley*.*

Scott didn't embark on a literary career until he was thirty-one—early middle age. But he was encouraged by the fact that, some years before, Horace Walpole, the fourth Earl of Oxford, had published *The Castle of Otranto,* merging medievalism and terror (the book opens with the hero's son crushed to death by a monster helmet falling from the skies) in what Scott himself lauded as "the first modern attempt to found a tale of amusing fiction upon the basis of the ancient romances of chivalry." His contemporary Maria Edgeworth (1768–1849), with such stories as *Castle Rackrent* (1800), also encouraged him to try his hand at a fiction set in the recent past. At first, this was mainly a commercial decision—a story based on real events promised good sales—but soon Scott realized that such tales were a chance to interpret history, to instruct as well as to entertain. As for an ideal setting, he wrote in *Waverley:* "There is no European nation which, within the course of half a century or little more, has undergone so complete a change as this kingdom of Scotland."

With the failure of the Jacobite uprising of 1745, in which the Scots tried to put their own king on the English throne, so much that was valuable to them had been stripped away. Scott's loyalty to the country of his birth was lifelong. Born in Edinburgh in 1771 to a strict Presbyterian lawyer father and a more outward-looking mother, he was only eighteen months old when he contracted polio—six of his eleven siblings were to die in childhood. To help him recover he was moved to the family farm on the border between Scotland and England, an isolated area alive with stories of adventure—his great-grandfather, "Beardie," had been a fervent Jacobite supporter who swore not to

---

* In a letter to her favorite niece, Anna Austen, dated September 28, 1814, Austen wrote: "Walter Scott has no business to write novels, especially good ones.—It is not fair.—He has fame and profit enough as a Poet, and should not be taking the bread out of other people's mouths.—I do not like him, & do not mean to like *Waverley* if I can help it—but fear I must." *Jane Austen's Letters,* 2d edition, ed. R. W. Chapman (London, 1952).

shave off his beard until the return of the "rightful" king, Bonnie Prince Charlie. Scott's childhood was full of accounts of these times, even though he returned to Edinburgh to complete his schooling (and endure electric shock treatment for his polio), to be admitted to the Scottish bar in 1792, aged just fifteen.

Although permanently lame, he recovered sufficiently to drill with a company of Edinburgh dragoons to repel an expected French invasion, and after several romantic entanglements and one failed love affair he was successful in a second, on Christmas Eve 1797 marrying Charlotte Charpentier, the daughter of a French refugee, a notably happy union that produced five children. In 1799 he became sheriff of Selkirkshire, then in 1806 chancellor of judicial court, a further promotion; he was settled and financially secure. All these years he had been collecting Scottish and German ballads (translating several of the latter), and in 1802–3 anthologized the local Border songs in three volumes. "By such efforts, feeble as they are," he wrote, "I may contribute somewhat to the history of my native country." He didn't just record and arrange; he edited texts and even put in stanzas of his own when he felt the originals fell short. It was his first experiment in altering the past to suit his wishes.

The anthologies proved popular and encouraged Scott to compose ballads himself, all of them imitations of medieval romances. *Marmion,* set in the sixteenth century, sold 28,000 copies over three years, *Lady of the Lake,* said to have inspired a highland revival, 25,000 copies in eight months. Crowds began to visit the sites of the scenes he had made up. His success, however, made him write too quickly. Poems like Byron's *Childe Harold,* set in more exotic surroundings than the Scottish border, were eclipsing him ("Byron beat me"), and he looked around for a new way forward. He opted to try prose fiction but was still unsure of himself, publishing *Waverley* anonymously and guarding his privacy so intensely that he was dubbed "The Great Unknown"—although his authorship was an open secret in the literary world.* The book has

---

* Seven of Scott's books were published in four volumes as a subset of the Waverley novels as "Tales of My Landlord." They were so titled because they were supposed to be stories collected from the (fictional) landlord of the Wallace Inn at Gandercleugh, in Midlothian, compiled by one "Peter Pattieson." One of the novels, however, is set partly in Constantinople! Scott's publisher, John Murray II, was sure the author was "either Walter Scott or the Devil," but Scott put him off the scent by saying he would prove he wasn't the begetter by reviewing the 1816 edition of the tales himself. He wrote a scathing article, calling one story "unusually artificial; neither hero nor heroine excites interest of any sort," and concluding that the real author was Scott's brother, Thomas. Murray was convinced.

been called the first bestseller (excluding the Bible), while Mark Twain even claimed that Scott's accounts so shaped the character of the American South that he was partly responsible for the Civil War (although one might have responded to Twain that the former slave Frederick Douglass, born Frederick Bailey, changed his name to one that honored a character in a Walter Scott poem).

With the book's profits, Scott bought, for £4,000, a farm on the river Tweed (the river that marks the boundary between Scotland and England), enlarged the main building into an impressive castle, acquired hundreds of acres of land, named his fortress "Abbotsford" after a nearby river, and fashioned himself a Scottish lord. The house was quickly filled with relics—the sword of the great Marquis of Montrose, Rob Roy's gun, Prince Charles Edward's hunting knives, even the keys of Lochleven Castle, found in the castle moat after Mary, Queen of Scots, had made good her escape in 1568, but also an elaborate system of air-bells (wind chimes) and revolutionary oil gas lighting. No expense was spared. As A. N. Wilson puts it, "When it came to his estates and his house, he was like a gambler held to the tables by an inescapable addiction."

And meanwhile the novels flowed, all his fiction completed in an astonishing fifteen years. There were stories with Scottish settings such as *Guy Mannering, The Antiquary, Rob Roy, The Heart of Midlothian* (in which much of the dialogue is in Lowland Scots, some editions carrying a glossary), *Redgauntlet* (his most autobiographical, and which refers to "the laudible habit of skipping"), *Old Mortality* (possibly his best, about the idea that rebellion against an unjust regime is the only way to secure religious liberties), and *A Legend of Montrose*. In his final years, to offset his publishing debts, he also dashed off other tales with non-Scottish backgrounds, such popular potboilers as *Ivanhoe* (the England of Richard the Lionheart), *Kenilworth* (the court of Elizabeth I), and *Quentin Durward* (fifteenth-century France). He even penned a biography of Napoleon, over six hundred pages and written with access to secret government papers six years after the emperor's death.*

---

* *The Times* of London extracted the book in its first-ever serialization; Scott's scathing view of his subject stirred controversy, and he was challenged to several duels (he declined). Bonapartistes were incensed. Louis Antoine Fauvelet de Bourrienne (1769–1834), a longtime confidante of Napoleon, expounded: "Sir Walter appears to have collected his information for *The Life of Napoleon* only from those libels and vulgar stories which gratified the calumnious spirit and national hatred. His work is written with excessive negligence, which, added to its numerous

Scott was honest and straightforward in his personal affairs but gave little time to overseeing his finances. He had entered into a secret partnership with his printer, from whom he never received a clear statement of his accounts. In 1826 the printer went bankrupt, and although Scott was not legally bound, he took on debts of more than £100,000 ($3.2 million now) and determined to pay off the money without outside help. In his journal he recorded quoting the Apothecary in *Romeo and Juliet*, "My poverty, but not my will, consents." Illness and stress both took their toll, and by 1832 Scotland's most influential novelist was dead, of typhus.

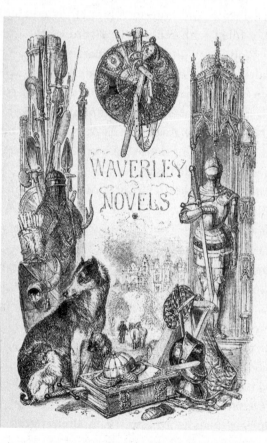

Title page of the Waverley novels, 1842–47, the Abbotsford Edition.

errors, shows how much respect he must have entertained for his readers. It would appear that his object was to make it the inverse of his novels, where everything is borrowed from history. I have been assured that Marshal Macdonald [a Scots émigré who served under Napoleon] having offered to introduce Sir Walter Scott to some generals, who could have furnished him with the most accurate information respecting military events, the glory of which they had shared, Sir Walter replied, 'I thank you, but I shall collect my information from popular reports.'" See *Memoirs of Napoleon Bonaparte* (Charleston: CreateSpace Independent Publishing Platform, 2015), ch. 2.

* * *

HORACE WALPOLE WROTE HIS Gothic tale by first creating a plot then adding the history. Scott chose the setting first, then spun his story, letting it unfold within the confines of actual events. When it came to adding a subtitle to *Waverley*, he considered "A Tale of Other Days," "A Sentimental Tale," and "A Romance from the German" (Germany just then being full of stories characterized by a "glorious national past shrouded in the mists of time" glow) before settling on "'Tis Sixty Years Since," a pointer that readers should expect not a straight retelling of the 1745 rebellion but an examination of what followed, of "those passions common to men in all stages of society," whatever their class or the period in which they lived. What he wanted to teach was that, faced with three courses of action in a crisis—cling to the past, reject it, or seek a compromise—the third way was best. There was no great ending in his scheme of history, just personal accounts to which readers could relate. History did not move forward; it simply moved.

To link the past to the present, he had to make that past convincing, so whether it was a blood-soaked tournament, a castle dungeon, or the inside of a farmer's cottage, the details had to be exact. He researched the color of uniforms, heraldic devices, even the eating habits of the time, anything that brought authenticity. Contemporaries praised him as a historian of genius. His descriptions of Border landscapes were so scrupulous that Stendhal would scoff that he must have had a researcher. Most readers agreed that the "genuineness" of Scott's backgrounds were among his greatest strengths, yet in part they were willing dupes. Much of the Scottishness was his personal creation, like the "missing" stanzas he had concocted for his anthologies. The Highland warrior in his tartan kilt, marching to the stirring sound of bagpipes, was a fantasy, and his associated emblems were either conjured (like the kilt) or were at best recent arrivals, like the bagpipe (an invention of ancient Egypt).

Where history was not being newly minted, it could be bent (after all, "fiction" means, in its Latin root, "shaping"). The cast of *Ivanhoe*, which includes Robin Hood and Friar Tuck, could never have been together at any one date; Charles II was never concealed at Woodstock; and in *Quentin Durward* the bishop of Beauvais comes to his sticky end thirty years ahead of time. Even the "Scottish" Highlands were basically Irish, but that mattered little to Scott's public. His books were huge successes, and half a century on, when Queen Victoria bought a Highlands estate, Balmoral, Prince Albert designed a suitable tartan, with no one protesting. Historical painting was already regarded as the highest pictorial genre, but now composers used Scott's stories for operas, children dressed in highland costume, and architects were inspired by his nationalism. Between 1824 and 1828 Windsor Castle was rebuilt in "authentic" Gothic style. As Hilary Mantel put it in her 2017 Reith Lectures, "All other possible Scotlands lost out to Walter's."

One should not be too critical. Scott, who defended his inventions and anachronisms as "necessary for exciting interest of any kind," won his readers' hearts by portraying the great crises that swept his country through the lives of ordinary people—and future historical novels, from *A Tale of Two Cities* to *Gone with the Wind* on to *Roots* and *Wolf Hall,* followed in his wake. In his day, little history was taught in schools, and knowledge of the past had to be gained through self-education; for most readers, the Waverley novels were the most pleasurable and effective way, and *Waverley* is probably still the best account of what life in the 1745 rebellion was like.

* * *

FOR A WHILE, it seemed almost impossible for novelists of any cut to escape Scott's influence (poets too: Byron professed in his diaries to have read all Scott's novels "at least 50 times," adding, "Wonderful man! I long to get drunk with him"). Robert Louis Stevenson (1850–94) was a direct disciple. In Italy, Alessandro Manzoni (1785–1873) wrote his masterpiece *The Betrothed* about Milanese society in the seventeenth century. In Russia, Alexander Pushkin (1799–1837) composed *The Captain's Daughter,* a love story set against a local rebellion, while in Germany Theodor Fontane (1819–98) started his first novel, a tale about the campaign of 1812–13, *Vor dem Sturm* ("Before the Storm"), a year before Tolstoy published *War and Peace.* In Spain Benito Pérez Galdós (1843–1920) also followed the struggle against Napoleon in *Episodios Nacionales,* part of a chain of forty-six novels written over forty years.

In the eighteenth century, as the writing of fiction gathered pace, authors liked to call their books "histories," as it conferred authority. Henry Fielding declared his *History of Tom Jones, a Foundling* (1749) just such a work on its title page, and began all eighteen "books" in the novel with a meditation on the reading and writing of history. He even included a chapter called "Of Those Who Lawfully May, and of Those Who May Not Write Such Histories as This." What he was providing was " 'true history'—fiction was what historians wrote."* He wanted it both ways: to enjoy the respectability of presenting a true story but also to make the point that, while history mattered, the best novels boasted a kind of truth that even the most authoritative histories could not claim. (It is no accident that Gibbon was a *Tom Jones* devotee.) Both Fielding and Defoe often included made-up historical documents, and in his preface to *The Life and Strange Surprizing Adventures of Robinson Crusoe* (1719) Defoe even declaimed that "the Editor believes the thing to be a just history of Fact; neither is there any Appearance of Fiction in it." But of course there was no editor, nor any journal: just Defoe's imagination. The first American novels began to appear in the 1780s and '90s, and their title pages regularly proclaimed: "Founded on Fact" or "A Tale of *Truth*." Homer might have made the same claim—were the person of Homer himself not a fiction.

In the eighteenth century, several people wrote both history books and novels, including Voltaire, Smollett, Goldsmith, Defoe, William Godwin, and Mary Wollstonecraft. Thereafter the boundary between the two forms became more fixed, and writers tended to settle on one form or the other—although Dickens wrote a children's history of England and D. H. Lawrence a textbook of European history.

In 1937, the Marxist critic György Lukács (1885–1971) published *The Historical Novel*. In it he argued that Enlightenment thinkers, in their attempt to portray the unreasonableness of absolutist rule, used historical inquiry as a weapon,† since "the lessons of history provide the principles with whose help a 'reasonable' society, a 'reasonable'

---

* Fielding's contemporary David Hume was once asked by a "young beauty" to send her some novels. Instead he dispatched three history books—including Plutarch's *Lives*—but made a point of telling her that they were novels and that "there was not a word of truth in them." She lapped them up, until she came to the biographies of Alexander the Great and Julius Caesar, both vaguely known to her. She at once returned the volumes, reproaching her mentor for deceiving her. See David Hume, *Of the Study of History* (1741).

† When in 1956 Lukács was arrested for his participation in the Hungarian uprising, a KGB officer asked him if he carried a weapon. Lukács reached into a pocket and handed over his pen.

state may be created." He cited Voltaire's *Henriade,* but it was Voltaire's successors who really established the novel as a contribution to history. Alexandre Dumas, Victor Hugo (who wrote *The Hunchback of Notre Dame* on his publisher's instruction to imitate Scott as closely as possible), Stendhal, Gustave Flaubert, Honoré de Balzac with his *La Comédie humaine* series (his panorama of French life in the years after the fall of Napoleon), and Émile Zola (who wrote a set of twenty historical novels) were the standard-bearers. Zola, of Italian parentage, was particularly proud that *zolla* in Italian means "clod of earth," in keeping with his aim to write naturalist stories.

The quality of writing varied. *The Three Musketeers* and its many imitations may have been "entertainment literature" (in the 1820s what in Britain are now called "Aga sagas" were known as "silver-fork novels"), but the major French realists, "that group of brilliant writers who invented the once-famous *tranche de vie,* the exact photographic reproduction of a situation or an episode," as Edith Wharton described them, were penning some of the greatest novels of the nineteenth century. "I want to write the moral history of the men of my generation—or, more accurately, the history of their *feelings,*" wrote Flaubert. Napoleon haunts many of their books, with Stendhal believing that the little corporal's history needed to be rewritten every six years; in his novel *The Red and the Black,* the hero, Julien Morel, lives according to Napoleon's maxims. Stendhal was not the only one obsessed. Hugo's father was a high-ranking officer in Napoleon's army until he was defeated in Spain. Balzac kept a bust of the emperor on his desk, its base emblazoned with the words "All that he did with a sword I will accomplish with a pen." He even started writing a novel under the title *The Napoleonic Battles.* It was never completed, but the stories of these encounters are scattered throughout his books, so much so that Napoleon is the most frequently cited character.

Balzac (1799–1850) found inspiration in Scott but also in James Fenimore Cooper (1759–1851), whose five "Leatherstocking Tales," classics of frontier and Native American life that included *The Last of the Mohicans,* appeared from 1823 on. Balzac conceived the idea of an enormous series that would provide a window on "all aspects of society." Although at first he called the books *Etudes des Mœurs* (Studies of Manners), they passed into history as *La Comédie Humaine,* enriched by more than two thousand characters. The project totaled eighty-five novels, and at his death at fifty-one he had a further fifty planned. He would revise each up to fifty times (this in the age of sweated typographers), at one point in a fit of creative energy spending twenty-six consecutive days at work, without once leaving his study. Zola praised his "messy creativity," but the overall quality is astounding, and he never doubted he was writing history, not just fiction.

Convinced that "the novel is the private history of nations," Balzac set out to take in the entire record of human achievement, a "universal illumination." In his preface to *Père Goriot* (1835), he declared that his "general plan . . . obliges [the author] to depict everything . . . just as he tries to represent human feelings, social crises, good and evil, the whole hotchpotch of civilization." Even so, he never goes beyond the year of his birth, the one exception being his homage to Cooper, *Les Chouans* ("The Silent Ones," the first novel he published without a pseudonym, in 1829, set among guerrilla fighters immediately after the French Revolution). Karl Marx said of him: "[He] was such a great novelist that many of his characters only reach their full development after he died." Indeed, on his deathbed Balzac called for the one doctor he could trust, Horace Bianchon—"Yes, that's it! Bianchon's the man I need! If only Bianchon were here!" But he was calling for the fictional doctor in *La Comédie Humaine*. The story is likely apocryphal, although it underlines that even in the moment of dying Balzac knew his characters would live on after him.

For Edith Wharton, "What was new in both Balzac and Stendhal was the fact of their viewing each character first of all as a product of particular material and social conditions, as being thus or thus because of the calling he pursued or the house he lived in (Balzac), or the society he wanted to get into (Stendhal), or the acre of ground he coveted, or the powerful or fashionable personage he aped or envied (both Balzac and Stendhal)." Some have made even greater claims. "Fiction is history, human history, or it is nothing," wrote Joseph Conrad. "But it is also more than that; it stands on firmer ground, being based on the reality of forms and the observation of social phenomena, whereas history is based on documents, and the reading of print and handwriting—on second-hand impression. Thus fiction is nearer truth. But let that pass. A historian may be an artist too, and a novelist is a historian, the preserver, the keeper, the expounder, of human experience."

But what kind of reality were these novelists uncovering? Not everyone agreed that they were historians. Thomas Carlyle might wheel over a barrowload of nonfiction books to Dickens to help draft *A Tale of Two Cities,* Zola might discover that pit horses lived and died underground and transfer such a detail to *Germinal,* and Tolstoy might consult the keepers of the Russian archives, but the priority was to tell a good story, not necessarily to get in the facts or get them right.

Most historical novelists will agree that their creations are fictional, and even when they include "real" people they may invent what they do and say. The historical novelist Thomas Mallon sums up the issue: "The fact-by-fact decision-making involved in composing mainstream historical fiction—what to change, when to leave well enough alone—is uncodified and imprecise, conducted on a sliding scale that's always a slippery slope." When in 1975 *Ragtime*—mainly set in the New York City area from 1902 until 1912—was published, its author, E. L. Doctorow, told an interviewer, "The book is a series of meetings that never took place." We have no evidence that J. P. Morgan ever discussed reincarnation with Henry Ford, as Doctorow has them do. On the other hand, Sigmund Freud and C. G. Jung's trip to America is well documented, as is the fact that they visited Coney Island. So, pressed his questioner, did Freud and Jung ride through the Tunnel of Love, as they do in the novel? "They do now," Doctorow replied. John Updike accused him of "playing with helpless dead puppets," but Doctorow was unrepentant. "The historian will tell you what happened," he said, "the novelist will tell you what it *felt* like"—a different kind of history.

* * *

IN 1981 THE GREAT French historian Emmanuel Le Roy Ladurie published an essay in which he examined the historical accuracy of one of Balzac's early novels, *Le Médecin de champagne* (The Country Doctor), set in the Dauphiné, a border province in southeast France, not far from Grenoble. Ladurie, who made his name with books based on the lives and times of small French villages, begins by criticizing Balzac's knowledge of the local dialect, economy, and geography, although "none of this really matters," since "despite these lapses, the essentials, as always with Balzac, are there from the start." We get the sawmill with its wooden troughs and its stripped fir trunks, the ramshackle cottages of the laborers in contrast with the houses of the better-off peasants, the vines, correctly staked *en hautains,* the herdsmen feeding bales

The great French realists, who used fiction to write history (clockwise from top left): Victor Hugo (who wrote The Hunchback of Notre-Dame *on his publisher's instruction to imitate Scott as closely as possible); Honoré de Balzac with his La Comédie humaine series, a panorama of French life in the years after the fall of Napoleon; Émile Zola, who wrote a set of twenty historical novels, subtitled "a natural and social history of a family under the Second Empire"; Stendhal, the pen name of Marie-Henri Beyle; and Gustave Flaubert were the standard-bearers. "I want to write the moral history of the men of my generation—or, more accurately, the history of their feelings," wrote Flaubert.*

of leaves to their flocks, and the baskets holding little cheeses hanging out to dry above every doorway. Balzac had done his homework. "A scrupulous anthropologist of today would be horrified at the hotchpotch this method produces," Ladurie comments. "But when Balzac wrote, there were no scrupulous anthropologists about."

Enter the book's leading characters, Pierre-Joseph Genestas, an ex-army veteran who takes up lodgings with Doctor Benassis, who is also the local mayor, having over ten years transformed the village into a thriving community. We are given an idealized picture of what can be achieved through farsighted altruism, but Balzac has weighted the scales. The village is highly untypical, with the real wretchedness of such places held at bay. Other details are supplied in full. "When it comes to recreating a way of life and its setting," Ladurie grants, "Balzac once more becomes a reliable and skilful observer. In describing interiors, especially dining-rooms, he has no equal." So what if the novelist is seemingly unaware that the Alps are generally covered in snow or that his village roofs are an impossible mix of shingle from the Alps, tiles from Provence, slate from Anjou, and thatch from everywhere else? The workshops established by Dr. Benassis are in full swing, and yet—

> after about 1815, people in the Alps were tending to move *down* not up. . . . Balzac paid no attention to that. Ignoring all the laws of historical gravity, he decrees that the new enterprises, which his correct observation of reality had suggested to his novelist's imagination, should be located halfway up a mountain. The economic growth in rural areas, which really did take place in the period 1815–35, is literally exalted by the author in a mood of Utopian creativity. . . .

And so the master historian's analysis continues, on the one hand Balzac getting many details meticulously correct (for instance, how peasant cultures dealt with death), on the other, a host of errors or incredible events, ranging from a far-fetched revolution in baking techniques, an out-of-the-way village where seventy houses are built in a single year, trees springing up spontaneously all over the mountain, and not so much as a snowflake falling. "In *six weeks,* the local population increases by several hundred! Pure science fiction!" writes Ladurie. "Balzac is hopelessly unrealistic: his fiction transcends reality and forgets even to keep within the bounds of possibility." And yet, "like many a visionary, Balzac *is* overdoing it—in the short term. But in the medium term, and *a fortiori* over the long term, he has not got it wrong." So to his final verdict: Balzac is a less than scrupulous anthropologist, a Utopian sociologist, an inaccurate geographer, but he makes up for this by being a first-class reporter and synthesizer of country ways. He "can do no more than take us by the hand and lead us to the threshold of village mysteries; he does not altogether succeed in taking us over it."

Few historical novelists do; but nor do many full-time historians.

However rich the archive material or the testaments of witnesses, all writing about the past has an element of conjecture. Too often we simply do not know for sure. According to Milan Kundera, "Fidelity to historical reality is a secondary matter as regards the value of the novel." The novelist who sets his or her story in the past can take two roads. One is to create as convincing an impression of the period as possible, so we believe in the story—even if it requires meddling with the facts. A conjoined consideration is to provide, in historian Brenda Wineapple's words, "the magical ventriloquism of historical novels," to which another admirer, Geoffrey Wolff, adds the "facts and artifacts, syntax and slang, costumes and customs, fads and prices, conventional wisdoms and bright ideas." Yet in his 1832 introduction to *The Talisman* Scott openly admitted that "considerable liberties have . . . been taken with the truth of history." While accuracy might be important, story and characters were the thing.

The other lies in not only trying to get every detail right, to be as scrupulous as a professional historian, but also not knowingly falsify anything. For the consumer, this still creates a problem. How much to believe? We remain reading a work of fiction, and even if an author (as some now do) adds a note explaining what is part of the historical record and what is not, we have in our hands something by definition made up, so that it is a special kind of history, history with benefits. We are back with Flaubert—"the history of their *feelings,*" the part of history that strict constructionists are inclined to omit or not to know.

Even accomplished writers of nonfiction worry they are missing out and ape the novelist's ways. In the third volume of *The Age of Roosevelt,* Arthur Schlesinger, Jr., devotes three pages to Dr. Weiss as he murders Huey Long (the controversial senator from Louisiana), reaching out to get inside the mind of his assassin, otherwise inaccessible, to capture the intensity of an individual passion that may have tilted the scales of history.

In a further attempt at an imaginative exploration of the past, in 1990 Peter Ackroyd published his immense biography of Dickens, including seven fantasy sections, in one of which he meets Dickens somewhere in time; when he describes himself as a biographer, his subject is made to reply mockingly: "Oh, biographers! Biographers are simply novelists without imagination." In the uproar following publication, Ackroyd defended his muddling of genres by saying, "Dickens saw reality as a reflection of his own fiction," but in the abridged 2002 paperback he eliminated the fantasy sections. Edmund Morris, after thirteen years of research and access to a living subject, Ronald Reagan, also introduced fictions into his 1999 biography, creating a mythical "composite" character who crosses paths with Reagan. For a prize-winning historian, it was quite a departure, as if he could employ fiction in a biography whenever he chose.

In the years since, the two forms of writing have continued to feed off each other. In her 2002 collection *On Histories and Stories,* A. S. Byatt notes that "recent historians like Simon Schama have made deliberate and self-conscious attempts to restore narration to history," and that, conversely, "the idea that 'all history is fiction' [has] led to a new interest in fiction as history." Schama has also been criticized for emphasizing story at the expense of argument.

It has been left to an American expert on Islamic history, Chase Robinson, and Britain's foremost military historian, Michael Howard, to add some welcome common ground. "Where does one draw the line," Robinson asks, "between non-fictional historical narrative which relies upon storytelling techniques that are usually associated with imaginative literature, and historical fiction, in which characters and stories are grounded in past events, particularly if the two projects share a common purpose—to edify, entertain or illustrate what their authors hold to be truths?" Howard simply says, "We're all having our stab at truth."

* * *

THE WORLD'S LIKELY BEST historical novel (not the bestselling—that is *Gone with the Wind*) is *War and Peace.** Its first draft was completed in 1863, and portions, under the title *The Year 1805,* were serialized in a Russian literary magazine between 1865 and 1867, although Tolstoy rewrote the entire book during this period and the first publication of the complete work wasn't until 1869. He had been mulling over writing a historical novel for some years, before deciding on Russia's tussles with Napoleon. He experienced war himself in the Balkans, the Caucasus, and the Crimea and was keen to examine its nature and causes.

---

* Soviet statistics for authors' popularity, up to the end of 1953, show that in copies sold Maxim Gorky came first with 71 million, then Pushkin with 68 million, followed by Tolstoy with 42 million. See R. H. Bruce Lockhart, *Your England* (New York: Putnam, 1955), p. 250.

One of his earliest biographers, Aylmer Maude, has suggested that *War and Peace* is not a historical novel in the true sense, since the story is set within the memory of the author's parents' generation. Tolstoy himself said that the best Russian literature did not conform to set rules and was reluctant to call his book a novel at all, instead regarding *Anna Karenina* as his first genuine work of fiction. Late in life, after a series of religious conversions, he grew ashamed of both books. *War and Peace,* Tolstoy said, was "not a novel, even less is it a poem, still less a historical chronicle." But he was ever contrary, and never offered his own definition. (Tolstoy is not alone in renouncing his early work: Gogol disowned both *Dead Souls* and *The Government Inspector.*)

Even before he left university Tolstoy had decided that his professors spent their time on trivial issues. He denounced theology and the teaching of dead languages as an accumulation that no reasonable person would want to know. History particularly irritated him as leaving out anything truly important: "History is like a deaf man replying to questions that nobody puts to him," he told one startled fellow student, when both were locked in a detention room for some minor act of insubordination. The more he researched into the past, the more he came to distrust accepted accounts. "History would be an excellent thing, if only it were true," he said, not jokingly but with bitterness.

By the time he settled on what was to become *War and Peace* he had already acquired a reputation as a war correspondent, particularly for his reports from the Crimea and his early Cossack stories. In 1861–62, he visited Western Europe and met Victor Hugo, who had just finished *Les Misérables,* which would greatly influence him (particularly the battle scenes). Shortly after his return, he started to plan his own novel. He spoke with men and women who had survived the 1812 French invasion of Russia and read widely on the subject. There are some 160 real persons in the book (out of 580 characters in all), Tolstoy's aim being, as he openly admits in the novel, to blur the line between fiction and history. In an early draft, he wrote that he really wanted to write about the history of Russia's war with Napoleon, but if he undertook the task without the help of fiction it would "force me to be governed by historical documents rather than the truth."

The latter parts of the novel are interspersed with essays about war, power, and history. Most of these lectures are hard going—Maxwell Perkins wrote to John Galsworthy in 1929 that he was reading the novel to his children "and won't permit skipping except those parts that give Tolstoy's theories of war"—and several editions remove the sections entirely. Others, even those published in Tolstoy's lifetime, moved the longer discourses to an appendix.

Leo Tolstoy in the 1860s. War and Peace came out in 1867–69. He wrote two different versions of the novel, starting on the second as soon as he finished the first. It was the second one that was published worldwide.

The second of the two epilogues is given up to Tolstoy's critique of traditional theories of history. The nineteenth-century "great man" theory claimed that pivotal episodes are the result of the actions of "heroes"; Tolstoy argues that such behavior rarely results in great events, which are the result of smaller incidents driven by the thousands of individuals involved. "In historic events, the so-called great men are labels giving names to events, and like labels they have but the smallest connection with the event itself." The wise man is not "tubby, dumpy" Napoleon, who believes he controls history, but the Russian General Kutuzov, who knows he doesn't. Come the great clash of armies at Borodino, Tolstoy spells out:

It was not Napoleon who directed the course of the battle, for none of his orders was executed and during the battle he did not know what was going on before him. So the way in which these people killed one another was not decided by Napoleon's will but occurred independently of him, in accord with the will of hundreds of thousands of people who took part in the common action. It *only seemed* to Napoleon that it all took place by his will. . . .

No wonder Anton Chekhov could write to a friend in 1891, "As soon as Napoleon is taken up, we get a forcing of effect and a distortion to show that he was more stupid than he actually was." But was Tolstoy writing history (good or bad), polemic, or fiction? On the book's first appearance, the liberal newspaper *Golos* ("The Voice") posed a question later repeated by many others: "What could this possibly be? What kind of genre are we supposed to file it to? Where is fiction in it, and where is real history?" Tolstoy himself explained in a letter to the editor of *Russkii Vestnik,* "the work is not a novel and is not a story, and cannot have the sort of plot whose interest ends with the dénouement. I am writing this in order to ask you not to call my work a novel in the table of contents, or perhaps in the advertisements either."

Any criticisms we have of Tolstoy's attempt to play the comprehensive historian should not blind us to the fact that in the most "fictional" parts of the novel he gives us what any professor of history would exchange his or her tenure for—scenes that capture indelibly what life was like in high-society and military Russia in the early nineteenth century. It is not just the realism of the battle scenes (the military writer General Mikhail Dragomirov advised his officers to use *War and Peace* as an indispensable handbook); in scenes like the madcap sleigh ride through the snow or the family wolf hunt or Natasha's folk dance Tolstoy gives us unparalleled social history and a deep insight into the years he is recounting.*

Memorably, Tolstoy tells what it was like as Napoleon advances on Moscow, and the city's inhabitants react in dread and panic, but we

---

* Nearly all the main characters are based on people Tolstoy knew in real life, especially his family members. Natasha, for instance, is based on his sister-in-law, Tatyana Andreyevna Behrs, who was sixteen when he himself married Sonia Behrs. Tatyana was a high-spirited teenager, already a great favorite of his, and very like her fictional counterpart. At one point, after taking poison after a love affair that was not going as she wished, she changed her mind about dying when another of her suitors called, receiving him politely and then rushing to her mother for an antidote.

learn this not by the use of archives or other sources but entirely by metaphor, that of the beehive. Here is part of that description:

Moscow meanwhile was empty. There were still people in the city—perhaps a 50th part of its former inhabitants still remained—but it was empty. It was empty in the sense that a dying, queenless hive is empty.

In a queenless hive no life is left, though to a superficial glance it seems as much alive as other hives. The bees circle about a queenless hive in the heat of the midday sun as gaily as about other living hives; from a distance it smells of honey like the others, and the bees fly in and out just the same. But one has to give only a careful look to realize that there is no longer any life in the hive. The bees do not fly in and out in the same way, the smell and sound that meet the beekeeper are different. A tap on the wall of the sick hive and, instead of the inane, unanimous response, the buzzing of tens of thousands of bees threateningly lifting their stings and by the swift fanning of wings producing that whirring, living hum, the beekeeper is greeted by an incoherent buzzing from odd corners of the deserted hive. From the alighting board, instead of the former winy fragrance of honey and venom, and the breath of warmth from the multitudes within, comes an odor of emptiness and decay mingled with the scent of honey.

No sentinels watch there, curling up their stings and trumpeting the alarm, ready to die in defense of the community. Gone is the low, even hum, the throb of activity, like the singing of boiling water, and in its place is the fitful, discordant uproar of disorder. Black oblong robber-bees smeared with honey fly timidly, furtively, in and out of the hive; they do not sting but crawl away at the sign of danger. Before, only bees laden with honey flew into the hive, and flew out empty; now they fly out laden. The beekeeper opens the lower chamber and peers into the bottom of the hive. Instead of black, glossy bees tamed by toil, that used to hang down, clinging to each other's legs, in long clusters to the floor of the hive, drawing out the wax with a ceaseless murmur of labor—now drowsy shriveled bees wander listlessly about the floor and walls of the hive. Instead of a neatly glued floor, swept by winnowing wings, the beekeeper sees a floor littered with bits of wax, excrement, dying bees feebly kicking their legs and dead bees that have not been cleared away . . .

So in the same way was Moscow empty.

* * *

THE ROLL CALL OF notable historical novelists, "literary" and "popular" both, even if restricted to recent times and to those writing in English, might begin: Mary Renault, Robert Graves, Anya Seton, Daphne du Maurier, C. S. Forester, Paul Scott, Rosemary Sutcliff, Jean Plaidy, Mary Stewart, William Golding, George MacDonald Fraser, Dorothy Dunnett, Georgette Heyer, Patrick O'Brian, Cormac McCarthy, Toni Morrison, Howard Fast, Colleen McCullough, Bernard Cornwell, Barry Unsworth, Beryl Bainbridge, J. G. Farrell, Thomas Keneally,[*] A. S. Byatt, Pat Barker, Philippa Gregory, Peter Ackroyd, W. G. Sebald (mixing genres within the same book), Gore Vidal, Joyce Carol Oates, Melvyn Bragg, Penelope Fitzgerald, Margaret Atwood, Rose Tremain, Peter Carey, Robert Harris, Sebastian Faulks, Iain Pears, Sebastian Barry, Sarah Waters, Andrew Miller, and Helen Dunmore. But already the list is unwieldy and limiting it to English-speaking novelists too restrictive. One wants to include the novels of Elena Ferrante, Gabriel García Márquez's amazing portrait of Simón Bolívar in *The General in His Labyrinth,* the thirty prose poems by Geoffrey Hill in *Mercian Hymns,* largely based in the eighth century, and many more.

In 1973 an entire book was published citing what its authors regarded as "better works insofar as literary excellence, readability, and historical value can be measured." The compilation, arranged chrono-

---

[*] Keneally's range of historical subjects is particularly diverse, covering inter alia the lives of Moses, Joan of Arc, and Stonewall Jackson, on through the treaty of Versailles in 1918, Tito's partisans in World War II, Napoleon's last years, and several novels about Australia's past. In 1980, I was fiction director at Hodder & Stoughton, and together with Ion Trewin, who had a similar responsibility for nonfiction, attempted to lure Keneally from his then publisher. I remember that when Keneally's agent, Tessa Sayle, sent both of us the proposal for a book about a little-known figure, Oskar Schindler, I ran down the corridor of our building in wild excitement at what I had read. But that was for a nonfiction account of the German hedonist who saved so many Jewish lives in World War II, so Ion took over as editor. Only as the writing progressed did Keneally decide that the story would be better as fiction, and the resultant novel, *Schindler's Ark,* won the Booker Prize in 1982, then in 1994 Steven Spielberg's film *Schindler's List* garnered seven Academy Awards. Keneally and Spielberg changed our view about "Good Germans."

logically, then topographically, *The World Historical Fiction Guide,* by Daniel D. McGarry and Sarah Harriman White (London: Scarecrow Press), lists 6,455 works.

To show how the genre has evolved, not only György Lukács but also critics like Fredric Jameson and Perry Anderson have argued that historical fiction has gone through phases. It begins, they argue, as a product of romantic nationalism. Scott (surprisingly, Lukács's favorite) introduced the epic costume drama, his storylines reflecting the battle between good and evil. Tolstoy introduced a different level of realism, interweaving public events and private lives but bending the historical evidence when it was inconvenient for his purposes.

With Balzac and Stendhal, Zola and Alexandre Dumas in France, H. Rider Haggard and John Buchan in England, the historical novel broadens to include a variety of registers, including not only highbrow and lowbrow but a wide range in between, setting it apart from other narrative forms. It no longer has a nation-building intention and can be sheer entertainment, but it predominates over all other kinds of story-telling down to the Edwardian era—taking in Ford Madox Ford, Anatole France, even Conrad. Twenty years on, by the interwar period, historical fiction fell out of fashion. The First World War stripped the

Toni Morrison's portrait on the jacket of her first (1970) novel, The Bluest Eye. *John Leonard, reviewing the book in* The New York Times, *wrote that it was "history, sociology, folklore, nightmare, and music."*

glamor from battles and high politics and made the melodrama of such fiction seem laughable, even tasteless. And the advent of modernism gave primacy to a different kind of consciousness. Only in the United States has the genre not been seen as recessive, so that William Faulkner (with *Absalom, Absalom!*), the later Thomas Mann (after he settled in America), and Thornton Wilder had notable successes, while *Gone with the Wind* sweeps all before it.

Although there were some exceptions (Virginia Woolf's *Orlando*, Joseph Roth's *Radetzky March*), the Second World War reinforced the prejudices of the First. At the more commercial level the form remained popular—one omnibus guide of the time lists more than six thousand new titles—but it was a considerable surprise when in 1951 Marguerite Yourcenar won a major literary award, the Prix Femina, for *Mémoires d'Hadrien,* about the Roman emperor. In 1960 came Lampedusa's *Il Gattopardo* ("The Leopard"), for Lukács an interlocking of the historical and the existential that defined what the genre could accomplish. About the same time, Naguib Mahfouz's Cairo trilogy took a bourgeois Egyptian family from 1918 to the nationalization of the Suez Canal, interweaving fictional characters and real historical figures as the narrative progresses toward national emancipation.*

It makes an unusual trinity, an unsocial semi-Belgian, a dead Sicilian prince, a little-known Egyptian, yet for some thirty years these were the jewels amid the gewgaws. Then, in the early 1970s, came a transformation, and today the historical novel is a highly respected form, with most leading fiction writers trying their hand. But the old ways have been reversed. Past and present may be freely interwoven; the author may appear in the narrative; historical figures may be central, not peripheral; stories may be counterfactual; or there may be multiple endings. Certainly in the Caribbean and in Latin America novelists have reinterpreted the past in notable ways, from Alejo Car-

---

* Chinese historians figure little in this book, but one notable figure is Shan Tianfang (1934–2018), a teahouse and later radio historian who would recite classic Chinese novels and events from the past as a performer of *pingshu,* formed in the Song dynasty (960–1279 A.D.), in which a narrator wears a traditional gown and sits behind a desk on which there is a folding fan and a wooden block, a form of gavel. He recites from memory a legend, most often a Chinese epic, using different voices, expansive gestures, and occasional commentary. From 1966 through 1976, Shan was exiled as a counterrevolutionary, but when he returned to his performances it was on radio, where more than 100 million Chinese tuned in to hear him. However, in recent years many of the great *pingshu* performers have died, and the tradition is fading. See Amy Qin, obituary of Shan Tianfang, *The New York Times,* September 19, 2018, B16.

pentier to Gabriel García Márquez or Mario Vargas Llosa, whose most admired novel, *The War at the End of the World* (1981), is about a provincial uprising in Brazil in the late nineteenth century that led to the slaughter of more than fifteen thousand peasants. The Russian author Vladimir Sharov helped pioneer what is called "magical historicism" in books like *Before and During* (1993), invoking real historical events and people (Tolstoy, Madame de Staël, Alexander Scriabin, Stalin) in a fantastic alternative chronology. In America the core experiences have been race (William Styron, Wallace Stegner, E. L. Doctorow, Alice Walker) or empire (Vidal, Thomas Pynchon, Don DeLillo, Norman Mailer) in tales of military tyranny, race murder, technological war, and genocide: history as a book of horrors.

Fiction has become a vital outlet for African American writers to pass on and interpret the past. Alex Haley (in *Roots: the Saga of an American Family*), James McBride (notably in his 2013 comic fiction *The Good Lord Bird*, about the abolitionist John Brown), Walter Mosley (in historical mysteries such as *Devil in a Blue Dress*, featuring his detective Ezekiel "Easy" Rawlins), and Colson Whitehead (with eight novels to date, preeminently *The Underground Railroad*) are just a few of those whose books recount and even reevaluate history. At their head, though, stands Chloe Ardella Wofford, otherwise known as the Nobel Laureate Toni Morrison.

Morrison (1931–2019) was born in Lorain, Ohio, the second of four children, to Black working-class parents, her father a sometime welder for U.S. Steel and her mother a homemaker and loyal member of the African Methodist Episcopal Church. When Morrison was about two, their landlord set fire to their house while the family was inside because they couldn't pay the rent. Her parents responded not with outrage or revenge but by laughing him into shame.

Young Chloe loved the singing at her mother's church, but in 1943, at the age of twelve, she converted to Catholicism, lured by its strong stories and works of art and by the enthusiasm of a Catholic cousin. "That's shallow," she would say. "But that's what it was, until I grew up a little older and began to take it seriously and then took it seriously for years and years and years." Critics have noted that Morrison never shied away from framing her sense of story, thought, and belief within a Catholic worldview. Her attraction to her new faith's "scriptures and its vagueness" led her to conclude it was "a theatrical religion. It says something particularly interesting to Black people, and I think it's part of why they were so available to it."

She soon acquired the nickname "Toni," based on her baptismal choice, an homage to St. Anthony of Padua. Over the years she became disaffected with the Church, especially its surrender of Latin to English Mass, and by 2007, her religious identity would be even more enigmatic; she spoke very much as having lapsed, yet as late as 2014 she affirmed, "I am a Catholic."

In high school, her favorite authors were not Fathers of the Church but Jane Austen and Leo Tolstoy, and she graduated from Howard University, a historically Black college in Washington, D.C., with a degree in English. She went on to an MA at Cornell, writing her thesis on Virginia Woolf and William Faulkner. Teaching and marriage (to a Jamaican architect she met after she had joined the staff at Howard) followed, and she was pregnant with their second son when they divorced in 1964. The following year she began her editing career at a textbook division of Random House, based in Syracuse, New York. In 1967 she moved on to Random House's general publishing division in New York City, becoming the house's first Black woman senior editor, and immediately began nurturing writers of color from Angela Davis to Gayle Jones—even to Muhammad Ali. "I was inspired by the silence and absences in the literature," she explained. "So many stories untold and unexamined." What made a book "Black," she came to believe, were unique elements of language, narrative, and religion. She said Black stories "are just told—meanderingly—as though they are going in several directions at the same time."

In 1974 she made a noteworthy attempt to collate those stories by producing *The Black Book,* an anthology of photographs, illustrations, essays, and other documents of Black life in America from the time of slavery to the 1920s. What struck her was how one-sided the record was; there was little that reflected how African Americans experienced their own lives.

By then she was already writing fiction, having joined a group of writers at Howard University, where she developed what would become her first full-length novel, *The Bluest Eye,* published in 1970. Set in the wake of the Great Depression, its protagonist is Pecola Breedlove, a poor young African American. After her father, in an alcoholic rage, burns their house down, she is taken in by neighbors, but eventually moves back in with her family. Isolated and neglected, she is convinced that if she had white skin and blue eyes she would be loved. One day, her father returns home drunk and rapes her. Driven insane by her terrifying ordeal, she believes that her wish *must* have been listened to and that she now has the skin and blue eyes of her dreams—a tragedy compounded, Morrison shows, by a dominant white culture that can conceive of beauty only in its own terms.

With her third novel, *Song of Solomon* (1977), which won the National Book Critics Circle Award, Morrison took a major step forward as a novelist, although—as with her next, *Tar Baby* (1981)—historical events, while they played an important part, were still not central. A play followed, based on the 1955 murder by white men of a Black teenager, Emmett Till. Then came *Beloved*.

A ghost story set after the American Civil War, the novel was inspired by the true account of an enslaved Black woman, Margaret Garner. Morrison had learned about her experiences while compiling *The Black Book*, coming across an 1856 newspaper article, "A Visit to the Slave Mother Who Killed Her Child." The work is dedicated to "Sixty Million and More," a reference to the Africans and their descendants who died as a result of the Atlantic slave trade, and while at one level a tale of evil, superstition, and phantasmagoria, it remains the most moving and empathetic account of the trauma of slavery in all American literature.

In April 1985, at the time Morrison was writing *Beloved*, a lifestyle magazine for Black women, *Essence*, asked her to contribute the concluding essay to its fifteenth anniversary edition. The result was "A Knowing So Deep," in which she wrote: "Anyone who doesn't know your history doesn't know their own." The year *Beloved* was published, 1987, Morrison described a process of "emotional memory" that found truth where the historical record fell short. She was not, however, simply writing about the pain of the Black American experience; she had a more ambitious program in mind.

In 1990 she gave a series of lectures at Harvard in which she argued that literary critics—mostly white, Protestant men—had presented the "classic" works of American literature as if they had been untouched by African American experience; this, she declared, was patently untrue. Further, these critics had contrasted the idea of "Americanness" with the image of "Africanness," as if the two represented opposite poles. There was an inherent racism in the way such guardians of American culture assessed such a canon, and Morrison urged authors to renounce the "white gaze" of the past and replace it with a new, unprejudiced view of what it is to be an American.

She conceived this all as a historical enterprise. An article in *History Today* in 2017 described the lectures: "She saw it as her task to reach back into America's past and to craft narratives that portrayed its history from an authentically Black perspective. This entailed not only recapturing the lived experiences of African Americans, but also revealing the physical and psychological damage that had been inflicted upon them by a dominant white culture."

Beloved would be the first of three novels (to be followed by *Jazz* in 1992 and *Paradise* in 1997) thematically devoted to "the search for the beloved"—Morrison has said that all of her writing is "about love or its absence"—but also charting Black history through African and American culture. As in every one of her books, the writing is passionate, fierce, and unforgiving: Morrison had wanted to title the third novel in her trilogy *War,* but was dissuaded by her editor.

In her eleven works of fiction (as well as in her plays, operas, and numerous essays), helping to write a new history of her country became her life's mission. A 2003 *New Yorker* profile quoted the Alabama-born poet Patricia Storace on that mission's success: "Morrison is relighting the angles from which we view American history, changing the very color of its shadows, showing whites what they look like in Black mirrors."

* * *

THE NOTION OF HISTORY as a nightmare, not in the United States but in the Soviet Union, was captured with equal force by Aleksandr Solzhenitsyn (1918–2008), the Russian ex–political prisoner who burst on the world's consciousness in 1962 with his short novel describing a single day in the life of a camp inmate, *One Day in the Life of Ivan Denisovich,* published in the Russian literary magazine *Novy Mir.** In 1945,

---

* The magazine's editor began to read a prepublication copy in bed. He was so overcome that he got up and put on a suit and tie to finish the story with what he felt to be the requisite respect. One of the few critics of the novel was Mikhail Sholokhov (1905–84), whose own novels, particularly the four-volume *And Quiet Flows the Don,* about the lives and fates of Cossacks from the revolution through the civil war and on to Stalin's collectivization, won him the 1965 Nobel Prize, the only Soviet-era writer not to be out of favor with the authorities when winning the award. Indeed, he was given the nickname "Stalin's scribe" for his years of political lobbying and government patronage.

while serving in the Soviet army, Solzhenitsyn had been arrested for writing mildly derogatory comments in a letter to a friend (he had called Stalin "the bossman" and "master of the house") and sentenced to eight years of hard labor, the normal punishment for anti-Soviet propaganda. He was assigned to a scientific research facility, then in 1950 transferred to a camp for political prisoners. After his sentence had run its course he was exiled to southern Kazakhstan, where he took up residence in a primitive clay hut, buying a Moskva 4 type-writer to record his experiences, burning all his drafts, and keeping a single version, secured in a complicated series of hiding places. In February 1956, in a period later called "The Thaw," Nikita Khrushchev made his famous denunciation of Stalin and officially revealed the existence of the gulag prison system. Not only was Solzhenitsyn exonerated, the Soviet leader personally approved his story's publication as a further way to discredit the Stalin era.

During his imprisonment in Kazakhstan, Solzhenitsyn had worked as a miner, bricklayer, and foundry foreman, experiences that formed the basis for his fiction. His alter ego, Ivan Denisovich Shukhov, wolfs down his starvation rations in the prison canteen, trudges off to work in below-zero temperatures, helps construct a pointless wall, and through the accounts of his fellow prisoners puts together an alternative history of the Soviet Union in deliberately toned-down descriptions, giving readers the chance to generate outrage themselves. The story was politically courageous and spiritually ambitious. (Unbeknownst to him, Primo Levi used a similar approach to capture the even more inhumane experience of the Nazi camps.) "Once you give up survival at any price," Solzhenitsyn declared, "imprisonment begins to transform your former character in astonishing ways." Reputedly, the poet Anna Akhmatova exclaimed on reading the novella in samizdat form,* "Oh my god, socialist realism has found its genius!" The general reaction to Solzhenitsyn so unnerved Politburo chiefs that they banned him from publishing any more work.

---

* By using carbon paper, a single typewriting session could produce as many as ten copies, which would be handed over to other readers, who might in turn duplicate the text and pass copies on. No matter how many distributors were arrested, samizdat could not be stopped, such was the hunger for it. A joke circulated in which a grandmother tried and failed to interest her granddaughter in *War and Peace*. Desperate, she retyped the massive novel to make it look like a samizdat reprint. See Martin Puchner, *The Written Word: The Power of Stories to Shape People, History, Civilization* (New York: Random House, 2017).

But Solzhenitsyn was too busy writing to stop. He would teach mathematics at a Moscow secondary school during the day but spend his nights engaged in new books. Three further novellas followed, then in 1968 came *In the First Circle,* a heavily autobiographical story about prisoners (*zeks*) who help security police track down undesirables by identifying their voices on the phone. In the same year he had another large novel released in *tamizdat* form ("publishing abroad"), with a note saying, "Published without the consent of the author." He had other personal experiences to mine. Around 1950, he had had a malignant tumor in his abdomen removed. In 1953 the cancer returned, and by year's end he was close to death. He was sent to a hospital in Tashkent, where the disease went into remission, but the experience formed the basis for *Cancer Ward.* I read both books while at college, and although *The First Circle* (its title in Britain) appeared only in a self-censored or "distorted" version—both novels had had to be smuggled to the West—I remember going round in a daze, feeling I had discovered a masterful new talent, telling me of worlds I never knew existed.

The Soviet authorities were aghast. The KGB ordered surveillance squads, stakeouts, death threats, bugging devices, and illegal seizures. In 1970 Solzhenitsyn was awarded the Nobel Prize, but he decided not to travel to receive it, fearing the authorities would not allow him to return. He was right. Not long after the ceremony, the KGB attempted to prick him with ricin, a fatally toxic poison, in a Novocherkassk store. Always expecting a knock on his door, he slept with a pitchfork near his bed. On January 7, 1974, the Soviet leadership met to discuss the fallout from his next work—*The Gulag Archipelago*—the microfilm of which he had smuggled to publishers in the West.

It was decided that the awkward laureate should be stripped of his citizenship and deported, bundling him off to Germany (with the connivance of the West German chancellor, Willy Brandt), from where he left briefly for Switzerland before settling in Vermont, his home for the next eighteen years—"the happiest of my life," he would say. He was able to collect his Nobel Prize. *The Gulag Archipelago,* three volumes in seven parts, has been called the most important work of history of the twentieth century. The books' overall title in Russian takes on a rhyming slang, *Arkhipelag Gulag,* giving it a sinister ring, as it came from a favorite phrase of a sadistic boss of one of the first gulags, a group of islands situated on the Solovetsky Islands, just south of the

Aleksandr Solzhenitsyn in Zurich in 1974, soon after having been deported and stripped of his Soviet citizenship in the wake of the Western publication of The Gulag Archipelago.

Arctic Circle. The tag *gulag* acquired a powerful resonance almost overnight, but at first it referred exclusively to the camps instigated after 1929 by Stalin. The *Washington Post* columnist Anne Applebaum, who in 2003 published a Pulitzer Prize–winning account of the gulag system, wrote that the word has come to signify "not only the administration of the concentration camps but also the system of Soviet slave labor itself, in all its forms and varieties: labor camps, punishment camps, criminal and political camps, women's camps, children's camps, transit camps." Even more broadly, she said, *gulag* has come to mean the entire repressive Soviet system, the set of procedures that prisoners once called the "meat grinder": the arrests, the interrogations, the transport in unheated cattle cars, the forced labor, the destruction of families, the years spent in exile, the early and unnecessary deaths.

Well over a million people died in the camps in 1937–38 alone, the Great Purge's most devastating years. Solzhenitsyn was inspired to write his account by the large number of letters and personal stories he received after *Ivan Denisovich* appeared, although at the time of publication he was unable to name most of his sources for security reasons. I had recently joined the publishing firm of William Collins, who had British rights to the books, and remember the excitement tinged with revulsion that met the opening *Gulag* volume as we eagerly read the first copies off the press. Here was vital, previously concealed history in the making.*

"Well, yes, he is an expert on history," said the Russian Federation's first president, Boris Yeltsin, somewhat derisively. Only what kind of history? Were these works fiction, memoir, political analysis, or documentary? It didn't matter. The Soviet past had been exposed as never before. By the time Solzhenitsyn left Zurich he had amassed a huge collection of documents. "I have to dismantle each stone in an account," he told an early interviewer, "then label it and be capable of finding it again so as to put it where it belongs. I'm far more of a mason than anything else—I was one, you know."

Meanwhile, secure in his country refuge in Vermont, he was clocking regular ten- or twelve-hour working days. From the age of nine he had been convinced he was to be a writer and by eighteen had begun planning a long account of the passing of imperial Russia and the early years of the Soviet Union. More than fifty years on, this became *The Red Wheel,* four sprawling novels in ten volumes and more than five thousand pages, published as *August 1914* (which appeared in 1971), *November 1916, March 1917,* and *April 1917.* Only the first volume enjoyed anything like his previous sales (the novels came with annotations and a long bibliography), and the final one has yet to be translated into English. Even Solzhenitsyn's best-known biographer, Michael Scammell, admitted, "History and polemic overpower the fiction, and for non-Russian readers the issues at stake don't appear to justify the effort of mastering them." Full of archaic words and phrases, stilted passages, and artificial-sounding dialogue, the narrative shares space with news clippings, long biographical set pieces, and other experiments, in the manner of John Dos Passos.

The great writer of realist fiction had become a bore, accused of

---

* As an instance of the book's freshness, it tells of a work crew in a camp in Kolyma, part of which is in the Arctic Circle, that was doing excavations when it came across a frozen-solid, ancient stream, immured with prehistoric fish and salamanders. Such historically important specimens never got to be studied. The workers who unearthed them ate the fish on the spot.

having evolved into a bitter and hardline nationalist, a tsarist, a Slavo-phile, even an anti-Semite. As so often in his life, he seemed intent to ape his hero, Leo Tolstoy, only now in the role of moral teacher. As with Tolstoy, such pontificating seemed inappropriate: Solzhenitsyn's first wife, Natalya Reshetovskaya, published an account detailing her ex-husband's extramarital affairs. Solzhenitsyn explained to her he took on lovers so he would have new material for his fiction. Of his liaison with a later lover, he told her, "You've helped me to create one novel. Permit me to allow her to help me create another"—an unusual if not unique example of a novelist creating history so that he could use it in his fictions.

In 1990, Solzhenitsyn's Soviet citizenship was restored, and four years later he and his second wife left America for west Moscow. He continued to write poems, short stories, and memoirs and was even given his own TV talk show, but the dominant impression was of a reactionary old man fulminating against the vapidity of Western cul-ture and at the same time venting his disillusion with post-Soviet Rus-sia. He longed for a strong republic and a return to traditional values. In 2007 President Vladimir Putin visited him, their views as one; by August the following year Solzhenitsyn was dead of heart failure, aged eighty-nine.

In 2010 the Russian government authorized a special edition of *The Gulag Archipelago* for use in schools—along with a teachers' manual explaining that Stalin acted in his country's best interests, to ensure its modernization; a recent TV contest to find the greatest Russian in his-tory ranked Stalin third behind the thirteenth-century nationalist Al-exander Nevsky and the reformist prime minister Pyotr Stolypin, assassinated in 1911; more than 50 million people voted. Meanwhile, a statue of Solzhenitsyn was unveiled in Moscow in 2018. On the cente-nary of his birth, in an encomium to the novelist, Scammell concluded: "He did more than any other single human being to undermine [the Soviet Union's] credibility and bring the Soviet state to its knees." No other novelist has so affected history.

* * *

WE STILL ASK, WHAT kind of history does fiction tell? That literary pu-gilist Vladimir Nabokov, spoiling for a fight, has written:

Can anybody be so naïve as to think he or she can learn anything about the past from those buxom best-sellers that are hawked around by book clubs under the heading of historical novels? What about the masterpieces? Can we rely on Jane Austen's picture of landowning England with baronets and landscaped grounds when all she knew was a clergyman's parlor? And *Bleak House,* that fantastic romance within a fantastic London, can we call it a study of London a hundred years ago? Certainly not . . . The truth is that great novels are great fairy tales.

People may still side with Nabokov, but in the main he has lost the contest, and we can leave him shadowboxing in an otherwise deserted ring. In a 2008 *New Yorker* article, Jill Lepore mused: "Historians and novelists are kin . . . but they're more like brothers who throw food at each other than like sisters who borrow each other's clothes." History, she points out (meaning not the past itself, but writing about it), is a "long and endlessly interesting argument, where evidence is everything and storytelling is everything else." She concludes, "In a way, history is the anti-novel, the novel's twin."

In a continuation of the argument, Hilary Mantel devoted the 2017 Reith Lectures, the annual BBC series that asks a leading figure to give a series of talks on a chosen subject, to examine the nature of writing about the past, either as fiction or as "history." Only, as Mantel quickly set out her stall, "history is not the past—it is the method we've evolved of organizing our ignorance of the past. . . . It's what's left in the sieve when the centuries have run through it."

Even then, she argued, evidence is always partial, and facts, while strong, are not stable: 99 percent of what happened or was thought is not available to us, and real history is "messy, dubious, an argument that never ends." In its recasting by a historian or novelist, facts should be seen as a stimulus to creative thought, not some truth in themselves, even though they are part of it: "My tendency . . . is to approach the received version with great skepticism and try to get the reader to challenge what they think they know." While "the great strength of historical fiction is that it allows you to find art in the common record," the novelist concentrates, if he or she is wise, on "what's *not* on the record. You're always looking for the untold story . . . for what has

Hilary Mantel in 2005 taken just before her appearance at that year's Edinburgh Book Festival. According to a 2012 interview with her in The Scotsman, *it was in 2005 that she set aside a book she had been working on, about Botswana, and began a novel she had promised her publishers—which became* Wolf Hall. *"The historical record," she argues, "is not a locked box to which only historians have the key."*

been repressed politically or repressed psychologically." She describes these untold stories as "the airy spaces where you swing on your flying trapeze."

We need fiction to remind us that the unknown—and the unknowable—still exert their force. Quoting St. Augustine, Mantel agreed with his comment that "the dead are invisible—they are not absent." Fiction about them asks its readers not so much to believe what is on the page but at least to consider it. "You can select, elide, highlight, omit. Just don't cheat." That doesn't mean the process of creating an invented world is corrupt, just that it introduces "a kind of wobbling into the fabric of reality." The reader becomes the novelist's ally in negotiating with that reality.

Oddly, of Mantel's fourteen books to date, only four have been historical novels. The first she completed, *A Place of Greater Safety* (the title refers to the grave), was repeatedly turned down by editors and was finally published in 1992, to excellent reviews. A host of contemporary novels followed, highly readable but wildly different in tone and subject matter, until her two Cromwell novels, *Wolf Hall* (2009) and *Bring Up the Bodies* (2012), with the final book in the trilogy, *The Mirror and the Light,* breaking sales records on its appearance in 2020. The fourth historical novel, *The Giant O'Brien* (1998), is concerned with people who had lived but who were not well known: the Irishman Charles Byrne (O'Brien), a freak over seven feet tall, and a Scottish surgeon, John Hunter (1728–93), one of the most distinguished scientists of his day, who in Mantel's vision has an insatiable desire to experiment on bodies and who covets the eventual corpse of the slowly dying Giant O'Brien.

Mantel has said her original intention was to write "a big, realistic novel" about Hunter, but instead she became inspired by O'Brien, who turns out to be a master storyteller, spinning yarns and retelling Irish myths to anyone who cares to listen. That bit is Mantel's fiction, although the massive bones of the giant can be viewed today at the Museum of the Royal College of Surgeons in London. In a note, she acknowledges that "this is not a true story, though it is based on one," and plays fair with her readers by saying that the real-life O'Brien couldn't have been like her giant. "As it is, the book announces itself from the first page as a fairytale about fairytales." It is a highly self-conscious exercise about the nature of storytelling and so not subject to the rules she imposes on her other historical novels.*

Mantel's lectures are witty and thought-provoking, and range widely. They deservedly won the Broadcasting Press Guild award as the best radio program of 2017. One constant theme is her insistence that a novelist may build on the facts but must not tamper with them: "In this world where false information flies about the planet at the speed of light, then the skills of the historian are more necessary than ever." Besides, "the reason you must stick by the truth is that it is better, stranger, stronger than anything you can make up." Hence her belief that one should write fiction about the past only "through honest negotiation with the facts and the power of the informed imagina-

---

* An ironic footnote: Maurice Girodias (1919–90), the founder of the Establishment-defying Olympia Press, eventually went bankrupt. The last book he published was in 1974—an erotic fictionalized biography called *President Kissinger: A Political Fiction.* He later faced deportation from the United States for issuing it. The prosecutor against Girodias naïvely stated, "I don't think you can take someone who is not fiction and build a fictionalized situation around him." See Erika Blair, "Famous Authors Who Wrote Filth," *Please Kill Me,* internet podcast, March 12, 2018. It may not be strictly relevant but is still pleasing to learn, from Ali Smith's preface to a new edition of Muriel Spark's *The Abbess of Crewe* (first published 1974), that the globetrotting nun, Sister Gertrude, is based on Kissinger.

tion." How does anyone know which bits are true? One must ask this of the historian as well as the novelist. History is not a science, it is a humanity, dealing in, and written by, "fallible, flaky human beings."

Try to change the facts, Mantel says, and you run into trouble. "Once you play around with history, it trips a whole load of consequences." Her purist view seems unassailable, although she has come under attack. "We really should stop taking historical novelists seriously as historians," argues David Starkey, an expert on the English constitution and long a leading authority on the Tudor period:

> The idea that they have authority is ludicrous. They are very good at imagining character: that's why the novels sell. They have no authority when it comes to the handling of historical sources. Full stop . . . I wouldn't dream of commenting on Hilary Mantel as a novelist; frankly I'd be grateful if she stayed off my patch as a historian.

Starkey does not cite any example of Mantel's misuse or ignorance of sources, and his comments, made in the run-up to a 2013 TV program alongside Mantel, smacks of Beatrix Potter's irate Mr. McGregor protecting his vegetables.

His fellow historian Eamon Duffy has quoted Starkey in a lecture where he also criticized Mantel for her presenting Cromwell as "wise, kindly, and formidably decent" rather than, as Duffy sees him, "an odious Tudor fixer," and her portrayal of Thomas More as "a sneering misogynist," an enforcer who so brutally tortured Protestants in his own home that his victims had to be carried out in chairs to their place of death. Duffy, an Irish Roman Catholic, argues that More was a great truth-teller who went to the stake for refusing to tell a lie and so prefers to accept More's own words, "Of all that ever came into my hands for heresy, as helpe me God, . . . never had any of them any stripe or stroke given them, so much as a fylype on the forhed." There seems little firm evidence either way, and even Duffy rounds off his lecture by admitting, "I have no doubt that in 50 years' time historians will still be debating what is fact and what is fiction in the Tudor past."

Is there any final judgment on fiction writers as significant historians? "The novel is history," contended Henry James, who believed it was the novelist's sacred office to write as a historian. But "Your real job, as a novelist," as Hilary Mantel concludes one talk, "is not to be an inferior sort of historian, but to recreate the texture of lived experience: to activate the senses, and deepen the reader's engagement through feeling." Thus, "if we want added value—to imagine not just how the past was, but what it felt like, from the inside—we pick up a novel." In the end, that is the most important addition to the historian's account. It gives us (if we choose to accept it) life from the inside—in the Tudor poet Philip Sidney's phrase, "the affects, the whisperings, the motions of the people."

CHAPTER II

AMERICA AGAINST ITSELF

Versions of the Civil War

———

All wars are fought twice, the first time on
the battlefield, the second time in memory.

—VIET THANH NGUYEN, 2017

ONE MOTIVE IN WRITING ABOUT THE PAST IS TO MAKE MONEY; AN-
other, to advance one's career; a third is to put on record an account
of what happened—perhaps to correct an earlier rendering. Some
episodes are so important to national or international understanding
that they are reconsidered endlessly, even obsessively—the two
world wars, the French Revolution, the life and loves of Henry VIII
(individual stories exert a special fascination: to date there are an estimated 128,000 books about Hitler, an extraordinary figure, yet the
Librairie Nationale in Paris lists more than twice that number on Napoleon).

A further subject that has amassed a mountain of literature is the
American Civil War, with the implications and origins of the war
still hotly contested to this day. Robert Penn Warren (1905–89), the
Southern poet and novelist who as a young man defended racial segregation, then recanted and lived his last forty years in the North,
wrote that it was, "for the American imagination, the great single
event of our history. Without too much wrenching, it may, in fact,
be said to *be* American history. Before the Civil War we had no history in the deepest and most inward sense." A white man's verdict,
certainly; but not least one can agree that it was by far the country's

deadliest conflict, resulting in 623,026 dead from all causes and 471,427 wounded, a total of 1,094,453 casualties.* More than ten thousand military encounters took place, spanning at least twenty states: one small town in Chesterfield County, Virginia, changed hands seventy-two times. In many respects, it has had the same defining character for American historians as the First World War for their British counterparts.

In 2011, to commemorate the 150th anniversary of the war's outbreak, *Time* magazine ran a special article. Its respected author, David Von Drehle, quoted from Lincoln's First Inaugural in 1861, a last-ditch effort to conciliate the South. In it Lincoln declared: "One section of our country believes slavery is right and ought to be extended, while the other believes it is wrong and ought not to be extended. This is the only substantial dispute." Lincoln had won the 1860 election with an Electoral College majority of 180 to 72 even though he received less than 40 percent of the popular vote and was not on the ballot in ten Southern states. He at once declared that he had no intention or power to interfere with slavery, only to restrict its expansion, but the South was not appeased (after all, as colonies, they had refused to ratify the Declaration of Independence until Thomas Jefferson removed the clause attacking the slave trade). Although four border states, Missouri, Kentucky, Maryland, and Delaware, remained part of the Union, seven others, seeing slaves as their most vital economic asset, banded together to form the Confederate States of America even before Lincoln took office in March 1861.

South Carolina, with the largest enslaved population, was the first to secede, on December 20, 1860, prompting one of its local politicians, James L. Petigru, to comment, "South Carolina is too small for a republic and too large for an insane asylum." Within two months, Mississippi, Florida, Alabama, Georgia, Louisiana, and Texas followed. After the war began, Virginia, Arkansas, Tennessee,

---

* This needs some perspective. The Taiping Rebellion of 1851–64, a very different conflict, cost more than 20 million lives, and four further rebellions, ending in 1877, a further 30 million, but that includes massive civilian casualties. The American Civil War figures, which are for combatants only, are probably higher than normally reckoned, since current estimates do not take into account the large number of official records lost in the burning of Richmond, for instance, nor all of the prisoners sent off to camps but who never made it through, nor women not at the front.

and North Carolina also seceded. (Kentucky officially joined the Union side only after the war was over, and Missouri, originally a slave state, remained neutral, although each sent thousands of men to fight, some on the Union side and some for the Confederacy.) The separatist territories covered a huge area, some nine hundred thousand square miles, and contained twelve million people, including nearly four million enslaved people and four million white women who were not allowed to vote.

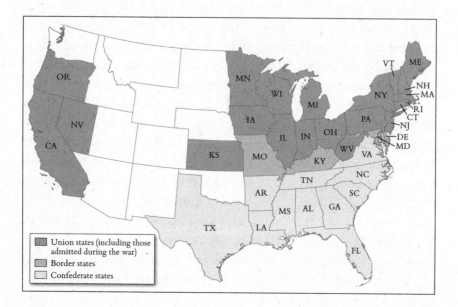

It was the leading Confederate general, Robert E. Lee, who named the American conflict the Civil War, although Northerners preferred to call it "the War of the Rebellion" and Southerners "the War of Northern Aggression." As often with great military encounters—the Battle of Waterloo is called "La Belle Alliance" in France, while the French also call the great engagement in 1870 (which the Germans call the Slaughter of Gravelotte) the Battle of St. Privat—even naming conflicts can be a partisan affair.

Hostilities are reckoned to have broken out on April 12, 1861, when Confederate forces opened fire on Fort Sumter in Charleston Harbor (the only casualty being a Confederate horse) and ended with fifty-eight-year-old Lee's surrender to forty-two-year-old Ulysses S. Grant at Appomattox, Virginia, on April 9, 1865. It cost the nation, then some 31 million, 2 percent of its people.

At the start both sides expected the struggle to end within ninety days, with one Alabama congressman saying he would mop up any blood that was shed with one of his pocket-handkerchiefs. On July 21, 1861, at Bull Run, the first land battle, when twenty-two thousand Confederate troops lined up against thirty thousand Unionists, the fighting was watched by crowds of onlookers, who traveled out from Washington with picnic baskets and champagne. A few enterprising vendors brought "pies and other edibles" to sell, flowers were stuck in gun barrels, multicolored streamers floated from saddles, and bottles of whiskey were passed around. But the war was anything but a sideshow. In the Battle of Shiloh alone (April 6–7, 1862), "a disorganized, murderous fist-fight," in one historian's phrase, more men fell—twenty-three thousand—than in the War of Independence and the war with Mexico combined. Weaponry had improved considerably since the last major conflict, the Napoleonic Wars, yet tactics had not evolved to keep pace. This new encounter was, to quote the historian Bruce Catton, "an all-out war . . . quite unlike the kind of war professional soldiers of the mid-nineteenth century usually had in mind," fought as an eighteenth-century conflict but with nineteenth-century weaponry. As a result, the carnage was horrendous, as both armies repeatedly marched head on, often uphill, into concentrated fire from entrenched fortifications. Frequently the noise of coughing drowned out the beating of the drums; yet from only a few miles away, sometimes because of the phenomenon of acoustic shadows, battles seemingly made no sound.

For every man who died from wounds, two succumbed to disease. Dysentery was the main killer, responsible for some ninety-five thousand deaths. The field at Shiloh was so covered in dead, said Grant, that it was possible to walk three hundred yards in any direction without touching the ground; at Antietam, noted General Joseph Hooker, whose Union forces were decisively defeated by Lee at Chancellorsville, "the slain lay in rows precisely as they had stood in their ranks a few moments before." Soldiers on either side felt they were encountering a new form of warfare—"we have seen the elephant," went the legend—something exotic, not encountered by most other people.*

A 10 percent casualty rate is considered a bloodbath, but Civil War battles often ended with three times that number—this despite the incompetence of the participants, an official study showing that Union troops fired one thousand rounds for every bullet that struck a Confederate soldier. Some 40 percent of the soldiers killed could not be identified; men took to scribbling their names on scraps of paper pinned to the backs of their tunics, so they might not be buried as unknown corpses.

Was the war triumph or tragedy, rebirth or mass murder? Could it have been avoided? What were its consequences? What really caused the two sides to fight? Was there a money motive? In 2011, a poll of 2,500 people across the United States revealed that two-thirds of white correspondents in the former Confederacy replied that the South had been principally motivated by "states' rights" rather than the issue of slavery, but for 160 years Americans have given a range of readings, depending on their perspectives and where they stood on the timeline. After Lee's surrender, the diarist George Templeton Strong confided: "They [the participants] can bother and perplex none but historians henceforth—forever." He wrote truer than he knew.

* * *

JAMES MCPHERSON, WHOSE *Battle Cry of Freedom* (1988) remains one of the best accounts of the war (particularly good on the leadup to the conflict), reckons it the most written-about event in American history. Another historian has calculated that it has led to some fifty thousand books. That estimate was made in 1995, and one can only guess how

---

* "To see the elephant" derives from the notion that an elephant was the most remarkable object one could take in at a traveling circus, itself a remarkable experience for most Americans. The first recorded definition of the phrase was in 1835: "to see or experience all that one can endure; to see enough; to lose one's innocence." See *The Veteran: Vietnam Veterans Against the War*, vol. 39, no. 1, Spring 2009. From the Civil War on, a related usage was "to see combat and death, especially for the first time." The metaphor endures. In the 1960s Eric Bagai, a former U.S. Marine, wrote "The Elephant," part of which runs:

We have seen the elephant.
We have gone, and by pure blind luck, returned,
Heroes, larger, no longer the same.
We are back, and we know the elephant. . . .
We've gone, and served, and somehow made it back.
Heroes? No. Just lucky, I guess.
But not the same. We've seen the elephant.

many more studies have been published in the quarter century since. Walt Whitman, for three years a volunteer nurse during the war, admitted: "Whatever we do, we must let our history tell the truth: whatever becomes of us, tell the truth." But people hold to different truths, and as Whitman later added, "The real war will never get in the books."

Over the decades since the war, a mix of other reasons has been put forward. For some, lists Von Drehle, it was the result of Northern aggressors brutally invading an independent Southern nation; or Northern Progress and Southern Decadence; or high tariffs setting off an economic war; or blundering statesmen too foolish to stop themselves; or the clash of industrial and agrarian cultures. Or it was an evil act that politicians failed to forestall; or war came because fanatics couldn't be contained; or it was all part of the Marxist class struggle; or the North wanted to stop Southerners moving westward, bringing slavery to yet more lands ("slavery haunted every step of Western settlement," writes the historian Jill Lepore). For Von Drehle, America has chosen to underplay the part that slavery played, "a massive case of amnesia."

Each notion had its advocates. For most of the hundred years after the war's conclusion, historians, novelists, and filmmakers "worked like hypnotists to soothe the post-traumatic memories of survivors and their descendants," in Von Drehle's words, cloaking the conflict in gallant myth. Denial played a large part, particularly in the South. First came the self-justifying accounts by Confederate leaders, and indeed most of the early books about the war were biographies or memoirs, officers on the same side often writing against each other.

In 1885 came Grant's bestselling two volumes of memoirs, in which, he said, he wished to "avoid doing injustice to anyone," but his most recent biographer, Ron Chernow, describes Grant's recollections as characterized by "breathtaking evasions." The same was true of the essays by other military leaders, who described their battles in elaborate detail but paid little attention to the conflict as a whole, let alone what one Yankee officer called "the tremendous n----- question."

An exception was *The Rise and Fall of the Confederate Government* (1881), a two-volume history by the ex-Confederate president Jefferson Davis, which he wrote a decade after his twenty-four-months confinement in a federal prison, where he was allowed no books but the Bible. It took him three years' research to complete what he described as "an historical sketch of the events which preceded and attended the struggle of the Southern states to maintain their existence and their rights as sovereign communities," but his account was even more partisan than earlier efforts, and he typically argued that "political demagogues" in the North had trumped up the slavery issue to acquire power. "Will you consent to be robbed of your property"—meaning slaves—he wrote, or will you "strike bravely for liberty, property, honor and life?" For him the Confederacy's defeat was a moral victory; though they were outnumbered, had far fewer arms, and by comparison with their opponents were grievously short of essentials (in the harsh winter of 1863, hundreds of men went without shoes and their feet froze to the ground) the South had fought with great courage to repel invaders whose dark satanic mills up north were the true exploiters.

Davis's views were part of a theory of Civil War history that became known as "the Lost Cause," a phrase taken from an 1866 book by a Richmond newspaper editor. The theory's followers embraced a set of beliefs that endorsed the virtues of the antebellum South and embodied a view of the war as an honorable struggle to maintain its independence while downplaying the actual role of slavery, which was presented as benevolent rather than cruel. After all, slave owners accounted for only 1 percent of the population. From this reading, the South emerged largely unrepentant, drawing strength from participants' memoirs, regimental histories, speeches at veterans' reunions, ceremonies at the graves of Southern servicemen, museums, archives, and the many paintings, songs, and films with Confederate sympathies. The Southern soldier was courageous and true; Southern armies were not defeated, just overwhelmed by numbers (Stonewall Jackson's men had hurled rocks at their foes when their ammunition ran out); and the Lost Cause's patron saint was Robert E. Lee. Commenting on Reconstruction in 1874, even Walt Whitman could declare without fear of being branded a bigot, "We have now infused a powerful percentage of blacks, with about as much intellect and caliber (in the mass) as so many baboons."

The United Daughters of the Confederacy, a powerful organization formed in 1894, set about monitoring school curricula so that their take on events would be taught throughout the South. Textbook publishers caved in to their demands, issuing different versions about the war, one for Northern pupils, another for the South. The United Daughters were also responsible for the erection of many of the Confederate statues that have caused such controversy in the present day.

By the fiftieth anniversary of the Battle of Gettysburg, in 1913, Woodrow Wilson—the first Southerner to become president since 1849 and a college historian before entering politics—was describing the terrorist organization the Ku Klux Klan as "an empire of the South," created by men "roused by a mere instinct of self-preservation."* In his anniversary speech at Gettysburg, he completely avoided any mention of slavery and once back in Washington issued an order segregating the city's federal offices. Two years after he spoke, the film *Birth of a Nation* premiered, a "great and vile movie," in Adam Gopnik's phrase. In it, D. W. Griffith presented the Klan as heroes, rescuing Lillian Gish from a vicious mob (white actors in blackface) bent on rape. Wilson is said to have commented: "It's like writing history with lightning. My only regret is that it is all so terribly true."

In 1929 Claude Bowers's *The Tragic Era,* a widely read work of history, provided an intellectual foundation for the system of segregation that followed Reconstruction—President Andrew Johnson's at best halfhearted attempts at reconciliation in 1865–68 and the North's undertaking to rebuild the South on antislavery principles. H. L. Mencken, ever the bigot, trumpeted: "The only thing wrong with Abraham Lincoln's Gettysburg address was that it was the South, not the North, that was fighting for a government of the people, by the people and for the people."

In 1939, a new Lost Cause drama achieved even greater impact than *Birth of a Nation:* David O. Selznick's *Gone with the Wind.* Margaret Mitchell's tale of plucky Scarlett O'Hara and the destruction of her "pretty world" had been the bestselling novel of all time;[†] now the film

---

* Six Confederate veterans from Pulaski, Tennessee, created the group on Christmas Eve, 1865, during the early days of Reconstruction, combining the Greek *kyklos* (κύκλος, circle) with "clan."

† It did have one rival. Harriet Beecher Stowe's *Uncle Tom's Cabin; or Life Among the Lowly* first appeared in newspaper installments from 1851 on. The two-volume book was an immediate bestseller, and not only in the States, for the British edition sold a million copies, three times its American number; in Russia it was the favorite childhood reading of both Tolstoy and Lenin, while Queen Victoria wept over it, and Heinrich Heine was reportedly so moved by its message that he converted to Christianity on his deathbed. Although not the most popular American novel of the nineteenth century (that accolade belongs to 1880's *Ben-Hur: A Tale of the Christ,* written by Lew Wallace, a Union general under Grant), it was the first American novel to be published in China and it energized antislavery movements in Cuba and Brazil (the last country in the world to have legalized slavery). Stowe's Uncle Tom, far from being the obedient old fool of stage adaptations, is a dignified figure who stands up for his race. Lincoln is said to have told Stowe that it was she who had started the Civil War by writing her tale. Stowe, a supporter of African repatriation who believed in a new Christian civilization in Africa, took pains not to

packed the movie houses. References to the Ku Klux Klan, which the novel calls "a tragic necessity," were omitted, and the opening title cards paid tribute to "a land of Cavaliers and Cotton Fields," a "pretty world" where "Gallantry took its last bow." Both Griffith and Mitchell/Selznick celebrate an antebellum South close to a heaven on Earth, then trace its fall into an anarchic postwar world of carpetbagging Northerners and malevolent, blundering freedmen. Such images were reinforced by leading historians such as William Archibald Dunning (1857–1922)

In 1913, commemorating the fiftieth anniversary of the Battle of Gettysburg, more than 50,000 veterans (8,750 of them Confederates) reunited and shook hands. "Elderly men wearing moth-eaten uniforms fashioned of blue and gray mingled and regaled one another with tales of their courage under fire" (Ari Kelman).

and Yale's U. B. Phillips (1877–1934), both of whom trumpeted the wickedness of the North, while teaching that Black people were "children" who could not appreciate the freedom that had been forced on them.

"Not surprisingly," writes Margaret MacMillan, "the old prewar South took on a golden glow, where men were gentlemen and women

---

vilify all Southerners or to present all Northerners as admirable, but despite her book's influence its popularity "stiffened the South's resolve to defend slavery and demonize the North." See David S. Reynolds, *Mightier Than the Sword: Uncle Tom's Cabin and the Battle for America* (New York: Norton, 2011). One might also mention the effect of Mark Twain's *Huckleberry Finn* and *Pudd'nhead Wilson* and their attacks on slavery, although they were not as influential at the time as they became later.

ladies, where gentility and courtesy marked relations among people, even between slave owners and their slaves." In this imagined world, "honor was inseparable from hierarchy and entitlement, defense of family blood and community needs." The Yankee victory ended this high civilization, and Reconstruction caused only loss and degradation. In 1877, Reconstruction was abandoned and Jim Crow established.*

What became known as the Dunning School, with its glorification of the Confederacy and opposition to Reconstruction, exerted a particularly virulent influence. Its views, says Eric Foner, "helped freeze the white South for generations." Many Southerners (and some from the North) received PhDs under Dunning then returned to the South, where they dominated the major history departments. A high school history of South Carolina, approved and promulgated by the state, has this entry on Reconstruction, typical of the textbook as a whole:

THE GREATEST PROBLEM

The sudden freeing of the Negroes would have brought serious problems even without the evil influence of the Carpet Baggers. There were more Negroes than whites in the State. The Negroes were uneducated. They had no knowledge of government. They did not know how to make a living without the supervision of the white man. They were so accustomed to

---

* The origin of "Jim Crow" (the practice of segregating and disenfranchising Black people in the United States) has been traced back to "Jump Jim Crow," a song-and-dance take-off of Blacks by white actor Thomas "Daddy" Rice in blackface. It first appeared in 1830 and was used to satirize Andrew Jackson's policies before being noted as a divisive force during the 1840s in the North, not the South, when railway cars were segregated.

Contrary to popular belief, blackface was not an American invention. In 1605, Ben Jonson wrote a masque, "The Masque of Blackness," specially commissioned by Anne of Denmark, the queen consort of King James I. It was performed in the palace at Whitehall, with Anne and five other ladies of the court all appearing in blackface. One observer noted: "Instead of Vizzards, their Faces and Arms up to the Elbows, were painted black, which was a Disguise sufficient, for they were hard to be known . . . and you cannot imagine a more ugly sight than a Troop of lean cheek'd Moors." *Memorials of Affairs of State from the Papers of Ralph Winwood,* vol. 2 (London, 1725), p. 44.

As for the end of Reconstruction, in 1876 the Democrats had won the intensely disputed presidential election, but neither candidate (Samuel J. Tilden, the Democrat, and the Republican Rutherford B. Hayes) commanded a clear Electoral College majority. So, in return for the Democrats not claiming victory, the Republican federal government slowly pulled its troops out of the South, formally ending the policy in 1877. It was a corrupt bargain in which the Republicans put power before principle and allowed the Democrats to condemn Black Americans to decades of further injustice.

being taken care of that they had no idea how to behave under freedom. They stole cattle and chickens and hogs, burned barns and stables. They were not willing to work. They were like children playing hookey the moment the teacher's back was turned. . . . They had nearly ruined the state during the years they voted.

The book was published in 1940 and has been regularly reissued, with only slight revisions. For years U. B. Phillips, the son of slaveholders, was the only scholar to examine the plantation economy, which he presented as benign and civilizing, the enslaved people being "submissive," "light-hearted," "ingratiating," and "imitative . . . serio-comic" figures. He also contended that slavery was not a lucrative system and would soon have disappeared on its own. This is a difficult position to defend, since in the decade before the war prices of slaves and land both rose by some 70 percent.*

But by the 1940s the North had generally accepted the South's racial attitudes. The South, went the adage, had lost the war but won the battle over its history. A synthesis of the process of Reconstruction based on Dunning's research dominated high school and college textbooks till the 1930s and was still widely accepted until at least 1945. In 1955, C. Vann Woodward pointed out in *The Burden of Southern History* that the South was the only part of the country to have lost a war, and as a result was drowning in nostalgia. More recently, William Safire, who served as Nixon's chief speechwriter, published *Freedom: A Novel of Abraham Lincoln and the Civil War* (1987), and Newt Gingrich, a presidential candidate in 2011–12, recycled the Lost Cause into a quartet of historical novels that served as a political outreach to Southern partisans. Meanwhile, Lee evolved from being an embodiment of the Southern cause into a national cult figure, "the realized King Arthur," deft surgeon to Grant's bloodthirsty butcher. The 1930s saw the publi-

---

* In 1931 the British playwright and poet J. C. Squire published a book of counterfactual essays, *If It Had Happened Otherwise*. One contributor was Winston Churchill, who wrote a chapter entitled "If Lee Had Not Won the Battle of Gettysburg," from the viewpoint of a historian in a world where the Confederates won the Battle of Gettysburg and then the Civil War, asking what would have happened if that were *not* so (the joke being that we know that it isn't). Thereafter, in this version of history, Lee supersedes Jefferson Davis and ends slavery in the Confederacy, an association of the English-speaking peoples prevents the Great War from breaking out, and Kaiser Wilhelm becomes the titular head of a peaceful United Europe.

cation of a four-volume hagiography by Douglas Southall Freeman (1886–1953), which came to be considered the definitive biography of Lee. Hardly mentioned was his hero's attitude to slavery beyond a throwaway line that his home state of Virginia represented the system "at its best" (Lee owned 250 human beings), nor that, during Reconstruction, he had opposed political rights for former slaves. Urged to condemn the Ku Klux Klan, he remained silent. Such facts took many more years to surface.*

The staying power of the Lost Cause version of history is all the more depressing given that 1935 saw the publication of the great Black activist and scholar William Edward Burghardt Du Bois's *Black Reconstruction in America,* a 768-page study that gave a sympathetic view of Reconstruction and vigorously challenged the anti-Black bias in the academy, not least showing the one-sidedness of the use of sources by Phillips and others. "The slave went free," he wrote, "stood a brief moment in the sun; then moved back again towards slavery." Americans couldn't understand the betrayal of Black people, he believed, if they didn't understand the enormity of that betrayal.

In its review, *The New York Times* commented: "There runs through the book a note of challenge which seems to point, in the author's mind at least, to the imminence of an inescapable and deadly racial struggle. 'There can be no compromise,' writes Professor Du Bois of the fight for absolute equality, for 'this is the last great battle of the West.'"

The book closed with a memorable final chapter, "The Propaganda of History," an indictment of the anti-Black take on events. "One fact and one alone," Du Bois wrote, "explains the attitude of most recent writers toward Reconstruction; they cannot conceive of Negroes as men." Despite excellent and widespread reviews, sales were modest, 1,984 copies from a first printing of 2,150, and although Du Bois's study is now regarded as a classic—a recent reviewer wrote that its author "looms over the study of African-American life like a cathedral over its close"—it was largely disparaged in white academic circles, and Du Bois found himself criticized for his attempt to fit the story of the end of Reconstruction into a Marxist framework and for his failure

---

* An edition of Hugo's *Les Misérables* (1862) in which all references to the evils of slavery had been omitted was such a hit with Lee's soldiers that they took to calling themselves "Lee's Miserables."

to use archival resources, in his day a near-impossibility anyway for a Black historian studying the South. The writings of his Black colleagues were likewise not taken seriously. Thus the Dunning-Phillips warhorse galloped triumphantly on into the 1960s, until at last civil rights groups successfully began to publicize its inaccuracies and to unseat its riders.

* * *

IN 1952, THE RESPECTED scholar Kenneth Stampp wrote an article in the *American Historical Review*. It began: "A survey of the literature dealing with southern Negro slavery reveals one fundamental problem that still remains unsolved. This is the problem of the biased historian." The prejudice spread beyond the issue of slavery or the heroism of Confederate soldiers into vilifying the commanders of the Union army. As a plainly irritated Grant had long ago complained:

> Our generals [have] had a hostile press, lukewarm friends, and a public opinion outside. The cry was in the air that the North only won by brute force; that the generalship and valor were with the South. This has gone into history, with so many other illusions that are historical.

Even if the slavery question was still not answered, at least a measure of revival in Grant's own reputation had begun in 1950, first with *Captain Sam Grant,* a sympathetic biography by Lloyd Lewis that took the Northern hero's story up to the brink of war in 1861; then, over a span of nearly a quarter of a century, Bruce Catton (1899–1978) produced a series of bestsellers that covered not only Grant but the war as a whole. Beginning with *Mr. Lincoln's Army* (1951), *Glory Road* (1952), and *A Stillness at Appomattox* (1953), the latter of which won the Pulitzer Prize, he continued with a second trilogy, and overall gave to the victors in blue something of the romance and aura that attached to the losers in gray; but he was also remarkably even-handed.

In *A Stillness at Appomattox* Catton describes the huge mine that exploded at Petersburg on July 30, 1864. It is a good example of his vivid style. "First a long, deep rumble, like summer thunder rolling along a faraway horizon" caught the attention of the Union soldiers waiting patiently to attack. There followed a swaying and swelling of the ground up ahead, with the solid earth rising to form a rounded hill, everything seeming very gradual and leisurely. Then the rounded hill broke apart, and a prodigious spout of flame and black smoke went up toward the sky, and the air was full of enormous clods of earth as big as houses, of brass cannon and detached artillery wheels, of wrecked caissons [ammunition wagons] and fluttering tents and weirdly tumbling human bodies . . . and all of the landscape along the firing line had turned into dust and smoke and flying debris, choking and blinding men.

Had he taken the details from a Union survivor? His books often read like personal memories, but with a heroic tint. In a sensitive account of Catton's career, the Yale historian David W. Blight recalls Catton agonizing in later years, asking himself if he had exploited the public appetite for an elevating myth that would obscure the terrifying reality of the killing fields—wondering whether he had indulged his readers, as well as himself, by telling what was in fact a gruesome story with such an eye for detail. Blight concludes that overall Catton had "a soft spot for secessionists and Confederate anti-statism" which in turn meant that he ignored the experience of African Americans, only belatedly acknowledging that their full emancipation remained "the profound . . . unfinished business" of the war. I recall attending a *New York Times* panel discussion in 2011 where Blight was one of the speakers. "Americans tend not to have an authentic sense of tragedy about our pasts," he told his audience. "We want our history to be triumphal. One hundred million Americans have a Civil War soldier somewhere in their family tree—'the Confederate in the attic,' something we can all share." Thus an abiding sympathy for the South together with an unquestioning optimism about America's place in the world contributed to a Panglossian story about the past. But even that story has many strands.

* * *

BY THE TIME THAT Freeman and Catton were midway through their long line of books, other views were being aired and establishing themselves: the Cambridge School, the St. Louis School, the Turnerian School, the Nationalist School, and the group, led by Charles Beard

(1874–1948, a professor at Columbia alongside William Dunning) that chose to emphasize the uneven distribution of wealth and the industrialization caused by the war. Beard and his co-author and wife, Mary, concentrated on those who had profited from the conflict and its aftermath; in their view, the eradication of slavery was directly linked to the rise of capitalism and the growth of the labor movement. Beard also said that if asked he could tell the entire story of the war without mentioning slavery except in a footnote.

This downgrading of the Black American experience continued with the revisionist school, led by Avery Craven (1885–1980) and the Illinois professor James Randall (1881–1953). As James McPherson sums up their view, this group "denied that sectional differences between North and South were genuinely divisive. Disparities that existed did not have to lead to war; they could have, and should have, been accommodated peacefully within the political system. But self-serving politicians . . . whipped up passions in North and South for partisan purposes. The most guilty were antislavery radicals. . . ." Randall saw the carnage of the First World War foreshadowed in the trenches and torched countryside of the Civil War, while Craven argued that the political system established by the Founders should have been resilient enough to accommodate the country's great diversity without the tragedy of war. It was the age of consensus history, in which most narratives about the nation were positive and a little self-congratulatory. But just *how* could peace have been accommodated? What would such an arrangement have looked like? It is hard to give a credible answer, yet such a theory won over many of the people searching to understand the conflict.

Even as Craven and Randall were propagating their views, other schools were challenging them. Energized by the Depression, the Southern Agrarians argued that Southern anti-materialism was necessary for the good of the country. The South was a principled, harmonious community, while Northern industrialists used the cloak of antislavery rhetoric to exploit the South for economic gain. Then in the 1960s came the "new political historians," a group that included figures like William Gienapp, Michael F. Holt, and Joel H. Sibley, which held that the tensions were based on differences like Protestantism or nativism, and that slavery was not the issue. When the antagonism became such that politicians could do nothing to assuage it, went the theory, the North and South blamed each other and war became inevitable.

These different takes reflect the times in which they arose. The "Nationalist" school gained heft after Civil War participants were no longer around to promote their cause; the "Marxist" and "Beard" claque, which stressed the crucial part played by economics, was at its most vocal during the Great Depression; the "Political" school, which aimed at a middle ground and avoided extreme interpretations, was the child of the consensus politics of the 1950s and the experience of congressional witch hunts that decade witnessed. Around 1990, the Comparative School argued that slavery's part in the Civil War could be understood only when compared to slavery in other parts of the world. This at least acknowledged that for decades slavery had been the elephant in the room—if not in the old soldiers' sense of seeing combat and death for the first time.

In 1947, the Black historian John Hope Franklin published *From Slavery to Freedom: A History of African Americans,* tracing African Americans from their beginnings in Africa, through slavery in the Western Hemisphere (over the course of 350 years, thirty-six thousand slave ships crossed the Atlantic), to the endless struggle for racial equality.* Allan Nevins built on his insights by examining the road to civil war in eight volumes starting in 1947. In the years since, scholars have explored almost every aspect of the conflict and its aftermath. In 1955, C. Vann Woodward published *The Strange Career of Jim Crow,* and a year later Kenneth Stampp, following up his 1952 call to arms, looked at the slave system from the perspective of the enslaved people themselves, extraordinarily for the first time, in his book *The Peculiar Institution: Slavery in the Ante-Bellum South.*

Ten of the first sixteen presidents owned slaves—Jefferson had a hundred and thirty, and although he penned, at the beginning of the American Revolution, "We hold these truths to be self-evident, that all men are created equal" he was to record in his *Notes on the State of Vir-*

---

* It is well to remember that slavery was practiced in Babylon, Egypt, Greece, Rome, Israel, Han China, and Japan, as well as by the Aztecs, Maories, Ottomans, and many European powers. It continues today in Mauritania, Mali, Niger, Chad, and Sudan. Exploitation is apparently a basic human trait, and subjugation as widespread as it is horrifying.

ginia (1785) that the future of the United States would never be secure unless the Black population could be removed. Although the importation of slaves from Africa had been outlawed by Congress in 1807, in the decades before the Civil War more than two million slaves were bought and sold. A really good male "specimen" could go at auction for as much as $1,750 (well over $40,000 today), and by 1860 one American in seven belonged to another. (In Colson Whitehead's carefully researched novel *The Underground Railroad* the main character, Cora, "was part of a bulk purchase, eighty-eight human souls for sixty crates of rum and gunpowder, the price arrived upon after the standard haggling. . . .") Of the South's nine million people, three and a half million were in servitude, nine out of every ten Black Americans being enslaved. The average life expectancy of a white man at birth was about forty-three, that of a Black slave about twenty-two (mainly due to undernourishment), and most slaves put in fourteen-hour days, if not more. To make their labor force work harder, planters beat them incessantly and imposed disciplines such as sexual humiliation, bodily mutilation, even waterboarding, which gives their conduct a depressingly modern resonance. Some 40 percent of those enslaved died within three years of their arrival in the United States.

At first, the North did not insist that the practice of slavery cease—only that it should not spread. In 1854, the just-formed Republican Party promised to restrict slavery in the new states and territories, so that free white laborers and farmers would not have to compete against slave owners. That same year, speaking about the institution, Lincoln declared, "If all earthly power were given me, I should not know what to do," and in his 1858 debates with racist senator Stephen A. Douglas he said outright: "There is no reason in the world why the Negro is not entitled to all the natural rights enumerated in the Declaration of Independence—the right to life, liberty, and the pursuit of happiness. I hold that he is as much entitled to these as the white man." But he was unable to use the Constitution as a formal document to end slavery, either during his brief time in Congress or after he became president. Letting enslaved people become equal citizens was impossible, because "the great mass of white people" would not countenance the notion.

It was not as if prejudice were restricted to the Southern states; as

Louis Menand has pointed out, "segregation began in the North, where it was the product not of the practice of slavery but of Negrophobia." As late as 1830, there were 2,254 enslaved people in New Jersey.* New York had slave auctions, slave whipping posts, and slave rebellions. "Prejudice at the North is much more virulent than at the South," declared the Black reformer William J. Watkins. Abolitionists agreed. Frances Trollope, the mother of novelist Anthony, spent time in the United States in the 1820s and wrote of the Americans she met: "Look at them at home; you will see them with one hand hoisting the cap of liberty, and with the other flogging their slaves."

There were others pointing the way. The great radical reformer Frederick Douglass (c. 1818–95), for twenty years enslaved and in the run-up to the war the most powerful African American in the country, declared the practice too monstrous for what he decried as the "whines of compromise." He was constantly at Lincoln's heels pushing him to take more of a stand. By the time of the 1860 election, Lincoln's public declarations had hardened: "Those who deny freedom to others deserve it not themselves." Yet the United States Constitution, written in 1787, conferred no such freedom upon African Americans, those enslaved being counted as "three-fifths of a person" in a famous compromise to give the South more seats in Congress. (Samuel Johnson had provocatively asked, "How is it that we hear the loudest yelps for liberty among the drivers of Negroes?")

When the Confederacy wrote its own Constitution, it proclaimed: "Our new government is founded on the great truth, that the Negro is not equal to the white man," and proclaimed its natural right to own human beings as property. To this Lincoln demanded that slavery be restricted, not abolished: hardly a libertarian response, in that this would have preserved slavery in the South, but he was trying to hold together a precarious coalition of Republicans, Northern Democrats, and Unionists from the border slave states that had not seceded. As McPherson says, "He was concerned—with good reason—that the first two parts of that coalition might break away if he took the kind of

---

* An 1850 census tallied the U.S. population as 23,191,876. Of these, 3,638,808 were African Americans, and the enslaved population numbered 3,204,313. As for Northern views, years later Malcolm X was to comment mockingly, "As long as you're south of the Canadian border, you're in the South."

bold action the radicals wanted." As Lincoln himself joked, but with underlying seriousness, "I hope I have God on my side, but I *must* have Kentucky."*

For more than two years Honest Abe, the Rail Splitter, the Ancient One, the Tycoon, the Great Emancipator—or, as Du Bois sympathetically described him, "the long-headed man with care-chiselled face who sat in the White House"—deliberated, even considering sending Black Americans back to Africa or, failing that, to tropical Latin America. On August 14, 1862, he met the first delegation of Black people ever to enter the White House and told them, with equal parts compassion and prejudice:

> You and we are different races. We have between us a broader difference than exists between almost any other two races. Whether it is right or wrong I need not discuss but this physical difference is a great disadvantage to us both, as I think your race suffer[s] very greatly, many of them by living among us, while ours suffer[s] from your presence. In a word we suffer on each side. If this is admitted, it affords a reason at least why we should be separated.

Up to the fall of 1862 it was official government policy that the war was being fought solely to restore the Union. "The hen is the wisest of all animals," Lincoln was to tell one of his generals, "because she never cackles until the egg is laid." He had no wish to seem a fool standing up for principles that couldn't be vindicated on the battlefield. Then, on September 22, 1862, after the Union success at Antietam, he felt able to proclaim that on January 1, 1863, "all persons held as slaves within any state [in rebellion] . . . shall be then, thenceforward, and forever, free." The order didn't free a single slave in the lands under Union control— Lincoln was permitting slavery to continue in such territories, putting off the day of reckoning—but it did give liberty to three million slaves in the Southern states. The announcement "set the South on fire."

From that point on, the North's ambitions had a moral purpose beyond the desire to preserve the states as one country. "The war was

---

* When Lincoln died, a Confederate five-dollar bill was in his pocket; one wonders why. But then he would steal away from the pressures of duty during the Civil War to see blackface shows.

ennobled," Lincoln told Congress. "In giving freedom to the slave, we give freedom to the free." The largest and wealthiest slave system in the hemisphere, one that had prospered for over 250 years, was coming to an end.*

Strategically, perhaps, Lincoln's announcement should have been a turning point but not in the minds of the American public, to whom the North continued to send mixed messages. While "saving the Union" united all parties, adding emancipation to the Union cause divided the nation as no other issue.

Even after the end of the war, the views of Southerners and "dough-faces," as Northerners with Southern principles were known, dominated the debate. Why did such opinions hold sway so long? McPherson gives one reason:

> When I entered graduate school in 1958, the historical reputation of the abolitionists was at a low ebb. The previous generation of historians had portrayed them as self-righteous fanatics who incited sectional conflict between North and South and brought on a needless civil war. . . . This image of the abolitionists persisted into the 1950s even as the tide of historical scholarship began to turn.

And yet it still seems surprising that generations of historians found it difficult to make slavery a paramount theme in any discussion of the

---

* In 1858, in a famous debate with Stephen Douglas, the Democratic candidate, over who should represent Illinois in the U.S. Senate, Lincoln confessed: "I am not, nor have I ever been, in favor of bringing about in any way the social and political equality of the white and Black races." But his views were not unchanging. Frederick Douglass made this final judgment: "Viewed from the genuine abolition ground, Mr. Lincoln seemed tardy, cold, dull and indifferent; but measuring him by the sentiment of his country, a sentiment he was bound as a statesman to consult, he was swift, zealous, radical and determined." *Frederick Douglass: Selected Speeches and Writings,* ed. Philip S. Foner (Chicago: Lawrence Hill, 1999), p. 616. More recently, the outstanding historian of Reconstruction Eric Foner has written, "The point is not that Lincoln was a modern egalitarian, but that unlike incorrigible racists such as his successor Andrew Johnson, he was capable of growth. As the war progressed, Lincoln's racial outlook evolved." Eric Foner, "The Not-So-Great Emancipator," *New York Times Book Review,* 25 June 2017, p. 14. Douglass had not been allowed to campaign for Lincoln, but at his second inauguration Lincoln greeted him at the White House reception not as "Mr. Douglass" but as "my friend."

In 1868, Ulysses S. Grant defeated Horatio Seymour for the presidency by the narrow margin of 304,906 votes out of nearly six million cast. Some 500,000 Black men, granted citizenship for the first time, took part—in effect, Black men won Grant the presidency. A grateful Grant must have realized, as Henry Louis Gates, Jr., has put it, "Black power, really, is in the ballot." Henry Louis Gates, Jr., and Paula Kerger, "Reconstruction: America after the Civil War," SXSW EDU conference, April 2019.

war. Possibly the North, intent on creating a lasting union, gave the South some leeway in portraying their history as a means of reestablishing themselves. "The decline of Civil War studies," Eric Foner wrote in his 1980 book *Politics and Ideology in the Age of the Civil War,* "was to some extent self-inflicted, for the subject had by the end of the 1950s reached a conceptual impasse."[*]

The 1960s, however, energized by the civil rights movement, witnessed a renaissance in the study of slavery, and a strong consensus called the "Fundamentalist school" emerged, among them Foner and McPherson. It holds that while slavery may have been the root cause, the North and South differed in fundamental ways: the former was a free labor society while the latter was committed to slavery and to extending its domain. Were new territories to be added to the Union as free states, the balance of power would shift to the abolitionists' side and the South would be compelled to change by democratic process. Foner in particular has argued that slavery was a form of organized labor, not just a system of racial domination, and that the North's victory, by identifying freedom with the ability to sell one's labor in the marketplace, reinforced the cultural hegemony of laissez-faire capitalism. Slavery led to the degradation of human beings into commodities. Giving up a slave was like giving up fossil fuels—divesting yourself of your most valuable commodity (indeed, in ancient Rome slaves were known as "human gold"). The Union Cause was just as much the subject of myth and reverence as the Lost Cause.

The various versions of Civil War history may mystify us now, but they reflected the times, the political winds, the communal needs and sensibilities—all these contributing factors that "tell it slant." Perhaps the efforts of the warring historians finally exhausted them, for by the end of the 1970s the subject again found itself relegated to the wings, part of "the overall crisis of academic history," in Foner's words, deriving from "an unprecedented redefinition of historical studies in which a traditional emphasis on institutions and events, politics and ideas, was

---

[*] When Foner was in ninth grade, so about fourteen, his history teacher, a Mrs. Bertha Berryman (affectionately known by her charges as "Big Bertha" after a famous gun of the First World War), described the Reconstruction Act of 1867, which gave the vote to Black men of the South, as "the worst law in all of American history." Foner argued the point, whereupon Mrs. Berryman told him: "If you don't like the way I'm teaching, Eric, why don't you come in tomorrow and give your own lesson on Reconstruction?" He did, and a lifetime's interest in the subject was born. Eric Foner, *Who Owns History?* (New York: Hill and Wang, 2002), p. 14.

superseded by a host of 'social' concerns" and new methods such as oral history and demography." But he also grants that the involvement of the social sciences has now helped historians of the war.

The Southern vision still persists, however. As the author and Harvard professor Henry Louis Gates has written, "the Confederacy didn't die in April 1865; it simply morphed." In 2010, the governor of Virginia issued a four-hundred-word Confederate History Month proclamation without a single mention of slavery, and films continue to give a romantic view of the old South. In October 2017, President Trump's chief of staff, John Kelly, opined that "a lack of an ability to compromise" had brought about the Civil War. This remark infuriated historians, who considered it "highly provocative" and "kind of depressing" that such a high-ranking figure should be so ignorant about his nation's past. But then there are few if any statues of the Black leaders of Reconstruction. In November 2020 CNN reported that only 16 percent of American high school students knew that the Civil War was fought over slavery. One constant in American history is its racism—even if that does not make the country unusual.

* * *

THE AMERICAN CIVIL WAR has come down to us in more than words. During the conflict, photography was in its infancy, but already it was shaping the course of history. The new art was advertised as the most accurate portrayal of a person, place, or thing, and in time of war people want to be fixed in memory, so that it became a technology of democracy. By the end of the first year of fighting, America had produced more than 25 million daguerreotypes. The demand for photos soared, especially *cartes de visite* (small portraits mounted on a card), and recruits would visit a studio before heading off to the front, having paid a dollar for their likenesses. At one popular New York studio, "the wait was sometimes hours long." Many soldiers died clutching pictures of their families—formed not just in daguerreotype (on silvered copper) but also in tintype (iron) and ambrotype (glass), more recent techniques that maintained the clarity of the daguerreotype but were faster and cheaper to produce.

However, by 1861 the notion of using the new medium to document events hardly existed. The first war photographer was an unknown American, attached to U.S. forces in the Mexican War in 1846. He was followed by three photographers who set out to cover the Crimean War (1853–56), forgotten now but important in helping define a new profession. It was still very much a new art form when in 1861 an established New York photographer named Mathew Brady wrote directly to the president asking permission to travel with the Union troops to record the Civil War for future generations. Lincoln agreed (he liked the camera, and over a hundred photos of him survive; one portrait by Brady became Lincoln's campaign button in 1864, while another graces the American five-dollar bill), and the young New Yorker set off with a state-of-the-art mobile studio that he had paid for himself. According to an authoritative account in militaryhistorynow.com, "This early photography method was first developed in 1839 by a French inventor named Louis-Jacques-Mandé Daguerre. It involved a rudimentary camera-like device that could project a scene onto a glass-encased polished metal plate that was treated with light-sensitive chemicals. The process, which could take up to ten minutes or longer to complete, required subjects to stand motionless for the duration of the exposure." As a result, Brady wasn't able to record battle scenes or anyone in motion, and his team of cameramen was learning on the job what a camera could accomplish in the rush of war—no photographs of cannons firing, bayonets thrusting, fortresses exploding, or the charges and countercharges of troops. (The first photograph of an actual battle, taken during the Franco-Prussian War of 1870, shows a line of advancing Prussian troops, from the approximate perspective of the French defenders.)

The early war photographers were an intrepid bunch all the same. In fact, during the First Battle of Bull Run in 1861, Brady let himself get so close to the fighting that he was nearly taken prisoner when the Union troops were overrun. (Officers had little time for journalists, regarding them as spies. As General Sherman noted: "These dirty newspaper scribblers have the impudence of Satan.") The technology was better suited to recording soldiers in noncombat mode. Brady took relatively few pictures (although often inserting himself in his photos, like Alfred Hitchcock in his films), instead installing himself in Washington and deploying more than twenty men into the field with traveling darkrooms, whose work he published under his own name. In all, his cameramen captured more than ten thousand images. No previous conflict had been so extensively photographed, and his work was the first coordinated attempt at photojournalism. Brady would even run an ad in the *New-York Daily Tribune* with the tagline, "You cannot tell how soon it may be too late," and at his carefully choreographed Washington studio one prop was a clock stopped at the ominous time of eight minutes to midnight.

One problem with Civil War photos is that Brady and his cameramen asked federal troops to strike poses as if they really were in action. The shutterbugs would rearrange persons and places in an attempt to create a more dramatic end product, and many of their images were later taken up as settled fact. They fudged identities and engaged in such misrepresentations as using the same scenes shot from different angles to depict different events. To take his classic photo "Home of a Rebel Sharpshooter, Gettysburg, July, 1863," Alexander Gardner, Brady's best-known photographer, dragged a soldier forty yards from a field to the rocks, carefully laid out his body, making sure the face was visible, and leaned a rifle on the rocks, all to present the most dra-

Dunker Church following the Battle of Antietam, September 17, 1862, one of the bloodiest encounters in U.S. history. At battle's end, the Confederates used the church as a temporary medical aid station. One nurse was so close to the fighting that a bullet went through her sleeve and killed the man she was tending. For many Americans exposed to the photo (taken by one of Matthew Brady's team), this was probably the first time they had seen images of dead soldiers, and must have brought home a new understanding of the war.

matic scene. Such attempts may have brought home how war looked, but they altered the historical record. In effect, they were frauds.

As well as battlefield reports, there were war paintings by such artists as Winslow Homer (working as a sketch artist for *Harper's Weekly*) and Eastman Johnson, or on-the-spot drawings of military actions by Alfred Waud and Edwin Forbes. The result was a body of evidence at that point unique in the annals of war reporting. But it was the photographs reaching the American public that had the most powerful effect. In his National Photographic Portrait Gallery, sited on the corner of New York's Tenth Street and Broadway, Brady opened an exhibit of photos by Gardner under the title "The Dead of Antietam." *The New York Times* commented: "Mr. Brady has done something to bring home to us the terrible reality and earnestness of war. If he has not brought bodies and laid them in our dooryards and along the streets, he has done something very like it." The philosopher William James spoke of how potent such pictures could be:

Only when some yellow-bleached photograph of a soldier of the 'sixties comes into our hands, with that odd and vivid look of individuality due to the moment when it was taken, do we realize the concreteness of that by-gone history.

* * *

WAITING IN THE WINGS was a historian ready to take advantage of all this material. In 1990, over five consecutive nights, PBS broadcast Ken Burns's account of the war. The original plan was for five one-hour programs; by the end the series had morphed into eleven and a half hours culled from 163 different sources. Burns made use of letters and journals, interviews, paintings, maps, quotations, and sixteen thousand contemporary photographs selected from more than nine hundred thousand in a mixed-media format, presenting an overview not only of the war but also the state of the country in which it was fought. More than 40 million Americans watched at least one episode during that heady week.

The stories were key. "After the Second World War," Burns has explained, "narrative fell out of fashion, and it was replaced by Freudian interpretation, later by a Marxist economic determinist interpretation, later by symbolism and deconstruction and semiotics, and later postmodernism and queer studies. They're all legitimate ways in, but strangely enough, the tortoise in this story that crosses the finish line long before the exhausted hare is narrative."

Starting his researches about 120 years after the war had ended, Burns had to solve how to convey the individual tales of thousands of participants. As far as witnesses went, there was no one left to talk to: the last surviving soldier had died in 1959. Burns turned to his frequent collaborator David McCullough to supply the narration, while celebrities such as Sam Waterston (as Lincoln), Jason Robards (Grant), Morgan Freeman, Garrison Keillor, Studs Terkel, George Plimpton, and even Arthur Miller gave voice to letters, memoirs, and news articles. Burns has added, in a personal moment, "My mom died when I was little, and a psychologist once said to me . . . look what I did for a living: I wake the dead."*

The filming was done before any script was put on paper. "We wrote constantly," Burns told me, "we never stopped writing, and rewriting again, which allowed a kind of fluidity that permitted this not to be a dry recitation of facts, not an exposition of an already arrived-at end, but rather the sharing with an audience of our process of discovery." In the end, his motivation was highly personal. "My attraction to any subject is based on what 'history' is mostly made up of—'story.' And I had been stunned by the way in which the centrality of the Civil War in American history had snuck up on me. I knew it intellectually; but its *emotional* centrality snuck up." That is why he filmed anew thousands of old photographs, taking as many as ten different new shots of a single image in order "to *listen* to the photograph."

He conducted all but one of the interviews himself, most notably with Shelby Foote, a noted novelist converted into a historian. Why give someone who had been primarily a fiction writer valuable airtime, when there were so many tried academics to call on? One evening in the 1980s, Burns had received a phone call from Robert Penn Warren, whom he had interviewed for an earlier documentary. "He said, in his wonderful Kentucky accent, 'Thinkin' about the Civil War. Thinkin' about, if you're gonna do it right, you have to interview

---

* In his autobiography, Colin Powell, when chairman of the Joint Chiefs of Staff under George H. W. Bush, writes of receiving videos of the series from Burns. "My family was so moved by the tapes Ken sent that I told the President how we had been glued to the television set for hours," Powell recalls. "He asked to see them. I sent the tapes to the White House, and he and Barbara were so impressed that it took forever for me to get them back."

Shelby Foote right away.' And that was enough for this wet-behind-the-ears novice to say, 'Okay.'"

Shelby Dade Foote, Jr. (1916–2005), was an original. His cultural roots lay in the Mississippi Delta, where he grew up, an only child born into a well-connected local family—his paternal great-grandfather was a Confederate veteran and a state politician. He attended the University of North Carolina for two years without graduating (he was not a model student but an insatiable reader, and on one occasion he spent an entire night closeted in the university library) before seeing army service during World War II.

His great boyhood companion and lifelong friend was the novelist Walker Percy (1916–90), whose great-uncle had been a Civil War hero. Both men set their hearts on becoming novelists, and Foote drafted his first fiction, *Tournament,* as early as 1939. Although it was turned down by Knopf as overly influenced by Joyce and Woolf, it was eventually published in 1949. The year after it appeared, Foote wrote to Percy: "I want to teach people how to *see*. I want to impart to them a 'quality of vision' (Proust's definition of style)." Besides Proust (he read *In Search of Lost Time* seven times) he was busy devouring Thucydides, Tacitus, and particularly Gibbon, whose narrative voice he admired especially. He planned to join them, writing Percy again in 1952: "Stand by: I'll tell you true—I'm going to be one of the greatest writers who ever lived." Percy held his tongue and cheered him on.

Four more novels followed in quick succession, including *Shiloh* (1952), a moment-by-moment depiction of that battle from the first-person perspectives of both Unionists and Confederates. The centennial of the Civil War was approaching, and on the strength of the impressive detail of *Shiloh,* Bennett Cerf, co-founder of Random House, commissioned Foote to write a short history of the conflict. The scope of the project swiftly outran its proposed length, but Cerf was understanding. The result was three hefty volumes, nearly three thousand pages in all, appearing in 1958, 1963, and 1974, together entitled *The Civil War: A Narrative.* Once the trilogy was completed, *The Dictionary of Literary Biography* commented: "It is possible to argue that no accounts of the great battles have ever equaled Foote's in their portrayal of relevant events and in their balance between the viewpoint and experience of commanders and common soldiers." As with Catton, Foote seems to be there alongside the soldiers. At Gettysburg, as

Pickett's men begin their charge, the men step from deep shade to bright sunlight and "the result was not only dazzling to the eyes but also added a feeling of elation and release." Then the enormity of their task dawns on them.

Foote wanted to allow events to unfold according to the logic of narrative flow rather than the demands of historical analysis. He describes a Union assault at Missionary Ridge, near Chattanooga, from the perspective of a Union colonel at Grant's command post, as he watches the "gallant rivalry" of the colors progressing up the ridge and compares them to a "flock of migratory birds" but then shifts focus: "That was how it looked in small from Orchard Knob. Up close, there was the gritty sense of participation, the rasp of heavy breathing, the drum and clatter of boots on rocky ground, and always the sickening thwack of bullets entering flesh and striking bone."

Modeling his work on the *Iliad*, with 214 chapters and an epic prologue, Foote still saw himself as an artist and not as an historian, or at best a "novelist-historian" who accepted "the historian's standards without the paraphernalia." The trilogy sold well and won noticeably good reviews, but professional historians were less impressed. This was the Civil War as literature and not as social science. Worse, not only had Foote omitted footnotes, critics claimed, but he had consulted just the 128-volume *Official Records of the War of the Rebellion* and published histories and memoirs. (This was a negligent criticism as well as unfair; in a persuasive bibliographical note appended to his opening volume, Foote gives a lengthy list of books referred to, including a thirty-volume history of the two navies during the war.) He was too intelligent not to give a nuanced view, but even so his conclusions were undisguised. He rejected slavery as a cause of the war; was sympathetic to the Lost Cause; presented Reconstruction, however honorable in intent, as a negative period; and was ambivalent about the emancipation of African Americans.

As a result, Foote had at best a mixed reputation by the time Ken Burns was assembling his group of experts and was not included in his first clutch. After Penn Warren's endorsement that changed, and Foote and Burns immediately hit it off. For his part, the author, now well into his seventies, was delighted to be recruited. He gave two initial interviews in his library in Memphis (his beloved copies of Dostoevsky in plain view), then took the production unit on a tour of Vicksburg,

Ken Burns (right) sits next to Shelby Foote, the Mississippi historian who dominated Burns's TV series on the Civil War. "[It] defined us for what we are and opened us for what we became."

site of a crucial Civil War battle. A year later Burns returned with a raft of new questions:

> I understood after a while that I was dealing with someone who had so internalized the Civil War—internalized it as a literary, a poetic, a linguistic, a geographical thing. He *knew*. He'd walked the battlefields, every single one of them. I'd toss questions out, rather like a grenade, and wait for the explosion to happen. [Shelby would say] "Oh, [he] had what he called four o'clock in the morning courage. That means you could wake him up at four o'clock and tell him that the enemy had turned his left flank and he'd be as cool as a cucumber."

Foote's contribution was vital. In an article in *Slate* published twenty years after the initial broadcasts, fellow historian James Lundberg described how the "shy Mississippi writer stole the show" with an endless supply of anecdotes, ending up a national celebrity, "the alpha anecdotalist," profiled in *Newsweek* and *People*. His books started selling a thousand copies a week, making him a millionaire. "Foote's face fills the screen," Lundberg wrote, "as he tells of a frightened Confederate sentry talking to an owl and you can smell the bourbon and pipe smoke and feel the terrible weight of Southern history in your living room." But while conscious of what the series had accomplished, Lundberg had one overriding concern: "Watching the film, you might easily forget that one side was not fighting for, but against the very things that Burns claims the war so gloriously achieved. Confederates, you might need reminding after seeing it, were fighting not for the unification of the nation, but for its dissolution."

Lundberg went on to argue that Foote, with his avuncular style and memorable anecdotes, speaking through his soft beard with a gentle drawl, creates an irresolvable tension at the center of a film series that attempts to give proper weight to racial conflict but that too often falls back on "grand pronouncements." After a careful fifteen-minute portrait of slavery's role in the buildup to the war, for instance, Foote tells the story of a "single, ragged Confederate who obviously didn't own any slaves." Asked by Yankee soldiers why he was fighting, the youth replies, "Because you're down here," which Foote rates "a pretty satisfactory answer." Foote's sympathies are with the underdog, and soon we are back in "the soft glow of nostalgia," appreciating the South's courtly leaders and its put-upon soldiery.

Is this a fair criticism? In my own interviews with Burns, he was at pains to argue the opposite. He believes that "for all the racial difficulties in the United States, before the Civil War, during the Civil War, and up to the present moment—we have in fact dealt with [race] better than any other country on Earth." His main criterion in making the series, he said, was

essentially to put our arms around the entire thing—as hopelessly romantic as that might have been—and to try to tell it as a story that we felt had been to some extent hijacked by previous popular culture manifestations of it. I mean, at least one thing, superficially: the two biggest Civil War films are *Birth of a Nation* and *Gone with the Wind,* all [sic] of which have it upside down;

that postulate that a home-grown terrorist organization, the Ku Klux Klan, was somehow a *hero*. We knew in our guts the opposite was true, and wished not so much to disprove the negative but to celebrate a complicated history of the Civil War that would permit northerners as well as southerners to invest in that story.

Burns has defended himself on Twitter. "Many factors contributed to the Civil War," he wrote. "One caused it: Slavery." He is not averse to notions of where he may have fallen short. He accepts that he might have focused more on the role of the radical Republicans in Congress, a group that during the war pushed through the crucial Thirteenth Amendment affirming emancipation, then after the war the Fourteenth and Fifteenth Amendments, and who would be at the forefront of Reconstruction. But going into the events after 1865 would have required "a whole 'nother film." As for the war itself, it provided Americans, "to an unmatched degree" with "the nation we became— including all the good stuff. Had secession succeeded, it's unlikely that there could have been a stable, tranquil coexistence between an inde-

W.E.B. Du Bois, a crucial interpreter of the war, yet for decades ignored or derided by the white establishment.

pendent North and South. Enslaved people would have continued running away. . . . There never would have been the sort of roisterous hodgepodge of wide-open energy that America became." Foote makes the point in the program that Americans perpetuate the grammatical error of saying "The United States is" rather than "are" as an unconscious sign of unity. "It made the country an actuality," he intones. "The Civil War defined us for what we are and opened us for what we became. It was the crossroads of our being—and it was a hell of a crossroads."

This strikes a convincing note, but it also introduces the suggestion of inevitable moral triumph, of an exceptional nation reborn, cleansed of its original sin of slavery and ready to shoulder its responsibilities in the continuing narrative of world history. David Blight tells us that "America is an idea that's always improvable," and so it has improved, to visible effect in our own lifetimes. The Civil War, in Walt Whitman's phrase, "condensed a nationality"; Burns's series captured that. But Blight warns: "Just now the idea of the American nation needs serious attention from historians." There is an element of self-congratulation, of unfettered optimism, as if we look back through nostalgic eyes. Eric Foner notes, "Americans have always had a highly ambiguous attitude toward history." And while the victory of the North marked the end of one great upheaval in the country's evolution and in some senses forged a nation, it heralded the beginning of another enduring battle: the civil rights struggles during a century or more of subjugation and violence meted out by whites to Blacks that came to a head in the 1960s and continue still in the era of Black Lives Matter.

Foner also contributed an essay to a book by historians commenting on the TV series, in which he notes that Burns devotes exactly two minutes to the years after the Civil War, that "Reconstruction" does not appear once (the five-hundred-page book based on the series mentions it just three times), and that the "facts" about Reconstruction—which after all turn the idea of the war as a unifying force on its head—have little meaning because they exist outside any historical context. He quotes the comment made by the literary critic William Dean Howells, "What the American public always wants is a tragedy with a happy ending."

That formidable African American author James Baldwin—born in 1924 to parents who left the South and settled in Harlem—wrote about the "90 years of quasi-freedom" that were misrepresented as "emancipation." He described the need to "free ourselves of the myth of America," the "most desperately schizophrenic of republics," and excoriated his country for having "spent a hundred years avoiding the question of the place of the Black man in it."

At the close of Burns's series, the Columbia University historian Barbara Fields comments that the end of the Civil War "was the moment that made the United States a nation—a real nation out of a theoretical nation." In this she was confirming what Foote and Burns believed—but then she adds, perhaps prophetically, "The Civil War can still be lost."

CHAPTER 12

OF SHOES AND SHIPS
AND SEALING WAX
The Annales School

———

The good historian is like the ogre of legend. Wherever he scents human flesh, he knows he has found his prey.

—MARC BLOCH, IN HIS LAST BOOK, *MÉTIER D'HISTORIEN*, LEFT UNFINISHED IN 1944

AROUND 8 P.M. ON JUNE 16, 1944, TEN DAYS AFTER THE D-DAY landings and a month short of his fifty-eighth birthday, the Resistance fighter known as "Narbonne" was taken in an open truck to a meadow surrounded by high bushes outside the village of Saint-Didier-de-Formans in eastern France. He was one of twenty-eight prisoners, handcuffed in pairs, pushed forward to face German machine guns, then mown down. An officer walked round the bodies and emptied his revolver into their heads and the napes of their necks. Each victim was stripped of identification and left where they lay. The next morning the local mayor buried the bodies.

Despite his advanced age, Narbonne had joined the Resistance in late 1942, but in March 1944 Vichy police captured him and turned him over to the Gestapo. He was taken to Montluc Prison, part of a fortress in the center of Lyon, where nearly four hundred prisoners were kept in cells intended for 120. Over several days, he was interrogated and tortured by the infamous "Butcher of Lyon," Klaus Barbie, but throughout the ordeal remained calm, giving up only his real name (to spread word of his arrest, including abroad, where he was known): Marc Léopold Benjamin Bloch—one of the most influential historians of the twentieth century.

Bloch died a Resistance hero, but he had already brought about a revolution. From 1929 till at least 1969, the magazine he co-founded, the *Annales,* changed the way that the past was recorded, as along with other French historians he widened the subject territory that historians could claim was within their remit. He is not only a highly appealing figure in himself; his breadth of vision showed that from economics to geography, weather conditions to birth statistics, the historian could roam where he or she pleased, taking in areas of study that had either been ignored or thought to be beyond his or her purview. He wrote of kings and generals but also of shoes and ships and sealing wax. Who knew that cabbage, a staple of diet since 4000 B.C., was made popular by the Celts?

An assimilated Alsatian Jew from an academic family (his father was a professor of ancient history at the Sorbonne), Bloch was born in Lyon in 1886 but studied in Paris, Berlin, and Leipzig, acquiring his professional spurs at a time that the discipline of history was profiting from government support. Scholarly journals sprang up and in 1896–97 the Sorbonne hosted the first course in historiography, overseen by Charles Seignobos and Charles-Victor Langlois, who became Bloch's teachers.* It was through them that he was told that historians should not concentrate on great men and great events but track the slow development of institutions and economic and social conditions, a view that would become his mantra in the years to come—*histoire totale,* as it became known. Another influential teacher, Henri Bergson, also based in Paris but at the Collège de France, argued that the past should not be divided into artificial chunks of time and space and that historians should develop "variable" measurements and wide boundaries that better fit an understanding of the human condition. As a third mentor, in 1900 a nonhistorian, Henri Berr, founded still another journal, the *Revue de Synthèse Historique,* arguing against academic specialization and in favor of all the human sciences being brought together in a grand synthesis.

For the young Bloch the years in Paris, from 1909 to 1912, were a heady time, working on his doctorate (on serfdom and emancipation in thirteenth-century France) surrounded by sympathetic scholar friends

---

* Not only Bloch's. In his collected essays, Fernand Braudel refers to their work *Introduction aux études historiques* (1898) as "this venerable book," adding that "for years it was a most authoritative work." See Fernand Braudel, *On History,* trans. Sarah Matthews (Chicago: University of Chicago Press, 1980), p. 8. From it, both he and Bloch learned to think in the long term.

in a major intellectual and cultural center of more than 2.5 million inhabitants. Toward the end of 1912, he secured his first teaching position,
a one-year appointment at the lycée in Montpellier, six miles from the
Mediterranean. The following autumn he moved to the lycée of
Amiens, a slightly larger city about eighty miles from Paris, again teaching children aged fifteen to eighteen. That year the twenty-seven-year-
old Bloch wrote a review of a book by Lucien Febvre (1878–1956),
criticizing its flamboyant style and language as well as the author's insufficient grasp of medieval social and economic history—unable to
foresee that he and Febvre would become close friends and longtime
collaborators.

Any further career plans were soon put on hold. When in August
1914 the Reich invaded Belgium, Bloch signed up for military service
"not joyfully but resolutely," a pudgy, myopic academic determined
to do his best fighting for his country. He was assigned with the rank
of sergeant to a regiment in the Meuse Valley, guarding bridges close
to the Belgian border. Bar a four-month secondment to Algeria, he
was on the front line for the rest of the war—after 1916, mainly in the
eastern Argonne—enduring heavy bombardment, poison gas, sickness
(he almost died of typhoid that opening winter), the regular death of
friends, extreme physical hardships, and numerous hair-raising encounters with the enemy. He learned to distinguish between percus-
sion fuse shells and time shells by the color of their smoke. In March
1916 he led a detachment of men on a charge to distract the Germans
from the main French attack on their trenches, an action for which he
was cited for bravery; on another occasion, undertaking a solo recon-
naissance, he had to crawl back to his lines under incessant German fire.
In the book he wrote about his experiences, *Souvenirs de guerre,* he likened being shot at to being cornered at a social gathering by a crank:
somewhat disconcerting. This was not braggadocio. Bloch was exceptionally cool in combat situations as well as being a superb officer, vigorous, knowledgeable, innovative, and, wrote his superiors, "possessing
unqualified authority over his men." He ended the war with the rank
of captain and the *Légion d'honneur,* France's top decoration.

With peace came a new academic posting, as assistant lecturer in
medieval history at the University of Strasbourg (the city having been
returned to France under the Treaty of Versailles). The university had
grown into a powerhouse under German control, and the French de-

cided to showcase it and attract the best scholars it could. The history faculty was before long one of the largest in France, and among Bloch's senior colleagues there was this "flamboyant" next-door neighbor— Lucien Febvre, whom he had met during the war when Febvre agreed to publish Bloch's first article. Bloch set down to work immediately, but on his furloughs to Paris he had other interests to pursue, and in July 1920 he returned to the capital to wed Simone Vidal, the daughter of one of France's leading experts in waterway navigation. The marriage produced six children.

Bloch was to remain in Strasbourg for seventeen years, a time of almost frenetic activity. He stood out as a teacher, his courses methodically presented and immensely erudite. Some students found him a distant and hypercritical figure, his prescribed reading lists dauntingly long and covering several languages, but for the most part he was cherished for his concern for his charges' and their families' welfare. He found himself more and more in sympathy with Febvre, whose energy matched his own. As Bloch's main biographer, Carole Fink, sums up, "There were, of course, significant temperamental differences between the reserved junior Bloch and the spirited elder Febvre. Nevertheless, this remarkable duo, with its force and its contrasts, left an indelible impression" on students and faculty alike.

Then there was their individual writing. In 1920 Bloch published his much-praised doctoral thesis "Rois et serfs." Four years later, making good use of his World War I experiences to analyze the role of rumors and false news, he wrote one of his most famous books, *The Royal Touch,* in which he examined the popular belief that had survived for more than eight centuries that kings could cure their subjects of scrofula (a tuberculous inflammation of the neck glands) simply by touching them. He asked why people accepted the rumor and how it shaped relations between a king and his people—a ground-breaking study that incorporated insights from medicine, psychology, social history, and cultural anthropology. He followed these books up with the even more revered *French Rural History* (1931), earning himself the tag "father of historical anthropology." He was determined, he announced, to "shatter" (*briser*) antiquated, falsely convenient categories or those that dwelt only on politics, war, and diplomacy. In the name of *"histoire humaine,"* he opposed all doctrines—particularly the over-disciplined approach preached by the Germans and system-builders like Oswald Spengler and H. G. Wells. He learned much from the writings of the French sociologist Émile Durkheim (who, like Henri Berr, wanted to unify all the relevant disciplines into a single social science) but had no time for Marx's all-encompassing theories.

His greatest influence, however, had come in 1929 with the founding of the journal first called (its name was to change several times over the years) *Annales d'histoire économique et sociale.** His co-editor was Febvre, and although the journal was published in Paris their base was in Strasbourg, which, with its central Rhenish location, active faculty, and excellent library, was a perfect workplace. The idea for the magazine had come to them in 1921, initially as an international review, but over eight years and numerous rebuffs they decided to make it a France-based journal, "a national review with an international spirit." That spirit was one "in which nothing would be out of bounds to the historian." It published contributions from the United States, Denmark, Czechoslovakia, England, Germany, Sweden, and North Africa (not, despite Bloch's hopes, from Italy) submitted by experts in sociology, ethnology, psychology, literary studies, and linguistics. Despite this collaborative attitude, the founders took on the brunt of writing, and between 1933 and 1938 they averaged sixteen and fourteen articles each, respectively, per year.

Febvre's life story in some ways mirrored Bloch's. He was born and brought up in Nancy, in northeastern France, although his roots and family were more in Franche-Comté (Besançon), on which he focused much of his future work. His father, a philologist, introduced him to ancient languages and significantly influenced his thinking. At twenty, Febvre decamped for Paris, to the École normale supérieure (as Bloch later did), and between 1899 and 1902 focused on history and geography. After graduation, he too taught at a provincial lycée, and again like Bloch spent the whole of World War I in the French army (based in Verdun). In 1917, Febvre had written to Henri Berr from the front:

---

* The original title ran till 1938, then was dropped for *Annales d'Histoire Sociale,* became *Mélanges d'Histoirs Sociale* between 1942 and 1944, then in 1945 *Annales d'Histoire Sociale,* until in 1946 it settled on *Annales: Economies, Sociétiés, Civilisations.* The *Historisch-Politische Zeitschrift* that von Ranke had founded lasted from 1832 to 1834, and the *Zeitschrift für Geschichtswissenschaft* from 1844 to 1848. The *Historische Zeitschrift,* founded in 1859, is the oldest scholarly historical journal to survive to the present day. It was followed by a host of French, English, and American counterparts, among them the *Revue Historique* in 1876, the *English Historical Review* in 1886, and the *American Historical Review* in 1895. None had the range and ambition of the *Annales.*

"I have a sense that social history will be the order of the day when peace returns and the painful and anguished period of social conflict and class upheaval begins." After the war, he found himself responding enthusiastically to the modernist movement, to T. S. Eliot and James Joyce and the new vision of his fellow Frenchmen.

In his first thesis, on King Philip II of Spain and the Franche-Comté (the province of eastern France that lies between Strasburg and Lyon, not then under French rule), published in 1911, he reconstructed the life of villagers and town dwellers by looking at historical events through the lens of geography and environment. By describing Franche-Comté's surroundings, he created an authentic portrait of medieval rural life, while also revealing the harm the French government had inflicted on the area. This approach would be a paradigm for his and Bloch's way of writing about the past.

Lucien Febvre in his garden at Souget, in the Jura. Fernand Braudel wrote of evenings listening to him as "we sat beneath the cedars in the garden in the gathering gloom." Febvre died in 1956.

The Annales School, as the magazine's contributors came to be known, grew to be the preeminent twentieth-century movement in historical scholarship. Friedrich Nietzsche had distinguished three approaches to history: the monumental, the antiquarian, and the critical. Such divisions made little sense to the staff at the *Annales*. The editors, "leftists with a socialist sensibility," set out a bold agenda that modestly embraced "the totality of the mental universe," in more practical terms all the social sciences, including currents such as microhistory (as eventually it came to be known, really being no more than writing that focused on small units of research, such as an event, community, individual, or a settlement). "There were forty of us there, barely out of uniform," wrote Febvre. "And we were advancing to meet one another with a sort of joyous spontaneity that we would never know again." Typical articles might focus on price and currency fluctuations in the Middle Ages or the effect of the arrival of precious metals from the New World on sixteenth-century Spain, but the magazine was also deeply interested in contemporary history, featuring articles on American society, the sociology of Nazism, and the economy of the Soviet Union. "Between the past and the present no firm partition," Febvre editorialized. "That is the anthem of the *Annales*."

Each blue-colored *Annales* edition was enthusiastically received, if by a small number of readers, rapidly gaining a warmer reception abroad than it encountered in France. By 1932 it was able to increase the frequency of its publications. It seems amazing that it could do so, for both founders had so many irons in the fire—teaching, books, articles for other publications, congresses, administrative duties, and their own families. (In 1933 Febvre founded and at first co-edited the *Encyclopédie française*, a major government-sponsored enterprise that was to run to twenty-one volumes.) Restive and ambitious, the two men were said to see eye to eye on all essential matters, but although each possessed a strong sense of fairness in dealing with the other, a history of continual harmony was part of a myth created by Febvre after Bloch's death. In fact their relationship was sometimes "deep and profoundly turbulent." Although each acknowledged the other's expertise, they had different personal styles, Febvre, the senior partner, more impulsive, Bloch more argumentative and penetrating. André Burguière, who was to write a history of the magazine, described them as being "like an old married couple."

Febvre's output of books was at least the equal of his younger partner's. They included *A Geographical Introduction to History* (1925), *Martin Luther: A Destiny* (1928),* *The Rhine: Problems of History and Economics*

---

* It is interesting that he should have written a biography, for his influential forbears Seignobos and Langlois had distanced themselves from the genre. Among French historians there was a tradition that individuals were not important; it was the structure of society that counted. So, while Febvre's doctoral thesis of 1911 was entitled "Philippe II et la Franche-Comté," the sub-

(1935), *The Problem of Unbelief in the Sixteenth Century: The Religion of Rabelais* (1937), *The Coming of the Book: The Impact of Printing, 1450–1800* (1958), and *A New Kind of History* (selected essays, English edition 1973).

Over the years, the *Annales* shifted from the socioeconomic to the sociocultural. "The world of yesterday is over." This succinct formula comes from Febvre's "Manifesto of the New Annales," which appeared in the opening pages of the very first issue. History expands, the magazine demonstrated, by taking in categories of material that hadn't been previously considered. Where could these new categories be found? A typical issue (November 1935) included remarks by Febvre defining the three essential approaches to a history of technology (investigate it, understand its progress, then understand its relation to other human activities), followed by an article by Bloch on "The Advent and Triumph of the Watermill in Medieval Europe," incorporating Febvre's criteria by pointing out the links between technology and more far-reaching social concerns. And as he inveighed against "the primacy of politics," Bloch became immersed in the retrieval and interpretation of village maps—indeed, maps generally, "the spatial representation of humanity's divisions"—and registers of landholdings that had been drawn up for tax purposes during various periods, material he saw as essential for analyzing French rural life. The magazine included notices about aerial photography; one colleague wrote about price history and the French Revolution, another about Taylorism, the factory management system pioneered in the late nineteenth century. There was the new subject of capitalism. Bloch concentrated not on "written testimonies" but on "vestiges of the past," such as tools, urns, coins, painted or sculpted images, funeral objects, or the remnants of buildings. These showed the "mentalities" of those who used them.

Bloch and Febvre were intent on examining human experience in the smallest possible narrative sections, but throughout the 1930s their disagreements multiplied: Febvre wanted a "journal of ideas," while Bloch began to voice practical complaints, being unhappy at the absence of regular meetings, delayed book reviews, inadequate communications with authors, and, after a decade of close collaboration, poor

---

title made the point that the book went far beyond traditional biography: "La crise de 1567, ses origines et ses conséquences: une étude d'histoire politique, religieuse et sociale." Even so, some two decades on he offered another individual life story with his study of Luther. Biography had not disappeared, but between 1930 and the mid-1970s it did suffer an eclipse.

liaison with his partner. Febvre was spending much of his time in Paris, having won a chair at the prestigious Collège de France in 1933, whereas Bloch was rebuffed by the college and had to wait several years before finally becoming a professor of economic history at the Sorbonne. (The stress evinced itself in his hands, which so seized up that they were almost paralyzed.)

Marc Bloch in his World War I military uniform and
in the last photo taken before his death, 1944.

They continued to write to each other often and at great length, not least because they wanted to avoid a bruising face-to-face encounter. However, neither man was willing to take over the magazine and run it on his own—or to bring about its demise. They submerged their differences and soldiered on. "The essential thing," Bloch wrote, "is that a team spirit should live among us." Fink describes Bloch at this point in his life:

At fifty, he was a distinguished-looking figure, small, compact, well groomed, and elegantly attired. His age was revealed in his balding, somewhat wrinkled countenance. A thick, bushy mustache stretched between his rather large nose and exceptionally narrow lips. His most striking feature was his pale eyes, which stared intensely from behind thick glasses, generally creating a serious expression but on occasion producing smiles of irony or genuine warmth. Bloch was a demanding but devoted husband and father. A heavy smoker, severely self-disciplined and nervous, in the privacy of his home [he] sometimes succumbed to sudden fits of anger which he ascribed to his "nasty character."

However, there were greater problems than Bloch's temper tantrums, for by 1938 the journal was laboring and its publishers had withdrawn their support. *Annales* was fighting for its life just as Europe drifted into crisis. When Germany annexed Austria that March, Bloch withdrew his contribution to a book honoring an illustrious Austrian medievalist, believing that "his nationality, his ideas, and his name" ought not be part of a work published in a Nazi-controlled Vienna. The following year saw the successful launch of the first volume of his two-book masterpiece *Feudal Society,* while he gave prestigious lectures in Brussels and Cambridge, but at the same moment the magazine was forced to go down to four issues a year. There were arguments with its publishers, culminating in disagreements over a special issue on Hitler's Germany. Bloch and Febvre decided they would forge on using their own resources. History was their mistress but also their master: that February, Franco toppled the Spanish Republic, then in March Czechoslovakia was dismembered and Nazi troops moved in. On August 24, Bloch, although exempted from active service because of his age, asked to be recalled to reserve duty. As war engulfed Europe, he found himself, in his fifty-fourth year, part of France's military force yet, as a middle-aged man, assigned pen-pushing duties, "paperwork and details." As he looked on in anguish and disbelief at the equivocations and ineptitude of his government in the face of German aggression, his patience broke, and during the three months after the fall of France he wrote in a "white heat of rage" one of his most personal books, *Strange Defeat,* an account of how his country had been overrun and a pungent assessment of his generation between the wars.

His next move was to take his wife and children, his eighty-two-year-old mother and a niece to nearby Clermont-Ferrand, where Strasbourg University had been exiled, and land a teaching job there. He was one of 310,000 Jews in France; the relocation could only be a temporary solution, and he appealed to the Rockefeller Foundation in the United States to support his family's rescue. It responded quickly, earmarking enough money for the New School to invite him to New York as an associate professor of medieval history. But over a year of pleas and bargainings, plans drifted, then floundered. Visas for his wife and younger children were promised, but he wanted to take his mother too, and she fell sick, too ill to travel. Nor could he get visas for his two elder sons, both of call-up age.

The fate of the *Annales* was also in question; with Bloch a non-Aryan co-proprietor, the magazine risked seizure or liquidation. On Easter Sunday 1941 Febvre wrote asking him to give up his position, and after initially refusing, on May 16, Bloch gave in. Febvre removed his friend's name from the *Annales* masthead, while Bloch transferred his family to Montpellier and took up a teaching position at the university there (not without its own difficulties: the dean of the Faculty of Letters, resenting a bad review Bloch had written, did his utmost to obstruct the appointment). Early the following February Bloch learned that German soldiers had occupied his Paris apartment, and within two months all his books had been appropriated. Anti-Jewish feeling was on the rise wherever he looked, and because of the threat of being physically attacked, Bloch was regularly escorted to his classes.

During these bleak months he was as busy as ever. He explored the roots of fascism and Nazism, read widely (particularly mysteries by Agatha Christie and Dorothy L. Sayers, while he even started to write a whodunnit himself). He sent love ballads to his wife. He also wrote four articles and several short reviews for the *Annales* under a pseudonym. Above all, he completed a draft of his book *Apologie pour l'histoire,* his answer to his son's question, "Tell me, Daddy, what is the use of history?" The book had two dedications—one to his mother, who had just died, and the other to Lucien Febvre, who may have run for cover but who was still a friend:

> Long ago we fought together for a larger and more human history. At this moment our common task is threatened. . . . The time will come, I am sure, when our collaboration can again as in the past be public and be free. In the meantime, on these pages filled with your presence, on my part it continues.

He was approaching his final act. By the end of 1942, France was almost completely under the German yoke, the increasing laws against Jews having cost Bloch his job, so that he was now out of work. The Nazis were becoming more brutal, more vengeful. The spate of new laws, roundups, and executions had stimulated the unification of the French underground. In early 1943, the three main nonconformist southern groups agreed to merge into the MUR (the Mouvements Unis de la Résistance); Bloch, still intensely patriotic and with a hatred of just standing by, decided to join them.

This was not an easy decision to put into action. He confided to his wife: "I didn't know it was so difficult to offer one's life." The underground, as with any successful resistance organization, was made up of tight networks based on personal contact and proven loyalties, and at first Bloch was not accepted. But he had colleagues within the Strasbourg faculty in Clermont-Ferrand whom he knew to be Resistance members, and eventually he was inducted (by a twenty-year-old philosophy student, Maurice Pessis) to work on a clandestine newspaper, Le Franc-Tireur. Its chief editor was to recall meeting

a gentleman of fifty, with a rosette in his buttonhole, a thin, refined face, silver-gray hair, and keen eyes behind a pair of spectacles. He was carrying a brief-case in one hand, a walking stick in the other. At first his manners were a little stiff, but, after the first few seconds, he smiled, held out his hand, and said politely: "Yes, I'm Maurice's 'colt.'"

Bloch was told to move to Lyon (his birthplace, which eased matters), where his first tasks were to deliver messages and newspapers. During these opening weeks, separated from his family, he lived in a series of furnished apartments, but he quickly proved his trustworthiness. As a result of arrests and of Resistance members moving on, by July 1943 he had risen to be Le Franc-Tireur's chief of the Rhône-Alpes region, its representative on the three-man regional directory of the MUR, organizer of the region's social services, and inspector of its ten départements. He and a handful of agents would decode and recode messages that they then delivered to other agents spread about the city, but his responsibilities multiplied and he was soon bringing order to a previously chaotic organization. He became "M. Blanchard," a traveling businessman. His wife could now visit and also send him food and clothing parcels.

He became mobile again, traveling to inspect units throughout the area. He wrote articles for *Le Franc-Tireur* and the more intellectual Resistance magazine *Les Cahiers Politiques,* as well as—perhaps inevitably—founding and editing an entirely new journal, *La Revue Libre.* But he was terribly exposed and easily recognizable. On the morning of March 8, 1944, a Gestapo car arrived in Bloch's neighborhood, and its occupants began asking about an elderly resident known as Blanchard. A local baker pointed them in the direction that Bloch, carrying a suitcase, had taken just minutes before. He was arrested on one of the city's bridges about nine o'clock. The next morning, the Gestapo raided his office and announced that they had discovered a receiving device and various papers that proved "the occupant was a member of the Resistance." In the course of that week there were about sixty further arrests of key MUR personnel. Had an insider betrayed them? It was never discovered. At least Bloch was beyond suspicion.

He was also beyond help. Following days of prolonged interrogation and torture, he spent four weeks in the prison infirmary in Lyon suffering from double bronchial pneumonia and debilitating contusions. To pass his remaining hours, he taught French history to a young *résistant.* As the Germans set about disposing of their mounting number of captives, they would drive off to isolated locations around Lyon, to avoid detection and retaliation by Resistance fighters. On the night of June 16, it took them less than twenty minutes to dispatch their twenty-eight prisoners in the field outside Saint-Didier-de-Formans. Miraculously, two of the men survived and were able to recount what had happened. Marc Bloch was not one of them. Eight weeks later, his death was officially established when his daughter Alice and his sister-in-law identified his personal effects—his spectacles, some pieces of his jacket and tie, and the three medals for bravery that he always wore.[*]

---

[*] Clive James has written a moving account of Bloch in his compendium *Cultural Amnesia.* It concludes: "He knew what he was up against. The drowning pool, the truncheon, the thumbscrew and the blowtorch: for an imagination like his, those things must have been almost as terrible in prospect as they were in actuality. But he risked it anyway." Clive James, *Cultural Amnesia* (New York: Norton, 2007), p. 62.

* * *

FEBVRE CARRIED THE *ANNALES* through the remaining months of the war and into the postwar period. Needing to secure his succession, he gathered younger colleagues such as Georges Friedmann (a Marxist and sociologist) and Charles Morazé onto the board while adding new collaborators from as diverse backgrounds as possible. The most notable was Fernand Braudel (1902–85).

This extraordinary historian was born in the small Meuse village of Luméville-en-Ornois in Lorraine, in northeastern France, and was always proud of his "peasant stock." For some years he lived with his paternal grandmother, although his father, a passionately anticlerical teacher of mathematics, was also an influence. Fernand fell in love with history early, while also writing poetry, although he initially wanted to study medicine until his father directed otherwise. Perhaps the frame of mind that had made him want to become a doctor influenced his love of analyzing evidence. André Burguière, who succeeded him as editor of the *Annales* magazine, supports this idea: "A latent Darwinism in his approach to societies," he says, might "be credited for his distinctiveness from the Annales tradition." Braudel's analytic method "borrows its principles of reasoning from the model of the biological sciences." Maybe; but as Alexander Lee, a fellow in the Centre for the Study of the Renaissance at the University of Warwick, writes, when Braudel came to compose his great works it was "in the manner of a novelist rather than of a historian proper"; in the preface to its first edition he even described himself as an *écrivain* rather than as an *historien*.

Braudel came to the Annales group late, in 1938, when already in his midthirties. After studying at the Sorbonne (where he came under the influence of the first French Marxists) he had spent eight years teaching in Algeria, becoming fascinated by the Mediterranean and its environs (inventing the term *geohistory*). Lee waxes lyrical about this extraordinary period in the young academic's life:

> He experienced his new environment in a manner comparable to that of many other French literary figures who took up life in the colonies at the same time. Able at last to see France from a distance, Braudel, like André Malraux, cast off his patriotism and opened his heart to wider possibilities. But like Antoine de

Saint-Exupéry, he also fell in love with the landscape, enchanted not only by the smell of the souks, the narrow streets and the scorching heat, but also by the romance of the desert and by the vast, rolling rhythms of the sea.

His outlook changed. He began writing his doctoral thesis on Phillip II and Spanish policy in the Mediterranean. His approach, however, was still rooted in traditional methods and he continued to concentrate on diplomatic history.

In 1930, while still in Algiers, he by chance met the historian Henri Pirenne (1862–1935). Pirenne's work was based on the idea that socio-economic, cultural, and religious movements were the result of underlying causes unnoticed in traditional approaches to investigating the past. In Lee's retelling, Pirenne "spoke of history as an adventure, rather than as a subject for research, and of the sea as a character, with its own personality and voice, rather than as a setting for human drama." It was after this, Braudel's wife was to recall, "that he began to dream of the Mediterranean in itself, of its ancient and fabulous history, so much more colourful and exciting in the imagination than the sad personality of Philip II."

In 1932 Braudel returned to France, to teach in various Paris lycées. In 1924 he had come across Lucien Febvre's *The Earth and Human Evolution,* and by 1927 the two were regularly exchanging letters. Febvre advised him to reverse his thesis subject, so rather than its being "Philip II and the Spanish Policy in the Mediterranean" the emphasis should be "The Mediterranean and Philip II." This led to Braudel concentrating on the sea as a historical space with its own special time span, a world of mountains, peninsulas, and geographical limits.

There was one more important posting in his education as a historian, one that allowed him to distance himself from Parisian intellectual rivalries. Early in the century a surprising number of French sociologists and economists had settled in Brazil, particularly around Rio de Janeiro and São Paulo, and in 1934 Braudel, along with the anthropologist Claude Lévi-Strauss, accepted an invitation to establish São Paulo's first university. He later said his three years there were the happiest period of his life. Certainly the mix of Lorraine, the North African years, and the South American experience helped him appreciate long-distance links. It was important, he said, to feel "surprise and distance—those important aids to comprehension are both equally necessary for an understanding of that which surrounds you—surrounds you so evidently that you can no longer see it clearly."

In 1937 he returned to Paris to concentrate on his doctorate, and found himself aboard the same ship as Lucien Febvre. By the time they reached port, Febvre had become something of a father figure to the burgeoning scholar, and advised on early versions of the book Braudel was writing. However, on June 29, 1940, the younger man, having been called up for military service, was captured by the Germans and spent more than five years in captivity, first at the Oflag XII-B camp in Mainz then in another camp near Lübeck in northern Germany.

The myth has arisen that it was while he was a prisoner that Braudel drafted his masterwork, the two-volume, 1,375-page history of the Mediterranean. That would have been a miracle of memory and composition, and it is only partly true. Even in prison he was allowed to exchange letters with Febvre, both writing to each other in code, while one of the German guards would pass on material that Braudel wanted from the local library, and he certainly had plenty of time to reflect on what he had already drafted. He also set up a "camp university," giving lectures to his fellow inmates, who nicknamed him "Magnifizenz." In his talks he liked to cheer his fellows by reminding them that the propaganda they were fed by their guards was "nothing but events" and that what counted was life in the long term, the slowly emerging structures that took years to put in place—a way of thinking that of course directly linked with his book ideas.

Even so, the bulk of his notes were at his home in France and he has recorded that he had begun work on a draft as early as 1923. "Moreover," his book's preface adds, "*The Mediterranean* does not date from 1949, when it was first published, nor even from 1947, when it was defended as a thesis at the Sorbonne. The main outline of the book was already determined if not entirely written by 1939, at the close of the dazzling early period of the *Annales* of Marc Bloch and Lucien Febvre, of which it is the direct result."

After the war Febvre (who during Braudel's "interminable imprisonment" had sent him provisions and in May 1945 invited him to lodge at his house) ensured that he should become leader of the second wave of Annales historians and would himself retire from the Collège de France in 1949, leaving the way for his protégé to take his place. Braudel worked frenetically on his thesis, and within two years was able to defend it before a board of leading French historians. All but one acclaimed it a triumph. "Bowled over by his daring sweep and its mastery of detail," writes Lee, "they recognised it immediately as a masterpiece." But its brilliance stemmed not so much from Braudel's scholarship as from his willingness to think and write like a novelist, its true importance lying "not in its elucidation of the Annales school's approach but in its demonstration of the power of the literary imagination."

Before long *The Mediterranean* was also taking the French reading public by storm, its author compared to historians from Thucydides to Gibbon. Braudel must have been particularly pleased when Febvre (to whom the first volume is dedicated) pronounced the trilogy a "perfect historical work . . . more than a professional masterpiece. A revolution in the way of conceiving history." Foreign readers were equally impressed. Hugh Trevor-Roper summed up the general view: "We are amazed by Braudel's range of illustration, his eye for detail, his power to select, animate, generalize. He seems to know every crease in these mountains, every island in that sea, every climactic freak, every human response to the problems which they pose." Colin Wells says nicely that "one gets the feeling, reading it, that here, perhaps, the inclusive and ever-inquisitive spirit of Herodotus has found new expression." As Braudel was to tell Eric Hobsbawm, "historians are never on holiday, on vacation. They are always, so to speak, on the job. Whenever . . . I get into a train, I learn something. And I think it is very important because this is another way of saying, 'be open to new phenomena.'"

In a 1996 seminar, the historian Alan Macfarlane suggested that Braudel's time as a prisoner of war had caused him to fuse his thoughts into a new synthesis, his helplessness and remorse at the defeat of his beloved France crucially shaping his most famous contribution to historical method, "the distinction between the three levels of time," comparable to "vertical thinking" in archaeology—the *longue durée,* being thousands of years, geological time in which one can chart long-term climactic changes; the *moyenne durée,* taking in decades or hundreds of years and covering economic and social occurrences, for example, the Industrial Revolution; and the *courte durée,* running from days to a year, a battle or an election, a *nouvelle sonnante* (a "matter of moment"), as Braudel named it, recalling a phrase used in the sixteenth century. As he described his personal evolution,

Fernand Braudel in 1937 during his time in Brazil, and in later years as doyen of the French Academy. "French school? A Frenchman hardly dares utter the phrase," he wrote in "The Situation of History in 1950."

All these occurrences that poured in upon us from the radio and the newspapers of our enemies, or even the news from London, which our clandestine receivers gave us—I had to outdistance, reject, deny them. Down with occurrences, especially vexing ones! I have to believe that history, destiny, was written at a much more profound level.

As soon as the first volume of *The Mediterranean* was published, he started on the second, which he envisaged as a single companion volume, to complement works by Febvre and others: instead, it ended up, twenty-five years on, as part of a massive undertaking without equal in twentieth-century history writing. Throughout, he enthusiastically made use of insights from other social sciences, downplayed the importance of "the jolts of short time" (he believed that narrative *was* important, but it should not be restricted to individuals' stories), and above all popularized the notion of the *longue durée*. This meant no more than "the long period," which in Braudel's hands came to signify a way of looking beyond the normal time periods that historians used, "thickening time" to focus on changes over two or three centuries, particularly in matters of geography and the environment, with their slow, almost imperceptible movements. This allowed historians to consider long-term patterns, the rise and fall of particular groups, or how changes in urbanism, language, travel, or the climate altered people's lives—but over centuries, not packaged into short-term periods. Political history was the froth of waves; the history that mattered was found far below the surface.

These were not in themselves new insights: David Hume, having read Montesquieu's *De l'Esprit des Lois* ("Spirit of the Laws") in 1749, had been converted to the view of history as a continuing process, governed by geography, climate, economic forces, laws, institutions, and religion, all of which could be affected to a limited extent but not controlled by the intervention of individuals. More recently, Jacob Burckhardt, in Germany, with *The Civilization of the Renaissance in Italy* (1860), and the Dutch historian Johan Huizinga, with *The Waning of the Middle Ages* (1919), had attempted to give a portrait of a whole culture. "There is also," adds Chris Wickham, professor of history at All Souls College, Oxford, "a traditional divide, still continuing, between a German preference for histories of political power, aristocratic identity, and socio-legal categories, and a French one for regional socio-economic and socio-political studies—the Belgians have for their part dominated economic history, though this is an area where all three national traditions meet." The phrase *l'histoire immobile* was actually coined by Braudel's successor, Emmanuel Le Roy Ladurie, forming the title of his inaugural lecture at the Collège de France.

Here Ernest Labrousse (1895–1988), although not a member of the Annales school, was an important influence and as chair of social history at the Sorbonne directed the theses of most of the third generation of Annales historians. In his two main books he had set down three headings that Braudel now picked up and expanded on: the time spans based on structure, conjuncture, and event. But in the younger man's hands these elements were forged anew. Braudel himself wrote: "History—perhaps the least structured of the sciences of man—accepts the lessons of its diverse neighbouring disciplines and endeavours to echo them in its own research."

From 1750 till the end of the Second World War, Braudel demonstrated, Europe's fate had largely been decided by demographics, and under his leadership his contemporaries continued to explore subjects usually outside their purview—"indirect" knowledge, such as the differing curves of population growth. France itself had been displaced from its prime position in Europe largely because its citizens were having fewer children. The same phenomenon was also seen in Ireland, where people married ever later, got drunk most Saturday nights, and so hardly ever touched one another—a startling but incontrovertible finding, but not a factor that those who wrote about the past had previously thought to research. (Although *The Mediterranean* suffers from a complete absence—not a single line—relating to religion: Braudel never sloughed off his father's agnosticism.)

Despite this odd blemish, the emphasis on social history influenced biblical scholars (especially in the United States, but only from the late 1970s on, when Braudel was finally published there). Certain questions were forcing themselves to the fore—such as whether the past had any systematically accessible story at all. The study of climate ("history without men") had previously been the job of climatologists, if anyone's. Now it was a legitimate area for historical research.

Braudel echoed the great Arab historian Ibn Khaldūn's complaint over the geographical convention by which Europe was designated a separate "continent" when it is more accurately a peninsula or adjunct to the great Eurasian landmass. Historians became less Europe-centric. Further, during this postwar period scholars recognized that most European languages were closely related to those of the Indian subcontinent. It was found that Icelanders are more than 70 percent Irish by gene (and almost entirely through the female side). Had Irish slaves ended up there? A prehistoric culture north of the Black Sea, known as the Kurgan (in Russian, "artificial mound" or "barrow"), suddenly got on the move and their descendants sent their languages as far as the Philippines and down through east India as far as Bengal—we know that this was so not through any conscious record but from the languages we speak. In Paraguay, Argentina, Bolivia, and Brazil, the main languages were Guarani and either Spanish or Portuguese and Dutch. In Haiti, they spoke heavily Africanized French. These were new areas, but the Annales group felt it their job to cover them.

Braudel followed up his Mediterranean book with a three-volume history of the preindustrial modern world, *Capitalism and Material Life,*

1400–1800, published from 1967 on in France and in English in 1979 (*The Structures of Everyday Life, The Wheels of Commerce,* and *The Perspective of the World*). Continuing to hew to the notion of the *longue durée,* Braudel claimed that there were long-term cycles in the capitalist economy that developed in western Europe in the twelfth century, with particular cities following one another as the matrixes of those rotations: Venice and Genoa, then Antwerp, next Amsterdam, and finally London in the mid-eighteenth till late nineteenth centuries.

Over the next two decades, a steady stream of shorter books followed, on a variety of subjects but all emphasizing the importance of slaves, serfs, peasants, and the urban poor: those on the margins of society. Such works helped cement the reputation of the *Annales* magazine, of which he was both director and editor, but Braudel, a man of great creative energy, was also determined to extend its reach. In 1947, along with Febvre, Charles Morazé, and, crucially, Ernest Labrousse, he obtained financing both from the French government and from the Rockefeller Foundation to found a special "Sixth Section" at the École Pratique des Hautes Études, helping it become the most important center for teaching and research in the social sciences in France. Fifteen years later he used Ford Foundation money to create the Fondation Maison des Sciences de l'Homme, an independent body that disseminated the *Annales* approach to the rest of Europe and beyond.

The net result of these quasi-political initiatives was that Braudel changed the magazine from being a small club for historians and economists to being of worldwide influence. But he did it in his own way; he was difficult to imitate and founded no school, had few pupils, and no disciples. André Burguière characterized him as paternalist ("he would take on staff who wouldn't have been hired by other magazines") and audacious, prone to changing his mind about people (such as Roland Barthes, whom he recruited but later came to loathe). Old habits of introversion and disciplinary quarrels once again assumed an upper hand, while the student uprisings of 1968 deeply offended Braudel, who stepped down from the magazine largely because of the protests, although he continued working for his foundations till shortly before his death in 1985, his place assured as one of the century's great historians.

* * *

A THIRD WAVE NOW took over, among them Emmanuel Le Roy Ladurie (b. 1929); François Furet (1927–97), like Ladurie an ex-Communist, and author of the classic *La Révolution Française* (1965–66); Philippe Ariès (1914–84), whose main interest was the French Revolution; Jacques Le Goff (1924–2014); Marc Ferro (b. 1924), an expert on Russia and the Soviet Union as well as cultural history; Jacques Revel (b. 1942), co-author of *The Vanished Children of Paris* (1991); and André Burguière (b. 1938), under whose editorship the magazine went from three thousand copies per issue to five thousand, a figure never since exceeded. Le Goff, the author of more than twenty books and one of the world's foremost medievalists, was formally named co-editor, and in 2014 rounded off his career with a volume very much in the Annales mode, *Must We Divide History into Periods?* ("I ask only that the Renaissance be seen in proper proportion, as a brilliant but superficial interlude.") Despite such a distinguished group, French historians fell behind other leading countries, not only in Europe but also in the United States, unable to organize themselves or make good use of the accumulation of new knowledge in their hands. But by then the principal work of its founders was done.

The most famous member of the school, Ladurie, was another whose life and career were shaped by the Second World War. For several months in 1942, his father, Jacques, was minister of agriculture in the Vichy government of Marshal Philippe Pétain. The family was of old Norman stock, descended from a former Catholic priest who gave up his vocation to marry a parishioner, and was ennobled by the king (though presumably not for that). The family had dropped the aristocratic "de" from their name for fear of being persecuted in the run-up to the revolution.

They continued to have a roller-coaster history. Jacques Le Roy Ladurie was politically conservative and in 1933 supported the quasi-fascist Greenshirts. After becoming a government minister he came into conflict with Pierre Laval over Nazi demands and in 1942 resigned, joining the Resistance and fighting for the Maquis around Orléans, at one point being arrested and beaten. This change of colors was not enough to prevent his imprisonment after the war for his time serving under Pétain, although six months later the High Court of Justice dismissed the charges in view of his Resistance activity. Although he was reelected as mayor of Les Moutiers-en-Cinglais, his participation in Vichy left a pall of shame over the family.

His historian son recalls supporting Pétain as a child, then living through his family's fall from grace. "I have remained fascinated since then with what we call decline and fall," he told one interviewer. "France is full of people who became very important, then became nothing. My fascination is probably due to the fact that my own family was once important and then became zero." His devoutly Catholic family had expected him to become a priest, then a soldier, then a businessman, but he decided instead to concentrate on being a historian. The leading role played by Communists in the Resistance, the willingness of traditional French elites to support the Vichy regime, and the seeming success of Stalin's planned economy and his "scientific socialism" led Ladurie to embrace Communism, and in 1949, aged twenty, he joined the Party and emerged a confirmed Stalinist. The PCF, as the French branch was called, showily advertised itself as the "party of 75,000 shot"—an allusion to the charge that between 1941 and 1944 the

Emmanuel Le Roy Ladurie, photographed at the Bibliothèque Nationale in 1987, when he was fifty-eight, and in 2014.

Germans had put to death seventy-five thousand French Communists (the true figure was ten thousand), but independent of this claim the PCF had acquired formidable prestige stemming from its Resistance role. Ladurie described his generation as traumatized: "If we are subjected to violence, we will in turn be violent towards others. It is like someone who is sodomized and then sodomizes others."*

He quickly made a professional hit with his doctoral thesis, *Les paysans de Languedoc,* published as a book in 1966. In this study of southern French peasantry over several centuries, he employed a huge range of information such as tithe records, wage books, tax receipts, and rent receipts to bring to life a far-off people's feelings—the history of *mentalités,* of mindsets and worldviews, all very much in the Annales style. Then came a major stroke of luck. Looking around for a new subject he delved into the local archives in Montpellier, his wife's hometown, where he had gone as a lycée teacher and later research fellow at the university. There he came across a reference to a fourteenth-century document, the detailed register of Jacques Fournier, bishop of Pamiers and a future pope (Benedict XII), who conducted a rigorous inquisition into possible Cathar heresies within his diocese, in particular in the village of Montaillou, set in a mountainous region of southern France. It was a research gold mine, but the ore still had to be brought to the surface. Le Roy Ladurie used the material as an anthropological study of how ordinary people lived and thought, detailing the criminal activities, sex lives, and family scandals of his villagers in a style as thrilling, said reviewers, as those of a soap opera. Published in 1975, *Montaillou: The Promised Land of Error,* was an international bestseller. The previously little-known village became a tourist destination, while Ladurie found himself feted as "arguably the best-known historian alive" and the "rock star of the medievalists."

Critics noted that the other central character besides Fournier him-

---

* When in 1949 Arthur Koestler's 1940 novel *Darkness at Noon* was published in French, Ladurie saw it as confirming the greatness of Stalin instead of the denunciation Koestler had aimed for. In the novel, a prominent Communist named Rubashov is falsely accused of crimes against the Soviet Union. Koestler had modeled his protagonist on Nikolai Bukharin, a prominent Old Bolshevik shot in 1938 after a show trial in Moscow in which, psychologically broken after months of torture, he confesses to an array of improbable charges. "Rubashov was right to sacrifice his life and especially his revolutionary honor," Ladurie wrote in a 1949 essay, "so that the best of all possible regimes could be established one day." Years later he admitted his mistake but added that at the height of the Cold War the atmosphere inside the Party was of *"une intensité liturgique."*

self, the village priest, Father Pierre Clergue, a confirmed womanizer who seems to have copulated with most of the females of Montaillou, came across as rather a hero for the historian. Clergue's doomed affair with the local *grand dame* and great beauty, the Countess Béatrice de Planisoles, forms one of the main storylines. Ladurie countered this criticism by arguing that he focused more than his predecessors on the quality of individual lives in all their oddness: the professional cartel formed by the *annalistes* was in danger of killing narrative history. The approach he favored was the kind that would extract the greatest interest from the smallest quantity of work. "When you are not young you need a digestible amount of data," he said, explaining that historians could be divided into two types: paratroopers, who comb vast tracts of territory, and trufflers, who snuffle about looking for particular gems. Ladurie felt he was both.

He followed *Montaillou* with other studies, most notably *Carnival in Romans,* which described social unrest at the 1580 Mardi Gras in the town of Romans, where such issues as religious warfare, population growth, inequities in taxes, and the carnival itself came into conflict. Then, in 1982, came *Love, Death, and Money in the Pays Doc,* in which he examined in detail an eighteenth-century Languedoc short story to ferret out what it revealed about life at that time and the potent oral traditions of the region.

Outside the steady stream of books, Ladurie's own life was filled with incident. Well known in France, where he wrote regularly for newspapers regardless of political affiliation, for a brief period he taught at Cornell, as well as taking classes at Princeton, Michigan, Stanford, and Pittsburgh. In 1955, he got married and the following year left the PCF after watching as Soviet tanks crushed the protesting citizens of Hungary who were, he wrote, merely demanding basic human rights. Communism, he concluded, was an inhumane, totalitarian ideology. He remained active in left-wing politics, standing for the United Socialist Party in Montpellier in 1957 but receiving just 2.5 percent of the vote. He finally left the Socialist Party in 1963, but he could not leave politics alone, and in late 1989, as a director of the Bibliothèque Nationale, tried to navigate between President Francois Mitterand's plan for a new national library and budget-minded critics of the plan. He failed to do so and was eventually fired.

In January 1978, he was a founding member of the Comité des intellectuels pour l'Europe des libertés, an anti-Communist grouping of liberal intellectuals opposed to the influence of the Communist Party on French culture. Still part of the Annales group, he championed microhistory, which was at the heart of his two-volume political history of France between 1460 and 1774. It was a harkening back to the first days of the *Annales,* although a number of other historians were making their mark at the magazine: Pierre Goubert (whose work on demography was to become a main ingredient in Annales history), Denis Richet, Maurice Agulhon, and Michel de Certeau were now the names that crowded its pages. There were also "outsiders" who may not have contributed articles but who influenced the magazine's contributors, people such as Michel Foucault, Michel Vovelle, and Philippe Ariès (whose main contribution was through his dazzlingly original work on collective attitudes toward childhood and death).

It is ironic that the Annales School is probably misnamed, the title originally a strategic accommodation to get economists and sociologists on board. "History is compiled with documents" had been an early rallying cry, although annals themselves were always but one source among many: "Total History" is still the more accurate title, as if the school were some all-purpose Swiss Army knife. In 1979, in an article in *Annales* marking the magazine's first fifty years, the house historian Jacques Revel asked: What was "the unity of an intellectual movement that has endured for a half century? What is there in common between the highly unified program of the first years and the apparent bursting apart of more recent orientations?"

Perhaps the unity of purpose that had distinguished the days of Febvre and Bloch was no more; but by the mid-twentieth century this supremely French revolution had changed the way people approached the past. Now historians were expected to join hands with experts from other disciplines; they were to think in sections of time far larger than they had before; and they were to be encouraged by the range of all that was set before them: the realization that no aspect of life was beyond their concern.

CHAPTER 13

THE RED HISTORIANS
From Karl Marx to Eric Hobsbawm

———

Under Marxism the future is well-known—
it is the past that is uncertain.

—POLISH SAYING

Among the young Communists [at university] we used to
joke: the Communist philosophers were Wittgensteinians,
the Communist economists were Keynesians, the
Communist students of literature were disciples of
F. R. Leavis. And the historians? They were Marxists,
because there was no historian that we knew of at
Cambridge or elsewhere . . . who could compete
with Marx as a master and an inspiration.

—ERIC HOBSBAWM

IN THE MID-1860S, KARL MARX WAS LIVING IN LONDON WHEN A LETTER arrived from his Leipzig publisher: "Dear Herr Doctor: You are already ten months behind time with the manuscript of *Das Kapital*, which you have agreed to write for us. If we do not receive the manuscript within six months, we shall be obliged to commission another author."

How different history might have been! Marx (1818–83) was ever the procrastinator, but he did eventually finish the first volume of his fateful undertaking, published in 1867. He did not live to see the planned second and third parts in print, but they were completed from his scrawled notes by his friend Friedrich Engels, who, stunned by how much had been left undone, stitched them together and published them in 1885 and 1894. A fourth volume, organized by the Czech-Austrian Marxist theoretician Karl Kautsky, appeared between 1905 and 1910. Although the books make frequent references to past events, they are primarily works of economic theory. Marx did write history, though, and he certainly influenced how it should be written, especially in the systematic study of social and economic factors. Of that influence, the conservative historian Hugh Trevor-Roper, not the most natural Marxist, noted: "He gave to our subject a new organizing philosophy and gave it at a time when it was most needed: when the material of history had become overwhelming and previous historical philosophies were running dry."

Marx's own first intellectual guide was the philosopher and anthropologist Ludwig Feuerbach (1804–72), whose 1841 book *The Essence of Christianity* advocated atheism and what became known as "historical materialism."* Marx first went to study at the Friedrich-Wilhelms-Universität in Bonn, where Hegel had once taught, then moved to Berlin to read law. By the start of the 1840s, still in his twenties (and already with a wife: ever keen to flout convention, he had married twenty-two-year-old Jenny von Westphalen when he was just eighteen), he was part of a group known as the Young Hegelians, which sought to restore the radical agenda embedded in Hegel's work. Marx developed a more down-to-earth version of how history develops, using Hegel's account of the unfolding of the spirit as history's endpoint: a far better world that would come into being once capitalism had been destroyed. In contrast to Hegel's high-flown theories, Marx held that history was driven by the material or economic conditions that exist at any particular time.

Marx's primary vocation was as a campaigning journalist. He began his career in January 1842 by writing for *Rheinische Zeitung,* a liberal newspaper. That November, Engels, two years his senior, stopped in at

---

* This term, so central to Marxist thought, argues that the material conditions in the way a society produces its needs determines how that society is organized and develops. Thus social classes and the relations between them, along with political structures and ways of thinking, are founded on economic activity. Marx never used "historical materialism" to describe his theory, but it nevertheless appears in Engels's 1880 work *Socialism: Utopian and Scientific,* to which Marx wrote an introduction.

the paper's offices in Cologne. Their lives thereafter would be inextricably combined (one historian has described them as "inseparable"—except when Engels went fox-hunting, an enthusiasm his friend did not share). Marx once observed of himself that no one had ever written so much about money and had so little. Not until he was past fifty did he have financial security, when Engels assigned him an annual allowance out of a family inheritance. At one point, Marx even contemplated becoming a railway clerk, but his application was rejected because of his poor handwriting. At another, he couldn't leave his house because he had pawned his only coat. His family fortunes would have collapsed entirely without Engels, who in November 1849 took on a day job in Manchester at his father's textile firm, which made it possible to support his friend on a regular basis. It was not just money he provided, for when Marx conceived a son by his family's servant, Lenchen Demuth, his otherwise happy marriage was saved by Engels claiming paternity.

During the 1840s, Marx edited and contributed to various political newspapers in Europe and won a reputation as a radical, in short order fleeing the Rhineland when state censors forced his paper to close, then getting himself expelled from Paris, Brussels, Cologne, and the French capital again, a serial exile. After joining him in Paris in 1848, Engels took him to England, and the two engaged in their first collaborations, *The Holy Family, The German Ideology* (mainly an attack on Feuerbach and the philosopher Max Stirner), and *The Poverty of Philosophy* (an attack on Pierre-Joseph Proudhon), in all of which Marx criticized his own earlier ideas as well as those of others. A recent biography describes his "passionately irreconcilable, uncompromising and intransigent nature," his unquenchable ferocity never more in evidence than when attacking his own side. Marx's despairing father asked in 1837, "Will you ever be capable of imparting happiness to those immediately around you?" It comes as little surprise that at Marx's funeral there were only eleven mourners.

Yet he did have friends, Engels above all. The two loved English seaside resorts, especially Margate and Ramsgate, in East Kent, and would go off together to watch Punch and Judy shows and Negro minstrels. And when Marx began his career in England, writing for *Diplomatic Review,* he took up with its editor, Dobson Collet, their families congregating weekly at each other's houses, to read together from Shakespeare. These meetings were even given a name, "The Dogberry Club," after the complacent constable in *Much Ado*.

From 1852 till 1862, Marx wrote a column for the New York *Daily Tribune,* which at the time had the largest newspaper circulation in the world. In all, he published 487 articles, totaling more than everything else he published in his lifetime. However, about a quarter were ghost-written by Engels, especially when Marx was ill, as he often was, suffer-

Marx, Engels, and Marx's three daughters. Swarthy when young, Marx was nicknamed "the Moor" at university; his wife, in letters to him, called him her "little wild boar." In contrast, friends called Engels "the General."

ing throughout his life from a variety of ailments, particularly a skin disease that caused him to break out in boils. "I hope the bourgeoisie will remember my carbuncles until their dying day," he wrote to Engels.

During 1847 and 1848 revolutions broke out across Europe—in France, Italy, Austria, Hungary, Prussia, and more. Over fifty countries were affected, the most widespread revolutionary wave in European history. It was time for Marx to show his hand. At the end of February 1848, alone in his study at 42 rue d'Orléans in Paris, "scribbling furiously through the night amid a thick fug of cigar smoke," as his liveliest biographer, Francis Wheen, describes it, he completed a twenty-three-page pamphlet: *The Communist Manifesto.* It stands as his signature text, yet it includes a ten-point program lifted almost verbatim from an earlier version by Engels, who titled his own draft "Fundamentals of Communism" and structured it as a catechism—twenty-five questions, each with a distinctive answer (making use of religious forms for political agitation was common). He became dissatisfied and wrote to Marx that it would be better to title "the thing *Manifesto*." So it came to be.

Focusing sharply on the 1840s, it describes capitalism as a force that would dissolve all national and religious identities, evolving into a universal civilization controlled by market imperatives. But before the proletariat could become conscious of its potential, capitalism had to modernize the world. Industrial production would mushroom, concentrating the two remaining classes into inherently opposed groups in anticipation of capitalism's demolition.

That was the central message, but intellectually the *Manifesto* was a terrible mess, as Timothy Shenk characterized it, "a hodgepodge of British economics, French politics, and German philosophy held together less by its internal coherence than by the force of Marx's will." Its author pretended to explain all history but had difficulty accounting for any particular event. And while he looked ahead to a new kind of society, he had no settled conception of what it would look like, for instance failing to foresee the two great forces of the twentieth century, Fascism and the welfare state.

The term *capitalism* is notably absent from the finished first volume of *Das Kapital*. Since Marx is capitalism's greatest critic, this is quite an omission. "Communism" derives from the French *communism,* which in turn developed out of the Latin roots *communis* and the suffix *-isme*—and was in general use long before Marx promoted it as an economic and political system. Yet "communism" is generally considered his brainchild, advocating class war leading to a society in which all property is publicly owned and each person is remunerated according to their abilities and needs. Exactly how it differs from socialism has been argued over ever since; like most writers of his time, Marx used the two terms interchangeably.

The idea of a classless society first emerged in ancient Greece. Following on, the fifth-century Mazdak movement in Persia would be described as "communistic" for disputing the favored position of the noble classes and for striving to create an egalitarian commonweal. At one time or another, various other similar communities have sprung up, generally under the inspiration of Scripture. Such ways of thinking have also been traced back to Thomas More, whose *Utopia* (1516) portrays a society based on common ownership of property. It was only later, following the French Revolution, that Communism emerged as a political doctrine. The term was first defined in its modern sense by the French writer Victor d'Hupay. His 1777 book *Projet de communauté philosophe* advises readers to "share all economic and material products between inhabitants of the commune, so that all may benefit from everybody's work."

What Marx and Engels did was to offer a new definition and popularize the word.* Yet for decades the *Manifesto* was ignored, until the early twentieth century, when it found readers ready to carry out its program. It was at that point that both *Das Kapital* and *The Communist Manifesto* acquired notoriety. "Marxism is still very young, almost in its infancy," Jean-Paul Sartre wrote as late as 1956. Despite this initial delay, no other text has had so much impact in so short a time.

Although Marx is inseparable from the idea of Communism, that was not his own way of thinking. On one occasion, he told his French son-in-law, "If anything is certain, it is that I am not a Marxist."† He relished being contrary. Writing in the *Rhineland News* in 1842, he launched a stinging attack on Germany's leading newspaper, the *Augsburg General News,* for publishing articles promoting a Communist perspective. The spread of such ideas would "defeat our intelligence, conquer our sentiments," he declared, an insidious process with no obvious remedy. Later he remarked that he was eager to get rid of the "economic crap" of *Capital* and concentrate instead on a biography of Balzac he had been planning. In 1848 he would make a speech denouncing as "nonsense" the very idea of a revolutionary dictatorship of the proletariat, even though that notion was central to his thinking.

---

* Before long, the enemies of Communism brought into play a host of other definitions, most of them extremely vague. At MI5, secret servicemen defined the word as taking in everything from "Comintern-controlled," "sympathetic to the Communist Party," "a man of Communist appearance," "known to hold socialist views," having "the appearance of a Communist Jew," even dressing "in a bohemian fashion."

† To be fair, this requires context. In 1880 Marx was assisting socialists in writing a program for the Worker's Party of France. But he had serious disagreements with them, in particular over demanding better work conditions and wages from the bourgeoisie. If urging such reforms from the capitalists was held to be Marxism, he said, then he wasn't a Marxist.

He liked to play with the past. And while one thinks of him as a political theorist, it would be a mistake to undervalue his role in the writing of history, most notably in those stitched-together four volumes that make up *Das Kapital* (a work that Marx wished to dedicate to Charles Darwin, whose theories of ceaseless struggle he greatly admired; but Darwin declined the honor). Gareth Stedman Jones, a recent biographer of Marx, has written:

> What is extraordinary about *Das Kapital* is that it offers a still-unrivaled picture of the dynamism of capitalism and its transformation of societies on a global scale. It firmly embedded concepts such as commodity and capital in the lexicon. And it highlights some of the vulnerabilities of capitalism, including its unsettling disruption of states and political systems. . . . If *Das Kapital* has now emerged as one of the great landmarks of nineteenth-century thought, it is [because it connects] critical analysis of the economy of his time with its historical roots.

In other words, what redeems *Das Kapital* is that it confirms Marx as "one of the principal—if unwitting—founders of a new and important area of historical enquiry, the systematic study of social and economic history."

* * *

IF ONE ACCEPTS THAT the most common synonym for Marxism is *historical* materialism, it is surprising how few works of Marxist history appeared before 1930. The first notable Communist historian after Marx is Leon Trotsky (1879–1940). He wrote over sixty books and extended pamphlets (a complete bibliography, compiled in 1989, runs to over 1,100 pages), including accounts of the Communist revolutions in France, Germany, and China, a history of the Spanish Civil War, and a remarkable autobiography, *My Life.* Most notable of all is his *History of the Russian Revolution,* published in English in three volumes in 1932. His writing is original, even unprecedented, within the Marxist tradition; whereas the way he wrote history is inseparable from his political career, he treated the facts of the revolution accurately, if from a highly partisan perspective.

"Trotsky" was a pseudonym, borrowed from the name of one of

his many jailers. He was born Lev Davidovich Bronshtein, from a family of well-to-do Jewish farmers living near the Black Sea. By early adulthood he would give up the whole tradition of "Jewishness," and it surprised people when late in life he supported the idea of an independent Jewish state. At ten, he was sent off to Odessa, to board with a cultivated relative. He developed a taste for opera, an enthusiasm for books, and an easy way with the liberal intelligentsia that passed through his guardian's home. He also grew into a social conscience, at one point taking part in a demonstration at his school after a teacher had picked on a boy simply because he was German. Bronshtein was suspended for an entire year for his insubordination. He was to write in his autobiography:

> Such was my first political test, as it were. The class was henceforth divided into three distinct groups: the tale-bearers and envious on one side, the frank and courageous boys on the other, and the neutral and vacillating mass in the middle. These three groups never quite disappeared, even in later years.

In 1896, aged seventeen, he was sent to Nikolaev in southern Ukraine to complete his education, and was introduced to socialist ideas. That December, in a meeting of young political enthusiasts, he challenged a woman student who had been awkwardly outspoken, saying, "A curse upon all Marxists, and upon those who want to bring dryness and hardness into all the relations of life!" The object of his attack, Aleksandra Sokolovskaya, fled the meeting in tears; but her arguments won the day. Shortly after, Bronshtein converted to Marxism—and Sokolovskaya became his first wife.*

The following spring, Trotsky's little group formed a clandestine organization, the South Russian Workers' Union, which held discussions and issued political leaflets, all written and run off by Bronshtein. The police arrested most of its members and Bronshtein found himself in prison, forced to endure several months of lice-ridden solitary con-

---

* Together they had two daughters, Zinaida and Nina, both of whom died before their parents. Nina fell to tuberculosis, cared for in her last months by her older sister. Zinaida followed her father into exile in Berlin. Suffering from tuberculosis (then a fatal disease) and also from depression, she committed suicide. Aleksandra disappeared in 1935 during the Great Purges, and although she emerged into society three years later Stalinist forces soon murdered her.

finement, then a transfer to another part of Ukraine, followed by Odessa for eighteen months, and finally four years in Siberia. He passed his days studying Marxist classics and holding discussions with other exiles. He also wrote a stream of essays on literary topics (Ibsen, Gogol, Zola), several of which were smuggled out and published in a liberal paper in Irkutsk.

Most Russian Marxists were exiled in Western Europe, not in their home country, and in the fall of 1902, feeling isolated, Bronshtein escaped his Siberian masters by hiding in a wagonload of hay and traveled across Russia to end up in London, where he hastened to meet Lenin, then in his early thirties and already regarded as a leading revolutionary. They became colleagues, taking long walks though the capital's streets, discussing how they could bring about a brave new world. It was about this time that Bronshtein took up his "party name" of Trotsky. He began to write for the underground Russian paper *Iskra*

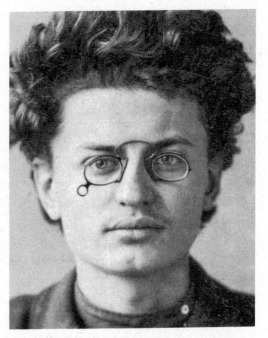

Police mugshot of Trotsky in 1905 after Soviet members were arrested. "Some said Trotsky had a Mephistophelian face. Actually he had the dark, pale face of a Russian Jewish intellectual: high brow, full lips, dense, curly hair, thick mustache, small pointed goatee, and weak, shortsighted eyes behind pince-nez" (Louis Fischer).

("The Spark"), which Lenin managed from a small office in Islington. Trotsky (using a second pseudonym, *Pero,* "feather" or "pen") regularly had to stand and watch Lenin edit his overwrought prose. His style improved.

The émigré group in England soon sent him to Paris, to give him experience, and there he met another young Russian, Natalia Sedova, who in 1902 became his second wife. She bore him two sons, both of whom, like his daughters, would die before their parents. Meanwhile, *Iskra* was riven with factions, and between 1904 and 1917 Trotsky worked hard to reconcile the different groups. This resulted in clashes with Lenin, who now referred to him as a "Judas," a "swine," and a "scoundrel." It's hard to believe that they were actually working for the same things, two idealistic young men (largely) trying to figure out what it was they held true.

By the time of the grandly named Second Congress of the Marxist Russian Social Democratic Party, held in Belgium in 1903, a group called the "Bolsheviks" (meaning "one of the majority") struck out on its own as a new political entity. Trotsky was not yet of their number, describing himself as a "non-factional social democrat." The following year he wrote, with remarkable prescience:

> Lenin's methods lead to this: the party organization at first sub-stitutes itself for the party as a whole; then the Central Com-mittee substitutes itself for the organization; and finally a single "dictator" substitutes himself for the Central Committee.

What he was describing was exactly the process of degeneration that would take hold of the Bolsheviks in the 1920s after their reach for power succeeded. They regarded their party as the "chosen" instru-ment of history, while other socialist groupings were either petty bourgeois or counterrevolutionary. It was an intolerance that had ter-rible consequences.

Trotsky himself was admired for his fearlessness, his tactical inge-nuity, his powers of oratory and his propagandist writing skills but was also seen as overbearing and sharp-tongued; those fighting for the cause made use of his skills but did not like him or trust him. At least all these Marxists agreed that their first task was to overthrow the tsar-ist regime and establish a new kind of government. On January 3, 1905, in a catastrophe known as "Bloody Sunday," a peaceful procession toward St. Petersburg's Winter Palace was confronted by government troops and some thousand people were shot down. The country was in turmoil, with strikes breaking out in the larger cities. That February, Trotsky returned to Russia, to St. Petersburg, to take up a half-public, half-clandestine life, yet one visible enough for him to become the popular tribune of the revolutionary left. He took over the newspaper *Russian Gazette,* increasing its circulation to five hundred thousand, and also co-founded *Nachalo* ("The Beginning"), which also proved successful in the frenetic atmosphere of the times. At one point he gave a speech to two hundred thousand people—about 50 percent of all the workers in the city. Just twenty-six, he was a leader of the first rank.

Tsar Nicolas II's forces regained control, however, and in the repression that followed thousands were killed or thrown into prison. Trotsky was tried on the charge of supporting an armed rebellion and sentenced to deportation to Siberia (again), only this time for life. But he escaped (again), being driven by a vodka-soaked peasant for a whole week through ferocious blizzards and across frozen tundra, reaching a safe house in London and setting down to write his first major work of history, *1905,* meticulously recounting the events of that tumultuous year.

In October 1908 he was asked to join the staff of *Pravda* ("Truth"), a biweekly paper for Russian workers, which he co-edited and which had to be smuggled into Russia. He continued at the paper for two years until it folded in April 1912. However, his main work was the development of his theory of permanent revolution, which sought to chart a path toward revolution for the bourgeoisie in especially backward countries. And of course that revolution was at hand in his backyard. Trotsky spent the war years first in Europe (managing to be deported from France to Spain for antiwar activities), then briefly in New York, working as a journalist—and writing a book against the war—but with the February 1917 uprising he returned to Russia. He traveled initially to Kiev, then to St. Petersburg (or Petrograd, as it had been renamed in 1914, to make the city sound less German), eager to be in the thick of things. It was a switchback ride. Lenin was in hiding and by August Trotsky was back in prison, but the tables turned and by September the Bolsheviks had a majority in the Petrograd Soviet. Trotsky, released from jail, became its chairman.

When in November the government, under the leadership of the onetime lawyer Alexander Kerensky, was overthrown and Lenin became national leader, Trotsky, although a newcomer to the inner circle of the Bolshevik leadership, was appointed foreign minister. He intended, he said in a rare flash of humor, to issue "a few revolutionary proclamations, then close shop." He led the Soviet delegation during the peace negotiations with Germany and by the end of 1917 was unquestionably the second man in the Bolshevik Party after Lenin. The scoundrel swine had won through.

In 1918, when civil war broke out over all Russia, he became minister of war, despite his lack of military experience. He was surprisingly good at his new job, creating a force of some million men—the Red Army—almost from scratch. For two years he lived in an armored train, his mobile political-military headquarters. As the historian and critic Irving Howe writes, "For intellectuals throughout the world there was something fascinating about the spectacle of a man of words transforming himself through sheer will into a man of deeds."

Trotsky was forty-one, at the apex of his power and fame. He had won decisive battles, so was seen as the organizer of victory in the civil war. While retaining overall control of the Red Army, he was put in charge of Russia's railroads while remaining the party's leading theoretician. But the country was to pay for the Bolsheviks' failure to think through the consequences of their power grab. Nothing turned out as they had hoped. Trotsky became their sometime conscience but also their apologist. In 1920, he published *Terrorism and Communism,* his most authoritarian book, not least in its identification of the Bolshevik Party with the destiny and interests of the working class. Reversing his insights of 1904, he argued that in desperate times it was necessary to *increase* the power of the ruling institutions. Robert Conquest, who has written authoritatively on Soviet history, is unyielding in his assessment: "He was, whatever his personal magnetism, a ruthless imposer of the Party's will who firmly crushed the democratic opposition within the Party and fully supported the rules which . . . gave the ruling group total authority." He not only ordered killings without remorse but even in his later years of exile his attitude toward Stalin's atrocities was that of a "loyal opposition."

Revolutions elsewhere in Europe all failed; the Russian economy was falling apart. Even Lenin was talking of his country as a "*deformed workers' state.*" After 1921 the Bolsheviks refused to allow any party but their own to function legally; the slide into despotism had begun. Lenin, who was to die in 1924, said in 1921 that Trotsky was "in love with organization" but over practical day-to-day politics "he hasn't a clue." However accurate that assessment, Trotsky certainly pursued an

In March 1903, Lenin wrote of Trotsky: "Unquestionably a man of rare abilities, he has conviction and energy, and he will go much farther." He did. Exiled by Stalin in 1929, he lived for four years on the Princes' Islands near Istanbul. Here he poses at his desk reading The Militant, *the newspaper of the Communist League of America.*

erratic course, occasionally lashing out at the deformations he witnessed, sometimes offering sharp analyses, at others retreating into depressed withdrawal. On the surface, he remained the most consequential and popular Bolshevik leader (although his "mistakes" were often mentioned by rivals), but in the private chambers of power he was excluded from decision-making. Meetings of the Bolshevik Central Committee were likely to find him engrossed in a French novel, ignoring the debates that swirled around him. At one gathering of the Politburo, Trotsky, unable to get his way, stormed out and tried to slam the door dramatically, but it was a massive metal structure, and he could only bring it to a close slowly, unintentionally underlining his impotence.

In 1922 Trotsky published an unlikely volume called *Problems of Everyday Life,* then the following year both *Literature and Revolution,* a major venture into literary criticism, and *The New Course,* a collection of essays exploring the character of Bolshevik bureaucracy. Many ranked him as Soviet Russia's foremost literary critic. He was still both the political leader and intellectual guide of the Left opposition, but

his growing criticisms of Stalin could have only one result (bar his stag-
ing a military coup, which he never seriously considered).

By 1928 Stalin had consolidated his power. Opposition from the
Left was crushed, while the Right was helpless. Trotskyist sympathizers were driven into exile and Trotsky himself, branded first a heretic,
then a "traitor," and finally, after a Moscow trial, an "accomplice of
fascism," was parceled off to a distant region of Asian Russia, Kazakhstan.

By the start of 1929 he was deported altogether, to begin years of
wandering, driven from country to country—Turkey, France, Norway, finally Mexico—at each resting post met by local Stalinists and
Fascists demanding he be sent away. His one weapon was his pen,
which he took up constantly, but in all these years he lived in danger of
assassination, and supporters provided him with bodyguards. Soviet
agents robbed the Trotsky archives in Paris and murdered a number of
his political associates (a headless body found floating in the Seine was
identified as belonging to his secretary), while Fascists ransacked his
Norwegian home. In May 1940 he almost lost his life when twenty
Communist hitmen raided his Mexico hideaway, shooting Trotsky in
his right leg (in all, their tommy guns let off three hundred bullets) and
abducting one of his bodyguards, whom they murdered. Nowhere was
safe, for Trotsky or his extended family. Back in Russia, his younger
son, Sergei, was charged with planning "a mass poisoning of workers";
when he refused to repudiate his father, he was shot. In 1938, Sergei's
elder brother, Sedov, died under mysterious circumstances in a Paris
hospital.

All the while, Trotsky was working to create a new movement
which, he forecast, would be loyal to the original principles of
Marxism-Leninism, and he kept writing, sometimes eighteen hours a
day. His finest books were composed in exile. *My Life* appeared in 1930,
The History of the Russian Revolution two years later. This last, enormous
work was completed in just thirteen months under exhausting conditions, mainly in Turkey, where he had no access to libraries. Despite its
length, the work is tightly focused on the months between February
and October 1917.

In its preface, Trotsky says he tried to be objective without pretending to be impartial, drawing a distinction between *neutrality,* impossible
for anyone not completely devoid of political belief, and *objectivity,* a

necessity for anyone who wanted to avoid being simply a propagandist. "The serious and critical reader will not want a treacherous impartiality," he adds, "which offers him a cup of conciliation with a well-settled poison of reactionary hate at the bottom, but a scientific conscientiousness which . . . seeks support in an honest study of the facts." But this needs to be taken with a large pinch of salt. Events may be presented accurately, but Trotsky was ever willing to suppress or misrepresent facts if his beliefs required it. He had a particular view of how the revolution triumphed and which groups and individual participants were responsible. One thinks of Tom Stoppard's play *Night and Day,* in which a seasoned journalist says of his paper, "It's not on any side, stupid, it's an objective fact-gathering organization," and a second character asks, "Yes, but is it objective-for or objective-against?" Trotsky was writing "objective-for."

If the *History*'s tone is epic (Trotsky writes about himself in the third person, and the 1977 edition is nearly 1,300 pages), the lifelong lover of literature could still skewer a character or convey a moment in a phrase. To take one example, describing Lenin at the Finland Station in 1917: He "endured the flood of eulogistic speeches like an impatient pedestrian waiting in a doorway for the rain to stop." The book ends before the revolution turned sour: Trotsky's is prelapsarian history, the revolution as an unfolding vindication of Bolshevik myth.

The indignity of having to defend himself against the slanders pouring out of Moscow led to bouts of acute depression, but while Trotsky did once contemplate suicide, in public he remained firm. In 1937, he wrote to an old political friend about the trials: "Indignation, anger, revulsion? Yes, even temporary weariness. . . . But . . . 'History has to be taken as she is'; and when she allows herself such extraordinary and filthy outrages, one must fight her back with one's fists." To his last day he held to the Marxist revolutionary idea.

That last day was fast approaching. On August 20, 1940, an agent of the Russian secret police given the alias of "Jacson" (an evident botched spelling, but nobody noticed) whose real name was Jaime Ramón Mercader del Río, inveigled his way into Trotsky's fortified home at Coyoacán, outside Mexico City, and proffered an article he said he had written on "the Russian question." The man had been dating one of Trotsky's assistants, so did not seem immediately suspicious. Trotsky agreed to look the essay over, and the two men repaired to his study, the visitor nervously clutching his raincoat. As Trotsky bent over the article, Mercader pulled out a cut-down ice axe (he appears to have been an experienced mountain climber), closed his eyes—a detail he later oddly admitted—and brought the murder weapon down on his victim's head. Trotsky let out a "very long, infinitely long" wail—"I shall hear that cry all my life," Mercader testified.* Though the axe had penetrated two and three-quarter inches into his skull, Trotsky leapt up, hurled everything he could lay his hands on and broke his assailant's hand. Members of the household came rushing in and seized Mercader, but Trotsky, despite his desperate state, was still thinking politically and told them not to harm his killer, for "he must be made to talk."

Taken to the hospital, Trotsky clung to life for another day. Then he was gone.

* * *

AFTER MARX'S DEATH, his writings started to be read across much of Europe, and throughout the late 1800s his disciples were partly responsible for several insurrections. Not one was successful, with the single exception of the revolution in Russia, which had an extraordinary impact on the spread of his ideas. Between 1918 and 1945, many intellectuals in the West (among them H. G. Wells, George Bernard Shaw, and Jean-Paul Sartre) either gave their support to the Soviet regime or joined their countries' emerging Communist parties, and following Germany's defeat the Soviet Union set up compliant governments in Central and Eastern Europe and indirectly championed the ascension of others in the Americas, Asia, and Africa, so that by 1985 one-third of the world lived under some version of Communism. With the dissolution of the Soviet Union in 1991, its ideology was quickly cast aside, and by 2020 only a handful of extreme socialist governments remained—in Cuba, North Korea, Vietnam, and Laos; even China makes little effort at appearing a Communist country now. Deng Xiaoping, its longtime leader until his retirement in 1992, pronounced pragmatically: "What does it matter what is the color of the cat provided it catches mice?"

Although many Marxist-inspired books have been published, rela-

---

* In 1943, Mercader was found guilty of murder by a Mexican court and given a twenty-year sentence. After serving his term (which included one attempt to spring him from jail), he moved to Czechoslovakia, thence in 1968 to Moscow, to be made a Hero of the Soviet Union, Gold Star—the equivalent of the Medal of Honor in the United States.

tively few have been works of history. Authors committed to Communism, such as Michel Foucault, Émile Durkheim, Simone de Beauvoir, Herbert Marcuse, and André Gide, were more interested in developing Marxist or socialist theory than in recording the past. Even Antonio Gramsci (1891–1937), who wrote more than three thousand pages of analysis during his years of imprisonment under Mussolini and was much influenced by the great theorist of history Benedetto Croce, concentrated on political ideology. Those Communist historians who succeeded in carving a career did so within the academy and generally did not win a wide readership.

There were some exceptions. György Lukács (1885–1971), primarily a literary critic but one whose work had important implications for how Communist historians should write, contributed what was almost a primer on Marxist development, *History and Class Consciousness* (1923), but because it departed from strict Soviet party lines he was summoned to Moscow and forced to disavow the book. In Italy, Renzo de Felice (1929–96), best known for his massive four-volume biography of Mussolini, was among 101 of his countrymen who sharply criticized the Italian Communist Party after it supported the Soviet repression of the Hungarian Uprising, and he severed his links to the Party. Of more influence internationally were Giovanni Levi and Carlo Ginzburg (born in the same month, April 1939). Both men had their thinking shaped by the social sciences and introduced their precepts into their respective universities, Turin and Bologna. Ginzburg, the author of over a dozen works of history, is best known for the delightfully titled *The Cheese and the Worms: The Cosmos of a Sixteenth Century Miller* (1976), which examines the beliefs of an Italian heretic of the sixteenth century.

This widening had an obvious political dimension. For instance, over its first forty years, the *Annales* magazine played a prominent but conflicted role in European cultural history. Many Marxist scholars were promoted in its pages, but some of its leading figures fought against them. It was a heady time to be a Communist intellectual in Paris, and there were several power centers. One key thinker was Louis Althusser (1918–90), a philosophy professor who exerted great influence on students during his thirty-five years at the École normale supérieure, an institution outside the public university system. His life was to be marred by tragedy. In 1980, he killed his wife, a former member of the French Resistance and a Communist activist, strangling her while not in full possession of his senses. He was declared unfit to stand trial and committed to a psychiatric hospital for three years, but well before mental illness consumed him he had been accused of teaching his students to look at criminal activity in a positive way, as having a revolutionary character. Even so, he was regarded as a prophet of a new world order.

On the other side of the city stood the *Annales*. After Fernand Braudel made the famous "Sixth Section" at the École Pratique des Hautes Études a power base, François Furet (1927–97) became something of a celebrity as president of what became the École des Hautes Études en Sciences Sociales (EHESS). Unlike the earlier tribal chiefs, Furet, an ex-Communist, never wrote a great book, yet he played an important part in French cultural and political life, mainly because through the *Annales,* the *Le Nouvel Observateur,* and other papers he led the attack on "the revolutionary catechism" of Marxist historians, whom he characterized as dogmatically Stalinist, inherently totalitarian and antidemocratic, even violent, rather than committed to true social reform. Communists in France who chose to write about past events certainly found life difficult.

* * *

GERMANY WAS FIGHTING ITS own history wars. In particular, a group of scholars that became known as the "Frankfurt School" has dominated Communist intellectual debate within the country since its founding in 1923 as an adjunct to Goethe University in Frankfurt, the first Marxist-oriented research center affiliated with a major German university. It was the brainchild of Felix Weil (1898–1975), a young Marxist who just after the First World War had written his doctoral thesis on the practical problems of realizing socialism. In 1922, in the hope of bringing together different trends of Marxism, he organized a symposium in east-central Germany, and the event was so successful that, using the money from his father's grain business, he set about funding a permanent institute. Lukács was an early supporter, and the fact that a year after the school opened he was forced by Moscow to repudiate his writings showed early on that Communist theorists departed from the party line at their peril.

The failure of revolutions in Western Europe, precisely in those nations where Marx had predicted success, coupled with the rise of Nazism in a country as technologically sophisticated as Germany, led many at the school to select from Marx's writings what might clarify contemporary social conditions that he himself had never experienced. As National Socialism became more threatening (most of the institute's members were Jewish), its founders moved—first to Geneva, then in 1935 to New York City. Only in 1953 was the institute formally re-established in Frankfurt, by which time several leading members, such as Marcuse and Erich Fromm, had decided to stay on in the United States.

Scarcely a single historian of note emerged from the institute. The school was inward-looking from its inception, preoccupied with nice-ties of theory and language. Even its insights were self-defeating. The one exception was Walter Benjamin (1892–1940), primarily a philoso-pher but who authored influential essays on the writing of history. A brilliant, tortured soul, he began a life of wandering exile in the early 1930s, aided by funds from the institute. When the Nazis stripped him of his citizenship, the French imprisoned him, a stateless man, in a camp near Nevers, in central Burgundy, but in January 1940 he was al-lowed to return to Paris. He planned to evade the Gestapo by traveling to neutral Portugal via Spain, and safely crossed the French-Spanish border to arrive in Catalonia and joined a group of fellow Jews. The Franco government put out an order for all runaway refugees to be rounded up and sent back to France. Expecting to be turned over to the Nazis, Benjamin killed himself with an overdose of morphine tablets. One does not know how his ideas would have evolved, but we are left with a compound of German idealism, Romanticism, and Jewish mys-ticism: not an easy mix, but of him more later.

Europe's revolutionary movements at this time saw themselves as perhaps the best chance of containing capitalism. Like most who ral-lied to the Communist banner, its members wanted to bring about a better, fairer world, and their idealism is in many respects easy to ad-mire (one thinks of the young Trotsky rushing to the aid of a bullied schoolmate). However, the baleful patronage of the Soviet Union had a shriveling effect, but then, as Martin Amis observed in an essay to mark the one hundredth anniversary of the October Revolution, "The chief demerit of the Marxist program was its point-by-point defiance of human nature." The historians of Communist Europe were hob-bled from the start.

* * *

ONLY ONE COUNTRY BRED a number of first-class historians who had wide influence beyond party boundaries, and that was Great Britain. In the early 1930s, its Communist Party (the CPGB) had just five thousand members, although its outreach was considerable, particularly in the trade unions.

In late 1946 a group of historians, friends, and members of the Party started regular London meetings, either in the upper room of the Garibaldi Restaurant in Saffron Hill or occasionally in Marx's shabby house on Clerkenwell Green. As Eric Hobsbawm, its most famous member, put it, the first decade of their existence was perhaps "where we really became historians." This evolved into the Communist Party Historians Group (CPHG) and eventually numbered some of the finest academics of the period, including Hobsbawm, Christopher Hill, Raphael Samuel, and E. P. Thompson.

Their first meetings were dedicated to the reevaluation of Arthur L. Morton's *A People's History of England,* published in 1938. Rather than spend their time teasing out the more recondite points in Marxist theory in the manner of the Frankfurt School, the group concentrated on considering events from the view of the oppressed, drawing out marginal voices from sources where they were barely mentioned. Eventually, so was their hope, their insights would empower people to emancipate themselves from the patronizing "high history" of monarchs, prime ministers, and other "great men" and cast aside the notion of Britain in constant evolution, rather than revolution.

Membership gradually reached three figures. Not all were professional historians, as the aim was to appeal to anyone interested in historical research. They arranged themselves into four main sections: ancient, medieval, the combined sixteenth and seventeenth century, and the nineteenth century. Using insights from the social sciences, they shared the approach of the Annales School but with the important difference that they applied Marxist principles to everything.

Almost immediately, it was asked whether membership in the CPGB might undermine academic integrity, and if so, in what way. This was unproblematic so long as members dedicated their work to subjects outside their Soviet mother party's existence. In late 1952 an anonymous article in *The Times Literary Supplement* questioned the historians' competence to teach at British universities due to their sympathies with or even loyalty to Moscow. This made the leading members of the CPGB keen to seek an escape from Stalinism, and that same year they founded their own magazine, *Past and Present*. Inveighing against "both idealism and the false god of objectivity," it created an immediate impression, becoming the most prestigious academic journal of history in the English-speaking world. "Brash and confident in wielding the best of the British Left's cultural arsenal," noted a historian of the group, "they welcomed open-ended dialogue with non-Marxist traditions." A *New Yorker* reviewer summed up: "The Communist Party never transformed Britain, as it had hoped, but the Historians' Group . . . has a fair claim to have transformed the profession of history."

That same article notes that in London's National Portrait Gallery hangs a painting of seven people set around a low table in a book-lined study: the editorial board of *Past and Present*. In keeping with their philosophy, many of the members carried out their projects from adult education institutions (such as workers' colleges or polytechnics), rather than the universities, although Oxford, and even more Cambridge, proved ideal recruitment centers. When in 1936 Hobsbawm went up to Cambridge, he found himself in the midst of "the reddest and most radical generation in the history of the university." One expounder of Communism's attractions was Maurice Dobb (1900–76), an economist at Trinity College who had joined the Party in 1920. He was notorious for long and dull lectures, with fewer attendees each class, but as a recruiter to Marxism he was unsurpassed. His home was so frequent a meeting place for his disciples that it was known as "The Red House." Among his students were Hobsbawm, Victor Kiernan (1913–2009), Amartya Sen (a Nobel Prize winner in economics), A. L. Morton (1903–87, from 1946 on the chair of the CPHG), and two other Trinity undergraduates, George Rudé (1910–93, an expert on the French Revolution) and the master spy Kim Philby.

At Oxford, Balliol College supplied the medievalist Rodney Hilton (1916–2002), Raphael Samuel (1934–96, co-founder of *Past and Present* and a pioneer of working-class history), and preeminently Christopher Hill (1912–2003). In 1931 Hill made an extended trip to Germany, where he witnessed the upsurge of the Nazis, later saying that the experience accelerated the leftward slant of his politics. In

1935, he undertook a ten-month sojourn in Moscow, where he became fluent in Russian and studied Soviet historical scholarship, particularly relating to Britain. After returning to England, he moved to the University College of South Wales and Monmouthshire. When the Second World War broke out, he enlisted as a private in the British Field Security Police, ending the war working in intelligence at the Foreign Office—an ironic posting, given that in later years MI5 scrutinized him as a possible traitor. As characterized by another Oxford historian, his hallmarks were, despite a persistent stammer, pithy sentences, high, bouncy black hair (which he dyed), and a legendary shyness. In years to come, Hill's colleague at Balliol, Richard Cobb, would object that his Marxist companion had no taste for pleasure; although Hugh Trevor-Roper, a natural conservative, would record that Hill actually did have a sense of humor: "I can't help liking the old wretch."

The other major historian in the group was Edward Palmer ("E. P.," as he was generally known) Thompson (1924–93), who be-

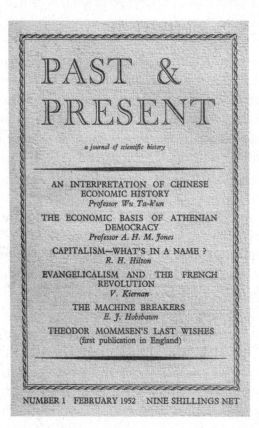

PAST & PRESENT

a journal of scientific history

AN INTERPRETATION OF CHINESE ECONOMIC HISTORY
Professor Wu Ta-k'un

THE ECONOMIC BASIS OF ATHENIAN DEMOCRACY
Professor A. H. M. Jones

CAPITALISM—WHAT'S IN A NAME ?
R. H. Hilton

EVANGELICALISM AND THE FRENCH REVOLUTION
V. Kiernan

THE MACHINE BREAKERS
E. J. Hobsbawn

THEODOR MOMMSEN'S LAST WISHES
(first publication in England)

NUMBER 1   FEBRUARY 1952   NINE SHILLINGS NET

The magazine broke even on a 400-copy run, two issues a year, each sixty to seventy pages. Unsuccessful at first, it became the most widely respected academic journal of social history in the English-speaking world. It would shed its Marxist connections only in 1958, joining mainstream history magazines such as Germany's Geschichte und Gesellschaft *and Italy's* Quaderni Storici.

sides his university work was a fervid campaigner against nuclear arms. He went to prep school in Oxford, then on to Cambridge, so was very much part of the elite he spent his adult life attacking, although in his writing he focused on the British radical movements of the late eighteenth and early nineteenth centuries. He wrote biographies of William Morris (1955) and William Blake (1993), was a tireless journalist and essayist, and published a poetry collection and a well-received novel, *The Sykaos Papers,* but by far his most important work is *The Making of the English Working Class* (1963). This massive book, nearly nine hundred pages (he "lacked the ability to express himself with brevity," noted Hobsbawm, his sometime rival), was a watershed in social history, judged by Tim Rogan in his recent history of the period as "the most widely read and most influential work of history published in English during the 20th century"—an extraordinary accolade, but one hard to rebut. By exploring working peoples' cultures through the previously neglected minutiae of their everyday lives, Thompson put together the first history of the working-class political left in the world. Reflecting on the importance of the book at its fiftieth anniversary, *Guardian* writer Emma Griffin explained how Thompson

> uncovered details about workshop customs and rituals, failed conspiracies, threatening letters, popular songs, and union club cards. He took what others had regarded as scraps from the archive and interrogated them for what they told us about the beliefs and aims of those who were not on the winning side. Here, then, was a book that rambled over aspects of human experience that had never before had their historian.

All the historical work produced by CPHG members came with a similar Marxist agenda. As Stephen Kotkin has pointed out in a *New Yorker* article, Rodney Hilton, the medievalist, wrote of the importance of small market towns, linking the replacement of feudalism by capitalism to the class struggles of the peasantry, whereas Hill depicted the English Civil War as a "bourgeois" revolution, casting the dissenters—the Levellers, Diggers, and Ranters—as proto-Bolsheviks. As he put it, "History was not words on a page, not the goings-on of kings and prime ministers, not mere events. History was the sweat, blood, tears and triumphs of the common people, our people."* But such an agenda had its shortcomings. Kotkin notes:

> The Marxist narrative was part of what made the work compelling, but it was a hindrance, too. Rodney Hilton's attempts to tie peasant uprisings to the eruption of a new mode of production proved a dead end. So have Christopher Hill's efforts to squeeze the English Civil War into the same scheme as the rise of capitalism. Only Thompson's work has had a lasting influence.

While Thompson, Hill, and Hilton were rooted in English history, one of their number had more global aspirations and a far greater inter-

Christopher Hill in January 1965, at the time of his appointment as Master of Balliol College, Oxford. He remained in the post until 1978.

---

* Hill's words are from his preface to an essay collection in honor of Dona Torr (1883–1957), one of the founders of the CPHG. For space reasons, I have had to omit a number of influential Communist or quasi-Communist historians, among them Torr; John Saville (1916–2009), an expert in nineteenth-century British economic and labor history; and two other Trinity College graduates, E. H. Carr (1892–1982), best known for his fourteen-volume history of the Soviet Union and *What is History?* and Raymond Williams (1921–88), the cultural theorist and literary critic. E. P. Thompson's wife, Dorothy (1923–2011), yet another Cambridge graduate, became an expert on the Chartist movement. It was truly a remarkable group.

national reputation—indeed, in his biographer's words, was for some years "the best-known and most widely read historian in the world." And so we come to the most remarkable historian of the CPHG, and the most troubling.

★ ★ ★

JUST BEFORE 4 P.M. on March 2, 2011, I made my way down the slopes of Parliament Hill to Nassington Road in north London, up the eight steps of a large Victorian house and into a brightly lit drawing room, to meet the ninety-four-year-old doyen of nineteenth- and twentieth-century history, Eric Hobsbawm. In his youth, just after the Second World War, he would appear to one contemporary, Karl Miller, as "lean, fair-haired, Jewish-looking, German-looking, lumber-shirted, trousers arrested by a leather belt." Or, as a plainclothes Special Branch officer who attended one of his university lectures reported to his masters: "slim build; eyes blue; pale complexion; hair light brown; long oval face; large nose and ears; thick lips." Bar the sporting of a bright mauve shirt, he looked much the same still. We talked for nearly two hours—about his teenage conversion to Communism, and the criticisms made of him for never attacking Stalin in a forthright way, even after Khrushchev's speech of 1956. Hobsbawm suggested I read Aldo Agosti, "although I am biased in his favor because he is an old friend," and we spoke about other Italian historians who had embraced Communism.

He was far from the "shy, ironic, whispering person," as he had once described himself, and more the cultivated yet unrepentant professor on whom Tom Stoppard based the Red Cambridge don of his 2006 play *Rock 'n' Roll*. After a while I worried he must be tired; he said he wasn't at all. His latest book, *How to Change the World* (2011), had been enthusiastically reviewed earlier that week, and only that morning he had finished a long article for the *London Review of Books*. He spoke self-deprecatingly, though firmly, and in good faith, it seemed to me; he was easy to be with. Afterward, I wrote that he had been scrunching the plastic cover of a magazine that had just arrived, and I hoped that wasn't a sign of his impatience at my questions. He replied: "I am afraid I tend to open packages whether or not I am talking to people at the same time. Sorry to have irritated you."

He was profoundly the author of the books I'd read on what he called "the long 19th century" (one of his most memorable and controversial concepts: another was "the invention of tradition") starting in 1789 and ending in 1914: a formidable trilogy—or quartet, if one includes the later *The Age of Extremes*. In 1958 the Vienna-born publisher George Weidenfeld had asked him to contribute to a forty-volume series on the history of civilization, and Hobsbawm, already with three smaller books behind him, was immediately enthusiastic. Gathering together every aspect of experience, the first volume, covering 1789 to 1848, related innovations in the arts and sciences to the economic demands of a new class, the bourgeoisie, whom he saw as both the cause and the consequence of political change. A sequel, in 1975, *The Age of Capital, 1848–1875,* described the creation of a world economy. A third volume, *The Age of Empire, 1875–1914,* published in 1987, charted examples of economic collapse, the free-for-all among imperialist powers to sweep up territory, and the internecine conflict ending in the world war of 1914–18. Hobsbawm would describe himself as "psychologically an unsystematic, intuitive, spontaneous historian, disinclined to plan," yet he produced four of the most consequent, interlocked works of cultural and economic history of the century. While he could play down the breadth of his knowledge, he was well able to explain his appeal:

> As a lecturer I know that communication is also [a] form of showbiz. We are wasting everyone's time if we cannot keep the attention of audience or reader. I have tried three ways of holding it: communicating passion (i.e., the writer's conviction that the subject is important), writing that makes readers want to read the next sentence—and the right dosage of light relief and soundbites.

The books received extraordinary tributes. The Scottish Old Etonian Neal Ascherson, a lifelong friend, wrote: "No historian now writing in English can match his overwhelming command of fact and source. But the key word is 'command.' Hobsbawm's capacity to store and retrieve detail has now reached a scale normally approached only by large archives with big staffs. . . . The engine inside his narrow head is a Rolls-Royce imagination." The *Spectator,* despite its right-wing agenda, described him as "arguably our greatest living historian—not only Britain's, but the world's." The paean was worldwide. Writing in

The New York Review of Books, Tony Judt judged him a cultural folk hero: "Hobsbawm doesn't just know more than other historians. He writes better, too." But he cautioned that Hobsbawm's bias in favor of the Soviet Union led him to disparage any nationalist movement as passing and weakened his grasp of parts of the twentieth century. Further, when it came to historical significance, economics mattered more than culture, men more than women, the West more than the Rest.

The criticisms of Hobsbawm's stance were hardly new, and he himself fanned the flames, wearing his obstinacy like a badge of honor. In a 1994 interview on British television, he said that the deaths of millions of Soviet citizens would have been worth it if a genuine Communist society had been the result: "In a period in which, as you might imagine, mass murder and mass suffering are absolutely universal, the chance of a new world being born in great suffering would still have been worth backing."

Eric Hobsbawm in January 1976. Just short of six feet, he yet weighed only 150 pounds. "You're as ugly as sin," his cousin Denis Preston told the teenage Hobsbawm, "but you have a mind."

Judt's article had specifically commented on this lack of repentance: "Hobsbawm clings to a pernicious illusion of the late Enlightenment: that if one can promise a benevolent outcome it would be worth the human cost. But one of the great lessons of the twentieth century is that it's not true. For such a clear-headed writer, he appears blind to the sheer scale of the price paid. I find it tragic, rather than disgraceful." That view was still relatively benign compared with the litany of criticisms that had formed over the years, particularly that Hobsbawm accepted the order to side with the Nazis against Britain and France following the Molotov-Ribbentrop Pact of 1939 and that, although he signed a historians' letter of protest against the Soviet invasion of Hungary,* he still supported the assault.

After my meeting with Hobsbawm, he wrote to me: "Of course I had ideas about Russian history including Soviet history, and keeping quiet about my ideas was frustrating, though I thought the reasons were convincing. For the same reason I didn't do any research on British labor history after World War I, because I thought the official line about the changes it underwent by the foundation of the CP in 1920 were tosh." In effect, he self-censored what he wrote. That reticence disappeared with the fall of the Soviet Union in 1991, and he was free to comment on Russian history in *The Age of Extremes* (1994). In some ways he is honest about his views, stressing that since Communism has not been accepted worldwide the sacrifices made in its name were not justified:

> Whatever assumptions are made, the number of direct and indirect victims must be measured in eight rather than seven digits. In these circumstances it does not much matter whether we opt for a "conservative" estimate nearer to ten than to twenty million or a larger figure: none can be anything but shameful and beyond palliation, let alone justification.

With regard to the 1930s, he wrote:

> It is impossible to understand the reluctance of men and women on the left to criticize, or even often to admit to themselves, what was happening in the USSR in those years, or the isolation of the USSR's critics on the left, without this sense that in the

---

* On February 25, 1956, Nikita Khrushchev's "secret speech" (broadcast to the world by the CIA) on the final day of the 20th Congress of the Communist Party of the Soviet Union, which revealed that the leadership had long been aware of Stalin's crimes, transformed the British Historians' Group from loyalists into vocal critics. Then that October Khrushchev ordered tanks into Budapest, and many left the Party, including E. P. Thompson, Rodney Hilton, Raphael Samuel, and John Saville. Christopher Hill also resigned in 1957 and Victor Kiernan in 1959, by which time almost all the intellectuals in the group had left. Hobsbawm, however, kept his membership up until shortly before the Party's dissolution in 1991.

fight against fascism, communism and liberalism were, in a profound sense, fighting for the same cause.

He even writes that he would have spied for Stalin had anyone bothered to ask, as it was "the only way to defeat Hitler." He saw directives from Moscow as the logos of History speaking through the Party. It was entirely consistent, then, that he should hold up the Bolshevik Revolution as civilization's hope, right through the atrocities. In a crucial paragraph of his final book, *How to Change the World,* he explained:

> I did not come into Communism as a young Briton in England, but as a Central European in the collapsing Weimar Republic. And I came into it when being a Communist meant not simply fighting Fascism but the world revolution. I still belong to the tail-end of the first generation of Communists, the ones for whom the October Revolution was the central point of reference in the political universe.

His views, he said, were "of someone who became politicized in 1931 and 1932 in Berlin and who has never forgotten it." There we have it. Communism not only gave him something to root for but a home. When he died in 2012, he was buried in London's Highgate Cemetery, a few yards from the grave of Karl Marx.

* * *

HE WAS BORN (a clerical error at his birth altering his surname), in Alexandria, a British sultanate of Egypt, in 1917—four months before the revolution and just twenty years from the death of Marx. His British father, Leopold "Percy" Hobsbaum, who had joined the British-run Egyptian postal service (and was incongruously the amateur lightweight boxing champion of Egypt—twice), was the hapless son of a cabinetmaker from London's East End who had migrated from Poland in the 1870s. Eric's mother, Nelly Grün, was Austro-Hungarian, the frail daughter of "a moderately prosperous Viennese jeweler." She was to earn money for the family writing short stories and a novel while working as a translator for the publishing firm that had issued her novel.

His parents, both non-observant Jews, moved to a defeated, impoverished Vienna when Eric was two, changing homes frequently to escape demands for rent. By the Depression, Hobsbawm recalls, "Politics in Central Europe had been reduced to two colors: brown for the anti-Semitic right, and red for the revolutionary left." When Eric was twelve, his father dropped dead of a heart attack; his mother died two years later from lung disease, "a devastating blow." Taken in by an uncle and aunt who lived in Berlin, Eric and his sister, Nancy, stayed two years in the city, living a precarious childhood in the last days of the Weimar Republic, where their rackety uncle worked for Hollywood's Universal Films. "We were on the *Titanic,* and everyone knew it was hitting the iceberg," Eric wrote in his autobiography (2003).

Later in the same book, he describes how his new family provided cold comfort. He "lived without intimacy," he wrote. But he became a Boy Scout, collected stamps, went on nature hikes, and immersed himself in books. He also became aware of the crisis facing his adopted country, with more than a third of the workforce unemployed and people fearful that their whole world order was about to collapse. He had no reason to put any faith in the capitalist system, but as that system came closer to falling apart, he decided he wanted to take some kind of personal action and so joined the youth section of the German Communist Party. "It was my most formative political experience." The Party gave him an almost ecstatic sense of identity.

Already he had witnessed the rise of Nazi Germany. In 1933, with Hitler voted in as chancellor, the teenage Hobsbawm had slipped flyers under apartment doors for the about-to-be-banned German Communists, his "first piece of genuinely political work." In his diary, written in German, he confessed to "a light, dry feeling of contraction, as when you stand before a man ready to punch you, waiting for the blow," then in his autobiography as an experience comparable to sex in its melding of "bodily experience and intense emotion." At one point he found himself alone in a streetcar with two Nazi storm troopers and was terrified they would set on him if they saw his Communist Party badge; at another, he concealed a duplicating machine under his bed for several weeks as SS thugs roared through the city searching out Reds to beat up. It was, he writes, "my introduction to a characteristic experience of the Communist movement: doing something hopeless and dangerous because the Party told us to." Elsewhere he observed,

"If I'd been German and not a Jew, I could see I might have become a Nazi, a German nationalist."

It was his Rosebud moment, the emotional underpinning of why he remained loyal to the Party, in his way, to the end. "The first thing to understand," he told an interviewer in 2004, "is that I grew up living under a volcano which was in the middle of erupting. In a world which had gone to bits, which had been a field of ruins in World War I. Which was expected to be another field of ruins in World War II." His Communism was "a tribal matter." "I could prove myself by succeeding as a known Communist, and in the middle of the Cold War," he would write. "I do not defend this form of egoism, but neither can I deny its force. So I stayed."

The family, who held U.K. passports, decided to move to Britain, though out of financial desperation rather than premonition; the first glaring public expression of hatred toward the Jews was not until April 1933, and by then the Hobsbawms had settled in London. Eric was sent to an excellent grammar school in Marylebone, in the West End, where, he claimed, he read his way through the local public library and "became conscious of being a historian at the age of sixteen," though more likely he chose the subject because he was good at it. (His schoolboy diaries show he was thinking instead of becoming a poet or a teacher.) He won an Open Scholarship to read history at King's College, Cambridge, took a double starred First, completed a doctorate (on the left-wing group the Fabian Society),* was elected to the prestigious Apostles debating group, and edited the undergraduate magazine, *The Granta,* where he was its main film critic and also wrote the first imaginative fantasy (well ahead of Len Deighton, Robert Harris, or Philip Roth) based on a Nazi-type Fascist takeover of Britain. Even as an undergraduate he gave classes in Marxism to other students and also joined the British Communist Party, earning himself an official MI5 file.

With the coming of war he served his second newly adopted country, although the authorities kept him away from the intelligence work

---

* The thesis, however, was judged "slick, superficial and pretentious" by the formidable economic historian R. H. Tawney and turned down by the Cambridge University Press. The Fabian Society, a group of radical intellectuals founded in the late nineteenth century, took their name from the Roman general Quintus Fabius Maximus (280–203 B.C.), whose nickname "the Delayer" stemmed from the tactics he employed when faced with a superior enemy, Hannibal: refusing open battle and wearing down opponents by guerrilla tactics until the moment came to attack.

he knew would best suit him, confining him to a sapper regiment, where his commanding officer noted that "he has a tendency to produce left-wing literature and to leave it lying about." He was also perhaps the first King's man to operate a road drill, dig antitank trenches, and attach explosive charges to bridges. When he was transferred to the Isle of Wight, MI5, fearing he might somehow gain access to "sensitive" military plans for D-Day, had him moved to another billet within days.

Mixing with ordinary citizens, he decided that for him Communism was "an ideal wish-fulfillment" rather than practical politics. Eventually demobilized, he returned to Cambridge, where he was elected a fellow, and in 1947 took up a post at London's Birkbeck College, an evening school for mature students that, exceptionally for the period, showed minimum signs of anti-Communism, although the unimpressive head of its history department, one R. R. Darlington, regularly barred him promotion.

Hobsbawm said that in the 1950s a milder version of McCarthyism took hold in Britain, and Marxist academics knew that their careers would be affected: "You didn't get promotion for ten years, but nobody threw you out." He was also denied a lectureship at Cambridge by political enemies (an old Cambridge mentor, the staunchly anti-Communist Russian émigré Mounia Postan, is said to have sent in "poisoned arrow" job references),* his applications to join the BBC were denied, and, given that he was also blocked at Birkbeck, spoke of how lucky he had been to have landed his post there before the Cold War really affected people's careers. But assessors and promotion committees also objected to his lack of interest in archival research, seen as the bedrock for most history-writing. As early as 1965, *Encounter* magazine was describing him as "a challenge to the profession."

---

* Various commentators have argued this, but Hobsbawm's biographer Richard Evans is doubtful: "Although I had heard that he [Postan] argued against [Hobsbawm's] appointment to a permanent position in Cambridge on more than one occasion, I couldn't find any written or first-hand evidence of this." Evans read an early draft of this chapter and was surprised I mentioned that Hobsbawm had written a book about chess. What was my source? I replied that in 2004 Hobsbawm had been interviewed by the Hungarian historian Iván Berend at the UCLA Center for Chinese Studies in Los Angeles. The transcript of the interview on the internet has Berend relating how Hobsbawm had told him he had written a book on chess, under the same pseudonym he used for his jazz book. Evans's reply: "Ha!! This is a comical misunderstanding by the Hungarian, who obviously mistook JAZZ for CHESS (try saying it with a Central European accent!)." So: no chess book, alas. Emails to the author, January 7, 2019, and July 17, 2019.

Even so, he became reader in 1959, professor between 1970 and 1982, and emeritus professor in 1982. If some promotions never came, or came late, by career's end he had been showered with recognition. His books were translated into fifty languages; he became an honorary fellow of King's, won the Wolfson History Prize, was made a Companion of Honor ("CH is for the awkward squad," he glossed), and a fellow of the Royal Society of Literature. He was even elected to the Athenaeum Club in Pall Mall, said to contain more bishops per square yard than anywhere else in the world except the Vatican. He was well aware of the irony that a lifelong Communist should be so garlanded. "Intellectuals are the chorus in the great drama of class struggle," he decided.

In 1943 he had married Muriel Seaman, a well-born fellow Communist, but by 1950 they had drifted apart, and to Hobsbawm's disgust and disbelief she took a non-Communist lover. They meandered on until divorcing in 1953. Hobsbawm was left on his own again, floundering and unsettled. One solace was jazz. The First World War had introduced this new musical form to many countries, even if by the 1930s Stalinists were denouncing "the culture of the Negroes," at one point banning saxophones and confiscating the instruments by the thousands. The British *Communist Review* railed against jazz, but Hobsbawm was impervious, seeing it as a form of unorganized cultural rebellion. As a teenager he had listened enrapt to Duke Ellington at a London club. Jazz at once brought him "wordless, unquestioning physical emotion." He loved to travel to Paris, to such haunts as the Club Saint-Germain and Le Chat Qui Pêche.* By the mid-1950s he was writing a jazz column for the *New Statesman* under the pseudonym Francis Newton, taken from the name of Billie Holiday's Marxist trumpet player. He spent time with aficionados and practitioners, "a sort of quasi-underground international freemasonry," as he called them. Before long his editor, Kingsley Martin, complained that his pieces were too technical, and what readers, mostly male middle-aged civil servants, really wanted was gossip about the demimonde where jazz flourished. Hobsbawm obliged, reaching into "the avant-garde

---

* While in Paris Hobsbawm began an affair with the wife of a good friend. To her surprise—she had been told by her doctor she was unlikely to conceive—she became pregnant and in 1958 gave birth to a son, Joshua. Hobsbawm sent money and continued to see his old girlfriend over the years, latterly making contact with Joss, as he was called, and happily introducing him to his own family.

cultural bohème" of London's Soho, sketching the "chicks" and "cats" among whom he passed his time.

It was in 1958, in the Star Club in Soho's Wardour Street, that he met Jo, a beautiful twenty-two-year-old part-time hooker with a drug habit and a young child in tow. They would see each other regularly for the next four years, united in their love of jazz and not just meeting for occasional sex: Hobsbawm would take Jo to the cinema, the ballet, and parties where he introduced her to friends. Even after the physical relationship had run its course, he kept in touch, sending her money until the end of his life. It was intrinsic to his nature to accept people as he found them, but seeing the world through the eyes of Soho's denizens was also important to how he viewed the past: that ordinary people and popular movements were the substance of history. In 1959 he published *Primitive Rebels: Studies in Archaic Forms of Social Movement in the 19th and 20th Centuries,* about peasants who took up as bandits and outlaws, and it remained one of his favorite books.

In the mid-1950s, he moved to Bloomsbury, near the West End clubs and the British Museum, then to Clapham, to a house he shared with Alan Sillitoe, the author of *Saturday Night and Sunday Morning* and *The Loneliness of the Long-Distance Runner.* Later, he spent half the year teaching in Manhattan, at the New School, ensconced in a Greenwich Village office above a jazz club. He also fell in love with the Vienna-born Marlene Schwarz, who in 1962 became his second wife and bore him two children. He acquired his first car, a large house in North London (for just under £20,000), and a holiday cottage in Snowdonia, up in the mountains of northwest Wales, where the Hobsbawms and other second-home writers and artists, soon nicknamed "the Welsh Bloomsbury set," willingly lived under "the sort of conditions we condemned capitalism for imposing on its exploited toilers." He was never a Communist activist. When Claire Tomalin, then literary editor of *The Sunday Times,* asked how he squared being a Communist with his lifestyle, he replied: "If you are on a ship that's going down, you might as well travel first class."

Hobsbawm spent much of his time traveling abroad. Early on, he had ridden on a Socialist Party newsreel truck during the 1936 Bastille Day celebrations in Paris at the height of the Popular Front; he crossed briefly into Catalonia during the Spanish Civil War; in Havana he once translated—extemporizing—for Che Guevara; and he formed many international friendships, particularly in Latin America and Italy. Meanwhile, his views were evolving. In the hostile environment of the 1970s and 1980s, Marxist historical scholarship experienced an abrupt decline. Hobsbawm was not immune. His commitment to inexorable "laws" of history was one with his disaffection with world capitalism, but in his final writings he gave up hope of libertarian socialism. "The socialism born of the October Revolution is dead," he recognized in 2003. And Marxism had, in the main, failed to capture the British working class, which was overwhelmingly liberal-radical rather than revolutionary. Communism overall, if not a blind alley, was at least a historical detour. And yet: "I have abandoned, nay, rejected it, but it has not been obliterated. To this day, I notice myself treating the memory and tradition of the USSR with an indulgence and tenderness. . . . The dream of the October Revolution is still there somewhere inside me." Richard Evans writes that Hobsbawm, "throughout his career as an historian, . . . was pulled one way by his Communist and, more broadly, his Marxist commitment, and another by his respect for the facts, the documentary record and the findings and arguments of other historians." In the end, he desired "historical understanding . . . not agreement, approval or sympathy."

Hobsbawm once said of Marxism that he wanted to love it "like one loves a woman." His admirers still insist his political allegiances never got in the way of his achievements, but they did. As Evans puts it, "Eric wanted to have his cake and eat it." In 2008, Tony Judt wrote a second eulogy, published four years before Hobsbawm's death; it ended with these words:

> Eric J. Hobsbawm was a brilliant historian in the great English tradition of narrative history. On everything he touched he wrote much better, had usually read much more, and had a broader and subtler understanding than his more fashionable emulators. If he had not been a lifelong Communist he would be remembered simply as one of the great historians of the 20th century.

* * *

DURING THE 1950s, AS the Cold War tightened its grip, governments in Britain and the United States became increasingly paranoid, sometimes with good reason. But more often there was no justification for the precautions taken. Only about twenty thousand people were ever members of the British Communist Party, less than 1 percent of the electorate, and but a handful were engaged in illegal or treasonous activities. Both Hobsbawm and Christopher Hill had their phones tapped, their correspondence intercepted, their friends and wives monitored. MI5 kept tabs on the activities of even suspected Communists, including the Oxford historian A.J.P. Taylor and the novelists Iris Murdoch and Doris Lessing (the last of whom they spied on for twenty years). At one point, Eric's sister Nancy and his uncle Harry were suspected.* The Communist Party's offices in King Street, Covent Garden, were extensively bugged, so peppered with hidden microphones that during a later renovation several fell out of the ceiling.

When in 1958 the Communist historian Raphael Samuel opened the Partisan Coffee House in Soho, the police planted informers disguised as chess players. The code name of one of the informants was "Ratcatcher." For over sixty years the government concentrated their energies on tracking British Communists, whether in the political sphere or outside it. MI5 was furious when Hobsbawm and others were allowed to broadcast on the BBC, and BBC employees have testified that their careers were impeded by a small red Christmas tree being stamped on their file, a symbol of political unreliability. Upward of 50 percent of all BBC staff were vetted without their knowledge, and even when this process was wound down in the late 1980s, between six and eight thousand positions (out of twelve thousand) were still being screened for security reasons.

In the United States the demonizing of far left sympathizers was far worse. Although the country's Communist Party (the CPUSA) never became a major player, it was a controversial group and gained some sympathy from the late 1940s on when Senator Joseph McCarthy started off a "red scare" in an attempt to stir up fear against Communist influence. Those who were imprisoned are in the hundreds, and some ten thousand lost their jobs. In many cases simply being subpoenaed by

---

* Hobsbawm, no. 211,764 on MI5's index of subversives, was refused access to his files when he asked for them in 2009. Many passages, sometimes whole pages, still remain redacted and an entire file on Hobsbawm has been "temporarily retained." The office of one MI5 unit had on a wall a framed letter from a prominent Communist with the postscript: "To MI5, if you steam this open you are dirty buggers." The unit classified this as "obscene post"; legally there was no duty to send it on, so they didn't.

the House Un-American Activities Committee (HUAC) was sufficient cause to be fired. By 1958 the party was down to three thousand members and had ceased to play a significant role in American life.

The first notable historical work by an American Communist was *Ten Days That Shook the World* by John Reed, his idealized account (not least, he spoke no Russian) of the Bolshevik Revolution that he had experienced firsthand, published early in 1919. The historian and diplomat George Kennan, no friend to left-wing causes, wrote: "Reed's account of the events of that time rises above every other contemporary record for its literary power, its penetration, its command of detail." It had a huge impact in the United States. Thereafter there is little by an American Communist historian or Communist sympathizer that is worth reading. The textbooks by Charles Beard (1874–1948), a quasi-Marxist, were widely bought, although by the 1950s his writings had been largely discredited.* Eric Foner's works on Reconstruction are outstanding, but when he strays outside his field, say in essays on the Rosenbergs or on post-1945 espionage, his judgments are questionable. For instance, he praises the American Communist Party as the paradigm for helping to redraw the boundaries of American freedom.

Ideology trumping any kind of objectivity has been the norm ever since Reed's journalistic salvo. In their authoritative 2003 study *In Denial*, John Earl Haynes and Harvey Klehr show how many historians of the American left (not all have been party members) have denied the truth and distorted the import of archival evidence about Communist history. Sympathy for the Soviet Union had mainly died away by the late 1940s, to rise again after the Vietnam War, when a new generation of radicalized scholars launched a ferocious attack on anti-Communism, discrediting those who criticized the Soviet Union; liberal anti-Communists became an endangered species in history departments.

From the late 1970s on, a determined group began to "normalize" what had occurred under Stalin by minimizing the number of his victims (not between three to over nine million, "just" tens of thousands, maybe a few thousand) and arguing that responsibility for the Terror lay with a bureaucratic process that had spun out of control. Fredric Jameson, a much-cited authority, in 1996 insisted that "Stalinism is dis-

---

* Beard was an unrelenting activist as well as a prolific author. The story goes that one day he was summoned to the office of the head of Columbia University, and on entering he asked, "Have you read my last book?" The president's reply was immediate: "I hope so."

appearing not because it failed, but because it succeeded, and fulfilled its historical mission to force the rapid industrialization of an under-developed country (whence its adaptation as a model for many of the countries of the Third World)."

Many of these new historians of American communism tied their research to their own radical sympathies, often openly acknowledging that it was driven in part by a desire to validate their political beliefs. They took the name "revisionists," in the uncontroversial sense that they were updating earlier interpretations, while traditional histori-ans were, in the words of Norman Markowitz, one of the American Communist Party's leading theoreticians, "triumphalists," "counter-revisionists," "right-wing romantics," and "reactionaries." It is true that most of the Communist parties of Western Europe and Canada did not suffer the ostracism and government scrutiny undergone by the CPUSA, but it is still astounding that a prominent historian could argue that criticisms of Communism were morally and politically un-justified.

As Haynes and Klehr write, "Far too much academic writing about communism, anticommunism and espionage is marked by dishonesty, evasion, special pleading and moral squalor." American Communists and those sympathetic to their worldview would often trash the infor-mation that other historians put forward. They not only poured scorn on criticisms of Stalin's reign of terror; the vast majority also disre-garded the Nazi-Soviet Pact (some defended it as necessary), refused to accept the details of the Katyn Forest massacre of 1940 (in which twenty thousand Polish prisoners were executed by the Soviet army), and argued that such figures as Julius Rosenberg, Klaus Fuchs, and Alger Hiss were never Soviet spies, despite the abundant evidence.

In addition, the CPUSA, while boasting of its independence from Moscow, for three-quarters of a century accepted huge financial subsi-dies, either in the form of precious stones and jewelry (known as "Moscow Gold") or as straight cash—to help start the CPUSA, John Reed was given valuables worth over one million rubles, then the rough equivalent of more than a million U.S. dollars.

The collapse of the USSR in 1991 and the partial opening of Soviet-era archives undercut the best efforts of the revisionists, but the story of American historians who were either members of the CPUSA or its sympathizers is a sorry one. Tony Judt's verdict is blunt: Communism was "a singularly dishonest confidence-trick whose consenting victims include its distant apologists in England and America, who enthusiastically sent others on the road to hell with the very best of intentions."

Seventy years after Marx's death, one-third of humanity lived under regimes inspired by his thought. Well over 20 percent still do. But let the last word go to Walter Benjamin, the extraordinary German theorist of history. In his main book *Theses on the Philosophy of History* he struggles to reconcile the Marxist idea of progress with the anguish of wartime Europe and produces a memorable gloss on a painting by Paul Klee, *Angelus Novus* ("The Angel of History"). Benjamin had purchased the work in 1921 for the equivalent of about thirty dollars. It became his most prized possession. The painting, he wrote,

> shows an angel looking as though he is about to move away from something he is fixedly contemplating. His eyes are staring, his mouth is open, his wings are spread. This is how one pictures the angel of history. His face is turned toward the past. Where we perceive a chain of events, he sees one single catastrophe that keeps piling wreckage upon wreckage and hurls it in front of his feet. The angel would like to stay, awaken the dead, and make whole what has been smashed. But a storm is blowing from Paradise; it has got caught in his wings with such violence that the angel can no longer close them. This storm irresistibly propels him into the future to which his back is turned, while the pile of debris before him grows skyward. This storm is what we call progress.

His reading may be fanciful and almost more than the image can bear (one has to stretch to see a "pile of debris" that "grows skyward" or a storm "blowing from Paradise"), yet it has great power, and one can appreciate his despair—the Marxist dream dashed.

CHAPTER 14

HISTORY FROM THE INSIDE

From Julius Caesar to Ulysses S. Grant

———

The man who plays a part in a historical drama
never understands its true significance.

—LEO TOLSTOY

HOW DOES ONE WRITE THE HISTORY OF EVENTS IN WHICH ONE HAS
taken a significant part? The cynical answer is by giving oneself as sympathetic or heroic a role as the facts can bear. Quoting the axiom, "History is written by the winners," Hilary Mantel then adds: "That's what
Robespierre meant when he said, 'History is fiction,'" while an African
proverb nicely runs, "Until lions have their historians, tales of the hunt
shall always glorify the hunters." Only: not quite. As Eric Hobsbawm
has argued, "The losers make the best historians." Herodotus came from
a conquered province, Thucydides had been relieved of his command
and sent into exile, and in the case of ancient Rome, it was the losers,
such as Varro and Cicero, who commandeered the narrative. Enraged
monks gave the Vikings bad press. The Earl of Clarendon (1609–74), author of the three-volume epic *History of the Rebellion and Civil Wars in England,* was also driven into exile, in his case for his bitter championing of
unpopular causes. After the fall of Constantinople in 1453, a wave of
Greek scholars emigrated to the West, bringing with them biased accounts of Ottoman brutality, and their version of events prevailed in the
West till well into the nineteenth century. Still, they are the exceptions;
most influential historians have written from a jumble of motives, of
which positioning themselves for posterity has been a common feature.

The professional historian and the memoirist rarely overlap—they lean in on the past at different angles. Memoirists shape their narratives from a self-declared personal perspective; it is *their* history first, even if also a chronicle of the times. But as Hobsbawm, who wrote his autobiography only after much cajoling, has further noted, "The basic thing about history is precisely that you take your distance," but adds that if you write about the times you have lived through, then "you are too close" and "you find it very difficult to distinguish from your actions and opinions at the time . . . you are writing about something in which you are emotionally involved."

There is a tradition of French statesmen writing history (as Louis XIV immodestly remarked, his biography was the history of his time) while Prosper-Olivier Lissagaray's *History of the Paris Commune* (1876) is notable as being written by someone who fought on the barricades and as a result had to go into exile (it seems, another tradition). But Lissagaray was, as he admitted, "neither member, nor officer, nor functionary of the commune." Alexis de Tocqueville's *Recollections,* published after his death, is a self-serving account, little read today. Charles de Gaulle's memoirs, though, while even more self-serving, are well worth a detour.

Italian statesmen, too, put pen to paper, the Germans not so much, although Bismarck wrote vast memoirs, still regarded as a masterpiece of German prose. At the end of the nineteenth century, the vogue began for the great to write poems as they fell from power—Pope Pius IX broke into verse when Italian troops stormed Rome in 1870, as did the Brazilian emperor Pedro II in 1889. Leon Trotsky, as already noted, wrote a self-justifying history of the Russian Revolution, but more remarkable is his *Diary in Exile,* during his last year in France, applauding history yet not realizing how it applied to him.

Among British contenders, Churchill stands alone as a statesman whose histories shaped peoples' judgment. David Lloyd George, prime minister during World War I, wrote about events in which he played a major role, but his memoirs are quarries, not influential works in themselves. Clement Attlee wrote *A Prime Minister Remembers,* which prompted A.J.P. Taylor to comment that it was remarkable how much a prime minister could forget. Roy Jenkins, a Labour Party politician of the 1970s, was a good historian, but with a caviar audience, and had little original to say. Nelson Mandela's autobiography *Long Walk to Freedom* (1995) is a valuable account of more than forty years of apartheid in South Africa but is ghostwritten. The leading military and political figures of world history have rarely had a second career as historians, although Xenophon's *The Persian Expedition,* while a military man's self-vindication, is also a major work.

In America, Ulysses S. Grant's two volumes reign supreme, while Frederick Douglass, who has been called the greatest American of the nineteenth century, wrote his own life three times, each draft with a slightly different purpose. George Washington would never have dreamed of writing his memoirs. Statesman George Marshall (1880–1959) refused (saying that the people of the United States had already compensated him), as did General Douglas MacArthur. Cleveland, Harrison, Hayes, Taft didn't take pen to paper; Wilson was too ill. Hoover did, boringly, as did George W. Bush. Dwight Eisenhower's *Crusade in Europe* and his two volumes of memoirs remain worth reading. Coolidge wrote an unthrilling memoir, Truman two mildly interesting volumes, Johnson's doorstopper was the work of his staff, Reagan's ghostwritten by Robert Lindsey. Nixon and Carter went on and on, seemingly unable to stop, a tradition continued by Bill Clinton, whose *My Life* weighed in at over a thousand pages. Obama's story is halfway told (*A Promised Land,* the first of two volumes, weighs in at 2.4 pounds, 768 pages), his memory aided by his regularly writing a journal. And we may have Donald Trump's account still to come. Today the retirement memoir is *expected*. But it was not always so. . . .

* * *

GAIUS JULIUS CAESAR WAS born on July 13, 100 B.C. (according to the modern calendar) to parents from the oldest aristocratic class in Rome. His first tutor was a Greek slave, Marcus Antonius Gnipho, respected for his Latin as well as his mother tongue, and Caesar had access to several well-stocked libraries in the days when, Alexandria apart, public collections didn't exist. Early on, he was inspired to compose his own works: Suetonius mentions a paean to Hercules and a tragedy, *Oedipus*. Tall and fair-skinned, with piercing black eyes,* Caesar learned to

---

* A modern rendering of Caesar as he might have been in real life is reproduced on page 398. Even more graphically, in 2020, a Toronto-based virtual reality specialist, Daniel Voshart, "harnessed artificial intelligence to create photorealistic, full-color portraits" of every Roman emperor who reigned from 24 B.C. to A.D. 284, basing them on classical busts and on descriptions by contemporary writers, such as Suetonius. Voshart's Augustus looks remarkably like the actor Daniel Craig; Caesar does not come off quite so flatteringly. See Mark Bridge, "Behold! AI Puts Flesh on the Busts of Roman Emperors," *The Times* (U.K.), August 31, 2020.

swim in the Tiber and handle weapons; he had yet to suffer the "falling sickness" (probably epileptic fits) of adulthood. Around 85 B.C., his father collapsed and died as he put on his shoes, and the teenager became head of the household. Within a year he broke off the betrothal his parents had arranged for him and married Cornelia Cinna, the daughter of one of the most powerful men in Rome. And so his precocious ascent began (he was too young for almost every early office he took), first to being a flamen, part of an elite priesthood that allowed him a seat in the six-hundred-strong Senate.

The city was soon caught up in a vicious civil war, from which Lucius Cornelius Sulla emerged triumphant, instigating a reign of terror. Caesar, at eighteen neither important nor rich enough to warrant falling victim to Sulla's proscriptions, was married to the daughter of one of the new dictator's main enemies, and Sulla ordered him to divorce her. Caesar refused and fled Rome, only to be captured by Sulla's men. It took his mother's special pleading for him to be granted a pardon. Sulla may have admired the young man's pluck. Caesar had not been especially interested in being a priest (in retrospect, he seems one of the most unlikely clergymen ever), but it was a respectable career, and he needed money to support his family. In 80 B.C., his standing won him a command in the army, after which he turned to legal advocacy, and within three years he was prosecuting important cases. He became known for the ruthlessness with which he took on former governors notorious for corruption and also for his oratory, delivered with impassioned gestures and in a distinctive, high-pitched voice. In 75 B.C. he had to be ransomed after being captured by Aegean pirates on his way to Rhodes.* The following year, he served with the governor of Asia, and on his own initiative raised a local army to defeat one of the commanders of King Mithridates of Pontus.

---

* For his ransom, the pirates demanded twenty silver talents—about a hundred thousand denarii, when a carpenter, say, would be paid fifty denarii a day, thus totaling what such an artisan might expect to earn over seven years. Caesar is supposed to have laughed at what he regarded as still a paltry sum, pledging instead to pay the pirates fifty talents of his own money. According to Plutarch, he held his captors in such contempt that when he lay down to sleep he would order them not to disturb him and lightly threatened to crucify the lot of them. During his thirty-eight days of captivity, he shared in their sports and exercises, writing poems and speeches that he would read aloud to the crew. On his release, he raised a fleet, pursued and overwhelmed his captors, took them to Pergamum, in western Turkey, and ordered their crucifixion, just as he had promised. To show his mercy, he had their throats cut prior to their being strung up, so sparing them a lingering death. Thus he learned early that the ultimate reach of political power is that it can put people to death.

Thereafter, even as his military exploits continued, office succeeded office, in the intricate musical chairs of Roman politics, which, to switch metaphors, were more a funnel than a ladder: 73 B.C., membership of the college of pontiffs; a year later, military tribune; 69 B.C., quaestor (a magistrate in charge of the treasury); 65 B.C., curule aedile (overseeing public buildings and festivals); 63 B.C., chief priest of the College of Pontiffs (the most powerful religious position in Rome); 62 B.C., praetor (both an army commander and a senior judge), then governor of Further Spain (Andalusia, western Spain, and most of modern Portugal). In 59 B.C. he became one of two consuls, the highest elected political office in the republic, and at forty-one years of age a member of the all-powerful First Triumvirate (as they were colloquially called, and even more unofficially "the three-headed monster"), alongside Gnaeus Pompey, the most distinguished commander of the previous generation, and Marcus Crassus, a financial magnate.

By then, Rome was the largest city in the known world, with a population of over a million. The *res publica*—literally, "the public concern," thus "the state"—ruled directly most of the lands in and around the Mediterranean: the entire Italian peninsula, southern Gaul, Sicily, Sardinia and Corsica, Greece, Macedonia and part of Illyricum (roughly modern Croatia and Bosnia and Herzegovina), Asia Minor, much of Spain and some of North Africa. Caesar was anxious for military adventure after his twelve months as consul, so he engineered an unprecedented five-year command that was to take in three of Rome's most important provinces, Gallia Cisalpina (northern Italy, from Venice on the Adriatic to Nice on the Mediterranean to Lake Geneva in the west and the Alps in the north), Gallia Transalpina (modern France, Belgium, the southern Netherlands, Switzerland, and Germany west of the Rhine), and Illyricum (Dalmatia): by the time his conquests were completed, a huge area. He was to capture eighty cities, subjugate three hundred nations, and fight three million men, killing a third of them.

Despite the fact that this period is probably the best documented in ancient history, we have but a fraction of Caesar's own writings—a real loss, as he was not only a leading public intellectual but also a prolific letter writer, able (according to Pliny) to compose, read, and listen at the same time and to dictate to his scribes four letters simultaneously— or, as Pliny claims, if otherwise unoccupied, seven letters at once.

Napoléon Dictating, *by William Quiller Orchardson, 1892. By 1823, two years after his death, four volumes of Napoleon's memoirs had appeared—some 1,600 pages, "Dictated by the Emperor at St. Helena to the Generals Who Shared His Captivity and Published from the Original Manuscripts Corrected by Himself."*

"The past resembles the future more than one drop of water resembles another," wrote Ibn Khaldūn, whose approach to history places him as the founder of historiography, sociology, and economics. Possibly uniquely for a historian, he appears on his country's currency—in 1994 he featured on the Tunisian ten-dinar banknote.

Richard Caton Woodville, War News from Mexico, *1848. By the eighteenth century, this was how most people got their "first draft of history" For the United States as a whole, it took some time to figure out what, in a republic, a newspaper was for; but by the 1780s there were hundreds of weeklies, and a decade on, their number was growing four times as fast as the population.*

Frederick Douglass is primarily seen as an abolitionist, orator, and statesman, but in his three autobiographies, Narrative of the Life of Frederick Douglass, an American Slave *(1845),* My Bondage and My Freedom *(1855), and* Life and Times of Frederick Douglas *(1881), he provides a compelling history of slavery in the United States as well as an authoritative account of Black American experiences during the Civil War.*

PRINTER'S COPY   79

History of the English-speaking Peoples.   Galley 90

Revise 26.6.9   for revise pp
gals 90·97

CHAPTER V
THE NORMANS

THE condition of England at the end of the reign of Edward the Confessor was one of widespread degeneracy in every sphere. The virtues and vigour of Alfred's posterity were exhausted. We see a strain of feeble and sterile princes, most of whom were short-lived, and who, except for Ethelred the Unready, died without children. Even the descendants of the prolific Ethelred died out with strange rapidity, and at this moment only a sickly boy and an aged man represented the warrior dynasty which had beaten the Vikings and reconquered the Danelaw. The remaining power of the monarchy was severely restricted by the Witenagemot. The main basis of support for the English kings had always been the select body of notables who regarded themselves as the representatives of the whole country. But at this time, this assembly of 'wise men' in no way embodied the life of the nation. It weakened the royal executive without adding any strength of its own. Its character and quality suffered in the general decay. As the central power declined, a host of local chieftains — the earls — disputed and intrigued in every county, pursuing private and family aims and knowing no interest of their own. Feuds and disturbances were rife. The Heptarchy had gone, but in its place had come now no unified nation, but only a multiple tribalism.

We may judge the manners of the court and royal family by this picture from the reign of Edward the Conf—

In local government, where the bishops and the earls presided over the county courts, and the Saxon shires and the social composition of the county are perhaps the best contribution of the Saxons to the future government of England, but be discerned.

If you go to your farm, you will find there plenty of salt meat, but you will do well to carry some more with you."

Taine's History of England, p. 30.

The people were hampered not only by the many conflicting petty authorities but by the deep division of custom between the Saxon and the Danish districts. Absurd anomalies and contradictions obstructed the administration of justice and the different scales of Wergeld applied to various classes were a perpetual cause of friction. The Island had ceased to count upon the Continent, and had lost contact with its progress. The defences, both of the coast and of the towns, were neglected. The Navy had made no advance in strength or efficiency, and Alfred's inspiration had died away. It was impossible to raise a strong army from the retinues of the quarrelsome earls. In social, moral, political, and military qualities the whole system was effete. Once again the Island had become an easy prey to fiercer and stronger races, and once again it stood in sore need of a stimulus from outside.

The only period of firm, clear-sighted and unified government which it had enjoyed in a hundred and twenty years had come from the Danish adventurer, Canute. He alone imposed a coherent polity upon the confused scene. He alone codified its laws and repaired its strength. But canute was gone.

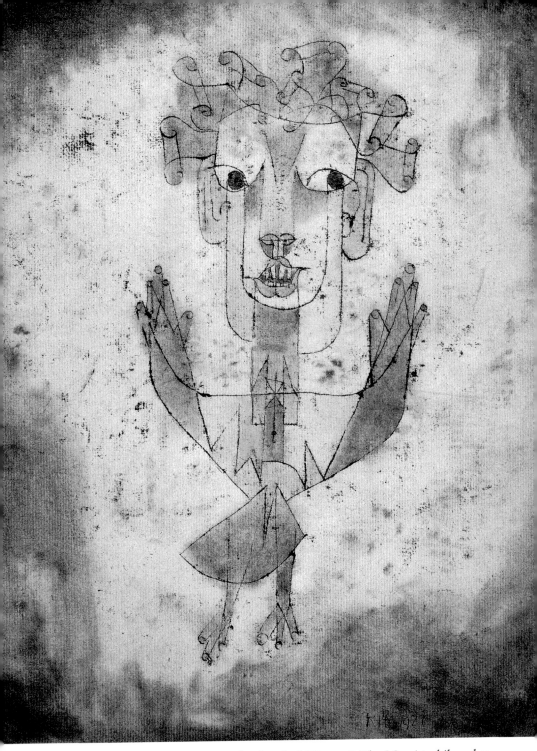

Paul Klee, Angelus Novus, "The Angel of History." The Marxist philosopher *Walter Benjamin purchased the work in 1921 and wrote of it: "[The painting] shows an angel looking as though he is about to move away from something he is fixedly contemplating. His eyes are staring, his mouth is open, his wings are spread. This is how one pictures the angel of history."*

David Starkey explains a late-sixteenth-century portrait of Richard III, on display at Hever Castle in Kent. "So much of academic writing is willfully obscure," he says. "It tries to exclude, whereas I don't think there is any shame in including people."

A.J.P. Taylor, with his trademark bow tie. "He had a special way with anecdotes, including a special way of smacking his lips, often as a signal that he was about to tell an important story. . . . The most noticeable thing about him was a permanent frown line—a sort of exclamation point—between the fierce circles of his eyes" (Kathleen Burk, Troublemaker).

Niall Ferguson in 1993. By then he led a group of young academics in the A.J.P. Taylor mold who became known as the Dial-a-Dons, willing and able to turn out articles in short order on any topic of the day.

David Olusoga, Mary Beard, and Simon Schama, who together presented the nine-part TV series Civilisations, *which told the story of art from the dawn of human history to the present. Schama fronted five episodes, Olusoga and Beard two each. Titian creations gambol behind them.*

Ken Burns after completing his World War II series for PBS. According to Stephen E. Ambrose, the bestselling historian, "More Americans get their history from Ken Burns than from any other source."

Henry Louis Gates, Jr., the bust of W.E.B. Du Bois behind him. How one folds one's arms is one of the clearest ways by which a person can be identified—as, whatever style one adopts, it doesn't change throughout one's lifetime—the kind of detail that has fascinated Gates in his studies of people.

For centuries, Caesar's writing was little read, not least because for a millennium it was ascribed to other authors. Several books of correspondence between Caesar and Cicero are irretrievably lost, while his speeches (other than fragments) and other compositions have likewise disappeared. Among the works missing are *A Collection of Maxims,* a two-volume compilation, sometimes described as a book of his favorite jokes; *On Analogy,* a treatise arguing for accuracy and simplicity in speech and writing, which he wrote while racing north from Cisalpine Gaul to rejoin an army in crisis; a long poem, *The Journey,* composed on active duty in Spain; his funeral oration for his paternal aunt Julia, dated 69 B.C.; and his *Anticato,* aimed to blacken the reputation of Marcus Porcius Cato, his bitter opponent during the civil war of 49 B.C. His favorite poems were burned on the orders of Augustus. At least we do have Caesar's ten books about his military exploits, *Commentarii Rerum Gestarum* (Reflections on Things Done), seven covering the operations in Gaul from 58 to 52 B.C. and three dealing with the civil war against Pompey from 49 to 48 B.C. After his death, several of his officers added four further books covering campaigns in Gaul in 51 B.C. and those in Alexandria and Asia, North Africa, and Spain. These too remain.

Caesar was still forty-one when he set out, not to return to Rome for nearly nine years, during each of which he took command in several major battles and sieges. Pliny says he led his army in fifty engagements altogether, Appian adding that thirty were in Gaul alone. Of the two major commanders with whom he is often compared, Alexander took part in only five pitched battles, Hannibal in more but not so many major ones. Alexander was dead at thirty-three; Hannibal fought his last engagement at forty-five. Caesar was still leading from the front after he was fifty, regularly placing himself in danger.

His accounts, besides Xenophon's the only detailed eyewitness records of any ancient warfare to survive, were immediately hailed as one of the great works of Latin literature, and he was considered among the best prose writers in Rome (after all, he had written a book about composing good Latin); even his sometime opponent Cicero, although his own style was more ornate, judged: "There is nothing better in the writing of history than clear and distinguished brevity." It was not just Caesar's concision. Apparently uncomplicated and direct in style, with a deliberately limited vocabulary aimed at a popular audience, his are not simple documents but highly sophisticated tracts, packed with clever wordplay and alliteration and with an ingenious structure. Any number of subjects catch his attention: the geography of Gaul and Britain, the British methods of fighting, a comparison of Gallic and German social customs, military details, and the political history of "hairy Gaul," among others.

Above all, his combat reports are exceptionally exciting. There are sieges and open battles, with first one side then the other holding the upper hand, guerrilla skirmishes, acts of great courage, forced marches in the dead of night, calamitous military errors (often critical situations he found himself in through his own poor judgment), deeds of astonishing cruelty and surprising mercy, mysterious portents, massacres and mass executions, unforeseen obstacles, sudden changes of weather or of allegiance, exceptional loyalty and gross betrayals. The *Commentaries,* as they are colloquially known, are (unless you are a teenager struggling to translate them) a wonderful read. They are the epic accounts of an army of the Roman people, in a period when Gaul was conquered and Roman rule extended to the Rhine in the east, the English Channel in the north, and the Atlantic coast in the west, a catalogue of extraordinary military success.

Caesar allows the story to speak for itself, even if he presents his campaigns as basically defensive. He once declared that an orator should "avoid an unusual word as a ship's helmsman avoids a reef,"* and his narrative keeps to that principle. It determinedly avoids purple prose (a phrase that comes from the Roman poet Horace, who compared such writing to patches of purple sewn onto clothes, a sign of wealth, and so pretentious), while he always refers to himself in the third person, probably to save whoever read out his reports in the Forum or the theater the daunting responsibility of impersonating him.

There is remarkably little material about Caesar himself. The first true autobiography was not written until St. Augustine and *The Confessions* between A.D. 397 and 400—the first book intended for publica-

---

* He has, though, a way with qualifiers. His most frequent adjectives are *aequus, iniquus, patens, apertus* (denoting features of the ground that are militarily significant); *turpis, pulcher* (to denote blame or approbation); *perpetuus* (continuity); *egregius, eximius* (to show admiration or praise); *incredibilis* (a favorite word—as it is today!—most often used to qualify *celeritas*); *repentinus,* indicating the unexpected, regularly applied to speed or surprise; and various words conveying the idea of comradeship. Adverbs are used to denote speed (*celeriter*), advantageousness (*commode*), and above all professional competence (*caute, industrie, diligenter*). Taken together, this can sometimes give off the whiff of a school report, even if a compelling one.

tion (still in existence, at least) that uses the word "I." Anything before that follows the form Caesar employs. It may be about his life, but it is written from a historian's perspective. Some details are given where Caesar was not himself present, which he wrote up from his officers' reports. Yet unlike Suetonius, say, who is almost obsessive about pen portraiture, or Tacitus, whose skill in catching people is remarkable, he barely touches on the character of his opponents (but then Winston Churchill's history of World War II has no remotely adequate portrait of Hitler). He avoids interpreting motives, rarely expresses praise or blame, and gives the minimum of information about the men whose activities he describes.

On the occasions that he does discuss motivation, it is to illustrate and explain people's subsequent actions. When, in a campaign near Atuatuca (modern Liège), after fifteen cohorts—some seven thousand soldiers—are cut off from the main army, surrounded, and hacked down to the last man, Caesar swears not to shave or cut his hair until he has avenged their deaths, and the depth of his feeling hits us with unexpected force. Yet even the uncompromising Caesar can find moments of humor. In book 6, covering his campaign in 53 B.C., he mentions an elk that lived deep in the German forests and had no knees, so that it was obliged to sleep leaning against a tree. Hunters, he tells us, sought to catch these animals by sawing almost completely through the trunk of a tree, so that when the elk leaned on it to sleep, tree and animal would topple over, the noise would alert the hunters, and the elk would be captured. Or so the great commander would have us believe.

Another time, in 47 B.C., King Pharnaces of Bosporus campaigned to reclaim territories lost by his father, Mithridates of Pontus, and Caesar was drawn away from his war against Pompey to deal with him. He came up against the rebel army near a hilltop town called Zela, in northern Turkey, and in short order routed them. The whole campaign took just a few weeks, prompting Caesar, in a letter to one of his agents in Rome, to quip, *Veni, vidi, vici*—I came, I saw, I conquered. The tone is more one of surprise than vainglory, but by the time Rome celebrated Caesar's unheard-of four triumphs, he had realized the worth of the epigram and it appeared on placards during processions through the city.

The obvious intent of the *Commentaries* was to present Caesar's exploits in the best possible light, but what he leaves out is instructive.

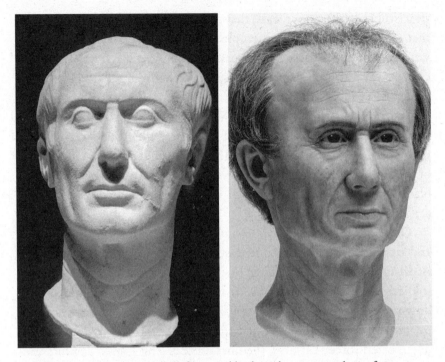

The "Tusculum portrait" (left), possibly the only surviving bust of Caesar made in his lifetime. During his major Triumphs, his troops sang of his mistresses in Gaul, warning Romans to lock up their wives because they brought with them their "bald adulterer." In 2019, the Dutch National Museum of Antiquities unveiled a reconstruction (right) showing what Caesar would have looked like—complete with a huge bump on his head. "Such a thing occurs in a heavy delivery," explained a physical anthropologist. "You do not invent that as an artist."

When around January 10, 49 B.C., Caesar famously crossed the Rubicon (no formidable waterway but a minor, shallow river just north of Rimini, although still the frontier boundary of Italy), he must have realized his actions were open to criticism, but he says little about what happened next, not mentioning the Rubicon at all. (The day before the fateful crossing he spent his time studying plans for a gladiators' school—before, wandering about in the dark, getting lost on his way back to camp.) We know from other sources that he had a short fuse; he once threw his baker into chains for serving substandard bread. Again, he visited the treasury in Rome, anxious for funds, as he had to pay a vast army over many months. A confrontation ensued between him and Metellus, a tribune, who barred his way. Caesar threatened to kill him, although every Roman citizen took an oath not to harm any tribune while in office. Onlookers were horrified, but eventually the official backed down, and Caesar went off with fifteen thousand bars of gold, thirty thousand of silver, and no fewer than 30 million *sestertii* (a loaf of bread cost roughly half a *sestertius*). His civil war history makes no mention of the affair.

In a further instance, describing his campaign against certain recalcitrant German tribes, he claims he stopped his advance as the Germans were herdsmen and not farmers, making it difficult for his army to live off the land; in fact, there was a long tradition of agriculture in the region. He sometimes writes admiringly of his subordinates beyond their deserts, because a particular officer was related to a family with which Caesar wanted to curry favor. When in 57 B.C. he took on and defeated the Nervii, a warlike Belgian tribe, he wrote that only five hundred of their army survived out of sixty thousand, and just three of their leaders out of six hundred, greatly inflated figures that were contradicted by his own comments in a later volume. He rarely gives a specific figure for his own casualties, although at one point he claims to have drowned 430,000 people, whom he drove into the marshes.* When he delivered the Egyptian throne to the twenty-one-year-old Cleopatra and her twelve-year-old brother, he does not add that the two siblings then wed each other, according to their country's tradition, or that shortly afterward Cleopatra had her brother poisoned.

---

* The Nervii were unusual in that alone of the major tribes they did not leave behind a city bearing their name—they must truly have been butchered to the last man. Plutarch claims that over a million Gauls were killed during Caesar's campaigns and as many more enslaved. Caesar's own estimates for the enemy dead in Gaul come nowhere near such figures, while on civil war casualties he is silent. Some in Rome accused him of our modern equivalent of genocide. Without doubt, Caesar could be ruthless, in the fashion of a Pompey, who in his early commands earned the sobriquet "the young butcher." On one occasion Caesar ordered that hundreds of prisoners have their hands cut off before they were set free. Against rebels in Cisalpine Gaul, he razed the homes and farms of his enemy, killing or enslaving their families, a tactic known as *vastatio,* the root of our words "waste" (as in "lay waste") and "devastation." But one reason that enemy towns surrendered to Caesar without a fight and that he was respected throughout his conquered territories was his general clemency. He often pardoned his enemies, even though a number would then sign up with other armies and oppose him again. Catullus wrote a poem criticizing Caesar—and found himself invited to dinner.

Some incidents are left unmentioned—not because Caesar had a sudden attack of modesty but because he wanted the spotlight to be on his military achievements, not directly on him (except that he wanted to convey that he emanated a mystical power, that he was unstoppable). As a young military tribune, he likely took part in quelling the uprising of 73–70 B.C., led by the famed gladiator Spartacus, yet he never mentions such a role. Again, during the civil war, he found that his 9th Legion, one of his most loyal, had mutinied, citing a range of grievances, not least that Caesar's clemency toward his defeated enemies was depriving his men of plunder. He rushed to where the 9th was camped and confronted the rebels, addressing them as *Quirites* (Gentlemen), as if they were no longer in the army, an implied threat that terrified them. His biographer Adrian Goldsworthy takes up the story:

> The proconsul's tone was stern and unrelenting as he explained that such a great conflict could not be hurried. He then announced that he intended to decimate the *Ninth,* an ancient punishment that involved selecting by lot one out of every ten men to be beaten to death by his comrades. The remainder would be dishonorably discharged from the army.

The veteran soldiers began to beg for mercy:

> Caesar knew how to work a crowd and gradually gave ground, finally saying that only 120 ringleaders would need to draw lots to choose twelve men to be executed. The selection is supposed to have been rigged to ensure that the names of the main troublemakers were drawn. However, Appian [a Greek historian from Alexandria, A.D. c. 90–c. 160] claims that one man who had not even been in the camp during the mutiny was included in the twelve. As soon as Caesar discovered this, he released the soldier and replaced him with the centurion who had tried to arrange the death of an innocent man in this way.

The *Commentaries* are silent on this entire incident.

Throughout his years campaigning, not just in Gaul but in England, Spain, and elsewhere, Caesar took pains to have his war reports regularly published, to remind the capital of his existence and to show his fellow Romans all he had achieved.* His commentaries were rushed to Rome in time to catch the first of the annual "theater games" in early April, where he could count on a large audience.

Caesar wrote to justify himself—certainly not to make money. Nor is there any notion that a prime objective was to chronicle the past. He wanted his words and deeds to be a matter of public knowledge, and his writings give ample evidence of how he liked to present himself, his weaknesses as a historian, as well as his strengths, and what he was trying to accomplish in his *Gallic Wars*. They were probably composed each winter when he was in Cisalpine Gaul and published each year just after the actual campaigns—a kind of dispatches from the front, the later books giving the impression of having been written hurriedly, for there is not the same careful word selection, and the narrative is more diffuse.

During campaigns, according to Plutarch, in the daytime Caesar would be conveyed to garrisons, cities, or camps, with one slave at his side to write from his dictation as he traveled. (He was the first to fold a roll into pages, for ease of dispatch.) Although no one knows exactly how he composed, Caesar would work with two secretaries at the same time, even when on horseback, a fondness for never wasting a moment that would make him unpopular in Rome, when during gladiatorial contests he would watch the shows while simultaneously dictating. One can imagine what he would have been like with a smartphone.

He hardly cared what people thought of him in his personal life, and from his earliest years reveled in standing out from the crowd. He had a notorious aversion to alcohol. When first he joined the Senate (or the "good men," as its leading members liked to dub themselves), he took to wearing his own version of the senatorial tunic, eschewing a belt and choosing long sleeves that reached down to the wrists and ended in a fringe. He was rumored to have had all his body hair re-

---

* Almost without exception, it was the wealthy elite in Rome who set to writing histories. It was, as ever, a matter of luck and timing who recounted your life story. All contemporary biographies of Cleopatra, for instance, were written by her enemies. In his account of the civil war, Brutus minimized his own role while playing up that of his uncle, Cato—a eulogy that infuriated Cicero, who promptly wrote a rejoinder. Caesar ordered Hirtius, who was to author his posthumous histories, to produce a book criticizing Cato, then used the account as the basis for his *Anticato*. But many tried their hand at authorship. Cleopatra—Greek for "glory of her race"—reportedly wrote on a range of subjects, from cosmetics and hairdressing to medicine and philosophy, while Mark Antony composed a book about drinking, of which he was a past master.

moved, and in his early years was very much the clotheshorse, his turn-out impeccable if eccentric (Cicero at first refused to take him seriously, believing that Caesar spent too much attention on his hairstyle). For jewelry, he shared with Cleopatra a lust for pearls, while throughout his life his sexual exploits and massive debts (he accumulated fortunes and gave fortunes away) were notorious.* He plucked his armpits and allowed the same license to his troops off-duty, saying his men would fight just as well even if they stank of perfume. "All my best troops are dandies," he said without concern.

Once it was clear that he had emerged triumphant from the civil war, Caesar's self-confidence knew little limit. He entered Rome near the end of July in 46 B.C. The Senate had already awarded him an un-precedented forty days of public thanksgiving, double the number he had earlier received for his victory over Vercingetorix, the Averni tribe's chieftain. In the days between processions—they lasted from September 21 till October 2—lavish feasts were provided, with as many as twenty-two thousand tables laid out at a sitting, for anyone in Rome to attend. Various traditions were upended so that he could be granted special privileges, including that in every procession he should be preceded by no fewer than seventy-two bodyguards. Parades of prisoners included Vercingetorix and Cleopatra's scheming sister, Arsinoe. Among the ac-companying athletic competitions and gladiatorial encounters five days were devoted to death struggles between animals, in which four hun-dred lions were killed, as were a number of giraffes, a beast never before seen in the city. At the Circus Maximus, two armies of captives, each of two thousand people, two hundred horses, and twenty elephants, fought to the death. Another sideshow was a naval encounter choreo-graphed in a specially flooded lake dug on the right bank of the Tiber. All these spectacles were intended to dwarf anything seen before.

And still the honors rolled in. Caesar was four times appointed dic-tator, in 44 B.C., *in perpetuo;* he presided over his own election to a sec-ond consulship, then to third and fourth terms, the last time without a

---

* "At one time in his life," wrote Thomas De Quincey, in an introduction to the *Commentaries* published in 1915, "when appointed to a foreign office, so numerous and so clamorous were his creditors that he could not have left Rome on his public duties had not Crassus come forward with assistance in money, or by guarantees, to the amount of nearly two hundred thousand pounds. And at another he was accustomed to amuse himself with computing how much money it would require to make him worth exactly nothing (i.e., simply to clear him of debts); this, by one account, amounted to upwards of two millions sterling."

The Assassination of Julius Caesar, *by Mariano Rossi (1731–1807).*
The moment has often been painted, but this version best captures the
muddle and uproar that must have characterized it.

colleague. The Senate named him censor for life and Father of the Fatherland, and his head featured on coins. He was granted a golden chair in the senate house, permitted to wear triumphal dress whenever he chose (along with a laurel wreath on his head, which hid his bald spot), and elevated into a semiofficial cult. His private house was bedecked with a triangular pediment, to make it look like a temple. Would he like to be declared a god?

It was all too much. Caesar remained extremely unpopular in certain high circles, and around sixty men began to plot his assassination. On the Ides of March* (the fifteenth) of 44 B.C., he was due to appear at a session of the Senate. Tillius Cimber, a heavy-drinking senator reputedly prone to violence, presented him with a petition to recall his exiled brother. Twenty other conspirators crowded around, pretending to submit their own petitions. As Caesar waved him away, Cimber grabbed him by the shoulder and pulled down his tunic.

---

* Thanks possibly to Shakespeare's reworking of Caesar's death, the Ides of March is a phrase forever associated with principled assassination and the opposition to tyranny. John Wilkes Booth used "Ides" as his code word for the day he planned to kill Lincoln.

At the same time, Servilius Casca, his dagger now in hand, came up behind Caesar and made a glancing thrust at his neck. Within moments, the entire pack was striking out. Caesar attempted to escape but, blinded by blood, tripped and fell; in a messy and almost bungled murder, the assassins continued hacking away as he lay sprawled on the lower steps of the atrium. There were so many hands gripping so many daggers that the conspirators lacerated one another—Gaius Cassius Longinus lunged at his victim, only to give Brutus a bad hand wound; another blow landed in a conspirator's thigh. Of the many thrusts, just twenty-three got home, although, according to Suetonius, a physician later established that only one wound, the second to his chest, proved fatal. The dictator's corpse lay on the Senate floor for nearly three hours before anyone dared move it. The room in which he was murdered was closed up, later to become a communal toilet. So ended the most famous assassination in history.

* * *

ONE OF THE MOST notable admirers of Caesar was Napoleon Bonaparte (1769–1821), who said that the great Roman's writings should be studied by any aspiring general (although he doubted the truthfulness of some of the *Commentaries*), and in exile on St. Helena produced a 238-page critique of his hero's campaigns. Napoleon would likewise use favorable descriptions of his battles to sell himself to his people, capitalizing on his victories to convey a persona associated with success and heroism, and his bulletins from the battlefield were published in newspapers throughout France. Letters were written that showed him as the victor, even when he lost battles. He also cheated at cards (a weakness shared with his eminent admirer Charles de Gaulle—even at solitaire); he had to win at everything.

He was interested in reading history, particularly Polybius and Plutarch, but at school won praise as a mathematician, his cast of mind being scientific. Yet in 1785, aged sixteen, he wrote *Clisson et Eugenie,* an autobiographical novella about a soldier and his lover. At military college, in one fifteen-month period, he filled thirty-six manuscript notebooks with his thoughts on artillery, philosophy, and history and later penned several short stories and political pamphlets. After his death there was an eager public for his writings: a book of seventy-eight maxims on the art of war and a volume of aphorisms were published, while his many letters appeared in various editions. One might think that Napoleon was confident enough of his place in history not to feel he had to write his version of events (during the French retreat from Moscow he had even burned the notes for an intended autobiography) but by 1823, two years after his death, four volumes of his *Memoirs* appeared, some 1,600 pages, "dictated by the Emperor at St. Helena to the Generals who Shared His Captivity and Published from the Original Manuscripts Corrected by Himself."

"My history is made up of events which mere words cannot destroy," runs one of his many sententious announcements. "Classic works are composed by rhetoricians, whereas they should be composed only by men of state or men of the world." According to the French historian Jacques Bainville, writing in 1933, "He even refashioned his historic remarks, writing them as they ought to have been uttered; and

Napoleon playing chess against his St. Helena companion de Montholon, who would deliberately lose to him.

they were thereafter repeated as he wrote them." As Anthony Burgess quipped in his novel *Napoleon Symphony,* "The vague historical, that's finished with; / Now the particularity of myth."

Few today read Napoleon's recollections, yet they rocketed to the top of the century's list of bestsellers. Like Caesar, Napoleon refers to himself in the third person and, self-righteous and argumentative, presents himself in the best light. However, even more than his predecessor he cannot refrain from puffing himself up. After the Battle of Lodi in 1796, for instance, between the French and Austrian armies, the Little Corporal* tells us, "This vigorous operation, conducted, under such a murderous fire, with all suitable prudence, has been regarded by military men as one of the most brilliant actions of the war." Caesar would have wanted a similar judgment made of his finest victories (and Lodi was not a decisive engagement), but he would never have stooped to self-congratulation.

It is still slightly surprising that Napoleon should be the subject of more books than Hitler or Jesus Christ. The *Encyclopedia Britannica* states that over two hundred thousand works have been written about him; French historians claim four hundred thousand. More volumes have been written with Napoleon in their title, according to Andrew Roberts, a recent biographer, than there have been days since Bonaparte's death. But Roberts does not tell us—nor do many of Napoleon's biographers, in fact—that Napoleon's memoirs are a peculiar testament. They begin in 1779 and end with the Italian campaign of 1806, so despite their length leave out the most crucial years of their author's career. Three further volumes, *Historical Miscellanies,* were later published, and here Napoleon is briefly quoted on the campaigns of 1813 and 1815, but these collections of conversations and remembrances are not by his hand. "Everything on earth is soon forgotten," Napoleon said, "except the opinion we leave imprinted on history." His own memoirs were his fingers on the scale.

---

* He earned this part-derogatory, part-affectionate nickname (which he liked and encouraged) after this battle because of his youth, his courage, and because he was said to be barely 5 foot 2 inches tall. According to most sources, however, he was 1.68 meters (5 foot 6), slightly above average height for the period. The contradiction exists due to the fact that French inches were different from English inches. Some paintings depict him alongside French grenadiers, usually the tallest soldiers in the French army, who tower over him. He is also caricatured as always having one hand inside his waistcoat, but such a pose was often used in portraits of rulers to indicate calm and stable leadership and was not specific to Napoleon.

* * *

CAESAR AND NAPOLEON FELT that they were writing for the record, their very use of the third person an indication that they wanted their accounts read as objective reports. That was never the intention of Ulysses S. Grant, commander of the Union army in the American Civil War and eighteenth president of the United States. Christened Hiram Ulysses (he later dropped his first name and substituted an "S," taken from his mother's maiden name of Simpson, to follow "Ulysses"), he was born into the two-room cabin, just twenty feet square, of a struggling tanner's family in Point Pleasant, Ohio. As a youngster he had to work hard both in the tannery "among the bloody skins and the giant rats that gnawed on them" and around the home (he perennially said that he preferred farming to any other occupation and came to love horses). In his memoirs he tells of one incident, when he was eight years old, that was to haunt him:

> A Mr. Ralston, living within a few miles of the village, . . . owned a colt which I very much wanted. My father had offered twenty dollars for it, but Ralston wanted twenty-five. I was so anxious to have the colt, that after the owner left, I begged to be allowed to take him at the price demanded. My father yielded, but said twenty dollars was all the horse was worth, and told me to offer that price; if it was not accepted I was to offer twenty-two and a half, and if that would not get him, to give the twenty-five. I at once mounted a horse and went for the colt. When I got to Mr. Ralston's house, I said to him: "Papa says I may offer you twenty dollars for the colt, but if you won't take that, I am to offer twenty-two and a half, and if you won't take that, I am to offer you twenty-five." It would not require a Connecticut man to guess the price finally agreed upon. . . . This transaction caused me great heart-burning. The story got out among the boys of the village, and it was a long time before I heard the last of it.

Classmates seized on Grant's first name, taunting him as "Useless," and the incident remained with him as a reminder that he was not a good businessman. Yet he was far from stupid academically, and his father ar-ranged for him to attend West Point, at a time when Congress was debating whether to abolish the academy. "Sam," as his new classmates dubbed him, after his initials and thus "Uncle Sam," spent his time there reading novels and drawing (he was also an accomplished artist) but miserably trying to learn French: cadets were expected to understand untranslated treatises on war by Napoleonic experts. Above all, Grant became a consummate horseman, the most daring in the academy. Crowds would gather to watch him turn a stubborn mount, often seventeen hands high (a hand is four inches, thus five feet eight inches, Grant's own height), into a calm and responsive animal. He loved to ride standing on a horse's back and gallop down the rough roads around his hometown by himself. At Grant's graduation, on July 1, 1843, the riding master placed a jump at the center of the ring, raised the bar higher than anyone had ever seen it, brought out a fractious horse that no one else could ride, and said, "Cadet Grant, take the jump." Uncle Sam went on to set a record that stood for twenty-five years.

Grant's memoirs are 1,231 pages long, yet only a small fraction is given to these early days. Two-thirds are taken up with the Civil War. He writes scarcely a page about events after the war ended, nor a word about his two terms as president. What is left is a masterful account of the Mexican War of 1846–48 (in which Mexico lost more than half its territory to the United States), then a distressed summary of the miserable six years that Grant had immediately following it. He started to drink whiskey to alleviate his migraines and won something of a reputation as a drunkard, until he was forced to resign from the army. His drinking bouts, which "furnished the only element of the spectacular" in Grant's personality—he would be sober for two to three months, then go on a two-day bender—go unmentioned in the memoirs, yet they serve as a leitmotif in Ron Chernow's 2018 biography, which charts Grant's "lifelong struggle with alcoholism."[*] Just once, on a bender in New York, was he so far gone that he was jailed for drunkenness.) He tried to work variously as a farmer in Missouri, a clerk in a custom-

---

[*] Chernow talks of Grant having the classic traits of an alcoholic (if a high-functioning one), in that he couldn't stop at a single glass, became jovial, stumbled round the room, slurred his words, and eventually turned sullen. In his study of the Civil War, Bruce Catton writes: "To do the army justice, it did not worry about Grant's drinking. A general who never got drunk was a rarity." See Bruce Catton, *A Stillness at Appomattox* (New York: Doubleday, 1953), p. 42. Grant never got drunk before a battle or during it. For an antidote to the accounts of these drinking binges, see "If Grant Had Been Drinking at Appomattox," James Thurber's comic take in *The Thurber Carnival* (New York: Harper Perennial, 2013), pp. 140–42.

house, a rent collector in St. Louis, a county engineer (even though West Point was the principal source of trained engineers in the country, Grant's job application was refused), and finally as a shop assistant in the family business, selling harnesses and other leather goods under the controlling eye of his two younger brothers, Simpson and Orvil.

In the severe depression of 1857, he was reduced to selling firewood in the street, and he had to pawn his gold watch for twenty-two dollars to buy Christmas presents for his children. He no longer owned a horse. In the words of another of Grant's biographers, William McFeely, "People talked of his vacant expression as he went down the long, long flight of stairs to work and climbed back up them to his house at the end of the day." Back in his hometown of Galena, in northwest Illinois, townsfolk would cross the street to avoid having to encounter his stooped, solitary figure. Then in 1861 began the Civil War—in Grant's words, "the most sanguinary and expensive war of modern times"—and at last he came into his own.

As soon as Charleston's Fort Sumter was fired upon, he volunteered, and the war "slid him back into uniform." He was thirty-nine. With help from old army friends, he wangled himself the surprising rank of colonel, and so began his meteoric ascent ("when he fought, he rose") until, in just three years, he had gone from chairman of a Galena recruitment meeting, his first new post, to being general in chief of the armies of the United States. Before long, the famous engagements of the war arrived—Belmont, Fort Donelson (the first important Union victory), Shiloh, Vicksburg, Chattanooga, Spotsylvania, Cold Harbor (8,500 casualties), and Petersburg, on to the fall of Richmond and Lee's surrender at Appomattox.

"The art of war is simple enough," Grant would explain. "Find out where your enemy is, get to him as soon as you can, and strike him as hard as you can, and keep moving on." At one point, in just seventeen days his army marched 150 miles and won five battles. He did not seem aware of his powers, yet his reputation grew, making him a hero, if of an unusual kind. By 1864 he was the most popular man in the United States. "Wherever he is, things *move*," declared Lincoln admiringly. In his book *The Mask of Command,* John Keegan argues that Grant invented "unheroic leadership." One of his staff, Charles Francis Adams, wrote to his father: "Grant is certainly a very extraordinary man. He does not look it and might pass well enough for a dumpy and slouchy little subaltern, very fond of smoking.* They say his mouth shows character. It may, but it is so covered with beard that no one can vouch for it." He scorned creature comforts, taking baths in a sawn-off barrel and allowing himself no servants, such that on one occasion, in February 1863, he wrote to his wife that by mistake his false teeth had been thrown away with his washing water.

Grant had a special gift for topography in reality or on paper. "His memory was astounding," records the dramatist and historian Elizabeth Diggs. "I think his preparation for the war came in childhood when he drove the delivery wagon loaded with skins from his father's tannery from the age of eight, through forests and across farmland over rutted paths that were not marked. He went alone and had to be lifted up to the high seat. People learned that he was always right about the best routes, and asked his advice." He was proud that he was "the best-travelled boy" in the West. He had the self-containment of an American frontiersman: a people watcher, who most often "padlocked his mouth," unless it was to chomp on a cigar, utterly concentrated on the matter at hand. He was ruthless on the battlefield, with a steely ability to send men to die and in negotiating surrenders would sweep aside any attempt at softening his stance from old West Point colleagues who were now his opponents. War meant fighting, and that meant killing, it meant annihilation. Herman Melville, who visited the Virginia battlefields in 1864 and even rode with Union cavalry pursuing Confederate guerrillas, captured in (not very good) verse "the silent General":

> *A quiet Man, and plain in garb—*
> *Briefly he looks his fill,*
> *Then drops his gray eye on the ground,*
> *Like a loaded mortar he is still:*
> *Meekness and grimness meet in him—*
> *The silent General . . .*
> *The resolute scheme of a heart as calm*
> *As the Cyclone's core.*

---

* Midwar, a newspaper printed in error that Grant liked cigars. Grateful citizens sent him box upon box, prompting him to switch from a pipe to a lifelong addiction to cigars; although he would try to cut down, he regularly got through two dozen a day. (Winston Churchill would smoke—or rather, chew—his way through ten a day, amounting to some 250,000 over his lifetime.)

Grant was far from being the dumb, inarticulate man of genius that he appeared in public, although it was a useful front. ("Pre-intellectual" was the historian Henry Adams's gibe; Grant was a figure who "would have seemed so even to the cave-dwellers.") He declared himself "unmilitary," continually stressing his simple nature, but he also used his memoirs to settle a few scores ("he appears to have clutched in his pocket a little squirming snake of resentment," T. J. Stiles writes). He also responded to negative criticism when he was accused of fighting civilians and soldiers alike, believing that he was a fair man, and was keen to record his memories of events, especially the Battle of Shiloh and the perceived brutality there. He stated, "The Northern troops were never more cruel than the necessities of war required." It was the evolution of weaponry and not Grant's ruthlessness that made it possible for the bullets of the Civil War—Minié balls weighing nearly two ounces—to be projected up to six hundred yards and still inflict the worst small-arms wound ever known in warfare.

Yet Grant was on occasion economical with the truth. He had been caught out at Shiloh and seriously misjudged his opponents' tactics but was not going to admit his mistake. He also makes no mention of his infamous General Order No. 11 of December 1862, barring Jews from his command.* Nor do the memoirs mention the burning of Atlanta on November 15, 1864—just its occupation. When, shortly after Lincoln's assassination and with Andrew Johnson the acting president, William Tecumseh Sherman, Grant's great friend and sometime rival, was officially reprimanded by a suddenly convened cabinet for exceeding his authority in treaty negotiations with the South, Grant records only that he, Grant, was "sent for" to attend the meeting, not that he had personally instigated it. Baring his soul was not his way.

Grant was also a practiced survivor—it is what makes the memoirs, in part, so riveting. During the Mexican War, for instance, in an attack on Monterrey, one of the largest cities in northeastern Mexico, he and his men were darting from house to house when they ran out of am-

---

* In the view of Diggs, who has written a play about Grant, he issued the order because of a conflict with his father, who was pushing for special treatment for himself and for several partners (all Jewish) who were war profiteers. "This made Grant furious. His father was always asking for favors and the only letters I have read where Grant is clearly angry are about this. At any rate, it was stupid and wrong to word the order the way he did. He 'made up' for it by appointing more Jews to important positions in his administration than any President till then." Letter to the author, April 7, 2016. He also developed close ties with Jews, going out of his way to speak in synagogues.

munition. Grant, on an unfamiliar horse, his left foot up behind the saddle, his right in the stirrup, his body protected by his mount's right flank, had to gallop full tilt past the Mexicans firing at him and was never hit. Ron Chernow puts this down to Grant's "preternatural tranquility" in the worst moments of combat.

During the Civil War, in Mississippi, while attempting to take the riverside garrison at Belmont, he was on his second horse of the day (the first having been shot from under him) and ambling alongside a nearby Union gunboat when he was attacked by Confederate troops. The horse "seemed to take in the situation," put his forefeet over the back of the bank, and with his hind feet well under him slid down the bank, stepped onto a single plank put out as a gangway to the gunboat, and carried his rider, the last man aboard, to safety.

Grant was at his best under pressure. A staff officer once witnessed a shell explode over him as he sat on a tree stump composing an order; the lieutenant general continued writing, and when he handed the communiqué over, its neat, uninterrupted script showed no sign that he had been disturbed at all. Grant was indifferent to danger. "Ulysses don't scare worth a damn," wrote one of his soldiers. In 1862, he wrote his wife, Julia, that he had already been in so many battles "that it begins to feel like home to me." Perhaps. Yet in later years Grant admitted he never liked the sound of cannon and so hated the sight of blood—the result of his recalling the carcasses and smells of his father's tannery, which reeked of the slaughtered animals—that he would not eat beef unless it was thoroughly well done, even burned to a crisp. He would not hunt or kill animals or birds; nor would he tolerate salacious stories or swearing and would walk away when either was unavoidable.

In August 1864, during the siege of Petersburg, he narrowly escaped being blown up by a bomb smuggled into his headquarters by a rebel—the "infernal machine" detonated an enormous explosion in an ammunition dump. On June 23, 1862, he escaped a prepared ambush only by luck, and also survived an assassination attempt while president. He was to have accompanied Lincoln to the theater on the night his leader was assassinated but cried off at the last moment. John Wilkes Booth had planned to kill them both.

Grant remained head of the army until 1868, when he was elected president. Those years after the Civil War, despite two terms in the White House, were an anticlimax. National hero he may have been,

Grant standing in front of a tent at Cold Harbor, Virginia, June 11 or 12, 1864. Only a man who had experienced so much defeat in his own life could have understood the psychology of defeated soldiers.

but his government was judged incompetent and corrupt, and his years in office were marked by financial scandals, glaring mistakes in foreign policy, and an almost complete lack of progress in national reconstruction. When his second term ended, in March 1877, he embarked on a two-year world tour (Joyce has Molly Bloom remember the thunderous salute that greeted Grant's flotilla when it reached Gibraltar). Political ambitions remained, but on his return home his hope of being nominated for a third term was soon dashed, for the Republicans selected James A. Garfield instead.

That failure precipitated a crisis. Simply, nearly sixty, Grant had little income, and—the schoolboy bartering for a young colt again—scarce talent for making any. Anxious to restore his finances, he was to fall victim to a classic Ponzi scheme.* In 1878, he moved to New York

---

* One thinks of Charles Ponzi in the 1920s and Bernie Madoff in more recent times, but such frauds have been perpetrated since the beginning of capitalism. According to some, the first such scam occurred in 1899, when William "520 Percent" Miller began operations in Brooklyn, New York. Miller forecast 10 percent a week interest and deployed some of the main characteristics of Ponzi schemes such as customers reinvesting the interest they made. He defrauded buyers out of a million dollars. But the scam against Grant preceded him by over a decade.

City to go into business with his son, Ulysses ("Buck") S. Grant, Jr., and a young venture capitalist named Ferdinand Ward, described by Ward's great-grandson Geoffrey as "a very plausible, charming, unobtrusive, slender person with a genius for finding older people and pleasing them."

At first, the firm of Grant & Ward did well, helped on by the war hero's reputation. Grant—in Edmund Wilson's words, "the incurable sucker," in Ron Chernow's, a "life-long naïf" who could not believe that dishonest people existed—took little part in the day-to-day running of the company, often signing papers without reading them, yet he boasted to his social circle that he was worth two and a half million dollars, so that family members and friends happily invested large sums of money. Ponzi schemes always come unstuck, sooner rather than later. By May 1884, Grant & Ward had failed. According to Mark Twain, the general lost $400,000, as well as a loan from William H. Vanderbilt of $150,000, made when Ward said that sum was needed to save the firm. The most telling act in terms of Grant's character was his insistence on repaying Vanderbilt even though the financier didn't want the money; Grant insisted because Vanderbilt said he had made the loan for him personally. It meant that Grant had to sell almost everything he had of value. An elderly relative who had scraped up savings of $1,000 was likewise bilked—in Twain's words, "Ward took it without a pang," spending investors' money on such visible self-indulgences as a mansion in Connecticut and a brownstone in New York City; he ended up in prison. Was Grant culpable too? The *New York World* ran a story headlined "Is Grant Guilty?"—with the implication that he was.

Grant's eminence rescued him, but by now he was to all intents destitute—reports said he had only $180 in cash—and once again he had to search about desperately for some way to provide for his family. Finally he agreed with a large publishing concern, the Century Company, to write four articles on important battles in the Civil War for one of their magazines. At that stage he had no inkling that a full-length book might earn him a sizable fortune, and in 1881, when Mark Twain had tried to persuade him to write his memoirs, he wouldn't listen. That he eventually did so was in large part due to the novelist, who had been introduced to him in 1866, during Grant's first term as president. By 1882, Twain, exasperated with his own publishers, had determined to publish his future books himself, which he did by setting up his nephew-in-law, Charles Luther Webster, as head of the new firm of Webster and Company. The enterprise started well, and after it had published *The Adventures of Huckleberry Finn* Webster handed his author and co-founder a check for $54,500—approximately $1.5 million in today's money.

"It had never been my intention to publish anybody's books but my own," declares Twain in his autobiography, but in November 1884 he had been walking home after giving a lecture when he overheard a passerby tell his companion that Grant had at last decided to write his memoirs. By this time, Twain had chatted with the general on several occasions, stopping by at Grant's home to shoot the breeze and share a cigar, so the very next morning he made sure to pay Grant a visit, only to find him in the very act of signing a contract with Century.

Generally a magazine publisher, the company was offering a flat 10 percent royalty on receipts. Twain immediately protested that the terms were "all wrong, unfair, unjust," and suggested that Grant should receive 75 percent of all profits and in addition that the publisher should pay running expenses out of the remaining fourth. Grant said he would feel like a robber if he insisted on such terms, and that anyway he doubted his book would bring in as much as $25,000 profit—the sum that William T. Sherman had earned from *his* memoirs, published nine years before. "It suddenly occurred to me," writes Twain, "that I was a publisher myself." He offered Grant a 20 percent royalty or 75 percent of the profits, and after several months' to-ing and fro-ing, a deal was struck.

Grant set to work, but on Christmas Eve 1883, stepping out of a rented carriage onto the frozen sidewalk by his home on Manhattan's East 66th Street, he fell and hurt his leg. This injury was soon compounded by a sore throat, eventually diagnosed as a malignant cancer at the root of his tongue. Newspapers said that the general's excessive smoking was to blame, but his principal doctor diagnosed a more likely cause: the shame and humiliation brought on by his disastrous investments. It was these mental miseries, he said, that gave the cancer its opening. At first, Grant dictated his memoirs, until it became impossible for him to use his voice. Because Twain was a famous writer and also Grant's publisher, a legend has grown up that he ghosted the work. That never happened; Twain facilitated and encouraged but never wrote a word. Grant had no need for him to do so.* As Sherman testified, "His expertise as a writer does not surprise me, for I have read hundreds of his letters and know too well his style and flawless effort at turning a phrase."

The memoirs in fact were a final stage in a process that began during the war and gathered steam in the decades thereafter. As he explained it,

> For the last twenty-four years I have been very much employed in writing. As a soldier I wrote my own orders, plans of battle, instructions and reports. They were not edited, nor was assistance rendered. As president, I wrote every official document, I believe, usual for presidents to write, bearing my name. All these have been published and widely circulated. The public has become accustomed to my style of writing. They know that it is not even an attempt to imitate either a literary or classical style; that it is just what it is pure and simple and nothing else.

Grant's prose has generally been praised for its pithiness and its lucidity—a sharp contrast with Lee's written orders and with other Civil War memoirs, which are weighed down by the fondness of the time for grandiloquent language. More than fifty years ago, Edmund Wilson, in *Patriotic Gore,* his study of the literature of the Civil War, delivered a judgment that has remained the litmus test:†

---

* In the early stages, Grant received help from Adam Badeau, a writer who had served as his military secretary during the last year of the war. Badeau severed relations well before the book was completed, having argued with Grant and his family about his fee and how he would be credited. After Grant's death, Badeau settled for $10,000—about $250,000 in today's money. He was never more than Grant's secretary and researcher, although he did write a three-volume biography of his former employer.

† In the course of his forty-two-page essay, Wilson mentions that the *Personal Memoirs* were one of the favorite books of Gertrude Stein and that she considered writing Grant's biography. She thought he might have been a great religious leader, Wilson reports: "It is not really difficult to understand what Gertrude Stein admired in Grant, what she must have felt she had in common with him: his impassivity, his imperturbability, his persistence in a prosaic tone combined with a certain abstractness which she regarded as essentially American. . . . She must have found in him a majestical phlegm, an alienation in the midst of action, a capacity for watching in silence and commanding without excitement." See Edmund Wilson, *Patriotic Gore: Studies in the Literature of the American Civil War* (New York: Oxford University Press, 1966), p. 140.

Grant's *Memoirs* are a unique expression of the national character . . . the *Memoirs* convey also Grant's dynamic force and the
definiteness of his personality. Perhaps never has a book so objective in form seemed so personal in every line, and though the
tempo is never increased, the narrative, once we get into the
war, seems to move with the increasing momentum that the soldier must have felt in the field. . . . Somehow, despite its sobri-
ety, it communicates the spirit of the battles themselves and
makes it possible to understand how Grant won them.

Grant frequently lacked confidence in his endeavors. Once the first
volume of the book was finished, whenever galley proofs went to the
author, a set was also sent to Twain, but he did not comment on them.
He eventually learned that Grant was disappointed that his literary
friend never expressed an opinion, so Twain hurried to put things
right. "He was venturing upon a new trade, an uncharted sea, and
stood in need of the encouraging word, just like any creature of common clay." As it happened, Twain had been reading Caesar's *Commentaries*, and was "able to say in all sincerity that the same high merits
distinguished both books—clarity of statement, directness, simplicity,
unpretentiousness, manifest truthfulness, fairness and justice toward
friend and foe alike, soldierly candor and frankness, and soldierly
avoidance of flowery speech. . . . Grant was pleased with this verdict.
It shows that he was just a man, just a human being, just an author."[*]

In his last year Grant was in constant pain and sometimes had the
feeling he was choking to death, so that he insisted that he sleep sitting
up. "If you could imagine what molten lead would be going down
your throat, that is what I feel when swallowing," he told his caregiv-
ers. All he could ingest was milk and cold soup. As one appreciative
reader has noted, "It is one of the great pictures of American history,
the cancer-wracked old man, writing all day out on the porch, under
blankets, his throat sealed after decades of cigars, unable to speak or
eat, and refusing morphine in order to keep his mind clear for writing

---

[*] One should not forget that Grant had a tart sense of humor. In his novel *1876* Gore Vidal tells
of Grant's disgust, when president, with Senator Charles Sumner and his outsize ego. Someone
informs Grant that Sumner does not believe in the Bible. Grant replies, "Only because he did
not write it."

Grant working on his memoirs in 1885. His style, he wrote, "is just what it is pure and simple and nothing else."

(he didn't refuse the cocaine-laced iced water, though)." The final chapters were written on pads held in his lap, his legs shaking with the effort.

Despite his plight, he wrote at great speed, sometimes completing fifty pages a day. In June 1885, as his condition worsened, the family moved to Mount McGregor, in Saratoga County, in northeastern New York State, to make life a little easier for him. Propped up on chairs and too weak to walk, Grant had one desire—to finish his history. He wrote its last sentence on July 18 and five days later he was dead.

The memoir was published in two volumes, the first on December 1, 1885, the second in March the following year. There were two editions, one in cloth at nine dollars and the other with calf binding at twenty-five dollars. Each copy contained what looked like a handwritten note from Grant. Twain came up with a plan to reach millions of veterans in the very weeks they were mourning Grant's death. Ten thousand salesmen, many Union veterans dressed up in faded uniforms and old medals, crisscrossed the North drumming up orders. The memoirs sold three hundred thousand sets, netting Grant's widow more than eight million dollars in today's money. The family fortunes were saved—with a good deal to spare.

In a letter to his favorite doctor, John H. Douglas, just days before he died, Grant wrote:

It seems that man's destiny in this world is quite as much a mystery as it is likely to be in the next. I never thought of acquiring rank in the profession I was educated for; yet it came with two grades higher prefixed to the rank of General officer for me. I certainly never had either ambition or taste for political life; yet I was twice President of the United States. If anyone had suggested the idea of my becoming an author, as they frequently did, I am not sure whether they were making sport of me or not.

CHAPTER 15

THE SPINNING OF HISTORY

Churchill and His Factory

———

It will be found much better by all parties to leave
the past to history, especially as I propose to write
that history myself.

—WINSTON S. CHURCHILL, COMMONS SPEECH, 1948

IT WAS AT WESTMINSTER IN 1948, ON THE FIRST DAY OF A NEW PARLIA-
ment, that the right honorable Member for Woodford made his famous retort about writing a history of the Second World War.* And
write that history he did, among his forty-three published works being
six volumes on the conflict, running 1,909,000 words from the end of
the First World War to July 1945. Published between 1948 and 1953,
they won him the Nobel Prize for Literature and were followed by his
four-volume *A History of the English-Speaking Peoples* (1956–58), for
which his Labour opponent Clem Attlee teasingly provided an alternative title, *Things in History That Interested Me.*

In a 1930s exchange with Stanley Baldwin, also in the Commons,
Churchill declared, "History will say that the Right Honorable Gentleman was wrong in this matter." (Broad grin.) "I know it will, be-

---

* His comment came in a long answer to a question about British foreign policy: "If we are to
go into the conduct and opinions of individuals between the two wars, as we are quite prepared
to do, I am very ready to do so. . . . In case at any forthcoming General Election there may be
an attempt to revive these former controversies, we are taking steps to have little booklets prepared recording the utterances, at different moments, of all the principal figures involved in
those baffling times. For my part, I consider that it will be found much better by all parties to
leave the past to history, especially as I propose to write that history myself." Hansard, vol. 446,
cc 529–622. The remark is often misquoted as, "History will be kind to me, for I intend to write
it," possibly because it was a repeated Churchill trope.

cause I shall write that history." He made a similar comment in January 1944 in an exchange of telegrams with Stalin. He liked repeating his best epigrams. Another favorite phrase was: "Let us go forward together," which he employed on nineteen occasions, usually as a call to unity. He used it at least once to his dog, a red-orange poodle named Rufus.

One may quibble about Churchill's place in the pantheon of national leaders who were also historians. In 2004, Bill Clinton's *My Life* prompted reviewers to reassess presidential memoirs, and the majority agreed that Grant's remain the gold standard—despite not writing about his time as president at all. Grant was not a professional author, whereas Churchill at once set out to earn his living by his pen. His collected works run to thirty-seven volumes, 5.1 million words written (as well as 6.1 million words spoken), more than Shakespeare and Dickens combined.

Politics was, as one biographer put it, the family business, but for much of the time Churchill's parliamentary salary counted for only 2.5 percent of his income, compared with literary earnings thirty times greater. Over the course of his ninety years he earned, in today's money, about forty million dollars, while spending sixty-five years in the House of Commons, for much of that time either as prime minister, cabinet minister, or leader of the opposition.

Churchill's father, Lord Randolph, was a glamorous aristocrat who at one time was the rising star of the Conservative Party, at thirty-seven chancellor of the exchequer. But, erratic and narcissistic, he overplayed his hand, making an ill-timed resignation. He also led a dissolute life, dying at forty-five, reportedly from syphilis but more likely from a rare brain disease that shared some of the same symptoms. It was a trying time for the family motto, *Fiel pero desdichado,* "Faithful but Unfortunate." "Faithless and feckless" would have been more appropriate.

Both Winston's parents were, in Muriel Spark's phrase, "famous for sex." Winston's beautiful heiress mother, Jennie Jerome of New York, had numerous affairs, including one with the obese Prince of Wales, and three husbands ("there was more of the panther than of the woman in her look," noted one admirer) and like her husband was profligate with her inheritance. Winston and his younger brother, Jack, had to work for their living: "The only thing that worries me in life is—

money," Winston told Jack. "We shall finish up stone broke." Indeed, though never "poor,"* on more than one occasion he was close to financial collapse (one reason that Churchill wrote so many books in the 1930s was his unsuccessful stock market speculation and gambling debts). He was born both at the top of the tree and out on a limb. Legally, his name was Spencer-Churchill, and this was what he answered to at school (to his frustration, as it meant he took a low position in alphabetical roll calls), but he soon relegated "Spencer" to form his middle initial, possibly because his father had once made a famous gibe against ambitious politicians who used double-barreled names to impress.

After school at Harrow (where, against school rules, he kept a bulldog, and would also, for a consideration, write essays for other boys) and military training at Sandhurst (it took him three attempts to get in, yet he graduated twentieth of 130 cadets—not, as he wrote in *My Early Life,* eighth out of 150), he was sent to India, to serve with the 4th Queen's Own Hussars. He had already written some articles based on a visit to Cuba in 1895 to witness the rebellion against Spain, the *Daily Graphic* paying him five guineas ($650 now) a pop, and keen on writing more inveigled himself as a correspondent for *The Daily Telegraph* covering the war between Turkey and Greece. Fifteen dispatches were published, and he turned these into his first book, *The Story of the Malakand Field Force,* which appeared in April 1898, while he was still only twenty-four.†

Back with his regiment in India, he completed his only novel, *Savrola,* in 1898, then the following year reworked his experiences with Lord Kitchener's expedition up the Nile for *The River War: An Historical Account of the Reconquest of the Sudan,* a thrilling narrative (Lieutenant Churchill had commanded a troop of lancers in the British Army's last

---

* The first time Churchill dialed a phone number himself he was seventy-three. It was to the speaking clock, which he thanked politely. See Andrew Roberts, *Churchill: Walking with Destiny* (New York: Viking, 2018), p. 11.

† Beatrice Webb, the famous social reformer, on meeting Churchill early in his career, described him as "a self-conscious and bumptious person with a certain personal magnetism, restless, shallow in knowledge, reactionary in opinions, but with courage and originality—more the American speculator in type than the English aristocrat." The book editor Maxwell Perkins concurred: Churchill seemed "much more like an American than an Englishman." See Maxwell Perkins, *Editor to Author: The Letters of Maxwell E. Perkins,* ed. John Hall Wheelock (New York: Scribner, 1987), p. 161. Lord Esher told Earl Haig: "His temperament is of wax and quicksilver." *Journals and Letters of Reginald, Viscount Esher,* ed. Maurice Brett, vol. 4, 1934, p. 121.

full cavalry charge against the Mahdi's sixty-thousand-strong forces at Omdurman). This was no longer just the reports of a war correspondent but a genuine attempt at history, buttressed by its author's reading of such writers as Samuel Johnson, Edmund Burke, Gibbon, and Macaulay—the last two of whom he could recite at length from memory, having as early as fourteen won a prize for reciting 1,200 lines of *Lays of Ancient Rome* without error. Lewis Namier would years later rebuke him for painting "imaginary pictures of what *may* have happened or what some people must have felt,"* but more importantly Churchill's direct experience of fanaticism in the Northwest Frontier and with the Mahdi in Sudan later helped him see the Nazi threat quite differently than other British politicians.

In late 1899, he sailed to Cape Town to cover the Boer War (at £250 a month, only £50 less than his annual pay as a soldier), taking with him six cases of wine and spirits for the three-week voyage. At Bloemfontein, his kit comprised an ox wagon "full of Fortnum & Mason groceries and of course liquor." Before long he was captured but made a daring escape. This led to *London to Ladysmith,* published five days before the relief of Mafeking, following a 217-day siege of the crucial British stronghold; amid much public rejoicing, his account sold fourteen thousand copies. He had been shot at on four continents.

All this time Churchill was looking around for a promising constituency as a way into Parliament and after one failed attempt was adopted as one of two Conservative MPs for Oldham. The vote of October 1900, dubbed "the Khaki Election," as it came in the middle of the Boer War, saw the celebrated war correspondent and POW swept into the Commons: "It is useless to preach the gospel of patience to me," he rejoiced. A grueling tour of the United States followed, but one that enabled him to write to his mother that in just two years he had earned £10,000—the equivalent today of $320,000—split between his lecture fees and the earnings from his five books, all this at a time when only a million Britons paid any income tax, so qualifying because they earned at least £160 a year.

Churchill was the best-paid British journalist of his day and one of

* In December 1897 he wrote to his mother of his journalism: "I very often yield to the temptation of adapting my facts to my phrases." See Carlo D'Este, *Warlord, A Life of Winston Churchill at War, 1874–1945* (New York: Harper, 2008), p. 74.

*A well-thatched Churchill bound for England on board a steamer in
Durban, South Africa, as a* Morning Post *war correspondent during the
Boer War. He achieved national hero status after his capture and
subsequent escape from the State Model School in Pretoria.*

a select league of financially successful authors. His next book advance,
for a two-volume biography of his father, was £8,000, negotiated for
him by Lord Randolph's flamboyant friend, the writer and "thundering liar" Frank Harris. By 1902, Churchill had thrown himself into the
research, writing the script in his flowing longhand, the last occasion
he was to compose this way. (He loved to write with what was known
as a Squeezer pen, which used rubber to suck up ink: "That is true happiness.") By the time both volumes had been published,* in 1905, he

---

* Not only does the biography defend his father and exalt his career, but throughout his life
Winston Churchill referred to him with awe (naming his firstborn after him), and spoke of
his wish that his father had not seen him as a failure. In November 1947 he dictated a short
story entitled "The Dream," based on his own experience, a dream he had had some weeks
before. In the tale he is in his studio at Chartwell, making a copy of a portrait of his father,
when Randolph suddenly appears in front of him, just as he was in his prime. In the conversation that ensues, he still has little good to say about his son, while Winston tells him he
makes his living as a writer and does not mention the two world wars or his part in them. "I
really wonder you didn't go into politics," Randolph muses. "You might even have made a
name for yourself." The apparition lights a cigarette, and as the match flares he vanishes. The
story is full of humor and pathos, the longing for parental approval clear, even after so many
years.

was part of the government, first as a junior minister in the Colonial Office, then in 1908 as a full cabinet member as president of the Board of Trade. He was thirty-three.

Provided with secretaries for the first time, he began dictating his letters (although he was never a good *long* letter writer), and proclaiming to others became his preferred method of producing books and articles, living, as he put it, "from mouth to hand," a man who "spoke his books and wrote his speeches." One cannot help seeing his methods of composition lovingly described in his protagonist in *Savrola:*

Successive cigarettes had been mechanically consumed. Amid the smoke he saw a peroration, which would cut deep into the hearts of a crowd; a high thought, a fine simile, expressed in that correct diction which is comprehensible even to the most illiterate, and appeals to the most simple; something to lift their minds from the material cares of life and to awake sentiment. His ideas began to take the form of words, to group themselves into sentences; he murmured to himself; the rhythm of his own language swayed him; instinctively he alliterated. Ideas succeeded one another, as a stream flows swiftly by and the light changes on its waters. . . . Could not tautology accentuate it? He scribbled down a rough sentence, scratched it out, polished it, and wrote it again. The sound would please their ears, the sense improve and stimulate their minds. What a game it was!

The essence of his oratory became not spontaneity but prior composition, ever since on April 22, 1904, speaking in the Commons, he lost the thread of his argument and had to sit down, acutely embarrassed. Thereafter he came to the House furnished with notes in case his memory failed him. Usually he ensured that it didn't, and up to 1904 he would prepare as if he were going on stage. He would walk around talking to himself or to one of his cats, rehearsing lines for later use. One of his most famous speeches, made to the Commons on May 13, 1901, he drafted six times, then memorized it. On one country-house weekend, he failed to appear at his hostess's table until teatime and was heard all day booming away in his bedroom, to the accompaniment of resounding knocks on the furniture. He took to copying his father's practice of using pauses while speaking, even fumbling in his pockets for a note he did not want or need. And some of his great phrases during the Battle of Britain were far from freshly minted.

The word patterns of "Never in the field of human conflict has so much been owed by so many to so few" (August 20, 1940) can be found in at least five of his speeches or writings between 1899 and 1920; the phrase "special relationship," for relations between the United States and its former colonial overlord, was coined by Ramsay MacDonald back in 1930, then neatly appropriated; and "Iron Curtain," first used

This cartoon, "A Choice of Characters," appeared in Punch *in 1912.*
It was captioned, "Let's see now; shall I go as Demosthenes, d'Artagnan,
Dan O'Connell-Leno, or merely the usual Daniel in the lion's den?"
A then thirty-seven-year-old Churchill was First Lord of the Admiralty
and already accustomed to many roles. Oddly, "The Writer" is absent.

by Churchill in a letter to Harry Truman on May 13, 1945, most likely originated in Nazi propaganda during the dying days of the Third Reich, to be reemployed for the famous speech against Communism at Fulton, Missouri, in March 1946.

"Blood, toil, tears and sweat" has a history to it too. Livy, Caesar, and Francisco Pizarro had all written of "blood, sweat and toil," Churchill making the effective addition of "tears."* Other phrases— "The Battle of the Atlantic," minted in March 1941, the almost talismanic "Some chicken. Some neck," and "Meeting jaw to jaw is better than war" (not "jaw-jaw is better than war-war," as often quoted) were his alone, as were neologisms such as "Middle East" and "summit." His famous 141-word "We shall go on to the end" speech of May 1940 was deliberately made up of short words or monosyllables, almost all derived from Old English, although *confidence* comes from Latin and *surrender,* one surely not chosen by accident, from the French. He had an estimated vocabulary of sixty-five thousand words, whereas most people possess less than half that number. It is also worth remembering that in 1952 political hopefuls could plan for average soundbites of twelve seconds; today they get four.[†]

Politics occupied Churchill until the end of the First World War, but from 1918 on, while a member of Lloyd George's coalition government (1918–22), he set about what was to be a five-volume, 823,000-word history of that war, *The World Crisis,* in large part a vindication of his role in it, especially the disastrous Gallipoli expedition of 1915, which had led to his resigning his position as First Lord of the Admiralty under a cloud. The books are impressive, all the more so for having been completed in his spare time, though they are far from his best work. "As with *Lord Randolph Churchill,*" judges Peter Clarke, whose study *Mr. Churchill's Profession* is devoted to assessing Churchill's writing career, "the author resorts both to outright suppression and to se-

---

* In 1611, John Donne had rhapsodized about "tears, or sweat, or blood," in a religious sonnet, and "blood and sweat and tears" features in a Teddy Roosevelt speech of 1897. The same list appears in *London to Ladysmith* and in a *Daily Telegraph* article Churchill wrote on General Francisco Franco of Spain. Clearly some of his best phrases were years in the making. Yet when Churchill made his speech in the Commons, it was not well received. See Andrew Roberts, *Churchill: Walking with Destiny* (London: Viking, 2018), p. 527.

† In contrast with Churchill's constant radio broadcasting—often having to repeat his Commons speeches, as they were not recorded at the time—Hitler virtually stopped broadcasting once the war started turning against him. The two men were different in almost everything; just about the only characteristic they shared was a hatred of whistling.

lective deletion, likewise unacknowledged, in the documents chosen."
The books were full of "truths, half truths and dubious assertions."
Churchill's cabinet colleague Arthur Balfour acidly described them as
"Winston's brilliant Autobiography, disguised as a history of the Universe." Nevertheless, they brought in £27,000—almost a million dollars today.

Such earnings were needed. Throughout his life Churchill spent at a
prodigious rate, his champagne intake, his whisky, his cigars (costing him
£13 a month—$750 now), his trips overseas, his grand home* with its
library of sixty thousand books, a circular outdoor pool kept heated all
year round, a special building to house his beloved collection of butterflies, and his large family all requiring sizable and regular injections of
capital. By 1920 he owed his bank £20,000 ($1.1 million now). So it is not
surprising that Churchill soon produced yet another book, *My Early Life*
(London, 1930; U.S. title *A Roving Commission*), one of his most graceful
pieces of writing, with much of it about what constitutes a good death.

Had his political career continued uninterrupted, such a regular
flow of literary endeavor may have been dammed, but from the "flapper election" of 1929 till the outbreak of war a decade later, Churchill
was out of office, with time to spare for yet two further projects. The
first was the biography of his ancestor the first Duke of Marlborough,
for which he received an advance of about a million dollars in today's

---

* In the 1920s, staff at Chartwell, his home in Westerham, near Sevenoaks in Kent, included
two kitchen servants, two pantry attendants, two housemaids, an odd-jobs man, a personal maid
for his wife, Clementine, a nursery maid for their youngest daughter, and two secretaries. Outdoors staff included a chauffeur, three gardeners, a farm bailiff, and a groom for polo ponies:
wages of some £2,000 a year. In 1935 alone, his bill for wines and spirits was £10 a week—about
three times the earnings of a male manual worker of the period, or enough to employ half a
dozen female domestic servants. But Churchill's income that year (a peak figure for him in the
1930s) was £16,312—over £375,000 today. To get an idea of his annual alcohol consumption,
David Lough, who has written a book about Churchill's finances, told NPR in an interview that
in 1908, the year he married Clementine, he ordered nine dozen bottles and seven dozen half-
bottles of Pol Roger 1895 vintage champagne; four dozen half-bottles of the 1900 vintage; six
dozen bottles of Saint-Estèphe (red) and seven dozen bottles of sparkling Moselle (white) wine;
five dozen bottles of port; six dozen bottles of whisky; three dozen bottles of twenty-year-old
brandy; three dozen bottles of vermouth; and four dozen of gin. "By 1936, he owed his wine
merchant the equivalent of $75,000 in today's money. He was also in hock to his shirtmaker, his
watchmaker, and his printer." Rich friends bailed him out, and at one point the government
settled his liquor bills. In old age, he told a group of young Tory MPs, "The secret of drinking
is to drink a little too much all the time." See interview by Andrew Roberts with Francis
Maude, July 26, 2016. The novelist C. P. Snow opined that Churchill could not have been an
alcoholic because no alcoholic could have drunk that much. In Churchill's own estimate, he
consumed half a bottle of champagne a day for forty-eight years; when he died in 1965, Pol
Roger put a black border around the labels of bottles exported to Britain. See David Lough, *No
More Champagne: Churchill and His Money* (London: Picador, 2015).

terms. The idea for the second came about during a visit to New York, in October 1929, when his publishers took him to a football game. What about, his editor Max Perkins suggested, a history of the British Empire? Churchill countered: "What about a history of the English-speaking race?" This duly became *A History of the English-Speaking Peoples,* a study that would be "about half-and-half British and American history." From their inception both enterprises grew like topsy, so that *Marlborough: His Life and Times* was published sometimes in two volumes, sometimes three, a total of one million words, and his history of the English-speaking peoples in four.

An early dictaphone was installed at Chartwell to help the process. Churchill gave the machine a test run on a day when he allowed all his typists a day off—but he never pressed the start button. When the machine failed to record anything, he banished it. He had a lisp, a distinctive slurring of some consonants, particularly pronouncing the letter *s* as "sh." In 1905, he asked the royal physician Sir Felix Semon to cut out what he thought was an extraneous ligament on his tongue, which Semon refused to do. Then, during the 1940s, he acquired several custom-made dentures, purposely designed to be loose-fitting—they did not quite connect with the top of his mouth—so that he could preserve the diction famous from his wartime radio broadcasts. The way the dentures fitted ensured that his lispy sibilants remained unaltered. He carried an extra set at all times—when angry, he would even throw his dentures across the room. His dental technician could tell how the war was going based on how much repair work he had to do.

Documents, dictation, and drafts were the "three Ds" of the Churchill production line. He would dictate anywhere, in train, car, or elevator, but preferably late at night, in his home, with a secretary (using a specially muffled typewriter to avoid disturbing his trains of thought) and a research assistant. Fortified by a good dinner (for his final snack before retiring, he liked a cup or plate of soup, and insisted, even at the Yalta Conference of February 1945, on operating on "tummy time"), he would pace up and down his study for several hours, a brandy or whisky and soda in hand, sometimes considering his words carefully, sometimes speaking at such a rush that his secretaries could hardly keep up. As Simon Schama said of Barack Obama, his eloquence was both his great gift and his great curse.

Churchill usually made amendments in the sober light of the following morning, over breakfast in bed. He would stay close to the original on matters of fact but tightened the prose, adding sharper nouns and adjectives. He wrote, he said, the way the Canadian Pacific Railway had been built: "First I lay the track from coast to coast, and after that I put in the stations." Once his draft had been sent to the printers, the galley proof of each night's work was returned to Chartwell for its author to mull over. The process was extremely costly for the publishers, since in his contracts Churchill had cannily insisted on a special provision that allowed for proofing costs to be met by them.

"*Marlborough* alone is a crusher," Churchill told his wife in January 1937, "then there are always articles to boil the pot!" He may have been a professional writer, but he was not a professional historian, and for the biography of his ancestor he established a modus operandi that was to serve him well for the rest of his life: getting other people to do the basic research and often to compose first drafts. In Volume One of *Marlborough* (published in 1933) he thanks Maurice Ashley, ultimately the author of several well-received books on seventeenth-century England, "who for the last four years has conducted my researches."

Ashley replied belatedly to such acknowledgments in a 1968 book, *Churchill as Historian,* in which he states categorically that page by page *Marlborough* bears Churchill's stamp: "Every word of it was originally dictated to his secretary, mostly in the small hours of the morning. . . . As his research assistant, I sat by in case he needed any facts supplied or verified, but he had such a marvelous memory that he rarely got them wrong." Churchill's powers of recall, as another aide has recorded, were "Napoleonic." Such a mode of writing may have been so, but as Peter Clarke observes, "The scholarly activity of 'writing history' has rather more to it than the exercises in delegation that can bring . . . an eloquent orator the better of an argument." For Churchill, the essential task was to generate the requisite rhetoric in a way that did no violence to the research that had been fed him. "Give me the facts, Ashley, and I will twist them the way I want to suit my argument," he said on one occasion, no doubt teasing his young researcher.[*]

---

[*] No doubt; although in April 1955, on the final weekend before leaving office for the last time, Churchill had the huge canvas of Peter Paul Rubens's "The Lion and the Mouse," which depicts a scene from Aesop's Fables, taken down from the Great Hall at Chequers, and, convinced that the mouse had been indistinctly painted and armed with his legion of paintbrushes, set about "improving" the work. Not only was the official record at his command to change but great works of art too.

From 1935 well into 1937 he took time off from his main commissions to complete *Great Contemporaries,* which was favorably received. He was adept at doing brilliant sketches of the not-quite first rank, while the element of play is there in nearly everything he wrote (in a lengthy disquisition on French character: "The Almighty in His infinite wisdom did not see fit to create Frenchmen in the image of En-

A liberated Frenchman lights Churchill's cigar following the German defeat. Churchill would give away the stubs to either his gardener at Chartwell or the news vendor at Crystal Palace, from whom he regularly bought an Evening Standard *but who always refused payment. He also had a love of unusual hats—he felt they were useful for cartoonists.*

glishmen. . . ."). Several months into 1938, he published a volume of his speeches warning of the Nazi menace, and the end of that year saw the final volume of *Marlborough,* which he shortened from 750 pages to 650—it was like "cutting off your fingernails and toes," he lamented.[*] He also started to mine the articles he had written for a collection, published in June 1939 as *Step by Step,* which again sold well. *A History of the English-Speaking Peoples* had barely been begun, yet by the time war was declared Churchill, working at a furious pace, had almost

---

[*] Ever loyal to his ancestors, he quoted the contemporary belief that Marlborough was so mean that he did not dot his *i*'s to save money on ink—but passed this off as commendable thrift!

completed the book, a million words written in a year and a quarter. For any writer, let alone one of the busiest politicians in the world, the output was phenomenal. There is a picture of a pig carrying a ten-ton weight on its back that Churchill drew for Clementine, having written twenty thousand words in just a few days during July 1932.

Some projects simply got left behind. He toyed with biographies of Abraham Lincoln and Giuseppe Garibaldi and always intended to write a book about Napoleon—the one writing project he really wanted to take on; if one types the word *Napoleon* into the Churchill papers at Churchill College, Cambridge, back come fifty-two relevant catalogue entries. Not incidentally, his first action on entering the Colonial Office in 1905 was to place a bust of Napoleon on his desk, and it later had pride of place at Chartwell. In 1928, he met Charlie Chaplin for the first time and suggested they make a film together about the young Napoleon, with Chaplin directing and playing the lead while Churchill would write the script, which he duly did (for the Korda brothers). Four years later, in January 1932, he told Robert Ballon, who was writing a biography of Bonaparte, that he would contribute a five-thousand-word introduction, but only on condition he had the right to reuse the material, "as he might one day write a book on the subject." In *A History of the English–Speaking Peoples,* ever the Francophile, he describes Napoleon as "the greatest man of action born in Europe since Julius Caesar." Until Churchill's own day, one presumes.[*]

A History was put aside with the outbreak of war and was finally published in four volumes between 1956 and 1958, the latter two completed when Churchill was over eighty. When he returned to the project in 1945 he found a massive rewrite was necessary and so set about organizing at least fifteen professional historians to help, a team that included Asa Briggs, whom in 2010 I interviewed at his home in Sussex.

Briggs had met Churchill's leading helper, a young Oxford history don, William Deakin, in Bletchley, where Briggs was a cryptographer and code-breaker. Deakin introduced Briggs to Alan Hodge (founder, along with Peter Quennell and Churchill's longtime lieutenant Bren-

---

[*] In January 2020 I asked his most recent biographer, Andrew Roberts (he was entering the lists as the 1,010th, Roberts reckoned), what quality Churchill most shared with his 1,009th biographer and fellow prime minister, Boris Johnson. "Audacity," he replied, and added that Churchill would regularly quote to himself Napoleon's words, in French (borrowed in turn from the great revolutionary George-Jacques Danton): *de l'audace, encore de l'audace, et toujours de l'audace.* Audacity, more audacity, and even more audacity.

dan Bracken, of *History Today*), and thereafter "most of my dealings went through him." Briggs was at that time specializing in modern European and English history. "I was sent material by Hodge, a printed version of Churchill's first attempts. My job was to scribble things in the side about factual accuracy, interpretation, and style."

What particularly surprised Briggs (later a Labour peer) was that Churchill took a decidedly radical approach to American history, mainly based on his reading of Charles Beard, the American radical-progressive, and his wife, Mary. Briggs, who was only twenty-four in 1945, recalled: "I was in the ridiculous position of saying his account was too left wing." Churchill appreciated candor and asked Briggs to elaborate. "I was prepared to change the perspective a little," Briggs said, "to tone down some of the things," but in the end Churchill's opinion prevailed. When the entire project was completed, Briggs received a check for £100—at a time when his annual salary was £400—but was never acknowledged in print.

But that is to jump ahead. In 1939, the Second World War was about to erupt, and for the next thirteen years the story of Britain's survival would be Churchill's chief literary endeavor. Even as he was working to forestall a German invasion, he was planning his history of the conflict. By 1940, the putative memoirs had become a Whitehall joke. That January, Lord Halifax forwarded Neville Chamberlain a long letter from Churchill (about lack of action in Scandinavia) with the note: "It's one more for the book!" Chamberlain's own comment was: "Of course I realize that the letters are for the purpose of quotation in the book that he will write hereafter." As Andrew Roberts, in his massive (and massively readable) biography, observes: "For Churchill, writing history was a natural adjunct to making it." The Churchill *très manqué* Boris Johnson adds, "Whatever Churchill said or did, he had an eye, like Julius Caesar, to the way he would report it." Indeed, the six *Second World War* volumes, over 4,200 pages, have been likened to Caesar's *Gallic Wars*.

More than ever before, a wide-ranging group of young researchers together with seasoned experts (including two retired generals—Hastings "Pug" Ismay and Henry Pownall) formed an impressive production line: Edward Marsh (his longest-serving parliamentary private secretary (PPS) to the prime minister: Churchill wrote the *Times* obituary of Marsh's lover, Rupert Brooke), Denis Kelly (an impecunious barrister who became his chief archivist), Leslie Rowan, John Martin,

Albert Goodwin, Professor R. V. Jones, Charles Wood (the main proofreader), Geoffrey Hudson, and above all William ("Bill") Deakin. The inner group called themselves "The Syndicate," but two successive cabinet secretaries, Edward Bridges and Norman Brook, not only facilitated Churchill's requests to use government papers but prepared vital drafts that sometimes—such as Brook's summary of the cabinet's war strategy in 1942—ended up in the relevant volume virtually untouched. "I am most profoundly grateful," Churchill wrote Brook. "The reconstruction . . . was a masterpiece." Jock Colville, the assistant private secretary for most of Churchill's postwar stint as prime minister, concluded: "I often think how difficult it will be for future historians to know what is 'genuine Churchill' and what is 'school of.' We are all fairly good imitators of his epistolary style now."

David Reynolds sums up: "What for shorthand we call 'Churchill's memoirs' are a complicated literary text—not entirely Churchill's work and not simply memoirs. Churchill's wartime minutes and telegrams formed the core, but these were interlinked with reminiscences he dictated at various times from 1946 and by drafts on the historical background from the Syndicate of research assistants." This often meant a dozen galley versions—the initial printer's bill for the first volume of the memoirs was £1,444 (more than $70,000 today). Many chapters were radically altered in the process. "I do not describe it as history, for that belongs to another generation," Churchill wrote in his opening preface. The Syndicate's contribution is one reason that the volumes are more than memoirs. He was operating as the head of a research group, with Chartwell (so aptly named) a veritable word factory, as he himself called it. "I'm not writing a book," Churchill admitted. "I'm developing a property." By the time he became prime minister again, in October 1951, four volumes had been published and a fifth was in the press. When the first appeared, most reviewers treated it as history rather than autobiography; none guessed it was the work of many hands. Denis Kelly, a key member of the Syndicate, has recorded that he was often asked how much the great man really wrote. That, he said, was "almost as superficial a question" as asking a master chef, "Did you cook the whole banquet with your own hands?"

Certainly Churchill did not chop the vegetables, and he did not set the table or mix all the sauces, but as Kelly implies he knew how to get a six-course meal on the table in the right order and at more or less the right time. He would coach his subordinates on writing, once issuing a directive ordering his staff to write in "short, crisp" paragraphs and to avoid meaningless phrases. Seeing Churchill tightening and clarifying a paragraph, Kelly wrote, "was like watching a skillful topiarist restoring a neglected and untidy garden figure to its true shape and proportions." Indeed, the Cambridge historian J. H. Plumb noted in 1969 how subsequent writers have adopted the phases Churchill used to structure the conflict: "Churchill the historian lies at the very heart of all historiography of the Second World War, and will always remain there." More recently, Andrew Roberts has elaborated this view: "It is said that journalism is the first draft of history, but his memoirs of both the world wars were the true first drafts of the histories of both those conflicts, setting many of the terms of reference for them for decades." Timing was in his favor; in the early volumes, he benefited from the absence of rival accounts. In the final ones, he could find shelter behind the verdicts of others.

"I have followed," wrote Churchill in the preface to the opening volume, "the method of Defoe's *Memoirs of a Cavalier,* in which the author hangs the chronicle and discussion of great military and political events upon the thread of the personal experiences of an individual." The books are full of personal anecdotes (arguably the most memorable parts), but also of directives (drawn from sixty-eight monthly volumes of minutes) and telegrams as well as other official documents, in early drafts simply strung together in chronological order, often with little connecting narrative. His researchers would rummage indiscriminately in government files, and key documents were frequently cut out and pasted into the text. (Wrote one assistant, typically: "I am afraid I cannot find Australia, but will have another search.") For most of the war and for the first three years of the peace, Churchill would be working on three volumes simultaneously, with inevitable drop-off in quality. There is insufficient connective tissue and in some volumes a surfeit of documents (which need to be read as closely as the text, for the two do not always tell the same story).

Volume One refers to an appendix that doesn't exist. Volumes Three and Five are particularly unbalanced. There is no overall guide to sources, further blurring the line between memoir and history. As *The Times,* reviewing Volume Two, noted, "An air of hurried composition makes the whole read more like a brilliant exercise in journalism." In the main, however, the books, for which the U.S. advance was $1.4 million (about $16.1 million now) and £555,000 in the United Kingdom (£16.7 million), sold worldwide in prodigious numbers, and the overall reception was exceptionally favorable. The opening volume was serialized by thirty-one newspapers in twenty-five countries, *Life* magazine paying half a million dollars for the U.S. rights. In North America alone, in hardback format up till 1954, over two million books were sold. The six volumes were, in the BBC's words, "the literary event of our generation," Volume Two "a book scarcely paralleled in literature" (New York *Herald Tribune*). Future volumes won similar praise.

At first, that is to say in February 1948, Churchill wanted his account to be called *Memoirs of the Second World War,* but his British and American publishers persuaded him that the word *memoirs* was off-putting. The tension between being an authoritative account of the war and a personal memoir remained throughout.* In his controversial diaries, Lord Moran, Churchill's doctor, muses, "One wonders whether, if the personal slant had been wanting, Winston would have troubled to write history. . . . Perhaps the truth can be found in between. Winston was a master of military and political narrative, but events had to march in the direction his case required." As the years since his books have gone by, so the judgment of historians has solidified that he "immensely" (as one put it) distorted the historiography of the Second World War. But then Churchill was not writing history, as he emphasized in his prefaces. Yet the importance of history was his inspiration: "The longer you can look back, the farther you can look forward," he told the Royal College of Physicians in March 1944.

* * *

FROM THE PERSPECTIVE OF the present century, Churchill's works have a dated air. For him the past was about heroism and grandeur, determined by the men at the top; his loyalty was to the story of how the

---

* In Britain, the 1914–18 war had been known as "The Great War," the terms *world war* and *weltkrieg* being employed in America and Germany, respectively. After September 1939, Whitehall statements referred simply to "the War." In 1941 Roosevelt popularized the phrase "the Second World War" to persuade American isolationists that they could not ignore the European struggle. The issue was not decided officially in Britain until 1948, when it became urgent to agree on a title for a series of official histories.

great and the good won through.* Sentimental maybe (he was famously so—no animal on his Chartwell farm was slaughtered for food once he'd said "Good morning" to it), partisan and writing with "an iron whim," he still produced some of the richest prose poetry of its kind ever written. On learning in October 1953 that he had been awarded the Nobel Prize, he received the news with "touching joy," although his mood turned to indifference on learning that it was for literature, not for peace. The Swedish Academy said it had given him the prize for "his mastery of historical and biographical description as well as for brilliant oratory in defending exalted human values."

Churchill's deepest objective in writing his war memoirs, says David Reynolds, "(apart from making money) was the search for vindication. Like most political memoirists, he wanted to show that he was right, or at least as right as it seemed credible to claim." Reynolds adds: "His goal, however illusory, was to unmake, or at least to remake, history—to pick up the pieces of 1944–1945 and build a stable, more peaceful Europe. Hence his reservations about Volume 6: nothing must be said about the evils of the past that could prejudice a better future." His account of the origins of the Cold War was written with one eye on his bid to transcend it, for all "the foul baboonery of Bolshevism."

What this actually involved was a series of omissions and fudges. A short list would include his simplification of the international scene in 1938, and the omission of any suggestion that he was in favor of German peace negotiations in 1939; his mistakes in tracking the German battleship *Tirpitz* or his backing of post-1943 Communist politicians in Italy; the brutal and possibly unfair way he replaced both Sir Archibald Wavell and Sir Claude Auchinleck as commanders in the Middle East; and his overstating his support for a cross-Channel invasion, when for many months, even years, he was against it. The Battle of Stalingrad receives hardly a mention, there is nothing on the three-year siege of Leningrad, and generally he shows little interest in the Eastern Front or

---

* *The History of the English-Speaking Peoples* even includes as historical fact the legend of Alfred the Great burning the cakes. When Bill Deakin pointed out that it was almost certainly untrue, Churchill told him, "At times of crisis, myths have their historical importance." See Andrew Roberts, *Churchill: Walking with Destiny* (London: Viking, 2018), p. 953. But then in a recent poll of three thousand English teenagers, about half said that Churchill was not a real person, although they were sure that Sherlock Holmes and Eleanor Rigby were. See *The Daily Telegraph*, February 4, 2008.

the Red Army. Japan excites intermittent comment, and he glosses over his complacency before the shameful surrender of Singapore (in Volume Two, the war in the Far East gets not a single mention). As Richard Crossman, reviewing the fourth volume of Churchill's Second World War history, warned: "The statesman who turns chronicler before he retires from active politics is always seeking to adapt the past to the conveniences of the present."

Churchill does not reveal how he paid millions of dollars to bribe Spanish generals to persuade Franco not to side with Hitler and ignores his accountability for the Bengal famine of 1943, when between 1.5 and 3 million Bengalis perished because they could not afford to buy food ("I hate Indians. They are a beastly people with a beastly religion" are Churchill's recorded words, voiced in exasperation in 1943, but not to be found in the war memoirs).* Over the six volumes, India and Spain, as well as Ireland, are given short shrift. Churchill's concern about the Holocaust is voiced, but in a cursory way, while the destruction of Dresden by the RAF receives but a single line.

That is a long list. Churchill could be careless, unbalanced, partisan, and self-protectingly selective. In partial mitigation, writing at the time he did, he had to consider the feelings of parliamentary colleagues, transatlantic summitry, atomic diplomacy, even the Cold War. He chose to omit or considerably tone down his true feelings about Charles de Gaulle and other leaders, national and international, of the immediate postwar years. In particular, the secrets of undercover actions were still sensitive to write about, thus the Special Operations Executive gets but a single mention and Ultra, the most important codebreaking initiative of the entire war, none.

In 1927, Churchill had been a member of the Baldwin cabinet that published Russian intercepts to justify breaking off diplomatic rela-

---

* In his 2018 biography, Andrew Roberts defends Churchill over this charge, pointing out that Bengal had been struck by a disastrous cyclone destroying all its rice. Normally the Raj would have imported food from Burma, but that country was occupied by Japanese troops and the bay was full of Japanese submarines. It was more important to feed the British Army than the locals because, had the Japanese broken through to India, far more would have died. Roberts also cites Churchill's many telegrams to the viceroy to sort things out, but hoarding by merchants awaiting rising prices could not be overcome. See Andrew Roberts, *Churchill: Walking with Destiny* (London: Viking, 2018), pp. 785–86; Yasmin Khan, *India at War: The Subcontinent and the Second World War* (Oxford: Oxford University Press, 2015). Roberts also discusses the bombing of Dresden (signed off on by Attlee, not Churchill), pointing out that an incompetent local *Gauleiter* had failed to provide sufficient air raid shelters and that the bombing was anyway not considered unusual at the time. See Roberts, *Churchill: Walking with Destiny*, p. 861.

tions, whereupon Moscow changed its methods and the British were unable to decrypt any more high-grade Soviet signals until 1944. In January 1948, Churchill had told the cabinet secretary that his memoirs should include at least some statements "implying that we were able to break the codes and cyphers of enemy powers" and asked that he should not be restricted by government diktat. Eventually, when the dangers were spelled out to him, he accepted the need for censorship. Thus when Bletchley Park decoded a Luftwaffe message outlining plans to invade Crete, Churchill ordered it to be sent to commanders in the eastern Mediterranean, but when it came to recounting this episode he implied that the information came from agents in Athens.

Because of the foreknowledge so often afforded by intercepts, Churchill has been accused of sacrificing lives to protect Ultra, such as leaving the citizens of Coventry uninformed when the city was bombed in November 1940, but decrypts show that the city was never named by the Germans as a target. A similar charge has been made over the attack on Pearl Harbor—that Churchill knew it was coming but kept silent to draw America into the war. On the night of the Japanese assault, December 7, 1941, he invited John Gilbert Winant and W. Averell Harriman, the U.S. ambassador and Roosevelt's envoy, respectively, to dinner at Chequers and had a radio brought in—evidence, one might surmise, that he knew what was coming. But in Churchill's account the news came as a complete surprise: "We had no idea that any serious losses had been inflicted on the United States Navy." The radio broadcast's mention of the attack followed several other news items ("a spectacular piece of bad news editing"), and it was left to the house butler, Frank Sawyers, to come into the room and announce, "It's quite true. We heard it ourselves outside." Whether or not Churchill knew about the attack beforehand, which remains very unlikely, that night he was euphoric.

* * *

DIPLOMAT, POLITICAL SCIENTIST, ACADEMIC, memoirist, and the author of nearly twenty books,* Henry Kissinger is not usually described as a historian. But as well as an early study of Metternich and Castle-

---

* One might add "would-be novelist." When in August 2014 I interviewed the former secretary of state, he admitted that in his twenties he had begun two works of fiction. They may never see the light of day.

reagh and a wide-ranging history of China, in 1980 he won the U.S. National Book Award in History for *The White House Years.*

In his foreword to that first volume of memoirs, he wrote:

> A participant's account of conversations can easily be *ex post facto* self-justification. (Dean Acheson once said that he never read a report of a conversation in which the author came out second best in the argument.) By a selective presentation of documents one can prove almost anything. . . . The participant in great events is of course not immune to these tendencies when he writes his account. Obviously, his perspective will be affected by his own involvement; the impulse to explain merges with the impulse to defend. But the participant has at least one vital contribution to make to the writing of history: He will *know* which of the myriad of possible considerations in fact influenced the decisions in which he was involved; he will be aware of which documents reflect the reality as he perceived it; he will be able to recall what views were taken seriously, which were rejected, and the reasoning behind the choices made. None of this proves that his judgment was right—only what it was based upon. If done with detachment, a participant's memoir may help future historians judge how things really happened.

There is some irony here: Richard Nixon is on record saying that he continued taping conversations in the White House so that Kissinger could not claim to be the main witness to what was said. And Kissinger years ago invited the editor of *Harper's,* Lewis Lapham, to a meal, in an attempt to enlist his sympathies for the Nixon administration. Arriving slightly late, the secretary of state apologized, then explained that he had been "editing" certain Department of State minutes, "which you have to do, if they're to be the way you want them." Yes, the participants in great events know much of the truth, but hoping for continual detachment from such witnesses is too much. "It is not history," Churchill countered. "It is my case."

CHAPTER 16

MIGHTY OPPOSITES

Wars Inside the Academy

———

The natural state of affairs between exponents
of the humanities is one of tension, suspicion,
rivalry and, all too often, enmity.

—CLIVE JAMES, 2007

Going for the largest game, creating an intellectual
sensation, striking a posture, sometimes at the expense of
truth, stating the arguments against a book or its author in
the most relentless, sometimes violent way, engaging the
interest of practically the whole literary population by
using every nook and cranny of journalism, carrying on a
bitter war of words in public but keeping friendships intact
in private, generally enjoying the fun of going against
the grain—all these features [are] prominent
in historical disputation.

—VED MEHTA, 1962

THIS CHAPTER CENTERS ON TWO CONTRARY AND DISPUTATIOUS BRITISH
historians who were leading figures in their day (roughly the last sixty
years of the twentieth century) and whose rivalry both shaped their
reputations and reflected the culture of their times. Most (not all) of
their books seem outdated now, but some of their work changed the
manner in which history was written, particularly the history of the

Second World War, and together they tell a story central to the way their profession was conducted. They are also irresistible to read about.

Almost a quarter century ago, I was at a party in London and found myself (as one does) talking to the deputy editor of *The Daily Telegraph*'s obituary pages. He told me how, sometime in the mid-1960s, one of his predecessors had mentioned to his editor that the paper had no obituary prepared for Hugh Trevor-Roper, one of the country's leading historians. "Whom do you suggest?" inquired the editor. His deputy ventured mischievously, "What about Taylor?" At that stage, the public rivalry between Trevor-Roper and A.J.P. Taylor had reached far beyond academe and become a topic for the chattering classes. The editor smiled. "Go with it."

Taylor was delighted to accept the commission, and before long a polished obituary was on the editor's desk, with each achievement in Trevor-Roper's career carefully tabulated, but by the article's end the eminent historian's reputation had been neatly reformulated. Editor and deputy felt they had a coup. Then the deputy pointed out that, well, they had no obituary of A.J.P. Taylor. There was a silence. The editor smiled. "Go with it," he said.

This time it was Trevor-Roper's turn, and an equally devastating assessment was delivered. As with all national papers, it was the custom for obituaries on file to be sent out to their authors for updating. One year a young assistant was given the task of sending out both the Taylor and Trevor-Roper proofs—only she got the contributors' addressees wrong: Trevor-Roper and Taylor each received their own obituaries—with the authors' names attached.

I tried to track down the details of the story, enlisting the help of both a past editor of the paper, Charles Moore, and the current obituaries editor, Andrew Brown, but conclusive evidence eluded them. I decided to let the matter rest. Why spoil a good tale? We do know that Taylor and his friend Malcolm Muggeridge drafted each other's obituaries, but for *The Guardian*. *The Telegraph*'s obituary of Trevor-Roper, who died in 2003 at the age of eighty-nine, is still available, possibly written by Taylor, perhaps rewritten after Trevor-Roper protested, if indeed that is what he did. Whoever the author, it makes interesting reading.

The son of an emotionally remote small-town rural doctor, Trevor-Roper was born on January 15, 1914, the middle of three children, in the small village of Glanton in the Cheviot Hills, close to Northumberland's border with Scotland. "He would never quite relinquish the image of himself as a countryman, and followed hounds well into middle age," said the paper but forbore to mention the stifling conditions of Trevor-Roper's early years. He was to confess to a "terrible, almost physical difficulty in expressing emotion," as he wrote to his future wife in 1953. "When I was a child I never saw, in my own home, any evidence of any emotion whatever." Precociously bright, he was garlanded with honors and offices throughout his career. A classical scholar at Charterhouse School, he went on to Cardinal Thomas Wolsey's foundation, Christ Church, "the grandest of the Oxford colleges," where he won the Craven, Hertford, and Ireland prizes but also had time for some high-spirited if minor debauchery (ritual debaggings, fountain-dousing, smashed glasses, and thrown food); during one riotous student dinner a companion inadvertently shot him in the thigh with an air pistol, while in another he himself hurled an empty magnum of champagne from a first-floor window, narrowly missing his friend Robert Blake, who was walking below.

He was by ancestry well born (a collateral ancestor, William Roper, was the son-in-law and biographer of Sir Thomas More), at home in high society, an epicurean, a regular bettor on horses, and an unlikely outdoorsman—in the words of The New York Times, "a sort of P. G. Wodehouse character with an avenging, steel-trap mind," and indeed his acquaintances included a Biffy Holland-Hibbert and a Euston Bishop. Burdened from an early age with circular spectacles to combat his nearsightedness, he briefly took up golf, striding the links in a loud check suit with plus fours, his neatly parted hair plastered to his forehead, ending in a quiff. He often traveled up to London for a night on the town; after one such occasion, while riding on the Underground, he gallantly offered his seat to a female passenger, only to find himself too drunk to stand. It is no accident that in his letters and diaries he presents himself as a mighty drinker; in 1941 he wrote in his journal: "There are three things on which I can get drunk: wine, the sound of my own voice, and flattery; and the greatest of these is flattery."

Appointed a research fellow at Merton, one of the wealthiest colleges in the university, in 1937 (and buying his first car, a 1927 Morris Oxford, to celebrate), Trevor-Roper never completed his doctorate, being recruited at the outbreak of the Second World War into the newly established Radio Security Service, a section of military intelligence. He was seconded to work alongside Kim Philby and broke the code of the Nazi secret service while lying in his bath during an air raid. When his superiors were unsympathetic to his ideas, he often went over their heads to people he knew in Churchill's inner circle, for he had already formed friendships in high places. Demobilized, he returned to Oxford, back to Christ Church, and over the years became a fellow of the British Academy, a national director of Times Newspapers, a peer of the realm (created Lord Dacre of Glanton by Mrs. Thatcher, "Dacre" after a branch of his family), Regius Professor of Modern History at Oxford (for all of twenty-three years, 1957–80), and finally master of Peterhouse, Cambridge (1980–87).

Writing success came early. By 1940, he had won accolades with his first book, a clever if polemical study of William Laud, the archbishop of Canterbury executed by Charles I in 1645 whom Trevor-Roper portrayed as a man of limited understanding, increasingly out of his depth. "Laud's clerical biographers," he wrote, "since they approach him on their knees, are naturally unable to see very far." Several churchmen duly reviewed the book in outrage and high dudgeon, but other reviewers took note of a singular new talent. And anyway, as his contemporary Eric Hobsbawm noted, "To doubt the theories of one's predecessors is as natural for historians as to develop a rolling gait for seamen, and as useful."

He "brought a fresh mind to whatever he tackled," said the *Telegraph* obituary, which in the course of twenty-nine paragraphs somehow managed to mention A.J.P. Taylor's name six times. It quotes the longtime friend turned archrival as having "once mischievously remarked" that Trevor-Roper had written but a single full-length book of real excellence, that one being a piece of reportage and detective work. This was a reference to *The Last Days of Hitler* (1947), a graphic and unsparing depiction of Hitler and his court of sycophants and psychopaths. In the final months of 1945, Trevor-Roper, still only thirty-one, was sent to Germany to verify claims that Hitler might still be alive, a matter of considerable sensitivity, as the Russians were spreading rumors that Hitler was being harbored in the British zone in Berlin for nefarious future use, or had been spotted in Dublin, disguised in women's clothing (mustache notwithstanding). Others claimed he was hiding in a Spanish monastery; or was living rough among the bandits of Albania; or had been secreted on a mist-enshrouded island in the Baltic; or had been spirited away by submarine to South America.

The strategy had a memorable name: Operation Myth. Given the authority of a major general and a pseudonym, "Oughton," Trevor-Roper traced several survivors of Hitler's staff (he even found his will, stuffed inside an empty wine bottle), and in his report showed that the Führer was indeed dead, having taken his own life, an account he developed into the book that made him a public figure and is still indispensable for anybody studying the final days of the Third Reich: "The primary documents were few, and these were in my hands." In 2017, *The Guardian* featured the work (at No. 32) as one of the hundred best nonfiction books of all time. None of his other works has proved so popular.*

Trevor-Roper's preferred form, however, came to be the long historical essay, into which "he would concentrate more pith than many writers bring to a book." Though never restricting himself to any one specialty, he was particularly acquainted with the history of the sixteenth and seventeenth centuries. "He might—perhaps he should—have written a great work on the English Civil War"—a calculated comment by the *Telegraph* obituarist, just barbed enough to suggest that Trevor-Roper had, in the court of academic opinion, fallen short. There was some truth in this, but from 1940 till his death in 2003 (as well as in the five books published posthumously) he authored distinguished work across a wide field. (Taylor once admitted that when he read one of Trevor-Roper's essays, "tears of envy stand in my eyes.") By the time he was forty-one, he was being paid a sizable retainer by the *Sunday Times* to write "special articles," which he did for more

---

* Some of the facts he unearthed still sound incredible: Hess would eat vegetables only if planted at full moon; Hitler was seized by such wild attacks of rage that he was known as *Teppich-beisser* (carpet-biter); at times he would lie prone on the floor and snap like a dog. Göring dressed completely in white silk and wore a stag on his head, with a swastika of gleaming pearls set between the antlers.

Trevor-Roper, had he lived, would have taken particular pleasure from the *Guardian* accolade; in 1995, A.J.P. Taylor's *The Struggle for Mastery* in Europe had made the top 100 in a similar *Times Literary Supplement* listing. But he was not universally esteemed. In Oxford, Maurice Bowra, the university's vice chancellor, wrote to Evelyn Waugh that "Trevor-Roper is a fearful man, short-sighted, with dripping eyes, shows off all the time, sucks up to me, boasts, is far from poor owing to his awful book, on every page of which there is a howler." The polymath Isaiah Berlin, often called "the world's greatest talker," also reported: "He doesn't have any human perceptions; he's all glass and rubber." Nor could he have endeared himself to his colleagues by buying, with money made from the Hitler book, a brand-new gray Bentley, which he would ostentatiously park in Christ Church's main quad, the largest in Oxford.

than thirty-five years, as well as contributing regularly to magazines such as the *New Statesman* and the *Spectator*.

Flagrantly old-school (he was one of the last Oxford dons to lecture wearing his professor's robes), he delighted in appearing fogyish and wedded to convention. He ensured that undergraduates who attended his lectures without a gown were evicted without appeal. By 1949, he had been forced to give up hunting, at which he was enthusiastic but inexpert and accident-prone (twice mounts rolled on him, on the second occasion breaking his back), and he even contrived to sell his hunting mare, Rubberneck, while holding a tutorial. He was an attentive teacher, telling his students that a useful test of lucidity was to translate a phrase from English into Latin, but he questioned the craving of undergraduates to be instructed in the history of continents outside Europe, believing that investigating the past without documents was pointless. "Perhaps in the future there will be some African history to teach," he said. "But at present there is none, or very little: there is only the history of Europe in Africa. The rest is largely darkness, like the history of pre-Columbian America; and darkness is not a subject for history."* Such a comment was not unusual at the time, but it still marks a terrible intellectual and ethical failing. It may not invalidate Trevor-Roper's best work, but even in his day it should have been possible to see how arrogant, circumscribed, and incurious such remarks were, evidence of a mind so convinced of the supremacy of European civilization that it didn't bother to examine what it was talking about. But Trevor-Roper did like to ruffle an audience.

---

* Jonathan Swift wittily wrote of such a mindset:

> *Geographers in Africa maps*
> *With savage pictures fill their gaps*
> *And o'er uninhabitable downs*
> *Paint elephants instead of towns.*

But Friedrich Hegel shared the same prejudices—African history, philosophy, and culture were "enveloped in the dark mantle of night." And Saul Bellow was to make a similar point. "Where is the Zulu Tolstoy, where is the Papuan Proust?" he asked—arguing that only great civilizations have great literature. Neither they nor Trevor-Roper was well-informed. The evidence was there had they cared to look. For instance, at the time that Western Europe was enduring its Dark Ages, Africa was enjoying a third Golden Age, with a great university at Sankoré, Timbuktu. In the sixteenth century, a Grenada-born ex-slave known as Leo Africanus visited the Mali city and was later commissioned by Pope Leo X to write a detailed survey of the whole of Africa. His account, completed in 1526, provided most of what Europeans knew about the continent for the next several centuries and was a possible inspiration for Shakespeare's *Othello*.

The truth was, as the *Telegraph* obituarist acknowledged, "Trevor-Roper was a stormy petrel who enjoyed routing his enemies, even if his love of excitement occasionally brought him low." He described himself as an "indigestible particle" among his fellow officers; one army colleague he typically put down as a "farting exhibitionist" who resembled "those baboons on Monkey Hill, exhibiting to all in turn their great iridescent blue bottoms." Once out of uniform he became equally indigestible and spent his adult life feuding. He could be warm to friends, generous and open-minded, but to those he scorned he was relentless. From at least 1950 on he aimed his sharpened darts at "the Mice"—dull, obscure, and unproductive history professors who detested, as he saw it, "Gaiety" and "Life." "The amount of man-hours wasted in useless research is depressing," he contended.

His first plunge into scholarly controversy came in 1953 with Lawrence Stone (1919–99) over the economic history of the seventeenth-century aristocracy in relation to the causes of the English Civil War. Stone had followed him both at Charterhouse and at Christ Church, where he had been his pupil, and was no colorless mouse but a gifted historian. In a long 1948 article in the *Economic History Review,* the younger man had attracted international recognition with his argument that the English nobility had seen their fortunes wane sharply in the lead-up to the war, but his case was marred by mistakes in both facts and interpretation; his thesis appeared to support the Marxist interpretation of history, of class struggle. Trevor-Roper had been working on the same material and realized that Stone had misunderstood the system of loans in the documents he had consulted.

At first he accepted the younger man's achievement with good grace, but he brooded and in 1951 wrote to a colleague, only half in jest: "I have decided to liquidate Stone." In a devastating rebuttal of the original article he came close to doing so, showing for example that the peerage's real income had been higher in 1602 than in 1534 and had grown substantially by 1641, the year before the war began. This led to a vehement squabble, not only in scholarly journals but in the print media generally. Other scholars entered the fray and the issue became an academic cause célèbre. Before long, Stone left England for Princeton. "He decided to get well known quickly," his tormentor aphorized, "and the terrifying thing is that he succeeded."

He further sharpened his polemical gifts with a caustic attack on

Arnold Toynbee, at that time in his late sixties with a worldwide reputation. Adam Sisman, in his biography of Trevor-Roper, sets the scene: "[Toynbee's] face had appeared on the cover of *Time* magazine. His 6,000-page, ten-volume *A Study of History* was . . . hailed as 'an immortal masterpiece,' 'the greatest work of our time' and 'probably the greatest historical work ever written.'" In all, the series (actually twelve in all), published between 1934 and 1961, surveyed twenty-six civilizations, arguing that the course of history followed certain laws. The two-volume abridged version had become a stand-out success; "as a dollar-earner," Trevor-Roper scoffed, "it ranks second only to whisky." Conscious that his criticisms would be controversial, he delayed publishing his broadside until he was sure the Regius Chair at Oxford was his; after that, he gave himself a green light. His choice of battle was the monthly review *Encounter,* then in its heyday. "Arnold Toynbee's Bible," he began, "has not been well received by the professional historians." He accused Toynbee of regarding himself as a Messiah replete with the whole baggage of the redeemer's life story: "the youthful Temptations; the missionary Journeys; the Miracles; the Revelations; the Agony."

Toynbee dared to have a theory of history, but his "study" was "huge, presumptuous, and utterly humorless," not only "erroneous" but even "hateful." There was more. "Toynbee's truly monstrous self-adulation combined with his fundamental obscurantism [does] indeed emotionally repel me," he wrote, by diligent use of a tape measure discovering that the index entry "Toynbee, Arnold Joseph" occupied twelve column inches, more than the listing for "history."

The article was described by the *Times Educational Supplement* as a "blistering philippic," and by the literary critic Martin Seymour-Smith as "one of the most savage and cruel yet justified and effective attacks on one historian by another ever written." Toynbee's reputation never recovered, the article in *Encounter* being the more deadly because its main weapons were derision and ridicule. "I don't think I have ever laughed so much as when reading your splendid piece on Toynbee," wrote Richard Cobb from Balliol. "I was invigilating an exam at the time & got furious looks from eager candidates." Several others wrote in the same vein, Taylor penning, "Your piece on Toynbee's millennium was the most brilliant thing I have read for many years." He then publicly praised the attack in the *New Statesman,* typically adding:

"The best thing in Trevor-Roper's article was the description of Toynbee's creed as 'the religion of mish-mash'; the phrase was mine."

There were other feuds, further victims, what Neal Ascherson has dubbed "a cauldron of discord": R. H. Tawney and the whole *Religion and the Rise of Capitalism* orthodoxy, E. H. Carr on his Communist-inspired determinism, the authors of the Warren Report on President John F. Kennedy's assassination (Trevor-Roper was convinced they had gotten it all wrong), even, in a heated exchange at Chequers, Margaret Thatcher, over her hostility toward a unified Germany. Reviewing a biography of Sir William Stephenson, an imperious presence in British wartime intelligence and reportedly the real-life inspiration for James Bond, he declined to list how many errors the book contained: "To make such a charge against this biographer would be unfair. It would be like urging a jellyfish to grit its teeth and dig in its heels." He was a mas-

Trevor-Roper as a young don and in his pomp. Ron Rosenbaum,
who interviewed him for his book Explaining Hitler, *wrote: "To look at him*
is to see skepticism embodied: from his waspish donnish demeanor (thin as
a rail in his Oxbridge tweeds, with a dyspeptically skeptical squint to the brow
beneath his snow-white thatch of hair) to the tart, elegantly acerbic, bone-dry
ironies of his speech and the touch of world-weary cynicism he might
have developed from serving in wartime British counterintelligence,
he does not seem the sort to have been easily mesmerized."

ter of controlled invective and took delight in choosing metaphors from the natural world he so loved. He nourished a lifelong enthusiasm for niggling the Scots, possibly because his Borders upbringing had formed such prejudices early, and he had a singular scorn for Catholics with closed minds, especially converts, cherishing a letter from Lord Birkenhead that castigated Evelyn Waugh in unrestrained terms, though he never quoted it in public for fear of "incurring the insane malice of his son," Auberon. He went out of his way to make sure that he and the senior Waugh never met, being unsure how either of them would react.

In 1977 he savagely attacked Richard Ellmann for defending Dr. Reinhard Hoeppli, a Swiss who was promoting the fantastical memoirs of the English baronet Sir Edmund Backhouse, about whom Trevor-Roper had written a book, *Hermit of Peking,* published the previous year. In his pursuit of personal vendettas, he took the cultivation of hatred to a high art: constantly brooding on slights and engaging in protracted correspondence. In the same issue of *Encounter* in which Trevor-Roper's attack on Toynbee appeared, Neville Masterman, a fellow historian, had taken him to task for violating the principles he had espoused in his 1940 study of Archbishop Laud:

> *I hate your tedious trouncings, Trevor-Roper,*
> *Laud's spirit in reverse now dwells in you.*
> *The irreligious inquisitor*
> *Is just as ugly as his opposite.*

Another Oxford colleague, A. L. Rowse, whom Trevor-Roper dismissed as "a Cornish egomaniac,"* asked him bluntly, "Why are you so

---

* Rowse was the son of an illiterate Cornish china-clay worker and would regularly make much of his humble upbringing. Trevor-Roper would have none of it. "Poor old Rowse," he wrote. "I fear he has never really transcended his social origins. That tongue which shoots out with such chameleon agility towards a ducal posterior never uncoils, in our little republic of letters, except to discharge the hoardings of a parish scold." See Paul Johnson, "Misfortune Made the Man," *Standpoint,* March 2014. Rowse was something else—having failed to be elected to a Cornish constituency, he thereafter referred to Cornish citizens as "the idiot people." In particular, he would frequently allude to the scurrilous chronicle that he kept for most of his life. "At breakfast in All Souls College he would tell colleagues, especially any who had displeased him, that they had been included in the entry written the night before: 'You're in it and you're in it.' His private jottings remained unpublished at his death, and those colleagues who read them agreed that full publication would require both courage and good legal advice" (John Clarke, *Oxford Dictionary of National Biography*). But the diaries did finally appear, in 2003, and described, inter alia, Trevor-Roper as "unforgivable" and Taylor as a "charlatan."

nasty to people?" Trevor-Roper himself, in a letter to his future wife, described his heart as "like a sea-urchin, prickly outside and untempting within." He was not without self-knowledge.

With so many battles to fight, it is amazing that Trevor-Roper published as much as he did. He followed his early volumes with *The Reformation and Social Change* (1967); *The Philby Affair* (1968); *The European Witch-Craze of the Seventeenth Century* (1970); *The Plunder of the Arts in the Seventeenth Century* (1970); and *Princes and Artists* (1976). He also edited *The Goebbels Diaries* (1978). His ambition, he said, was to produce a book that "someone, one day, will mention in the same breath as Gibbon." He brooded on a comprehensive treatment of the English Civil War ("the English Great Rebellion," he called it), but it never got written.

One reason was that he allowed himself to be distracted by the constant stream of newspaper commissions, writing introductions to books by other people, TV appearances, and his many personal battles, all of which limited the time for sustained research. He knew better than anyone that he should have written more. Even Mrs. Thatcher scolded him for not finishing enough books. "On the stocks? *On the stocks?* A fat lot of good that is! In the shops, that is where we need it!" In a letter he admitted:

> The trouble is, I am too interested in too many things. . . . And then, there are the delights of idleness: of walking in the country, of scratching the noses of horses, or the backs of pigs; of planting and lifting and cutting trees (I *love* trees) . . . or the pleasures of convivial, social life: of slow monosyllabic conversation, over beer and cheese and pickled onions.

It was not that Trevor-Roper was lazy: his papers contain at least nine almost-completed manuscripts. One, a biography of the seventeenth-century Huguenot physician Théodore de Mayerne, was published posthumously, and more may still follow. He was also, among his other gifts, an energetic correspondent, pouring into his letters some of his wittiest and wisest observations. The columns he wrote for the *Spectator* in the late 1960s and early 1970s under the pseudonym Mercurius Oxoniensis were tongue-in-cheek classics. His repeated denials of their authorship fooled no one. As the *Telegraph* obituary had it, "Few men alive could have written such a scathingly witty commentary on the affairs of the university, and none could have done so in such a flawless pastiche of seventeenth-century English prose." Reviewing a selection of his correspondence in 2014, David Cannadine reckoned their author "probably the greatest letter-writer of what Noel Annan called 'our age,' corresponding with almost anybody who was anybody, and in a style that was both inimitable and incomparable." But that was the writing of squibs, however delightful or provoking; full-length books were a different category.*

As the Peterhouse historian Brendan Simms (b. 1967), reviewing Trevor-Roper's life story, wrote, "Part of the explanation [for the relatively slender publishing record] lies in the demands made on him by his temperamental wife, Xandra." In 1954, Trevor-Roper had married the daughter of Field Marshal Earl Haig, the First World War commander, a woman seven years his senior. It was a genuine love match, as his letters attest. However, over the years she came to mock her husband's inability to produce the masterpiece he so often claimed he was on the point of finishing. "Our attic is crowded with Chapter Ones. Never a Chapter Two," was her regular sally.† In that regard, the *Daily Telegraph* obituary had made fair comment.

* * *

IT IS TIME TO return to the long-running dispute Trevor-Roper had with Taylor and to take a measure of his adversary. One thinks of the lines from *Hamlet,* V, scene 2, ll. 59–62: "'Tis dangerous when the baser nature comes / Between the pass and fell incensed points / Of mighty opposites." In certain respects the two men had much in common—both were children from the north of England, both loved fast cars

---

* In October 1992 I wrote to Trevor-Roper asking to publish some of his letters. (I was then publishing director at Hodder & Stoughton.) He replied, in his elegant hand, "A dreadful thought! I hope that if any of my friends or correspondents have kept any of my letters, they will not give them to a publisher! I can assure you that, anyway, they would be of no general interest. Please forget so unfortunate an idea!" I should have realized from the many exclamation marks that he wished to be courted further, but I dimly took his refusal at face value. By now, two fat volumes of his letters have appeared (in 2006 and 2014), to wide acclaim. I went off and instead commissioned a biography of Alan Taylor, written by his last postgraduate pupil at Oxford, the American historian Kathleen Burk.

† Lady Alexandra had a quick tongue. When in 1979 her husband was offered a life peerage, he thought of refusing the honor, but she told him, "Think of the people it will infuriate." That settled the matter.

and good wine, both were convinced of their own outstanding cleverness, both were quick to take offense, and above all both loved to be at the center of a good argument (the historian Donald Cameron Watt would refer to Taylor's "notorious outbursts of eccentricity and *animus academicus*"). But the differences were plainer to see, from their childhood on.

Alan John Percivale Taylor was born on March 25, 1906, in an upmarket seaside resort called Birkdale (just north of Liverpool and west of Manchester), the only surviving child of Percy and Constance Taylor, comfortably-off left-wing intellectuals. In that respect, both A.J.P. and Trevor-Roper had privileged upbringings, though Taylor's family was by far the more sustaining. His home evolved into a bastion of left-wing radicalism, with his mother a well-heeled revolutionary. As a young boy Alan was precocious, well read, and spoiled—in the Lancashire idiom, a "clever-clogs." After school in York (during which he played a word-perfect Puck in *A Midsummer Night's Dream*) he applied to Balliol College, but when asked during a formal dinner for his views on what should be done with Oxford in a Communist society, he replied: "Blow it up after I have gone down." He had to settle for Oriel, where his parents provided him with the rare luxury for an undergraduate of a sports car, a fishtailed, air-cooled, two-seater Rover. He took up bow ties, horse riding (an activity he shared with Trevor-Roper, though he never went hunting), rowing (surprisingly, given that he was five feet five inches tall, he took No. 2 position in the Oriel second boat), voraciously read Agatha Christie and P. G. Wodehouse, watched Charlie Chaplin films, took to good whisky and even better wine (hock for preference)—and became a Communist Party member. In 1926, two years on, he broke with the Party over what he judged its lame response over the general strike. Just as likely, the theories of Marxism bored him.

The history faculty at Oxford was the largest of the arts schools, with some 30 percent of undergraduates reading the subject, mainly focused on medieval and early modern. In the 1920s, probably a fifth of all undergraduates at Oxford failed to take any kind of degree. By contrast, in 1927, having chosen the reign of Richard II as his special paper, Taylor graduated with a First (he expressed surprise at this success), but he had little idea of what to do with it. In one of his autobiographical essays, he tells the following story to describe the trajectory of his career:

A Galician priest was explaining to a peasant what miracles were.

"If I fell from that church tower and landed unhurt, what would you call it?"

"An accident."

"And if I fell again and was unhurt?"

"Another accident."

"And if I did it a third time?"

"A habit."

His own version of his life, he would tell people, was just such a chapter of accidents, but then so was history as a whole. This eventually earned him the soubriquet "the chance-minded historian," although that was still some way off. Having graduated, he moved to London as a clerk in his uncle's solicitors' office, which specialized in representing figures on the left such as Ramsay MacDonald and H. G. Wells. His parents continued to silver-line him, installing him in an expensive six-room apartment on the edge of Hampstead Heath, complete with a housekeeper. On his uncle's advice, he also put his name down for the Inner Temple, intending to qualify as a barrister.

The law did not hold him long, however, and by 1928 he was off to Vienna to research that city's links to British parliamentary radicals before the 1848 revolutions. He stayed there two years. When that adventure reached a dead end, he switched to reading up on Italian unification, returning home in 1930 to become an assistant lecturer at Manchester University, at that time the best place in Britain at which to study history.

After a year, an important mentor came into his life in the form of the parliamentary historian Lewis Bernstein Namier (1888–1960), who arrived in Manchester as professor of modern history after having made a name for himself with surveys of political life under George III. Namier was a naturalized Polish Jew who had come to England in 1907, studied at Balliol, and was to make writing about British history his life's work. To E. H. Carr, Namier was "the greatest British historian to emerge on the academic scene since the First World War"; to C. V. Wedgwood, "the best historical writer in our time." He now became Taylor's colleague, handing over drafts for Taylor to improve, calling him his "friendly critic," and adding that the younger man seemed to have "green fingers" when it came to rooting out evidence for his imaginative theories about the past. "To a quite remarkable degree," argues Namier's biographer Linda Colley, "Taylor has written the books that Namier planned to write." Taylor for his part acknowledged that Namier was "for many years a central figure in my life" but then, in his customary way, added: "If anything he was my pupil, not I his."

His main teacher, he insisted, was A. P. Wadsworth, deputy editor, eventually editor, of *The Manchester Guardian*. When Namier tired of writing regular reviews for the paper, he encouraged Taylor to take over, as he would again over his *New Statesman* and *TLS* journalism. To begin with the growing amount of extracurricular writing Taylor took on was a distraction: his first book, *The Italian Problem in European Diplomacy, 1847–1849,* did not appear until 1934. But after that there was no stopping him. In all, he published twenty-three books, a large number of essays, and an unbelievable nearly 1,600 book reviews. Writing, as the second of his three biographers, Kathleen Burk, points out, was his "primal urge," a form of obsessive-compulsive behavior to which he was prone throughout his adult life. Over the years, he wrote about history and politics in *The Manchester Guardian* and *The Observer,* about politics and history in the *New Statesman,* and about anything he fancied in the *Sunday Express,* as well as in a mix of other tabloids, the *Daily Herald,* the *Sunday Pictorial, Reynolds' News,* the *News Chronicle,* and the *Sunday Graphic.* If they paid, he would provide. "Most of his writing for the really popular press was tripe, and he knew it," said *The Guardian* of his work late in his career. "He was exploiting his fluency and cashing in on his fame."

In 1938, he became, to his delight (after two earlier attempts to return to Oxford had failed[*]), a fellow of the wealthiest foundation

---

[*] On one of his early applications, for a fellowship at Corpus Christi, its president said sternly, "I hear you have strong political views." Taylor replied: "Oh no, President. Extreme views weakly held." One might question this. From his teens to the end of his life he was in tune with the way the Soviet Union saw the rest of the world and was disappointed in 1945 when Britain chose the United States as its ally. He was opposed to Communism and to capitalism, seeing the latter as both immoral and unstable. The phrase "The Establishment" was a Taylor coinage, made in 1959. He campaigned, among many causes, for nuclear disarmament and opposed the British policy on Suez and its participation in the Korean and Vietnam wars. He was against Britain joining the EEC (predecessor to the EU) and NATO and wanted its withdrawal from Northern Ireland. In one of many speeches against nuclear power he called pro-nuclear MPs "murderers." He was not one for holding limp opinions.

in the university, Magdalen College, a post he held till 1976. (Hugh Trevor-Roper was one of the other candidates.) During the war he served in the Home Guard, then in 1945 published *The Course of German History,* a bestseller in both Britain and the United States; its success also marked the beginning of the breakdown in relations between Taylor and Namier, who had planned to write a similar study. Namier had become known as a Leviathan bore, memorably caricatured as Dr. Wenceslaus Bottwink in Cyril Hare's *An English Murder.* "Once let this fellow start talking, there was no stopping him," one character complained. Taylor, though acknowledging a huge intellectual debt to his Manchester friend, also portrayed him as a self-important windbag, totally blank on any history not about the shifts and transitions in political power, uninterested in fiction, music, the theater—or television, of course. Further:

> Though his collected works make up a formal [had he meant "formidable," one wonders?] array on the shelves, none of them is the finished masterpiece which he hoped to write. . . . It was a strange thing about this great man that, while he could use both the microscope and the telescope to equal effect, he never managed the middle range of common day. He was tremendous when he dissected each detail of some seemingly trivial transaction; and just as powerful when he brought the whole sweep of a century or a continent into a single lecture. But he could not provide sustained narrative. His work lacked movement, which many find the stuff of history. It was ponderous and immobile, like the man himself.

No one could make the same criticisms of Taylor. From the very beginning of his writing career, he was "good at interesting people in history, making it seem attractive, even fun." His lectures both at Manchester and Oxford were scheduled especially early in the morning, as they were always crowded out. "I'm a straight narrative historian; I like telling stories," he would explain. He told one journalist colleague, "No use writing history if you can't make it as exciting as a good novel. Actually it's more exciting." He added, "Better not write books at all, if they're just going to gather dust on the shelves of a library. Use short sentences. Then put in the odd long one. Stress *people.* Build up character. . . . Have fun. Enjoy yourself. You should be grinning with delight after a hard day's writing."[*]

He was never afraid to pronounce judgment, and readers loved his doing so, even if it made fellow practitioners wince. His skill was to take reasonably well-known areas and make readers see them differently. He further said of himself, in one of his many autobiographical essays: "I am not a philosophic historian. I have no system, no moral interpretation. I write to clear my mind, to discover how things happened and how men behaved. If the result is shocking or provocative, this is not from intent, but solely because I try to judge from the evidence without being influenced by the judgements of others."

So did he have no message, no agenda? His own answer to that question was dispiriting: "As I once wrote about Bernard Shaw, I had a great gift of expression and nothing to say." Stefan Collini, a professor of intellectual history at Cambridge, has little truck with this:

It's a characteristically Taylorian remark in some ways. It contains some truth; it's doubly self-referential, since he is also citing his own writing; and it sacrifices measured judgment (about himself and Shaw) to the pleasures of epigrammatic exaggeration. . . . The writing was attractive in the surface, all paradox and anecdote, yet in the end it could come to seem intellectually dull and even to convey a somewhat philistine view of the world. Ideas don't matter, culture doesn't matter much, even most people don't matter that much. Things happen; politicians respond; outcomes are unpredictable.[†]

---

[*] At Magdalen one of the fellows was C. S. Lewis, whom Taylor believed "professed an urgent Low Church piety which he preached everywhere except in the college common room." To puncture Lewis's pretensions, Taylor took to proposing that the college chapel be turned into a swimming pool.

[†] Robert Skidelsky, the acclaimed biographer of John Maynard Keynes, told me: "Historians may be read for their thoughts, but remembered for their style. Originality is much overrated." Email to the author, February 26, 2019. A student at Jesus College, he got to know Taylor when a postgrad at Nuffield College and later in London. Another of those who studied under him was Paul Johnson, later editor of *The New Statesman*: "You arrived at his house, Holywell Ford, in the grounds of the college, on the dot of the hour, never a second before or after, and the typing within stopped and a growly voice said 'Enter!' Then you got a full, crowded hour, and left again on the dot. The typing (of a *Sunday Express* diatribe, probably) resumed before you had closed the door. . . . If you want to know what he looked like, go to Bruges where more or less every man over 40 looks like A.J.P. . . . He could be sharp. Once, while I was reading my essay,

That is but part of the story. Denis Mack Smith, in later years an emeritus professor at All Souls, Oxford, was given the task of reviewing *The Struggle for Mastery in Europe.* "It . . . could have been written only by someone who combined great learning with tremendous confidence in his own judgment," he concluded. "Even though the demands of accuracy may inhibit his more brilliant and exciting sallies, he manages to be as provocative as his material will allow. . . . It is refreshing these days to find a historian who shows so little hesitation in leaping to his conclusions." In similar language the military historian Michael Howard wrote in the *New Statesman:* "How refreshing it is to read a historian who is not afraid of patterns, epigrams and judgments!"

Besides his TV and radio appearances and his political campaigning, Taylor was traveling widely (although pointedly never to the United States, his bête noire), had a cameo part in the 1981 film *Time Bandits,* and was the historical consultant to both stage and film versions of *Oh! What a Lovely War.* "That Jansenist leprechaun, Mr. A.J.P. Taylor," Rebecca West christened him. "A jack-in-the-box," pronounced *The New Yorker.* "The most famous historian of his generation," judged his fans.

Taylor was far from averse to home charms. One thinks of the Balliol College saying, "The eyes which have coldly assigned praise and blame shine when there are sausages for tea." By 1931 he had married the first of three wives, Margaret Adams. The original ceremony at Marylebone Town Hall ended abruptly when Taylor was asked to assent to the customary commitment. "No," he replied tersely and strode from the building. A few weeks later the couple tried again, and this time the function passed off without incident. Not so the mar-

---

he suddenly snapped, 'What, precisely, were the provisions of the 1909 Lloyd George budget to which you refer, so grandly and glibly?' I failed to give a satisfactory reply (not easy) and got a tremendous rocket." Paul Johnson, "A.J.P. Taylor: A Saturnine Star Who Had Intellectuals Rolling in the Aisles," *The Spectator,* March 11, 2006. Another student, less hardworking and somewhat perplexed, unable to find an agreeable homework idea to present to his unpredictable tutor, complained, "It's no good going to that bloody man with an essay cribbed from his own books; he's against it, even if he thought of it himself." "The Seventh Veil," *The New Statesman,* September 28, 1957. Separately, in 2019 Stefan Collini published a fascinating study, *The Nostalgic Imagination* (Oxford: Oxford University Press, 2019) in which he showed that some of the most prominent and influential literary figures of the twentieth century—T. S. Eliot, F. R. Leavis, William Empson, and Raymond Williams, among others—attempted to make a hostile takeover of history departments in the U.K. in an attempt to annex history and promote English literature as the presiding discipline in the arts. Luckily, they failed.

riage. Margaret was regularly love-struck. The first object of her affections was one of Taylor's students, the darkly handsome Robert Kee, later a fine historian and broadcaster in his own right, but although he was stalked by Margaret over several months, he soon tired of her advances; her infatuation and likely cuckolding became the common talk of Oxford, though, and hurt her husband deeply.

Luckily for the marriage, Kee went off to war. Then in late 1946 the Taylors became involved with a thirty-two-year-old Welsh bard: Dylan Thomas, until that moment down on his luck, and his wife, Caitlin. The couple stayed with them for a month. Margaret proceeded to bed the already alcoholic poet (he would down between fifteen and twenty pints of beer a day), and amid a humiliating ménage à trois Taylor's earnings would barely have reached the family home before Thomas was spending them. Margaret's own savings went the same way. Thomas, whom Taylor detested, not least for his cruelty, was overheard to say: "I'll have to see if I can squeeze Maggie's left breast and get some money." Caitlin was happy to reap any benefits that came her way.

Taylor and Margaret divorced in 1951. His second wife was Eve Crosland, the sister of the future Labour minister Anthony Crosland, his third a Communist historian from Hungary, Éva Haraszti. Between them all they produced eight children—Margaret four, Eve a further two, and Éva two from a previous marriage. Taylor's work rate may have been in his genes; it was also necessary. But by the early 1950s his freelance income exceeded his university salary, and as his celebrity grew soon multiplied.

Then in 1961 came *The Origins of the Second World War*. Taylor loved publicity—Trevor-Roper quotes him as admitting: "I would rather be mentioned as A.J.P. Taylor the notorious sexual pervert than not be mentioned at all"—and he reveled in thinking the unthinkable. What if Hitler had never intended to go to war in 1939? What if he operated within a national tradition formulated by Tirpitz, Hindenburg, and all the way back to Bismarck? What if Britain's appeasers had played a poor diplomatic hand with unappreciated adroitness? Such questions, together with Taylor's inflammatory conclusions about events still fresh in the minds of his readers, with its argument for appeasement as a rational political strategy and its portrayal of the war as an "accident" caused by the errors of politicians and diplomats, and Hitler as a "normal leader," set off a huge controversy. No matter that after the book's appearance no historian would write about the origins of the conflict in the same way, for it changed the terms in which the war's causes were debated. A. L. Rowse wrote in his defense that the author's enfant terriblism was founded in his wish to provoke and that this was a weakness that led him to say silly things.* His Dutch friend Pieter Geyl also spoke up for him, saying, "After one has said the worst about Taylor—that *The Origins of the Second World War* is dreadful history— still he remains in many ways the best historian at present writing in England." Such comments were not enough to put out the firestorm of criticism.

In the aftermath of the furor, his "special lectureship" at Oxford was not renewed when it ran out in 1963, nor was any new university post forthcoming. Taylor got in touch with journalists, telling them he had been "sacked," which was not true and angered other historians in Oxford. He should have known better—should have foreseen, not least, that waiting in the wings was his long-time rival, Hugh Trevor-Roper, acknowledged expert on Hitler and the Third Reich, avenger of the historically unsound.

* * *

THE ARGUMENTS BETWEEN THE two men had begun in 1957 when the post of Regius Professor of History at Oxford fell vacant. Despite their differing political beliefs, they had been genial colleagues since the early 1950s, but the professorship was the crown, the sine qua non of their profession; both men wanted it and campaigned hard to get it. The vice chancellor, Alic Halford Smith, consulted about the appointment, chose Taylor, and told the new Conservative prime minister Harold Macmillan so, but Smith then fell ill, and his successor J. C. Masterman immediately began pushing Trevor-Roper's claims; a number of other Oxford dons felt that Taylor's essays in the popular press were "demeaning" and also lobbied against him. A confused Macmillan asked Lewis Namier to come and see him. Namier telephoned Taylor, who made it plain that he would not forswear popular journalism

---

* Not least, regarding Hitler's long-term plans, the book mentions *Mein Kampf* just four times—for the simple reason that Taylor had not read it. Trevor-Roper, in contrast, had slogged through the tome in 1938, in the original German, as the English translation, first published in 1933, was an anodyne abridgment carefully censored by the German authorites.

if awarded the prize. That was enough; Namier went to Downing Street and recommended Lucy Sutherland (1903–80), a much-respected economic historian who was principal of Lady Margaret Hall, one of Oxford's few women's colleges. But Sutherland did not want to give up her college role, and so the Chair was taken from under her. Instead Macmillan gave the post to Trevor-Roper. Taylor never spoke to Namier again (his old colleague twice attempted a reconciliation, once from his deathbed, but without success), while in public he declared that anyway he would never have accepted an honor from a government that had "the blood of Suez on its hands." In private, he never forgave Trevor-Roper for accepting a position he believed should have been his. Before the year was out he would get his revenge, reviewing his rival's essay collection, *Men and Events* (*Historical Essays* in Britain). "It seems like an original work," he summed up, "and will enable Mr. Trevor-Roper to conceal for some time the fact that he has not yet produced a sustained book of mature historical scholarship." But that was just an opening shot.

Trevor-Roper's succeeding to the Regius professorship provided the backdrop to a further spitting contest, when he disparaged Taylor's *The Origins of the Second World War* (1961) in another *Encounter* article. He described his onetime colleague's philosophy as one where there were no heroes or villains; for the author under review, he summarized, "the real determinants of history are objective situations and human blunders." No one who so discounted the role played by character could possibly see what kind of person Hitler was. Trevor-Roper considered it a supreme folly to regard the Nazis as anything but evil (Hitler was "a gangster solely intent on power"), while Taylor's attack on this belief was the core of his book.

How had Mr. Taylor come to such a pass? "In spite of his statements about 'historical discipline,' he selects, suppresses, and arranges evidence on no principle other than the needs of his thesis; and that thesis, that Hitler was a traditional statesman, of limited aims, merely responding to a given situation, rests on no evidence at all, ignores essential evidence, and is, in my opinion, demonstrably false. This casuistical defence of Hitler's foreign policy will not only do harm by supporting neo-Nazi mythology: it will also do harm, perhaps irreparable harm, to Mr. Taylor's reputation as a serious historian."

At this point in his article, Trevor-Roper switched to the matter of the Regius Chair, and the fact that he had been recommended over Taylor by Namier as being a preferable academic candidate. Trevor-Roper speculated:

> Is it, as Mr. Taylor's friends prefer to believe, mere characteristic *gaminerie,* the love of firing squibs and laying banana-skins to disconcert the gravity and upset the balance of the orthodox? Or does Mr. Taylor perhaps suppose that such a reinterpretation of the past will enable us better to face the problems of the present? Theoretically this should not be his motive, for not only does Mr. Taylor, in his book, frequently tell us that the past has never pointed the course of the future, but he has also assured us recently, in the *Sunday Express,* that the study of history can teach nothing, not even general understanding: its sole purpose, he says, is to amuse; and it would therefore seem to have no more right to a place in education than the blowing of soap-bubbles or other forms of innocent recreation.

Previously, Taylor had never replied to negative comments by critics. From that moment on, he took every opportunity to denigrate his rival's character or scholarship, beginning with a contemptuous attack in the following September issue of *Encounter.* Even the title was a study in how to put someone down: "How to Quote—Exercise for Beginners." He compared statements made by Trevor-Roper to corresponding passages in the book. Each juxtaposition made hay over some mistake Trevor-Roper had made. The last one read, "The Regius professor's methods of quotations might also do harm to his reputation as a serious historian, if he had one."

Trevor-Roper riposted in kind, publishing a scathing rebuttal: "If Mr. Taylor had been able to convict me of any 'quotations' comparable with his own version of the German documents . . . or if he had shown my summary to be as inconsistent with his theories as he so often is with himself . . . I should be ashamed. But if these 'exercises' represent the sum of his answer to my criticism, I am unmoved." And so the dispute roiled on, gaining ever more column inches, because the point-scoring was such fun to read.

This reached a climax when the two were brought together to debate on television, under the chairmanship of Robert Kee, on July 9,

1961. Their differences in style in front of the cameras even showed in how they addressed each other: Trevor-Roper called his opponent "Mr. Taylor" or just "Taylor," while Taylor spoke of Trevor-Roper as "Hughie." Both men repeated the charges they had made in print—about the other's reputation as a historian—if they had one: each was obviously pleased with such a line, and also aware that saying it once more in front of the cameras would make good television. A viewer of the exchange commented: "Trevor-Roper gave me the impression of spluttering flame under the withering impact of Taylor's mind. Taylor would pinch his nose and take off his glasses as though he had an ulcer or was in pain . . . while Trevor-Roper appeared nervous, his mouth a little jumpy, his hands writhing. As far as I was concerned, Taylor stole the show." Although Trevor-Roper is generally believed to have lost the contest on points, subsequent research has endorsed his view that Hitler had a consistent ideology that needed to be taken seriously and was not simply reacting to events, as Taylor argued.

The dispute continued beyond the reach of television. Interviewed in late 1962, Trevor-Roper was unabashed: "Odious though Hitler was, he had an arguable policy and a real mind, a powerful mind." And: "For me, Taylor's book [on the Second World War] is . . . a worthless one." The media portrayed their disagreements as a battle between generations. Yet Adam Sisman, who wrote biographies of both men, corrects the myth that they were enemies. They largely respected each other and remained on cordial terms, for all the mudslinging. In a letter Trevor-Roper wrote to Sisman in 1991, commenting on Taylor's autobiography, he concluded: "He writes as if public applause was necessary to his self-esteem, the real measure of his worth; which I found depressing." And yet in January 1994 he declared outright: "[Taylor] *ought* to have been made Regius Professor and it was not an accident, or an error, but a crime that he was not."

Trevor-Roper and Taylor's feud took in figures such as A. L. Rowse, Alan Bullock, and E. H. Carr, while other notable historians of the time included Herbert Butterfield, Pieter Geyl, Veronica Wedgwood, G. R. Elton, and the medievalists V. H. Galbraith and R. W. Southern, some of whom sent potshots from the sidelines. The arguments spread across the Atlantic; in 1962, in an exhaustive two-part *New Yorker* article covering just short of one hundred columns (ninety-four pages, in the days of copious magazine advertising), the Indian writer Ved

Mehta, who himself had read history at Oxford, investigated this vexed world of "arrows of cleverdom" to uncover the "tomatoes and onions of controversy" (somehow an appropriate mixed metaphor).

He found himself appalled at what he called "the stuffy little parishes of self-importance" that he discovered in London, Oxford, and Cambridge universities. There was major work being done in other places in Britain—Alan Bullock began at Leeds, John Burrow at Sussex, Christopher Hill at the University of South Wales, Taylor and Namier at Manchester—but all these figures gravitated toward the three main centers. Only it was not just historians who gave themselves up to "devoted altercation." In architecture, the traditionalist

A.J.P. Taylor (left), Robert Kee (center), and Hugh Trevor-Roper.
Taylor commented on not getting the Regius Chair: "It is not my fault that Hugh got the chair for political reasons. Most people, including Hugh himself, thought it should have gone to me."

and poet John Betjeman took on Nikolaus Pevsner, belittling him as "Herr Professor Doktor," whom he saw as a baldly categorizing academic of Teutonic thoroughness, while to Pevsner, Betjeman was a frivolous dilettante. Art historians, in Trevor-Roper's own words, were "*genus irritabile* if ever there was one, with their blow-pipes and arrows steeped in *wourali* [curare] poison." The very year of the television debate between Trevor-Roper and Taylor had also seen a spectacular war of words between C. P. Snow and F. R. Leavis over the existence of two disconnected cultures, science and the arts. The *Spectator* was first to publish those splenetic diatribes but after several weeks closed the debate by announcing: "Controversy on matters of intellectual principle frequently has the disadvantage of obscuring those issues which it is intended to lay bare."

It took Mehta, an outsider, to see how such factionalism led to a greater truth:

> The smallness of English intellectual society, the availability of space in newspapers and periodicals of the better class (indeed, their encouragement of controversial material), the highly individual and belligerent nature of English scholars—all have made England the perfect country for such energetic pursuits. . . . In a sense, to follow any of the proliferating controversies to its roots was to discover oneself writing about the intellectual life of a people.

* * *

IN 1980 TREVOR-ROPER'S LIFE changed. He departed Oxford for Peterhouse as its new master, having been handpicked by a small group in the college whom he spoke of initially as the "Peterhouse mafia," later as "a gaggle of muddle-headed muffaroos bumbling and fumbling blindly after each other in broken circles." The whole episode is an odd one. He had mostly gotten his way in Oxford, but he now met his match, accepting the blandishments of Maurice Cowling (1926–2005), who presided over the "Peterhouse Right" with a mixture of affability and spite. (This is not an unfair description; he himself in his role of tutor advised his students to tackle liberals with "irony, geniality and malice.")

Cowling had it in his head that Trevor-Roper was a right-winger who would keep the college an all-male establishment. In fact, the new master was appalled to find that the college fellows made up an all-male enclave, prone to wear mourning on the anniversary of General Franco's death, attend parties in SS uniform, and insult Black and Jewish guests at high table. "They live in their comfortable little mouse-holes squeaking quietly to themselves about the shocking advance of liberal theology in the 19th century," he wrote to a friend.

The professors of his new college were "a grim Druid Church," he considered, adding, "dons in general, I fear, *are* boors." And often bores as well. For Trevor-Roper, his time as Master led to extreme personal misery, exacerbated by vindictive infighting that included a campaign to drive him from the college. Ironically, although he earned the nickname "the noble refrigerator" (while he dubbed Cowling, with more wit, "our college death-watch beetle"), his stewardship won the approval of the majority of the dons, and he brought about several much-needed reforms. He was to write to an Oxford friend: "The Fellows of Peterhouse have now been brought to order, if not to life."

Meanwhile, the books continued: *Renaissance Essays* in 1985; then *Catholics, Anglicans, and Puritans* in 1987, the latter containing the provocative index entry for "Peterhouse":

> high table conversation not very agreeable . . .
> four revolting Fellows of . . .
> main source of perverts . . .

It was not hard to give the lines a modern interpretation. Then, in 1983, came the incident that was to define Trevor-Roper's career. Early in the year, *Stern* magazine paid 9.3 million deutsche marks for the German rights to an extraordinary discovery (supposedly, in a hayloft)—what were claimed to be the diaries of Adolf Hitler. Rupert Murdoch, who had taken over *The Times* in 1981, purchased the English-language rights and asked Trevor-Roper (for a five-figure sum) to travel to Zurich, where the diaries were secreted in a bank vault, to examine them (for a few hours only) and adjudge their authenticity. Trevor-Roper had no illusions about Murdoch—"he aims to moronize and Americanize the population . . . wants to destroy our institutions, to rot them with a daily corrosive acid"—but he proceeded to make "an egregious ass of himself" (the *Telegraph* obituarist's phrase), writing in *The Times* that the diaries were not only genuine but "the most important historical discovery of the decade."

His error derived from a prior "expert" having declared the diaries' handwriting genuine. He was also told that the paper had been tested and shown to be of the right date and that the provenance of the diaries had been established. None of this turned out to be true; it had all been orchestrated by the perpetrators of the hoax. The sixty volumes were the work of a small-time German crook and prolific fraudster named Konrad Kujau and should have been immediately seen as faked. The pages were made of paper, ink, and glue of postwar origin, while the handwritten volumes were full of inaccuracies and anachronisms and contained banal, unrealistic entries such as "Must get tickets for the Olympic Games for Eva," descriptions of flatulence and halitosis ("Eva says I have bad breath"), and the revelation that Hitler had no idea what was happening to the Jews. The initials "AH" appeared at the bottom of every page, so unlikely that it was another warning signal, but Trevor-Roper persuaded himself that the Gothic script, which he could hardly read, was indeed Hitler's. Neal Ascherson parses his mistake as the result of "a sort of innocence, rather than the famous arrogance." Whatever the wellsprings for his error, a fortnight after this assessment he tried to retract his authentication, but it was too late, Murdoch famously telling his *Sunday Times* editorial team: "Fuck Dacre. Publish."

The British press had a field day. *Private Eye,* ridiculing Trevor-Roper as "Hugh Very-Ropey," devoted two pages to what became a public shaming: "Hitler's diaries [as translated from the original Belgian] 'genuine' says Goebbels's gardener's great niece," chortled the magazine. And in a 1991 five-part ITV drama-documentary based on Robert Harris's 1986 book *Selling Hitler,* Trevor-Roper's character was portrayed by a dithering Alan Bennett. Trevor-Roper's torments did not end there. He had made many enemies at Peterhouse, and now came the payback. He was ever, in the words of one of his friends, "a scholar who played with fire," and he was made to suffer "incurable burns from the lightning he had himself brought down." Soon the tale went around that the dean of his college had named his dog "Diaries," and would take it out for morning constitutionals that would lead unerringly toward the Master's Lodge. "Diaries!" the academic would shout, urging his hound to heel.

Even though the essays he wrote after the debacle, while he was in his seventies, are among his best work, Trevor-Roper's one great public misjudgment dogged him for the last twenty years of his life and even beyond the grave; the day after he died, *The Times,* although writing of one of its most loyal directors, headlined his passing: "Hitler Diaries Hoax Victim Lord Dacre dies at 89."*

In an obituary written the week after Dacre's death, Paul Johnson offered a surprisingly moving envoi. Trevor-Roper, he said, was a case of "redemption by misfortune." Brilliantly gifted, for much of his life he had devoted himself to his career of social climbing and the exercise of "virtuoso malevolence," and he had flourished mightily. But when his fortunes turned sour, a new man emerged, more sensitive, gentler, and his end was "strangely edifying." Commenting on the Hitler fiasco, Johnson wrote that he was amazed that Trevor-Roper could ever have fallen into such "an obvious media trap":

> The idea of Hitler keeping a diary, that endless hostage to fortune, is almost inconceivable to anyone who studied his mentality and record. Clearly, Trevor-Roper knew much less about Hitler than his reputation suggested. But then *The Last Days* had been written many years before. Trevor-Roper was also wrongfooted by his close financial connections with Murdoch and his papers.

At this point his eulogy moves up a gear:

> Though I had never liked Trevor-Roper, I felt so sorry for him that I wrote him a letter begging him not to let the scandal pull him down. . . . Of course he never quite recovered his reputation. He will always be known as the professor who authenticated the Hitler diaries. But in a profound sense, he improved morally after this catastrophe. And his regeneration enabled him to face other personal calamities, especially the death of his wife, which left him, to his surprise, dreadfully lonely and forlorn, and his debilitating blindness. When we met, as we occasionally did, I always found him friendly and amiable, which I never had

---

* Thirty years on, in April 2013, *Stern* magazine announced that it had given the forgeries to Germany's federal archives. "The fake Hitler diaries are documents of the past," declared the president of the archives in a joint statement with *Stern,* with a colleague adding, "These documents are of great significance to past history and the history of the press. Everything you read in the papers that is cold coffee by tomorrow, we preserve for eternity." The forger then publicly asked for the forgeries to be returned to him; without success. *The New York Times,* April 24, 2013.

done before. The malice seemed to have gone, completely. . . .
Thus fortune, or the fates, or divine providence, or whatever
God watches over us, moves in mysterious ways, and History
marches on.

There is another obituary to note, this one for A.J.P. Taylor, that
appeared not in *The Daily Telegraph* but in its Sunday sister publication
for September 16, 1990, nine days after Taylor's death. It is balanced,
warm, appreciative and in no way diminishing. Its author is Hugh
Trevor-Roper.

CHAPTER 17

THE WOUNDED HISTORIAN

John Keegan and the Military Mind

———

Every man thinks meanly of himself for not having
been a soldier. . . . Mankind reverence those
who have got over fear.

—SAMUEL JOHNSON

A NUMBER OF WRITERS HAVE PRODUCED CLASSIC LITERATURE UNDER extreme physical distress. Laurence Sterne (1713–68) wrote *Tristram Shandy* while in the throes of advanced tuberculosis, suffering "the most violent spitting of blood mortal man [ever] experienced." Samuel Johnson, from his earliest years wracked by twitches and convulsions, in the intervals of intelligible speech would make alarming sounds, sometimes giving a half whistle, sometimes clucking like a hen; while both his hearing and eyesight were defective—"My eye is yet so dark that I could not read your note," he once admitted. Neither of these writers was a historian, though. Others were. David Hume, like Gibbon, was grossly fat, reported to crush the chairs he sat on, while he also suffered from tuberculosis and a skin condition that distorted his face. Ulysses S. Grant initially dictated his memoirs, then, as cancer "choked his voice, in agony he wrote on," the most famous deathbed testimony in American letters.

William Hickling Prescott (1796–1859), robbed of sight from his student days, conducted his entire writing life in the shadow of severe disability. Few people know of his achievements, which include the seminal *Conquest of Mexico* and *Conquest of Peru,* but during his lifetime he was hailed as America's Thucydides and his country's first great "scientific" historian (because of the importance he attached to original sources, all of which had to be read aloud to him).* Francis Parkman, Jr. (1823–93), author of *The Oregon Trail: Sketches of Prairie and Rocky-Mountain Life* and the monumental seven-volume *France and England in North America,* suffered from a debilitating neurological illness. He was often unable to walk and for long stretches he too was all but blind. F. W. Maitland (1850–1906), author of what is considered the best book on English legal history, suffered from both tuberculosis and diabetes. Thomas Woodrow Wilson (1856–1924), the twenty-eighth U.S. presi-

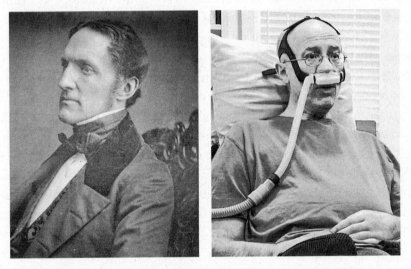

William Hickling Prescott (left), "America's Thucydides," who despite almost total blindness completed eleven books, and Tony Judt, who despite Lou Gehrig's disease went on producing new work almost till the end.

dent, had dyslexia but wrote several well-received works. The British Tudor expert David Starkey was born with clubfeet, had to overcome polio, and suffered a breakdown when only thirteen. John Henrik Clarke (1915–98), an African American from Alabama, completed twenty-seven works such as *Africa in the Conquest of Spain* and a two-

---

* Prescott was hit in the left eye by a thrown crust of bread during a student affray at Harvard. Within the year he had lost sight in that eye, and at the same time acute rheumatic fever reduced his right eye's vision to almost nil. His poor vision shaped the way he fashioned his prose. His writing often displays the mnemonic tricks of oral literature, and the strongly rhythmical sentences sometimes actually scan, especially in the battle scenes—he was aping Homer.

volume *History of Africa*. Though he was totally blind toward the end of his life, he still managed new work.

All historians, unless their deaths are sudden and unexpected, have a period at the end of their lives when they may still be productive but are ill or physically impaired. Perhaps the most moving example is the British writer Tony Judt (1948–2010), author of a highly praised history of Europe since 1945, *Postwar* (2005). Three years after that book appeared, he was diagnosed with amyotropic lateral sclerosis (ALS), known as Lou Gehrig's disease, a progressive motor-neuron breakdown that causes the nervous system to cease functioning. Over time, patients lose the ability to move but their minds are functioning as they always have. Judt likened it to "progressive imprisonment without parole." By October 2009, he was paralyzed from the neck down. Nevertheless, the last two years of his life saw a creative outpouring, with a short book, *Ill Fares the Land;* a set of essays, *The Memory Chalet;* and a further, untitled work in which he talked through his planned intellectual history of the twentieth century. He told an interviewer: "There have been people who have said to me, 'Tony, you are so lucky. More than anyone you live the life of the mind. It could have been so much worse.'" His response: "Hello! Are you from Planet Zurg? This is one of the worst diseases on Earth. It is like being in a prison which is shrinking by six inches each day."

* * *

HOW DID SUCH DRAWBACKS influence what these writers of history wrote? How did they rise above them? This chapter is devoted to John Keegan, who contracted tuberculosis as a schoolboy. When he died in 2012, NBC declared: "He was simply the best war historian of his era," but his significance is greater than that, for he refashioned how military history is written.

Keegan was born in May 1934, one of four children of cultured but financially constrained Roman Catholics. Both his parents, Frank and Eileen, were of Irish heritage, his father initially a PE specialist (he had played rugby for London Irish, one of the capital's top teams, and also boxed for the army), then an inspector of schools around Streatham in south London. The area was one of the most densely populated of the city and with the outbreak of war was judged a likely target of air attack. Its schoolchildren were among the first to be moved to the countryside, and before 1939 was out the Keegans (eight in all, including Keegan's maternal grandfather and a nanny) had decamped to rural Somerset in England's southwest. Frank Keegan's responsibilities widened to being a billeting officer, and as an "essential user" he retained his car; his elder son would often accompany him on his travels—not always straightforward, as to confound likely invading Germans all rural signposts had been uprooted.

For John, it was a time of almost unbridled happiness, marked by his discovery of the "secret world" of the English countryside. Not a bomb was dropped within thirty miles of his home. "It was simply as if the war was not," he recalled in *Six Armies in Normandy*. But the conflict was still very much part of his imaginary world. He would play with toy models of Blenheim and Hurricane planes, read and reread a complete set of Ministry of Information pamphlets on the war effort or articles on military subjects torn from *Picture Post,* or consult yet again an out-of-date *Jane's Fighting Ships*. He could recite the characteristics of most early models of British Army equipment by heart.

Frank Keegan was an enthusiastic amateur artist, having early on been an apprenticed draftsman. He also collected cigarette cards, his favorite series being on the regiments of the British Army (he was a particular expert on Waterloo, and engendered John's early interest in the battle).* He would research each regiment's histories and paint—in pastels and watercolors, never oils—from his prize set. His elder son was to share his interest in British uniforms his whole life.

School for John meant King's College, Taunton, undemanding and enjoyable. Then, suddenly, in late 1943, America came to England. GIs of the nascent D-Day invasion force poured into the Somerset countryside, bringing packets of Spearmint, Hershey bars, and Jack Frost sugar cubes, flung idly, generously, from the backs of jeeps. And there were the vehicles themselves: gleaming four-wheel-drive juggernauts, bulldozers (a machine previously unknown in Britain), amphibious trucks, and gigantic transporters. "I had my first sight of a method of war I had not dreamt." So began his long love affair with things American.

---

* Mary, the elder of Keegan's two sisters, recalls sharing with him an early admiration for Napoleon, but John's views changed over the years. His grandfather bequeathed him a miniature bronze of his longtime hero, but after their father died, rather than take hold of the statuette, John declared with some force, "I won't have that man in my house!" The bust is now in Mary's home.

Within six months this first batch of heroes had taken to the air: "The noise!" Keegan was to recall. "Hundreds of aeroplane engines directly overhead. The grinding sound crushed you to the ground. I knew something extraordinary was happening." Within a further twelve months Europe had been liberated. The family returned to the pitted streets of south London, acquiring a five-bedroom house opposite Streatham Common. Sometime in 1946 John's right hip began to ache. Consultants diagnosed mycobacterium tuberculosis or orthopedic tuberculosis, a potentially deadly disease, and he was sent to a clinic for children in Surrey, where he stayed for several months (a spell that, according to an interview Keegan gave to *The Daily Telegraph,* included spending the glacial winter of 1947 "in an open-air ward with snow drifting under the iron beds; at night, he recalled, the nurses lowered canvas screens that flapped and banged in the winter gales 'like the sails of a man-o'-war'"). "As summer heightened, I began to smell. Even I noticed it." Eventually he was moved to an adult male ward, an outpost of St. Thomas' Hospital, in central London. His younger son, Matthew, describes what he encountered:

At first, confined to bed in an open-air ward, even during one of the country's harshest winters for decades, he was then encased in a plaster corset from his shoulders to his thighs during the hot summer months during the second year of his treatment—"I spent many weeks in a kind of daze," he wrote later. The endurance of being encased was every bit as bad as how it was applied. "The Gallows," as this iron frame was referred to, was used to suspend a child from its upper part leaving their feet just touching a metal plate in its center. The patient would be slowly rotated while bandages soaked in wet plaster-of-Paris were applied.

John would be allowed home at Christmas, but he was ordered to lie flat, encased in plaster, one of the house's solid wooden doors having been taken from its hinges to form a makeshift bed in the dining room. After nine years of treatment he left hospital for good, with a hip immobilized by a bone graft. The episode not only changed Keegan physically—he was left with one leg shorter than the other, while by middle age his back began to curve, so that in later years he was almost bent double—but he also experienced a metamorphosis intellectually. The hospital staff realized they had a precocious teenager on their hands, and visitors too rallied to the clever adolescent. The chaplain helped with Latin and Greek, the hospital schoolmistress (there was such a person, herself a polio victim) with his French, which became very good. Not only did he continue to read like a boy possessed (not least, all the novels of Thomas Hardy), but his fellow inmates offered another, possibly unique education. Many were Cockneys, from the poorer areas of south London. Possibly for the benefit of "Johnnie," as they called him, they were relentlessly cheerful, scornful of anything but self-help. For Keegan, they exhibited "moral decency, personal integrity, and almost unreasoning refusal to admit the fact of their illness." He spent two years in their company, many of them having fought in the war and sharing with him what life was like for an ordinary trooper in the thick of battle. From his hospital bed, the Second World War gave him a special band of brothers and a bank of wartime experiences that shaped his attitude toward armed conflict.

It also helped save him from his disease. Whether the complaint is named consumption, phthisis, "the romantic disease," scrofula, the King's evil, Pott's disease, the White Plague, *mal du siècle,* or the now

John Keegan (left, with toy rifle!) at age eleven, with his sister Clare, a school friend, and his father in Taunton, 1945

more accepted TB, in the twentieth century an estimated hundred million died from a bacterium that has been killing humans for over five thousand years. As a direct result of wartime research to combat infection suffered by the wounded, a team from Rutgers University in New Jersey isolated an effective antibiotic, streptomycin. On November 20, 1944, it was first administered to a critically ill patient. The effect was extraordinary. The man's disease was visibly arrested, the bacteria disappeared from his saliva, and he quickly regained full health. In the following years a succession of anti-TB drugs appeared, and Keegan was one of the beneficiaries.

He returned to school (Wimbledon College, in southwest London), and to a thriving home life, full of jokes and fun and newspapers. The family was formidably clever, both his sisters getting good Oxford degrees, while there were regular outings to the theater, exhibitions, and the National Gallery. "Despite having little money," his sister Mary recalls, "we felt unusual and privileged. We thought we were so lucky." However, she adds, "When John came back to us he was so thin and without leg muscle." Francis, by eight years the younger brother, was a natural athlete, and the family learned to downplay his sports achievements when his invalid brother was present.

Despite the lost school years, Keegan won a state scholarship to Balliol College, Oxford, known by its admirers as "the best teaching college in the world" (the university's tutorial system is thought to have originated there), where he chose military history as his special subject. Deeply well read and deeply humorous, the "shrunken boyman" was caricatured by his fellow students in a Balliol Rhyme, a college tradition for newly arrived members:

> *I am Keegan. I am quite*
> *The laughing, limping Jesuite.*
> *I bed at dawn, I rise for tea*
> *(Regular S.J.* ... *Clause Three)*

---

* To be a Jesuit meant, strictly, belonging to the Society of Jesus (formed in 1534 by Ignatius of Loyola), although to be charged as "Jesuitical" meant that one was given to clever argument and equivocation, in the manner associated with Jesuits. This short doggerel aside, Keegan was inclined to gentler religious orders. His parents, in their Somerset years, could not afford to enter him for Downside School, run by Benedictine monks, but he was to send both his sons there.

"It was the most brilliant generation," Keegan told an interviewer in 1998. Many of his contemporaries were older than normal undergraduates, had served in the war, and seemed to "have had a spell cast over them. They spoke of the officers they'd known with such admiration, and that touched me." He added, "The friends I made at Oxford . . . made me conscious of having missed something." A recurrence of his TB made him lose several months of study, and he had to take an extra year over his degree.

Keegan thought of himself as no more than "slightly disabled," and in 1952 he reported for his medical examination for national service. But "the doctors laughed when they saw my orthopedic scars," and he was declared permanently unfit for the military. The failure stung. His father had been for three years a gunner on the Western Front during the First World War and been gassed; although that experience marked him ever after, "he felt better about himself for having been a soldier." John Keegan felt less of himself for knowing he could never be one, and would recall the pacifist hero of L. P. Hartley's 1953 novel *The Go-Between* being told by his gardener that the happiest time of his life was between 1914 and 1918, "when all of us mucked in together" enduring the sharp end in Flanders: "His gaiety had a background of the hospital and the battlefield. I felt he had some inner reserve of strength which no reverse, however serious, would break down."

Instead, Keegan applied for a newly instituted grant funded by a philanthropic American graduate of Balliol, and in the summer of 1957 he traveled to America to explore the battlefields of the Civil War. Installed in a friend's apartment overlooking New York's Union Square, he found a country "booming, in wealth and in enjoyment of world power." He learned to love its landscape and much of its culture: film directors like John Ford (*The Searchers* was a favorite), Edward Hopper's paintings, and authors such as Whitman and Chandler.

On his return to the U.K. he worked for two years as a political analyst at the U.S. embassy in London. The Royal Military Academy at Sandhurst was expanding its academic department, which for Keegan was perfect timing; he became a lecturer there, moving to a creosoted wooden bungalow buried in woods near the base's training ground, and was to stay at Sandhurst for the next twenty-five years. In 1960, aged twenty-six, he married Suzanne, daughter of a German mother, Ingeborg Vogt, and Thomas Everett, a popular Somerset doctor; together they had four children—like John's own family, two boys and two girls.

In charge of the history department from 1959 to 1969 was Brigadier Peter Young, a charismatic ex-Commando and the author of several well-received military books; Young co-opted Keegan to help him, and the writing seed was planted. Keegan's great friend at university, Maurice Keen, who had married his sister Mary, introduced him to a languid, raffish Irishman named Anthony Sheil. Sheil's mother was a Canadian heiress, his father a successful racing trainer outside Dublin. Anthony had spent the war in Canada, but in 1945 was sent to Ampleforth, the austere Benedictine academy on the Yorkshire moors, from where he too went up to Oxford, although for much of his time there he could be found at nearby racetracks. After university, Sheil devoted himself to gambling, and to the end of his life exhibited a mastery of the horseracing world, but in 1962 he deserted the turf for his other love, books, and opened a literary agency. Following Keen's introduction, he was soon exhorting Keegan to try his hand at individual authorship. Three early volumes followed: *Waffen SS: The Asphalt Soldiers* (1970), *Barbarossa: Invasion of Russia, 1941* (1971), and *Opening Moves: August 1914* (1971). Then in 1976 came the longed-for breakthrough.

The Face of Battle was hailed by the Cambridge historian J. H. Plumb in *The New York Times* as "a brilliant achievement," and in a twin accolade in *The New York Review of Books* as "totally original." For the revered academic C. P. Snow it was "the most brilliant evocation of military experience in our time." Even fellow historians were in awe: "This without any doubt is one of the half-dozen best books on warfare to appear in the English language since the end of the Second World War," wrote Sir Michael Howard, Emeritus Fellow of All Souls, Regius Professor of Modern History at Oxford, Robert A. Lovett Professor at Yale, and founder of the Department of War Studies at King's College, London.

What was so impressive? Keegan's originality was to focus on the practical mechanics of war and examine popular myths about men in combat. After a long introduction about the nature of warfare, he analyzed three battles, all involving British troops but taking place in different periods, 1415, 1815, and 1916, describing them from the position of the men at the "point of maximum danger." In doing so, he conveyed what the experience meant for the participants, whether facing an arrow cloud at the Battle of Agincourt, the spinning musket balls at Waterloo, or the bursts of machine-gun fire and streams of flame of the Somme. "Nobody describes a battle as Keegan does," wrote Niall Ferguson in *The Sunday Times*.

His research felled several sacred cows. The arrows of the English archers at Agincourt, for example, were not decisive, as had been assumed. Of their opening volley, Keegan wrote,

> Four clouds of arrows would have streaked out of the English line to reach a height of 100 feet before turning in flight to plunge at a steeper angle on and among the French men-at-arms opposite. These arrows cannot, however, given their terminal velocity and angle of impact, have done a great deal of harm. . . . For armour, by the early fifteenth century, was composed almost completely of steel sheet, in place of the iron mail.

The trapped French were bludgeoned to death by charging archers, not slaughtered by arrows. Even mail was no protection against strong-armed men stabbing away at their foe in the neck, eyes, armpits, and groin through gaps in their opponents' armor. Almost six thousand Frenchmen lost their lives out of some fifteen thousand troops.

What distinguished Keegan's account was not only his grasp of narrative and his deep research. He acknowledged in his introduction that he had "not been in a battle, nor near one, nor heard one from afar, nor seen the aftermath," but that made him determined to write about what actually takes place on a battlefield rather than give a commentary of who might be winning or losing or outline the geometry of military maneuvers. How exactly did an outnumbered and disheveled English army slaughter the French in 1415 to the point there were "heaps of dead"? How were Napoleon's renowned cavalry attacks repulsed by men on foot? Great historians pose simple, important questions, then give clear, simple answers. Keegan asked: Why do men in battle not do the sensible thing and just run away? What could have propelled a man out of a rat-infested trench to walk into the machine guns of no-man's-land of World War I? Such an approach was transformative. As Plumb concluded his review, "One learns as much about the nature of man as of battle." For Keegan, teaching young cadets their future business, understanding the beastliness and chaos of war, its sights, sounds, and smells, was a moral priority.

* * *

THE FACE OF BATTLE was a bestseller.* Over the next eleven years it was followed by six further books, of which the most notable were *Six Armies in Normandy* (1982) and *The Mask of Command* (1987), the latter, following Keegan's six months at Princeton as a visiting fellow, a study of generalship that showed he could be as perceptive about commanders as those commanded. "The leader of men in warfare," he wrote, "can show himself to his followers only through a mask, a mask that he must make for himself, but a mask made in such a form as will mark him to men of his time and place as the leader they want and need." Class was far less important than character.

In the spring of 1979 I became editorial director of Hodder & Stoughton in London and invited Anthony Sheil to lunch. To my surprise, he said he was looking to move John Keegan from his current publisher, and would I be interested? It was not a hard question to answer, and for the next eight years I was his editor. I have rarely looked after an author with greater pleasure.

John had strong views, and a temper (he came to abominate the IRA, and for someone with Irish ancestors seemed sometimes to hate that whole nation). Sheil told me that "John has very vigorous views of people," and so he did—on one occasion he almost came to blows with a fellow member of the Garrick, the famed London gentleman's club. "I'm very rebellious by nature. . . . I fly off the handle very quickly. I'm super-critical," Keegan told an interviewer in 1987. But that anger fueled much of his writing, expressed in a moral indignation at how war could so often have been avoided. In my experience he was always generous, modest, humorous—and, not least, extravagantly courteous to women. A friend who met him at a literary event wrote me years afterward to say, "By the 1990s he was bent over at the waist in a way that looked dangerously painful, but he stood for every woman who approached the table where he was signing." Indeed, he lived his whole

---

* Some fifteen years on, a *Daily Telegraph* reader wrote in to attest that train crews on London's Northern Line were devotees of the book. Letter, *The Daily Telegraph*, January 20, 1990.

adult life in sharp discomfort, and took quantities of painkillers to keep him going; but by the end of his life he had simply worn out his spine.*

* * *

SHORTLY AFTER *THE FACE OF BATTLE* was published, Keegan applied for the position of professor of the history of war at Oxford, but the powers that be felt that he had too little experience in archival research and would be out of his depth in supervising graduate students. It was an odd decision, for the previous incumbent, Norman Gibbs, had no interest at all in military history (his main contribution to history was the definitive work on Reading Priory), while his predecessors had all been self-trained historians. The rejection rankled. Keegan's Sandhurst salary was not large for a family of six, and for years he had severe financial difficulties, at one point narrowly avoiding bankruptcy. Then one day in the mid-1980s his friend Max Hastings confided that he had been offered the editorship of *The Daily Telegraph,* the conservative upmarket newspaper highly respected for its overseas reporting. "Can I be your defense correspondent?" Keegan asked. "Of course" came the reply, and so in 1986, aged fifty-one, he started what he called "my second career."

Keegan's first experience of being in a war zone had begun in the winter of 1983, when he accepted a commission to visit Lebanon's capital from *The Atlantic,* whose editor was an admirer: ten thousand dollars for ten thousand words, more than half a normal year's pay. It was a dangerous assignment, as Beirut was by then a wilderness, with rival gangs roaming the streets, at a time of "ammunition affluence." Keegan's safety was further threatened by his befriending Patrick Cockburn of the *Financial Times.* Cockburn, who had survived childhood polio, also limped, so the shuffling duo would make their way across the ravaged city, and whenever the novice reporter asked his award-winning compatriot how close gunfire was, Cockburn would

---

* Keegan made light of his health problems, but they were always with him. One day we were discussing *The Magic Mountain,* Thomas Mann's book about (among other things!) TB sufferers, and I foolishly asked him if he knew A. E. Ellis's 1958 novel *The Rack,* which covers similar territory. It was Ellis's only work of fiction, but an extraordinary one. Graham Greene wrote of it: "There are certain books we call great for want of a better term, that rise like monuments above the cemeteries of literature: *Clarissa Harlowe, Great Expectations, Ulysses. The Rack* to my mind is one of this company." Keegan said he knew exactly where the novel was on his bookshelves and frequently looked at its spine with a shudder.

squint through pebble glasses and laconically reply, "Difficult to say." It wasn't, and on several occasions the firing was close enough that they were in considerable danger.

Keegan of course survived, to produce, over the next fourteen years, six major works: *The Price of Admiralty* (covering war at sea, the title taken from Kipling, "If death be the price of admiralty, Lord God we ha' paid it in"), *The Second World War*, *A History of Warfare* (dubbed in *The New Yorker* "a masterpiece properly so-called," and a further

Keegan circa 2000, photographed by his son Matthew. Considering his high standing and widespread popularity, he was frequently criticized in his later years—for backing the United States in Vietnam, his support of the Iraq War, and his attacks on Carl von Clausewitz, the Prussian military strategist.

move away from financial worries, bringing in for the U.K. rights alone an advance of £150,000), *The Battle for History, Warpaths,* and *The First World War*. In addition, he completed a short biography of Churchill, a TV series (with his Sandhurst colleague Richard Holmes), and an accompanying book (John Gau's *Soldiers*), as well as contributing to another (*Churchill's Generals*). He continued to be an original thinker, inveighing for instance against the futility of studying human conflicts without considering geography. Only 30 percent of the world's dry land is suitable for the waging of war, he pointed out; the rest is "either too high, too cold or too waterless for the conduct of military operations." He was a master of the telling detail, observing that in the naval engagements of the early nineteenth century the French never heaved their dead overboard in time of action because "a

Catholic widow needed the evidence of burial of her husband's body if she was to remarry."

And his narrative style was peerless. Of the atmosphere aboard a wooden warship at the Battle of Trafalgar (1805), for instance, the last great encounter between such vessels but also the bloodiest and most decisive, he noted: "The smell of . . . pine pitch and tar run hot between the cracks of the timbers . . . the fibrous odour of hemp from the cables: the sweet tang of vegetable-oil paints," and also the sound of the timbers "moving with and working against each other in a concerto, sometimes a cacophony, of creaks, groans, shrieks, wails, buzzes and vibrations." He could also be controversial; he thought the Vietnam War justified (if not the manner in which it was fought), approved the bombing of Kosovo, and backed the invasion of Iraq to topple Saddam Hussein. He counted the controversial U.S. secretary of defense, Donald Rumsfeld, a friend. But whatever his beliefs, his Gulf War commentaries were widely regarded as the most authoritative in British journalism.

Going further back into the past, Keegan believed that the First World War was "unnecessary . . . a mystery," and in *A History of Warfare* wrote with unconcealed hostility about Carl von Clausewitz (1780–1831), who famously saw war as "the continuation of political intercourse with the intermixing of other means." For Keegan, war was "at the heart of human history" yet not a "natural" activity and had become ever more unthinkable. His years at Sandhurst and the empathy of his writing gave him a special position. "Soldiers treat me as a privileged interlocutor," he revealed. "They tell me things they don't talk about . . . breaking the rules of war, shooting the people you shouldn't shoot."

But writing constantly about conflict took its toll. In *The Face of Battle* he speaks of "the military historian, on whom, as he recounts the extinction of this brave effort or that, falls an awful lethargy, his typewriter keys tapping leadenly on the paper to drive the lines of print, like the waves of a Kitchener battalion failing to take its objective, more and more slowly toward the foot of the page." When a friend of mine, Alan Judd, asked him why he had rushed the end of his account on the First World War, where only fifty pages cover the final stages of the war in the east, the tremendous German offensive of spring 1918, and the game-changing Allied counteroffensive that brought the conflict to an end, he admitted that he had finished the book as quickly as possible, as he found the casualties so harrowing.[*]

Keegan would say that his mind was a compost heap, from which he would later take out the digested ideas. But some of these were never fully considered. The combined occupations of journalist and author meant that he came to write too quickly, and toward the end of his career his books verged on potboilers. Friends of his who were also leading military historians—Antony Beevor (who studied under him at Sandhurst), Max Hastings, who in 2000 used his contacts at the Ministry of Defence to get Keegan a knighthood "for services to military history," and Michael Howard—each noticed how little original research he was doing. "All his books are worth reading, and have something interesting and original to say," Howard sums up. "It is a pity that he never got an academic appointment that would have given him the time and opportunity to spend more time on reflection."

But there was one primary source that he consulted again and again—himself, and his experience recovering in hospital with common foot soldiers. When in 1993 *The Battle for History* was published, Brian Bond, professor of military history at King's College, London, noted that Keegan had "an admiration for warriors." Certainly, for Keegan soldiers were not as other men. That L. P. Hartley novel again: "Life was meant to test a man, bring out his courage, initiative, resource; and I longed, I thought, to be tested." Keegan, the "unabashed English Romantic," the lover of Kipling, whose chosen desert island book was John Buchan's *The Thirty-Nine Steps,* even admitted "the allure that the warrior life exerts over the male imagination." (He entered his elder son, Matthew—fruitlessly, as it turned out—for the Irish Guards.) Michael Howard believes that what distinguishes Keegan is the moral passion he brought to his subject. "For him war *mattered*—

---

[*] Keegan could also make mistakes, or at least be cavalier or sloppy. Invited to deliver the 1998 Reith Lectures, titled "War and Our World," he argued that the threat of disease had ended, even though some thirty-three thousand children perish daily from curable sicknesses worldwide. There are—as with Herodotus, Churchill, Gibbon—errors of fact, of interpretation, even of judgment. He described the Normandy landings, for instance, as "the greatest military disaster Hitler had yet suffered in the field," despite the German defeat at Stalingrad and the collapse of the Eastern Front. This so angered the Russians that in 2015 a decree was issued to have Keegan's books withdrawn from schools and libraries, as they were evidence that Keegan had Nazi sympathies. Antony Beevor, whose books were also singled out (see chapter 20), replied that the Russian government was "trying to control the history of the past" due to its current isolated geopolitical position. That is likely true, but in Keegan's case it was still something of an own goal.

mattered terribly." So did his Catholicism, which profoundly affected his approach. Howard again: "This gave to his writing a certain quality of grandeur missing in even the best of his competitors. . . . John was a *good* man. Perhaps it prevented him from being a great historian—or perhaps it made him one."

The flow of commissions never dried up. Besides further books (*The Iraq War,* an *Atlas of World War II*), Keegan readily undertook numerous articles and lectures, in Britain and the United States. In 1995, he joined five American historians at the White House to advise Bill Clinton on what to say for the fiftieth anniversary of VE Day (an assignment of which he was perversely proud), then in 1998 was chosen to deliver the fiftieth-anniversary Reith Lectures. His last book contract was for two separate volumes, the first on wartime intelligence, the second an overview of the American Civil War, the subject he had studied since his student days. The first, *Intelligence in War: Knowledge of the Enemy from Napoleon to Al-Qaeda,* appeared in 2003, but while preparing the second he had a knee operation and developed gangrene in a toe on his right foot. By the time it was properly diagnosed his condition was critical and he had to have his right leg amputated above the knee. For several months he was confined to the hospital. Recovered, he started work again, albeit from a wheelchair at his desk, but his manuscript, when delivered, was under length, and he had to expand it considerably. It was a difficult time for him, and the normally reserved Sheil reckoned the book's second completion "an extraordinary feat of courage, discipline, and resolution." *The American Civil War* was finally published in 2009.

A month after he finished the extended version Keegan suffered a stroke. His prognosis was so dire that his doctors stopped feeding him and focused on making his last hours comfortable. Three times he was given the last rites, yet once again he staged a recovery, and when I last saw him, in March 2011, at his family home in a small Wiltshire village close to the Somerset-Dorset border, he was planning a book about the Second World War in Italy. As with his hospital fellows, he was completely free of self-pity.

Bedridden for almost three years, he died on August 2, 2012, aged seventy-eight, of natural causes. Wars are fought not only on the battlefield.

CHAPTER 18

HERSTORY

From Bān Zhāo to Mary Beard

———

Men have had every advantage of us in telling their
own story. Education has been theirs in so much higher
a degree; the pen has been in their hands.

—JANE AUSTEN, *PERSUASION*, 1817

Gender. n. a grammatical term only. To talk of persons or
creatures of the masculine or feminine gender, meaning of
the male or female sex, is either a jocularity (permissible
or not according to context) or a blunder.

—FOWLER'S *DICTIONARY OF MODERN ENGLISH USAGE*, 1940

"FAMOUS FEMALE HISTORIANS" IS A WEBSITE DEVOTED TO THE BEST OF
their kind worldwide. There are some bizarre entries: the photo accompanying the medieval Italian specialist Carol Lansing (b. 1951) is of Katharine Hepburn, and the list includes Georgiann Makropoulos (b. 1943), an American wrestling historian, and Dorothy Dietrich (b. 1969), "the first and only woman to have performed the bullet catch in her mouth." At the same time, omitted are such historians as C. V. Wedgwood, Antonia Fraser, Jill Lepore, Amanda Foreman, Mary Beard, Brenda Wineapple, and anyone born before 1806. The women who do make the cut run to a strangely precise 397, and the site makes it clear there are thousands who might have been included.

Only recently could such a listing even have been contemplated. For centuries, reading and writing were reserved for the power holders in what worldwide were patriarchal societies.* The first woman to be taken seriously for works about the past was the Chinese writer Bān Zhāo (A.D. 45–116). Her family had been part of the imperial court for three generations. Zhāo had elder twin brothers, Bān Chao, who became a well-known general, and Bān Gu, a poet who followed his father as the editor of *Hanshu,* a history of the first two hundred years of the Western Han dynasty. Some scholars believe Bān Zhāo was already contributing to this ambitious undertaking by the time her brother took over: from internal evidence, it is likely she was responsible for about one-fourth of the whole. We know she was mainly responsible for the section on astronomy as well as the "Eight Tables," a list of the careers of the senior officials of the dynasty.

In A.D. 89, a high-born child was installed as emperor, and power fell to his mother, Dowager Empress Dou, and her family. Bān Gu was part of this inner circle. In 92, the Dous were arraigned for treason, the empress lost her influence, male members of the family committed suicide, and their collaborators were sentenced to execution. Bān Gu died in prison, leaving much of his writings unfinished. Bān Zhāo had been married off while a young teenager and had several children, but after the early deaths of her husband and Bān Gu she took over her brother's work. Later, the emperor made her a kind of court supervisor of education, in charge of tutoring his queen, his various mistresses, and the many ladies-in-waiting.

In one of her books, *Lessons for Women,* Bān Zhāo advises women (ostensibly her own daughters) to be submissive and accept that their husbands could have concubines while they must remain faithful—although she does recommend that married women should try to educate themselves, so that they might better serve their husbands and in so doing survive long enough to become powerful dowagers. She certainly did. According to her deftly shaped apologia,

---

* One should give an honorable mention, however, to an earlier well-born figure, Princess Ennigaldi, the daughter of King Nabonidus, who from 556 to 539 B.C. ruled as the last king of the Neo-Babylonian Empire. She founded the world's first museum, situated about 490 feet southeast of the famous ziggurat of Ur in southern Iraq. In 1925, an archaeologist named Leonard Woolley discovered a remarkable collection of artifacts, from many different times and places, yet expertly organized and even labeled, using tablets and clay cylinders. Ennigaldi's museum was created about 530 B.C., but we know nothing about her bar this, her one great gift to world history.

Bān Zhāo as depicted in a book of woodcut prints from the late seventeenth century containing imagined portraits of heroes and heroines from Chinese history.

I, the unworthy writer, am unsophisticated, unenlightened, and by nature unintelligent, but I am fortunate both to have received not a little favor from my scholarly Father, and to have had a cultured mother and instructresses upon whom to rely for a literary education as well as for training in good manners. More than forty years have passed since at the age of fourteen I took up the dustpan and the broom in the Cao family [the family into which she married]. During this time with trembling heart I feared constantly that I might disgrace my parents, and that I might multiply difficulties for both the women and the men of my husband's family. Day and night I was distressed in heart, but I labored without confessing weariness. Now and hereafter, however, I know how to escape from such fears. . . .

She ends by resorting to verse:

Succeed in pleasing the one man/And you are forever settled.
Fail in pleasing the one man/And you are forever finished.

Her account neatly captures the position of women in Confucian China. Yet beyond the books that dealt with historical matters she also delved into mathematics and wrote essays, poetry (including the delightful "Ode to the Sparrow"), and a travel memoir, even rising to become court librarian. A crater on Venus is named after her; one fancies she would have been pleased.

Bān Zhāo was the exception to the rule that men write history—histories about men. After her, there is no woman historian of note until the tenth-century dramatist, poet, and canoness Hrotsvit of Gandersheim (935–1020), in Lower Saxony, who not only wrote six well-regarded plays but also an epic in Latin on the Holy Roman Emperor Otto I. Clearly aware of the prejudices against her sex, she said she "put womanly weakness aside and summoned manly strength to her prudent heart." She hasn't had a crater named after her, but a minor planet orbiting the Sun, asteroid 615.

Anna Komnene (1083–c. 1155), a remarkable Byzantine scholar who wrote an authoritative account of her father's imperial reign, has nothing in the heavens bearing her name, but she was a considerable star, not only as a physician, hospital administrator, and biographer but also a princess who, when virtually under house arrest, presumed to write military history. For many years Komnene believed that, as the eldest of Emperor Alexios I's seven children, she would succeed him, but to her disgust saw her younger brother John become emperor instead. When, in the story that has come down to us, her husband, Nikephoros, refused to do away with her sibling, she was so infuriated that she raged that she should have been the man and he the woman.[*]

Banished to a convent after attempting to stir up revolt, in 1148 Anna began a political and military account of her father's years in power, 1081–1118, with the deliberately epic title *The Alexiad*. Much in the style of Thucydides, she provides insight on the conspiracies and

---

[*] Anna's lurid reputation is mainly the work of Edward Gibbon, who in 1788 described how, "stimulated by ambition and revenge," she plotted her brother's murder. According to Gibbon, her history "betrays in every page the vanity of a female author," as if he himself were innocent of such a failing. Subsequent chroniclers swallowed his story. "A woman so intrepid as to write history, that most masculine of genres, *must* have been power-hungry enough to wish . . . that she had 'the long member and the balls,'" writes Barbara Newman acidly. "Byzantine Laments," *London Review of Books,* March 2, 2017, p. 21, reviewing Leonora Neville, *Anna Komnene: The Life and Work of a Medieval Historian.*

wars between Alexios I and the West, describing weaponry, tactics, and battles with vivid enthusiasm. She is particularly good on the First Crusade, her account being our one eyewitness view from Byzantium. According to Charles Diehl's influential 1906 work *Figures Byzantines,* she exhibited "the fury of Medea" and, bitter to the end, refused her brother's forgiveness. Her book's prologue also features a disarming essay on the difficulties of composing history:

> My material . . . has been gathered from insignificant writings, absolutely devoid of literary pretensions, and from old soldiers who were serving in the army at the time that my father's accession. . . . I based the truth of my history on them by examining their narratives and comparing them with what I had written, and what they told me with what I had often heard, from my father in particular and from my uncles. . . .

Thereafter the locker is empty. One reason for the scarcity of women historians from ancient Roman times on was their exclusion from learning Latin, the language of literature. There were always a few exceptional females proficient in classical languages (Cleopatra was probably one, but she never tried her hand at history), but for centuries a formal education in Latin set apart a group of individuals who could share information in what amounted to an esoteric code, and among those shut out were the vast majority of otherwise literate women, however voraciously they read.

Compounding and underscoring that conspiracy was the low opinion men had of women. Herodotus mentions them just 375 times, and although he refers to various powerful queens like Artemisia and Pheretime, his history also includes oddities like the beard-growing priestess of Pedasa and the Mendean woman who is said to have had public sex with a goat. Apart from Sappho, we possess almost no female voice from the ancient world. One of the rare pieces of expository writing by a woman in antiquity was by one Gnathaena, a courtesan in late fourth-century B.C. Athens; her list of instructions on how to behave when visiting an exclusive house of prostitution was actually catalogued in the Great Library of Alexandria.

In *The Odyssey,* Telemachus informs his mother, Penelope, that "speech will be the business of men" and sends her upstairs to her weaving. Aristotle saw women as defective men and, as Thucydides's Pericles famously puts it in his funeral oration, addressing Athenian women who have been left war widows: "A woman's best fame is to be as seldom as possible mentioned by men, either for censure or for praise." Athenian prostitutes had their own way of protesting at such diminishment. As St. Clement of Alexandria noted, they would "have figures in erotic postures engraved on the soles of their sandals so that they could leave an impression of their obscene etchings as they walked along."

Ancient Rome was no better. Juvenal in his *Satires* (late first century A.D.) abhorred "the woman who is forever referring to Palaemon's *Grammar* and thumbing through it . . . or who quotes lines I've never heard." The distaff side of humanity refused to let their brains waste away, however. For instance, the 1333 painting "Annunciation with St. Margaret and St. Ansanus" by the Gothic artists Simone Martini and Lippo Memmi, now housed in the Uffizi Gallery in Florence, shows the archangel Gabriel informing Mary that she is about to give birth to the son of God, but she keeps her thumb in her book, so as not to lose the place. Life mirroring art, a Venetian who spent her adult life in France, Christine de Pizan (1364–c. 1430) was dubbed the first professional woman of letters in Europe. Both her father and her husband were dead from the plague by the time she was twenty-five, so she was forced to take up writing to feed her three children. By 1405 she had completed her most famous works, *The Book of the City of Ladies* (*Le Livre de la cité des dames*) and *The Treasure of the City of Ladies* (*Le Livre des trois vertus*). The first of these records women's past contributions to society, the second advises them how to show themselves to advantage in male company.

Clever women were a threat to men, thus the myriad stories of women's vanity, their tendency to lying, and their weak intellects, tales against them multiplying through the centuries. According to *The Hammer of the Witches,* a 1486 work commissioned by the Papacy, woman "is an imperfect animal, she always deceives . . . she is an inescapable punishment, a necessary evil, a desirable calamity, a delectable detriment, and evil of nature." A seventeenth-century law in the state of Massachusetts declared that women would be treated as witches were it proved that they had lured men into marriage via the use of high-heeled shoes. And so it went. One can pick examples of prejudice or subjugation almost at will; between 1580 and 1640, for instance,

Christine de Pizan instructing her son (who seems to have lost a sock). The scene is from The Queen's Manuscript, *her collected writings, which has several portraits of her engaged in intellectual pursuits, a highly unusual subject at the time. The work was commissioned by Isabel, the queen of France, and completed in 1414.*

only about 10 percent of women in the diocese of London could write even their signature. In Benjamin Franklin's time (1706–90), three in five women in New England couldn't sign their names, and those who could were not able to actually write—signing is mechanical, writing an art. As Joan Acocella says, "until the eighteenth century, a female writer who had bold ideas, especially ideas that might be considered socially disruptive, was widely regarded as foolish or insane." The world's male historians meanwhile in their works systematically snuffed out hundreds of women, their accomplishments, their bravery, and even their notoriety.

Sophie Brahe, second sister of the astronomer Tycho Brahe, is one example of a woman whose achievements have been appropriated. Another is the eleventh-century Italian physician Trotula, who gained both fame and respect in her own lifetime for treating women's ailments. By the next century, a male historian, assuming someone so accomplished couldn't be a woman, changed her pronoun and name to the masculine form. In the twentieth century, her gender was reversed, but her occupation was downgraded to midwife. Textbooks abound with scientific discoveries credited to men, even when a woman was a co-discoverer or made the first breakthrough. The seventeenth-century New England poet Anne Bradstreet wrote:

> If what I do prove well, it won't advance,
> They'll say it's stolen, or else it was by chance.

According to Charlotte Gordon, introducing an edition of Mary Shelley's *Frankenstein,* "Experts declared that women were inferior to men in all areas of human development and could not be educated beyond a certain rudimentary level. Whereas men possessed the capacity for reason and ethical rectitude, women were considered foolish, fickle, selfish, gullible, sly, untrustworthy, and childish." Not only was it legal in England for a husband to beat his wife (so long as it was with a stick no thicker than his thumb), men were encouraged to punish any woman they regarded as unruly. A Buddhist text describes woman as the "emissary of hell."

Even up to the fifteenth century, the life of any woman was unlikely to be written until centuries later, and prejudice toward women as neither intellectually serious nor fit subjects for biography endured into the 1940s. "If you happen to have any learning, keep it a profound secret," Mary Wollstonecraft recalled a father telling his daughters as late as 1774. His contemporary Samuel Johnson concurred: "A man is in general better pleased when he has a good dinner upon his table, than when his wife talks Greek." And when in 1776 Abigail Adams begged her husband, John, in a letter, to "remember the ladies" in the nation's new code of laws, the second president of the United States was not persuaded. "Depend upon it," he wrote back, "we know better than to repeal our Masculine systems."

In *Northanger Abbey* (1803), Jane Austen's heroine confides that she finds history uninteresting: "It tells me nothing that does either not vex or weary me. The quarrels of popes and kings, with wars or pestilences, in every page; the men all so good for nothing, and hardly any women at all—it is very tiresome." The argument is carried on in *Persuasion* (1818). When Anne Elliot argues that women are more constant than men, Captain Harville replies: "All histories are against you. . . . But perhaps you will say, these were all written by men." Anne can only agree: "Men have had every advantage of us in telling their own story," she says. Austen's contemporary, the scandal-ridden Georgiana Cavendish, Duchess of Devonshire (1757–1806), confided in her journal that history was not history at all but something that looked very much like it unless one knew the truth.

* * *

CHANGE CAME, BELATEDLY AND SPORADICALLY. Most women historians of any note continued to come from the upper or aristocratic classes. One typical example—although deeply her own person, and irrepressible—is Lady Mary Wortley Montagu (1689–1762). She was brought up in considerable luxury at Thoresby Hall in Nottinghamshire. To supplement the meager tutoring she received from a governess she loathed, she used her father's formidable library to "steal" her education, teaching herself Latin, still a language reserved for men. Clever, witty, and beautiful, she had two prominent suitors by her early twenties: Edward Wortley Montagu, a legally trained diplomat, and the memorably named Clotworthy Skeffington. Mary's father, now Marquess of Dorchester, pressured her to marry Skeffington, who was heir to an Irish peerage, in reply to which Mary promptly eloped with her diplomat. They married, and in 1716 Wortley was appointed British ambassador to Turkey. After accompanying him to Istanbul, she wrote a series of letters home (including several to her friend Alexander Pope) about the Ottoman Empire, which, when posthumously published, became an inspiration to other women travel writers.

During her time there she recorded her experiences in a Turkish bath, where one group of local women, horrified when they saw Montagu's elaborate underclothing, exclaimed that "the husbands in England were much worse than in the East, for [they] tied up their wives in little boxes." In general, she dismissed the European travel literature of her day as "trite observations . . . superficial . . . [of] boys [who] only remember where they met with the best wine or the prettyest women." The letters regularly underline the fact that they presented a different (and, as Montagu believed, more accurate) description than that provided in other records: "You will perhaps be surpriz'd at an Account so different from what you have been entertained with by the common Voyage-writers who are very fond of speaking of what they don't know." She was also an accomplished poet, and her ode "Constantinople," written in heroic couplets, describes Britain and Turkey through the centuries, depicting knaves, dandies, adulterers, politicians on the make—anyone in the capitals she knew who was colorful.

Two others to show the new revolutionary spirit, in historical writing as in much else, were Mary Wollstonecraft (1759–97) and Anne Louise Germaine de Staël (1766–1817). Wollstonecraft, a philosopher and novelist of guile and strength, is remembered mainly for her travel accounts and for *A Vindication of the Rights of Women* (1792), but in 1794 she published *An Historical and Moral View of the French Revolution; and the Effect It Has Produced in Europe*. The British historian Tom Furniss calls it the most neglected of her nineteen books, making use of her considerable gifts as a reporter.

In the wake of an unhappy love affair with the married and highly unstable Swiss artist Henry Fuseli, Wollstonecraft, still staunchly unmarried at thirty-three, had traveled to Paris in 1792, eager to take part

Mary Wortley Montagu in Turkish dress, and
Madame de Staël in one of her characteristic turbans.

in the exceptional events that she had already celebrated in her *Vindica-tion of the Rights of Men* (1790), written to rebut the Whig parliamentar-ian Edmund Burke's condemnation of the turbulence in France. That December, she saw the former king, Louis XVI, being led off for trial before the National Assembly, and to her surprise found "the tears flow[ing] insensibly from my eyes, when I saw Louis sitting, with more dignity than I expected from his character, in a hackney coach going to meet death. . . . Though my mind is calm, I cannot dismiss the lively images that have filled my imagination all the day." She was a commit-ted republican but believed what she saw with her own eyes.

She was to stay in the French capital for more than two years. Al-though without formal training as a historian, by the use of journals, letters, and documents she was able to describe how ordinary people in France reacted to the revolution, and her book acted as a counterbal-ance to the intense antirevolutionary mood in Britain, which viewed its old adversary as a nation gone mad. Calling the uprising a "glorious *chance* to obtain more virtue and happiness than hitherto blessed our globe," Wollstonecraft argued that it arose from social conditions that made a people's rebellion inevitable.

Her previous books had won her literary celebrity, yet she received little support from fellow intellectuals and many mocked her, while her life was marked by misfortune. During her time in Paris she fell deeply in love with an American adventurer, Gilbert Imlay, and gave birth to a daughter, Fanny. At first they were happy, even amid the excesses of the Terror, but Imlay's absences and Mary's reproaches took their toll. In April 1795, Imlay having evidently lost interest in her and moved to England, Wollstonecraft returned to London to at-tempt a reconciliation, but he woundingly rejected her. Twice she tried to take her life, first by ingesting laudanum, then by an attempted drowning. On both occasions she was saved, after which she accepted that her time with Imlay was over. By 1797 Mary had begun an affair with the philosopher, political journalist, and religious dissenter Wil-liam Godwin. When she became pregnant again, they married so their child might be legitimate (their daughter would marry Percy Bysshe Shelley and write *Frankenstein*), but at the birth Mary's placenta broke apart and became infected. After several days of agony, she died of septicemia. She was just thirty-eight.

In 1982, working for the British publisher Hodder & Stoughton, I commissioned the biographer Richard Holmes, already the author of an award-winning biography of Shelley, to make a series of journeys in France and Italy and in writing about them link his adventures with famous travelers from the past. The result was *Footsteps: Adventures of a Romantic Biographer,* and the second of his subjects was Wollstonecraft, whose adventures he compared to his own experiences of the student uprisings in Paris in 1968. "Mary's story in France astonished me," Holmes concluded his account. "Her courage and tenacity, as well as her marvellous honesty as a witness to her own revolutionary experiences, made her a woman in a million. She was exemplary in a way that completely altered my conception of what 'the revolution' was about." He then quotes from the last published of her books, *Letters Written*

Mary Wollstonecraft as painted by John Opie, circa 1797.
Dress, Wollstonecraft believed, should "adorn the person and not rival it."
At the time she sat for this portrait, Wollstonecraft was pregnant
with her daughter Mary (later the author of Frankenstein),
whose birth was to cost her mother her life.

During a Short Residence in Sweden, Norway, and Denmark, in which Wollstonecraft rhapsodizes about the independent farmers of the Scandinavian far north:

> I want faith! My imagination hurries me forward to seek an asylum in such a retreat from all the disappointments I am threatened with; but reason drags me back, whispering that the world is still the world, and man the same compound of weakness and folly, who must occasionally excite love and disgust, admiration and contempt.

Her bereaved husband, William Godwin, said it was the kind of book that made one immediately fall in love with its author.

***

MADAME DE STAËL MAY not have been so lovable, but she was at least as formidable. For Byron, she was "the first female writer of this, or perhaps of any age," while the great French nineteenth-century compilation *Biographie Universelle* dubbed her "the feminine Voltaire." A Frenchwoman of Swiss origin, de Staël was an eyewitness to the Enlightenment, the French Revolution, the Terror, and Napoleon's rise and fall.* She was the principal critic of Bonaparte (whom she likened to Machiavelli), and when he banished her from France, she moved to Germany. "I did not know what would become of me." A witty and brilliant conversationalist and formidable life force, she often dressed in flashy and revealing outfits (especially flamboyant turbans), even as she threw herself into the political and social life of her times. Her lovers included Count Narbonne (made minister of war in 1791 through her influence), Talleyrand (made foreign minister, again through her patronage), and the novelist Benjamin Constant. Her partnership with Constant made them one of the most lionized intellectual couples of their time, while in 1814 a contemporary observed that "there are three great powers struggling against Napoleon for the soul of Europe: En-

---

* Perhaps surprisingly, de Staël and Wollstonecraft never met, even though their circles overlapped. A certain backstory would have put them at odds. In 1788, Wollstonecraft translated de Staël's father Jacques Necker's work *De l'importance des opinions religieuses.* This should have brought the two women together, but Wollstonecraft then went on to write *A Vindication of the Rights of Women,* in which she not only lambasted de Staël's acceptance of Rousseau's condescending attitude to women in *Emile,* but dedicated her book to de Staël's lover Talleyrand.

gland, Russia, and Madame de Staël." Tolstoy credits her in his epilogue to *War and Peace* as one of the "influential forces" that shaped the way people lived. Chateaubriand and Wellington both attended her deathbed.

Her complete works run to seventeen volumes, including novels and accounts of her travels, with emphasis on passion (she found Austen's novels contemptible) and opposing those in power. Among her works are two historical novels, *Delphine* (1802; it particularly enraged Napoleon) and *Corinne* (1807), which examines the forces holding back women's artistic creativity in two very contrasting cultures, England and Italy. She also published *On Germany* (1813; she used Tacitus's title deliberately, even though it was a country which at that time did not exist, while also introducing a new word, *Romanticism*), and a two-volume study of the French Revolution. Appearing posthumously in 1818, this last book sold sixty thousand copies in its first year of British publication. One crossed her at one's peril.* Talleyrand observed tartly that she enjoyed throwing people overboard just to have the satisfaction of fishing them out of the water, while a further Byron verdict runs: "In her own house she was amiable. In any other person's, you wished her gone, and in her own again." Elsewhere, he wrote simply, "She ought to have been a man." As it was, she joined Wollstonecraft in pioneering a new approach to history, a female one.

★ ★ ★

A GENERATION ON, LUCY AIKIN (1781–1864), part of a distinguished family of Unitarians, wrote more than twenty books (some under the pseudonym Mary Godolphin) encompassing poetry, memoirs, and three influential historical works, each of two volumes, on the courts of Elizabeth I, James I, and Charles I. She so easily might never have picked up her pen. According to Geri Walton, her biographer, "Although her family had literary tendencies, she initially appeared not to have the skills to learn to read." Her flailing attempts resulted in her grandmother naming her the "little dunce." Luckily, in time Aikin did learn—not only English but French, Latin, and Italian. And her books were read. Despite their hardly mentioning the Spanish Armada or the

---

* In exile on St. Helena, Bonaparte reflected that he might never have ended up there had he tried harder to get her on his side. "I made a mistake," he dictated, "Madame de Staël raised more enemies against me in exile than she would have done had she stayed in France."

English Civil War, her view of life at court has the whiff of an insider's firsthand knowledge, and her *Memoirs* of both James and Charles won a wide enough following, even in their American editions, that both were quickly reprinted.

Aikin lived most of her life in the bosom of her family. So too did a warmhearted Suffolk spinster, Agnes Strickland (1796–1874). One of six sisters in a brood of nine, she published several immensely popular works of biographical history, of which the best known is the twelve-volume *Lives of the Queens of England*. Her father gave his daughters a literary education, believing that the female mind should be "strengthened," if only to take part in rational conversation with men. He died early, so his children took to writing to keep their family afloat (only one, Sarah, did not become an author). Agnes's penmanship was unusual in that her elder sister, Elizabeth, helped with research and did much of the writing too (out of the thirty-three English queens featured, nineteen were her work), but she adamantly refused all publicity, so Agnes was put forward as sole creator. As she was gregarious and reveled in becoming a celebrity, the arrangement suited everyone. Only Queen Victoria seems to have guessed that the books were the work of two separate pens.

The Dictionary of National Biography is harsh in its entry on Agnes. "Miss Strickland," it states,

> was laborious and painstaking, but she lacked the judicial temper and critical mind necessary for dealing in the right spirit with original authorities. This, in conjunction with her extraordinary devotion to Mary Queen of Scots and her strong Tory prejudices, detract from the value of her conclusions. Her literary style is weak, and the popularity of her books is in great measure due to their trivial gossip and domestic details.

Others are more generous. Antonia Fraser, introducing a 1972 facsimile edition of the *Lives of the Queens,* reckons Strickland an important figure in that "she founded a whole new school of vivid utterly readable history, aimed to capture the general reader who felt himself inadequately served . . . either by the pedantic scholar or the over-imaginative historical novelist." One suspects that the "general reader" was more often "*herself,*" as the books focus on female subjects and are full of information about dress, manners, and diet. But Strickland also broke new ground in that she based her *Lives* wherever she could on unpublished official records, contemporary letters, and other private documents that previous biographers had neglected. When researching the consorts of Henry VIII, for instance, she applied for the obligatory permission to consult state papers, which was refused by "the midget Whig" Lord John Russell, who in short order was to become prime minister. However, the obstacle was removed through intensive political lobbying, and both Agnes and Elizabeth were given the access they needed. When Agnes died in 1874, a year before her self-effacing sister, the inscription on her tombstone read: "Historian of the Queens of England."

So a woman had written a bestselling work of history—several, in fact, as well as a dozen books for children. But Agnes was still a creature of her time. When a reviewer in the *Spectator* attacked her for having turned to writing because her attempts to find a husband had proved fruitless, she replied loftily:

> The infelicity of celebrated literary women in the married state forms a heavy list. That some exceptions may be found is certain; but, indeed, it cannot add to the comfort of a husband if his wife's time is so occupied. A female author is wiser to remain unmarried. . . .

Generally, however, the tide was turning—that is, men could no longer keep the world of letters to themselves, and women throughout Western Europe and North America took to writing history in increasing numbers, their works being reviewed with respect, even if Nathaniel Hawthorne could write in 1855, "America is now given over to a damned mob of scribbling women."

* * *

"MILITARY GLORY! IT WAS a dream that century after century had seized on men's imagination and set their blood on fire." So opens *The Reason Why*, an account of the charge of the Light Brigade, published in 1953 and an immediate bestseller. I quote from a first edition, originally priced at fifteen shillings, bequeathed me by my parents. The author was not a man but a woman, Cecil Blanche Woodham-Smith (1896–

1977), part of a well-known Irish family that sent her to a special school for officers' daughters in Bath, until she was expelled for the most minor of misdemeanors, absconding from class to visit the National Gallery. After a spell at a French convent and then studying English at Oxford, she married a London lawyer, George Woodham-Smith, and wrote a series of pseudonymous potboilers before embarking on a biography of Florence Nightingale (1950) that took her nine years to research but sold more than 260,000 copies in hardback and established her reputation.

Women have long been presumed to be uninterested in or no good at writing about war and combat,* but Woodham-Smith's next book was *The Reason Why,* and it proved more popular still. She later explained how she wrote her account of the fateful charge itself, working for thirty-six hours without stopping until the last horse was felled; she then poured herself a large Scotch and slept soundly for two days.

Two more notable works followed, *The Great Hunger: Ireland 1845– 1849* (1962), about the famine that killed over a million people and drove as many more to emigrate to America, and the first volume of a biography of Queen Victoria, once again making telling use of primary sources. By the time she died she had proved that women could research in depth, then deliver great narrative history—and about military matters too. But she was an odd duck. Alan Bennett wrote of her:

> Cecil was a frail woman with a tiny bird-like skull, looking more like Elizabeth I (in later life) than Edith Sitwell ever did (and minus her sheet-metal earrings). Irish, she had a Firbankian wit and a lovely turn of phrase. "Do you know the Atlantic at all?" she once asked me and I put the line into [his play] *Habeas Corpus* and got a big laugh on it. From a grand Irish family she was

---

* Evidence suggests this is generally true—even C. V. Wedgwood covers her major battles in just a page or two, and while Barbara Tuchman's *The Guns of August* is highly authoritative, her book on the Vietnam conflict is her least convincing. "Even more than in fiction," says the military historian Antony Beevor, "men tend to write about men and women tend to write about women, presumably because they understand their own sex better." "Big Books by Blokes About Battles," *The Guardian,* February 6, 2016. On the other hand, Margaret MacMillan has written authoritatively on the First World War, as has Lyn MacDonald, particularly on the battles of the Somme and Passchendaele. Women began writing on war in significant numbers during the 1960s with the turn toward a "multidisciplinary approach that embeds war in its political, social, cultural and personal contexts." Julia Lovell, "Military History: Not Just for Men," *The Guardian,* September 30, 2011. Other pioneers include Joanna Bourke and Amanda Foreman. However, they remain underrepresented in the annals of war.

quite snobbish; talking of someone she said: "Then he married a Mitford . . . but that's a stage everybody goes through."

Much of her career overlapped with that of the most distinguished woman historian of her time: Veronica Wedgwood (1910–97), who flourished over five decades from the 1930s to the 1970s. She too came from a privileged background; her great-great-great grandfather was Josiah Wedgwood, the eighteenth-century Staffordshire potter, and her father, to whom Ralph Vaughan Williams dedicated his London Symphony, chairman of railway administration during the Second World War. Her mother was a novelist and travel writer.

After gaining a First in Modern History at Oxford, Wedgwood began her writing career in 1935, with a life of the Earl of Strafford (1593–1641), the brilliant, tragic adviser to King Charles I and a major figure in the period leading up to the English Civil War. "The biography was very feminine and sentimental," she told an interviewer in 1962. Her second book, published when she was twenty-eight, was a study of "that squalid struggle," as she called it, *The Thirty Years War* (1938). The historian Sir George Clark was accustomed to say that no first-class work of history was ever written by anyone under thirty. C. V. Wedgwood (her nom de plume; like Woodham-Smith, she preferred to hide her gender, being aware of the prejudices against women) was an exception.

A biography of the founder of the modern state of Holland, *William the Silent* (1944), followed. She also fitted in a biography of Oliver Cromwell (1939; she argued that one of his major weaknesses was his Welsh genes) and, ten years later, *Richelieu and the French Monarchy*. She is best remembered, though, for two major works on the English Civil War, *The King's Peace* (1955) and *The King's War* (1958), in which she depicted its sheer confusion and the impossibility of coordinating events in three countries, Wales, Scotland, and England, once any central order had broken down.

According to her old Oxford tutor, A. L. Rowse, for whom she was "my first outstanding pupil," her work early on displayed "not only a mastery of research but maturity of judgement, with a literary capacity not common in academic writing. She wrote indeed to be read." *The New York Times* was condescending: "Miracles do happen. A generation ago the young English woman historian was often tethered to a dry theme until she had nibbled it bald. Today she dares much more to select a major subject." Unusually, thirty years after Wedgwood wrote her biography of Strafford, she published a revised, far more critical version. In the earlier edition she judged him a "sincere, brave and able man," but after reviewing newly available family papers she concluded he was certainly brave but greedy and unscrupulous.

It was a typical respect for the evidence. Wedgwood was a conscientious historian, relying on primary sources and on seeing for herself the locations she wanted to describe. "I enjoy the unexacting company of the dead," she once remarked of her addiction to churchyards. She would walk around battle sites and put herself through the same weather and field conditions as her subjects, and was later at pains to point out that Cromwell, for instance, had no military experience and that most of those who fought in the civil war were "talented amateurs" when it came to battlefield strategy, not professional soldiers.

Simon Schama refers to her "elegant, surprisingly astringent mind," but generally she kept her opinions to herself. She belonged to no school but was swimming in a crowded pool. She had intended a civil war trilogy but never completed it, probably discouraged (in Rowse's view), by the venom academics injected into her subject. She stayed clear of contentious subjects, and was wary of the heavy theorizing and academic nitpicking that characterized the writing of many of her contemporaries. That was not her way. As she explained, she was interested in how things happened rather than why. "I have tried to describe the variety, vitality and imperfections as well as the religion and government of the British Isles in the 17th century, *deliberately avoiding analysis* [her emphasis], and seeking rather to give an impression of its vigorous and vivid confusion," she wrote in *The King's Peace*.

According to *The Economist,* she "had a novelist's talent for entering into the character of the giants of history" and openly defended the poetic nature of her craft, conceding that all style brings with it the possibility of distortion. "The whole value of the study of history," she explained, "is for me its delightful undermining of certainty, its cumulative insistence of the differences of point of view. . . . It is not lack of prejudice which makes for dull history, but lack of passion."

Ever courteous and devoted to good works (she was president of both PEN and the Society of Authors as well as being "on every prize committee," as she put it), Wedgwood was also a successful lecturer and broadcaster; her books included *Montrose* (1952), a short biography of the brilliant Scots general who supported Charles I; two collections of essays, *Velvet Studies* (1946) and *Truth and Opinion* (1960); and two translations, a biography of Charles V by Karl Brandi (1939) and *Auto-da-Fé* by Elias Canetti (1946). Her last undertaking was a two-volume introduction to world history, of which she had completed the first volume, *The Spoils of Time* (1984), when ill health cut her work short. Canetti tells how he got to know her when she sought him out after reading his novel in German:

> Veronica was short and dark and a little on the heavy side, not at all your usual Englishwoman. She explained her appearance by her Celtic forebears. She was very quick on the uptake, remembered everything, reacted sharply; in England, where there are so many stodgy people, she was certainly the very opposite, someone with whom you could never be bored. But she was never confident of her effect on others, and always had the feel-

Cecil Blanche Woodham-Smith (left) and Veronica Wedgwood (right). Both were formidable, the former said to resemble Elizabeth I in her mature years, Wedgwood to have "a novelist's talent for entering into the character of the giants of history."

ing of not being taken seriously. . . . She wasn't physically attractive, her face was too broad and flat, her expression piteous,
her movements rather graceless, but her voice was warm and
rich and sonorous. If one had heard her only, perhaps then one
might have fallen in love with her, and, as I gradually learned,
there was in fact more than one man who had fallen for the
charms of her voice and her background. But they weren't men
of the kind she was looking for, she admired great historical figures . . . she lived, much more than is usual for historians, *their
lives,* vicariously. She had an instinct for passion and certainty.

Canetti, an eager womanizer, was not at his most perspicacious. At
a time when women were calling attention to themselves in many areas
where before they had been all but invisible, Wedgwood flouted conventions in her personal life, for almost seventy years living openly
with Jacqueline Hope-Wallace, a civil servant, and when tramping
around battle sites or at their shared house in the Sussex countryside
would wear manly clothing. Politically, however, she kept a low profile during the decades that feminist movements were popular.

Other women historians were more militant. According to the standard histories, by 1913, Feminism (originally capitalized) was already a
household term in the United States. In Britain during the First World
War, more than a million women were newly employed outside the
home—in munition factories, engineering works, the police—and in
1918 the Representation of the People Act gave near-universal suffrage
to men and suffrage to women over thirty. In 1928, a further act extended equal voting rights to both sexes. By 1930 nearly all developed
countries had followed suit, although French women did not receive
the vote until 1945, the Swiss not until 1971. But political evenness was
not the same as cultural equality. In 1963, Betty Friedan's *The Feminine
Mystique* voiced the acute frustration women felt in having to follow
their college graduations by becoming "homemakers." Over the following decade, "Women's Liberation," a term first used the year after
Friedan's book appeared, became an accepted phrase (though the French
equivalent, *libération des femmes,* had established itself back in 1911).

The feminism of the 1960s, fueled by the new climate, was joined
by increased female enrollment in higher education, including history
courses, and what became known as "feminist history" sought to in-

clude gender in everything that historians came to study. Two particular issues it attempted to address were the exclusion of women from the way history was presented and the negative portrayal of women in past writing. In October 2000, Susan Pedersen, a historian at Columbia University, set out the case:

> If we take feminism to be that cast of mind that insists that the differences and inequalities between the sexes are the result of historical processes and are not blindly "natural," we can understand why feminist history has always had a dual mission—on the one hand to recover the lives, experiences, and mentalities of women from the condescension and obscurity in which they have been so unnaturally placed, and on the other to reexamine and rewrite the entire historical narrative to reveal the construction and workings of gender.

Feminist historians pointed to the lack of references to women in standard texts. A pioneering study, *Hidden from History* by Sheila Rowbotham, was followed by detailed investigations into women's lives, including employment, trade unionism, family life, and sexuality. But there were dangers; as Hilary Mantel wrote in a 2013 article, "Often, if you want to write about women in history, you have to distort history to do it, or substitute fantasy for facts; you have to pretend that individual women were more important than they were or that we know more about them than we do." This is a valuable corrective, but "history" had already been distorted by the minimization and outright exclusion of women, and the new approach transformed writing about the past, much to the better. A new generation began to be published: Rosalyn Baxandall (1939–2015), Linda Gordon (b. 1940), Camille Paglia (b. 1947), Virginia Nicholson (b. 1955), Amanda Foreman (b. 1968)—who produced a TV series on the history of women; and old hands rediscovered: Betty Behrens (1904–89), Gerda Hedwig Lerner (1920–2013), even the archconservative, intellectually formidable Gertrude Himmelfarb (1922–2019). As the Pulitzer Prize winner Carolyn Kizer (1925–2014) wrote:

> *We are the custodians of the world's best-kept secret:*
> *Merely the private lives of one-half of humanity.*

There was still much to do. From the late 1960s on, the women's liberation movement had great impact. In early 1970, an article in the underground newspaper *Rat* introduced the neologism "Herstory,"* which spawned women-centered presses, such as Virago, along with T-shirts and buttons, as well as becoming an accepted term in academia. But in these early days of radicalism too many works by women historians were spoiled by repetitive political rhetoric.

While this revolution was in progress, one of the twentieth century's most celebrated historians, Barbara Tuchman (1912–89), was busy carving out a career. "So gorgeous was the spectacle of the May morning of 1910," runs the opening sentence of her book *The Guns of August,* "when nine kings rode in the funeral of Edward VII of England that the crowd, waiting in hushed and black-clad awe, could not keep back gasps of admiration." She had no fear in writing about men, nor about how women had been treated by historians; in *A Distant Mirror* she states unequivocally, "Any medieval woman whose life was adequately documented would be atypical."

Like others in the first wave of great women historians, she came from a highly privileged background. When her book appeared, Tuchman was described in the press as a late starter, a fifty-year-old housewife, mother of three daughters, and wife of a well-known New York physician. That was true but misleading. She was descended from two of the most prominent Jewish families of New York City. Her grandfather Henry Morgenthau, Sr., had been Woodrow Wilson's ambassador to Turkey in the First World War and her uncle Henry Morgenthau, Jr., had been FDR's treasury secretary for more than a decade. Her father, a publisher, sportsman, and philanthropist, founded an international banking house. Her childhood homes were a brownstone on the Upper East Side, where a French governess read aloud from the French classics, and a Connecticut country house complete with outhouses and stables. Her fellow historian Robert K. Massie tells in his foreword to the 1994 reissue of *The Guns of August* how her father for-

---

* The social historian Robin Morgan believes that the word's debut was in the byline of her article "Goodbye to All That," in the first issue of *Rat* after it was taken over and "cleansed" by women. She identified herself, she says, as a member of W.I.T.C.H., decoding the acronym as "Women Inspired to Commit Herstory." See Robin Morgan, *The Word of a Woman: Feminist Despatches, 1968–9* (New York: Norton, 1994). The movement led to an increase in the popularity of other disciplines, freshly minted as "femistry" and "galgebra."

bade any mention of Franklin Roosevelt at the dinner table. One day the adolescent daughter made some social faux pas and was ordered to leave the room. Sitting up straight, she replied: "I am too old to be sent away from the table." Her father was lost for words; she remained in place.

Soon she was off to Radcliffe College, the female coordinate of Harvard, studying history and literature, but skipped her graduation ceremony, choosing instead to accompany her father to the World Monetary and Economic Conference in London, where he headed the U.S. delegation. She spent 1934–35 in Tokyo (including a month in China) as a research assistant at the Institute of Pacific Relations, then became an apprentice writer at the progressive weekly *The Nation*, which her father had purchased to save it from going under. Still in her early twenties, she was next off to Valencia and Madrid to cover the Spanish Civil War. A first book culled from these experiences, *The Lost British Policy: Britain and Spain Since 1700*, was published in 1938.

On June 14, 1940, the day Hitler entered Paris, she married her doctor boyfriend, who was about to enlist as a soldier and told her it was a poor time to start a family. His new wife replied: "If we wait for the outlook to improve, we might wait forever." The first of three daughters was born nine months later. For much of the next decade Tuchman raised her family while fitting in her next two books. First came *Bible and Sword* (1956), a necessarily unfinished history of Britain's relationship with Palestine, Jews, Arabs, the Turks from Seljuks to the Ottomans and on to the founding of Israel. This was followed by *The Zimmermann Telegram* (1958), an account of the attempt in 1917 by the German foreign minister, Arthur Zimmermann, to lure Mexico into war with the United States and so distract America from entering the European conflict. Tuchman's thesis at Radcliffe had been returned to her with the note, "Style undistinguished," and *Bible and Sword* had collected thirty rejection slips before finding a publisher, but now she was writing with literary flair and wry humor, and reviewers noticed.

The Guns of August (1962), which analyzed the political ploys and intrigues that culminated in World War I, was her fourth book and the one that made her a celebrity, securing a durable niche on bestseller lists and her first Pulitzer Prize. Massie goes so far as to describe it as "one of the finest works of history written by an American in our [twentieth] century." It was followed in 1966 by a collection of interlinked essays, *The Proud Tower: A Portrait of the World Before the War, 1890–1914* ("the book I most enjoyed doing . . . 1914 was really the moment when the clock struck for our century"), and *Stillwell and the American Experience in China, 1911–45* (1971), a biography of General Joseph Stilwell, "Vinegar Joe," the hard-driving American officer who played a major role in China during World War II, a work that won her a second Pulitzer. Then came a study of an entirely different period, *A Distant Mirror: The Calamitous Fourteenth Century* (1979); *The March of Folly: From Troy to Vietnam* (1984), a collection of sketches about mature countries that get things woefully wrong; and *The First Salute: A View of the American Revolution* (1988). There was also a short book about China (1972) and a volume of essays about history (1981)—a fine tally in a little over forty years of writing.

She inhabited the libraries of America and Europe: "I was blissful as a cow put to graze in a field of fresh clover and would not have cared if I had been locked in for the night." Yet some professional historians bridled at her success. She never took an advanced degree and did not teach at a university until after her reputation was secure. She was a natural storyteller, providing lively narratives rather than delighting in fresh archival material. In the words of one critic, she was "not a historian's historian; she was a layperson's historian who made the past interesting."

She herself argued that not having to observe the esoteric demands of academia had been her liberation. In an essay at the time *A Distant Mirror* was published (selling more than half a million copies in under five months), she defended her view of the past: "Academics—most academic medievalists—no longer give you a picture of a whole society, because they are focusing on very small areas, monasticism, or castles, or knives and forks, or whatever it may be. It's very difficult to find any book written in the last 25 years that gives you a sense of the *whole*." She provided that along with sharp character portraits. Thus, in *The Guns of August,* we read of Alfred von Schlieffen, architect of the German war plan, "Of the two classes of Prussian officer, the bull-necked and the wasp-waisted, he belonged to the second," while the French commander-in-chief Joseph Joffre is dissected in a sentence: "Massive and paunchy in his baggy uniform, . . . Joffre looked like

Santa Claus and gave an impression of benevolence and naïveté—two qualities not noticeably part of his character." She ever delighted in the telling phrase.*

By the last decade of her life, the history establishment had fallen into line. In 1978, Tuchman was elected a fellow of the American Academy of Arts and Sciences, and the following year was elected the first female president of the American Academy of Arts and Letters. She became a trustee of Radcliffe College, a lecturer at Harvard, and in 1980 won the National Book Award for *A Distant Mirror,* the same year she was invited to give the Jefferson Lecture, the government's highest honor for achievement in the humanities. It was entitled "Mankind's Better Moments." It must have been one of hers.

* * *

TUCHMAN'S RANGE OF INTERESTS was unusually broad; among other subjects, she wrote on the Middle Ages, the Renaissance, the American Revolution, the year 1900, and the Vietnam War. By the time her book on Stilwell was published, women historians were not just writing about issues central to their experience but alighting on almost any subject—a 1999 book of essays devoted to women historians writing about women noted that its twenty authors had chosen to cover arms and economics in the Third Reich; the salons and shops of eighteenth-century France; European peace movements; German historians of the nineteenth century; France's Third Republic; life in Mombasa, Kenya; the construction of citizenship in the United States; and crime and society in early modern Seville—as wide a range as one could imagine.

Even so, one of the difficulties for researchers on women was the fact that archives and libraries often did not catalogue their material in a coherent way. If, say, a student was keen to learn about a soldier's life during the U.S. Civil War, many books provided such information; but if she wanted to know what a woman's day-to-day existence was like, she had to read through diaries of women who stayed at home

---

* John F. Kennedy was influenced by *The Guns of August* during the Cuban missile crisis. The book had just been published, and he told his brother Bobby: "I am not going to follow a course which will allow anyone to write a comparable book about this time [and call it] *The Missiles of October.*" Tuchman's focus on the First World War's "miscalculations" not only influenced JFK's policy over Cuba; he also ordered that White House conversations should be tape-recorded, laying the foundations for the incriminating Nixon tapes a decade later.

during the war or find the scattered autobiographies of nurses or spies or even women who fought dressed as men. Researchers found that women's writings had been lost in family correspondences catalogued under male members' names. Many historical documents reflected an elite male viewpoint, making an unbiased or well-sourced analysis more difficult. It took time for women's history to catch up.

The most obvious successor to Barbara Tuchman in prestige and popularity has been Doris Kearns Goodwin (b. 1943), who unusually among women historians owes her success to two acts of paternalism. The first was a family one. The daughter of Irish immigrants, she developed an enthusiasm for baseball and in her childhood was a devoted Brooklyn Dodgers fan, as was her father. At work during the day, he was unable to attend games, so instructed her to document them from the radio and replay all that had happened once he returned home. She cited this as her first experience as a historian. Baseball became a lifetime passion.

Her second experience of paternalism came from her going to Washington, D.C., in 1967 as a White House fellow during the presidency of Lyndon B. Johnson. Johnson was interested in hiring her as his assistant, but she had just written an article in *The New Republic* titled "How to Dump Lyndon Johnson," while he had also discovered that she was active in the anti–Vietnam War movement; so the job in the Oval Office quickly melted away. Yet she was not sent home in disgrace. "I thought for sure he would kick me out of the program," she later recalled, "but instead he said, 'Oh, bring her down here for a year and if I can't win her over, no one can.'" She found herself assigned to the Department of Labor, and after Johnson had decided not to run for reelection he brought her back to the White House as a member of his staff.

Kearns was not to become Kearns Goodwin until her marriage in 1975 to Richard N. Goodwin, a speechwriter under both Kennedy and Johnson. After LBJ left office, she taught government at Harvard for a decade, during which time she helped Johnson draft his memoirs. Their conversations together launched her writing career, her first book, *Lyndon Johnson and the American Dream* (1977), becoming a *New York Times* bestseller.

She was also juggling three young sons and writing her second book, *No Ordinary Time: Franklin and Eleanor Roosevelt: The Home Front*

Barbara Tuchman and Doris Kearns Goodwin. Goodwin was encouraged by the example of Barbara Tuchman, not only because she wrote political and military history but because of her belief that "you have to tell a story from beginning to middle to end and pretend you don't know how it turns out, because you can only know what people at the time know."

in *World War II;* in 1995 it won the Pulitzer Prize for History. Further bestselling biographies followed, among them *The Fitzgeralds and the Kennedys: An American Saga* (1987), *Team of Rivals: The Political Genius of Abraham Lincoln* (2005—the basis for Steven Spielberg's Academy Award–winning film *Lincoln*), and *Leadership In Turbulent Times* (2018), drawing upon the four presidents she had studied closely—Lincoln, the two Roosevelts, and Johnson—to show how they recognized leadership qualities within themselves and were perceived as leaders by others.

Her focus was narrow, but it ran deep. And although her writing could be slapdash at times ("Restlessly descending to the street, [Lincoln] passed the state capitol building. . . ."), her judgment was sure and usually expressed in a readable and authoritative style. Her best book, *Team of Rivals,* was, she wrote, a story of Lincoln's political genius revealed through his extraordinary array of personal qualities that enabled him to form friendships with men who had previously opposed him; to repair injured feelings that, left untended, might have escalated into permanent hostility; to assume responsibility for the failures of subordinates; to share credit with ease; and to learn from mistakes. He possessed an acute understanding of the sources of power inherent in the presidency, an unparalleled ability to keep his governing coalition intact, a tough-minded appreciation of the need to protect his presidential prerogatives, and a masterful sense of timing.

This is almost Johnsonian—Samuel Johnson, this time. Lincoln's wife, Mary, Goodwin tells us, "possessed what was then considered an unladylike interest in politics." Many might still consider writing about the hurly-burly of Washington infighting a man's game, but Goodwin has proved an exception to such traditions.

In 1997, she published a memoir about her early years and the deaths of her parents, her mother when Doris was fifteen, her father when in her twenties. She explained: "I think it made me want to tell stories of people who were dead to somehow bring them back to life. . . . It is stories that keep people alive. That's where my ambition for history came from." As one reader reflected on the book's reception: "She could write a washing machine manual and I'd probably still gobble it up. She has a gift of conjuring up the past so vividly, so real, so believable, that you feel as if you're right there with her as it's happening."

There was one embarrassing blip. In January 2002, Goodwin was shown to have used several earlier works without attribution in writing *The Fitzgeralds and the Kennedys*. In explanation, she said she had mixed up quotations from the books mentioned with her own notes, and that she had never intended to pass off the writing of other people as hers. The principal author whose work was plagiarized (there were at least two others), Lynne McTaggart, accepted a sum of money in settlement soon after the book was published not to reveal the use of her work; new endnotes were added to the paperback edition, as well as a paragraph to its preface declaring McTaggart's study the "definitive" biography of Kathleen Kennedy. But Goodwin never admitted she had plagiarized anything. *Slate* magazine reported that Goodwin's book on the Roosevelts had also used multiple passages from other peoples' books. Goodwin said she had taken notes from various sources and forgot that certain quite long passages were not her own.

The fallout was considerable. Goodwin was removed from the Pulitzer Prize board and resigned her position as a regular guest on the news program *PBS NewsHour*. She ended up hiring a political consultant, Robert Shrum, to solicit media support; a group of prominent historians, headed by Arthur Schlesinger, Jr., signed a letter to *The New York Times* proclaiming that Goodwin "did not, she does not, cheat or plagiarize. In fact, her character and work symbolize the highest standards of moral integrity." Within a decade, her reputation had largely recovered: Goodwin remains a popular figure, and the overall quality of her writing has seen her through.

* * *

WHEN GOODWIN FIRST APPEARED as a TV pundit, no woman historian on either side of the Atlantic had fronted a history series. Now there is a long list—Bettany Hughes (whose debut series, broadcast in 2000, was the first to be hosted by a woman), Francesca Beauman, Wendy Beckett, Helen Castor, Tessa Dunlop, Amanda Foreman, Ruth Goodman, Suzannah Lipscomb, Lucy Moore, Cassie Newland, Janina Ramirez, Hallie Rubenhold, Amanda Vickery, Sandrine Voillet, Anna Whitelock, Kate Williams, Lucy Worsley, and Clare Wright. Such a roll call may already be out of date, so rich is the seam of talent.

Most famous among them, and most controversial, is the Cambridge classicist Mary Beard (b. 1955).* The only child of an architect father and a feminist headmistress, she went to a private girls' school where she was taught poetry by Frank McEachran, the man who inspired the character of Hector in Alan Bennett's play *The History Boys*. "McEachran was terribly influential," she related. "He taught us reams of English poetry, which we had to learn for financial reward. So it was

---

* Only by interests and influence is Beard related to Mary Ritter Beard (1876–1958), the American who played an important role in the women's suffrage movement and pioneered the field of women's history, writing several books, including *On Understanding Women* (1931), *America Through Women's Eyes* (1933), and *Woman as Force in History* (1946). She also collaborated with her husband, Charles, on several seminal works, most notably *The Rise of American Civilization* (1927), a radical text that combined political, economic, and cultural histories with an overview of America's national character. Churchill read their books, somewhat indiscriminately, to inform himself about U.S. history.

50p for *Prufrock* and some enormous sum (which he never had to pay out) for *The Wreck of the Deutschland*." She also studied French, German, Latin, and Greek. "Bright kids at that age do like doing things they're good at," she has explained. "I was an intellectual control freak, and Greek was quite good for that—you could be good at it. You could *master* it." A born nonconformist with a formidable brain, she acquired a taste for taking risks and also a tendency to fall for older, slightly dangerous men. There were plenty of "scrapes," she admits. "Playing around with other people's husbands when you were seventeen was bad news. Yes, I was a very naughty girl."

She was awarded a place at Newnham College, Cambridge, then a single-sex college, but before going up joined a summer dig where archeologists were uncovering a Roman settlement not far from her home in the market town of Shrewsbury, nine miles east of the Welsh border. "The guy who was running the excavation was really keen to say, 'Look, everybody wants to see the glories of Roman civilization. But how was the city used when the Romans were gone?'" She too took to asking how ordinary people experienced life. Before university, she had not been especially caught up in feminist issues, but at Cambridge the inequities of gender were unavoidable. "Most of the people who taught us in the faculty were blokes," she says. "There were only twelve per cent women among the students, and you thought, 'Actually, there is an issue here.' You go into a dining hall of a men's college and everybody's portrait was a bloke." She attended women's groups and campaigned to open up the university to women.

Beard left Cambridge in 1979, for King's College, London, completing her PhD in 1982, "The State Religion in the Late Roman Empire: A Study Based on the Works of Cicero." Two years later, she returned to Newnham as a fellow (a telling term), one of only three women within the classics faculty out of a total of twenty-six; before long, she was the only female left. The following year, she published her first book, *Rome in the Late Republic*, co-authored with Michael Crawford (b. 1939), a professor of ancient history at Christ's College. Two years later she married Robin Sinclair Cormack, a specialist in Byzantine art sixteen years her senior, with two children from a previous marriage. Together they had two more, Zoe and Raphael, now respectively a historian of South Sudan and a scholar of Egyptian literature. They bought an apartment in London, with Robin teaching at the Courtauld Institute of Art, Mary lecturing at King's.

In 1980 she had published a pioneering paper on the Vestal Virgins (the celibate priestesses who looked after the sacred flame in the Roman Forum), using techniques borrowed from anthropology to ask original questions about their role. By decade's end she had completed three further studies on aspects of Roman life, but they were co-authored with fellow scholars and did little to advance her reputation. The family was financially strapped, so she had to work hard, teaching a trio of subjects: archaeology, ancient history, and Latin literature. She had little time for writing books, as so many of her colleagues were doing, and the word went around, as she passed her fortieth birthday, that she was squandering her talent. Beard was aware of the gossip. "You would have said: 'Pity about Mary, she looked so promising.'"

When she did turn to writing under her name alone it was not a heavyweight academic tome but *The Good Working Mother's Guide* (1989), advice on interviewing a nanny, on maternity benefits, on managing housework—"pay for as much help around the house as you can afford"—and the best way to hand-express milk. "It seemed a fun

Mary Beard around 1978.

thing to do," she explains, although it also showcased her pedagogical bent. She started writing pieces for the *London Review of Books* and *The Times Literary Supplement,* so trenchant and well informed that the editor of the *TLS* asked her to take over its classics coverage. "Book reviews are perfect," Beard says, "for a woman with two kids under three who has no time for the big projects, but who wants to keep the intellectual wheels rolling." It also had the bonus of being a fast turnaround: "You could see the fucking thing in print the next week. Not like writing an article for the *Journal of Roman Studies.*" Further, it suited her tendency to argue from unusual angles and make thought-provoking connections between the ancient and the contemporary.

In one piece she wrote in August 2000 for the *London Review of Books,* in part a highly critical review of Randy Thornhill and Craig Palmer's book *A Natural History of Rape,* she acknowledged that she too had been assaulted. While traveling through Italy as a graduate student, she had met an architect taking the night train from Milan to Naples. He offered to upgrade her ticket to a bed in his two-berth sleeping car. It was not until she was alone with him in their compartment that she realized that her Good Samaritan was not being altruistic; within minutes he had removed her clothes and had sex with her. "To all intents and purposes," she wrote, "this was rape," but she did not describe it as such at the time, telling friends it was a "seduction" and herself that it had been *her* seduction of *him.* Her experience was "relatively harmless"—she never gave consent to what happened, but he did not use force. "I'm absolutely fine. I still take Italian trains." But deciding how to talk about such an experience was complicated: "Rape is always a (contested) story, as well as an event. . . . It is in the telling of rape-as-story, in its different versions, its shifting nuances, that cultures have always debated most intensely some of the most unfathomable conflicts of sexual relations and sexual identity." This was not a subject that any previous female historian had broached.

In another *LRB* article, where a group of contributors each gave their views on the terrorist attacks of September 11, 2001, Beard argued that one should try to understand the terrorists' ideology. It served little purpose to decry the strikes as cowardly, she wrote, or just to write off the perpetrators as malevolent terrorists: "There are very few people on the planet who devise carnage for the sheer hell of it. They do what they do for a cause." The assaults should be comprehended not merely as an atrocity but as a response to Western foreign policy—"however tactfully you dress it up, the United States had it coming."

At once, the magazine was inundated with emails from incensed readers who felt Beard was suggesting that everyone caught in the Twin Towers had deserved to die. Her immediate reaction was to hold her tongue; then she realized that she had written something that, even if it had been misunderstood, had greatly upset people—she had used the wrong language. She wrote back to each of her critics, trying to spell out clearly what she had meant. To this day, she remains in contact with some of those correspondents.

In 2005, egged on by a new editor at the *TLS* (Peter Stothard succeeding Ferdinand Mount), she agreed to try a weekly blog and so began the highly informal *A Don's Life*, which was soon getting forty thousand hits a day. These accounts of her studies, travels, and domestic life have included the future of #MeToo, her views on book blurbs, David Beckham's tattoos, and one-night stands.

She was surprised by the column's success and taken aback again after, to expand her audience, she took to using Twitter. "When I started, I thought, oh help. This is a cheap, tawdry, debased form of journalism, blah blah. I have come to find that it's a hugely interesting form of journalism in the most surprising way. I can use the layers of the web to take people to places that would never appear in a broadsheet." Broadcasting was a different matter—as early as 1994 she had appeared on radio and television, popular programs like BBC's *Question Time, A Point of View, Weird Thoughts, Open Media;* she has also made TV documentaries including a three-part series, *Meet the Romans with Mary Beard,* a BBC series that aired in 2012 and had her hypothesizing about the day-to-day workings of an impressively preserved communal toilet in the port city of Ostia, a commune of Rome.

After *The Good Working Mother's Guide,* her next sole-authored book had been a biography (2000) of a previous female don at Newnham, the early twentieth-century classicist Jane Harrison. Since then she has sped up, writing about the Parthenon (2002), *Pompeii: The Life of a Roman Town* (2008); *Laughter in Ancient Rome: On Joking, Tickling, and Cracking Up* (2014); *The Roman Triumph* (2007; about the ritual military victory parade); *SPQR: A History of Ancient Rome* (2015); *Women and Power: A Manifesto* (2017); and *Civilisations: How Do We Look* (2018), based on a reboot of the Kenneth Clark television series *Civilisation.*

She started to contribute to *The New York Review of Books, The Guardian,* the *Daily Mail.*

Her writing has kept its deep learning but is ever accessible, even conversational. *SPQR* was a bestseller, and one can see why. A typical passage:

> In one of the Roman world's most quoted jibes, the satirist Juvenal, writing at the end of the first century CE, turned his scorn on the "mob of Remus," which—he claimed—wanted just two things: "bread and circuses" (*panem et circenses*). As the currency of that phrase even now shows, it was a brilliant dismissal of the limited horizons of the urban rabble, presented here as if they were descendants of the murdered twin: they cared for nothing but the chariot racing and food handouts with which the emperors had bribed and effectively depoliticized them.

In 2004, Beard became a full professor of classics at Cambridge, then was elected a visiting professor at Berkeley for 2008–9, where she delivered a series of lectures on "Roman Laughter." She is perpetually in demand. In 2014, she gave a lecture at the British Museum titled "Oh Do Shut Up Dear!" in which, with "amiable indignation" (according to Rebecca Mead, who interviewed her for a profile in *The New Yorker*), she explored the many ways that men have silenced outspoken females since the days of ancient Rome. A columnist for *The Spectator,* Beard noted, currently ran an annual competition to name the "most stupid woman" to appear on the current-affairs show *Question Time.* Beard's take: "There have always been men who are frightened of smart women." After an appearance on that same program, in August 2013, following an exchange with an audience member about the effect of immigration, she received death threats; she recovered enough to say she would have felt worse had someone "been through one of my articles and pointed out that all the footnotes were wrong." They very rarely are—although she's been known to correct her own judgments.

Her breakthrough book, *Pompeii,* came out in 2008 and debunked myth after myth. She contended that the ancient city was not "frozen in time" but rather for centuries had been "disrupted and disturbed, excavated and pillaged," even bombed during the Second World War.

Looked at critically, one could ferret out vivid clues to the lives of ordinary people, from hapless lovers to flophouse guests pissing in their beds. Janice Hadlow, then controller of BBC Two, read the book on holiday and urged Beard to turn it into a TV program, telling her: "You've complained there are loads of wrinkly, crusty old men presenting documentaries and no women over 35, and now I'm offering you the chance—you're not going to tell me you're not going to do it, are you?" It was the beginning of a new career. Hitherto, her readers had numbered in the thousands; the documentary was watched by 3.4 million. Typically, Beard introduced her audience to a boastful graffito scrawled on the wall of a Pompeii bar that claims: "I fucked the landlady." History was about real life.

As a young don, Beard was the kind of female colleague that the men she worked with liked—"a woman who answered back. Feisty, a bit gobby," as she puts it. This, she says, was partly a useful front to fit into a coterie of male colleagues. "I got the best out of them by being pushy. It was a strategy, but also a strategy that felt like me." On one occasion, having written in an article that the classical philologist Eduard Fraenkel was a notorious groper whose youthful prey included both Iris Murdoch and Mary Warnock, she added that mixed with her sisterly outrage was "a certain wistful nostalgia" for the "erotic dimension of classical pedagogy." When all hell broke loose (again), among her ripostes was: "Isn't intellectual life about having an argument?"

Beard has altered how women writers of history are seen and also the way history itself is being written. Among the questions now being asked are: What happens to our vision of the past when gender becomes a central concern for historical analysis? In what way is "women's history" distinct from the broader study of history? Are the techniques of such an approach any different from those of all historians? Are we even asking the right questions? A recent *Guardian* profile described her as "a celebrity, a national treasure, and easily the world's most famous classicist." She has become, it said,

> a standard-bearer for middle-aged women, and beloved by the young—indeed, by anyone who wants to be seen in terms of their ideas, not their looks; anyone who think it's cool to be smart; and by those who relentlessly ask questions and never reject a contrary opinion out of hand. . . . One reason Beard is

so widely beloved is that her interventions in public life—whether one agrees with her or not—offer an alternative mode of discourse, one that people are hungry for: a position that is serious and tough in argument, but friendly and humorous in manner, and one that, at a time when disagreements quickly become shrill or abusive, insists on dialogue. . . . When she engages with those who challenge her, on Twitter or on *Question Time*—when she argues her case with humour and knowledge, when she listens to the views of the other side, when she takes no shit—she is making the whole world her undergraduate.

Meanwhile, she remains "the classical world's most irreverent star turn." Readers of *Prospect,* the British general-interest monthly magazine, recently voted her the world's seventh most significant thinker—behind the Indian economist Amartya Sen and Pope Francis but above Peter Higgs, the Nobel Prize–winning physicist. In person, Beard's need for reassurance and regular limelight can make her difficult company at times, but her intelligence ensures that her words dance on the page. Like Dorothy Dietrich, with whom this chapter opened, she catches bullets between her teeth. When Beard was first abused by Twitter trolls, the winner of a Poetry Society national youth slam, Megan Beech, put out a YouTube ode that shows why so many young people admire her. Its opening lines crackle with life:

> *When I grow up I want to be Mary Beard,*
> *A classy classic classicist*
> *intellectually revered.*
> *Wickedly wonderful and wise*
> *full to the brim with life,*
> *whilst explaining the way in which Caligula died*
> *   on BBC prime time.*

* * *

IN OCTOBER 1928, VIRGINIA WOOLF was staying at Beard's Cambridge college to deliver a series of lectures. The talks were an account of women authors up to that date, although what they had written was mainly fiction. The lectures were later published as *A Room of One's*

Own, the title a reference to her demand, "Give her [a woman writer] a room of her own and five hundred a year [modern equivalent: $32,000], let her speak her mind and leave out half that she now puts in, and she will write a better book one of these days." In one of the lectures, Woolf imagines a sister for William Shakespeare, one Judith, a woman with talent equal to her brother's but who could not, because of society then, achieve the same success. Judith's life abounds in tragedy—first forced by her family into an early marriage, she escapes to London in the hope of becoming an actress but is spurned by every theater she approaches. She becomes pregnant and in a fit of despair kills herself. Later in the essay, Woolf brings back Judith's ghost to tell any young women in the audience that they have the power to assume the voice Judith never had.

If a real-life Judith Shakespeare had turned to writing history any time up to sixty years ago, she might not have had such a miserable end (particularly if born into the same class as a Wedgwood, a Tuchman, a Woodham-Smith, a Longford), but she would have struggled to have been published or taken seriously. In those five decades, however, we have witnessed a near-total recasting in the way women are written about and how women can impart their views on the past, given the confidence and opportunity. It has truly been a revolution, over little more than half a century, as important as any other since Herodotus.

CHAPTER 19

WHO TELLS OUR STORY?

From George W. Williams
to Ibram X. Kendi

It is the responsibility of the Negro writer
to excavate the real history of this country . . .
to tell us what really happened.

JAMES BALDWIN, 1963

History is a weapon with which we fight.

MANNING MARABLE, 2006

Early on in *Invisible Man*, Ralph Ellison's classic 1952 novel about African American displacement, a Black doctor who has recently returned from the trenches of the First World War has the ear of the book's young protagonist. "I'm a student of history, sir," the man tells him. "The world moves in a circle like a roulette wheel. In the beginning, black is on top, in the middle epochs, white holds the odds, but soon Ethiopia shall stretch forth her noble wings! Then place your money on the black!" This is a tenable view of world history, but the trouble is that the doctor is mad, quite mad. In Ellison's writing, anger and pained irony are always close bedfellows.

The telling of the full history of the African diaspora, and particularly of Africans in the United States, is a vexed subject, made the more so because for centuries white scholars have ignored and disparaged Black historians. However, even before Southern authors began spinning their version of what life was like in the Confederacy, there was a desire by Black writers to wrest back control of their story and by so doing give a fuller account of America as a whole, one that accurately reflected the nation's founding sin, stripped of antebellum myths, and accorded full due to the enslaved Black people who over many generations had helped build the country.

What are the uses to which the writing of history is put? And, for any Black writer, what should be the balance between the drive of ideology and the narrative of history? It took some time before such questions became paramount. Throughout the eighteenth century, the status of Africans, whether in England or the Americas, was seldom anything other than as slaves, and very few could even write.

Although slave narratives and history-laced poems appeared as early as the 1740s (some six thousand former slaves from North America and the Caribbean wrote accounts of their lives, of which about 150 found their way into print), the first of these historians published in the late nineteenth century. Two notable women authors were Elizabeth Keckley (1818–1907), who published *Behind the Scenes; or, Thirty Years as a Slave and Four Years in the White House* (she worked for Mary Todd Lincoln), and Josephine Brown (1839–74), the youngest child of abolitionist William Wells Brown, who wrote a life of her father, *Biography of an American Bondman*. Not long after them came the first major historian of Black America.

In 1882, George Washington Williams (1848–91) published his *History of the Negro Race in America from 1619 to 1880,* prompting W.E.B. Du Bois, writing twenty years later, to describe him as "the greatest historian of the race."

The only child of two former Pennsylvania slaves, Williams was a Civil War veteran, minister, politician, lawyer, and journalist. He grew up with little education except "learning about Jesus," as he put it. During the Civil War, once the government allowed Black men to enlist, the fourteen-year-old Williams joined the Union army and went on to serve in the Indian Wars before a gunshot wound to the chest forced his discharge. In 1870, he enrolled in a theological college in Massachusetts and four years later won an undergraduate place at Harvard. After graduation, he became a pastor in Roxbury, Massachusetts, and over the next five years grew impatient at the slow pace of social reform. "The time has come when the Negro must do something," he wrote. He retired from church work and started a newspaper but, financially straitened, had to give up the venture after only eight issues.

He next turned to politics, and having moved with his wife and child to Ohio, he won election to its state legislature, all the while immersing himself in researching his people's story. His two-volume his-

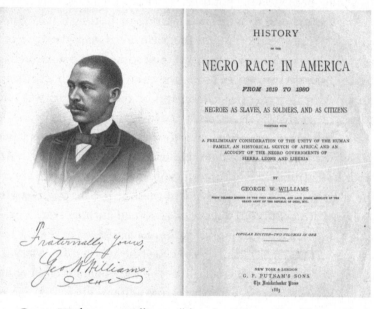

George Washington Williams, "the greatest historian of the race"

tory, published in 1882, is the first overall account of that trajectory, and in its thousand pages it strikes only one obvious unrealistic note—at the end of its opening paragraph:

> During the last half-century, many writers on ethnology, anthropology, and slavery have strenuously striven to place the Negro outside the human family; and the disciples of these teachers have endeavored to justify their views by the most dehumanizing treatment of the Negro. But, fortunately for the Negro and for humanity at large, we live now in an epoch when race malice and sectional hate are disappearing beneath the horizon of a brighter and better future.

Would that it were so. The book is still an important primary source and is remarkably percipient. For instance, in 1947, when Howard

University professor John Hope Franklin (1915–2009) described in *From Slavery to Freedom* the splendor of West African kingdoms before the advent of the Atlantic slave trade, he was only repeating what Williams had written. By the 1960s, most historians agreed that slavery was the root cause of the Civil War and that the failure of Reconstruction was the result of actions by both Southern white supremacists and overaggressive Northerners; both insights had been Williams's. The same applied when historians started to highlight the role of women and Black people in the abolitionist movement: Williams had recorded them all. In *Black Reconstruction in America,* Du Bois celebrated how people of African descent had created their own system of education in the South during Reconstruction: Williams had made the point fifty years earlier. This remarkable writer blazed a trail that decades later other historians were only just beginning to follow.

Williams's life and work take us to the heart of the issue that has dogged Black historians: that the story of their race has been so misrepresented, when covered at all, that they have had to concentrate their efforts in setting that story straight—all the more necessary when that history concerns the subjugation of an entire race. And inasmuch as Black people have experienced appalling injustices, their historians are urged not only to see themselves as combatants in the fight against racism but also to bear witness, to be a conduit to a new version of the historical record. It's about history as a living organism and a never-ending, day-to-day fight for control.

* * *

JUST HOW TO BEAR witness was the question—as shown by the writings and career of Booker T. Washington (1856–1915; the "T" stood for "Taliaferro," an impressive middle name that means "ironcutter" in Italian). Born, as he put it, "in a typical log cabin," he was a former slave who founded the Tuskegee Institute, a college for Blacks in Alabama that began as a one-room shanty filled with thirty students and by the time of his death had 1,500 undergraduates and a hundred well-equipped buildings. (Ralph Ellison, an alumnus, wrote about his days there in *Shadow and Act.*) Following Frederick Douglass's death in February 1895, Washington, who deeply admired Douglass and wrote a reverential biography of him, proclaimed him the foremost spokesman for Blacks in America; he published five books in one of which he re-

ferred to Blacks as "a new people . . . a new Negro for a new century";
his second volume of autobiography, *Up from Slavery* (1901), reached a
wide audience and inspired the charismatic Marcus Garvey to become,
in Garvey's words, a "race leader."

The years 1895 to 1915, writes the Black historian Wilson Jeremiah
Moses, "may be identified as the age of Booker T. Washington." For
most of his career, Washington supported civil rights and empower-
ment causes across the South, yet in a speech in Georgia on September
18, 1895, that became known as "the Atlanta Compromise," he said
that he accepted segregation and disenfranchisement, as if Black people
required some finishing touches of the evolutionary process: "It is at
the bottom of life we must begin, and not at the top."

The address won national acclaim (it was said to have moved Blacks
in his audience to tears), and other Black leaders seemed to agree that
to advance the status of African Americans it was necessary to complete a "civilizing" process. A young Du Bois even sent Washington a
telegram: "Let me heartily congratulate you upon your phenomenal
success in Atlanta—it was a word fitly spoken."

Such approbation did not last for long. Eight years later, Du Bois
published *The Souls of Black Folk,* a collection of fourteen essays in which
he wrote, "The time is come when one may speak in all sincerity and
utter courtesy of the mistakes and shortcomings of Mr. Washington's
career," and unequivocally criticized Washington for being "a compromiser," arguing that Blacks should be fighting for equal rights and higher
opportunities, not meekly accepting the status quo. He also wrote for
the first time about what he called his "double consciousness"—of
being "an American, a Negro; two souls, two thoughts, two unrecon-
ciled strivings; two warring ideals in one dark body."

While Washington believed that Black people should concentrate
on helping themselves through education and success at business rather
than opposing segregation, Du Bois was advocating a frontal assault on
injustice, quoting Douglass's line, "Power concedes nothing without a
demand. It never did and it never will." At the American Negro Academy in 1897, he openly rejected Douglass's appeal for Black Americans
to integrate into white society. Black Americans formed "almost a nation within a nation"—larger than Canada or the Netherlands, almost
as large as Turkey—and were "the hope of the world."

Yet ten years later, despite their differences, Du Bois and Washington managed to come together to co-author an influential work, *The Negro in the South*. The volume contained four essays, two by each man, Washington discussing Black economic development both during and after slavery, Du Bois writing in more general terms about economic and religious Black Southern history. The book was an unlikely compact, but Washington was a calculating, ambitious figure who knew when an alliance was in his interests, while Du Bois, in the words of W. J. Moses, "frequently championed apparently opposing positions, sometimes within the scope of a single paragraph." It would take several years before Teddy Roosevelt would warn a colleague to be "careful of that man Du Bois," as he was "dangerous," presumably for his left-wing views; or for Du Bois to evolve a philosophy that embraced a Marxist view of history, liberalism, Afrocentrism, and a lack of reverence for American democratic traditions.*

* * *

FOR HIS BOOK ON RECONSTRUCTION, Du Bois traveled through the Jim Crow South, searching for every primary source he could get his hands on, although only seeing half of what was available (this is also why there are so many lengthy excerpts in the book—he was helping to create a public archive of the period). Inevitably for his time his many works were short of archival resources, but soon a cluster of eloquent Black historians emerged keen to dig further. Three in particular, one from the First World War period and the years that immediately followed it, the other two his natural successors, set themselves to correct the gaps and distortions in the official records. The first is Carter G. Woodson (1875–1950), known as the "Father of Black History." Overlapping with him are Joel Augustus Rogers (c. 1881–1966), who has been described as "perhaps the most beloved and influential of the vin-

---

* In the light of his later beliefs, as a young man Du Bois chose some odd bedfellows. He considered Otto von Bismarck a model for Black leadership, and while he acknowledged that "no lie ever stood between him and success," Du Bois overlooked the Iron Chancellor's hosting the Berlin conference of 1884–1885, where European colonizers partitioned Africa on the pretext that they were bringing civilization to the continent. "I did not understand at all, nor had my history courses led me to understand" that colonialism had exploited Africa, Du Bois wrote. He had trained by studying German philosophy and admitted, "I was blithely European and imperialistic in outlook." Du Bois's intellectual mentor was William Lloyd Garrison (1805–79), who held that slavery—or more broadly, racial discrimination—had "imbruted" Black people, making their cultures, psychologies, and behaviors inferior to those of whites. In time Du Bois evolved away from that belief, just as he did from colonialist sympathies. But it did take time.

dicationists," and John Henrik Clarke (1915–98), who pioneered the creation of Pan-African studies in the late 1960s and went from scholarship to activism.

Woodson was one of nine children of formerly enslaved parents, a poor Virginia family who in the years following the end of Reconstruction needed him to bring in money, even as a young teenager, first as a sharecropper, then as a coalminer, before he left to get himself educated. He began his formal education at the age of twenty, passing through a series of schools before he qualified as a teacher, and in 1903 took up the position of school supervisor in the Philippines, working for the U.S. War Department. He next set off traveling through Africa, Asia, and Europe before winning a place at the University of Chicago. He completed his master's degree there, then received a doctorate at Harvard, only the second African American to do so, Du Bois being the first. The photographs we have of him show a broad-browed, handsome young man with an intense gaze and a determined, set mouth, both accurate clues to his ambitions. He was acutely aware that Black people were not included in history books and determined to write a record that would ensure "the world [would] see the Negro as a participant rather than as a lay figure."

In 1915, Woodson helped establish the Association for the Study of Negro Life and History, based in Chicago. The following year he founded *The Journal of Negro History* (now *The Journal of African American History*), which quickly demonstrated that Black history was a legitimate subject for scholars. The publication of the magazine coincided with the arrival in the United States of Marcus Garvey (1887–1940); Woodson would become a regular columnist for Garvey's *Negro World*. It was a time of rising Black self-awareness expressed in movements such as the Harlem Renaissance and Garvey's Universal Negro Improvement Association. Woodson became an active campaigner, rechanneling ideas that had been a staple of the rhetoric of nineteenth-century Black leaders— Negro improvement, race progress, African civilization. The last was a particular concern: *Civilization* had become a fashionable word during the late eighteenth century (despite Samuel Johnson refusing to include it in his dictionary, for all Boswell's urgings), and Woodson now invoked it.

The months between May and September 1919 saw the so-called "Red Summer," so named because the federal government, fearing

Communist influence on the Black Civil Rights movement, sat back as white supremacists ran riot. It was a time of intense racial violence, mainly in the South, and hundreds of Black people lost their lives in riots in more than three dozen cities across the country. In the face of widespread disillusionment, Woodson redoubled his efforts, writing: "I have made every sacrifice for this movement. I have spent all my time doing this one thing and trying to do it efficiently."

He became affiliated with the Washington, D.C., branch of the NAACP (the National Association for the Advancement of Colored People) and was soon backing a proposal by Du Bois to boycott any business that failed to "treat races alike." In a letter dated March 18, 1915, in response to a letter from the NAACP chairman, who questioned so aggressive a strategy, Woodson wrote, "I am not afraid of being sued by white businessmen. In fact, I should welcome such a lawsuit. It would do the cause much good. Let us banish fear. We have been in this mental state for three centuries. I am a radical. I am ready to act." "White businessmen" gave him a wide berth.

In 1920 Woodson formed Associated Publishers, the first such Black company in the United States, which made possible books about Black people that other publishers turned down. Six years later, he introduced Negro History Week (now Black History Month), held every February, a date chosen in honor of two significant birthdays: Abraham Lincoln's on the 12th and Frederick Douglass's on the 14th. The more than five thousand documents that he donated to the Library of Congress—letters, diaries, articles, and court testimonies—became a vital resource. Not least, they attest to the fact that by the 1850s Black leaders were supporting schemes to settle Black Americans in such sites as Upper Canada, Haiti, Mexico, Liberia, and the Niger Valley.

Some contemporaries ostracized Woodson because he insisted that Black ethnic culture be defined as a separate category of history, but he was unswerving. Helped by a Carnegie grant in the early 1920s, he purchased a 3,380-square-foot terraced house in Washington, D.C., and turned it into a research center, with his own small living space on the top floor. Even in his seventies he would go into the streets, where he distributed posters, stopping off at local schools to talk about his work to anyone who would listen. The neighborhood children nicknamed him "Bookman." Dorothy Porter Wesley, herself an important figure in the construction of Black archives, stated that Woodson would teasingly decline her regular dinner invitations by saying, "No, you're trying to marry me off, but I am married to my work."

He wrote fifteen books, among them *The Negro in Our History* (1927), which has sold more than ninety thousand copies. "Has the culture of the Negro anything in common with that of the Western nations," he asked, "or is the Negro merely imitative, as is often asserted by many writers?" His answer, of course, was that the Black man had a proud history of his own. But that complex story was intimately connected with that of other races. "We should emphasize not Negro history, but the Negro in history," he declared.

As the philosopher and educator Alain Leroy Locke wrote of the book's fourth edition: "Designed to 'present to the average reader in succinct form a history of the United States as it has been influenced by the presence of the Negro in this country,' [it] has borne the brunt of the movement for the popularization of Negro history." But it was not really the book itself that made such an impact: that was the entire life and work of its author.

* * *

IMMEDIATELY AFTER THE END of the Second World War there were plenty of books about race in America, by both Blacks and whites. In 1945, Richard Wright (1908–60) published *Black Boy,* a half autobiographical, half fictional account of his hardscrabble Mississippi childhood that sold more than half a million copies. In 1947, the Black historian John Hope Franklin produced an authoritative study that traced African Americans from their beginnings in Africa. Allan Nevins and Kenneth Stampp published in this period as well. In the 1950s, C. Vann Woodward wrote a seminal essay called "The Burden of Southern History," and his *The Strange Career of Jim Crow* (published in 1955, then twice updated), which recounted race relations in the United States from before the Civil War through the protests of the 1960s, was judged by Martin Luther King, Jr., to be "the historical bible of the Civil Rights Movement."

These writers were never, as the Princeton historian Eddie Glaude puts it, "just one homogenous blob." Some were nationalist in their orientation, others asserted the value of Black experience, others still were liberal and reformist. How each writer plotted the facts was conditioned by ideological positioning. Williams was very different from

Franklin, Garvey from Du Bois. Each was doing a certain kind of political work, but it might be toward compiling an archive, using history to justify a particular point of view, or forming connections in the historical record that had been previously overlooked or underplayed.

One crucial way historians and scholars differed was in how race, nationality, culture, and identity were articulated. Blackness was in some ways linked to geography, although in contentious ways that led to heated debate about such terms as African American, African, Black, Negro, and Disparic. The Senegalese cultural theorist Léopold Sédar Senghor and Caribbean intellectuals such as Derek Walcott and Aimé Césaire championed what became known as the Négritude movement, focused on French colonial exploitation from the 1930s through the 1950s. In Césaire's words, Négritude was a direct repudiation of "civilizationism"—the belief in a single standard of human accomplishment—and "the simple recognition of the fact that one is Black, the acceptance of this fact and of our destiny as Blacks, of our history and culture."

The term *African American,* on the other hand, although traceable as

Two of the giants among Black historians: Carter G. Woodson (left), who founded Black History Month, and John Henrik Clarke, who helped found the Harlem Quarterly, the Black Academy of Arts and Letters, and the African-American Scholars Council.

far back as 1835 (the related term *Afro-American,* which enjoyed a brief popularity in the 1960s, has an 1831 citation in the *Oxford English Dictionary*), came to prominence as part of a 1980s movement led by the Baptist minister Jesse Jackson (b. 1941) to call Black people in the United States by a name that linked the two continents.

Jackson had an earlier writer to thank for extrapolating the history of such a connection: Joel Augustus Rogers, whose books on the African diaspora established vital connections between the life of Black people in the Americas and their African forebears. Self-educated and self-published, Rogers researched in six languages and sixty countries to write more than ten volumes on Black people in world history, paying for the printing himself because no mainstream publishing house would do so. One of eleven children of mixed-race parents, in 1906 he emigrated from his home in Jamaica to settle in New York City, where he became part of the Harlem Renaissance. His first book, *From "Superman" to Man,* published in 1917, attacked notions of African inferiority, dramatizing his argument in a dialogue between an educated Pullman car porter and a bigoted but tractable passenger, a senator from Oklahoma. In the course of the novel the Black porter persuades the senator of the nobility of the Black past.

Rogers continued to be the leading spokesman pointing out the lack of scientific support for the notion that any one race was superior to another. In popular volumes such as *100 Amazing Facts about the Negro, Sex and Race,* and *World's Great Men of Color,* he wrote about outstanding Black people and their achievements. Several famous figures, he told his readers, including Aesop, Cleopatra, and Hannibal, were not white, as generally assumed, but Black (he was "an accomplished ironist").

In *Nature Knows No Color-Line,* Rogers developed his argument a stage further, postulating that color prejudice evolved from the struggles between two physiologically different groups and grew to become a specious rationale for domination, subjugation, and warfare. Societies, he contended, created myths and biases to justify their own interests at the expense of other groups. It was ironic, given the supposed inferiority of Blacks, that the civilization of Egypt had lasted longer than any other known to man—about ten thousand years, reaching its height before European settlements arrived on the scene. What Rogers called "the bran of history," the disregarded, unexplored happenings in the world, showed that many ancient African civilizations had been the matrix of Western civilization. America owed its Black population respect as well as equality.[*]

* * *

ROGERS DIED IN 1966, on the eve of the Black Studies revolution. In his lifetime his books circulated mainly among his fellow Black people. I first learned of him through an article written in 2013 by John Henrik Clarke, the third in the trio of Black historians who did so much to explore the narrative of the Black diaspora. Unlike Rogers, though, Clarke was part of the educational mainstream, even if both men began life as outsiders.

Born plain John Henry Clark in 1915, he was the youngest son of an Alabama sharecropper and a washerwoman (nearly all the major Black historians before 2000 came from poor families), and when he was four his parents moved to Columbus, Georgia. "I grew up with a lot of lap time, a lot of slap time," he told an audience in 1995. He recalled how the woman who taught him in fifth grade, Eveline Taylor, one day stopped him from taking part in the normal playground ragging and led him into her classroom. There was something special in the way he would go off by himself to read, she told him. "Stop playing the fool," something he often did, he well knew, in an attempt to be accepted. "It's no disgrace to be right when everybody else thinks you're wrong. Better to march into hell than to follow a bunch of fools into heaven." As so often with stories of childhood, this may be an embroidered memory, but the point is he was seen as unusual.

His secondary education completed, he left home during the Great Migration, the time from 1910 to 1970 when African Americans moved from the Southern states to the North in search of work and a better life. "At eighteen you can pursue all kinds of fantasies," he would explain. He stopped briefly in Chicago before settling in New York, where within weeks he went to visit Arturo Alfonso Schomburg, the

---

[*] Like Williams and Woodson, Rogers was not writing in a void, of course. Of his early years, the great South African leader Nelson Mandela relates: "I did not yet know that the real history of our country was not to be found in standard British textbooks, which claimed South Africa began with the landing of Jan Van Riebeeck at the Cape of Good Hope in 1652. It was from Chief Joyi [Zwelibhangile Joyi, an authority on African tribes] that I began to discover that the history of the Bantu-speaking people began far to the north . . . and that slowly over the millennia we made our way down to the very tip of this great continent. However, I later discovered that Chief Joyi's account of African history, particularly after 1652, was not always so accurate. . . ." Nelson Mandela, *Long Walk to Freedom* (New York: Little, Brown, 1994), p. 21.

Puerto Rican historian who was to mentor two generations of Black scholars. "Son," Schomburg told him, "go study the history of your masters"—by which he meant the largely untold past of the African people. Clark started to read in earnest. He also changed his second name from his baptismal "Henry" to that of the radical Norwegian playwright Henrik Ibsen, whom he greatly admired, and added an "e" to his surname (he never explained why).

Between 1941 and 1945 he served in the U.S. Armed Forces ("I was one of the worst soldiers the Army ever had—but I was a wizard at administration"), before returning to New York, where he joined the Harlem History Club ("which taught me the political meaning of history") and the Harlem Writers Guild. He also attended various elite institutions, taking courses at Hunter College, the New School of Social Research, and both New York University and Columbia University, although he never graduated. At the same time he started out on the road to becoming a prominent figure in the Black Power movement, working odd jobs to support himself.

He was co-founder and editor of the *Harlem Quarterly* (1949–51), co-founder and first president of the African Heritage Studies Association, and a founding member of the Black Academy of Arts and Letters and the African-American Scholars' Council. In 1956 he began teaching at the New School for Social Research, while from 1964 to 1969 he served as the director of the Heritage Teaching Program in Harlem. In 1969 he was appointed professor of Black and Puerto Rican Studies at Hunter College, a department for which he served as founding chairman, and was also a visiting professor at Cornell—all this without a high school diploma, let alone a doctorate (a distinction he was finally awarded in 1993, at the age of seventy-eight).

His writing included six books, such as the influential *Marcus Garvey and the Vision of Africa* (1974) and *My Life in Search of Africa* (1999), as well as editing anthologies by African Americans and publishing his own short stories and poetry. In 1996, his story "The Boy Who Painted Christ Black" was filmed as part of the 1996 HBO production *America's Dream*. This still left him time to be the book review editor of the *Negro History Bulletin,* the associate editor of the magazine *Freedomways,* and a feature writer for the *Pittsburgh Courier,* one of the country's leading Black newspapers.

Producing work of high quality in so many fields made him a significant figure, but what chiefly marked him out was his attack on the accepted ways of teaching Black history, methods he branded as Eurocentric and biased. "When they take away your human being-ness, they take away your nation-ness," he believed. "Once you're taken from the geography of your origin and forced to live in a state designed by others, you're still the slave to the man who's astute enough to control the container called 'the state.'" (Say those sentences out loud and you'll get the rhythms of his speech.) In an essay he wrote toward the end of his life, Clarke wrote:

> Africa and its people are the most written about and the least understood of all of the world's people. This condition started in the fifteenth and the sixteenth centuries with the beginning of the slave trade system. The Europeans not only colonialized most of the world, they began to colonialize information about the world and its people. In order to do this, they had to forget, or pretend to forget, all they had previously known about the Africans. . . . The history of the modern world was made, in the main, by what was taken from African people.

At the heart of all he did was his pride in his people and his anger at their suppression. Here it helped that among his other gifts he was a formidable speaker. A freshman at California State University, attending a talk by Clarke in 1982, recalled years later: "I was right there. I could see some Paul Robeson in him, a touch of Du Bois, a bit of Malcolm X and a whole lot of my granddaddy. . . . He had my grandfather's Southern sophistication, his preacher's cadence and his complete mastery of 'the word.' Clarke's word was, however, not Scripture but history."

For him, being a historian went hand in hand with his political beliefs. He admired Marcus Garvey (unlike Du Bois, who dubbed Garvey "either a lunatic or a traitor") and was a close friend and adviser to Malcolm X, about whom he wrote an early biography. Clarke was a convinced socialist and an unremitting critic of capitalism. The much-vaunted March on Washington for Jobs and Freedom of August 28, 1963, during which Martin Luther King, Jr., delivered his "I Have a Dream" speech, he regarded as "Showbiz Liberation, a great rehearsal for a show we didn't put on the road." His primary message was that the purpose of history-teaching—"I know that being a good classroom teacher was my best work"—was to make African Americans develop a pride in themselves.

On September 21, 1997, aged eighty-two, he married Sybil Williams, his assistant for over a decade. The following year he died of a heart attack, but not before she had helped move his books and documents to the Atlanta University Center and to the Schomburg Center for Research in Black Culture, now part of the New York Public Library. By then African American history was safely recorded and available in more than 110 research centers around the country.

***

IN 1948 PRESIDENT TRUMAN banned discrimination in the military; in 1954, as a result of the Supreme Court decision in *Brown v. Board of Education,* which ruled that separate schools for whites and Blacks were inherently unequal, states were required to offer equal opportunities. Then in 1957 President Eisenhower signed legislation that empowered the Justice Department to intervene and file injunctions where Black people had been denied the right to vote in federal elections.

Protest continued to push legislators to act. On May 4, 1961, thirteen Freedom Riders—seven Black and six white, including the future civil rights icon John Lewis—embarked on a tour of the American South to protest segregated bus terminals. During the days that followed, their bus was attacked, a mob set on them with chains and pipes and baseball bats, and a bomb was thrown at them. In Jackson, Mississippi, they were arrested for trespassing in a "whites-only" facility and sentenced to jail. The U.S. Supreme Court reversed the convictions; that autumn a law was passed prohibiting segregation in interstate transit terminals.

The 1963 March on Washington was an international news story that highlighted demands by American Blacks, and on July 2, 1964, President Johnson, completing legislation initiated by President Kennedy, signed a wide-ranging act that guaranteed equal employment for all, limited the use of voter literacy tests, and instructed federal authorities to ensure public facilities were integrated. The following year, Johnson took the 1964 Act several steps further, heralding a "Second Reconstruction." Walter Mosley, in his 1994 Easy Rawlins novel *Black Betty,* set during the early days of JFK's presidency, captures the moment by having Rawlins say: "I tried to think of better things. About our new young Irish president and Martin Luther King; about how the world was changing and a black man in America had the chance to be a man for the first time in hundreds of years." So it must have seemed.

When on April 4, 1968, King was assassinated, the riots that followed forced the Johnson administration to pass a further act, this time one that forbade housing discrimination based on race, sex, national origin, or religion. One more step forward. And yet this would be the last legislation enacted during the civil rights era.

* * *

BETWEEN 1500 AND 1900, some four million Africans were shipped off to island plantations in the Indian Ocean, eight million were transported to various Mediterranean countries, and about eleven million reached the New World. Throughout the years in which Black Americans have been fighting to take control of their history, writers in those other countries, "people of color," not necessarily Black, have contributed their own testaments, particularly on the history of colonialism, and several have profoundly affected the debate within the United States about Black history.

One of the most memorable of these took on race at a tangent and was all the more effective for that: Cyril Lionel Robert (ever reduced to "C.L.R.") James's *Beyond a Boundary,* published in 1963. James (1901–89) was a Black Trinidadian, born eight miles from the island's capital, Port of Spain; the tint of his skin was important, given the various social strata in the islands were based on fine color differences. His twin loves were literature (*Vanity Fair* holding an extraordinary, possibly unique, place; from the age of *eight,* he says, he re-read Thackeray's satire of British society on average every three months) and cricket, the game that soon became his main preoccupation, in that he either played it—at a level just short of international class—or commented on it in print or on the radio his whole life.

He wrote almost thirty books, a play about the Haitian revolutionary Toussaint L'Ouverture (staged in London's West End and starring Paul Robeson), while his 1936 novel *Minty Alley* was the first work of fiction by a Black Caribbean man to be published in Britain. He was also a well-known historian and political activist, a founding father of

Black Nationalism whose first publication was the provocative *The Case for West Indian Self-Government*. He toured the United States giving lectures before being deported in 1953. "Thackeray, not Marx, bears the heaviest responsibility for me," he wrote, but he was characterized as an "anti-Stalinist dialectician" who would go on to write *World Revolution* (1937), a history of the Communist International that was praised by both Trotsky and George Orwell, and the equally acclaimed radical history *The Black Jacobins: Toussaint L'Ouverture and the San Domingo Revolution* (1938). He became something of a hero in the Caribbeans, Britain, and the United States.

It was *Beyond a Boundary*, however, his book on cricket, that made his reputation and has even been lauded as the best book on sports ever written, not least because it went, as his pun intended, beyond sport's boundaries. What sets it apart is that James saw cricket through the prism of race, examining "the social passions which were using cricket as a medium of expression" at a time when the Caribbean islands were producing some of the world's most famous cricketers, all of them men of color, within a sport that played a vital role in both British and Caribbean lives and that in each country was ruled by whites determined to keep the social order from changing.

Interspersing stories from his own life with portraits of leading West Indian players, James wrote about figures such as Sir Learie Constantine, a cavalier batsman and fearsome fast bowler who became Britain's first Black peer and was also a leading figure in the passing of the country's 1965 Race Relations Act. Another portrait is of Sir Frank Worrell, a stylish right-hand batsman and deceptive left-arm seam bowler who in 1960 became the first Black captain of the West Indies team for an entire series—largely due to the vigorous campaign that James conducted on his behalf. At the end of his career Worrell became a noted educator, was appointed a Jamaican senator, and in 1964 was knighted by the Queen. James uses him to make several political points.

Thus one of the most influential histories of race relations was a book about sports, but one, as James proudly described it, "within a frame of reference that stretches east and west into the receding distance, back into the past and forward into the future." Some of James's sentences still resonate today: "Social explosions take place when most of the fundamental causes of dissatisfaction have been removed and only a few remain," he wrote, a particularly timely comment now; and:

C.L.R. James (left), who wrote about sport as a way of writing about Black experience as a whole; and Manning Marable, who set up African American studies departments at five different American universities.

"To establish his own identity, Caliban, after three centuries, must himself pioneer into regions Caesar never knew." The curse of being such an "exotic savage" became for James not only a badge of honor but a revolutionary project.

★ ★ ★

TWO YEARS BEFORE *Beyond a Boundary* appeared, a psychiatrist and political theorist from the French island of Martinique (a former slave colony based on sugar production) published one of the most important books about colonization to appear in the twentieth century; not surprisingly, the French government banned it. I didn't read Frantz Fanon's *The Wretched of the Earth* (*Les damnés de la terre*) until 1969, my last term in college, by which time Fanon (1925–61) was recognized as a major influence on the civil rights, anticolonial, and Black consciousness movements. He dubbed the United States "a nation of lynchers."

An earlier, more autobiographical book, *Black Skin, White Masks* (1952, the same year Ralph Ellison's *Invisible Man* was published), had examined the Black psyche in a white world as well as racial differences in history; his current biographer Adam Shatz called the book "his great study of the 'lived experience of the black man.'" *The Wretched of the Earth,* by contrast, focuses on colonial injustices and has relatively little history in it, but it is still in this, his best-known work, dictated in haste as he lay dying from leukemia, that Fanon makes his case for a reframing of how we write about the past:

> It is a question of the Third World starting a new history of Man, a history that will have regard to the sometimes prodigious theses which Europe has put forward. . . . So, comrades, let us not pay tribute to Europe by creating states, institutions and societies which draw their inspiration from her.

The Wretched of the Earth, with its faith in the "revolutionary spontaneity" of the peasantry, would become the theoretical foundation for many revolutions and inspire leaders such as Steve Biko in South Africa, Che Guevara in Cuba, and Malcolm X in the United States. For the last sixty years, no writer on Black history has been able to ignore it.

This raises two important points. While the accounts by Black historians share a robustness and breadth, they deploy their writing in a variety of ways. For instance, the history of race relations in America is not the same as Black history. Second, minorities get a raw deal in most accounts, specifically those by white male writers from Europe or North America, but Black people are only one such minority; there are several others. The debate in the United States between African Americans and white Americans tends to crowd out disadvantaged groups such as Latinos, Asians, and Native Americans. It may not feel like it, but Black campaigners have been exceptional in the attention they have received.

* * *

WHATEVER THE RELATIVE BALANCE between racial minority stories, from the 1960s on American historians were illuminating almost every area of Black experience—from before the slave trade began, in Africa then in America as indentured servants or prisoners of war or being forced into slavery from pirate raids; then their lives up to the American Revolution; and on, through the antebellum period, the Haitian Revolution (the only slave revolt that has led to an independent country), the Civil War, and post-Reconstruction.

There would be books on the 1921 Tulsa Race Riot (when white racists burned an entire Black neighborhood to its foundations), Black religious life, their businesses, military experience, prison history, and encounters with the law. Studies would flow on African American labor relations—in 1925 Charles H. Wesley (1891–1987), in a famous Harvard dissertation, soundly rejected the then-dominant assumption that Black people were lazy and incapable of skilled work. There were writings on education, housing, health, and culture—thus the Harlem Renaissance, Blacks in the arts, the birth of Black Power. Myriad volumes examined the First Great Migration, from 1910 to 1940, then the Second (roughly from 1941 to 1970), Jim Crow, disenfranchisement, and the battle for civil rights. Black history became mainstream.

Black women historians continued to make their voices heard. Anna Julia Cooper (1858–1964) memorably defended her race's womanhood in *A Voice from the South,* published in 1892. "The colored woman of to-day," she wrote (significantly, *before* Booker T. Washington's Atlanta address; she herself had been born into bondage), "occupies, one may say, a unique position in this country. . . . She is confronted by both a woman question and a race problem, and is as yet an unknown or an unacknowledged factor in both." Cooper has another of her aphorisms printed in every U.S. passport: "The cause of freedom is not the cause of a race or a sect, a party or a class—it is the cause of humankind, the very birthright of humanity." Another female scholar, Helen G. Edmonds (1911–95), who wrote *Black Faces in High Places: Negroes in Government* (1971), became the first Black woman to second the nomination of a U.S. presidential candidate when she backed Dwight Eisenhower at the 1956 Republican Convention.[*]

Several Black historians have won significant prizes. What follows is inevitably something of a roll call, but it is an impressive one: David Levering Lewis (b. 1936) was awarded a Pulitzer for each part of his two-volume biography of Du Bois, in 1994 and 2001. Frank M. Snowden, Jr. (1911–2007), a professor of classics at Howard University, was acclaimed for his studies of Black people in the ancient world. Arnold Rampersad (b. 1941), for his two-volume life of Langston Hughes,

---

[*] Because of Lincoln, most Blacks were Republicans until Franklin Roosevelt's presidency: by 1936 only 28 percent of the Black vote was Republican. This change was underscored in 1960, when Kennedy made his famous phone call to Coretta Scott King while her husband, Martin, was in prison. The biggest source of resistance to civil rights legislation came from what was known as "the solid South," reliably Democrat-voting until Lyndon Johnson's agenda lost those states. For his "I Have a Dream" speech, King appropriated sections of the 1952 Republican Convention speech by the Reverend Archibald Carey, another Black pastor.

the great poet at the heart of the Harlem Renaissance; Nell Irvin Painter (b. 1942), recently retired from Princeton University, notable for her works on Southern nineteenth-century history and, in *The History of White People,* her discussion of Black/white sensibilities; and Thadious M. Davis, of the University of Pennsylvania, author of *Southscapes: Geographies of Race, Region, and Literature* (2011), are just three others who reached the heights of their profession. In 2019, Jeffrey C. Stewart (b. 1950), a professor at the University of California, won a Pulitzer for his life of Alain Locke, the "Father of the Harlem Renaissance." Alex Haley (1921–92) not only collaborated with Malcolm X in the writing of his autobiography but also published *Roots: The Saga of an American Family,* which as a TV series was a sensation, reaching more than 130 million viewers in the United States. And preeminently there is Henry Louis Gates, Jr., who though he describes himself as primarily a literary critic has won a substantial following for books like *The African-American Century* (2000), *Life Upon These Shores* (2011), and *Stony the Road* (2019). Like a number of other historians, Black and white, he has gained celebrity status thanks to his ability to complement rigorous research with his skill at making highly popular TV documentaries.

Given this impressive roster, it is salutary to realize that at the time Eric Foner (a white New Yorker, b. 1943) went to high school not a single textbook mentioned a historian of color by name, and even at Columbia he never had a Black historian teach him. Black colleges were thriving by then, but instruction in African American history hardly existed. When in 1969 the subject was finally introduced to his university, Foner was asked to run the course, and later he chaired the committee that hired Columbia's first head of African American Studies—the Black scholar Manning Marable.

In the summer of 2008 I was asked to be the editor of Marable's long-anticipated biography of Malcolm X. He had already taken more than twelve years to conduct his research, and he needed an out-of-house editor to help him see the project through. Although we could hardly have been more different in background, race, or life experience, working with him over several drafts was a pleasure, and I treasured the friendship.

Then one day over lunch he announced some highly distressing news. Born in Ohio but of émigré West Indian stock, Manning had been diagnosed with sarcoidosis, generally known as sarcoid (literally, "flesh-like"), a little-studied disease caused by an overreaction of the body's immune system. It is ten times more common in Caribbeans of color and in African Americans than in white Americans, he explained, and is also prevalent among Scandinavians, although no one knows why. His lungs were affected, and he had been told that he needed a double lung transplant.

As we raced to finish his script, Manning struggled to contend with a nagging cough, shortness of breath, and the disciplines imposed by his oxygen machine. He also had to check into New York Presbyterian Hospital for the operation, only to be told on no less than five occasions, having been required to stay there overnight, that the required new lungs had turned out to be unusable—a record number of delays, according to the hospital's records, for any patient.

By the end of August 2009 a third draft was sent off to Viking, his publisher. Midway through the following year Manning was at last given the lungs he needed, and for a time it looked as if everything had turned out well—he even told his in-house editor at Viking that he would be back working on the book in three weeks or so. However, complications set in, and on April 1, 2011, Manning died from pneumonia, a month short of his sixty-first birthday. Three days later, Viking published *Malcolm X: A Life of Reinvention,* which immediately went onto the bestseller lists (it sold over seventy thousand copies in its American hardback edition), was shortlisted for the Pulitzer Prize for biography, and won the Pulitzer history award outright.

Before this, Manning had authored some two dozen other books, all on the African American experience, while in 1993 he had founded the Institute for Research in African-American Studies at Columbia University. He also served as the founding director of similar programs at no fewer than four other universities (Colgate, Purdue, Ohio State, and Colorado), all of which combined his work as a historian and his commitment to political activism. In 1998 he established the Black Radical Congress, a grassroots network of African Americans devoted to bringing about racial equality and social and economic justice.

For a historian, what is the proper balance of one's work as a scholar and political activism when the subject is race, a topic so dependent on history for a proper understanding? For Manning, the two marched hand in hand. In 2006 he wrote, "Historical knowledge drawn from the reservoir of past collective experience is absolutely vital to the task of imagining new racial formations for African Americans and for all Americans." In an essay published in 2009, he described the conditions of Blacks in America as a "paradox of integration" in which, although there was a visible middle and political class, "millions of African-descendant Americans remain stigmatized and excluded from employment, quality health care, education and home ownership relative to whites . . . combined with continuing incidents of police brutality and mass incarceration of young blacks." He concluded: "A new Black Panthers may soon be on the political horizon." But just what kind of uprising might be imminent neither he nor his fellow Black historians could predict.

★ ★ ★

THERE ARE CERTAIN ICONIC periods of time—the forty-three seconds it took for the "Little Boy" atomic bomb to fall from the *Enola Gay* onto Hiroshima on August 6, 1945, the three hours on July 4, 1776, that it took fifty-six delegates to sign the American Declaration of Independence; or the eight minutes and forty-six seconds it took Minneapolis police officer Derek Chauvin to crush the life out of George Floyd on May 25, 2020. No matter that Little Boy actually took 44.4 seconds to fall and missed its aiming point; or that the Declaration was drafted and passed on July 2, revised on July 4, and not fully signed until August 2; or that prosecutors later revised the time Chauvin had his knee on Floyd's neck to be exactly nine minutes and twenty-nine seconds.

News of memorable moments spreads quickly. "Die-ins" have taken eight minutes forty-six seconds as their staged length, and marches and gatherings worldwide have used that timing to mark moments of silence, vigils, even traffic slowdowns. George Floyd's memorial on June 4, 2020, ended with mourners standing for 8:46 in commemoration. "Eight minutes 46 seconds" even has its own Wikipedia entry. His agonizing, slow-motion killing marked a hinge moment in history and was part of a confluence of events: the COVID-19 epidemic, which particularly struck down Blacks and Latinos; an economic crisis that underlined the gap between rich and poor; a sharp increase in social tensions (a video of a white woman frantically reporting to the police that she was being harassed by a Black man, a totally innocent birdwatcher in New York's Central Park who had asked her to put her dog on a leash, went viral; the incident occurred on the same day as the death of Floyd); open racism in the White House; and a series of incidents of police brutality against African Americans, all playing out in real time, in public on social media, combined to bring about a perfect storm. Black Lives Matter was borne aloft.

The original movement had begun seven years earlier, in July 2013, when three women activists created a hashtag of the three words, seventeen months after George Zimmerman, a twenty-eight-year-old white self-appointed vigilante who had shot an African American teenager, Trayvon Martin, was acquitted of all charges. Following the deaths of two more African Americans, the teenager Michael Brown in Ferguson, Missouri, and a forty-three-year-old father of six children, Eric Garner ("I can't breathe"), in New York City, Black Lives Matter became associated with street parades and the number of protests grew, so that by January 2017 at least 1,889 Movement for Black Lives (M4BL) marches and demonstrations had taken place across the world.

When George Floyd was killed, his death was seen "not just as a murder* but as a metaphor" of Black repression, and an estimated fifteen million to twenty-six million people participated in protests throughout the United States (with the percentage of white protesters nearly three times the percentage of Black ones), making the movement, which now includes more than sixty organizations, one of the largest in America's history. One's eye tends to glide over numbers, but these figures are extraordinary, suggesting a new era in the world's awareness of injustices toward Black people.

Such a moment makes special demands on those who interpret the past, because one of BLM's basic beliefs is that the history of African Americans has to be largely recast, as it is still a racist account. On July 17, 2020, the Society for Historians of the Early American Republic (SHEAR) hosted a discussion via Zoom on "Andrew Jackson in the Age of Trump." It focused on a paper by Daniel Feller, a sixty-nine-year-old professor at the University of Tennessee at Knoxville. The other panelists (all of them white) lambasted Feller for his interpretation of the historical record, for his criticisms of female scholars ("incompetent" was just one of the words he used), and for his references to Jackson's reputation for slaughtering "redcoats and redskins," which they saw as an unacceptable slur.

---

* In April 2021 Derek Chauvin, the former Minneapolis police officer, was found guilty of all three charges brought against him: second-degree unintentional murder, third-degree murder, and second-degree manslaughter. At the time of writing, no appeal has been lodged.

Following the broadcast, the society's president formally apologized for the panel's lack of diversity and for Feller's use of objectionable language, but further condemnations followed. In an article on the front page of the arts section of *The New York Times,* the fracas was seen as representing "a long-overdue racial reckoning within the white-dominated historical profession," with implications "of how history gets written, and by whom." Seth Rockman, a historian at Brown University who had recently co-authored a diversity report for the forty-five-year-old body, viewed the dispute not just as an interpretive disagreement of America's seventh president and his legacy but also as "a broader struggle within a tight-knit scholarly community over how to produce an inclusive American history capable of rising to the challenges of 2020." Another historian, Elizabeth Pryor from Smith College, added that the whole idea of writing history was "to generate new scholarship, to understand what we study—and where we are as a country—better."

That challenge had been taken up even before the explosion of feeling that followed George Floyd's death. The previous August *The New York Times Magazine* had launched the 1619 Project, an initiative in partnership with the Smithsonian Institution geared to the four-hundredth anniversary of the arrival of the first enslaved Africans in the Virginia colony in 1619 (thus, in its view, the "nation's birth year"). "It is finally time to tell our story truthfully," the magazine declared on its cover page. The project, it went on, was intended "to reframe our country's history . . . placing the consequences of slavery and the contributions of black Americans at the very center of the story we tell ourselves about who we are."

Originally the idea was to produce a one-off issue of the magazine, but it quickly evolved into a more ambitious venture, including live events, a special section in the paper, a high school curriculum, a book, and a multi-episode podcast. "1619" was spray-painted on a toppled statue of George Washington. The opening essay in the magazine was by the woman who conceived the project, Nikole Sheri Hannah-Jones, a forty-three-year-old investigative journalist known for her coverage of civil rights. "America wasn't a democracy until Black Americans made it one," she wrote.

The United States is a nation founded on both an ideal and a lie. Our Declaration of Independence, signed on July 4, 1776, proclaims that "all men are created equal" and "endowed by their Creator with certain unalienable rights." But the white men who drafted those words did not believe them to be true for the hundreds of thousands of black people in their midst. "Life, Liberty and the pursuit of Happiness" did not apply to fully one-fifth of the country.

People lined up in the streets of New York to purchase copies. But the articles immediately sparked criticism. The Princeton historian Sean Wilentz, an expert on the Revolutionary era, circulated a letter objecting to the project, and to Hannah-Jones's contribution in particular, as activism in the guise of writing history. His draft acquired four other signatories—James M. McPherson, Gordon Wood, Victoria Bynum, and James Oakes, all leading scholars of the period, and all white. The letter* duly appeared in *The New York Times* that December, voicing "strong reservations," making several factual corrections, and accusing the project of putting ideology before historical understanding. It particularly challenged the notion that the American War of Independence had been fought primarily because the colonists were determined to safeguard slavery.

Jake Silverstein, the magazine's editor, wrote an extensive rebuttal in which he defended the accuracy of the reporting and declined to issue any corrections: "Out of slavery—and the anti-Black racism it required—grew nearly everything that has truly made America exceptional," he wrote. But in March 2020 the version of the article online was changed; it now reads that safeguarding slavery was the prime motive for fighting the British only "for some of the colonists," and the references to 1619 as the country's "true founding" or "moment [America] began" disappeared from the digital display copy without any reason being given.

In an opinion piece in *The New York Times* published more than a year later, as arguments about the original feature persisted, the paper's conservative columnist Bret Stephens took his colleagues to task:

---

* According to a well-informed article in *The Atlantic,* the refusal of other historians to become signatories, despite their misgivings about some claims made by the magazine, was evidence of a divide over whether the letter focused on correcting inaccuracies or on discrediting the project more broadly. See Adam Serwer, "The Fight Over the 1619 Project Is Not About the Facts," *The Atlantic,* December 23, 2019.

These were not minor points. The deleted assertions went to the core of the project's most controversial goal, "to reframe American history by considering what it would mean to regard 1619 as our nation's birth year."

That same month Leslie M. Harris, a respected historian at Northwestern University who had been one of the issue's fact-checkers, wrote that several of its authors had ignored her corrections. "I listened in stunned silence," Harris wrote in the first line of her essay, "as Nikole Hannah-Jones . . . repeated an idea that I had vigorously argued against with her fact-checker: that the patriots fought the American Revolution in large part to preserve slavery in North America." According to Harris, slavery in the colonies faced no immediate threat from Great Britain, so colonists wouldn't have needed to rebel to protect it. Yet she added that, in her view, what had appeared in the magazine was still a much-needed corrective to prevailing narratives. "I was concerned that critics would use the overstated claim to discredit the entire undertaking," she wrote. "So far, that's exactly what has happened." She saw the newspaper as asking for a second telling of a nation's past—perhaps the only example in all history—the first version written by white historians, the second predominantly by Black ones.*

As Adam Serwer observed in *The Atlantic,* "The 1619 Project, and Hannah-Jones's introductory essay in particular, offer a darker vision of the nation, in which Americans have made less progress than they think, and in which black people continue to struggle indefinitely for rights they may never fully realize." Much of American history, in Serwer's view, has been written by scholars who offer ideological claims in place of rigorous analysis. "But which claims are ideological and which ones are objective is not always easy to discern."

---

* Following Stephens's article in *The New York Times,* some 1,400 letters were sent to the paper about the issues raised. One reader commented: "By the time Gordon Wood and Sean Wilentz were publishing their first, highly acclaimed books on pre-Civil War America, in the early 1970s and mid-1980s, respectively, academic historians had begun, finally, to acknowledge African American history and slavery as a critical theme in American history. But Wood and Wilentz paid little attention to such matters in their first works on early America." But Wilentz has also stated, since circulating his letter, "Each of us . . . think that the idea of the 1619 Project is fantastic." Another reader made the reasonable point: "We must see the 1619 Project in the context of decades of such incomplete and misleading 'history' lessons. Some degree of rhetorical excess may be necessary to correct the narrative."

It seems plain in hindsight that some of those who worked on the magazine feature were careless in their research and insufficiently open about admitting their mistakes. They cost their project a great deal in terms of credibility and support. (Perhaps inevitably, by September 2020 Donald Trump was declaring that he would cut off federal funding to any public school using the 1619 Project in its curriculum. He even established a much-derided "1776 Commission" to help "restore patriotic education to our schools.") At the same time, it was still an extraordinary piece of journalism, one that opened the eyes of many thousands of their readers to the history of slavery in America, a country that, while proclaiming itself the land of liberty, justice, and equality for all, has spent much of its history ensuring that large portions of its population are unfree and unequal and treated unjustly.

The feature won both a National Magazine award and a George Polk Award; the article that drew the most attention and the most criticism was Hannah-Jones's. She herself felt a measure of satisfaction: "I know when I talk to people, they have said that they feel like they are understanding the architecture of their country in a way that they had not." In May 2020, she received a Pulitzer Prize. Then, on June 28, she again had the cover story in *The New York Times Magazine,* a ten-page article headlined "What Is Owed," which set out the case for the United States paying reparations to its Black citizens for "four hundred years of racialized plundering." The essay ranged widely and made a powerful statement; this time no letters of correction followed. The issue was published just a month after George Floyd's death.

Whatever one's view, the magazine's two articles and the book they spawned, *The 1619 Project: A New Origin Story* (2021), appeared at a time when the United States in particular wanted to learn what Black historians could tell them about race. In recent years several publishing imprints have been established in the United States and abroad to foster and promote Black American writing. Foremost among them is One World, an imprint of Penguin Random House, whose publisher and editor-in-chief is Chris Jackson. The advice he gave to the first raft of writers he took on was not to let themselves be boxed in: "I just told them to bring me their biggest ideas," he says, "and not to think about what would make a great Black book or whatever. The lens that we have is a way in which we can claim the entire world."

Nikole Hannah-Jones:
"Nobody wants to get over slavery
more than Black folks."

Elizabeth Hinton:
"Are we going to take this
moment for a real reckoning?"

In this, the future of interpreting the past will be in the hands of writers such as Isabel Wilkerson, the first African American woman to win a Pulitzer Prize for journalism. It took her fifteen years to complete her highly praised study *The Warmth of Other Suns* (2010), the complex story of African American migration, but little over half that time to write her next, *Caste: The Origins of Our Discontents,* which Dwight Garner, reviewing the book in *The New York Times,* lauded as "the keynote nonfiction book of the American century thus far." Driving her on, Wilkerson told Ken Burns, was her realization that "the fundamental facts about millions of people are just not known by so many others. . . . How do you fit all Americans into this concept of 'us'?"

The range of subjects covered by current Black historians is impressive. To name just three: Martha S. Jones, of Johns Hopkins University, started out as an activist lawyer before she turned to studying history and in 2007 published *All Bound Up Together,* about women's rights in African American culture, then in 2018 *Birthright Citizens,* a history of birthright citizenship as it has affected Blacks, and *Vanguard* (2020), which studies how Black women have fought for equality over the decades. Allyson Hobbs, who occupies a similar position at Stanford, published her first book in 2014, an examination of racial passing—largely based on a cousin who although classified as African American was accepted ("passed") as a white woman—but for the last five years has been extending her reach in *The New Yorker,* one week writing on Muhammad Ali, the next on the Scottish song "Auld Lang Syne" ("long, long ago" in English). Two of her current projects are *To Tell the Terrible,* a history of sexual violence toward Black women, and *Far from Sanctuary,* which examines the history of the automobile through the eyes of Black motorists. And in 2017 Kelly Lytle Hernández, a history professor at the University of California, published *City of Inmates,* an ambitious cultural study of the dysfunctional Los Angeles prison system from 1771 to 1965; the book has won four major prizes.

For several years now, the bestseller lists have been uncommonly filled with works about race in America or about the "African diaspora." *White Fragility, Between the World and Me, How to Be an Antiracist, So You Want to Talk About Race, The Color of Law,* and *Begin Again: James Baldwin's America and Its Urgent Lessons for Our Own* are just six such. Then there is the Black academic Ibram Xolani Kendi, who in June 2020 had three books simultaneously among the top twenty in the country. He was born Ibram Henry Rogers; when he married, in 2013, he adopted the surname Kendi (meaning "loved one" among the Meru people of Kenya), while he dropped his middle name, Henry, after learning about Prince Henry, the fifteenth-century Portuguese explorer who sponsored the first slave-trading voyages to West Africa. In its place, he chose Xolani, Zulu for "peace."

Both Kendi's parents, New Yorkers who in 1997 moved to northern Virginia, were influenced by the Black Power movement and by liberal theology but over the years became members of the bourgeoisie. Kendi attended Stonewall Jackson High School (named after the Confederate general), where he won a competition with an essay deriding poor Blacks who had not "made it." The memory still haunts Kendi, who confesses he was in thrall to "racist ideas disguised as middle-class striving."

His breakthrough as a writer came with *Stamped from the Beginning: The Definitive History of Racist Ideas in America,* a well-written, near six-hundred-page account telling the story of race through the lives of five major American figures: Cotton Mather, Thomas Jefferson, William Lloyd Garrison, W.E.B. Du Bois, and Angela Davis. In 2016 it won the National Book Award for Nonfiction (I gulped it down in one sitting). His next book, *How to Be an Antiracist,* also a No. 1 bestseller, is more a

Ibram X. Kendi, who had three books on the bestseller lists simultaneously.

Eddie Glaude, Jr., who used James Baldwin's writings as a way of commenting on today's racial divisions.

polemic than a work of history but still a thoughtful study (one U.S. publisher, Penguin Random House, has asked all its senior staff to read the book). It argues that to do nothing in the current climate is to be racist—for Kendi there is no middle ground. But as Henry David Thoreau wrote: "You must speak loud to the hard of hearing."

Given the slow evolution in self-confidence that Du Bois and others navigated, it was almost with throw-back honesty that Kendi admits in *Stamped from the Beginning:* "I held racist notions of Black inferiority before researching and writing this book. . . . I did not fully realize that the only thing wrong with Black people is that we think something is wrong with Black people." At first, he never intended to write the account he did but rather to rework his doctoral thesis, a history of the origins of Black studies in higher education in the late 1960s—only his first chapter came out ninety pages long, and he recognized that he had something quite different he wanted to say. Now, at thirty-nine, a professor at Boston University (he holds Elie Wiesel's old chair) and the founding director of its Center for Antiracist Research, Kendi has already begun his next book, tentatively titled *Bones of Inequity,* about the history of racist policies enshrined in the American legal code. Like *Stamped from the Beginning,* it will be a storytelling narrative, this time detailing the history of voter suppression, redlining (the practice of mortgage lenders of drawing red lines around portions of a map to indicate neighborhoods in which they will not make loans), gerrymandering, and other practices that still cast their shadow.

* * *

AMONG SEVERAL HISTORIANS, POLITICAL scientists, and intellectuals, there has been a backlash to this sudden emphasis on racism. Some people contend that Black historians are giving their agenda a priority that presents history askew—and that the focus suggests narcissism, as if everything in American history is about race, with Black people purely and only victims. They point out that more than 43 percent of African Americans are now middle-class or higher.

In turn, antiracists have passionately defended their territory. In the summer of 2020 the Democratic Socialists of America's New York City chapter invited the Black political scientist Adolph Reed, professor emeritus at the University of Pennsylvania, to speak before a Zoom audience. His argument, already expressed in various essays, was that the Left had become preoccupied with race and was not paying sufficient attention to class. To be successful, he contended, working-class and poor people of all races should band together. Race as a construct was overstated; it missed parts of the whole picture.

Hearing of the invitation, members of the chapter were outraged. How could such a figure be allowed to speak when he downplayed racism "in a time of plague and protest"? Providing such a platform, one group of objectors said, was "reactionary, class reductionist and at best tone deaf." Reed and his sponsors agreed to the lecture being canceled. Thus, as a *New York Times* report had it, "perhaps the nation's most powerful Socialist organization rejected a Black Marxist professor's talk because of his views on race."*

Despite this irony, and the literal and metaphorical "canceling" of Professor Reed's talk out of political animus, African Americans have

---

* Back in 1970, I applied to Shelter, the UK's help-the-homeless organization, to be manager of its London office. During the subsequent interview I asked naïvely why Shelter didn't combine with other charities—for the blind, the mentally impaired, the war-damaged—to create one single, truly powerful lobbying organization. The woman interviewing me was scathing. "Bugger the blind," she spat out, which I interpreted as her way of saying that only by putting your energies into the single cause that galvanizes you can you ever achieve anything. Other charities could look after themselves.

long been suspicious of both Communism and Socialism. In 1931 Du Bois voiced the feelings of many—that Black people should ideally align themselves with working-class interests, but only when the white working class showed up in support of the fight against racism:

> American Negroes do not propose to be the shock troops of the Communist Revolution, driven out in the front to death, cruelty and humiliation in order to win victories for white workers. They are picking no chestnuts from the fire, neither for capital nor white labor. . . . Negroes perceive clearly that the real interests of the white worker are identical with the interests of the black worker; but until the white worker recognizes this, the black worker is compelled in sheer self-defense to refuse to be made the sacrificial goat.

Maybe in 2021 "Socialist Revolution" would be a more appropriate stalking horse, but such sentiments still hold. Blue-collar whites are not noticeably antiracist and pro-equality. As for Du Bois, he died aged ninety-five in Accra, Ghana, on the eve of the March on Washington in 1963, having been invited to Africa two years before by the Ghanaian president Kwame Nkrumah to put together, in Du Bois's words, "an encyclopedia not on the vague subject of race, but on the peoples inhabiting the continent of Africa." He became a Ghanaian citizen (not least, an important symbolic underlining of African American and Caribbean interest in Africa), but left his final project, *Africana,* unfinished. It was completed by Henry Louis Gates and Anthony Appiah in 1999.

African American historians come under enormous pressure to testify about Black experience; it may be the locus of their concern, but that is also where the academic marketplace has been, at least from the 1970s on. Such a choice is sensible yet can be limiting. "Afrocentrism," as Cornel West, the widely published director of Afro-American Studies at Princeton and Harvard, has noted, "is a gallant yet misguided attempt to define an African identity in a white society perceived to be hostile. It is gallant because it puts black doings and sufferings, not white anxieties and fears, at the center of discussion. It is misguided because . . . it reinforces the narrow discussions about race."

The African American author Bob Herbert, from 1993 to 2011 an opinion columnist for *The New York Times,* says: "My entire life I've refused to become obsessed with race, to put myself in a box, always covering Black stories, civil rights—'urban issues,' to quote the term they use." He believes it is vital not to succumb to such restrictions. In 2014 he published *Losing Our Way,* a deeply researched survey of the working poor and middle class in America, and how they are being left behind in the twenty-first-century economy. As he explains, "You have these parameters you feel you have to stay within, and it constricts you. I know so many Black writers who will write only about Black subjects."

When one thinks of other groups who have suffered great prejudice—women, for instance—such a singleminded focus is less common. The injustices women have endured are searing enough: excluded from education, denied rewarding work, and obliged by law to surrender their possessions and finances to a husband's control. But still (except of course for women of color) they were never continually brutalized, or defined as three-fifths of a person, as the United States Constitution designated slaves in 1787. Women were seen as inferior to men, but never less than human, and as soon as they approached a position of relative educational equality they did not confine themselves to issues of gender. Cecil Woodham Smith, C. V. Wedgwood, and Barbara Tuchman all wrote bestsellers about war, Doris Kearns Goodwin about American presidents, Mary Beard about Ancient Rome, Amanda Foreman about British and American relations during the American Civil War. What strikes one immediately, though, is that all these writers, as well as such figures as Elizabeth Longford, Antonia Fraser, Linda Colley, Margaret MacMillan, and Jill Lepore, come from privileged families, which gave them the confidence and the opportunity to write on a broad canvas. Other women from a whole range of backgrounds would reframe their gender's history, and some have certainly been activists for the women's cause, but for almost two hundred years women have selected whatever subject they chose.

Maybe Black historians confine themselves by writing within the box, as Bob Herbert termed it, but no other such group—not Communist historians, who are more concerned to interpret the past to conform to their vision of the future; nor Latin American or Middle Eastern historians, both of whose pasts are highly contentious; nor religious proselytizers, wishing to promote the one true path to heaven; nor even Jewish historians narrating their race's persecution over the centuries, write from such pain and exploitation, such shared trauma. However, Black Studies programs differ from history departments; they are often more involved in acts of protest. Modern-day historians for the most part write and teach, however committed their beliefs, and demonstrate on paper. "Of course you can take to the streets," Eric Foner comments, "but you don't need a PhD to do that." He then adds: "Still, this is a fascinating moment to be an African American historian."

A telling example of how commitment within the academy currently shows itself is *Begin Again: James Baldwin's America and Its Urgent Lessons for Our Own* by Eddie Glaude, Jr. "My dad was a postman," he says. "He harnessed the anger he felt by joining the American Postal Workers Union, became a shop steward and then a national officer. But he continued to deliver the mail." In his own life, Glaude opted for academia because, he says, "I wanted to think in public with others. There's a political arc to my work, but I don't see a distinction between my university work and activism. Being a writer tests out my particular interpretation of pragmatism. That's my choice; but I don't cease being a person living in a particular community at the same time; it doesn't stop me being a citizen." In 2016 he told an interviewer:

> Colleges and universities are the places where you cultivate the habits of courage or you learn the habits of cowardliness. When the students [at Princeton, where he teaches] responded to the non-indictment of Darren Wilson [the police officer who shot Michael Brown in Ferguson in 2014] and marched on Prospect Avenue, later organized a die-in response to all of the deaths at the hands of police, and finally sat in at Nassau Hall and in President Eisgruber's office, I was so proud, smiling like the Cheshire Cat from ear to ear. They asserted a sense of possession of this institution, not that they should be thankful to be at Princeton, but to claim the University as their own, and I just love that. To force it to reach for its better angels.

Glaude's new book is an eloquent plea against Trump's America, in which he uses Baldwin's post-1963 texts to argue that the United States is not "fundamentally good and innocent" and that the country can either continue to pretend that it offers equal opportunities to all or can begin a third founding, "something as radical as the second." Glaude, a protégé of Cornel West's, notes "a tendency—particularly in white America—to make a little bit of progress and then congratulate ourselves, then use it as an excuse to not keep pushing." De Tocqueville called it the United States' "perpetual utterance of self-applause," Glaude "the ideology of Anglo-Saxonism," in which the identity of white Americans is inextricably bound up "with the story of America; if we tarnish that, people will ask, 'What is left?' " He goes on:

> Our history suggests that we're not going to do very well, that we're going to tinker around the edges, and another generation will have to go through this haunting ritual of Black grief and suffering again, that my child is going to have children, and he's going to have to explain to *his* children what is happening in the world. . . . We'll find ourselves on a racial hamster wheel, just running in a circle.

Glaude quotes from Baldwin's 1972 book *No Name in the Street,* written in "profound disillusionment" soon after Martin Luther King's assassination: "To be an Afro-American, or an American black, is to be in the situation, intolerably exaggerated, of all those who have ever found themselves part of a civilization which they could in no wise honorably defend—which they were compelled, indeed, endlessly to attack and condemn—and who yet spoke out of the most passionate love, hoping to make the kingdom new, to make it honorable and worthy of life." He cites Baldwin's revolutionary inversion—that the problem in America is not the Black man "but this belief on behalf of white people that they matter more."

Glaude's conclusion is grim: "At the core of this ugly period in our history is the idea that who 'we' are as a country is changing for the worse—that 'we' are becoming unrecognizable to ourselves." For that reason he is not "overly hopeful," although he admits to "a blues-soaked hope—not a kind of easy optimism, but one that recognizes the darkness, recognizes the failure, yet one that shows an undying faith in our capacity to be otherwise."

Aligned with this forecast is the notion that Black historians are being presented with an unusual opportunity, and are keen to seize it. Nearly a quarter century ago John Henrik Clarke foresaw such a moment. His words may sound rhetorical, but he meant them as pragmatic. "In the twenty-first century," he wrote, "there will be over one billion African people in the world. We are tomorrow's people. But, of course, we were yesterday's people, too. With an understanding of our new importance we can change the world, if first we change ourselves."

★ ★ ★

FOR A RISING GENERATION of scholars living through the current moment of political and racial polarization, the stakes are high. In August 2020 I spoke with Elizabeth Hinton, another young Black historian carving out a reputation. After completing her doctorate under Eric Foner at Columbia, she helped Manning Marable research Malcolm X's life before leaving for Harvard and later Yale; in 2016 she published *From the War on Poverty to the War on Crime,* a study that forced a national conversation. Her next book, due out in 2021, looks at the Black political rebellions of the late 1960s and early 1970s. At first she thought of becoming a criminal defense attorney, but personal issues (a cousin was in and out of prison for most of her childhood) and the questions that remained unanswered after completing her master's thesis together guided her into writing African American history. She sees Black Lives Matter as marking a potential epiphany for the United States: "In all the repression and racism there are new opportunities. Are we going to take this moment for a real reckoning?"

Hinton says she is currently taking risks in what she writes because "risks are OK now in a way they wouldn't have been before BLM became a buzzword." When she was researching her dissertation fifteen years ago, she had to make the case for why the history of the War on Crime (President Lyndon B. Johnson's 1965-minted phrase for a national focus on crime control) and the rise of the prison system mattered. Now terms like "white supremacy" and "systemic racism"—long invoked within Black Studies—have gone mainstream. The current reckoning with the history of racial inequality and injustice has pushed discussions so that racism is accepted as a fact of American life today, not a relic of the past. "As a result," she says, "I don't have to spend as much time 'proving' that racism exists in my writing."

Hinton has her own take on whether her country can right itself. "It's tough, right? Is American history a story of continual progress, in which eventually we'll realize the principles of our founding fathers, or is it fundamentally undemocratic? Can America ever be a postracial society?" She is hopeful, as in the present moment "more people recognize that Black history is important, are interested in what Black historians have to say—they want to hear from us."

* * *

AS A FINAL WORD, I will allow myself a measure of optimism, perhaps all the more open to question in that what follows was penned by a white man, a Jewish New Yorker (Aaron Sorkin) writing at the turn of the century. Back in April 2000, when the TV series *The West Wing* was regaling audiences with an implausibly sympathetic White House run by Democrats, one episode told of the attempts of a Black lawyer, Jeff Breckenridge, to become Assistant Attorney General for Civil Rights. His candidacy runs into trouble when he contributes an approving blurb to a book, *The Unpaid Debt,* that argues that the U.S. government should repay African Americans the sum (conservatively calculated) of 1.7 trillion dollars, a position that causes considerable embarrassment to the administration. Breckenridge is called in to see Josh Lyman, the deputy White House chief of staff, and their discussion becomes heated.

Breckenridge tells him: "You can't kidnap a civilization and sell them into slavery. No amount of money will make up for it, and all you have to do is look, two hundred years later, at race relations in this country." He asks Lyman if he has a dollar bill, and Lyman obligingly takes one out. "Look at the back," Breckenridge says.

> The seal, the pyramid, it's unfinished. With the eye of God looking over it and the words *Annuit Coeptis*. He, God, favors our undertaking. The seal is meant to be unfinished, because this country's meant to be unfinished. We're meant to keep doing better. We're meant to keep discussing and debating, and we're meant to read books by great historical scholars and then talk about them. Which is why I lent my name to a dust cover.

CHAPTER 20

BAD HISTORY

Truth-Telling vs. "Patriotism"

———

"I suppose history never lies, does it?"
said Mr. Dick, with a gleam of hope.
"Oh dear, no, sir!" I replied, most decisively.
I was ingenuous and young, and I thought so.

—CHARLES DICKENS, *DAVID COPPERFIELD,* 1850

My daughter noticed it first, while in Budapest for a sport-ing event. There, in a downtown park known as Szabadság tér (Liberty Square), stands a memorial to the 1944 Nazi occupation erected by the government in 2014, the country's "Holocaust Year." An example of modern Hungarian kitsch, the statue depicts a bronze imperial eagle (Germany) swooping down on the archangel Gabriel (patron and sym-bol of the Magyar nation) and glorifies the smaller country's courage in defending its Jewish population during the Second World War. Just a few feet away, locals have erected a countermonument: photos of Jewish loved ones, on commemorative piles of stones, mainly in mem-ory of those eliminated during the war. The action group Eleven Emlékmű (Living Memorial) cleans the items and has put out two white chairs next to their memorial to symbolize alternative forms of dialogue. They also organize public meetings in the park to protest against what they call the government's "falsification of history," pointing out that in 1944 nearly four hundred thousand Hungarian Jews were deported by the Nazis, mostly to Auschwitz, with the coop-eration of the Hungarian authorities, complicit in a genocide that wiped out 70 percent of the country's prewar Jewish population.

Switch countries and affiliations, and a different government made its attempts to refashion history. In the same year, 2014, on the fiftieth anniversary of the Vietnam War, the Pentagon decided to "provide the American public with historically accurate materials" with which to honor veterans. Sadly but perhaps not surprisingly, the extensive website largely described a courageous and honorable engagement that would be unrecognizable to many of those who fought in the war—scant mention of mistakes by generals, the deaths of many thousand noncombatants, or the years of violent protests and heartfelt arguments. Within months, the Pentagon did change some entries, so that the description of the My Lai atrocity, for example, was revised to read "American Division Kills Hundreds of Vietnamese Citizens at My Lai"—even if the word *massacre,* as the incident is more usually described, was still omitted. But the impulse was the same: to erase unwelcome facts from the record. That impulse is far from being controlled: as recently as February 2020 the Columbia University historian Matthew Connelly wrote how under President Trump "vital information is being deleted or destroyed, so that no one—neither the press and government watchdogs today, nor historians tomorrow—will have a chance to see it." Emily Creighton, a lawyer for the American Immigration Council, has described as "mind-boggling" the planned destruction of records detailing the U.S. government's treatment of undocumented immigrants. "It's almost as though we are, you know, erasing our nation's conscience."*

Most countries have supplied bits of "history" to order. From the recounting of the Spanish Armada (valiant small British ships against massive Spanish ones) to heroic tales of the Battle of Britain, British history is crowded with myths. The French thought themselves the decisive factor in the outcome of the First World War; many in the United States have only a hazy notion of who helped them win the

---

* When state-sanctioned history is knowingly falsified, people often find ways to correct the official record. In Poland under Communism, schools were made to teach that in the Second World War the Red Army rushed to Warsaw's defense, but every household taught its children that the army slowed its advance across the Vistula to let the Germans annihilate the (pro-Western) Home Army. When Solidarity gained sway, a special exhibition was mounted called "Blank Spots in Polish History," correcting the missing chapters. In contrast, the present Polish government has outlawed any mention of the country's participation in the Holocaust, intent on removing from cultural institutions any reference to this aspect of its citizens' behavior. It fired Warsaw historian Barbara Engelking from the advisory board of the Auschwitz Museum for asserting that two-thirds of the Jews in regions under German occupation were murdered directly or indirectly by Polish neighbors and police officers.

Second. For decades, Israelis were taught that most Arabs who fled their country in the wake of the 1948 war left voluntarily, the opposite of the truth. Kwame Nkrumah, president of Ghana from 1960 to 1966, commissioned huge murals to show European scientists being instructed by African predecessors, a fiction he deemed necessary for national self-respect. Rome's founding fathers are cousins to King Arthur, and when its emperors fell, their statues were pulled down and their likenesses on coins were erased. The Romans even had a phrase for such spoliations: *damnatio memoriae*, "the condemnation of memory."

The past could be eradicated or it could be invented. The world recognizes Charles XIV of Sweden, but there have been only eight kings called Charles, the first six having been fabricated sometime in the sixteenth century to bring dignity to the royal line and to fill an awkward gap—a transfusion of plausible names into the blood deficiency of history. Similarly, there are at least two nonexistent popes—there was never a John XX, and as for Pope Joan, she supposedly reigned, disguised as a man, between A.D. 855 and 858, her gender discovered only when she had a baby while in office (reportedly giving birth during a procession as she tried to mount a horse, in a lane originally known as "The Sacred Way" but smartly retitled "The Shunned Street"). It is said that a mob bound her feet to her mount's tail, then stoned her to death as she was hauled along the cobbles.* For centuries, her existence was widely believed, until the story was discredited in the seventeenth century by Parcelles, a French Huguenot; because of his religion, his account was placed on the Index, so could never be read by Catholics, many of whom continued to believe in their female pope.

History has ever been a harbor for dishonest writing, a home for forgers, the insane, or even "history-killers" who write so dully they neutralize their subjects. Direct witnesses can be entirely unreliable. The travelogue of the thirteenth-century explorer Marco Polo covering his years in China, which he dictated while in prison in Genoa to a romance writer who was his fellow inmate, is about two-thirds made up—but which two-thirds? Scholars are still debating. On July 14,

---

* The legend was certainly imaginative. It suggested that subsequent popes were subjected to an examination whereby, their having sat on a so-called *sedia stercoraria* or "dung chair" containing a second hole, a cardinal had to reach up and establish that the new pope had testicles, before announcing *"Duos habet et bene pendentes"* (He has two, and they dangle nicely). See Catherine Clément, *Opera, or The Undoing of Women* (University of Minnesota, 1999, p. 105).

1789, Louis XVI's game-book entry reads: *"Rien"*—this on the day of the storming of the Bastille. Dean Acheson, when writing his memoirs, which were published as *Present at the Creation,* reportedly called a friend to corroborate his memory of an important meeting. The friend said his description was accurate except for one detail: Acheson hadn't been present. Gerald Wellesley, the seventh Duke of Wellington, was an attaché in St. Petersburg in 1912, attending the imperial maneuvers, when amid great excitement he was brought over to an unimaginably old Frenchman who claimed that when a small child he saw Napoleon. "He was a very tall man, your honor, with a long yellow beard." Evidently to this sage any invading emperor should be gigantic and Viking-like, and wishful thinking did the rest. Auschwitz survivors of Joseph Mengele's vile experiments recall him as tall and blond and fluent in Hungarian. In fact, he did not speak that language and was relatively short and dark-haired. The director of the Yad Vashem Holocaust memorial in Israel has said that most of the oral histories collected there were unreliable, however honestly contributed.

Those instances can be ascribed to the quirks of human memory. Actual fakery, though, has a long history. Tacitus begins his *Annals:* "The histories of Tiberius and Caligula, of Claudius and Nero, were falsified, during their lifetime, out of dread—then, after their deaths, were composed under the influence of still festering hatreds." In England in the sixteenth century, it was common to include made-up stories about your ancestors in the hope of achieving greater social standing. Late in the seventeenth century, a hack writer, Gatien de Courtilz de Sandras, wrote the bogus *Memoirs of M. d'Artagnan* of the recently slain commander of the Musketeers. The book proved immensely popular and established the real d'Artagnan's name. Encouraged, de Sandras went on to fabricate the memoirs of another two dozen celebrities. After 1945, the British wallowed in a number of myths of how the country had all pulled together valiantly during the world war, preserving Britain's place as one of the Big Three powers—what the military historian Michael Howard has called "nursery history," as sent up by the 1960s satirical revue Beyond the Fringe in its sketch "Aftermyth of War."[*]

---

[*] In July 2012 the History News Network in the United States held a contest to determine "the least credible history book in print." After voting by readers, *The Jefferson Lies* by David Barton was judged the winner, narrowly edging *The People's History of the United States* by the left-wing historian Howard Zinn.

Hardly a single nation or country has not molded its history to advantage. The most famous history of Japan, the eighth-century *Nihon Shoki* (Chronicles of Japan), has so many fabrications that it has been described as "one of the greatest historical frauds ever perpetrated," yet still carries authority and has been used as a tool by various administrations during Japan's history. China, however, may hold a special place in the forging of the past. In 1926 the respected academic Gu Jiegang revealed that for millennia much of his country's history had been falsified, with a line of faux historians searching for genealogical, historical, and philosophical sanctions for their particular political programs. It was not only Confucius who had made up an ancient China "that had no basis in fact" to advance his theories of the future; for two thousand years before the birth of Christ running to the first quarter of the third century A.D., his countrymen invented what they thought China's past should be. "The more remote from a given event," wrote Professor Gu, "the more detailed . . . the information about that event." In his multivolume *An Exposition of Spurious Literature* (1929), he outlined how extensive this collective forgery was:

> The commonly accepted chronology for Chinese history covers a period of 5000 years (according to the apocryphal literature this period is extended to 2,276,000 years!). But if we eliminate the evidence drawn from spurious history, or the history that rests on spurious literature, this chronology must be contracted to something like 2000 years—in other words, to about half the traditional figure.

Gu's was by no means the first exposé to appear in China, but it was the most widely accepted, and he was asked by colleagues to write an authoritative survey of his country's past, to correct what he characterized as "the muddled account-book of Chinese history." Perhaps wisely, he declined, limiting his work just to the exposure of forgeries. This might seem a supreme example of falsifying the past, but in fairness one could have handed the professor the works of Geoffrey of Monmouth or Livy and he would have had a field day exposing their imaginings.

Omission is another way to get history wrong: H. G. Wells's bestselling book *The Outline of History* leaves out any mention of Romanticism or the Enlightenment (although it includes a chapter on flying dragons). Even experienced historians can be bamboozled. Heinrich Friedjung (1851–1920), a historian who had studied under Mommsen and von Ranke, around 1908 testified in the trial of certain Slav nationalists charged with cooperating with foreign governments. He appeared for the prosecution in good faith, but the authorities had faked much of the evidence, and he was taken apart by the defense counsel.*

This world of false facts leads to the vexed history of David Irving (b. 1938), often described as the most skillful preacher of Holocaust denial in the world today. To be clear: the key claims of such denial are that the Allies dreamed up the Holocaust as a way of demonizing Nazi Germany. Jews were eager participants, as they could prey upon people's sympathies to extort money from Germany to establish the state of Israel. The Holocaust is at best a huge exaggeration, if not totally fabricated. Hitler had no official policy of exterminating the Jews. Irving is not alone in his views. In 2005, the president of Iran, Mahmoud Ahmadinejad, reportedly said that the extermination of six million Jews during World War II was "a myth." The vast majority of people find such blindness to the truth abhorrent, but Irving has influenced—and energized—thousands and continues to do so, though his light has dimmed.

In 1942, his father, an officer in the Royal Navy, was aboard a light cruiser in the Barents Sea when a U-boat sank it; Commander Irving survived but deserted his family after the catastrophe. Cast largely upon his own devices, the young David began his infatuation with Hitler early, partly as a result of the skepticism aroused in him by cartoonish portrayals in the British press. His twin, Nicholas, says that his

---

* Another handicap for historians has been the loss of vital evidence, particularly important documents. In November 2019, *Lapham's Quarterly* listed (p. 142) ten major lost archives, including the Library of Alexandria, the House of Wisdom, the Mayan Codices, and the National Library of Cambodia. Ramesses II, with his "sneer of cold command," chipped off the names of all the pharaohs who had built great buildings before him and substituted his own record, so there is a history, just a fudged one. Chinese war studies (China was the first country to have such) existed c. 1200–1000 B.C., but probably were written down about 500 B.C., yet kept so secret that one major record vanished for 1,200 years, only to turn up in an excavated tomb in 1972. The confessions of Walter Raleigh took four hundred years to surface. An unknown manuscript of the English poet Thomas Traherne (c. 1637–1674) was picked off a bonfire in the 1960s. Only in 2003, in Rouen, did papers show that Edward V (1470–1483) had been born out of wedlock. It has recently been released that the British government was protecting the Republican freedom fighter Michael Collins (1890–1922) during the Irish War of Independence (which is why he was able to cycle through Dublin quite openly). At least all these papers did finally turn up. Anthony Sampson's *The New Anatomy of Britain* (1971) reports that there are government files on the Napoleonic Wars still judged unreleasable.

brother has been a provocateur since his youth. In his teens, he won a school prize and insisted that he be presented with a copy of *Mein Kampf,* hoping to have photographers capture the occasion of Britain's chancellor of the exchequer, Rab Butler, handing him the book on speech day. (The school—Brentwood—had the last laugh, substituting a German-Russian technical dictionary.)

Irving continued to exhibit his sympathies at university, where he studied engineering and economics before dropping out, for financial reasons. He headed for Germany, and for a time was a steelworker in the Ruhr. It was there that he learned of the firebombing of Dresden and began to research the episode, writing thirty-seven articles on the bombing for a German magazine. These formed the basis for his first book, *The Destruction of Dresden* (1963), an international bestseller. Most reviewers praised the work, particularly the prodigious use of primary sources, which Irving could read in the original. But as he was later to complain, the Establishment hardly warmed to his branding of Churchill ("a corrupt politician") as a war criminal. Not only did he find it impossible to get a job in academia, but he said that his elder brother John, an officer in the Royal Air Force, found himself summarily dismissed. Irving was bitter.

He is now the author of some thirty books on the Second World War, nearly all revisionist history, including *Hitler's War* (1977), in which he finally acknowledges the Holocaust but claims that Hitler was the dupe of subordinates. Each book is a curate's egg, containing excellent research but also much history gone bad. And of course the point about the curate's egg, the subject of an 1895 Punch cartoon, is not that there aren't good bits but that the bad bits corrupt the whole.

Even the evidence Irving displayed in his book on Dresden has been found to be distorted. He wrote that those killed numbered between 100,000 and 250,000—lower than the Nazi estimate of 500,000 but much higher than other published figures. He quoted a Nazi document that said that 202,400 people were known to have died and predicted that another 250,000 corpses would be found. Over the next thirty years he gradually adjusted these estimates, to 50,000–100,000. The latest estimate (not his) is 22,700–25,000, the outcome of a five-year study by a panel of German historians.

In 1996, Irving's reputation was further confounded after he brought an unsuccessful libel action against the American historian Deborah

Lipstadt and her publisher, Penguin, for labeling him a Holocaust denier. Professor Richard Evans, then chairman of the history faculty at Cambridge, gave ferocious testimony: "It may seem an absurd semantic dispute to deny the appellation of 'historian' to someone who has written two dozen books or more about historical subjects," he said. "But if we mean by historian someone who is concerned to discover the truth about the past, and to give as accurate a representation of it as possible, then Irving is not a historian." He went on: "Irving is essentially an ideologue who uses history for his own political purposes; he is not primarily concerned with discovering and interpreting what happened in the past, he is concerned merely to give a selective and tendentious account of it to further his own ideological ends in the present. The true historian's primary concern, however, is with the past. That is why, in the end, Irving is not a historian." The judge, Charles Gray, made a different distinction, allowing that "as a *military* historian, Irving has much to commend him," and that his knowledge of World War II was "unparalleled," but whereas an incompetent historian might make random errors, Irving consistently misconstrued his material all in one direction: to exonerate Hitler and minimize the Holocaust. He finally ruled that Irving was a Holocaust denier, an anti-Semite, and a racist and that he had "persistently and deliberately misrepresented and manipulated historical evidence."*

There are important issues here. First, any historian has the right, not to deny the Holocaust, but to challenge statements about it; otherwise, as the Spanish newspaper *El Mundo* put it, there is a "criminalization of opinion." Indeed, some twenty years ago the *Historikerstreit* (historians' dispute) was an intellectual and political argument in West Germany about the way the Holocaust should be interpreted. The *Historikerstreit* spanned the years 1986–1989, pitting left-wing intellectuals against those of the right. So—are certain parts of history off-limits to historians? Maybe there is a time limit before which certain questioning is not acceptable? Or has writing history become linked to a criterion of truth-telling that radically differs from the histories of Herodotus, Thucydides, Caesar, and Gibbon?

* In July 2012, I spent two hours interviewing Irving in his borrowed apartment (he no longer had enough funds for a home of his own, he told me) off Kew Gardens in southwest London. Afterward, unasked, he sent me a one-page summary of our meeting. It contained three factual errors.

There is a whiff of a dangerous orthodoxy here. This whole conversation may be distasteful, Irving a racist and malefactor (in 2006 he served eleven months in an Austrian prison), but is his doctoring of the evidence or the foul nature of his prejudices enough to disqualify him from being a historian? How unreliable a historian do you have to be before you are no longer a member of that fraternity?

* * *

MOST COUNTRIES AT ONE time or another have been guilty of proclaiming false versions of their past. The late-nineteenth-century French historian Ernest Renan is known for his statement that "forgetfulness" is "essential in the creation of a nation," his positive gloss on Goethe's blunt aphorism, "Patriotism corrupts history." But this is why nationalism often views history as a threat. What governments declare to be true is one reality, the judgments of historians quite another. "History always emphasizes terminal events," Albert Speer commented sharply to his American interrogators just after the end of the war. He hated the idea that the earlier achievements of Hitler's government would be eclipsed by its final disintegration.

Few recorders set out deliberately to lie; when they do, they can have great impact, if only in certain parts of the world. Japan is a prime example. Its contentious years began in 1931 with two officers of the locally garrisoned Japanese Kwantung Army in the south of China setting off an explosion on a railway line in Manchuria, in China's northeast. Within days, the Japanese seized the Nationalist capital of Nanjing and between December 1937 and January 1938 went on a six-week rampage, massacring three hundred thousand Chinese civilians and raping more than twenty thousand women (both figures are Chinese estimates and are likely exaggerated, but since no records were kept, exact numbers are unknown). Chinese soldiers in civilian clothes were marched to execution sites where they were gunned down en masse. Women were assaulted in front of their families; streets were filled with rotting corpses as Japanese soldiers hauled away cartfuls of loot; children were casually murdered. The appalling episode has been the subject of heated exchanges in the Japanese media at least since the early 1970s, after the publication of a book of interviews with survivors. Even conservative scholars put the death toll as at least forty thousand, although between one hundred thousand and two hundred thousand is more likely.

There were other war crimes: the inhumane treatment of prisoners, including live vivisections performed on captured American airmen; Asian prisoners and civilians killed for the purpose of eating them; Asian women (and some Europeans) forced to become sexual slaves, under the chilling euphemism of their being "comfort women"; experiments carried out on Chinese prisoners by Unit 731, the Japanese army's covert germ warfare division;* the brutal sacking of Manila; planes that dropped infected fleas on Chinese settlements, causing a local plague; the use of poison gas; and both the Bataan Death March and the "Death Railway," in which the savage treatment by Japanese and Korean guards, including starvation diets and merciless hard labor, led to the deaths of more than twelve thousand Westerners and possibly one hundred thousand Asians. An American missionary captured part of the 1937 massacre in Nanjing on film; one scene shows Japanese soldiers enjoying a competition in which a dozen Chinese civilians are lined up in single file and a soldier fires a rifle point-blank at the first prisoner, to see how many bodies the bullet will penetrate.

The Japanese were guilty of crimes that even the Nazis did not commit, trading in opium to finance its puppet governments, and—also in China—forced evacuation of vast areas of population. For these and other misdeeds, the International Military Tribunal for the Far East, in session from May 1946 to November 1948, issued seven death penalties and sixteen sentences of life imprisonment. In the years to come, the country's reputation would be further besmirched as it became known that some two hundred thousand young women, taken against their will from South Korea (mainly: the territory was annexed

---

* The unit carried out experiments from 1937 to 1945, operating on its victims without anesthetics and infecting them with lethal diseases to see how long it would take them to die. It was based in Harbin, the largest city in the Japanese puppet state of Manchukuo, now northeast China, and was officially known as the "Epidemic Prevention and Water Purification Department of the Kwantung Army." The facility itself was built between 1934 and 1939 and officially adopted the name "Unit 731" in 1941. Some three thousand men, women, and children were tortured in Harbin alone, and that figure excludes victims from other similar sites, such as Unit 100, which went by the obfuscating appellation "the Warehouse Disease Prevention Shop." The Japanese government funded the unit up to the end of the war. Instead of being tried for war crimes, the researchers in Unit 731 were granted immunity in exchange for the research data they gathered, which was co-opted into the U.S. biological warfare program. See Charles Burris, "Myths of 'the Good War,'" k12.tulsaschools.org/charlesburriswebpages/world-war-ii/.

by Japan from 1910 to 1945), Taiwan, Indonesia, and the Philippines, were submitted to sexual slavery and sexual violence. The women were stripped of their names and called by the names of flowers. One survivor, Kim Bok-dong (1926–2019), has said: "On weekdays, I had to take fifteen soldiers a day. On Saturdays and Sundays, it was more than 50. We were treated worse than beasts." Both the army and the navy trafficked women in all areas occupied by Japanese troops, where they provided medical inspections, built facilities, established fees, and determined the "durability or perishability of the women procured."

How would a postwar Japan reconcile itself to such knowledge? Its people remained largely ignorant of the country's responsibility (when Bok-dong returned home, aged twenty-two, she lied even to her family about what had happened), as they were of the invasion of China in general, and tended to see themselves only as victims. Nevertheless, in 1945 the Allied occupation forces instituted a reeducation program to teach the conquered citizenry "the truth" about the war. Throughout December of that year, the major newspapers were required to publish a series of articles drafted by General Douglas MacArthur's headquarters, and for ten weeks Japanese radio ran a serial program called "Now It Can Be Told."*

The American occupation of Japan, known as "Operation Blacklist," came to an end in April 1952, having begun in August 1945. A handful of historians felt free to write accounts in which they insisted on dealing with all aspects of the war, but they were outnumbered by memoirs of former soldiers, mostly noncommissioned or low-ranking officers, extolling the bravery of ordinary Japanese and often criticizing the military leadership's conduct of the war. This contributed to the self-perception of the Japanese—"victim consciousness." There were films, novels, even an opera, all poring over the wartime years. In the latter half of the 1950s, led by Japanese Marxist historians, a lively discussion (*rondan bunka*—"debate culture") started up over war responsibility. Scholars within Japan began to pose awkward questions about the country's behavior: not only about "comfort

---

* Or at least some of the truths. The Civil Information and Education Section of the American initiative ("a misnomer, if there ever was one," comments the author Ian Buruma acidly) prohibited the Japanese media from criticizing the Allied wartime and occupational forces, including making any mention of the dropping of atomic bombs on Hiroshima and Nagasaki. See Ian Buruma, "Expect to Be Lied to in Japan," *The New York Review of Books,* November 8, 2012, p. 34.

women," but about previously unknown cases of bacteriological experiments. Nevertheless, it was an ill-informed debate, as only from about 1970 on did studies of Japanese wartime atrocities become available to the public.

Then came the backlash. Nationalist historians began to question whether the Nanjing Massacre ever happened, and in October 1999 an alternative textbook for schoolchildren, *Kokumin no rekishi* (The History of a Nation) was released, extolling Japan's record while vehemently attacking those who publicized wartime outrages. The founder of this faction, a fifty-three-year-old professor of education at Tokyo University named Nobukatsu Fujioka, declared that past events were not a fixed tabulation: "History is not just something that involves the discovery and interpretation of sources. It is also something that needs to be rewritten in accordance with the changing reality of the present." His predecessor as the revisionists' intellectual leader, Tanzan Ishibashi (1884–1973), "wanted to use history to transform the relationship between the State and the people"—so the books children read in school became a central battleground. Fujioka and the "Liberal School" began their counterattack against the "dementia of the defeated" with a series of articles, which snowballed into the four-volume *Kyokasho ga Oshienai Rekishi* (History That Is Not Taught in Textbooks); by May 1997, the first two books in the series had sold nine hundred thousand copies. Following up, the *New History Textbook* of 2001 not only carefully avoided using words denoting aggression but played down both the Nanjing atrocity (presenting it as a "spring-break party for the soldiers that got a little out of hand," in the words of one commentator) and what Japan did to POWs or civilians, focusing instead on atrocities committed by other nations.

* * *

THE JAPANESE HISTORIAN MICHIKO HASEGAWA has posed the question: "Why is it that people do not look at history honestly?" Her words invite an ironic response, given that Hasegawa is a leading revisionist, intent on arguing that the atrocities committed by the Japanese military during the 1930s and 1940s never occurred or at least have been greatly exaggerated. Her stance mirrors that of a large number of Japanese scholars, politicians, and teachers. A 1989 article by the Japanese commentator Rikki Kersten put all this into context:

Japanese revisionism . . . contended that the attack on Pearl Harbor, and invasion into China and other parts of Asia were not acts of aggression. . . . The underlying objective of historical revisionism is to blur the distinct line that exists between the victims and the aggressors. By depicting Japanese war criminals as victims (of western imperialism), revisionists want their school children to memorize prewar Japan as a heroic nation that struggled to free its Asian neighbors from Western aggression.

But this makes records of the past subject to the nation's self-image, demanding that it fulfill the goal of "making Japanese proud," whatever the facts. It fosters patriotism by self-delusion. One might argue that all wars require a heroic narrative, to inspire soldiers to risk their lives and, after the conflict has ended, to make them and their survivors feel they have not suffered or died in vain. Such a comforting comes at great cost. As John Carey has said: "One of history's most useful tasks is to bring home to us how keenly, honestly, and painfully, past generations pursued aims that now seem to us wrong or disgraceful." That is not how Japan's governments have seen it. To this day, they have not prosecuted a single war criminal. Shirō Ishii, who headed Unit 731, avoided all punishment; his successor became head of Japan's first commercial blood bank. Kishi Nobusuke, who ran his country's war economy and was imprisoned as a Class A war criminal, went on to be prime minister from 1957 to 1960, as did his grandson, Shinzō Abe, in two separate spells in power.

From 1985 on, Japan's political leaders have made a point of visiting the Yasukuni Shrine in downtown Tokyo, where the remains of more than a thousand war criminals are buried, including fourteen Class A felons. Next door to the shrine is a museum that almost completely reiterates the revisionist view of Japan's wartime history. The Nanjing Massacre is referred to as "an incident"; once the Japanese forces had cleared up the problem, "residents were again able to live their lives in peace." In one set of panels, Hitler's ambitions are explained as "trying to reclaim the territory lost in World War One." The Holocaust is not mentioned.

In February 2007 the prime minister, Abe, declared that his administration had found no evidence that the government had coerced women who had served as sex slaves to Japanese soldiers and that his party would move to downgrade a 1993 statement that admitted state involvement over the issue. He would also seek to repudiate the judgment of the International Military Tribunal for the Far East about Japan's war crimes; there was something noble about his country's war years, he said, and its involvement had had the goal of liberating Asia from Western imperialism.

*An American officer, Captain Chan from San Francisco,
with captured "comfort women" of the Japanese garrison
at Myitkyina, Burma, August 14, 1944.*

In September 2007 Abe resigned his post for "health reasons" (although some commentators said it was partly due to his losing the battle over revisions to history textbooks), but he later staged a comeback, becoming prime minister again in 2012, then was reelected in 2014 (on the slogan "Take back Japan!") and once more in 2017. In October 2013 his education minister ordered a school board to use a conservative textbook it had rejected, and two months later the same minister proposed new screening standards, requiring school textbooks to include nationalist views of the war years and the deletion, for example, of the military's throwing grenades into caves where Okinawan civilians were hiding, then forcing them to commit suicide rather than surrender.

In the years since, efforts for change have sped up, and Abe could let himself be photographed on a fighter plane with the same number—731—as the plant where Chinese prisoners were used as experiment subjects. In October 2014 Abe's government once again asked for a partial retraction of the nearly two-decades-old UN report on comfort women, but the report's author refused to comply. Since then, Abe has responded in some measure to all the international criticism; in August 2015, in a carefully worded televised address, he admitted that Japan had inflicted "immeasurable damage and suffering" when it "took the wrong course and advanced along the road to war." At the end of 2015, Japan finally made a formal apology and promised $8.3 million to provide care for any comfort women still living—as of March 2020, there are eighteen survivors, most in their nineties.

The historian Eri Hotta wrote in her 2014[*] study *Japan 1941: Countdown to Infamy,* "Despite the efforts of some individual citizens, academics, and journalists to have a more honest debate, it is difficult to deny that Japan's official impulse has been to look away from what is undesirable and unpleasant in its history." *The Japan Times* further remarked, "There's nothing wrong with fostering patriotic pride, but it should be for the wonders of Japanese art and literature, its premodern civilization, not for its 20th-century nationalism." Meanwhile, the Japanese press, notoriously docile, has continued to place "the national interest" ahead of the public's right to know. Yet without full disclosure history recedes into myth and becomes a form of propaganda.

When Abe first became prime minister, he asserted: "It is not the business of the government to decide how to define the last world war. I think we have to wait for the estimation of historians." But that is just what he has *not* done. Japan is a democracy, in many ways a thriving

---

[*] That same year saw the publication in Japan of a sixty-one-volume official biography of Emperor Hirohito. Against the evidence that Hirohito supported the 1937 invasion of China and the use of chemical weapons there and that he backed the attack on Pearl Harbor, or even that his refusal to admit defeat in 1945 condemned tens of thousands to die in Hiroshima and Nagasaki, the history presents him as "a benign, passive figurehead," a puppet of his country's militaristic leaders.

one (in December 1997, on the anniversary of the Nanjing Massacre, a citizens' parade walked peacefully through Tokyo behind a lantern bearing the Chinese characters for "to commemorate"), but while there is open debate about the issues that continue to bedevil Japan's history, the government is setting the agenda. This is understandable, but a tragedy.

It may seem in some sense unfair to pick on Japan for the way it has airbrushed its past, given that there is scarcely a nation that has not to some degree massaged accounts of its history. And as the distinguished Canadian historian Margaret MacMillan points out:

> It can be dangerous to question the stories people tell about themselves because so much of our identity is both shaped by and bound up with our history. That is why dealing with the past, in deciding which version we want, or on what we want to remember and to forget, can become so politically charged.

But unless Japan can accept full responsibility for all it inflicted through colonialism and war, it will be living with a false past. And the cost of that? As Ryōtarō Shiba (1923–96), one of Japan's foremost novelists who lived through the Second World War and its aftermath, wrote: "A country whose textbooks lie . . . will inevitably collapse." One might also quote the respected literary critic John Lukacs: "It is true that a good man can write bad history. It is not true that a bad man can be a good historian."

* * *

"I KNOW IT IS the fashion to say that most of recorded history is lies anyway," wrote George Orwell in 1942, reflecting on pro-Franco propaganda in the aftermath of the Spanish Civil War. "I am willing to believe that history is for the most part inaccurate and biased, but what is peculiar to our own age is the abandonment of the idea that history *could* be truthfully written." The problem continued to trouble him. Three years later he went further: "Already there are countless people who would think it scandalous to falsify a scientific textbook, but would see nothing wrong in falsifying an historical fact." Chief among the culprits, of course, were the falsifiers of the Soviet Union, in particular Vladimir Ilyich Ulyanov, known as Lenin (1870–1924), and Joseph Vissarionovich Stalin (1878–1953).*

Lenin presided over Soviet Russia from 1917 till his death, but Stalin (a name he came up with, from the Russian word for "steel") had usurped much of his authority even before his final illness. As it was, Lenin had already put in place the basic institutions of the Stalinist regime, a state committed to totalitarian rule based on the party, the army, and the secret police; the soviets (workers' councils) in whose name the Bolsheviks had seized power, had been rendered impotent. Starting with the Red Terror of 1918, Lenin and Stalin shared responsibility—by enforced famine, brutal imprisonment, mass killing, ethnic cleansing, or assassination—for the deaths of twenty million of their fellows. In one of the peak periods of Stalin's era, 1937–38, seven million were arrested (Party leaders were given quotas of "enemies" to be turned in), with a million executed and two million dying in concentration camps. At that year's height, 1,500 people were being shot every day. "Ten million," Stalin told Churchill was his tally for the dead, holding up both palms in the Kremlin in 1942, but that figure has been reckoned low, given the vast numbers who perished in what has come to be called the Holodomor ("hunger-death").† (Coincidentally, Lenin and Stalin even shared the same cook—the grandfather of Vladimir Putin.)

In her history of Eastern Europe, Anne Applebaum writes of the "peculiarly powerful combination of emotions—fear, shame, anger, silence—[that] helped lay the psychological groundwork for the im-

---

* Thus the situation that Orwell satirized with his vocabulary of state power and deception—Big Brother, Hate Week, Newspeak, doublethink, and the Thought Police: "The past was erased, the erasure was forgotten, the lie became the truth. . . . Every record has been destroyed or falsified, every book has been rewritten, every picture has been repainted, every statue and street and building has been renamed, every date has been altered. And that process is continuing day by day and minute by minute. History has stopped. Nothing exists except an endless present in which the Party is always right." George Orwell, *Nineteen Eighty-Four*, bk. 1, ch. 7.

† The historian Timothy Snyder puts the death toll of civilians alone—and just for the period 1933–45—at fourteen million. Between 1932 and 1933, such were people's desperation that at least 2,505 Ukrainians were found guilty of cannibalism. Timothy Snyder, *Bloodlands: Europe Between Hitler and Stalin* (New York: Basic Books, 2010). The purges were documented by the British historian Robert Conquest, who in a celebrated limerick favored a neat rhyme over strict historical accuracy:

There was a great Marxist called Lenin
Who did two or three million men in.
That's a lot to have done in,
But where he did one in
That grand Marxist Stalin did ten in.

position of a new regime," Stalin's Soviet Union. The completeness of the state, the pervasiveness of every institution from kindergarten schools to the secret police, put an end to independent historical inquiry. In this brave new world (Orwell described Soviet commissars as "half gramophones, half gangsters"), historians were not just to do Stalin's bidding; if in his eyes they failed to do so, their lives were ruined and often shortened. For instance, Boris Grekov (1882–1953), director of Moscow's Russian History Institute, had seen his son sentenced to penal servitude and, in terror, made wide-ranging concessions to the Stalinist line, writing books and papers to order. Mikhail Rostovtsev (1870–1952), an authority on the ancient history of South Russia and Ukraine, fled the country in 1918, ending up in the United States, teaching at Yale. In his later years he suffered from acute depression, the fate of many of his expatriates.

Mikhail Pokrovsky (1868–1932) was one of the most influential Soviet historians of the 1920s and an early member of the revolutionary movement. Following the Bolshevik seizure of power, he became deputy chief of the government's department of education and edited several major historical journals, presenting semiofficial reinterpretations of the Russian past. Despite such loyalty, Stalin repudiated his work as insufficiently appreciative of the role of great men in history as well as its "lack of patriotic fervor." Many of Pokrovsky's colleagues were charged with encouraging ideas that were "anti-Marxist, anti-Leninist, essentially liquidatorist, and anti-scientific."*

Another leading historian, Yevgeny Tarle (1874–1955), a founder of

---

* A suitable metaphor for these times comes in Michael Dibdin's thriller *Ratking*. In the novel, the public prosecutor explains local conditions to Police Commissioner Aurelio Zen:

> A ratking is something that happens when too many rats live in too small a space under too much pressure. Their tails become entwined and the more they strain and stretch to free themselves the tighter grows the knot binding them, until at last it becomes a solid mass of embedded tissue. And the creature thus formed, as many as thirty rats tied together by the tail, is called a ratking. You wouldn't expect such a living contradiction to survive, would you? That's the most amazing thing of all. Most of the ratkings they find . . . are healthy and flourishing. Evidently the creatures have evolved some way of coming to terms with their situation. That's not to say they like it, of course! In fact the reason they're discovered is because of their diabolical squealing. Not much fun, being chained to each other for life. . . . What we're dealing with is not a creature but a condition, the condition of being crucified to your fellows, squealing madly, biting, spitting, lashing out, yet somehow surviving, somehow even vilely flourishing!

Ratkings were first detected in Germany back in 1564, but this description fits the historians who served Stalin from 1918 on. Michael Dibdin, *Ratking* (London: Faber, 1988), pp. 80–81.

the Moscow State Institute of International Relations, Russia's university for future diplomats, was one of a group of prominent historians accused of hatching a plot to overthrow the government; he was arrested and sent into exile. At the same time (1934–36) the Politburo of the Russian Communist Party focused on national history textbooks, and Stalin set scholars to writing a new standard history. The state became the nation's only publisher. Orwell had it right in *Nineteen Eighty-Four,* where the Records Department is charged with rewriting the past to fit whomever Oceania is currently fighting. The ruling party of Big Brother "could thrust its hand into the past and say of this or that event, it never happened—that, surely, was more terrifying than mere torture and death."

Odd to think that Hitler and Stalin never met. Margaret MacMillan, whom I have already quoted on Japan's history, puts Stalin's approach in perspective:

> Dictators, perhaps because they know their own lies so well, have usually realized the power of history. Consequently, they have tried to rewrite, deny, or destroy the past. Robespierre in revolutionary France and Pol Pot in 1970s Cambodia each set out to start society from the beginning again. Robespierre's new calendar and Pol Pot's Year Zero were designed to erase the past and its suggestions that there were alternative ways of organizing society. The founder of China, the Qin emperor, reportedly destroyed all the earlier histories, buried the scholars who might remember them, and wrote his own history. . . . Mao went one better: he tried to destroy all memories and all artifacts that, by reminding the Chinese people of the past, might prevent him from remodelling them into the new Communist men and women.

Stalin too wrote his own version of events, contributing part of a "short course" on the history of the Soviet Communist Party. In his teens, *vozhd* (the boss), as he liked to be called, had been a budding poet, and now he contributed verse for the national anthem, improved on several poets' translations, and even made changes to the film script of Sergei Eisenstein's *Ivan the Terrible.* He was a master of what could be done with language; under him, the euphemism "extraordinary events" was used to cover any behavior he considered treasonable, a phrase that covered incompetence, cowardice, "anti-Soviet agitation," even drunkenness. When, in January 1924, *Pravda* divulged that Leon Trotsky was "ill," this was taken as a sure sign of his imminent removal. The great Polish poet Zbigniew Herbert was to refer to Stalin ironically as "the Great Linguist" for his corruption of language.

Uncle Joe himself died peacefully, aged seventy-four, on March 5, 1953, after three decades of bloody rule. Three years later, after the 20th Party Congress, his successor, Nikita Khrushchev, announced a special session in which he gave delegates a four-hour "secret speech" denouncing the former leader and providing a radically revisionist account of Soviet history that included a call for a new spirit in historical work. Practitioners were admonished to upgrade their methods, to use documents and data to explain rather than simply proclaim past Bolshevik views, and to write a credible account—one that would include setbacks, confusions, and real struggles along with glorious achievements.

So began a "thaw" that saw Stalin repudiated throughout the Soviet Union, political prisoners released, and prison camps dismantled, ushering in a season of "free thinking" that, for instance, saw the publication of Solzhenitsyn's *One Day in the Life of Ivan Denisovich* and *Not By Bread Alone,* Vladimir Dudintsev's bestselling 1956 novel about a teacher of physics who invents a labor-saving machine that is rejected by bureaucrats because the innovation runs up against Soviet dogma. Khrushchev even set up a commission to protect defamers of Stalin. One high school history teacher staged a mock trial of Stalin in his class, while activists in Moscow put on an evening of poetry and music performed by and in honor of gulag survivors. By early 1955, lively discussions centered on the journal *Voprosy istorii* ("Problems of History"). "You still had to toe a Marxist line," Dominic Lieven, a Cambridge professor specializing in Russian history, says, "but by the 1970s in many cases you could get away with quoting Lenin in the introduction and then providing much valuable info and ideas in the text." Academics were allowed room for maneuver, so long as it was exercised discreetly and deniably, but they were not free of political controls regarding what material they saw, their links with historians overseas, and what they could write. They had to observe a code of conduct—*poniatiia,* literally "concepts."

Ever since Martin Luther showed what could be achieved through

the printed word, governments have attempted to control what is published (even Cervantes had to apply for a royal license). The distinguished poet Anna Akhmatova (1889–1966) was never a political
activist, yet her police file grew to almost a thousand pages. After literary figures wrote to Khrushchev on her behalf, she was allowed to
publish openly and not just in samizdat, but her epic poem *Requiem,*
about people's suffering under the Great Purge, was still regarded as
dangerously candid and finally appeared in the USSR only in 1987.
Solzhenitsyn was exiled and his work banned, while Khrushchev
rounded on Dudintsev, saying his novel was "false at its base" and accusing its author of taking "a malicious joy in describing the negative
sides of Soviet life." Dudintsev was shunned and reduced to poverty.

For other members of the Politburo, the thaw, such as it was,
seemed too much. In October 1964 Khrushchev was toppled and Leo-
nid Brezhnev took his place. Many innovations were reversed. Other
conservative leaders followed—Kosygin, Andropov, Chernenko. In
1968, during Czechoslovakia's Prague Spring, this same process of
opening up for a bit, then closing down again, repeated itself. Prisoners
from the Stalinist period were released, some writers were rehabili-
tated, and recent events were reexamined with more openness. Then
the tanks came. As became typical for Soviet historians, in March 1974
P. V. Volobuev, director of the Institute of History and a leading figure in new history-writing, was fired; a book of essays suggesting that
Russia was a backward country in 1917 was condemned. It was not
until March 1985, when Mikhail Gorbachev took charge, that the writing of history was given a measure of freedom from government control. As David Remnick relates in *Lenin's Tomb,* his prize-winning look
at the Soviet Union morphing into modern Russia,

> Something had changed—changed radically. After some initial
> hesitation at the beginning of his time in power, Gorbachev had
> decreed that the time had come to fill in the "blank spots" of
> history. There could be no more "rose-colored glasses," he
> said. . . . The return of historical memory would be his most
> important decision, one that preceded all others, for without a
> full and ruthless assessment of the past—an admission of mur-
> der, repression and bankruptcy—real change, much less demo-
> cratic revolution, was impossible. The return of history to

personal, intellectual, and political life was the start of the great reform of the twentieth century.

Remnick relates the story of Yuri Afanasyev, a "calculating man" who in his early days had successfully used the system to better himself. "For more years than I care to remember," Afanasyev told a TV audience, "I was up to my neck in shit." A specialist in French historiography, he looked, with his bullfrog neck and barrel chest, more like a high-school football coach or perhaps a Russian Norman Mailer. He joined Gorbachev's campaign for the "return of history" and in 1986 wangled a key appointment as rector of the Historical Archives Institute. Soon he was giving public lectures criticizing Stalin and introducing new academic faces. He insisted that professional scholars and not the Central Committee should be the country's principal historians. "As long as such things still exist," he told Remnick, "there will still be the idea that history should be made not in the archives and universities and by writers, but rather at Party conferences and committees. That way history remains a handmaiden of propaganda and an extension of policy rather than a sphere of knowledge on the level of science or literature."

Boris Yeltsin, who served as first president of what was called the Russian Federation from 1991 to 1999, allowed yet further freedoms. The old textbooks became so completely devalued that history examinations had to be postponed throughout the Soviet Union. (In Estonia and Ukraine, laws were introduced that made writing bad history a prosecutable offense.) By 1989, Remnick notes, books had appeared in Russian schools with chapters on the Soviet period that resembled Solzhenitsyn more than the approved texts of previous generations.

Historians who had previously been obedient Communists felt emboldened to come out in their true colors. Particularly notable was Dmitri Volkogonov (1928–95), whose father had been arrested and shot in Stalin's purges and whose mother had died in a labor camp during the Second World War. In 1945, the orphaned Volkoganov, aged seventeen, joined the army, and over some four decades rose to the rank of colonel general and the positions of special adviser for defense to Yeltsin and head of the Soviet military's psychological warfare department. More than this, he was a talented historian, and in 1988, after years of research in secret archives, published an outspoken biography of Stalin that acknowledged his subject's strengths but also frequently contradicted official versions of events and argued persuasively that it was only under Stalin that the Soviet Union became the "dictatorship of one man." He continued with lives of Trotsky (1992) and Lenin (1994), making full use of similar never-before-seen archive material. The breakthrough was even more remarkable in that Soviet historians did not write biographies, far less psycho-historical works.* All three of Volkoganov's books had an immense impact.

For non-Russian authors too it appeared to be open season to spend time in the many previously closed archives. Orlando Figes was one of a relatively small group (Antony Beevor, Anne Applebaum, Laurence Rees, and Adam Zamoyski among them) who made their way to Moscow (rarely St. Petersburg) in search of treasure. "Intellectually, the end of communism was a liberation for historians," Figes recorded. From 1984 to 1987, he spent weeks researching in the State Archive of the Russian Federation:

> The system worked on the principle of [their] preserving everything but admitting the existence of only those materials cleared for publication by Soviet historians. All our requests for documents were vetted by a woman from the KGB [the main security agency]. As foreigners we had to work in a separate reading room, without access to the canteen, so that we would not come into contact with Soviet historians or archivists, who might help us with our work. There was just one flaw in the system:

---

* They were translated by the genial British historian Harold Shukman. In 1987, as publisher of Hutchinson, I commissioned Shukman to take on Andrei Gromyko's memoirs. These had been published in Russia while Gromyko was chairman of the Presidium of the Supreme Soviet (in effect, number two to Gorbachev), and had reportedly enjoyed a two-million-copy first printing. From 1939 on, he had spent his career as the wiliest of politicians, and I traveled to Moscow to see if he might expand on the selected memories he had employed for Russian consumption. Inside the Kremlin (after passing by his desk, laden with twelve phones, eleven of them black, one red—for what?) I cautiously presented him with a list of questions. Gromyko spoke excellent English (he had been ambassador in London), but had insisted that my list be translated into Russian, and his advisers had duly complied. One of the questions was about the Prague Spring of 1968, the uprising in Czechoslovakia that had been brutally quelled but which Gromyko had not so much as mentioned in his book. Utterly humorless, he studied the translated memo, then asked, "What is this Czech mattress that you wish me to consider?" I never did get any extra paragraphs.

the reading room for Soviet researchers shared a toilet with the room for foreigners. In those days I was a smoker, so I'd go there frequently and chat with Soviet historians and archivists, who liked my Western cigarettes and were happy to find out for me the numbers of the files I needed.

Another visitor, Jonathan Brent, editorial director of Yale University Press, persuaded the archivists to allow him to publish their documents, employing them as co-editors, so that they would be paid royalties in U.S. dollars. Brent stipulated that the books would be available in Russian, an important tactic, as already nationalists were protesting that their archives were being plundered by foreigners wanting to blacken Soviet history by focusing on its darkest areas. He negotiated subsidies for the Russian publication of a series of books the university produced, leaving it to the publishers to decide what they wanted to add or remove. By the end of 2009, fourteen of the twenty books in the Yale series had appeared in Russian—although of course there were many cases where archivists sold the same documents to several publishers.*

Antony Beevor was another supplicant foreign scholar who traveled to Moscow to undertake research, in his case into Russian military archives. He had to promise to submit material, aware that if the authorities disagreed with what he finally wrote, he would not be allowed back. When his award-winning *Berlin: The Downfall 1945* appeared in a Russian edition it was criticized for focusing on atrocities committed by the advancing Red Army. His *Stalingrad* (1998) was also published in Russia, with a foreword (not cleared or even known about by Beevor) warning readers that much in the book was wrong. But this was not enough. In 2015 the Russian army announced it was forming

---

* Other accommodations are more sinister. In 2005, husband and wife Jon Halliday and Jung Chang published *Mao: The Unknown Story,* based on interviews with many of Mao's close circle who have never talked before. As their publishers proudly announced in their 2006 catalogue, the book was "full of startling revelations, exploding the myth of the Long March and showing a completely unknown Mao. He was not driven by idealism or ideology; his intimate and intricate relationship with Stalin went back to the 1920s, ultimately bringing him to power; he welcomed the Japanese occupation of much of China; and he schemed, poisoned, and blackmailed to get his way. After Mao conquered China in 1949, his secret goal was to dominate the world." Every single file in the Russian archives, as quoted in the book, has been removed on request by the Chinese government.

"*Whom you photograph, how you frame it—it's all choices*," notes Hany Farid, a photo-forensics expert. "*So we've been fooling ourselves. Historically, it will turn out that there was this weird time when people just assumed that photography and videography were true. And now that very short little period is fading. Maybe it should've faded a long time ago.*" Under Stalin, photos were regularly doctored to omit political figures who had fallen out of favor. Here, Kliment Voroshilov, Vyacheslav Molotov, Stalin, and Nikolai Yezhov stroll along the banks of the Moscow-Volga Canal in April 1937. Within two years, Yezhov had been arrested, tortured, and shot. The photo was reproduced in 1940 in a volume published in Moscow in celebration of Stalin's sixtieth birthday, with Yezhov eliminated.

Sometimes figures were removed to make the main person appear more powerful. Here Chairman Mao inspects soldiers of the Red Army, but in the doctored photo an official has been moved back and Mao's figure enlarged.

Stalin's artists were not alone. When on May 7, 1945, Germany officially surrendered, photos of General Eisenhower holding up the pens with which the surrender was signed were taken both with and without his driver and supposed mistress, Kay Summersby. In versions released to the press, her presence behind Eisenhower's right shoulder was eliminated by publishing only those photographs in which she cannot be seen.

a special commission to open up its archives to refute the "lies" Beevor had perpetrated, and in the same year the regional education ministry in Sverdlovsk, near the Ural Mountains, issued a decree telling school and university libraries to "check the availability of works" by Beevor and to "take measures to remove them from access by students and teaching staff." The ministry claimed that his books "misinterpret information about World War II events, contradict historical documents and are infused with stereotypes of Nazi propaganda." The titles had been published by the Open Society foundations of the American billionaire George Soros, the ministry went on, organizations known to meddle in Russia's internal affairs. The criticisms were taken up in 2015 by the upper house of parliament in Moscow, which set forth a list of "undesirable" organizations recommended for banning, including the Soros foundations. Neither Beevor's nor other suspect historians' books (for instance, those by John Keegan) can now be bought in Russia.

Such official diktats continue; the Russian edition of Yuval Noah Hahari's *21 Lessons for the 21st Century* (2018) had whole sections rewritten without the author's knowledge to eliminate criticisms of government behavior. Yet that same government has declared censorship illegal.

* * *

BY 2015 THE LAISSEZ-FAIRE policies of Boris Yeltsin had long been revised by the controlling hand of Vladimir Putin, who took over as prime minister in August 1999[*] and is now in his fourth term as the country's president. His views of his country's recent history were clear. The Soviet Union was the last, not the first, European country to sign a deal with Nazi Germany: Western deals with Hitler were the real disgrace. In September 1939 the Soviet Union did not attack Po-

---

[*] That same year, South Africa, trying to recover from years of apartheid, formed a Truth and Reconciliation Commission, which offered amnesty to government officials and anti-apartheid fighters who came forward to acknowledge past crimes. The commission reflected the government's conviction that national self-understanding was more important than punishing people, and that the uncompromising exposure of historical evils is a prerequisite to national reconciliation. Eric Foner, "'We Must Forget the Past': History in the New South Africa," *Yale Review* 83 (April 1995): 1–17. Germany has also made great efforts to grapple with the events of 1939–45, even coining a word to describe such coming to terms with issues of collective culpability— *vergangheitsbewältigung,* which combines *Vergangenheit* and *Bewältigung* to produce a twenty-three-letter expression that translates as "struggle to overcome the negatives of the past."

land; it merely protected territory abandoned by the collapsed Polish state. And so the defense of Stalin's diplomacy has continued.

From the start, Putin appreciated the effectiveness of historical rhetoric for his nationalist agenda, particularly if it played to popular nostalgia for the Soviet Union, the collapse of which was a humiliation for most Russians. This was a point emphasized by Orlando Figes in a recent article on Putin's approach to controlling the historical record as far as Russians are concerned. As he summarizes their situation: "In a matter of a few months they lost everything—an empire, an ideology, an economic system that had given them security, superpower status, national pride, and an identity forged from Soviet history."

Polls in the year that Putin came to power showed that three-quarters of his people regretted the breakup of the USSR and wanted Russia to win back lost territories such as the Crimea and eastern Ukraine. As Figes argues, they were resentful about being told they should be ashamed of their history. They had been raised on the Soviet myths: the great liberation of the October Revolution, the first five-year plan, the collectivization of agriculture, the defeat of the Trotsky-ites, and Soviet achievements in culture, science, and technology. Why should they feel guilty? Today even Soviet-era secret police uniforms are on sale. Putin promptly created his own version of history, combining Soviet myths (sans their Communist baggage) with stories from the Russian Empire before 1917, and when the centenary of the revolution came his government studiously ignored it.

Recently the Norwegian novelist Karl Ove Knausgaard was commissioned by *The New York Times Magazine* to travel through Russia and report what he found. He concluded:

With each year that passes they try to reduce the significance of 1917. They do this because in their ideal version of events there *was* no revolution! They are trying to establish an unbroken link between the czars and Stalin's Russia. According to the current narrative, foreign spies and traitors provoked us into killing one another a hundred years ago. That must never happen again. Therefore we have to stand together, therefore we must all follow Putin's banner, therefore we must forbid all opposition, therefore we must even sacrifice our civil rights, because it must never happen again.

Putin has not denied Stalin's crimes (on the contrary, on several occasions he has publicly acknowledged them)* but urges that they should be set against Uncle Joe's achievements, above all victory in the Great Patriotic War of 1941–45. It makes for an odd balancing act. In 2015 a gulag museum was opened in Moscow, but most labor camps and mass graves have not been commemorated and are gradually being destroyed or removed. As the Russian emigré Masha Gessen has written, "every museum, indeed every country, ultimately aims to tell a story about the goodness of its people." But Gessen can still talk of a "mafia state ruling over a totalitarian society" without it seeming a gross overstatement.

In June 2007, during a nationally televised conference of high-school teachers in Moscow, Putin grumbled about the confusion he saw in the way that Soviet history was taught and called for well-established criteria. The following then took place:

CONFERENCE PARTICIPANT: In the past two decades, our youth have been subjected to a torrent of the most diverse information about our historical past. This information [contains] different conceptual approaches, interpretations, or value judgments, and even chronologies. In such circumstances, the teacher is likely to . . .

PUTIN (INTERRUPTING): Oh, they will write, all right. You see, many textbooks are written by those who are paid in foreign grants. And naturally they are dancing the polka ordered by those who pay them. Do you understand? And unfortunately [such textbooks] find their way to schools and colleges.

In his concluding speech, Putin told the history teachers:

As to some problematic pages in our history—yes, we've had them. But what state hasn't? And we've had fewer of such pages

---

* Thus, for instance, in November 2010 the long-simmering debate between Moscow and Poland about who should bear responsibility for the massacre of more than twenty thousand prisoners of war by the Soviet secret police in the Katyn forest near Smolensk in 1940 was resolved by the Duma condemning the massacre, which for the first time blamed Stalin for ordering it. The murders were "a crime by the Stalinist regime and the Soviet Union, a totalitarian state. . . ."

than some other [states]. And ours were not as horrible as those of some others. Yes, we have had some terrible pages: let us remember the events beginning in 1937, let us not forget about them. But other countries have had no less, and even more. . . . All sorts of things happen in the history of every state. And we cannot allow ourselves to be saddled with guilt.

Four days after the conference, the Duma introduced a law authorizing the Ministry of Education to decide which textbooks should be published and which used in Russian schools. Not long after, a chapter was added to textbooks about Crimea's glorious return. In theory, competition in the school textbook market exists, but in reality the Kremlin is motivated as much by avarice (an approved book may have print runs of up to a million) as by ideology and has heavily promoted an educational publisher called Enlightenment, whose chairman is a friend and onetime judo partner of Putin's; meanwhile the administration has shut down rival companies or banned competing textbooks. It has also turned out that one of the leading textbooks, *The Modern History of Russia, 1945–2006: A Teacher's Handbook,* had been commissioned by the government itself, which had issued the following guidelines about how authors should evaluate the national leaders of these years:

> Stalin good (strengthened vertical power but no private property); Khrushchev bad (weakened vertical power); Brezhnev good (for the same reasons as Stalin); Gorbachev and Yeltsin bad (both destroyed the country, although under Yeltsin there was at least private property); Putin the preeminent ruler (strengthened vertical power and private property).

According to Figes, the main author was Alexander Filippov, deputy director of a think tank connected to the administration, but the chapter on "sovereign democracy" was written by Pavel Danilin, a Kremlin propagandist reportedly without a history degree or any teaching experience. Danilin explained in an interview:

> Our goal is to make the first textbook in which Russian history will look not as a depressing sequence of misfortunes and mistakes but as something to instill pride in one's country. It is pre-

cisely this way that teachers must teach history and not smear the Motherland with mud.

He also put out a warning on his internet blog to any history teachers unhappy about his message:

You may ooze bile but you will teach the children by those books that you will be given and in the way that is needed by Russia. It is impossible to let some Russophobe shit-stinker (*govnyuk*), or just any amoral type, teach Russian history. It is necessary to clear the filth, and if it does not work, then clear it by force.

The first use of actual violence in the service of Putin's control of history came on December 4, 2008, when masked men from the Russian General Prosecutor's Office forced their way into the St. Petersburg offices of Memorial, a civil rights group that since 1987 has pioneered research into Stalinist repressions. The men confiscated the organization's twelve hard drives containing information on more than fifty thousand victims of repression and other documents from 1917 to the 1960s. In September the following year a Russian historian researching German prisoners of war sent to Arctic gulags was arrested, his apartment searched, and his entire personal archive confiscated. He was told he faced up to four years in jail. Russia's FSB intelligence agency also arrested a police official who had handed over archive material to the professor. A human rights campaigner in the Arkhangelsk region where the gulag was situated commented: "What we are seeing is the rebirth of control over history. The majority of Russians don't have any idea of the scale of Stalin's repression." In January 2018, the Culture Ministry withdrew the distribution license for *The Death of Stalin,* Armando Iannucci's black comedy about the Soviet leader and his immediate circle.

A leading member of Memorial points out that today's power is very rational—it doesn't shut everyone up. "There is freedom of expression and speech. There are shelves of anti-Putin books in the stores." That optimistic view was uttered at the end of 2011, however. Since then, Putin, who doesn't care if his critics think he is "on the wrong side of history," has become ever more intent on a single narrative, controlled by the Kremlin, about what Russia was, which means he will continue to deny the full complexity of its history, molding a collective memory through propaganda, the media, and officially sanctioned books.

In an essay first published in 1990, Eric Foner concluded:

Sometimes . . . history serves mainly to rationalize the status quo. History can degenerate into nostalgia from an imaginary golden age, or inspire a utopian quest to erase the past altogether. And it can force people to think differently about their society by bringing to light unpleasant truths. In today's Soviet Union, it is playing all these roles and more.

But whatever the intentions of Putin's campaign, the current regime's attempt to alter the historical record is hardly realistic. The opening of the archives, the publication of their documents, and the work of organizations like Memorial have made that infeasible. Although the archives are no longer as easy to consult as for a short time they were, they cannot return to their former shut-off state. However, as long as the government promotes self-serving patriotic myths, bad history will continue to be written and propagated.

Yet it cannot prevail, and an incident in Putin's own history suggests why. From 1985 to 1990, he served in the Dresden, East Germany, section of the KGB, stationed at the organization's mansion at 4 Angelikastrasse. From November 9, 1989, on, as the Berlin Wall was being hacked down, the thirty-seven-year-old's job was to feed a raging furnace in the basement of the building with the documentary evidence of Soviet espionage activities. So great was the volume of papers that the furnace eventually broke down.

It is not easy to burn great bundles of paper. There may not be enough air, and it takes time. Thick wads should be machine-compressed, or they will burn too hot and fast and may damage the flue. Thus Putin, along with his colleagues in the Stasi, the East German secret police, were forced to shred many documents, but the few machines they had, of poor East German make, rapidly broke down too, and thousands of papers had to be hastily torn up by hand and stuffed into sacks.

With Germany again united, the government decided to fund an attempt to put all this material together again, some 16,000 sacks containing an estimated 600 million scraps. Forty employees have been painstakingly sorting through the fragments for decades, an exercise in *Aufarbeitung*, a concept that roughly translates as "working through the injustices of the past." "Sometimes you're lucky," says one, "and the documents were only torn in half." Many scraps are not much bigger than a U.S. quarter, and early on it was reckoned that it would take several more decades to produce significant results by hand. The Stasi alone left behind just under seventy miles of paper as well as more than 1.4 million photos, videos, and tape recordings along with an astonishing 39 million index cards in what *Der Spiegel* has dubbed "the horror files." Since 1995, government "puzzlers" have managed to reassemble the contents of just five hundred sacks, around a million pieces of paper, but enough to have named and shamed two high-ranking East German officials who had been secretly recruited by the Stasi. And help is at hand: five years ago a new computer system, an "unshredder," was enlisted. It virtually reconstructs the documents by looking for matching colors, fonts, and torn edges, ruled or plain paper, handwritten or typed; even so, it is reckoned that completing the work will take many years hence.

Not all the truths of the past will be uncovered, but a good number will be. Francis Bacon famously said that truth is the daughter of time, not of authority. Alexandr Solzhenitsyn was once asked what would happen after the end of Soviet Communism. His reply: a long, long period of healing. That would seem the more realistic judgment, so pernicious and enduring is bad history.

CHAPTER 21

THE FIRST DRAFT

Journalists and the Recent Past

—————

Histories . . . are a kind of distilled newspapers.

—THOMAS CARLYLE, 1841

I suppose, in the end, we journalists try—or should try—to be the first impartial witnesses of history. If we have any reason for our existence, the least must be our ability to report history as it happens.

—ROBERT FISK, 2005

SAMUEL PEPYS (1633–1703) WAS AN ENGLISH NAVAL ADMINISTRATOR who sat in Parliament and rose to be secretary to the Admiralty under Charles II and James II, so was witness to a lot of history. The journal he kept, 3,102 pages in the coded original, runs from 1660 until 1669— thus Pepys from age twenty-seven to thirty-six—and ends only because he feared he was going blind from farsightedness and astigmatism, conditions that could have been ameliorated by good eyeglasses, which would have enabled him to continue. Early on he discovered he had a flair for vivid description. Around 1651, he even wrote a novel, or part of one, a romance called *Love a Cheate,* but destroyed the manuscript in a fit of tidiness, or "humour of making all things even and clear in the world." That was never an issue with the diaries. On September 2, 1666, Lords day, he made the following entry:

Some of our maids sitting up late last night to get things ready against our feast today. Jane called us up, about 3 in the morning, to tell us of a great fire they saw in the City. So I rose, and slipped on my nightgown and went to her window, and thought it to be on the back side of Markelane at the furthest; but being unused to such fires as fallowed, I thought it far enough off, and so went to bed again and to sleep.

Hardly the energetic foraging of an adventurous reporter, but so begins Pepys's celebrated record of the fire that raged for five days and destroyed much of the city, including around 1,300 houses, reducing 436 acres to ashes and leaving seventy thousand Londoners homeless. Pepys was at last roused from his bed and, boarding a small boat by St. James's Park, he and his wife watched the town's devastation:

So near to the fire as we could for smoke; and all over the Thames, with one's face in the wind, you were almost burned with a shower of Firedrops. This is very true; so as houses were burned by these drops and flakes of fire, three or four, nay, five or six houses, one from another. When we could endure no more upon the water, we [went] to a little alehouse on the Bankside, over against the Three Cranes, and there stayed till it was dark almost and saw the fire glow. . . . We saw the fire as only one entire arch of fire from this to the other side of the bridge, and in a bow up the hill for an arch of above a mile long; it made me weep to see it.

Later, Pepys returned home and buried a large hunk of Parmesan cheese in his next-door neighbor's garden for safekeeping; as always, we get great events followed by intimate moments. At one level this is a private diary entry, raw evidence for future historians to weigh alongside other accounts—the diary of John Evelyn (1620–1706), for instance: "The stones of Paules flew like Granados, the Lead mealting down the streetes in a streame." At another level, it is far more than that, as is Pepys's account of the Great Plague, which over eighteen months in 1665 and 1666 killed almost a quarter of London's population. In Claire Tomalin's setting phrase, the diary provides "an unequalled record of the events of the time."

Though he was not writing for contemporary publication, Pepys took steps to preserve all he wrote. Apart from carefully transcribing each entry from the notes he made, he also had the pages bound up and must have known that eventually someone would discover them. They were finally decoded and published in the nineteenth century; only the diary of Anne Frank may rival them in influence.*

How to place Pepys as a recorder of events? Journalist, diarist, belle-lettrist, or historian? Such labels do not get us far. One might as well call Herodotus a foreign correspondent or Julius Caesar a war reporter. What is important is how Pepys's times come alive in his record of them. As Robert Latham—editor of the definitive edition of the diaries—has remarked, his accounts, "agonizingly vivid—achieve their effect by being something more than superlative reporting; they are written with compassion. As always with Pepys it is people, not literary effects, that matter."

Authors of journals can protest too much about the intimate nature of their jottings. Many diaries tell us only of private histories, but others, such as Queen Victoria's unflinching description of Prince Albert's death, are more than raw material. Jumping through the centuries, from the secret notes of Procopius (A.D. 500–554) to the diaries of the Labour cabinet member Richard Crossman (1907–74), private records have given us insights that few professional historians have matched. As Jane Austen was well aware, gossip is a real way of knowing. In the late 1980s, I persuaded Tony Benn, the onetime deputy leader of the Labour Party who went on to become its Grand Old Man, to publish diaries he had been writing from his early twenties, and the eleven volumes that appeared, covering 1940 to 1990, are the fullest insight into his party's daily workings that we have. The Italian journalist Oriana Fallaci wrote a diary of her time reporting the war in Vietnam (*Nothing, and So Be It,* 1972) expressly so it could be published, and she is obviously not the only one. Even Anne Frank wrote two versions of

---

* Harold Nicolson, himself a noted diarist, missed most of the point but not all of it when he recorded: "To my mind Pepys was a mean little man. Salacious in a grubby way; even in his peculations there was no magnificence. But he did stick to his office during the Plague, which was more than most men did. It is some relief to reflect that to be a good diarist one must have a little snouty sneaky mind." See Harold Nicolson, *Diaries and Letters, 1945–62* (London: William Collins, 1968), p. 113.

her diary. The first, called either "Kitty" or "diary a," begun on her thirteenth birthday when she received a diary among her gifts and consisting of her original reflections, was intended for herself; the second, called "the Secret Annex," was version b, considerably tidied up, with parts added to, names changed, and sections rewritten (thus more a memoir in the form of diary entries), the one she intended for publication. After the war ended, more than two thousand diaries were collected by the National Office for the History of the Netherlands.

★ ★ ★

DIARIES ARE ONE WAY to write history; recording the previous day's events for a newspaper is another. The day after the Great Fire of 1666 broke out, *The London Gazette,* which had begun publication the year before and had a monopoly of sorts, was seen as the voice of the government (indeed, it was edited by politicians), and the paper's suspiciously abbreviated account of September 3 caused people to fear that the seeming news blackout was part of some cabinet conspiracy, or even a foreign invasion (in fact, the paper's premises had simply been destroyed the first afternoon of the fire).

In Pepys's time, journalism had started up again after being in hibernation for centuries* but in any modern sense was still in its infancy. (Pepys kept a lion cub and an eagle that fouled his house "mightily," but no paper had reached the stage where it would write about *that.*) The concept of a professional newspaperman is relatively recent, even though as long ago as 1495 an enterprising Dutchman called Wynkyn de Worde (his true name) had set up a printing press in London's Fleet Street at "the sign of the Sun" in St. Bride's Churchyard. By 1536 monthly newssheets were appearing in Venice, in manuscript, and were read aloud in certain parts of the city, typically narrating how it was faring in its war against Turkey. To purchase a copy of the newssheet cost a *gazzetta* (about a quarter of a British penny), and over the years the paper took on the name of the coin. In England, at the time of the Spanish Armada, any scrap of news about Francis Drake and

---

* Julius Caesar had encouraged reporters in the first century B.C., and Acta Diurna, the daily journals of the time, came to record even the commonest events. They were written under the direction of the magistrates and placed in Rome's Hall of Liberty. After Caesar's death, the privilege of publishing Acta Diurna was withdrawn, and from then until the early sixteenth century newspapers disappeared.

Martin Frobisher's attempt to defeat the Spanish was eagerly awaited, so the government published a newssheet under the title of *The English Mercurie*. Around the same time, the Fuggers of Augsburg, in southern Germany, a mining and banking family so prominent in western Europe that it took over many of the assets and political connections of the Medici, relied on reports on current affairs from a wide-ranging circuit of correspondents and confidential agents, creating the first modern global news service. Later, in the early eighteenth century, the bishop of Trent sorted and bound various loose manuscripts and gave them the name *Fuggerzeitungen*, "Fugger newsletters," but even late into the century there were no "journalists" as we would currently define the profession.

The public's longing for information was initially fed by newssheets like the *Mercurie* that were a mix of public pronouncements, private letters, even tavern songs, and this led to the establishment of postal routes, private back channels—and yet further newssheets, concentrating on trade reports and stories about politics, sometimes set out in type, sometimes copied by hand. Britain's first daily was the work of a printer, Nathaniel Butter, who in 1608 had published the first quarto of *King Lear*. Sometime in 1620 Butter was imprisoned for issuing a pamphlet claiming that the Holy Roman Emperor, Ferdinand II, had been born of an incestuous relationship. While Butter was in prison, a newssheet arrived in London from the Netherlands, a single folio dated December 2, 1620, and described as a *coranto*, a word associated both with "courier" and "current." The sheet contained a report of the coming battle between Ferdinand II and Frederick V of Bohemia, whose wife was the daughter of James I of England, so there was the prospect of Britain getting involved. As soon as Butter was free again he applied for and was given a license to publish *corantos* of his own, and on September 24, 1621, his first offering, entitled *Coranto, or, News from Italy, Germany, Hungarie, Spaine and France,* went on sale. Printed on one side only, it was just a few short paragraphs—all foreign reports, since as a result of a government order back in 1586 no domestic news could be printed for public circulation.

Butter soon became more ambitious, the following year publishing his *Weekly Newes,* with issues ranging from eight to twenty-four pages, from the start numbering and dating each edition, and introducing headlines and scandalous stories ("The strangling and death of the great *Turke,* and his two sons . . ."). By October 1632 the Privy Council ordered Butter to stop publishing, as the ambassadors of both France and Spain had complained, and the unfortunate printer found himself in prison yet again. He was to die, impoverished, in 1664, but his innovation could not be repressed; indeed, throughout the English Civil War two "newsbooks" were published, *Mercurius Britannicus* in London and *Mercurius Aulicus* in Oxford. They were tendentious and biased but provided a solid background of fact.

Even so, printing the news ("newly received or noteworthy information, especially about recent or important events, and previously not known," as one London journal defined it) was a dangerous business: in 1663, a printer called John Twyn ended up with his head skewered on a pike on East London's Ludgate Hill and his limbs dispersed across the capital's other gates for publishing an innocuous-sounding pamphlet suggesting that citizens should have a larger role in governing. The majority of these early sheets played it safe, their news, according to Jill Lepore, "mostly old, foreign, and unreliable." Some seventeenth-century papers, however, could have graced the pages of the most sensational of present-day tabloids, one typical story running:

> A perfect mermaid was, by the last great wind, driven ashore near Greenwich, with her comb in one hand and her looking glass in the other. She seemed to be of the countenance of a most fair and beautiful woman, with her arms crossed, weeping out many pearly drops of salt tears; and afterwards she, gently turning herself upon her back again, swam away without being seen any more.

Geoffrey of Monmouth couldn't have put it better. Soon other newspapers (a word that entered the English language only in the 1660s) arrived in tandem with that other great boon to literacy, the coffee shop. In 1772, Daniel Defoe published his *A Journal of the Plague Year,* a fictional account of the pandemic of 1664–66 that purported to be a factual record, and declared on his opening page: "We had no such thing as printed newspapers in those days to spread rumours and reports of things, and to improve them by the invention of men, as I have lived to see practiced since." But this was a sheer marketing ploy to boost sales of his account amid all the other plague histories being published. There were newssheets enough, even in Pepys's day.

With the permanent lapsing of censorship in 1695 new publications sprouted up, and by 1712 London alone had twelve different papers, by the mid-1730s thirty-one—six dailies, twelve tri-weeklies, and thirteen weeklies—with a combined weekly circulation of one hundred thousand, each individual copy being read by up to twenty people in the main coffeehouses and taverns. Fleet Street, off the Strand, where many papers had their offices, became known as "Tippling Street." The social commentator Lewis Mumford recorded that "the swish and crackle of paper is the underlying sound of the metropolis."

In 1890 the author John Pendleton published a charming memoir of British journalists entitled *Newspaper Reporting in Olden Times and Today,* capturing the romance of mid-nineteenth-century journalism. It begins with these lines from William Makepeace Thackeray's 1850 novel *The History of Pendennis:*

> They were passing through the Strand as they talked, and by a newspaper office, which was all lighted up and bright. Reporters were coming out of the place, or rushing up to it in cabs; there were lamps burning in the editors' rooms, and above, where the compositors were at work, the windows of the building were in a blaze of gas. . . .
>
> "Look at that, Pen," Warrington [a fellow journalist who befriends Pendennis] said. "There she is—the great engine—she never sleeps. She has her ambassadors in every quarter of the world—her couriers upon every road. Her officers march along with armies, and her envoys walk into statesmen's cabinets. They are ubiquitous. Yonder journal has an agent, at this minute, giving bribes at Madrid; and another inspecting the price of potatoes at Covent Garden; Look, here comes the foreign express galloping in. . . ."

Small wonder that Pendleton dubs the typical journalist of the mid-nineteenth century "the daily historian of the time."

The British enthusiasm for newspapers was mirrored in the United States. Its first paper was *Publick Occurrences, Both Foreign and Domestick,* the opening issue of just three pages published in Boston on September 25, 1690—about six by ten inches in size. It forthrightly proclaimed its aims: "That something may be done towards the Curing, or at least the Charming of that Spirit of Lying which prevails among us, wherefore nothing shall be entered but what we have reason to believe is true." The editor, Benjamin Harris, was a former publisher who had fled England four years before after issuing seditious pamphlets and ending up in jail. Harris soon ran afoul of the New World's authorities too, particularly with gossip about the king of France and a critical account of Native American troop atrocities. Declaring "high Resentment and Disallowance of said Pamphlet," officials ordered the paper be "suppressed and called in," making it America's first to be closed down.

The first paper to be continuously published, *The Boston News-Letter,* arrived in April 1704. During its early years, it dealt mostly with items from London journals detailing English politics and wars in Europe. Otherwise it was filled with bulletins listing ship arrivals, deaths, sermons, political appointments, fires, and accidents. One of its most spectacular stories was of how Blackbeard the pirate had come by his death in hand-to-hand combat on the deck of a frigate that had attacked his own ship. For the new country as a whole, it took some time to figure out what, in a republic, a newspaper was *for,* but by the 1780s there were hundreds of weeklies, and, a decade on, their number was growing four times as fast as the population.

"In the early nineteenth century," writes Nicholas Lemann, from 2003 to 2013 dean of Columbia University's graduate school of journalism, "[Alexis de] Tocqueville treated the new country's proliferating newspapers as a species of 'association,' which functioned as organizing tools to influence politics and government, not as gatherers and purveyors of information." And it is true that for much of their existence—in America, at least—newspapers were funded by political parties and had no pretense of presenting both sides of an issue. That changed around the time Adolph Ochs bought *The New York Times* (1890s) and coined the phrase "without fear or favor." The so-called objective press grew out of two seemingly unrelated developments just before the turn of the century—the streetcar, which brought people into city centers, and department stores, which allowed them to browse for goods in a "democratic" setting and required full-page ads in newspapers to lure them.

In the mid-1890s, the circulation war between Joseph Pulitzer's *New York World* and William Randolph Hearst's *New York Journal* gave rise to the phrase "yellow journalism"* (some articles appeared in yellow ink) to describe the sensational reports both papers resorted to in the scramble for readers. The most lurid stories tended to be on the domestic front, but foreign news was also presented in the most dramatic terms possible.

At first, overseas reports consisted of unpaid letter-writers from abroad. Newspapers were also dependent on appropriating stories from foreign journals, their staff rushing to collect valuable copy from ships new into port. Oddly, despite there being no editors, and certainly no reporters, newspapers printed a greater percentage of foreign news than at any time since, an overseas story frequently taking up the entire front page.

Beginning in the early nineteenth century, however, a new kind of contributor emerged, the special correspondent—men such as Henry Crabb Robinson (1775–1867), Coleridge's good friend and the first Briton to be based abroad specifically as a foreign correspondent, reporting on Napoleon's campaigns in Spain and Germany for *The Times* of London; George Wilkins Kendall of the New Orleans *Picayune,* who covered the 1846 Mexican War; Henry Morton Stanley, who (after somehow having managed to fight on both sides in the American Civil War) in 1871 found Dr. David Livingstone for the *New York Herald;* and George Smalley of the *New-York Tribune,* who became famous for organizing teams of reporters.

* * *

PERHAPS THE JOURNALIST WHOSE writing most influenced history as well as recording it was the *Times* foreign correspondent William

---

* Erwin Wardman, the editor of the *New York Press,* was the first to give the term a public airing. He never defined it at all precisely; it may have evolved from an earlier smear campaign where he had transposed "new journalism" into "nude journalism." Wardman had also used the phrase "yellow kid journalism," a reference to *Hogan's Alley,* a comic strip about a bald child in a yellow nightshirt which both papers ran. Horace White, another revered American journalist (most notably, at the *Chicago Tribune*), tried to be more specific: "This phrase is applied to newspapers which delight in sensations, crime, scandal, smut, funny pictures, caricatures and malicious or frivolous gossip about persons and things of no public concern." Nicholas Lemann, "Can Journalism Be Saved?" *The New York Review of Books,* February 27, 2020, p. 39. It was newspaper writing such as this that is said to have prompted Søren Kierkegaard (1813–55) to comment: "If my daughter became a prostitute, I would never give up hope. . . . But if my son became a journalist and remained one for three years, I would give him up as lost."

Howard Russell (1820–1907). Russell's reputation was made during the twenty-two months he spent covering the Crimean War, which raged from October 1853 to February 1856 and ended with Russia losing to an alliance of the Ottoman Empire, France, Britain, and Sardinia. His dispatches covered the Charge of the Light Brigade and the Siege of Sevastopol, during which he coined the phrase "the thin red line" to describe the British troops. Florence Nightingale would tell how she became a wartime nurse from reading his reports.

The best account of Russell's career is by John Simpson (b. 1944), himself an outstanding correspondent for fifty years with the BBC while for much of that time also working as *The Spectator's* foreign editor; on top of which he is the author of sixteen books (four fiction), mainly drawing on his time as a reporter. He provides a succinct and appealing history of the opening years of foreign correspondents in *News from No Man's Land* and *We Choose to Speak of War and Strife.**

Simpson begins by describing Russell as "one of the finest journalists who ever wrote a dispatch; yet he had no training whatever for the job." Born outside Dublin in 1820 into "a mildly disorganized, perpetually hard-up middle-class" family, Russell went to Trinity College in Dublin and emerged with no clear idea what to do next; he even thought to enlist in the army but was persuaded out of it by his grandfather. As Max Hastings describes him in somewhat Olympian tones, "he seems to have been a rumbustious, cheerfully combative young man, prone to the usual range of adolescent enthusiasm for whiskey and modest riot." A cousin who worked for *The Times* was sent to Ireland to cover elections in the capital and, realizing he was shorthanded, hired Russell to help him; and so a career was born. The neophyte journalist arrived late for his first assignment, to cover a local riot, but, thinking imaginatively, went to the local hospital to check the casualties coming in from political meetings across the city. The report he filed was dramatic enough to land him a job at *The Times* in London as

---

* In 1989 I asked Simpson to write about the events of that year, from the breaching of the Berlin Wall through the fall of Nicolae Ceauşescu in Romania and ending with the release of Nelson Mandela on February 11, 1990. The resultant book, *Despatches from the Barricades,* was published just six weeks after Mandela walked free. During its production, John asked that his name on the cover be made smaller—the only time any author has asked me that. Years later, we were having tea together, and I noticed he was shifting uncomfortably in his seat. He explained that his buttocks (I wonder what word he would have used on air) contained shrapnel fragments from one of his war reporting adventures. He was never comfortable sitting still.

a parliamentary reporter, and he started there in 1842. He discovered that he was paid only when Parliament was in session, so he supplemented his earnings by enlisting as a part-time barrister. For a while he even forsook *The Times* to work for a higher salary (he had just married) for *The Morning Chronicle,* covering the Irish potato famine.

Somewhat to his surprise, *The Times* reclaimed him, and his first overseas posting came in July 1850 when he was sent to report on a brief military conflict between Prussian and Danish troops, receiving a slight flesh wound for his troubles. Then in 1854 his editor sent him to Malta; the government, wanting to show its support for France and Turkey in their dispute with Russia over who controlled sites in the Holy Land, deployed an army unit to the island to make its point. The crisis escalated, and Russell moved on to Gallipoli, filing a report criticizing the poor medical facilities for the troops. In the mid-nineteenth century *The Times* enjoyed unique prestige, and Russell was authorized to accompany the expeditionary force as far as the Mediterranean. At that point, the British commander, Lord Raglan, refused to give any of the press official recognition or help them in any way.

Russell, however—in Simpson's account, "charming, funny and without any form of snobbery"—was welcomed by the regular soldiers, and even eventually by the generals. His first notable dispatches were from Bulgaria (where the troops broke off their advance), reporting a cholera epidemic and the medical staff's complete inadequacy in confronting it. Nothing he wrote was spiteful or unfair (he passionately wanted Britain to succeed), but it was incendiary. He praised Raglan's courage and industry but gave example after example of the commander's inability to manage a large army: Raglan himself scarcely disagreed with the verdict but still longed to send him packing.

Russell sympathized with the sick and injured on both sides, and his reports—one of them written in an account book seized from a Russian corpse—detailed the sufferings of the Turks, Russians, and French, not just the British. He wrote with real insight, providing facts that no one else reported in narratives full of precise detail more compelling than any other journalist was filing. And *The Times* gave him plenty of space. Most of his letters—he was, literally, a correspondent—appeared in the paper two to three weeks after he sent them, and sometimes five or six reports would appear on the same day. Of the early stages of the war, he later admitted, "I did not then grasp the fact that I had it in my power to give a halo of glory to some unknown warrior by putting his name in type." He became completely accepted by the troops with whom he mingled. A foot soldier in the Crimea described him as "a vulgar low Irishman" who "sings a good song, drinks anyone's brandy and water and smokes as many cigars as a Jolly Good Fellow. He is just the sort of chap to get information, particularly out of youngsters." Although he despised the term *war correspondent,* Russell almost single-handedly invented what such a reporter should be. And he was telling his readers a story as had never before been brought back from any battlefield to any newspaper.

In October 1854, at Balaclava (near Sevastopol on the Black Sea), he watched the Charge of the Light Brigade from a ridge above the battle-field. As soon as it was over, he rode down to talk to survivors, going from tent to tent to find out what had happened. He remained in the field longer than any other correspondent. Eventually he returned to his tent back at headquarters, with a splitting headache and having eaten nothing all day. The "heart-stricken spectator" then sat down on his horse's saddle (there were no chairs) and typed out four thousand words, "the biggest story of his entire career." The dispatch took nine-teen days to reach London, and appeared on page seven, the main news page, under the headline: "The War in the Crimea," bylined simply "From Our Special Correspondent." It began:

> If the exhibition of the most brilliant valour, of the excess of courage, and of a daring which would have reflected lustre on the best days of chivalry can afford full consolation for the disas-ter of today, we can have no reason to regret the melancholy loss which we sustained in a contest with a savage and barbarian enemy.

Russell went on to explain that the charge was made against enemy guns without support of infantry. "We could hardly believe the evi-dence of our senses! Surely that handful of men are [*sic*] not going to charge an army in position!" But so they did, sweeping forward in two long lines, going faster and faster as they approached the Russians:

> At the distance of 1,200 yards the whole line of the enemy belched forth, from thirty iron mouths, a flood of smoke and

flame, through which hissed the deadly balls. Their flight was marked by instant gaps in our ranks, by dead men and horses, by steeds flying wounded or riderless across the plain. The first line is broken, it is joined by the second, they never halt or check their speed for an instant; with diminished ranks, thinned by those thirty guns, which the Russians had laid with the most deadly accuracy, with a halo of steel above their heads, and with a cheer which was many a noble fellow's death-cry, they flew into the smoke of the batteries, but ere they were lost to view the plain was strewn with their bodies and with the carcasses of horses.

At his home in Lincolnshire, Alfred Tennyson read the dispatch and reshaped its details (from "a mile and a half" into "Half a league, half a league, half a league onward") into one of the most recited poems in the English language. Even without Tennyson's help, Russell's reputation was set for life. His dispatches marked the first time that the British public could read what war was really like, and such was the outrage that the government was forced to reevaluate its treatment of troops and Florence Nightingale was inspired to revolutionize battlefield care. A fellow journalist working for *The Daily News* reckoned that Russell's reports "brought home to the War Office the fact that the public had something to say about the conduct of wars, that they were not the concern exclusively of sovereigns and statesmen." His articles were read aloud in the House of Commons and did much to bring down the government early in 1855. Russell was being hailed as "the most famous newspaper correspondent the world has ever seen," probably with more influence than any journalist before or since.

He remained in the Crimea (where Tolstoy was a fellow correspondent) until the last British soldier departed, sailing for home in July 1856. Just ten days after returning in triumph, he packed up again to cover the coronation of Tsar Alexander II in Moscow, to be followed by stints that included the Indian Mutiny (1858) and the Austro-Prussian (1866) and Franco-Prussian wars (1870–71). Through 1861–63 he was in America, reporting on its civil war, for £1,200 a year plus expenses, with the new president Abraham Lincoln receiving him with, "The London *Times* is one of the greatest powers in the world. In fact, I don't know anything which has more power—except perhaps the Mississippi." He was not immune to flattery, he drank too much and was a showoff ("overeating and excessive drinking were his chief vices," confirms Amanda Foreman), but his reports were unclouded by laziness or by nationalism. Often he ran so late with his dispatches that he nearly missed the mailbag; twice during the Civil War envelopes containing his copy had to be stuck on the outside of bags already sealed and about to head on their way.

The Times had declared its support for the secession of the South while Russell was sailing across the Atlantic on his way to America, but he was soon to reveal to readers how much he loathed slavery and told his editor that he was unwilling to report on the Southern side (later, on another wartime assignment, he refused to stay with the Prussians when they besieged Paris, because he thought their behavior barbaric). He was in Baltimore, during a tour he made of the South, when news came of the fall of Fort Sumter, heralding the outbreak of hostilities.

Caricature of William Howard Russell from Punch *magazine, 1881.*

His account of the headlong flight of the Union Army after the First Battle of Bull Run led to his suffering a torrent of animosity (even as army officers agreed to the accuracy of all he had written) and he found himself excoriated by both sides. Depressed, he returned home in April 1863, leaving others to write about the war.

Even so, he never seemed to stop. He took over the editorship of *The Army and Navy Gazette,* holding the post till 1903; published a novel, *The Adventures of Doctor Brady;* and kept reporting on a whole range of subjects—an attempt to lay a transatlantic cable, the marriage of the Prince of Wales (who became a lifelong friend), the Austro-Prussian War, the later stages of the 1879 Anglo-Zulu War (this time for *The Daily Telegraph*), and the Paris Exposition of 1889. By his early forties he may have been "a vain, middle-aged man with a cocked nose, blue eyes, grizzled hair, and a double chin," but his carefully composed "first drafts" had as lasting an influence as anything written by his contemporaries. As the esteemed foreign correspondent Patrick Cockburn has written, "Journalists are sometimes patronisingly congratulated for providing 'the first draft of history,' though often the first draft is better than the last. There is [a] credibility about eyewitness reporting before it has been through the blender of received wisdom and academic interpretation."

* * *

THAT PHRASE ABOUT JOURNALISM being the first draft of history has been variously attributed (in fact, the coinage was employed by several writers as early as 1905),* yet whatever the provenance the notion that journalists are writing a form of history has endured, even as its value remains uncertain. The notion arose at a particular time when so-called

---

* For years it was thought the author was *The Washington Post*'s publisher, Philip L. Graham (1915–63), but long before him an article of December 5, 1905, in *The State* in Columbia, South Carolina, uses it. "What is 'news' today will be history tomorrow," it began. "No one would be bold enough to deny that history is one of the most essential branches of modern education, yet the proposition that the study of the news of the day is of equal value, is, indeed, but a part of the study of history, would probably be challenged by many. Those who value history as a study cannot consistently, however, deny to the study of news an equal value, for it is plainly apparent that the happenings of today are but the progress of history. . . . If the 'news' as it is published is so inaccurate, so untrustworthy, how does it happen that it stands the fiery ordeal of time and historic investigation? The newspapers of this morning . . . will some day be eagerly sought in libraries as the foundation of the history of the wonderful year 1905. The newspapers are making morning after morning the rough draft of history."

objective journalism was in its ascendancy and the profession wanted to dress itself up in a finer suit of clothes. Either way, it is history making—or history recording.

When Russell was writing, readers of *The Times* and the *Telegraph* hung on his words. And the public's appetite for news was insatiable. By the 1880s, Britain had fifteen morning papers, nine evening, and 383 weeklies, of which fifty were local to London. Yet in 1894, Charles A. Dana, editor of *The New York Sun,* who early in his career was a correspondent on Horace Greeley's *New-York Tribune,* pointedly noted the "comparatively new" profession of journalism, even as foreign correspondence was embarking on its glory days.

Journalism of that period is well captured in an entry from the *Chicago Tribune*'s 1928 encyclopedia: "If to this business of getting out a great daily newspaper there still clings any of the aura of romance which once surrounded all newspapers and all newspapermen, it is the foreign correspondents who get the greater share of it." The news— two world wars, Communist revolutions, the emergence of global interdependence—was of towering significance. It was journalists in the field who first told not just of the Light Brigade's charge, but in the years to come the My Lai massacre and the 2014 Ebola epidemic in West Africa.

These were newspapermen (rarely women), not at first TV journalists. For a decade after its founding in 1922, the BBC held that news was best left to newspapers; as the *Guardian* journalist Ian Jack notes, the role of the radio news bulletin was to encourage people to buy newpapers, and one broadcast even began: "Good evening. Today is Good Friday. There is no news." By the mid-1930s, however, the BBC had set up a small news department (but employed no reporters), and it was a BBC reporter (Richard Dimbleby) who covered, on air, Chamberlain's fateful return from Munich in 1938. The game was afoot.

For most of the twentieth century, the reputation of correspondents was unsurpassed, and star journalists would follow up their daily reports with books on the same subjects they had been covering for their papers. Some enterprising writers ignored newspapers and set to work researching books at once. Most famous of these is Eric Blair (1903–50). He was born with a silver pen in his mouth; his great-grandmother was the daughter of the Earl of Westmorland, and his father worked for the Indian Civil Service, in the Opium Department. After a term at Wellington College ("beastly"), he went on to Eton, which unexpectedly he rather enjoyed (he was taught French by Aldous Huxley). His parents lacked the money to send him to university, so he enrolled in what would become the Indian Police Service, choosing to be sent to Burma, to a backwoods area where he was responsible for some two hundred thousand people; he also acquired a mustache and tattoos on his knuckles, not his choice but traditionally done, he was told, "to protect against bullets and snakebites." He was to draw on his time there for his essays "A Hanging" and "Shooting an Elephant." ("Of course he shot the fucking elephant," his second wife, Sonia, was to remark.)

Back in London, he began to investigate the deprived areas of the capital, and for a period went native, dressing as a (somewhat unconvincing) tramp. He recorded his experiences in "The Spike," his first published essay in English, and also in his first book, *Down and Out in Paris and London* (1933). In 1928 he had moved to a working-class district of Paris and began to write novels, although he was more successful as a journalist. *Le Progrès Civique,* a left-wing paper, accepted three of his pieces, dealing, respectively, with unemployment, twenty-four hours in the life of a tramp, and the beggars of London. Poverty was to become Blair's consuming subject—central to everything he wrote until his book on the Spanish Civil War.

At the end of 1929, after nearly two years in Paris, Blair returned to his parents' house, set in a coastal town in Suffolk. It was to be his home for the next five years, while he wrote reviews and worked as a private tutor. "Here was he, supposedly a 'writer,' and he couldn't even 'write!'" he was to bemoan in his autobiographical novel *Keep the Aspidistra Flying* (1936). He didn't look like a rakish reporter. One acquaintance dubbed him "Laurel," after Stan Laurel the comedian, and generally he was seen as a figure of fun. "He was awfully likely to knock things off tables, trip over things," said a friend. Stephen Spender described him as having real entertainment value "like . . . watching a Charlie Chaplin movie." Unbowed, he continued to mix teaching with forays up to London, where he would explore its seamier side, on one occasion deliberately getting himself arrested so that he could write about Christmas in jail (after two days in a cell he was ingloriously set free). David Taylor, one of his biographers, notes: "Practically everyone was agreed on the faint air of 'unreality' that Orwell [Blair] carried around with him, his bouts of abstraction."

By 1932 Blair had finished *A Scullion's Diary,* as *Down and Out* was first called. T. S. Eliot rejected it for Faber and Faber ("We have no conviction . . . that this is the right point of view from which to criticize the political situation at the present time"), but Victor Gollancz, a German immigrant who in 1927 had formed his own publishing company, offered an advance of £40 (a little over $7,500 now, so not inconsiderable). Blair decided not to publish under his own name, to avoid his time as a tramp embarrassing his family, but at first left the choice of pseudonym to Gollancz, although he put forward P. S. Burton (which he had used when tramping), Kenneth Miles, H. Lewis Allways, and George Orwell, all conjured from his imagination. That last suggestion won the day because Blair felt it was "a good round English name." *Down and Out* appeared in 1933 and was moderately successful. When Gollancz turned down his next effort, *Burmese Days,* fearing potential libel suits, Blair was disheartened, and although Harper & Brothers took on the book in the United States, he decided to turn in earnest to fiction.

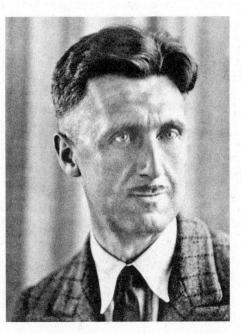

George Orwell in the 1940s. An article in The Guardian *on May 6, 2017, was headlined, "George Orwell's Spanish civil war memoir is a classic, but is it bad history?" It argued that he provided only a partial, partisan version, yet also acknowledged that, "for many thousands of people,* Homage to Catalonia *is the only book on the Spanish civil war that they will ever read."*

He was to publish six novels in all, including *Animal Farm* (1945)[*] and *Nineteen Eighty-Four* (1949; British advance £300), but there were to be two further works of reporting. Gollancz had suggested that Orwell spend time looking into conditions in economically depressed northern England. This led to *The Road to Wigan Pier* (1937), Orwell's classic survey of working life in industrial Lancashire and Yorkshire.[†] He spent February 1936 in lodgings over a Wigan tripe shop, visiting homes to witness how people lived, and researching housing conditions and wages. He also ventured down a local coal mine and consulted public health records. He went on to visit Liverpool, South Yorkshire, and Barnsley, attending meetings that ranged from Communist Party enclaves to rallies for the fascist Oswald Mosley. (Such research led to his being put under surveillance by the Special Branch—for twelve years.) Gollancz himself contributed a foreword.

Finally, during a burst of creative writing that embraced nonfiction, fiction, and essays totaling some two million words, Orwell wrote *Homage to Catalonia* (1938), a first-person account of his six months fighting for the Republicans in the Spanish Civil War containing an uncensored view of what he saw of Communism in action. (Gollancz, a Communist fellow traveler, would refuse to publish the book.) "I've come to fight against Fascism," he told a compatriot early in 1937. With his Eton cadet corps and Burmese police training, in a matter of days he was made a corporal, although he quickly became disenchanted with the distortions of the Communist press. After spending time in Barcelona, instead of joining the Interna-

---

[*] In a telling article in *The New York Times,* Laurence Zuckerman records how the book has fared since: "Many people remember reading George Orwell's *Animal Farm* in high school or college, with its chilling finale in which the farm animals looked back and forth at the tyrannical pigs and the exploitative human farmers but found it impossible to say which was which. That ending was altered in the 1955 animated version, which removed the humans, leaving only the nasty pigs." The film's undisclosed producer was the Central Intelligence Agency, which worried that Orwell's critique of both the capitalist humans and Communist pigs might have an unhealthy effect on audiences. After Orwell's death in 1950, agents were dispatched to buy the film rights from his widow so that its message could be made more overtly anti-Communist. Laurence Zuckerman, "How the C.I.A. Played Dirty Tricks with Culture," *The New York Times,* March 18, 2000.

[†] In a 1943 interview, Orwell explained that the "pier" itself was long gone: "At one time, on one of the little muddy canals that run round the town, there used to be a tumble-down wooden jetty; and by way of a joke someone nicknamed this Wigan Pier. The joke caught on locally, and then the music-hall comedians get hold of it, and they are the ones who have succeeded in keeping Wigan Pier alive as a by-word."

tional Brigades, as he had originally planned, he decided to return to the front in the Aragon Mountains. Hugh Thomas, who wrote an authoritative history of the conflict, describes Orwell's account as a book about war in general rather than about the Spanish Civil War, but that is unfairly limiting, and Thomas went on to admit that he had gotten more out of *Homage to Catalonia* than all the academic works he consulted.

"No one who was in Barcelona then, or for months later, will forget the horrible atmosphere produced by fear, suspicion, hatred, censored newspapers, crammed jails, enormous food-queues and prowling gangs of armed men," Orwell wrote, aiming at immediacy rather than an overview of the conflict. The dangers were real enough; he was shot in the throat by a sniper and was lucky to survive, and his association with POUM (the Workers' Party of Marxist Unification) put him on the authorities' wanted list. The police in Barcelona ransacked the hotel room where he and his first wife Eileen were staying, but they allowed her to stretch out undisturbed on her bed as they searched, thereby overlooking the two passports stuffed under the mattress. The Orwells thus had the papers they needed to escape by train into France and back to England. They returned to Wallington, where Orwell became the proud owner of several goats, a rooster called Henry Ford, and a poodle puppy christened Marx. He settled down to homestead duties and writing up his experiences in Spain.

Because of the fame of his two best-known novels and his groundbreaking essays, Orwell is not usually considered a historian, but his three works of contemporary reporting have been more read than any other work of English social history of the period or any personal account of revolutionary Spain.* Even the original seed for *Nineteen Eighty-Four* lay in the Spanish Civil War. Orwell imagined that the Soviet Communists shared "the same objective" of fighting fascism. Instead, he "witnessed the communist media's rewriting of history"—an

---

* I am tempted to include Mark Twain as a writer who has influenced our ideas about the past. As a novelist he surely has, but as a reporter much less so, despite travel books like *The Innocents Abroad* (1869), *Roughing It* (1872), and *Life on the Mississippi* (1883). Yet he was acutely interested in the past, and instigated a history game with his family, "Mark Twain's Memory-Builder," in which, having knocked pegs into the driveway of his Hartford, Connecticut, home that measured years in feet, he would test his daughters on whether they could see the Norman Conquest at the base of the driveway or Victoria's reign up near his study.

experience that convinced him that tyranny is always opposed to "objective truth."

* * *

DURING THE SECOND WORLD WAR Orwell broadcast regularly for the BBC ("where I wrote enough rubbish . . . to fill a shelf of books"), but the radio reporting of the war years was chiefly memorable for the "glory days" of Edward R. Murrow (1908–65), notably his broadcasts from London during the Blitz. To quote Patrick Cockburn again, "Of course, there may be a certain *déformation professionnelle* involved in the reporting of wars. When doing so in Afghanistan, Syria, Libya or Iraq, it is difficult not to convince oneself of the significance of whatever skirmish one is describing. This failing is almost impossible to avoid, because everybody is prone to exaggerate the importance of an event in which others are being killed." That may be true of present-day reporting, but it is hard to undervalue the nightly contributions of such American radio commentators as Murrow, working for CBS. During the war he recruited a team of correspondents in six European capitals and made a point of "meaning, not speed." They were known as "the Murrow Boys," including the future historian William L. Shirer and, despite their nickname, one woman, Mary Marvin Breckinridge. Murrow, with his signature introductory and signoff phrases, "*This* is London" and "Good night, and good luck," and his courage in broadcasting through falling bombs, had an enormous impact, as did his team, described by Harrison Salisbury as "the finest news staff anybody had ever put together in Europe." Murrow's broadcasts during the worst bombing raids could be surprisingly reminiscent of Pepys's description of the Great Fire of London:

> The fires up the river had turned the moon blood red. The smoke had drifted on till it formed a canopy over the Thames; the guns were working all around us, the bursts looking like fireflies in a southern summer night. The Germans were sending in two or three planes at a time, sometimes only one, in relays. They would pass overhead. The guns and lights would follow them, and in about five minutes we could hear the hollow grunt of the bombs. Huge pear-shaped bursts of flame would rise up into the smoke and disappear. The world was upside down.

Radio, invented in 1912, was a powerful new way to convey history, whether reports on events only a few minutes old, in the Pepys fashion (Ken Burns calls this "the specific gravity of journalism," or "near-history"), or more considered broadcasts, marinated in time and by perspective. Even so, Murrow and the other leading journalists were constantly frustrated by management interference. In Murrow's case, CBS News staff in Washington, D.C., or New York constantly sought editorial control of overseas news, and once World War II was over the in-depth coverage that Murrow provided was largely ignored.

Writing for newspapers could be just as frustrating. "The bigger and richer and more powerful the journalistic institution the more bureaucratic its way of dealing with its own best people, the more distant and aloof its management," recalled David Halberstam in *The Powers That Be*. In 1952, Graham Greene was a foreign correspondent in French Indochina. In 1955 he wrote a novel about the war there, *The Quiet American,* in which he explains that every story he sent in had to be cleared by French censors before the telegraph operator would pass his piece on; when it arrived in Britain, the copy then had to be OK'd by government censors before it could be delivered to his newspaper. Finally, the editor "fixed" the story to fit the paper's position on the war. Greene wrote that he could tell the truth about what he was experiencing only in his novel; his newspaper stories were so much fiction.

There were many other notable foreign correspondents both before and after Greene, of course—Winston Churchill, for example, or Martha Gellhorn (1908–98), whose reporting talents eclipsed those of her husband, Ernest Hemingway, and which she exercised until well into her eighties, traveling to report on the U.S. invasion of Panama in 1989 and poverty in Brazil in 1995.* Earlier she had covered the "evil stupidity" of nations at war—the Spanish Civil War, the Second World War (her 1940 novel *A Stricken Field* contains, among its other qualities, a brilliant re-creation of war-torn Prague), the Six-Day War, and the

---

* In 1992, as program director for the Cheltenham Festival of Literature, I invited Gellhorn to join John Simpson and Max Hastings to discuss war reporting. Gellhorn and Simpson became fast friends. I also took to visiting her for evenings at her London apartment, where I would drink wine while she consumed a bottle of whiskey. One night in 1997 I took her to the Royal Geographical Society to hear Tom Stoppard talk about his play *The Invention of Love*. By that time she had great difficulty in seeing, so we sat in the front row, only a few feet from the platform. Twenty minutes in, she stretched into the Gladstone bag she had brought with her and removed a huge pair of binoculars, which she trained unerringly on Stoppard, for a memorable moment stopping him in his tracks.

expansive war in Vietnam, Laos, and Cambodia that raged from November 1, 1955, until the fall of Saigon on April 30, 1975. "I have witnessed modern war in nine countries," she wrote in an extraordinary report in January 1967, "but I have never seen a war like the one in South Vietnam."

Journalists will get things wrong, all the more likely given that they are writing under pressure of a deadline. Missiles are being fired at them from every direction, and they manage to spot one or two. Writing about events as they occur is categorically different than looking back at them with the luxury of many sources and the knowledge of the end result.* "It is a difficult business," John Simpson admitted in his book about the tumultuous happenings of 1989, "writing about events which have only just taken place." He also noted, "There were times when it was harder to understand what was going on, when being on the spot, than by reflecting on events in the peace of one's own home, reading the newspapers and watching the news on television."

This must have seemed particularly true of so complex and drawn-out a conflict as the war in Vietnam, but several journalists, mainly but not exclusively American, first reported events as they happened, then in their books proffered second and third drafts of history. As William Hammond has noted in his recollections as a journalist, the tools and access available to correspondents increased greatly during these years. Innovations such as cheap and reliable handheld color video cameras and the proliferation of television sets in Western homes allowed him and his colleagues to portray conditions more vividly and accurately than ever before. Additionally, the U.S. military allowed unparalleled access for journalists. Reporters exceeded four hundred at the height of the war (sixty-eight would be killed before the conflict finally wound down). It has been said that perhaps the one plus to emerge

---

* The *New York Times* journalist Herbert Matthews (1900–77), for instance, in February 1957 sought out Fidel Castro in his mountain retreat and came back to report that Castro was a lot of things, none of them Communist: "[His] program is vague and couched in generalities, but it amounts to a new deal for Cuba, radical, democratic, and therefore anti-Communist." This mistake was recalled years later during a Cuban parade down New York's Fifth Avenue in which marchers carried a banner reading: "Castro. I got my job through *The New York Times*." Another infamous error of judgment was perpetrated by the *New York Times* journalist Walter Duranty, who won a Pulitzer in 1932 for his coverage of the Soviet Union but overlooked both the famine in Ukraine and the fact that Stalin was on his way to becoming the second biggest mass murderer of the twentieth century. To this day the Pulitzer committee has to fend off demands to withdraw his award.

from the debacle is a body of literature unsurpassed by the prose writing from any other war (poetry is a different matter); works of fiction such as *A Rumor of War* (1977) by Philip Caputo, *Fields of Fire* (1978) by James Webb, and Tim O'Brien's *Going After Cacciato* (1979) and *The Things They Carried* (1990). The 1960s and 1970s are seen as the "golden age" of journalism. Seven nonfiction writers were particularly notable for their histories: the Americans Stanley Karnow, Frances FitzGerald,

Virginia Cowles and Martha Gellhorn (both center), two Second World War correspondents who after the war wrote a play, Love Goes to Press, *about two journalists, seconded to a press camp in the Italian countryside during 1944, who are beautiful, witty, talented, and better at their job than their male counterparts.*

David Halberstam, Gloria Emerson, Michael Herr, and Neil Sheehan and the British author Max Hastings.*

Probably the most influential history of the war of its time is by Stanley Karnow. Early in his career he was based in Paris as a correspondent for *Time*, then in 1958 was assigned to Hong Kong as bureau chief

---

* One aspect of *The New York Times*'s roster of reporters is that for years it assigned correspondents for a limited three-year tour, not wanting "experts" in the area (unlike, say, the broadsheet British papers). They wanted instead curious, skeptical reporters who had a good general knowledge but would not indulge in inside stories of limited interest to their readers. A person who came upon a new assignment with a fresh eye would notice (so the thinking went) aspects of a country that experts might gloss over. Today, in a time of financial constraints, the three-year limit is no more.

for Southeast Asia. Within a few weeks he had arrived in Vietnam at a time when the American presence was still minimal. The following year, he reported on the first two American deaths in Vietnam, and over two decades he would cover the conflict for *Time, The Washington Post,* and five other news organizations. As his obituary in *The New York Times* in 2013 noted, he interviewed fighters, villagers, refugees, North and South political leaders, the French, and the Americans, researching a people and a war poorly understood until he drew upon these experiences for *Vietnam: A History,* published in 1983. It coincided with a thirteen-part PBS documentary series that won six Emmys, a Peabody, and a Polk and was the highest-rated documentary at the time for public television, with an average of 9.7 million viewers per episode. Like Frances FitzGerald, Karnow also appeared on Nixon's "enemies list."

Karnow's other books included *Mao and China,* which in 1973 received a National Book Award nomination; *In Our Image: America's Empire in the Philippines* (1989); and *Paris in the Fifties,* a memoir published in 1997. As his obituary in the *Los Angeles Times* noted, "He was known for his precision and research—his Vietnam book reaches back to ancient times—and his willingness to see past his own beliefs." Over the years, other journalists who have turned their field reports into successful books have shared those gifts. Max Hastings, who published his account of the Vietnam War in 2018, using many of his own experiences, was asked what the best part of being a military historian was. "The compliments I have valued most," he replied, "have been from veterans who say, 'Yes, that's how it was, how it really felt.' "

Day-to-day reporters grasp that touchstone more easily than most academic historians, but there is a downside. Now, in the new social media landscape, people are not just writing on a twenty-four-hour cycle but on a deadline-this-very-minute routine, which reduces time for reflection and turns journalists into little more than town criers. They are also writing in a polarized society, so the notion of "objective" reporting is under attack. The generally shared antiwar beliefs of the reporters writing about Vietnam makes one wonder whether journalists are capable of being impartial. "There is no such thing as Objective Journalism," was Hunter S. Thompson's opinion. "The phrase itself is a pompous contradiction in terms." But that view is too extreme. When a reporter's goal is to be as objective as possible and that goal is joined with writerly craft, one can get pretty close to the truth. What one needs is time to judge that truth in the cold cast of thought.

* * *

JOURNALISTS QUESTION WITNESSES, ONLOOKERS, victims, perpetrators, survivors. Citing the words of those at the center of stories is their stock in trade. As quotations expand, they can take on a life of their own, and with the evolution of recording devices a new kind of testament emerges: oral history. In 1997, the Supreme Court of Canada ruled that such histories were just as important as written testimony, and around the world historians have endorsed that finding. Many universities now boast oral history programs.

Preeminent among current oral historians is the winner of the 2015 Nobel Prize for Literature, Svetlana Alexievich (b. 1948). Until she won the prize she was little known outside Belarus and the former Soviet Union, although she had published several books in English, among them *The Unwomanly Face of War* (1985); *Chernobyl Prayer: A Chronicle of the Future* (1997); and *Zinky Boys: Soviet Voices from the Afghanistan War* (1990), made up of interviews she carried out with soldiers and their widows and mothers about the war of 1979–90 (the title refers to the sealed caskets made of zinc in which dead soldiers were returned home). These were soon joined by *Secondhand Time: The Last of the Soviets* (2013), a wide-ranging review of people whose lives had been affected by the Soviet Union's collapse, based on interviews conducted between 1991 and 2012. In 2019 an English version of an earlier book appeared, *Last Witnesses: An Oral History of the Children of World War II,* thirty-four years after its Belarussian edition was published.

In 1976, four years after graduating from university in Belarus, Alexievich became a correspondent for the Minsk literary magazine *Neman* and started to specialize in narratives based on witness testimonies. She has stated that she has spent most of her writing life asking one big and very Russian question—why doesn't people's suffering translate into freedom?

Her books owe much to the ideas of a fellow Belarusian writer, Ales Adamovich (1927–94), who felt that the best way to describe the horrors of the twentieth century was not by putting them into a novel, where they might be seen as made up, but through recording real-life testimonies. His documentary novel *I'm from the Burned Village,* about villages burned by German troops during the World War II occupation of Belarus, was the main influence on Alexievich's writing—a style that's been called a "collective novel"—that weaves together several narratives, often from first-person points of view. "Reality has always attracted me like a magnet," she says. "I wanted to capture it on paper. So I immediately appropriated this genre of actual human voices and confessions, witness evidences and documents." People read Russian novels not for the happy endings, she said, but "because there is great catharsis in great pain and then something that is sublime."

Her first book was culled from more than two hundred monologues, all by women—soldiers, doctors, partisans, nurses, mothers, wives, and widows—who grew up in Stalin's Russia and were among the roughly one million Russian women involved in fighting the Great Patriotic War of 1941–45 but whose experiences had never been revealed. She includes stories of women who enlisted in the army right after school. ("The only time we were free was during the war. At the front," one woman told Alexievich.)

In a long review article, *The Economist* commented that "some tales were blood-curdling—like that of a 16-year-old nurse who bit off the smashed arm of a wounded soldier to save his life, and days later volunteered to execute those who had fled the field. Other stories were heartbreaking, like that of a girl who first kissed her beloved man only when he was about to be buried. . . . Even so, the censor demanded cuts, such as the story of a young partisan woman who drowned her crying baby to avoid alerting German soldiers."

Those cuts are restored in the new edition—as are her altercations with the censor, who was particularly taken aback by the description of menstruation on the front line. "Who will go to fight after such books?" he demanded. "You humiliate women with a primitive naturalism. . . . You make them into ordinary women, females." She was tried for defaming the Soviet army in *Zinky Boys,* as its testimonies destroyed most notions of military heroism. The court acquitted her.

Explaining *Secondhand Time,* about a country of 143 million people yearning for some kind of restoration after the sudden swing from Communism to capitalism in the 1990s, Alexievich says: "I sought out people who had been permanently bound to the Soviet idea. . . . They couldn't just walk away from History, leaving it all behind and learning to live without it." Her work has been called both journalism and history, but it defies easy labeling. She has said that her aim is "the transformation of life—everyday life—into literature," "a history of human feelings," and that she is writing "novels in voices," editing her transcripts, as Orlando Figes, who has tracked Alexievich's career, has written, into "a spoken literature that carries all the truth and emotional power of a great novel." Only nothing has been invented. For her, the nightmares of the twentieth century make fiction impossible. "The witnesses must speak," she said in her Nobel acceptance speech. On announcing Alexievich's victory, the Swedish Academy proclaimed: "She transcends journalistic formats and has pressed ahead with a genre that others have helped create," a new literary form described as "a history of emotions—a history of the soul, if you wish . . . the everyday life of the soul, the things that the big picture of history usually omits, or disdains." Yet remembering can feel pitifully inadequate when held against lived experience. "So I've told you," says one interviewee, a Leningrad survivor. "Is that all? All that's left of such horror? A few dozen words . . . ?"

Svetlana Alexievich: "a diminutive woman with a kind, round face and eyes that show empathy and humor" (Rachel Donadio). At a press conference in Minsk when her Nobel was announced, Alexievich, whose books have been translated into nineteen languages, said that the Belarusian authorities pretend that she doesn't exist.

Alexievich has now received more than two dozen awards, both from her own country and internationally, although as her fame has increased abroad her popularity in Russia has fallen away, and the state-controlled Russian media greeted the Nobel, Masha Gessen has said in a profile, with "an outpouring of vitriol reminiscent of Soviet newspapers' reactions to most of the earlier Russian-language Nobels" (Boris Pasternak, Solzhenitsyn). But "no one was chasing after me with a Kalashnikov," Alexievich acknowledges. As Gessen notes, unlike some Belarusian intellectuals who have been arrested or have "disappeared," she has been protected by her international reputation. Wearying of tales of war, as of 2018 she has been working on two new projects, one on aging and another on love, but also adding to new editions of her books material that was either suppressed by the authorities or self-censored.

With her success has come criticism. Her books are repetitive, some say; she can be heavy-handed, her justifications grandiose ("I track down the human spirit"), her editing imprecise, for she sometimes melds one person's testimony into another's. But her achievement is still extraordinary. Reviewing *Last Witnesses* in *The New York Times,* the Ukrainian novelist Sana Krasikov wrote, "Alexievich is a master at employing the withheld detail to undercut the unfiltered sentimentalism of a narrator, or adding a poetic sting to an otherwise prosaic entry." Certainly Alexievich's narratives do not make comfortable reading, which is largely the point. In her book about Chernobyl, a young woman describes watching her husband, a firefighter, die from radiation poisoning:

At the morgue, they said: "Want to see what we'll dress him in?" I do! They dressed him up in formal wear, with his service cap. They couldn't get shoes on him because his feet had swelled up. They had to cut up the formal wear, too, because they couldn't get it on him, there wasn't a whole body to put it on. It was all—wounds. The last two days in the hospital—I'd lift his arm, and meanwhile the bone is shaking, just sort of dangling, the body has gone away from it. Pieces of his lungs, of his liver, were coming out of his mouth. He was choking on his internal organs. I'd wrap my hand in a bandage and put it on his mouth, take out all that stuff. It's impossible to talk about. And even to live through. It was all mine. My love. They couldn't get a single pair of shoes to fit him. They buried him barefoot.

There are many passages equally harrowing. Each of her four books has taken between five and ten years to write and represents the voices of between two hundred and five hundred interview subjects. According to Figes, the practice of oral history took longer to establish itself in the Soviet Union than in the West, and as a result it was never recognized by the Soviet Academy of Sciences, so could not be accepted as part of professional historical research. In Stalin's time, the oral recollections of veterans who had taken part in the Revolution were recorded as part of the official history of the party, but the disorderly, potentially upsetting memories of ordinary people were never the government's business to compile.

Alexievich is unique among Nobel laureates for having written books based entirely on interviews. The headline of a *Los Angeles Times* article announcing the prize called her a reporter, a classification she finds almost insulting. She just "happens to use some tools of journalism," she says. In Russia, the line between fiction and nonfiction is often blurred, so that her books get described as *proza,* literary fiction, and the border between journalism and literature is viewed as sacrosanct. Not so in the world at large, where she can be celebrated both as a journalist and a historian.

CHAPTER 22

ON TELEVISION

From A.J.P. Taylor to Henry Louis Gates, Jr.

————

Modern history's another name for television.

—PRESIDENT JOSIAH BARTLET, *The West Wing*

A DISEMBODIED VOICE INTONES SOLEMNLY: "ATV PRESENTS AN experiment. Can a brilliant historian talking about a fascinating subject hold the attention of a television audience of millions for half an hour? That is the question, and the answer lies with you. Our subject is the Russian Revolution, this evening's theme The End of the Czars, our historian, Alan Taylor, Fellow of Magdalen College, Oxford."

The curtains part, and Taylor, by then in his early fifties, makes his way a trifle diffidently onto the bare stage of what had once been a cinema, the Wood Green Empire in north London. He is wearing a buttoned-up tweed jacket, jersey, tie, and a slightly bemused expression. He stops, rubs his hands,* and nods to an unseen audience. "Umm . . . Good evening," he says. "In the last days of December 1916, a small group of Swiss university students had an evening meeting and an exiled Russian politician living in Switzerland gave them a talk on the coming revolution. . . ."

So began, with this mention of Lenin, the first-ever history lecture on television. It was Monday, August 12, 1957, from 6:00 to 6:30 P.M.

---

* Taylor never quite worked out what to do with his hands. During the first fifteen seconds of starting this opening lecture, he rubbed them together, tucked them into his pockets, took them out again, stuck them behind him, then fiddled with his watchband. Such fidgeting continued whenever he talked alone or on a naked stage, and changed only in the 1970s, when he often stood next to a prop, which constrained him. See Kathleen Burk, *Troublemaker: The Life and History of A.J.P. Taylor* (New Haven: Yale University Press, 2000), p. 393.

Some months before, the head of Associated Television (part of Independent Television's network), Lew Grade, keen to find something suitable for the dead period of Sunday afternoons, was told that the answer might be a certain professor at Oxford. "He's a great historian," went the recommendation. Grade's reaction was lukewarm. "I'm not sure I fancy that. But I'd like to meet him." Taylor, duly summoned, explained that he would like his first talk to be on Russian history. "Well," said Grade, a noted popularizer, "that will be very difficult for the public to understand. Why don't you tell me a little about it?" Grade's family had come from Russia, but he sat astonished as Taylor regaled him with a mass of stories he'd never heard before. "It was put so simply, and was so understandable," Grade later explained. "You knew that here was a star, an unusual kind of star."

It was far from being Taylor's introduction to broadcasting. As early as March 1942 he made the first of several appearances on *The World at War—Your Questions Answered,* broadcast by BBC Forces Radio. (In those days and on up through the early 1950s, radio was believed by most broadcasting policy makers to be a more important medium than television. It was certainly the more easily available.) After the war, the controller of BBC TV felt the need for a program that would stimulate discussion rather than merely convey information and would at the same time entertain—his model being based on American programs that primarily involved talking heads. Thus, from 1950 to 1954, Taylor was a panelist on the political discussion program *In the News,* which became so popular that he would boast that he (not it) was "capable of emptying pubs on Friday nights."* Maurice Richardson, *The Observer*'s TV critic, commented on one program that the "team seemed not only on the verge of, but actually, losing their tempers with each other over the desirability or otherwise of the House of Lords. . . . Anyway, it was first-class television." But the talk began to descend into the crevices of party politics, and Taylor became increas-

---

* At the beginning of the 1950s, television sets in Britain were an unusual item—only 350,000 households owned one. Taylor himself wrote: "Few middle-class people had them and certainly no intellectuals. Most of the viewers came from the more prosperous, skilled working class— taxi-drivers . . . artisans, waiters and such like." A.J.P. Taylor, *A Personal History* (New York: Atheneum, 1983), p. 196. By 1960, nearly three quarters of the population did. Following the Queen's coronation in 1953, a must-watch event, the proportion of households with sets went up rapidly, from 14 percent in 1952 to 31 percent in 1954. By 1955, some 30 million households had sets.

ingly unhappy, in one episode declining to acknowledge the other panelists at all. Then, toward the end of another live transmission, he announced he wasn't going to utter another word. The press dubbed him "the sulky don," while the BBC responded by dropping him. An internal memo revealed that it regarded him as a loose cannon and had misgivings about him as a broadcaster. "Taylor's method is to shock," the note contended, "an appropriate method for an audience of under-graduates but a dangerous one for a listener without background. I don't think he has begun to tackle the question of history in broadcast-ing. We'll do all right with the really good men, but Taylor is second-rate—or at least has made himself so."

This was all part of a general BBC angst about how history could be dealt with effectively in broadcasting, for which it had no immediate answer beyond wanting historians on air to be "dependable." But if the government-funded BBC doubted Taylor, independent broadcasting did not. From 1955 he moved, to become a panelist on Independent Television's rival discussion program *Free Speech,* where he remained until the series ended in 1961, complete with the same fellow panelists he had had at the BBC. Then came the invitation to address the nation. By the mid-1980s, Taylor had delivered more than forty such lectures. His achievement was the unscripted monologue, and whereas that form of TV soon became more sophisticated, his talks never changed, despite the new medium's impatience with "talking heads." He might fidget with his jacket cuffs (his collar crowned with a signature polka-dot bow tie), beetle his bushy eyebrows, and interlace his fingers, but he continued to address the camera directly, without rehearsal, notes, photographs, teleprompter, or any editing, finishing on time to the second (he kept one eye on a large clock mounted behind the camera). And still people watched "this cocky, lizard-like little figure," as *The Observer* would describe him, his audiences climbing to more than four million, many of them half-wanting to see him fall off his high wire.[*]
As he explained his sartorial taste to his onetime pupil Paul Johnson:

---

[*] He lost his footing just once. In July 1977 he was recording a lecture on the First World War: "I got so involved that I went on too long and overran my stopping time. Instead of making a quick end I lost my nerve and broke off with an apology, a thing I have never done before. We made a reasonable end afterwards, but it was not the same thing. I have always said there is one thing I can do well and without a mistake, and that is to lecture on television. Now I have slipped, I shall never be so confident again." Alan Taylor to Éva Haraszti, letter of July 29, 1977, *Letters to Éva, 1969–1983* (London: Century, 1991), p. 355.

"Don't like Bohemians, so won't wear sports jackets and flannel bags. Don't want to be stuffy and wear dark suits. So I have them make me three-pieces in corduroy. Just right."

He was the personification of the engaged, nonstop-talking professor, by turns combative and wry, polemical and anecdotal. "I am the aboriginal Talking Head," he would say. Taylor would test his listeners with subjects that TV analysts would have reckoned surefire turnoffs. "Ladies and Gentlemen," he began one talk, "you probably know the story of the man who saw a giraffe and said, 'There ain't no such animal.' This is what I feel about Disraeli"—and he was up and running, albeit by the end of his career sandwiched between late-night wrestling and episodes of soapy *Dr. Kildare.*

Despite his earlier animosity toward the BBC, Taylor returned to the corporation for a series of lectures in 1961, although he continued to give talks for ITV. His final series was *How Wars End,* for Channel 4 in 1985. By then, history programs in both Britain and America had been transformed. Documentary footage was a must, as were interviews, while a narrator was often required to appear on location, retracing firsthand the terrain of the events under review. Or there would be no historian on camera at all, only visual images backed by an anonymous voice-over.

In 1969, Thames TV, part of the ITV franchise, commissioned *The World at War,* a twenty-six-hour documentary on the Second World War narrated by Laurence Olivier. At the time of its completion in 1973, at a cost of £900,000 (more than $130 million today), it was the most expensive factual series ever made. Widely praised, it also highlighted some of the dangers when interpreting the past on television. Peter Foges, now a history professor at Brooklyn College in New York, contributed to a program for the BBC about the making of the series. "Allied wartime propagandists had sliced Hitler's speeches to ribbons, emphasizing climactic moments to make him look mad, but Thames TV discovered uncut tapes well over an hour long showing his speeches to the party faithful in full. They were much more complex than we expected, starting sotto voce in monosyllables interspersed with long silences before slowly building. They were Wagnerian."*

---

* Having gained a BBC reputation as the in-house Hitler expert, Foges was asked to show uncut speeches and action footage to Alec Guinness, who had been cast to play the Nazi leader in a BBC drama. "I sat with him in a cutting room showing him hours of film while he made

One might add that the accelerated speed of prewar newsreel footage must have helped create a comic, Chaplinesque impression. This is Ron Rosenbaum's point in *Explaining Hitler:* "Herky-jerky, sped-up newsreels made him almost impossible to take seriously, and contributed to the deadly serious error of underestimating the threat he posed."

Television, in other words, could form and perpetuate myths or versions of events either through technical inefficiencies, a particular agenda, or simply taking the easy option. As the *New York Times* critic Charles McGrath has argued, "TV is seldom good at developing character and feeling—there isn't enough time, usually—and so it resorts to shortcuts, to little loops of what amount to emotional porn. Moments suffused with feeling but almost empty of content."

There is a scene in Ron Howard's 2008 film *Frost/Nixon,* after the final interview, when the American journalist James Reston, Jr. (played by Sam Rockwell) gives vent to what he sees as the distorting effects of television. "The first and greatest sin—or deception," he says, "is that it simplifies. It diminishes. Great complex ideas, tranches of time, whole careers become reduced to a single snapshot. . . . That was before I really understood the reductive power of the close-up. Because David [Frost] had succeeded that final day in getting for a fleeting moment what no investigative journalist, no state prosecutor, no judiciary committee or political enemy had managed to get: Richard Nixon's face swollen and ravaged by loneliness, self-loathing and defeat." This is not a record of Reston's own words but those of the film's screenwriter, Peter Morgan; nonetheless it rings true. The real-life interviews won the largest audience for a news program on American television. It was not just an event but history-in-the-making—or at least a certain kind of history.

Images have a powerful effect but so too does sound. Foges, who also worked for the BBC, recalls a corporation ordinance stating that music in documentaries had to be carefully monitored, with recorded music used only if it was played in real time with what was appearing

---

notes. 'See that? Look where he puts his left hand/foot/thumb. Let me see it again.' I had to run stuff back and forth as I watched one of great actors of my time construct a role from detailed empirically derived observation. When I watched the taped drama some months later I could see the masterly way he had absorbed and physically regurgitated what he had seen and heard." Email to the author, October 7, 2018. Thus an actor gave a truer version of Hitler in full flood than the edited tapes of the documentaries.

on screen. In America, CBS ordered a similar restriction, underlining the point that music could be a manipulative tool, as shown by Nazi propaganda. Then again, A.J.P. Taylor maintained that once David Lloyd George started to rely on a microphone, his hold over audiences left him; it is a mistake to underestimate the power of the unmediated human voice. Margaret Thatcher learned to lower her voice, as early broadcast microphones were designed for male voices and distorted female voices profoundly, while Donald Trump, when interviewed in a TV studio, will request special filters that modulate tone and add effects.

Different problems arise for a news reporter, whose "first draft" most often reaches its audience after going through many hands—usually a collaborative effort, but not in a good way. "When an action is captured on film," noted Hilary Mantel in her 2017 Reith Lectures,

> it seems we have certainty about what has happened. We can freeze the moment. Repeat it. But in fact, reality has already been framed. What's out of shot is lost to us. In the very act of observing and recording, a gap is opened up between the event and its transcription. Every night as you watch the news, you can see story forming up. The repetitious gabble of the reporter on the spot is soon smoothed to a studio version. The unmediated account is edited into coherence. Cause and effect are demonstrated by the way we order our account. It gathers a subjective human dimension as it is analysed, discussed. We shovel meaning into it. The raw event is now processed. It is adapted into history.

In an essay about a contentious police shooting in Cincinnati in 2015, the long-serving *New Yorker* writer David Denby makes the point that in videos, as against a single photograph, "events *flow* in time; one thing happens after another, without editorial shaping or emphasis. The inexorable forward movement brands the events in consciousness and shapes our reactions." In Britain, during the miners' strike of 1984–85, a bruising confrontation took place between the strikers and the police at a coking plant in South Yorkshire. Footage showed the police charging first, the picketers throwing stones afterward; BBC News broadcast these events in reverse order. That may have been an honest mistake, but we know that various governments worldwide make controlling the media a priority and try to ensure that their state news outlets provide audiences with regime-friendly information. In 2011, during Egypt's so-called January 25 Revolution, state TV stood steadfastly behind President Hosni Mubarak and played old videos of an empty Tahrir Square in downtown Cairo rather than broadcast the true-life images of the hundreds of thousands protesting there. One recalls Paddy Chayefsky, who wrote the darkly satirical film *Network* in the 1970s, describing TV as "an indestructible and terrifying giant that is stronger than the government."

When in 1953 the BBC first broadcast a news bulletin on television, it featured the voice of the newsreader but not the reader himself. Richard Baker, the announcer in question, later explained: "It was feared we might sully the stream of truth with inappropriate facial expressions." Programs about historical events seemed, at first, the special province of British television (where they were known as the "heritage industry"), but other countries have caught up. In America, the History Channel was launched on January 1, 1995, and its owners, A&E (a unit of the Disney conglomerate), soon had a Spanish version running. Over the next eight years similar channels were set up in Italy, Australia, Scandinavia, India, and elsewhere, and on October 26, 1996, a channel devoted to history was introduced to the United Kingdom.[*]

* * *

FOR THE MOST PART, television still relies on the expert narrator. In the United States, as early as 1961 Harry Truman agreed to participate in a series about his presidency, which three years later became twenty-six

---

[*] In the last three decades Continental European companies have started to make excellent history programs (although *The Sorrow and the Pity,* a two-part documentary by Marcel Ophüls, about French collaboration in 1939–45, was made back in 1969; initially banned, it was not shown on French television until 1981). At the History Makers International conference in 2012, French and German documentary filmmakers discussed how they had pioneered the coloring of Second World War newsreels. At Q&A time, I asked if bringing color to old Pathé footage wasn't doctoring the historical record. The French producer replied that yes, in a way it was, but one had to set against this the benefits. For instance, there was film of an American landing craft on D-Day, and the camera showed a GI pushing the man in front of him to get down into the water. Once color was added, one could see on the GI's fingers the gold of his wedding ring. This was lost in the original black and white but added a strong emotional charge. Peter Jackson's 2018 documentary on World War I, *They Shall Not Grow Old,* further shows how powerful such footage can be. "Their humanity just jumped out at you," Jackson says of the restored and newly colored images. See Mekado Murphy, "Bringing World War I Back to Life," *The New York Times,* December 17, 2018, C1.

half-hour programs reaching about 70 percent of American house-holds. Although there was an overall narrator besides Truman and plenty of archival footage, American Cinema Editors named him the outstanding television personality of 1964.

Most presenter-led classics have been on British TV—Taylor's lectures, Kenneth Clark's 1969 series *Civilisation,* and Robert Kee's *Ireland: A Television History* in 1980. By far the most popular subject for history programs now is the Second World War—especially featuring the Nazis. "I always tell my younger producers that the Nazis pay our salaries," says Janice Hadlow, who was to preside over some of television's most successful history productions. Known as "Hitler Porn," such programs usually get about twice the audience of other history output. Part of the reason may be that there is good war footage available, but mainly it's because there's such a strong music hall–type villain. Television has moved away from kings and queens, prime ministers and presidents, wars and disasters, toward social history. Narrative history programs today find their main home on cable. But for the whole period 1980–2015 the most celebrated presenter on U.K. television was a Tudor historian, David Starkey, partly because he was an excellent broadcaster and partly because he cultivated a reputation as a rebarbative commentator who spoke truth to power ("You're looking for a character who *pops,*" says Hadlow).

His background could not have been more different from the feted historians of previous decades. He was born on January 3, 1945, his parents working-class Quakers, both often unemployed. His father was for some time a foreman in a washing-machine factory, his mother a cotton weaver, although she also scrubbed floors to bring in money. They lived in a council house in Kendal, Cumbria, where they had moved from Oldham in the 1930s in the hope of finding work. His father was a gentle if often frustrated man whom Starkey hardly knew, his mother dominant and electrically bright, "with a will that made Margaret Thatcher look like a wimp. . . . In particular she was mistrustful. She disliked most people and I suppose passed that on to me."

He was their only child, born after ten years of marriage, and at first badly disabled. Walter Scott, Byron, Joseph Goebbels, and Oswald Mosley, high achievers all, each had a clubfoot; both Starkey's feet were afflicted, and, before long, he came down with polio as well.

"There was a huge pall over my childhood, as for the first five years I was in and out of hospital having operations." He wore leg braces (although he shows no sign of lameness now), could not engage in sports, and felt "different." By eleven he had read almost all Dickens and most of Arthur Mee's *Children's Encyclopedia*. At thirteen he suffered a nervous breakdown, or at least a series of psychosomatic illnesses, and for six months was confined to home. Back at school, the only time he was popular was the day he won a debating competition for his house.

The penny-pinching ways of his parents made him determined to avoid the same life: "I actually remember thinking: I WANT OUT." He found that his best subjects were physics, chemistry, and mathematics, although "my problem was I'm not a natural mathematician. The only time I'm really interested in numbers is when they have a pound sign in front of them." He had fantasies about becoming an architect and turned to history almost by accident.

His mother's influence was crucial. He has described her as the impetus behind his drive, but also as "monstrous," a Pygmalion who wanted her son to realize her own frustrated hopes. It was a relief when he won a scholarship to Cambridge, where he fell under the influence of G. R. Elton, the Tudor historian and, for Starkey, the father/mentor he never had.* "There were two really dominant figures in the history faculty: Jack Plumb and Geoffrey Elton. Plumb had already handpicked Simon Schama, and so I suppose I gravitated to Elton." Thus began his great interest in the Tudors and their best-known monarch—at least fifteen of his books and five of his TV series have been devoted to Henry VIII and his wives, mistresses, and children. "It's a kind of Goldilocks period," he says, "in which you've got just enough information but not too much."

After gaining a good First, completing his doctorate (inevitably, on Henry VIII's inner household), and several years teaching at Cambridge, Starkey went to the London School of Economics, his home from 1972 to 1998. A major reason for the move was the capital's gay scene. As Starkey told an interviewer: "Oh, that magic moment of

---

* Starkey has said that with age Elton became short-tempered and self-important. When in 1983 his old tutor received a knighthood, Starkey strongly criticized one of his essays. Elton reciprocated by writing a dismissive review of an essay collection that Starkey had edited. Starkey was to regret the incident ever happened and told me that he regarded his mentor as "a great teacher." Interview with the author, September 26, 2017.

coming to London and someone taking your pants down for the first time. . . . I had many memorable moments on Hampstead Heath. They were like scenes from a *Midsummer Night's Dream*." He claimed to be an "excessively enthusiastic advocate of promiscuity," although it may also have been a way of liberating himself further from his mother, who was aghast at his homosexuality. Then in 1994 at a bar in the LSE he met James Brown, a young book designer twenty-seven years his junior, and their relationship lasted till Brown's death in 2015.

He had made his first appearance on television back in 1977, with the flamboyant presenter Russell Harty in a series entitled *Behave Yourself*. (Neither of them did.) Starkey found that he enjoyed the medium. In 1984, he was a prosecution witness in an ITV program *The Trial of Richard III* (the defendant was acquitted on grounds of insufficient evidence). National fame arrived in 1992 with Radio 4's *The Moral Maze*, a discus-

David Starkey at a "British Values" conference in Beckton, London, in 2015.

sion program similar to Alan Taylor's *In the News*, only here Starkey debated moral questions, not political ones. Michael Buerk is quoted in a *Guardian* interview as recalling in his autobiography, *The Road Taken*, that when Starkey joined the program he was "a relatively impecunious historian at the LSE, frustrated and angry. He had not written a big book and had largely lost out in the venomous world of academic politics. He was pretty venomous himself on air. . . . He had no sense of restraint and would sometimes get completely carried away." Buerk often had to shout, "Shut up, David!" On one occasion Starkey shouted an obscenity right back. "I suppose in those days there was a sense of trying to make my mark," he acknowledged. "I do have this very powerful extrovert streak, I like performance. I like dancing on the public stage."

Starkey left the program after nine years; it had been moved to an evening spot, and besides, he was getting bored. It was also a strain. "I'd wake up in the middle of the night after a program and think, 'Oh my God, did I really say that?'" By this time the *Daily Mail* had branded him "the rudest man in Britain," a sobriquet that he gleefully reckoned added considerably to his earning power. And earn he did. From 1995 he enjoyed three years at Talk Radio UK as host for his own weekend show, making him a bona fide celebrity. In 2000 he wrote and narrated a series on Elizabeth I and the following year one on Henry VIII, both great ratings successes. Then in 2002 he signed a £2 million contract with Channel 4 to produce twenty-five hours of television on a history of English kings and queens from Anglo-Saxon times on. This made him the highest-paid TV host in Britain in terms of hourly rate—£75,000 every sixty minutes. He bought a home in Highbury in north London, an eighteenth-century manor house in Kent, and a sizable hideaway in America in a small town on the Chesapeake and indulged in a chauffeur-driven Daimler. His fellow historian Margaret MacMillan, perhaps wistfully, described him as "rich as a Tudor monarch."

The fact is that Starkey writes well and lucidly and broadcasts superbly. The core of history, he believes, is narrative and biography. "So much of academic writing is willfully obscure. It tries to exclude, whereas I don't think there is any shame in including people." Much of academia has looked askance at his celebrity, but he takes the same view of television's advantages as A.J.P. Taylor:

> If you want to ask, "Do I wish to publish a 400-page book with a university press that has a print run of 1,000 and sells for £65?" the answer is no. It's not that I dismiss universities—I am still a member of one, a fundraiser for one—but the notion that the only respectable form of scholarship is obscurity is something I find utterly and totally damaging.

Starkey is in his mid-seventies now, and has acquired a new *nom de guerre*, "one of Britain's best-loved historians." Not that he has ceased to sound off on controversial subjects. He has described the Catholic Church as "riddled with corruption," criticized Prime Minister Tony Blair as "shallow and silly," likened the Queen to Joseph Goebbels, compared the head of the Scottish Parliament, Alex Salmond, to "a Caledonian Hitler," and damned the practice of history itself for becoming "feminized" by "aggressive women." He has also railed against those who prioritize the historian over history, but when in 2017 we lunched together, despite knowing my book's purpose, he was courtesy itself and talked generously and expansively.

He was never, really, the rudest man in Britain, but in July 2020 he became possibly the most reviled. In his regular column for the British magazine *The Critic,* he wrote about "the repeated claim of BLM that the slave trade was genocide or mass murder. It wasn't of course, otherwise there wouldn't be so many blacks in North America or the West Indies." In an online interview recorded on June 29, he repeated his argument, only this time saying, "there wouldn't be so many damn blacks in Africa [*sic*; he had meant to say "America"] or Britain, would there?" It was a single added word, usually the mildest of epithets, but to the British public, newly sensitized to the swampland of racist speech, it was hard to think of a more objectionable thing to say.

Starkey was swiftly dropped by his publisher, HarperCollins, and resigned or was fired from his honorary posts at Fitzwilliam College, Canterbury Christ Church University, the Mary Rose Trust board of trustees, the editorial board of *History Today,* and his fellowships at the Royal Historical Society and the Society of Antiquaries of London. The special medal awarded to him by the Historical Association was withdrawn, and two other universities, Lancaster and Kent, announced they were reviewing Starkey's visiting professorships.

Most hurtful must have been the ending of his relationship with Fitzwilliam, where he had been a student, a research fellow, and a bye-fellow, and with which he had been closely associated for more than fifty years. "It was a bad mistake," he said in a prepared statement. "I am very sorry for it and I apologize unreservedly for the offense it caused. I have paid a heavy price for one offensive word with the loss of every distinction and honor acquired in a long career." Seemingly unaware that the words he had used marked him as a bigot, he went on to argue, unconvincingly, that in any event he was referring to the "damn" number of Black people, not the people themselves.

Unsurprisingly, he was soon back to his exuberant self. In his next column for *The Critic,* he denounced the word "blacks" as having "become a totem or fetish. Used in any other than a wholly favourable sense it is an immediate indicator of racism and its user must be punished accordingly." Then in mid-September 2020, in an interview in *The Daily Telegraph,* he continued to attack the Black Lives Matter movement and expanded on his "three-day divestiture," accusing his detractors of "Salem-style puritanism. . . . Racist has become the equivalent of heretic. . . . We've been here before. This is Robespierre." He already had a new literary agent, he said, and had started writing an autobiography. "It's going to be called '*Damned*,'" he told his interviewer with some glee. It is too early to know whether David Starkey will ever climb back to any position of popular esteem, but it seems unlikely.

One recalls the warning given him by his mother. "Your tongue," she told him, "will be the ruin of you."

* * *

"SIMON SCHAMA AND I were lucky in our timing," Starkey says of his days riding high. "We were the historians around when television decided to spend big money on history programs." In 2002 the £2 million he was paid was for five years' work; the following year, Schama accepted £3 million (around $5.3 million) for writing three books and two accompanying television series, then the biggest advance ever given a TV historian. In 1991, Schama's book *Dead Certainties* had looked at two well-publicized deaths a hundred years apart and pointed out how much the two had in common, exploring the historian's inability "ever to reconstruct a dead world in its completeness however thorough or revealing the documentation," and speculating on "the teasing gap separating a lived event and its subsequent narration." If his doubts still remained, he had found the confidence to overcome them.

For Schama, telling stories came as to the shtetl born. His mother, "a mix of protectiveness and ferocity, both Spitfire and Hurricane," was from an Ashkenazi Jewish family, his father of Sephardic Jewish background. Together they would regale him with their families' past—a relative who broke wild mustang horses, another who traded spices in Istanbul, forebears who were Hasidic lumberjacks on the Lithuania-Belarus border—engaging him early in what Schama describes as "that fantastic paradoxical mystery when you are in the company of the dead."

He almost never made the company of the living. His mother called him "the accident," and in the early stages of her pregnancy wanted to do away with him altogether. But he was safely born in February 1945, to join a sister fourteen years his elder, and grew up a not particularly religious Jew in a kosher London home, and as a teenager spent time on a kibbutz. It was the story of the Jews, he says in the opening moments of his TV series on Jewish history, that made him want to be a historian.

His family was constantly moving, from its East London home to Southend-on-Sea in Essex, then back to London again. In a 2009 interview Schama would describe his early life spent in a removals van, as his father was always broke: "There was one kind of business my Dad wasn't good at. Unfortunately, it was business." When he was five, he contracted lockjaw and was unable to speak for eleven months but quickly made up for it; in his early years he was constantly reprimanded at school for speaking out of turn. Talk was the family currency. His parents "basically communicated by mutually agreed interruption,"[*] but their garrulity had its pluses. From the ages of thirteen to fifteen, he read aloud nearly all of Shakespeare with his father, who took for himself the parts of both Shylock and Portia.

In 1957 he won a scholarship to Haberdashers' Aske's Boys' School in Hertfordshire, an awkwardly named establishment founded in 1690 that is frequently proclaimed the best school in Britain. From there he progressed to Christ's College, Cambridge, to study history under J. H. Plumb, an argumentative popularizing socialist turned rabid right-winger who detested "scientific history" and advocated strong

---

[*] The description is a carefully honed line from a one-man show of 150 minutes that Schama put on in London, Edinburgh, and Sydney (aided by a pianist/singer and an actor in the roles of both Schama and Donald Trump). In May 2019 he performed (in bright red shoes with blue laces) before a packed house at the Theatre Royal Haymarket, one moment lampooning his father belting out, "There's No Business Like Show Business," the next imitating his mother singing the next verse. Could Thucydides or Gibbon have done that? "Clearly," wrote Schama afterward, "my life to this point has been a complete waste." Simon Schama, "I'm on Tour, Singing. Yes, Seriously," *The Spectator,* June 15, 2019.

Simon Schama (center) with Clive James at Cambridge, circa 1970.
According to James, "Anyone afraid of what he thinks television
does to the world is probably just afraid of the world."

narratives. (Plumb would have sympathized with the narrator of one of John O'Hara's stories, who tells us: "My children call history 'social science,' and hate it.") Plumb's own supervisor had been George Macaulay Trevelyan, a great-nephew of Lord Macaulay who was once crowned "the master storyteller of 20th-century British Liberalism." Schama duly took note. In 1991 he wrote an essay for *The New York Times Magazine* entitled "Clio Has a Problem," in which he warned that professional historians were hobbling themselves by setting expertise above plotlines and drama.

Schama took a starred First and settled down to an academic career, initially at Cambridge, where he became a fellow and director of studies, then at Oxford, where he specialized in the French Revolution. His first published book was as a junior partner to two other academics in putting together *The Cambridge Mind: Ninety Years of the Cambridge Review, 1879–1969,* a compilation put out by a revered journal he had himself edited in 1968 and 1969. Then in 1973 he was asked to complete a history of the Jews left unfinished by its author, the British Jewish historian Cecil Roth, who had died. Schama energetically tried to take on the commission, but "for whatever reason the graft wouldn't take."

Instead his first book as a stand-alone author was *Patriots and Liberators,* originally intended as a history of the French Revolution and a reworking of his doctoral thesis but which morphed into a study of the Netherlands from 1780–1813, "a tale of a once-powerful nation's desperate struggle to survive the treacheries and brutality of European war and politics." This was followed by *Two Rothschilds and the Land of Israel* in 1978, then a move to Harvard to take up a history chair and marriage to Virginia Papaioannou, a geneticist from California, with whom he has two children.

Teaching and family preoccupied Schama, and it wasn't until 1987 that he wrote his next book, again focused on Dutch history and its golden period in the seventeenth century, *The Embarrassment of Riches*. It marked his evolution into an art historian, and several future books followed that interest, including *Rembrandt's Eyes* (1999), *Hang-Ups* (2005), and *The Power of Art* (2006). However, it was a major work of history that cemented his reputation. In 1989 he published *Citizens*, an exploration, nearly a thousand pages long, of the revolution in France, from the years that led up to it until 1794. In what *Publishers Weekly* called a "sprawling, provocative, sometimes infuriating chronicle that stands much conventional wisdom on its head," Schama argued that the revolution did not produce a "patriotic culture of citizenship" but was *preceded* by one. His research was dazzling, delving into almost every area of life. He wrote about festivals and food, exhibitions and executions, people's hidden motives, and the savagery of crowds with an erudition that marked the study as something special in the way historians recorded events. "This is no ordinary book," wrote Lawrence Stone in *The New Republic*. "His chronicle is, after all, a stunningly virtuoso performance." Hugh Trevor-Roper complained of his "displays of erudition"; young historians should not show off. But it was a bestseller.

In 1993, after thirteen years at Harvard, Schama moved to Columbia as professor of both art history and history. During this period arose the internet; his website declared him "historian, writer, art critic, cook, BBC presenter but not necessarily in that order." In an interview he was asked to sum up his life in six words and replied: "recklessness undeservedly rewarded by good fortune." In 1995 he was appointed art critic for *The New Yorker*, a position he held for three years, by which time he had bought a Jaguar convertible and developed a taste for good cigars and expensive shoes. He became a (fairly engaging) crooner, an adept cook, and a covert writer of short stories.

His television work began with a five-part series based on one of his most interesting projects, *Landscape and Memory* (1995), in which he examined the relationship between physical environment and folk memory, roaming through an impressive range of digressions personal and cultural. The book won numerous prizes. In 2000 he returned to the United Kingdom to produce TV documentaries on British history. He wrote and presented the series himself, to excellent reviews and ratings. His idiosyncrasies—his sometimes fey delivery ("you do shout a lot when you are an amateur on television"), the Schama shoulders, seemingly with an energetic life of their own, his inclination to be matey ("It's all news to us, chum," some fourteenth-century Scottish nobles get paraphrased; while Thomas Becket is "a cockney, a street fighter and as tough as old boots under the cowl")—are minor irritants set against the intelligence of the commentary; he is our companion and our authority. Janice Hadlow, who oversaw the series, describes him as "slightly noisy" and "a strong flavor."

The project, expanded to fifteen episodes that cover the country's history up until 1965, went on to become one of the BBC's bestselling documentary series on DVD and a success on the History Channel in the United States. Other series, with books to accompany them, followed in regular procession, while Schama became a frequent pundit on the political scene, particularly on British and Israeli issues. By the time he wrote *The Story of the Jews,* a book trilogy to accompany another TV series, his jocular way with words had been widely recognized, sometimes critically but more often with affection and applause. David Nirenberg, a professor of medieval history at the University of Chicago, acknowledged that "Schama understands the simplification necessary for narrative. . . . His stress is on 'story,' not 'history': fascinating vignettes and felicitous formulations are his trademarks, and his gift is engagement through detail." He's done sixty television programs to date. The next series he's plotting, or maybe a book, will be about tribalism and nationalism—"a behavioral history, taking in sport and much else."

Schama is well aware that he has been criticized for presenting a dumbed-down, highly oversimplified view of the history of nations (even David Starkey calls their joint output "the higher tosh") and has taken pains to justify his approach. As long ago as 1998, in a joint interview with Martin Scorsese for the magazine *Civilization,* he admitted: "There were many hundreds of years in which history was never anything except popular. Unfortunately, though, the professors came along. [*Laughter.*]" Since then he has regularly argued that the effective historian has always been a performer. In a speech entitled "History Beyond the Page" given at the Van Leer Jerusalem Institute in December 2017, he started off by playing Aaron Burr's lines from Lin-Manuel Miranda's astoundingly successful musical *Hamilton*:

> *How does a bastard, orphan, son of a whore and a*
> *Scotsman, dropped in the middle of a*
> *Spot in the Caribbean by providence, impoverished, in squalor*
> *Grow up to be a hero and a scholar?*

An entirely accurate summary, he said, as was the history in the rest of the musical. But why can't hip-hop be history? Herodotus's writings, after all, were performed before thousands at pan-Olympic festivals in a metrical chant, accompanied, most likely, by dancing, lyres and woodwind; the great Greek historian was speaking to an audience, not to a readership. Thucydides too wrote to be read out loud, with his great passages of direct speech. So it is not too great a jump to the Public Theater in downtown Manhattan, or to the Theatre Royal Haymarket in London.

History as a form of theater has continued—Bede's histories retain the character of orally transmitted folklore—but not long after Bede that tradition withers away, and Europe had to wait many centuries before recounting the past again reached a nonliterate mass audience: In 1595, when *Henry VI, Part 1* was put on at the Rose in Southwark, the groundlings paying just two pence to attend. After Shakespeare, history goes between covers again, although Walter Scott brings the past to a broad audience, as do the many other great narrative novelists.

And so the tradition goes on, sometimes submerged beneath the waves of the academic sea, sometimes triumphantly rising, as with Churchill, a theatrical genius in his writing—"no one channeled Shakespeare's tetralogies better"—and on to A.J.P. Taylor. But since Taylor we have become conditioned by a professional, academic way of writing, confined by the conventions of scholarly discourse. Only now are theatrical events like *Hamilton* returning us to a preliterate world.

Schama's argument is obvious enough; his documentaries are a way of describing the past as it is shown best. "The academy is under siege," and if historians are to enter the public consciousness they must find the language to do so successfully. Just as popular history without scholarship is trivial, so academic accounts without a sense of audience do not merit a hearing. "Alas," wrote Thomas Carlyle, Schama's frequent hero, "what mountains of dead ashes, wreck and burnt bones, does assiduous Pedantry dig up from the Past Time, and name it History." That was Schama's point.

* * *

IN 2018 BBC 2 aired a nine-part series pointedly titled *Civilisations,* to mark it out as a broader inquiry than Clark's 1969 series *Civilisation.* Schama hosted five programs, the other four being divided between Mary Beard and David Olusoga, a forty-eight-year-old Nigerian specialist in military history, race, and slavery. The films won a large audience but came in for criticism, for instance over Mary Beard telling the tale of a youth who, thousands of years ago, supposedly ejaculated over a nude statue of Aphrodite. She describes this dramatically as "rape," telling her audience: "Don't forget, Aphrodite never consented." The British satirist Craig Brown spoofed her in a *Private Eye* piece, "Mary Beard: Julius Caesar Revealed":

> MARY: He is the most famous—and the most notorious!—
>   Ancient Roman of the lot. As famous in his day as
>   Beyoncé—
> *Cut to footage of Beyoncé*
> or Posh or Becks
> *Cut to footage of David and Victoria Beckham*
> are in ours. When his name is mentioned we think of
>   power, victory . . .
> *Cut to footage of Donald Trump's inauguration*
> and betrayal!
> *Cut to photo of Michael Gove behind Boris Johnson*
> Yes, Julius Caesar changed his own world in unimaginable
>   ways—and he's left a pretty big mark—
> *Cut to a splodge on the wall of a housing estate*
> —on ours!

And so it continues, through three hilarious columns. This is not entirely Beard's shtick: Schama's series on Britain had Edward I referred to as the "Hammer of the Scots"—cue shot of a hammer striking an anvil—then we are told he was called "the Leopard"—and on lopes a leopard. But Beard has had to contend with a continual barrage of adverse comments, usually giving back as good as she gets.

Several years before *Civilisations* aired, three senior British academics gave their views about history on TV. Keith Thomas, the Oxford professor best known for *Religion and the Decline of Magic,* spoke of the damage done to "diligent" scholarship by "eye-catching academics." Sir Richard Evans, then Regius Professor of History at Cambridge, wrote: "It's when historians . . . appear on Question Time, host chat shows or write newspaper columns that they become real celebrities; and, as some of them have found out, you become a celebrity at your peril." The third, Tony Judt, by 1987 professor of history at New York University, condemned "the rise of a counterfeit currency of glib 'popular' articulacy: in the discipline of history this is exemplified by the ascent of the 'television don,' whose appeal lies precisely in his claim to attract a mass audience in an age when fellow scholars have lost interest in communication"—the very skill Schama was advocating historians must reclaim.

So what might have gone wrong? Nicholas Hytner, who directed Alan Bennett's play *The History Boys* in both the theatrical and film versions, puts it succinctly: "There is a thin line between a sparkling intellect and a flashy one." In Bennett's play historians who appear on television are treated harshly. Bennett himself began as a historian, winning a place at Oxford to study the subject, then writing a doctoral thesis on the finances of Richard II. He stayed on as a medieval specialist but was neither a good teacher nor a popular one, and it was a relief when he teamed up with Jonathan Miller, Peter Cook, and Dudley Moore for *Beyond the Fringe,* their hit revue of the 1960s.

In the sixty-odd years since then, Bennett has written more than thirty plays and TV scripts, but *The History Boys,* which began at the National Theatre in London in 2004, is the first to tackle head-on how to teach history. Set in a northern grammar school much like Bennett's own, it focuses on an elderly teacher who believes in the value of knowledge for its own sake and whose classroom style is subversive and freewheeling. He finds himself pushed aside by a dynamic supply teacher, a too-clever-by-half younger man known simply as "Irwin," who tells the students that "the wrong end of the stick is the right one. A question

has a front door and a back door. Go in the back, or better still, the side."
He tells them ways of doing this: subvert the normal historical assumptions. Argue that those who had been genuinely caught napping by the attack on Pearl Harbor were the Japanese and that the real culprit was President Roosevelt. Create interest, which is more important than truth. "History nowadays is not a matter of conviction. It's a performance. It's entertainment. And if it isn't, make it so."

By the play's end, Irwin has slid easily into a career as a presenter of TV documentaries. As he tours the medieval abbey of Rievaulx, in northern Yorkshire, he justifies his role: "Ours is an easier faith. Where they reverenced sanctity we reverence celebrity; they venerated strenuous piety; we venerate supine antiquity. In our catechism old is good, older is better, ancient is best with a bonus on archaeology because it's the closest history comes to shopping."

Reviewing his performance, he has a moment of self-criticism, but also finds himself in conversation:

> IRWIN: Meretricious, of course, but that's nothing new.
> MAN (ONE OF HIS OLD PUPILS, NOW GROWN UP, AND
>   WHO HAS OBSERVED THE FILMING): I've forgotten
>   what meretricious means.
> IRWIN: Eye-catching, showy; false.
> MAN: But you were a good teacher.
> IRWIN: The meretricious often are . . . on television
>   particularly.

We now know that the character of Irwin was chiefly based on the academic, author, and TV personality Niall Ferguson, and the arguments about World War I that Irwin hails as admirable counterintuitive creativity (perfect for landing that Oxbridge scholarship)—that Britain was as much to blame as Germany, that soldiers exulted in trench-warfare killing—come directly from Ferguson's 1998 book *The Pity of War,* even repeating lines from the work. A friend told Ferguson, "You should feel flattered—using your methods, Irwin got all his boys into Oxbridge!"

Irwin is not Scottish, whereas Ferguson attended Glasgow Academy, his father a doctor, his mother a physicist, and he won a scholarship to study history at Magdalen College, Oxford, emerging with an inevitable First. As a teenager, he had inhaled A.J.P. Taylor's TV lectures, and Taylor's study of the First World War was an early favorite. At Oxford, he became a belligerent Thatcherite, drinking and partying hard and taking delight in taunting anyone from the left. He deliberately chose Norman Stone, a fellow Scot and Glasgow Academy alumnus as well as one of Thatcher's closest advisers, to mentor him. Both men responded to Taylor's iconoclastic sensibility and devil-may-care fondness for the spotlight.

Niall Ferguson (left) giving the Barclays Wealth Lecture on
"The Ascent of Money" at the Hay Literary Festival in 2009.
By Alan Bennett's own account, the character of Irwin in
The History Boys *(right) was chiefly based on Ferguson.*

The book that emerged from Ferguson's dissertation, *Paper and Iron,* was his first venture into counterfactual history, a deeply analytic study of hyperinflation in Weimar Germany that postulated what the country would have looked like had it been governed on Thatcherite principles. Even as he researched (learning German by meeting Stone at his local pub at eleven in the morning to read Nietzsche and Hegel over pints of Irish stout), he turned to journalism, mainly for *The Daily Mail* and *The Daily Telegraph,* joining a group of young academics in the A.J.P. Taylor mold who became known as the "Dial-a-Dons," willing and able to turn out articles in short order on any topic of the day.

In the words of the London *Sunday Times,* Ferguson soon became "about as networked as they come," his "every opinion . . . delivered with utter certainty." *The New York Times* crowned him the "enfant terrible of the Oxbridge historical establishment," a "one-man book factory . . . the brightest kid in the debating club" who "pulls all-nighters in the library and ferrets out facts no one thought to uncover." While possibly guilty of "authorial overstretch," he defied categorization and was still an accomplished and imaginative scholar. Adam Gopnik in *The New Yorker* pointed to his "sometimes shaky taste. . . . He so often gets things just a bit 'off' "; but the magazine, back in 1999, still devoted a long and admiring profile to him.

Teaching posts at Oxford and Cambridge were followed by a move across the Atlantic. He is now a senior fellow at the Hoover Institution at Stanford but has also taught at Harvard, the Harvard Business School, and New York University; he has held a professorship at the London School of Economics and been a visiting fellow at China's Tsinghua University. Ferguson became notorious for his contrarian contention (among many) that empire-building is a positive good and that the United States should enthusiastically pursue such a role. Yet his unique marketing factor, he says, is that he knows about money. Historians don't understand finance, he claims, particularly the centrality of the bond market. This has led to his making several TV programs on such subjects. He has hosted eight TV documentary series in all, including *Empire* (2003), *The Ascent of Money* (2008), which won an International Emmy Award, and *Civilization: Is the West History?* (2011), in which he developed the idea of six "killer apps" that for five centuries elevated the West above the rest of the world: property rights, science, competition, the consumer society, medicine, and the work ethic, notions that are now being taken up by China, threatening the West's hegemony. In 2004, he was named as one of *Time*'s hundred most influential people in the world. In 2012 he presented the annual Reith Lectures on BBC radio. He was also an adviser to John McCain during his U.S. presidential campaign in 2008, supported Mitt Romney in 2012, and was a vociferous critic of Barack Obama. Poking fun at the left has remained a constant enthusiasm.

His last book was *The Square and the Tower,* in which he argued the central importance of social networks in human history. As so often, it received a mixed reception. "The scientific credentials of network theory are highly questionable," sniffed *The New York Review of Books,* but criticism has rarely worried him. "The point is to stir things up a bit," he told me over a lively dinner in early 2019 that included a very passable Henry Kissinger impersonation (he is great company, whatever his views). "Don't be boring. Be controversial." Ferguson is currently writing the concluding volume of Kissinger's authorized biography, a project that originally was discussed between Andrew Roberts and Kissinger before they each backed away from working together. But future books for the time being are unlikely; as opposed to television, they no longer have sufficient influence to interest him. And he has enough on his plate, with regular newspaper columns, several companies he helps run, and five children. In fairness, the Irwin of Alan Bennett's imagining is a very pale imitation.

Bennett's introduction to *The History Boys* quotes a review of *The Pity of War* by the Oxford don R. W. Johnson:

> Anyone who has been a victim, let alone a perpetrator, of the Oxbridge system will recognize Niall Ferguson's book for what it is: an extended and argumentative tutorial from a self-consciously clever, confrontational young don, determined to stand everything on its head and argue with vehemence against what he sees as the conventional wisdom—or worse still, the fashion—of the time.

Bennett adds: "It has always struck me that some of the flashier historians, particularly on television, are just grown-up versions of the wised-up schoolboys who generally got the scholarships." Further:

> The doyen of TV historians, Simon Schama, is in a league of his own . . . but the new breed of historians—Niall Ferguson, Andrew Roberts and Norman Stone—all came to prominence under Mrs. Thatcher and share some of her characteristics. Having found that taking the contrary view pays dividends, they seem to make this the tone of their customary discourse. A sneer is never far away and there's a persistently jeering note, perhaps bred by the habit of contention.

One wonders whether Bennett absolves Schama because the two men's political views are aligned. There is also an irony here. Bennett objects to "history provocation," but in writing about his own undergraduate years, he attributes what he achieved at Oxford to having divined the "journalistic side to answering an examination question: . . . in brisk generalities flavoured with sufficient facts and quotations to engage the examiner's interest and disguise my basic ignorance." Bennett says that as a university don he passed on these same tricks of the trade to his students. The meretricious Irwin had more than one source.

* * *

IN THE UNITED STATES, television history differs from that in Britain. It may import contrarian polemicists and one-person narrators, but it prefers to rely on the detached authority of a David McCullough or a Ken Burns. McCullough, now eighty-eight, has narrated seventeen TV documentaries, five by Burns and three with Burns's younger brother Ric. Together they have changed the way TV history is presented.

The Burns brothers were born in 1953 and 1955 and have worked together on several series, but Ken is the more celebrated. His documentaries include *The Shakers: Hands to Work, Hearts to God* (1984), *Huey Long* (1985), the eleven-and-a-half-hour *The Civil War* (1990), *Baseball* (1994), *Jazz* (2001), *The War* (2007, on World War II), *The National Parks: America's Best Idea* (2009), *Prohibition* (2011), *The Roosevelts* (2014), *The Vietnam War* (2017), which took ten years to make and cost about thirty million dollars, *The Mayo Clinic* (2018), *Country Music* (2019), *Hemingway* and *Muhammad Ali* (both 2021), as well as lesser-known films on the painter Thomas Hart Benton, Thomas Jefferson, and Mark Twain. Already it stands as an extraordinary body of work, but Burns's company, Florentine Films, has documentaries, each on an American subject, planned all the way to 2030, with topics ranging from Benjamin Franklin to Lyndon B. Johnson, Barack Obama, Winston Churchill ("Thank God that he had an American mother," Burns adds), the American criminal justice system, and African American history from the Civil War to the Great Migration.

The Burns brothers are descended from an American Revolutionary War physician on one side and the Scottish poet Robert Burns on the other. Their parents were Lyla Smith (*née* Tupper) Burns, a biotechnician who died when the brothers were children, and Robert

Kyle Burns, a cultural anthropologist who taught at the Universities of Delaware and Michigan—although it is a family joke that he never finished his doctoral thesis.

On Ken's seventeenth birthday his parents gave him an 8-millimeter camera to shoot a documentary about an Ann Arbor factory. He went on to work as a cinematographer for the BBC and for Italian television and studied under the photographer Jerome Liebling. Then in 1977, having made some further shorts, he adapted McCullough's book about the construction of the Brooklyn Bridge. In 1981 the film won an Oscar nomination. Four years later, Burns's documentary on the Statue of Liberty would do so as well.

Critics have carped that these and other films Burns made are typical of a cameraman trying to tell a story—overlong, sappy, nostalgic, and with higgledy-piggledy narratives, the ultimate triumph of length over content. Further, he has chosen over time to neglect professional historians—*The Civil War* featured twenty-four of them, his 2007 film on the Second World War fifteen, *The Vietnam War* (2017) just two out of seventy-nine commentators, and *Country Music* one. But it is difficult to argue with his series on the Civil War, begun in 1985, which received more than forty major film and television awards. Viewership averaged just shy of 14 million each evening, making it the most-watched program ever to air on PBS. "There's never been anything quite like it before on television," wrote the critic John Leonard. "So much death and eloquence." According to Steven Ambrose, the best-selling historian, "more Americans get their history from Ken Burns than from any other source."

The late 1980s and early 1990s had seen the release of several innovative documentaries, with Claude Lanzmann's 566-minute chronicle of the Holocaust, *Shoah,* Errol Morris's *The Thin Blue Line* (about a man sentenced to death for a murder he did not commit), and Michael Moore's *Roger and Me* (the story of General Motors shutting down auto plants in Flint, Michigan) leading the way. But Burns created something new, what has been called, in its Civil War incarnation, a "semi-mythical narrative," more reminiscent of the immersive experience of the 1922 silent American documentary *Nanook of the North,* about an Inuit family in the Canadian Arctic. He wants his audience to "surrender to narrative," he says. "*Then* and *then* and *then*" is "about as good a thing as has ever been invented."

Ken Burns (left) in 2019, talking about his documentary The Holocaust and the United States, *and Henry Louis Gates, Jr., during an award ceremony for the W.E.B. Du Bois Medal at Harvard University in 2013.*

For George F. Will, writing the week Burns's series debuted, it was a "masterpiece of national memory. . . . Our *Iliad* has found its Homer." He went on: "You see a 19th century photograph, black-and-white, of course, of a black man's back. It is hideously covered with scars left by a lash. Burns's camera does not dwell; the narrative does not even mention what we have briefly seen. Burns knows how to blend passion and delicacy: reticence can be its own emphasis." The director found himself, at thirty-seven, recognized as not just an uncannily gifted storyteller but the nation's unofficial documentarian-laureate. In 2017 a *New Yorker* profile listed the items Burns now always carries in his pants pocket: a button from the uniform of a soldier who was part of the D-Day landings, a silver heart, and a minié ball picked up at Gettysburg.

The series also cemented in the public consciousness what has become known as the "Burns style," bringing old photographs to life by slowly zooming in and tracking from one image to another. For example, in a photograph of Confederate soldiers, the camera might scroll across their faces before coming to rest on the one who is currently the subject of the narrative. (In 2002, Steve Jobs invited Burns to visit Apple, and a few months later Apple's iMovie program enabled the user to add a smooth zoom motion to photos or video clips, for "the Ken Burns Effect.") For viewers, *The Civil War* resembled a wonderful collage, a huge number of stories set side by side, setting off elements in common and forming unexpected connections. In a recent *New Yorker* profile, Burns describes his films as exercises in "emotional archeology" that aspire to be works of art. "We just happen to work in history," he says. Indeed he does. Speaking for myself, at the end of this long survey of historians, I believe his most effective documentaries rank with many of the best works of written history from the last fifty years. John Burrow rounds off his book on the history of histories with an even greater plaudit for the Civil War series: "Considered as the presentation of an epic theme on a grand scale this has claims to be the outstanding work of history of the late twentieth century."

★ ★ ★

OTHER FILMMAKERS HAVE FOLLOWED in Burns's wake, notably Henry Louis Gates, Jr. (b. 1950), who has been a staple of PBS screens for more than a decade. Scholar, journalist, and institution builder, he is also director of the Hutchins Center for African and African American Research at Harvard University, where he has taught since 1991. At first, Gates won a fine reputation with books such as *The Signifying Monkey* (1988), a work of literary criticism based on the trickster figure of Yoruba mythology (Gates's ancestors came from West Africa); *Loose Canons* (1992), in which he wrote that the role of African American studies was "to redefine how the nation defines itself"; and a literary memoir, *Colored People* (1994), starting from his childhood in the mill town of Piedmont, West Virginia, where he was called "Skip" from the time he was born.

His interest in history started early:

The day we buried my father's father, Edward St. Lawrence Gates, was July 3, 1960. I stood in front of his casket holding my father's hand and looked at how astonishingly white my grandfather was. I thought he looked ridiculous and I was going to laugh. Then I heard a noise. My father was weeping. [Later, he] took us back to the Gates family home and showed us an obituary of Jane Gates, an "estimable colored woman." He said, "I

never want you to forget this woman. She is your oldest ancestor." Before I went to bed I looked up the word *estimable*. The
next day I asked my father for a composition notebook and I
started to record our family history. I was 9 years old.

In the years before college, he was expected to become a doctor
(just as Braudel had been), but by the time he applied to Yale his personal statement had a very different focus. "My grandfather was colored, my father was Negro, and I am black," it began, and ended, "As
always, whitey now sits in judgment of me, preparing to cast my fate.
It is your decision either to let me blow with the wind as a non-entity
or to encourage the development of self. Allow me to prove myself."
A quarter-century later, he was to write, "I wince at the rhetoric today,
but they let me in." He took a degree in history and after graduation
went on to work as the London correspondent for *Time,* then earned a
PhD in English literature at Cambridge University. A MacArthur Fellowship soon followed. Today he is the recipient of no fewer than
fifty-three honorary degrees.

Gates has taught at Cornell, Duke, and Yale, as well as at Harvard,
continually pushing for African Americans to be recognized and promoted. Balance is all; he insists that both Western and African or African American aesthetic principles be used to explicate a text. In his
classes, Gates will set his students up for debate, one team putting forward the arguments of Booker T. Washington—say, his line that "the
biggest mistake the Negro made was to pursue elective office before he
was ready for it"—while the other team argues the more assertive
views of Du Bois. "I don't just say Booker was an Uncle Tom. . . . I
like to teach Black history in relation to *American* history," he says—
not in isolation. Gates is proud of the African and African American
Studies Department he runs at Harvard, which he built with the help
of what he always refers to as "the Dream Team," which originally
included the noted scholars Kwame Anthony Appiah (with whom he
completed Du Bois's *Encyclopedia of Africa*), Evelyn Brooks Higginbo-
tham, Cornel West, and William Julius Wilson. When Gates arrived in
1991 there were only two faculty members; today Harvard's is one of
the premier departments in the field, with more than forty faculty.

His academic career led naturally to his writing books, but another world was waiting in the wings. Gates never studied film at university but considers himself "a movie junkie" and gradually succumbed to its lures. "I love storytelling," he explains. "My father was a great story-teller, and my mother used to write obituaries for the local newspa-per." Thus he inherited two traditions, the oral and the literary. In 1969 he sat spellbound watching Kenneth Clark's *Civilisation* series and in 1973 was entranced by Jacob Bronowski's *The Ascent of Man.* "I thought, 'Man, if only I could have a job like that—and tell people's stories.'"

He says that being an academic still shapes his primary identity, but by the mid-1990s he was making television documentaries—a further way of being a historian, of teaching people about the past. In 1995 he presented a program in the BBC/PBS series *Great Railway Journeys* that documented a three-thousand-mile trek through Zimbabwe, Zambia, and Tanzania, each showing him in fashionable and often colorful clothes and with his distinct, lopsided gait—at the age of fourteen Gates suffered a hairline fracture in his hip while playing touch foot-ball, and as a result he walks with a cane and an elevated shoe, his right leg being an inch and a half shorter than his left.

These journeys were followed by two seasons of *African American Lives* (2006 and 2008), in which as co-producer and presenter he traced the lineage of more than a dozen African Americans employing genea-logical and historical data, although he reckons he is continually learn-ing on the job how to put history across (and not just Black history). "I see myself as a student and am still growing. I study Simon Schama and Niall Ferguson" (whose house in Cambridge, Massachusetts, he bought: "First thing I did was knock all the walls down to get rid of all that rightwing ideology"—although the two are good friends). Each documentary filmmaker, he has discovered, has a personal signature, like a voice. He doesn't say what his own signature might be, but as one British interviewer observed, "The guy has charisma by the bucketful."

In 2010, he hosted *Faces of America,* a four-part series that examined the genealogy of a dozen North Americans of mixed family back-grounds; then in 2014 came another series, *Finding Your Roots,* with the professor serving as the viewer's main guide. "It floats my boat," he confesses, "to break down barriers between us—we're all immigrants." The average African American, he points out, has 24 percent European ancestry. Other conclusions can be surprising. "Since the day Martin

Luther King was killed," Gates noted during his 2002 documentary *America Beyond the Color Line,*

> the Black middle classes have almost quadrupled, but the percentage of Black children living on or below the poverty line is almost the same. Two nations, but they're both Black and they're both defined by economics, and never the twain shall meet. In fact, the class divide in the Black community is now seen by some as a permanent aspect of our existence. . . . The most ironic outcome of the Black Civil Rights movement has been the creation of a new Black middle class which is increasingly separate from the Black underclass. . . . If Martin Luther King came back, he'd say we need another civil rights movement built on class, not race.

Gates's 2013 documentary *The African Americans: Many Rivers to Cross* ranged over five hundred years of African American history. He then made a list of ten subjects to film next, including a series on the Great Migration, a history of the Black Church in America, and Reconstruction, but beginning with the Great Civilizations of Africa. Then, after the 2016 election of Donald Trump following two terms of the first Black president in American history, Gates felt the pressing need to tell the story of the backlash against the dramatic progress African Americans had made in the years immediately after the Civil War ended in 1865. He thus flipped the original order and in 2019 presented *Reconstruction: America After the Civil War,* a four-hour study of Reconstruction and its aftermath, those twelve crucial years when two thousand Black people served at almost every level of government, only to be followed by nearly a century of Jim Crow segregation. Forty-four historians took part in the series, and after each day's shoot, says Gates, "we would choose a nice restaurant, drink a lot of wine," and he and the crew would analyze what they had done, with everyone chipping in.

The depth of research and also the science involved in Gates's programs are a world away, say, from the investigation undertaken by Alex Haley for what Haley called his "faction" novel *Roots: The Saga of an American Family,* a mix of fact and fiction published in 1976 and made into a twelve-hour television series the following year. After Haley's death, Gates, who had been a friend of his, said that *Roots* was "a work of the imagination rather than strict historical scholarship." Gates has supplied the scholarship. In 2016, after he had interviewed Seattle Seahawks quarterback Russell Wilson and showed that his lineage reached back to 524 A.D. and Saint Arnulf of Metz, a Frankish bishop, Gates exulted: "Alex never had a story like this!"

Gates, who uses three DNA companies to research people's genealogy, likes to quote Harry Truman's remark, "The only thing that's really new is the history you don't know." He considers Ken Burns's Vietnam series the greatest documentary he has ever seen, and he and Burns often team up at festivals and on television panels. Burns refers to Gates as "my backup and my muscle," but even he was surprised when, brought together for a *Finding Your Roots* episode, Gates showed him that his ancestors had been slave owners. "He found on my mother's side a character named Eldad Tupper, a Tory who fought for the British in the Revolution."

"Now, God help me!" Burns exclaimed in mock horror, having first reacted in disbelief that past members of his family had been involved in the slave trade. "This is the thing I'm most ashamed of!"

Gates replied with a laugh: "Genealogy giveth, and genealogy taketh away."

Such programs have an uncritical, almost psychiatrist's couch air, unlike Gates's academic writing. "I adjust my voice depending on the audience," he explains in his defense. "But, really, I don't see any contradiction between the registers." It's still all about telling stories.

In a 2016 interview at the Brooklyn Academy of Music, Gates was asked to sum up his books and articles, his teaching and political activism, as well as his television programs. He didn't hesitate to find the common theme: "I've tried in all my work to represent the question, 'Who are we?'"

AFTERWORD

―――――

Professionals do well to apply the term "amateur" with
caution to the historian outside their ranks. The word does
have deprecatory and patronizing connotations that
occasionally backfire. This is especially true of narrative
history, which nonprofessionals have all but taken over.
The gradual withering of the narrative impulse in favor of
the analytical urge among professional academic historians
has resulted in a virtual abdication of the oldest and most
honored role of the historian, that of storyteller.

―C. VANN WOODWARD, 1975

A FRIEND OF MINE, AFTER READING THROUGH A DRAFT OF THIS BOOK,
asked, did I think people were writing better history now? I think we
are. "But," said Simon Schama when I mentioned this view to him,
"what are your criteria for 'better'? Deeper research? More imaginative storytelling? I don't think you can improve on, say, Fernand Braudel, whose books can sometimes become prose poems. Does one find
anyone like that now? No. Not combining that panoramic scholarly
research and intense literary power."

Even so, one can reasonably argue that history has advanced over
time—that is, those who write or attempt other re-creations of the
past are getting better at uncovering and describing what really went
on. In the long run, works of history seem to be moving ahead, adding
to an expanding body of knowledge, as we tend to think science does.
(In 2008, the Nobel Prize–winning physicist Murray Gell-Mann even
posited that it was only a matter of time before laws of history would
be found, like the laws of science.)

Most of the history programs made for television, for instance, by leading filmmakers would not have been possible even fifty years ago. Both Gates and the Burns brothers are the beneficiaries of major advances in technology. Dangers exist, and given the concerns about disinformation on social media and the emergence of a new "postfactual" world in which the facts—those precious building blocks for historians—are under constant attack it sometimes seems that we are no longer able to support a meaningful structure of information. Henry Louis Gates for one believes that "we live in a world with way too much information." But history itself can offer perspective here; fears about "fake news" and the manipulation of facts have been around for a long time. What is undeniable is that whatever the drawbacks of the internet, the growth in cheap computing power and the development of large historical data sets also means that scholars can pool their research findings with unparalleled ease as well as use new instruments of research to unearth material only dreamed of until recently.*

For sure, television can be guilty of trivializing the past, but there's much good programming, which, far from appealing to the lowest common denominator, promotes an interest in history, making scholarly ideas attractive to a general audience. One wonders what historians from past ages might have achieved had they been armed with a camera, a crew, and a generous budget. Gibbon might stride down the Appian Way, no doubt in silver boots, or Herodotus and Thucydides become the Taylor and Trevor-Roper of their day; Julius Caesar presents a history of war, while Tolstoy makes his own multipart series for a rival channel; W.E.B. Du Bois fronts a series about Black historians; and Matthew Paris, Geoffrey of Tours, and Voltaire collaborate on a history of gossip. Many in these pages might have made successful TV presenters.

* * *

CERTAINLY, WRITING "HISTORY" HAS changed considerably over the decades. I have chosen to give the last word to one of the great Ameri-

---

* At the end of 2019, an article in *The Guardian* reported that "calculating the patterns and cycles of the past could lead us to a better understanding of history" and so might help us prevent future crises. According to Peter Turchin, a professor of ecology and evolutionary biology, anthropology, and mathematics at the University of Connecticut, historical theories can now be tested against large databases, and "the ones that do not fit—many of them long cherished—will be discarded. Our understanding of the past will converge on something approaching an objective truth." One can't help but think that this seems an optimistic claim. See Laura Spinney, "History as a Giant Data Set: How Analyzing the Past Could Help Save the Future," *The Guardian*, November 12, 2019.

can recorders of the past, William Hickling Prescott, author of *History of the Conquest of Mexico*. In 1829, in a review of Washington Irving's *Conquest of Granada,* he considered the question of what a historian should ideally be, concluding that such a paragon

> must be strictly impartial; a lover of truth under all circumstances, and ready to declare it at all hazards: he must be deeply conversant with whatever may bring into relief the character of the people he is depicting, not merely with their laws, constitution, general resources, and all the other more visible parts of the machinery of government, but with the nicer moral and social relations, the informing spirit which gives life to the whole. . . .

He was not done yet:

> He must be conscientious in his attention to geography, chronology, etc., an inaccuracy which has been fatal to more than one good philosophical history; and, mixed up with all these drier details, he must display the various powers of a novelist or dramatist, throwing his characters into suitable lights and shades, disposing his scenes so as to awaken and maintain an unflagging interest, and diffusing over the whole that finished style without which his work will only become a magazine of materials. . . . He must be—in short, there is no end to what a perfect historian must be and do. It is hardly necessary to add that such a monster never did and never will exist.

ACKNOWLEDGMENTS

———

In his autobiography, first published in 1926, the Chinese historian Gu Jiegang admits that he had written a previous memoir—when he was twelve. One of its themes was entitled "Would That I Might," and its third chapter began "Would that I could read through every book under heaven." His grandfather cautioned him that quantity should not be his prime consideration, while his grandmother laughingly joked that he might be as undiscriminating in his selection as "the blind cat that didn't even know she was dragging a *dead* chicken."

In researching and writing this book I have sometimes wished that I too could have read everything in history, but I have been stopped from dragging in dead chickens by the help and advice of many generous friends and advisers. Because of the length of the book I have rarely asked anyone to read more than a chapter or two, so I am thanking people for their generous input into specific chapters; they are free to criticize the others.

For the preface and general discussions: Dr. Kevin Jackson, Stuart Proffitt, Joe Klein, Alice Mayhew, Prof. Martin Brett, Tim Dickinson, Prof. William Taubman, Prof. Lord Peter Hennessy, Prof. Sylvia Nasar, Prof. Dora Weiner, Prof. Valerie Hansen.

For Overture: The Monk Outside the Monastery: Dr. Dominic Aidan Bellenger, Prof. Christopher Brooke, Dr. Simon Johnson, Prof. James Clark, Thomas Jackson.

For chapter 1, The Dawning of History: Prof. Geoffrey Hawthorn, Dr. Jeremy Mynott, Prof. Paul Cartledge, Dr. Mark Ringer, Dr. Richard Buch.

For chapter 2, The Glory That Was Rome: Stacy Schiff, Prof. Donald McDonough.

For chapter 3, History and Myth: Prof. John Barton, John Wilkins, Fr. Gerald O'Collins.

For chapter 4, Closing Down the Past: Prof. Chase Robinson, Prof. Alan Mikhail, Prof. Richard W. Bulliet.

For chapter 5, The Medieval Chroniclers: Prof. Paul Freedman, Prof. Chris Given-Wilson, Baron Melvyn Bragg.

For chapter 6, The Accidental Historian: Prof. Marcello Simonetta, Dr. Stella Fletcher.

For chapter 7, William Shakespeare: Clare Asquith (Countess of Oxford and Asquith), Rachel Eisendrath, Felix Pryor, Prof. Jean Howard, Ron Rosenbaum.

For chapter 8, Zozo and the Marionette Infidel: Prof. Paul Cartledge, Dr. Richard Holmes, David Bodanis.

For chapter 9, Announcing a Discipline: Prof. Edward Muir, Prof. James Clark.

For chapter 10, Once Upon a Time: Dame Hilary Mantel, Nina Darnton, Prof. Eamon Duffy.

For chapter 11, America Against Itself: Prof. Harold Holtzer, Dr. Brenda Wineapple, Jeremy Garron, Bill Woodward, Charles Perkins.

For chapter 12, Of Shoes and Ships and Sealing Wax: Prof. Robert Darnton, Prof. André Burguière, Prof. Jacques Revel, Dr. Romain Bertrand, Joelle Stockley.

For chapter 13, The Red Historians: Prof. Eric Hobsbawm, Prof. Harvey Klehr, Prof. Sir Richard Evans, Julia Hobsbawm.

For chapter 14, History from the Inside: Dr. Brenda Wineapple, Elizabeth Diggs, Joshua Mark.

For chapter 15, The Spinning of History: Dr. Piers Brendon, Prof. Andrew Roberts, Allen Packwood, Mary Lovell, Lady Jane Williams, Lord Asa Briggs, Secretary Henry Kissinger.

For chapter 16, Mighty Opposites: Paul Johnson, Adam Sisman, Baron Robert Skidelsky, Prof. Kathy Burk.

For chapter 17, The Wounded Historian: Prof. John Elliott, Matthew Keegan, Mary Keen, Francis Keegan, Anthony Whittome, Sir Antony Beevor, Sir Max Hastings, Dr. Felipe Fernández-Armesto, Prof. Sir Michael Howard.

For chapter 18, Herstory: Lady Antonia Fraser, Dr. Alice Kessler-Harris, Prof. Amanda Foreman, Professor Dame Olwen Hufton, Sarah Dunant, Annette Kobak, Virginia Nicholson.

For chapter 19, Who Tells Our Story?: Prof. Eric Foner, Prof. Elizabeth Hinton, Prof. Farah Jasmin Griffin, Prof. Eddie S. Glaude, Prof. Leith Mullings, Kevin Sack, Bob Herbert, Professor Jesse W. Shipley, Joe Klein, Kevin Doughten, David Denby, Melanie Locay.

For chapter 20, Bad History: Bill Woodward, Dr. Olga Kucherenko, Prof. Orlando Figes, David Irving, Prof. Norman Stone, Michael Žantovský, Sir Antony Beevor, Jeremy Garron, Pippa Wentzel, James MacManus.

For chapter 21, The First Draft: John Simpson, Liz Trotta, Shelby Coffey, Frances FitzGerald, William Pitt, Lewis Lapham.

For chapter 22, On Television: Prof. David Starkey, John Farren, Ken Burns, Dr. Libby O'Connell, Janice Hadlow, Bernard Clark, Prof. Peter Foges, Prof. Simon Schama, Prof. Niall Ferguson, Prof. Henry Louis Gates, Jr.

I am also indebted to Magdalene College, Cambridge, for making me a Visiting Scholar in 2012, to Cambridge University Library, The New York Public Library, the Society Library of New York (although I do wish they would change the signs above low-slung doorways from 'Duck or Complain' to 'Duck or Grouse'), and the Downside Abbey library. In each case both the institution and the people who work there have been helpful beyond the call of duty.

The lines from Megan Beech's poem "When I Grow Up I Want to Be Mary Beard" from her book of the same title are reprinted by kind permission of her publishers, Burning Eye Books.

The entire manuscript was read and commented on by John Darnton, Mary Sandys, and David Henshaw, to all three of whom I am extremely grateful. Bill Woodward, whose books with Madeleine Albright I have been responsible for editing, read several of my chapters and corrected me accordingly—noting of one piece of abrasive dialogue by Walter Mosley that I mischievously quoted, "Love this, but what Mosley can get away with, you cannot." At the Robbins Office, David Halpern, Rachelle Bergstein, Janet Oshiro, Jessica Hoops, Ian King, and Alexandra Sugarman all read parts of the book and helped in innumerable other ways. Alexandra, for instance, turned out to be an adept juggler; I am not sure how this improved the actual material, but it certainly added to the gaiety of nations. At Simon & Schuster, I feel very lucky in my editor Bob Bender and his assistant, Johanna Li, as well as in my publicity guru, Rebecca Rozenberg, and am also grateful to Dana Canedy and Jon Karp for their support. I wish my old friend and publisher, Susan Kamil, had lived to see this book in print, having over innumerable suppers been part of its evolution.

Martin Schneider was the most eagle-eyed and conscientious of copyeditors, and Cecilia Mackay a revelation as an innovative picture researcher; their contributions were crucial. Cheryl Hunston was again my scrupulous indexer. Iain MacGregor, then of Simon & Schuster UK, came up with the title. In Britain, I am blessed in my publisher, Alan Samson, and the rest of his team at Weidenfeld. Then there is Kathy Robbins, my wife and agent. How to say thank you for all she has done and continues to do, helping, teasing, objecting, remembering, cajoling, inspiring (and adding in the margins of the pages small dancing figures in green ink, to ameliorate any critical comments)? Certainly without her this history, and my history, would have been entirely the poorer. In this of course I am biased, but may at least be ending this book with one undeniable, objective truth.

NOTES

───────

PREFACE

3 **"A man sets out to draw"**: Jorge Luis Borges, afterword to *El hacedor* ("The Maker," from the Scots word *makar*, meaning "poet"), 1960.

4 **thirty-seven chosen texts**: According to Burrow's friend Geoffrey Hawthorn, in conversation with the author, 2 May 2012.

4 **"Almost all historians"**: John Burrow, *A History of Histories* (New York: Knopf, 2009).

4 **"Every man of genius"**: Edward Gibbon, *The Miscellaneous Works of Edward Gibbon, Esq.: With Memoirs of His Life and Writings*, vol. 3 (London: John Murray, 1814), p. 56.

5 **"Historical consciousness is neither"**: Wilson Jeremiah Moses, *Afrotopia: The Roots of African American Popular History* (Cambridge: Cambridge University Press, 1998), p. 17.

5 **"Aristotle was born"**: Robert Pogue Harrison, "A New Kind of Woman," *The New York Review of Books*, 25 April 2013. Harrison was taking some liberties with his "is said." The original reads, *"Bei der Persönlichkeit eines Philosophen hat nur das Interesse: Er war dann und dann geboren, er arbeitete und starb."* ("Regarding the personality of a philosopher, our only interest is that he was born at a certain time, that he worked, and that he died.") Thus Heidegger didn't mention Aristotle by name (though the comment did occur during a seminar on Aristotle). And the "let's move on" kicker is missing.

6 **"History does not refer"**: James Baldwin, "The White Man's Guilt," *Ebony*, August 1965.

6 **"the hallmark of the amateur"**: G. R. Elton, *The Practice of History* (Sydney: Sydney University Press, 1967). See also Martin Chanock, "Two Cheers for History," *The Cambridge Review*, 26 January 1968, pp. 218–19.

7 **"Of course not"**: Interview with Eric Hobsbawm, 2 March 2011.

7 **"Every nation, every people"**: Arnold Toynbee, *A Study of History* (Oxford, U.K.: Oxford University Press), first published in two volumes, 1947 and 1957, new abridged edition 1987.

7 **"sheer volcanic literary eruptions"**: *The Guardian*, 9 December 1999. Schama's other choices were: *The Police and the People: French Popular Protest, 1789–1820* by Richard Cobb, *Decline and Fall of the Roman Empire* by Edward Gibbon, *The Defeat of the Spanish Armada* by Garrett Mattingly, *The Ordeal of Thomas Hutchinson* by Bernard Bailyn, *London: A Social History* by Roy Porter, *The Mediterranean and the Mediterranean World in the Age of Philip II* by Fernand Braudel, *The Face of Battle* by John Keegan, *The Cheese and the Worms: The Cosmos of a Sixteenth-Century Miller* by Carlo Ginzburg, and Tacitus's *Annals and Histories* (although he told me he would remove Tacitus now!).

OVERTURE

9 **"However evolved our methods"**: Ryszard Kapuściński, *Travels with Herodotus* (London: Allen Lane, 2007), p. 272. Kapuściński died in January of that year, the book having been published in Polish in 2004.

9 **"a poet among historians"**: Dominic Aidan Bellenger and Simon Johnson, eds., *Keep-*

ing the Rule: David Knowles and the Writing of History (Stratton-on-the-Fosse, U.K.: Downside Abbey Press, 2014), p. 7; and Dominic Aidan Bellenger, *Monastic Identities* (Stratton-on-the-Fosse, U.K.: Downside Abbey Press, 2014), p. 137.

9 **"one of the great oaks":** Dom Alberic Stacpoole, *The Ampleforth Journal,* vol. 80, part I (Spring 1975), p. 75.

9 **"unsurpassed":** Norman F. Cantor, *Inventing the Middle Ages* (New York: Morrow, 1991), p. 324.

9 **The Festschrift opens:** W. A. Pantin, "Curriculum Vitae," *The Historian and Character and Other Essays* (Cambridge, U.K.: Cambridge University Press, 1963).

10 **the most important relationship:** Maurice Cowling, *Religion and Public Doctrine in England,* vol. 1 (Cambridge, U.K.: Cambridge University Press, 2003), p. 132.

11 **Knowles began his autobiography:** All the quotations from Knowles, unless otherwise cited, are from the unpublished autobiography held at Downside Abbey.

13 **"with enthusiasm, if without great skill":** Dom Adrian Morey, *David Knowles: A Memoir* (London: Darton, Longman & Todd, 1979), p. 23.

14 **virtually as a second son:** Nicholas Vincent, "Arcadia Regained?" *Keeping the Rule,* ed. Bellenger and Johnson, p. 50.

14 **"This failure to serve":** Morey, *David Knowles,* p. 301.

19 **"a storm-centre":** Abbot Chapman's letter is quoted by Knowles in his autobiography, third version.

22 **Knowles came to believe:** Morey, *David Knowles,* p. 88.

23 **Nobody knows for sure:** Adrian Morey, note attached to Knowles's autobiography, dated 1977. Morey, ever the loyal Benedictine, had little time for Kornerup or for Knowles's memoir: "This is a saddening work for anyone who admired and had affection for its author. . . . The Kornerup chapters [are] absurd, when they are not shocking." To an objective eye the autobiography is moving and disturbing, certainly, but fascinating in the insights it provides.

24 **two of Knowles's heroes:** Knowles's literary executor, Christopher Brooke, has noted: "He was a great admirer of Macaulay, strangely for a monk." Christopher Brooke, interview, *Making History,* 10 March 2008.

24 **"Had Cicero written on monasticism":** Nicholas Vincent, "Arcadia Regained?" *Keeping the Rule,* ed. Bellenger and Johnson, p. 43. See also Janet Burton, "After Knowles," *Keeping the Rule,* p. 119.

25 **"He came nearer":** Cowling, *Religion and Public Doctrine in England,* pp. 154–55.

26 **by 1540 every monastery:** G. W. Bernard, "The Dissolution of the Monasteries," *Keeping the Rule,* ed. Bellenger and Johnson, p. 211.

26 **"one of the historical masterpieces":** Kenneth Clark, *The Other Half: A Self Portrait* (London: John Murray, 1977), p. 196. The two men were close friends.

26 **"These two books were written":** Cantor, *Inventing the Middle Ages,* p. 311.

27 **"When once a religious house":** Knowles, *Historian and Character,* p. xxviii.

CHAPTER 1. THE DAWNING OF HISTORY

29 **"The conversion of legend-writing":** R. G. Collingwood, *The Idea of History* (Oxford: Oxford University Press, 1946).

29 **"Exiled Thucydides knew":** W. H. Auden, "September 1, 1939," first published in *The New Republic,* 18 October 1939; first published in book form in Auden's collection *Another Time* (1940; repr. London: Faber and Faber, 2006).

30 **"Epic, which was invented":** Adam Nicolson, *Why Homer Matters* (New York: Macrae/Holt, 2014).

30 **"the audience burst into tears":** Herodotus, *The Histories,* translated by Walter Blanco and edited by Walter Blanco and Jennifer Tolbert Roberts (New York: Norton Critical Editions, 1991), 6.21, p. 435. Further references are given in the text.

32 **"the noble lie":** Plato, *Republic,* book 3, 414e–15c, where Socrates speaks of the parable of the metals.

32 **Above all, he asks questions:** Jessica Mary Priestley, *Herodotus and Hellenistic Culture: Studies in the Reception of the Historiae,* unpublished doctorate in the Cambridge University Library, p. 45.

32 **He is the world's first travel writer:** The list is Justin Marozzi's, from his *The Way of Herodotus: Travels with the Man Who Invented History* (New York: Da Capo Press, 2008).

32 **"a typical wanderer":** Kapuściński, *Travels with Herodotus,* pp. 79–80. In 2002, Kapuściński spoke in New York City about his career. Among those in the audience was Susan Sontag, who suggested that he had gotten it wrong; he should have opted for the companionship of Thucydides, not Herodotus. In the view of most others, Kapuściński had a similar cavalier attitude to facts as his Greek hero, so he got it right in choosing Herodotus!

"Pictographs or it didn't happen."

32 **southern Russia, and Georgia:** Although see also O. K. Armayor, "Did Herodotus Ever Go to Egypt?" *Journal of the American Research Center in Egypt* 15 (1980): 59–71. Some historians bracket Herodotus's claims to have "been there" with Baron von Münchhausen's fantasy memories.

34 **to instill a sense of the past:** Donald Lateiner, *The Historical Method of Herodotus* (Toronto: University of Toronto Press, 1989), pp. 189, 5, footnote.

34 **"illicit eroticism":** Marozzi, *Way of Herodotus,* p. 6.

34 **Herodotus notes:** *The Histories,* 2.2–3, 35.

37 **"The most lasting":** John Gould, *Herodotus* (New York: St. Martin's Press, 1989), p. 134.

37 **In the first four "books":** This summary is taken from Encyclopedia.com.

38 **the old techniques:** Joshua Foer, *Moonwalking with Einstein: The Art and Science of Remembering Everything* (New York: Penguin, 2011).

39 **As for the noun *history*:** Lateiner, Historical Methods of Herodotus.

39 **"father of history":** Marcus Tullius Cicero, *De legibus,* 1.i, 5.

39 **"string-along style":** Aristotle, *Rhetoric* 1409a, 28–36.

40 **His inexactness is particularly evident:** Lateiner, *Historical Method of Herodotus,* p. 223; and Michael A. Flower, "The Size of Xerxes' Expeditionary Force," *The Landmark Herodotus,* pp. 819–22.

40 **"If we had to give an *a priori*"**: Arnaldo Momigliano, "The Place of Herodotus in the History of Historiography," Rome: Editioni di Storia e Letteratura, 1960, p. 32. But Momigliano considered Herodotus the superior of Thucydides in his understanding of the causes of war, because of his open mind and wider mental horizon.

40 **"picks up the notebook"**: Michael Ondaatje, *The English Patient* (New York: Vintage, 1993), p. 16.

41 **"I had leisure"**: *The Landmark Thucydides: A Comprehensive Guide to the Peloponnesian War*, ed. Robert B. Strassler (New York: Free Press, 1996), 5.26.5. Further references are given in the text.

41 **"in almost impossibly difficult Greek"**: Mary Beard, "Which Thucydides Can You Trust?" *The New York Review of Books*, September 2010, p. 52.

42 **"Thucydides is one"**: Thomas Hobbes, introduction to *The Peloponnesian War*, "To the Right Honorable Sir William Cavendish" (1628; repr. New York: Gale Ecco, 2010).

42 **"the grand summation"**: Friedrich Nietzsche, "What I Owe to the Ancients," *Twilight of the Gods*, quoted in Burrow, *History of Histories*, p. 50.

42 **"analytically concentrated"**: Simon Schama, *Scribble, Scribble, Scribble: Writing on Politics, Ice Cream, Churchill, and My Mother* (New York: HarperCollins, 2010), p. 106.

45 **"a rebarbative critic"**: Schama, *Scribble, Scribble, Scribble*, p. 389.

45 **"He wanted to know"**: Simon Schama, "Roughing Up the Surface," *Civilization*, February/March 1998, p. 88.

45 **the first Western author:** James Romm, "Be Spartans!" *London Review of Books*, 21 January 2016, p. 13.

48 **The Greeks worshipped memory:** Foer, *Moonwalking with Einstein*, p. 125.

49 **Writing allowed prose to happen:** John H. Finley, *Thucydides* (Cambridge: Harvard University Press, 1942), p. 258.

51 **"It was once common to contrast"**: Ford, *The Landmark Herodotus*, p. 818.

51 **"The difference between the mind"**: Will Durant, *The Life of Greece* (New York: Simon & Schuster, 1939). Although a bestselling author, Durant craved scholarly respectability, which may have led him to be hard on Herodotus and more accepting of Thucydides as a "scientific historian."

51 **"Sir, if Herodotus was"**: Peter Green, "On Liking Herodotus," *London Review of Books*, 3 April 2014, p. 29.

CHAPTER 2. THE GLORY THAT WAS ROME

52 **"One may think him bold"**: Michel de Montaigne, "The Art of Conference (or Conversation)," *The Complete Essays of Montaigne*, ch. 8, 1588.

52 **"The distinction . . . is not in the one"**: Aristotle, *Poetics*, 1451a–b. Plato's *Republic* does not mention history once.

53 **"When did historians"**: Eric Foner, *Who Owns History?* (New York: Hill and Wang, 2002), p. xvii.

53 **fewer than 20 percent:** Lionel Casson, *Libraries of the Ancient World* (New Haven: Yale University Press, 2001), p. 51.

54 **"a military man's vindication"**: Burrow, *History of Histories*, p. 53; see also Robin Lane Fox, ed., *The Long March: Xenophon and the Ten Thousand* (New Haven: Yale University Press, 2004). In some settings, students of the classics are accorded a special day off every March 4 in Xenophon's honor.

54 **"When the men in front"**: Xenophon, *Anabasis*, Digireads.com, 2009, 4.2.

55 **"I have neither received"**: Xenophon, *Anabsasis*, 7.7.44–46.

55 **"In order to fill the long time gap"**: Anthony Everitt, *The Rise of Rome: The Making of the World's Greatest Empire* (New York: Random House, 2012), pp. xxxi, 20. See also Robert Hughes, *Rome: A Cultural, Visual, and Personal History* (New York: Knopf, 2011), p. 15.

56 **Latin literature did not get under way:** L. D. Reynolds and N. G. Wilson, *Scribes and Scholars: A Guide to the Transmission of Greek and Latin Literature* (Oxford: Oxford University Press, 1991), p. 18.

57 **"Once made captive"**: Horace, *Epistles*, bk. 2, and *Epistles to the Pisones*.

59 **"for him Asia had been"**: Burrow, *History of Histories*, p. 69.

59 **"It is not a historian's business"**: Polybius, *The Histories*, trans. Ian Scott-Kilvert (London: Penguin, 1979), II, 56. All quotations from Polybius are taken from this edition.

61 **"are not simply the storehouses"**: Mary Beard, *London Review of Books*, February 1990, p. 11.

62 **its first public library**: Casson, *Libraries of the Ancient World*, p. 22; see also Ernst Posner, *Archives in the Ancient World* (Boston: Harvard University Press, 1972); and Felix Reichmann, *The Sources of Western Literacy: The Middle Eastern Civilizations* (Westport, Conn.: Greenwood Press, 1980).

62 **"Why would the historian"**: Stendhal, *The Charterhouse of Parma*, trans. John Sturrock (London: Penguin, 2006), p. 111.

63 **"an Ian Fleming trying to pass"**: Colin Wells, *A Brief History of History* (New York: Lyons Press, 2008), p. 33.

64 **"Yonder is a city"**: Sallust, *The Jugurthine War/The Conspiracy of Catiline* (London: Penguin, 1964), 37.3.

64 **"Latin is a rather chunky language"**: Daniel Mendelsohn, "Epic Fail?" *The New Yorker*, 15 October 2018, p. 92.

65 **some two dozen crown-octavo volumes**: M.L.W. Laistner, *The Greater Roman Historians* (Berkeley and Los Angeles: University of California Press, 1947), p. 77. Laistner points out that Macaulay's collected works fill only "twelve stout volumes," but that the English historian was ever busy with public affairs and died at fifty-nine.

67 **"Here are the questions"**: Titus Livius (Livy), *The History of Rome*, bk. 1, 1–14.

68 **"shall we put it down to"**: Josephus, *The Jewish War*, Bk. III, ch. 8, pa. 7.35. See also Ralph Ellis, *King Jesus: King of Judaea and Prince of Rome* (Cheshire, U.K.: Edfu Books, 2008), p. 248.

69 **"No destruction"**: Josephus, *The Jewish War*, IV, 423–30.

70 **"The luckiest traitor ever"**: Mary Beard, *The New York Times*, 1 April 2018, p. 8.

70 **"Over the course of a glittering career"**: Tom Holland, *Dynasty* (New York: Doubleday, 2015), p. xxi.

71 **"Our style of dress"**: Tacitus, *Agricola*, ch. 1, para. 21.

71 **"They rob, kill and plunder"**: Tacitus, *Agricola*, ch. 1, para. 30.

71 **"It is no part of my purpose"**: Tacitus, *Annals*, III, 65.

72 **"Once killing starts, it is difficult"**: Tacitus, *Histories*, I, 39.

72 **"The desire for glory"**: Tacitus, *Histories*, IV, 6.

72 **"The more numerous the laws"**: Tacitus, *Annals*, trans. Ronald Syme, vol. 1 (Oxford: Oxford University Press, 1958; repr. 1985), III, 27.

72 **"Benefits are acceptable"**: Tacitus, *Annals*, IV, 18.

72 **"The scene lived up to its horrible associations"**: Tacitus, *Annals*, I, 60.

73 **"His character passed through"**: Tacitus, *Annals*, VI, 51.

75 **describes how the Nazis**: Christopher Krebs, *A Most Dangerous Book: Tacitus's Germania from the Roman Empire to the Third Reich* (New York: Norton, 2011). The phrase "a most dangerous book" was coined by Arnaldo Momigliano in *Studies in Historiography* (New York: Harper and Row, 1966), p. 112.

75 **"the beauty of the Roman style"**: Plutarch, "Demosthenes," *Delphi Complete Works of Plutarch* (Delphi Classics, 2013), vol. 12.

77 **"Question 49"**: Plutarch, *Moralia*, trans. Frank Cole Babbitt (Boston: Harvard University Press, 1936), Loeb Classical Library, vol. 4.

CHAPTER 3. HISTORY AND MYTH

79 **"Bibles laid open"**: George Herbert, "Sin: Lord with what care," 1633.

79 **"the world's bestseller"**: John Updike, "The Great I Am," *The New Yorker*, 1 November 2004, p. 100.

79 **more than five hundred translations:** See Daniel Radosh, "The Good Book Business," *The New Yorker,* 18 December 2006, pp. 54–59.

79 **a superheroes version for children:** Charles McGrath, "Thou Shalt Not Be Colloquial," *The New York Times,* 24 April 2011, p. 3.

80 **wildly beautiful flights:** Matthew Parris, *The* (London) *Times,* 25 November 2015, p. 32.

80 **"Slight Inconsistency Found in Bible":** *The Onion,* 3 March 1999.

81 **he was arguing:** Adam Kirsch, "What Makes You So Sure?" *The New Yorker,* 5 September 2016, p. 74.

82 **"If we think of [the Bible]":** Richard Elliott Friedman, *Who Wrote the Bible?* revised edition (New York: Harper, 1989), p. 5.

82 **"Imagine assigning four":** Friedman, *Who Wrote the Bible?* pp. 53–54. In this and the previous paragraph I have largely followed Friedman's exposition.

82 **evidence of an extremely skilled:** Friedman, *Who Wrote the Bible?* p. 60.

83 **his or her heroes perfect:** David Edwards, *A Key to the Old Testament* (London: Collins, 1976), p. 201.

"I'm concerned about my legacy—kill the historians."

84 **"His task was both to record history":** Friedman, *Who Wrote the Bible?* p. 134.

86 **"All of the texts":** Friedman, *Who Wrote the Bible?* p. 208.

87 **Paul's word:** Frank Kermode, "A Bold New Bible," *The New York Review of Books,* 15 July 2010, p. 40.

89 **"bawling and scratching one another":** *The Prose Works of Andrew Marvell,* vol. 1, 1672–73, ed. Annabel Patterson (New Haven: Yale University Press, 2003), p. 158.

89 **Many claim that these further gospels:** Peter Nathan, "How Many Gospels Are There?" *Vision,* Winter 2012, available at vision.org/how-many-gospels-are-there-169.

90 **"a wise man who did surprising feats":** This summary is by Craig L. Blomberg, in *Jesus Under Fire: Modern Scholarship Reinvents the Historical Jesus,* ed. Michael J. Wilkins and James Porter Moreland (New York: Zondervan, 2010), p. 40.

90 **Matthew was a Galilean:** Charles Herbermann, "St. Matthew," *Catholic Encyclopedia* (New York: Robert Appleton Company, 1913).

91 **"weird . . . reminds me":** Harold Bloom, *The Shadow of a Great Rock: A Literary Appreciation of the King James Bible* (New Haven: Yale University Press, 2011), p. 248.

91 **"gloomy ferocity":** Frank Kermode, *The Genesis of Secrecy: On the Interpretation of Narrative* (Boston: Harvard University Press, 1979).

91 **"Many have undertaken":** Luke 1:1–4, New International Version.

94   **"The New Testament represents Jesus"**: Terry Eagleton, *How to Read Literature* (New Haven: Yale University Press, 2013), pp. 64–65.

94   **"terrified of being tarred"**: Diarmaid MacCulloch, "The Snake Slunk Off," *London Review of Books,* 10 October 2013, p. 9.

94   **"John the novelist"**: Bloom, *Shadow of Great Rock,* p. 264.

95   **"John everywhere is at pains to tell"**: Donald Foster, "John Come Lately: The Belated Evangelist," *The Bible and the Narrative Tradition* (Oxford: Oxford University Press, 1991), p. 124.

95   **Where Matthew, Mark, and Luke:** Foster, "John Come Lately," p. 114.

95   **narrative itself begins:** Frank Kermode, *The Sense of an Ending: Studies in the Theory of Fiction* (Oxford: Oxford University Press, 1970).

95   **"The Old Testament is the literature"**: John Barton, *A History of the Bible* (New York: Viking, 2019), p. 145.

96   **"We are perfectly ready to accept"**: Thomas L. Thompson, *The Bible in History: How Writers Create a Past* (London: Cape, 1999), p. 236; see also pp. 38, 120, 388 (U.S. title: *The Mythic Past: Biblical Archaeology and the Myth of Israel*); and Baruch Halpern, *The First Historians: The Hebrew Bible and History* (State College: Pennsylvania State University Press, 1996).

97   **"rollicking, silly nonsense"**: K. A. Kitchen, *On the Reliability of the Old Testament* (Grand Rapids, Mich.: Eerdmans, 2003), p. 454.

98   **"extraordinary fiction"**: Ruth Margalit, "Built on Sand," *The New Yorker,* 29 June 2010, p. 42. Margalit concludes: "In the long war over how to reconcile the Bible with historical fact, the story of David stands at ground zero."

99   **an exodus from Egypt:** David Plotz, "Reading Is Believing, or Not," *The New York Times Book Review,* 16 September 2007.

99   **"proof that Israelites ever invaded"**: Plotz, "Reading Is Believing."

99   **"The language of political propaganda"**: Thomas L. Thompson, *The Mythic Past: Bible Archaeology and the Myth of Israel* (New York: MJF Books, 1999), p. 193.

99   **helped change and determine:** Thompson, *Bible in History,* p. 193.

99   **"They are talking about"**: Thompson, *Bible in History,* p. 104; see also pp. 122, 136–39, 164, and 207.

100 **"quite incoherent and self-contradictory"**: Philip R. Davies, *In Search of "Ancient Israel": A Study in Biblical Origins* (London: Bloomsbury, 1992), p. 18.

100 **"most of the 'biblical period' consists"**: Davies, *In Search of "Ancient Israel,"* p. 26.

100 **"religious commitments should not"**: Davies, *In Search of "Ancient Israel,"* p. 19 footnote.

100 **"there is probably not a single episode"**: Barton, *History of the Bible,* p. 25.

100 **"although he likes"**: The Rev. Professor John Barton, email to the author, 9 April 2017. Barton is professor emeritus of the Interpretation of the Holy Scripture at Oriel College, Oxford.

100 **"There is *no evidence*"**: Giovanni Garbini, *History and Ideology in Ancient Israel* (London: SCM Press, 1988), p. xv.

100 **"the 'minimalist' view"**: Simon Schama, *The Story of the Jews: Finding the Words 1000 B.C.–1492 A.D.* (New York: Ecco, 2017).

100 **We can take from it political history:** William G. Dever, *What Did the Biblical Writers Know and When Did They Know It?* (Grand Rapids, Mich.: Eerdmans, 2002).

CHAPTER 4. CLOSING DOWN THE PAST

101 **"I did not get my picture"**: Ludwig Wittgenstein, *On Certainty*, trans. Denis Paul and Elizabeth Anscombe (New York: Harper, 1972), Proposition 94.

101 **"asserted the liberty of conscience"**: Edward Gibbon, *The Decline and Fall of the Roman Empire,* ch. 50.

101 **"Despite the lapse of fifteen hundred years"**: Israr Ahmad Khan, *Authentication of Ha-dith: Redefining the Criteria* (Washington, D.C.: International Institute of Islamic Thought, 2010).

102 **They created empires:** Max Rodenbeck, "The Early Days," *The New York Times Book Review*, 6 January 2008, p. 17.

104 **with oral communication:** Chase F. Robinson, *Islamic Historiography* (Cambridge, U.K.: Cambridge University Press, 2003), p. 10.

106 **"A little inaccuracy sometimes saves":** Saki (H. H. Munro), "Clovis on the Alleged Romance of Business," *The Square Egg and Other Sketches* (London: Bodley Head, 1924), p. 160.

108 **an *akhbari* was one who wrote:** Franz Rosenthal, *A History of Muslim Historiography* (Leiden: E. J. Brill, 1968), p. 3.

108 **"A spreading inkpot":** Richard W. Bulliet, *Islam: The View from the Edge* (New York: Columbia University Press, 1994), p. 8.

108 **"the further in time":** Tom Holland, *In the Shadow of the Sword* (London: Little, Brown, 2012), p. 25 and ff.

109 **The notion that, a fresh era:** D. S. Margoliouth, *Lectures on Arabic Historians* (Delhi: Idarah-Adabryat-1Delhi, 1977), p. 41.

109 **the very word *Qu'ran*:** Holland Carter, "From Islam, a Book of Illuminations," *The New York Times*, 11 November 2016, C19.

110 **"axial text . . . an end and a beginning":** Tarif Khalidi, *Arab Historical Thought in the Classical Period* (Cambridge: Cambridge University Press, 1994), p. 7.

110 **"It is as if historiography":** James Westfall Thompson, *History of Historical Writing*, vol. 1 (New York: Macmillan, 1942), p. 339.

110 **"as toilsome reading as I ever undertook":** Thomas Carlyle, *On Heroes, Hero-Worship, and the Heroic in History* (Berkeley and Los Angeles: University of California Press, 1993), p. 56.

110 **Continuity was essential:** Marshall G. S. Hodgson, "Two Pre-modern Muslim Historians: Pitfalls and Opportunities in Presenting Them to Moderns," *Towards World Community*, ed. John Nef, Springer online, 1968.

112 **is obsessed with the past:** Khalidi, *Classical Arab Islam*, p. 59.

113 **"The different paths are like":** Margoliouth, *Lectures on Arabic Historians*, p. 54.

116 **"Let him who examines this book of mine":** Ṭabarī, *The History of al-Tabari*, trans. Franz Rosenthal (New York: State University of New York Press, 1989), 1: 6–7.

117 **For that reason, he is more:** Margoliouth, *Lectures on Arabic Historians*, p. 16.

117 **the wise man is like a jeweler:** Tarif Khalidi, *Arabic Historical Thought in the Classical Period* (Cambridge: Cambridge University Press, 1994), p. 94.

117 **"thought seemed to rest":** Joseph Conrad, *The Secret Agent* (New York: Everyman, 1992), p. 89.

117 **Hanbalism was not a legitimate school:** Rosenthal, *The History of Al-Tabari*, introduction.

118 **"under the stimulus":** H. G. Wells, *The Outline of History* (London: George Newnes, 1920), vol. 2, p. 431.

119 **"incrementally innovative":** Robinson, *Islamic Historiography*, pp. 134, 60.

120 **"the dust that swirls":** Shihab al-Din al-Nuwayri, *The Ultimate Ambition in the Arts of Erudition: A Compendium of Knowledge from the Classical Islamic World*, ed. and trans. Elias Muhanna (New York: Penguin, 2016). See also Kanishk Tharoor, "Aphrodisiacs? Search This Medieval Encyclopedia," *The New York Times*, 29 October, 2016.

120 **"It should be known that the discussion":** Ibn Khaldūn, *The Muqaddimah: An Introduction to History*, trans. Franz Rosenthal, abridged N. J. Dawood (Princeton, N.J.: Princeton University Press, 1967), vol. 1, pp. 77–78.

120 **"It deals with such conditions":** Ibn Khaldūn, *Muqaddimah*, vol. 1, p. 35.

121 **"The entire world":** Ibn Khaldūn, *Muqaddimah*, vol. 1, p. 386.

121 **a compendium entitled "Secret of Secrets":** For a discussion of whether a genuine history of political thought is even possible before the seventeenth century, see Regula Foster and Neguin Yavar, eds., *Global Medieval: Mirrors for Princes Reconsidered* (Boston: Harvard University Press, Ilex Foundation, 2015).

121 **"What Thucydides was":** Thompson, *History of Historical Writing*, p. 359.

121 **"undoubtedly the greatest work":** Encyclopædia Britannica, 15th ed., vol. 9, p. 148; see also Arnold J. Toynbee, *A Study of History*. Toynbee is little read now, and one

should be careful with his pronouncements. He finds more than twice as many civilizations in history as Oswald Spengler did in his influential *Decline of the West* (1918).

121   **"more brilliant than a well-arranged pearl"**: Walter J. Fischel, *Ibn Khaldūn in Egypt: His Public Functions and His Historical Research (1382–1406)* (Berkeley and Los Angeles: University of California Press, 1967), pp. 28–29.

121   **"For on the surface history is no more"**: Ibn Khaldūn, *Muqaddimah,* vol. 1, p. 1.

122   **"These things are not strictly relevant"**: Robert Irwin, *Ibn Khaldun: An Intellectual Biography* (Princeton: Princeton University Press, 2018), p. 118.

124   **"most high-ranking governors"**: Patricia Crone, *Medieval Islamic Political Thought* (Edinburgh: Edinburgh University Press, 2004), p. 315.

125   **"cured of the temptation of office"**: Ibn Khaldūn, *Le Voyage d'Occident et d'Orient* (Paris: Sinbad, 1980), p. 103.

125   **"I was inspired by that"**: Ibn Khaldūn, *Le Voyage d'Occident et d'Orient,* p. 142.

125   **"The Negro nations are, as a rule"**: Ibn Khaldūn, *Muqaddimah,* vol. 2, pp. 57–61, 117.

127   **"He stands out"**: Wells, *Brief History of History,* ch. 5.

128   **"The encyclopedia's impartiality"**: Amir-Hussein Radjy, obituary of Ehsan Yarshater, *The New York Times,* 21 September 2018, B12.

128   **"Whoever imitates a people"**: Malise Ruthven, "The Islamic Road to the Modern World," *The New York Review of Books,* 22 June 2017, p. 24.

CHAPTER 5. THE MEDIEVAL CHRONICLERS

129   **"The best portraits are perhaps"**: Thomas Babington Macaulay, "Machiavelli," *Critical and Historical Essays,* vol. 2 (London: Longman, 1883).

130   **When he saw how much had been destroyed**: David Markson, *This Is Not a Novel* (Berkeley, Calif.: Counterpoint, 2001), p. 70. But then in today's climate virtually the second book in every library in the world is irreparably deteriorating because of brittle paper and acid content.

130–31 **"has recently been . . . analysed"**: Chris Wickham, *Framing the Early Middle Ages: Europe and the Mediterranean, 400–800* (Oxford: Oxford University Press, 2005), p. 8.

131   **"Trollope with bloodshed"**: Burrow, *History of Histories,* p. 198.

132   **"his bearing was so full"**: Charles G. Herbermann et al., eds., *Catholic Encyclopedia* (New York: Robert Appleton, 1910), vol. 7. See also entry for Gregory of Tours.

133   **"When King Clovis was dwelling"**: Gregory of Tours, *History of the Franks,* book 1, ch. 40.

134   **"small class of books"**: Frank Stenton, *Anglo-Saxon England* (Oxford: Oxford University Press, 1971), p. 187.

136   **One account has it**: *Lesser Feasts and Fasts* (New York: Church Publishing, 2018).

137   **miracles, miracles, miracles**: Wells, *Brief History of History,* p. 57.

137   **"what I was able to learn myself"**: Bede, *Historia ecclesiastica gentis Anglorum,* p. 6. He makes similar remarks at two other points in his prologue.

138   **"What makes a nation"**: Eric Hobsbawm, lecture delivered to the American Anthropological Association in 1991; see also Richard J. Evans, *Eric Hobsbawm: A Life in History* (London: Little, Brown, 2019), p. 553.

140   **"a tapestry of lies"**: Ben Macintyre, "France May Be Sending Us a Tapestry of Lies," *The Times* (London), 20 January 2018. See also Andrew Bridgeford, *1066: The Hidden History in the Bayeux Tapestry* (New York: Walker, 2005), p. 8; and David Beinstein, *The Mystery of the Bayeux Tapestry* (Chicago: University of Chicago Press, 1987).

140   **"judge from some New York district"**: F. Scott Fitzgerald, "Echoes of the Jazz Age," November 1931.

143   **"You see!"**: Tom Stoppard, *Arcadia* (New York: Samuel French, 2011), pp. 49–50.

144   **"only a person ignorant of ancient history"**: William of Newburgh, *Historia rerum Anglicarum* (The history of English affairs), Book I, preface.

144   **No other contemporary chronicler**: A. W. Ward, ed., *The Cambridge History of English Literature* (Cambridge: Cambridge University Press, 1908).

145 **The most important Anglo-Norman:** C. Warren Hollister, *Henry I* (New Haven: Yale University Press, 2001), p. 9.

147 **He is still well worth reading:** Rodney M. Thomson, *William of Malmesbury* (Woodbridge, Suffolk: Boydell & Brewer, 2003).

147 **"He respected God too little":** William of Malmesbury, *Gesta Rerum,* p. 557 ff.

148 **"lively and demotic and sometimes macabre":** Burrow, *History of Histories,* p. 234.

148 **"There was in this church":** *Chronicles of Matthew Paris: Monastic Life in the Thirteenth Century,* ed. and trans. Richard Vaughan (Gloucester, U.K.: Alan Sutton, 1986), p. 17.

149 **Paris was recording events:** Hugh Chisholm, ed., "Matthew of Paris," Encyclopaedia Brittanica, 11th ed. (Cambridge: Cambridge University Press, 1911), pp. 888–89.

150 **"like trying to de-vein Gorgonzola":** Burrow, *History of Histories,* p. 232. As a wise teacher once told me, historians are little appreciated because their research tends to destroy myths.

151 **"its gains had largely melted away":** Thompson, *History of Historical Wrtiting.*

151 **he knew little of his subject's childhood:** Janet Nelson, *King and Emperor: A New Life of Charlemagne* (London: Allen Lane, 2019).

152 **"Since, at some point in the future":** Jean Froissart, *Chroniques,* Book I, p. 7.

154 **"Froissart, write that down":** Jean Froissart, *Oeuvres,* ed. Kervyn de Lettenhove, 25 vols. (Brussels, 1867–77), pp. xv, 167, xvi, 234.

154 **He loves the flourish and display:** Burrow, *History of Histories,* pp. 254–56.

154 **"He did not inquire":** Will Durant, *The Reformation* (New York: Simon & Schuster, 1957), p. 76.

154 **he shortcuts real thought:** Johan Huizinga, *The Autumn of the Middle Ages* (Chicago: University of Chicago Press, 1996), pp. 347–48.

154 **As to those supposedly dark ages:** Dan Piepenbring, "Hunky, Virile Consumers, and Other News," *The Paris Review,* 13 July 2015.

155 **Chroniclers, on the other hand:** Chris Given-Wilson, *Chronicles: The Writing of History in Medieval England* (New York: Hambledon and London, 2004), p. 126.

CHAPTER 6. THE ACCIDENTAL HISTORIAN

156 **"Princes should have more":** Antonio Pérez, *Aforismos de las Relaciones y Cartas Primeras y Segundas de Antonio Perez* (1787; repr. Charleston, S.C.: Nabu Press, 2011).

156 **It was the first modern analytical study:** Fuerter, quoted in Thompson, *History of Historical Writing,* p. 498. See also the introduction by Tim Parks to *The Prince* (New York: Penguin, 2009); and Felix Gilbert, *History: Choice and Commitment* (Cambridge: Harvard University, 1977), p. 135.

157 **helped usher in a revolution:** Dominique Goy-Blanquet, "Elizabethan Historiography and Shakespeare's Sources," in *Cambridge Companion to Shakespeare's History Plays,* ed. Michael Hathaway (Cambridge, U.K.: Cambridge University Press, 2002), p. 57.

158 **"gradually settling into oligarchy":** Patrick Boucheron, *Machiavelli: The Art of Teaching People What to Fear,* tr. Willard Wood (New York: Other Press, 2020).

159 **"put seven times to the torture":** Voltaire, "Of Savonarola," ch. 87, p. 166.

162 **"air of one who felt":** Will Durant, *The Renaissance: A History of Civilization in Italy from 1304–1576 A.D.* (New York: Simon & Schuster, 1953), p. 418.

162 **"These were not places":** Miles J. Unger, *Machiavelli* (New York: Simon & Schuster, 2011), p. 102.

163 **"This Lord is of such splendid and magnificent bearing":** Machiavelli, *Legazioni, Commissarie, Scritti di Governo,* 4 vols. (Rome, 2006), vol. 2, p. 125.

164 **"Little by little this Duke is slipping":** Pasquale Villari, *The Life and Times of Niccolò Machiavelli,* 2 vols., trans. Linda Villari (London: T. F. Unwin, 1898), p. 364.

165 **"I have on my legs":** Claudia Roth Pierpont, "The Florentine," *The New Yorker,* 15 September 2008, p. 87.

166 **"connoisseur of depravity":** Erin Maglaque, "Free from Humbug," *London Review of Books,* 16 July 2020, p. 37.

167 **"Come evening, I return"**: *Lettere Familiari di Niccolò Machiavelli,* ed. Edoardo Alvise (Florence, 1893), pp. 308–9.

167 **"Politics, these days, is no occupation"**: Aristophanes, *The Knights,* a satire on social and political life in Athens in the fifth century B.C.

168 **"is in point of Morality"**: Frederick II, der Grosse, King of Prussia, *Anti-Machiavel, or, An Examination of Machiavel's Prince, with Notes Historical and Political, published by M. de Voltaire* (London: T. Woodward, 1761), p. v.

169 **"we are much beholden"**: *The Works of Francis Bacon,* 1884, vol. I, book 2, p. 223.

170 **"The *Prince* claimed to put"**: Erica Benner, *Be Like the Fox: Machiavelli in His World* (London: Allen Lane, 2017), p. xv. A contrary view published recently is Philip Bobbit, *The Garments of Court and Palace; Machiavelli and the World That He Made* (New York: Grove, 2013), which makes its subject sound like Dick Cheney. See also Sarah Dunant's well-researched historical novel *In the Name of the Family* (New York: Random House, 2017). The recently published *Machiavelli: His Life and Times* by Alexander Lee, a plodding 762 pages, is best avoided.

170 **"a sponsor of the Higher Cheneyism"**: Garry Wills, "New Statesman," *The New York Times Book Review,* 4 August 2013, p. 12. See also Bobbitt, *The Garments of Court and Palace.*

170 **"For Macchiavelli"**: Simon Schama, *Wordy: Sounding Off on High Art, Low Appetite and the Power of Memory* (London: Simon and Schuster, 2019), p. 261.

171 **Roman historians would chiefly:** Burrows, *History of Histories,* p. 279.

172 **"Thus [states] are always descending"**: Niccolò Machiavelli, *Florentine Histories,* book 5.

173 **Niccolò, now almost sixty:** Maurizio Viroli, *Niccolò's Smile: A Biography of Machiavelli,* trans. Antony Shugaar (New York: Farrar, Straus and Giroux, 2002), ch. 1.

CHAPTER 7. WILLIAM SHAKESPEARE

174 **"Think ye see"**: William Shakespeare, *Henry VIII,* Prologue, ll. 25–27.

174 **"It is he who has etched"**: Peter Saccio, *Shakespeare's English Kings: History, Chronicle, and Drama* (1977; repr. Oxford: Oxford University Press, 2000).

174 **"not only a poet but a historian"**: Beverley E. Warner, *English History in Shakespeare's Plays* (New York: Longman, 1906), p. 3.

175 **"In the absence of newspapers"**: Jonathan Bate, *Soul of the Age: A Biography of the Mind of William Shakespeare* (New York: Random House, 2009), p. 322.

175 **"In Italy the peripatetic"**: Simon Schama, *Wordy: Sounding Off on High Art* (London: Simon & Schuster, 2019), p. 234.

175 **historical texts, chronicles, and chapbooks:** Louis B. Wright, *Middle-Class Culture in Elizabethan England* (Ithaca, N.Y.: Cornell University Press, 1965).

176 **The chorus in *Henry V*:** Ivo Kamps, "Shakespeare's England," *A Companion to Shakespeare's Works: The Histories* (Oxford: Blackwell, 2003), p. 8.

177 **"There is as much history in *Macbeth*"**: Samuel Taylor Coleridge, *On Shakespeare and Other Poets and Dramatists* (Charleston, S.C.: Nabu Press, 2011). In the original text, Coleridge omits the Roman numeral after Richard but it is clear that he is referring to *Richard II.*

178 **"a little like taking George C. Scott's words"**: Stacy Schiff, *Cleopatra: A Life* (New York: Little, Brown, 2010), pp. 7, 300.

179 **"Business first, pleasure afterwards"**: Charles Dickens, *The Pickwick Papers* (London: Chapman and Hall, 1838), p. 412.

180 **Alison Weir has pointed out:** Alison Weir, *Richard III and the Princes in the Tower* (London: Vintage, 2014). Her original study was published in 1992 but has been updated: "I feel that there is an even stronger case to be made against Richard III—and this from someone who, for a quarter of a century, thought he was much maligned!"

180 **Richard's heroic end:** Janis Hull, "Plantagenets, Lancastrians, Yorkists, and Tudors,"

in *Cambridge Companion to Shakespeare's History Plays,* ed. Michael Hathaway (Cambridge, U.K.: Cambridge University Press, 2002), p. 98.

180 **"Something in us":** Stephen Greenblatt, *Tyrant: Shakespeare on Politics* (New York: Norton, 2018).

181 **"the one place":** James Shapiro, *The Year of Lear: Shakespeare in 1606* (New York: Simon & Schuster, 2015), p. 11. See also "Is Shakespeare History?" *In Our Time,* a program on BBC Radio 4 with Melvyn Bragg, 11 October 2018.

183 **"of all beastly and filthy matters":** The words of a contemporary preacher at St. Paul's Cross, an open-air pulpit in the grounds of Old St. Paul's Cathedral. Bate, *Soul of the Age,* p. 16.

183 **"in the month of January, 1596":** Garry Wills, "Shakespeare and Verdi in the Theatre," *The New York Review of Books,* 24 November 2011, p. 34.

184 **Scripts were bought:** William J. Humphries, "How Did Shakespeare Make His Money?" *The Author,* Winter 2016, p. 119.

184 **women's parts make up only 13 percent:** Garry Wills, *Verdi's Shakespeare: Men of the Theater* (New York: Penguin Books, 2012).

185 **"When he was writing *Hamlet*":** Bob Dylan, speech given at the Nobel Banquet, 10 December 2016.

186 **"the first time":** Henry Ansgar Kelly, *Divine Providence in the England of Shakespeare's Histories* (Cambridge: Harvard University Press, 1970). The discussion of the *Henry VI* trilogy is based on Kelly's book.

187 **"When is it right to rebel?":** John F. Danby, *Shakespeare's Doctrine of Nature: A Study of King Lear* (London: Faber, 1949).

187 **small inaccuracies and anachronisms:** For a considered if dyspeptic account of Shakespeare being "careless," see J.A.K. Thomson, *Shakespeare and the Classics* (London: Allen and Unwin, 1952).

187 **"In order that a drama":** Samuel Taylor Coleridge, "Shakespeare's English Historical Plays," *Shakespeare, With Introductory Matter on Poetry, the Drama, and the Stage* (New York: Amazon Digital, 2015).

188 **"The greater the artist":** Ron Rosenbaum, in conversation with the author, August 2014.

188 **In *Henry V,* Harry boasts:** Bate, *Soul of the Age,* p. 223.

189 **"I am Richard II":** For a discussion of whether Elizabeth ever said this, see Bate, *Soul of the Age,* pp. 263–67.

189 **"If, despite such screening":** Wills, *Verdi's Shakespeare.*

190 **"To go fishing for subjects":** Paola Pugliatti, *Shakespeare the Historian* (Basingstoke, U.K.: Macmillan, 1995), p. 36.

192 **Hamlet and Laertes:** Bart Vanes, "Too Much Changed," *The Times Literary Supplement,* 2 September 2016, p. 14.

192 **"Why, I can smile, and murder":** *Henry VI, Part III,* Act III, scene ii, ll. 182–95.

193 **"the emergence in the seventeenth century":** Terry Eagleton, *Humour* (London: Yale University Press, 2019).

194 **"We know / enough":** *Henry V,* Act IV, scene i, ll. 129–45; the king then gives a forty-line reply!

194 **Schama reckons the encounter:** Schama, *Wordy,* p. 237.

CHAPTER 8. ZOZO AND THE MARIONETTE INFIDEL

195 **"The arch-scoundrel . . . has finally":** *The Letters of Wolfgang Amadeus Mozart (1769–1791)* (New York: Hurd and Houghton, 1866), vol. 1, in a letter to his father of 1778.

195 **"'He is a disagreeable dog, this Gibbon'":** *The Correspondence of James Boswell with James Bruce and Andrew Gibb, Overseers of the Auchinleck Estate,* ed. Nellie Hankins and John Strawhorn (New Haven: Yale University Press, 1998), p. 298.

196 **"nothing more than a tableau":** Voltaire, *Works,* vol. 16a (New York, 1927), pp. 250–51.

196 **the form of literature:** See John Lukacs, *The Future of History* (New Haven: Yale University Press, 2011), p. 5.

196 **"History is the most popular":** Lukacs, *Future of History*, p. 5.

196 **"a fighter, without tenderness":** Lytton Strachey, "Voltaire and Frederick the Great," *Books and Characters French and English* (New York: Harcourt, Brace, 1922).

197 **"The character of every man":** Pomeau, *Voltaire and His Times*, vol. 1 (Oxford: Voltaire Foundation, 1985), p. 4.

197 **"not with the eye of a devout seer":** Thomas Carlyle, *The History of Frederick II of Prussia*, 8 vols. (1858–65; repr. London: Chapman & Hall, 1897).

197 **"an open sesame":** Will and Ariel Durant, *The Age of Voltaire: The Story of Civilization*, vol. 9 (New York: Simon & Schuster, 1965), prologue.

198 **"thin, long, and fleshless":** Norman L. Torrey, *The Spirit of Voltaire* (1938; repr. New York: Russell and Russell, 1968), p. 21.

198 **Voltaire was allowed books, furniture, linen:** Durant, *Age of Voltaire*, p. 36.

199 **"No authors ever had so much fame":** James Boswell, *The Life of Samuel Johnson*, ed. Percy Fitzgerald (London: Sands & Co.), vol. 1, p. 355.

199 **"with hair like golden flame":** Roger Pearson, *Voltaire Almighty* (New York: Bloomsbury, 2008), p. 57.

"How much more history is there?!"

200 **"His whole intelligence":** letter from Gustave Flaubert to Mme Roger des Genettes, quoted in P. N. Furbank, "Cultivating Voltaire's Garden," *The New York Review of Books*, 15 December 2005, p. 69.

200 **"To hold a pen":** Voltaire, letter to Jeanne-Grâce Bosc du Bouchet, comtesse d'Argental (4 October 1748). The remark also appears in a letter to Marie-Louise Denis (22 May 1752).

202 **"I cannot be away from him":** René Pomeau, *La Religion de Voltaire* (1958; repr. Paris: Nizet, 1995), p. 190.

202 **"I was overwhelmed":** Voltaire, *Memoirs*, p. 41.

203 **"I have found a port":** *The Works of Voltaire: A Contemporary Version with Notes by Tobias Smollett*, vol. 1 (London: E. R. DuMont, 1901), p. 22. It is unclear whether the remark is Voltaire's or Smollett's.

203 **"I soon felt myself attached to him":** Voltaire, *Memoirs*, p. 45.

204 **In a rage:** Voltaire, *Memoirs*, p. 23.

206 **which critics judged a revelation:** F. C. Green, introduction to Voltaire, *The Age of Louis XIV* (London: J. M. Dent, 1961), p. vii.

207 **he was enunciating:** See Page Smith, *The Historian and History* (New York: Knopf, 1964), p. 31.

207 **"Elizabeth, during her confinement":** Voltaire, *Essay on the Manners and Spirit of Nations,* vol. 3, p. 40.

207 **"Without haste or effort he swings":** Virginia Woolf, "The Historian and the Gibbon," *The Death of the Moth and Other Essays* (New York: Harcourt Brace, 1974), p. 85.

208 **"I shall be coming":** *Love Letters of Voltaire to His Niece,* ed. and trans. Theodore Besterman (Oxford: Oxford University Press, 1958).

208 **"a fat little woman":** Louise de l'Epinay, *Memoirs and Correspondence,* trans. J. H. Freese (London, 1899), vol. 3, p. 178.

209 **"animals . . . with little or no intelligence":** Voltaire, *Lettres d'Amabed, Septième lettre,* 1769.

209 **"a philanthropist masquerading":** Peter Gay, *Style in History* (New York: Basic Books, 1974), p. 29; see also Ian Davidson, *Voltaire in Exile, 1753–78* (New York: Grove Press, 2004), p. 6.

211 **"with the pomp, the dignity":** *The Letters of Edward Gibbon,* ed. J. E. Norton, vol. 1, 1750–73 (New York: Macmillan, 1956), no. 388, p. xi.

211 **it became a choice item:** *Studies on Voltaire and the Eighteenth Century: Edward Gibbon, Bicentenary Essays,* ed. David Womersley (New York: Oxford University Press, 1997), p. 297.

212 **"I don't want to die":** *The Letters of Edward Gibbon,* vol. 1, 18 December 1757, p. 80.

212 **"fifteen times because it comes":** The same letter, 18 December 1757, p. 79.

213 **not his head but his bare buttocks:** Lytton Strachey, *Books and Characters* (Cheltenham: Orchard Press, 2008) and *Portraits in Miniature* (London: Chatto, 1931).

214 **"The body in Gibbon's case":** Woolf, *Death of the Moth,* p. 90.

215 **"fat Tory landowners":** "Dish and Dishonesty," *Blackadder the Third,* first broadcast 17 September 1987.

216 **"in the prime of her short-lived beauty":** Young, *Gibbon,* pp. 44–45.

216 **"It has been observed":** Henry Fielding, *The Adventures of Tom Jones,* p. 62.

217 **"half a Frenchman":** Jorge Luis Borges, "Edward Gibbon, Pages of History and Autobiography," *Selected Nonfictions.*

218 **Gibbon knew that all accounts of the past:** Gerald Rose, "Shakespeare as an Historian: The Roman Plays," *Fidelio,* vol. 13, Fall 2004.

218 **his writing set in train:** Jim White, "Onan off the Playing Field," *The Daily Telegraph,* 20 March 2005.

219 **"overpaid the labor of ten years":** Will and Ariel Durant, *Rousseau and Revolution* (New York: Simon & Schuster, 1931), p. 800.

219 **the young Maggie Tulliver:** George Eliot, *Mill on the Floss* (London: Collins cleartype), p. 150.

219 **"In history I decided to begin":** Winston Churchill, *A Roving Commission: My Early Life* (New York: Scribner, 1930), p. 111.

220 **increasing use of italics:** *Gibbon and the "Watchmen of the Holy City": The Historian and His Reputation, 1776–1815,* ed. David Warmersley (Oxford: Clarendon, 2002), p. 1.

221 **"It is very true":** Lord Sheffield, *The Miscellaneous Works of Edward Gibbon Esq,* 1814, vol. I, p. 278.

221 **As Virginia Woolf remarks:** Woolf, *Death of the Moth,* pp. 82–83.

222 **Many people have written pastiches:** Paul Hendrickson, author of *Hemingway's Boat,* lecture, Macaulay Honors College, CUNY, 2 November 2011.

222 **"Many experiments":** Will and Ariel Durant, *Rousseau and Revolution,* p. 800.

222 **Five Horsemen of the Apocalypse:** Ian Morris, *Why the West Rules—For Now: The Patterns of History and What They Reveal About the Future* (New York: Farrar, Straus and Giroux, 2010).

223 **The resultant decline**: Rose, "Shakespeare as an Historian."

223 **the wickedness of priests**: Gay, *Style in History*, p. 12.

223 **"Such is his eagerness"**: Roger Bradshaigh Lloyd, *Christianity, History, and Civilization* (Madison: University of Wisconsin Press, 2008), p. 44.

225 **"What he could not understand"**: Virginia Woolf, *Death of the Moth*, p. 112.

225 **"Both [Edmund] Burke and [Samuel] Johnson"**: Young, *Gibbon*, pp. 74–75.

226 **"I can part with land"**: *The Letters of Edward Gibbon*, vol. 3, letter to Lord Sheffield, 20 January 1787, p. 61.

226 **"Should you be very surprised"**: *The Letters of Edward Gibbon*, letter to Lady Sheffield, 22 October 1784, p. 10.

227 **"Poor France!"**: Letter to Lord Sheffield, 9 April 1791, in H. H. Milman, *The Life of Edward Gibbon with Selections from His Correspondence* (Paris: Baudry's European Library, 1840), p. 232.

227 **"the lives or rather the characters"**: Letter to Lord Sheffield, 6 January 1793, *The Letters of Edward Gibbon*, vol. 3.

CHAPTER 9. ANNOUNCING A DISCIPLINE

228 **"Why should history"**: Simon Schama, speech at National Book Festival, Washington, D.C., 26 September 2009.

228 **The emergence of a historical consciousness**: Lukacs, *Future of History*, p. 3.

228 **"the most popular historian"**: Peter Gay and Victor G. Wexler, eds., *Historians at Work*, vol. 3 (New York: Harper & Row, 1975), p. 88.

229 **The rapid development**: Alberto Manguel, *A History of Reading* (London: Flamingo, 1997), p. 231.

229 **from being solely an aristocratic entertainment**: Manguel, *History of Reading*.

230 **The nineteenth century has been called**: Joan Acocella, "Turning the Page," *The New Yorker*, 8 October 2012.

231 **"The so-called 'chancery double'"**: Stefan Zweig, *Beware of Pity* (New York: New York Review of Books, 1976), p. 246.

233 **"the more warm-hearted"**: John Clive, *Macaulay: The Shaping of the Historian* (New York: Vintage, 1975), p. 259.

234 **"A presence with gigantic power"**: John Moultrie, "The Dream of Life," *Poems*, 2 vols. (London, 1876), I, pp. 421–42.

234 **at Cambridge he left**: Clive, *Macaulay*, p. 59.

234 **"My father"**: Lord Macaulay, letter to his sister Hannah, 30 July 1831, *The Life and Letters of Lord Macaulay*, ed. Otto Trevelyan (New York: Harper, 1875).

235 **"By the way, Tom"**: *Morning Chronicle*, 26 June 1824.

235 **"a bumptious youth"**: Clive, *Macaulay*, p. 139.

235 **"I have quite forgiven"**: Margaret Macaulay, *Recollections*, 27 November 1837, pp. 59–60.

238 **"the reconstruction of a decomposed society"**: H. V. Bowen, *The Business of Empire: The East India Company and Imperial Britain, 1756–1833* (Cambridge: Cambridge University Press, 2006), p. 203.

238 **"something like what would ensue"**: Fanny Macaulay to Margaret Macaulay, February 1834, Huntington MSS.

239 **"I am a changed man"**: Robert E. Sullivan, *Macaulay: The Tragedy of Power* (Cambridge: Harvard University Press, 2009), p. 131.

239 **"became almost invisible to him"**: Sullivan, *Macaulay*, p. 127.

240 **"undertake some great historical work"**: Letter to Thomas Flower Ellis, 30 December 1835.

240 **Winston Churchill memorized them**: Winston Churchill, *My Early Life*, ch. 2.

240 **"the Revolution which brought"**: Macaulay to Napier, 20 July 1838, Napier Correspondence, pp. 264–65.

241 **The Temple essay used**: Macaulay, *Critical and Historical Essays*, p. 415ff.

242 **"I shall be a rich man"**: Sullivan, *Macaulay*, p. 315.

243 **self-conscious to the point of obsession:** Schama, *Scribble, Scribble, Scribble*, p. 110.

243 **He developed an almost operatic possessiveness:** Owen Dudley Edwards, *Macaulay* (New York: St. Martin's Press, 1988), p. 26.

243 **"How dearly I love":** Macaulay to Hannah and Margaret, 7 June 1932, Trinity Correspondence.

243 **"It is quite impossible":** Schama, *Scribble, Scribble, Scribble*, p. 111.

244 **"The history of England":** Lord Macaulay, essay on James Mackintosh's *History of the Glorious Revolution of 1688*, in *Critical and Historical Essays*, vol. 2, p. 206.

245 **The Victorian man of letters:** Terry Eagleton, "A Toast at the Trocadero," *London Review of Books*, 18 February 2018, p. 10.

245 **"Ranke is the representative":** Lord Acton, "The Study of History," *Lectures on Modern History* (London: Macmillan, 1906), pp. 32–33. See also G. P. Gooch, *History and Historians in the Nineteenth Century* (London: Longmans, Green, 1913), p. 12; and George G. Iggers and James M. Powell, *Leopold von Ranke and the Shaping of the Historical Discipline* (New York: Syracuse University Press, 1990), pp. 1–10.

245 **"Ranke is to historians":** Edward Muir, "Leopold von Ranke, His Library, and the Shaping of Historical Evidence," *Syracuse University Library Associates Courier* 22, no. 1 (Spring 1987): 3.

246 **This was a convincing argument:** Wells, *Brief History of History*, p. 227.

247 **"a weapon of war":** John Barker, *The Superhistorians: Makers of Our Past* (New York: Scribner, 1982), p. 183.

247 **Without an independent government:** Muir, "Leopold von Ranke."

248 **"books, or rather":** Leopold von Ranke, *Collected Works* (Sämtliche Werke), 53/54, p. 227.

248 **Down to the eighteenth century:** Susan Cramer, "The Nature of History: Meditations on Clio's Craft," *Nursing Research* 41, no 1 (1992).

249 **"I have been here in Rome":** Leopold von Ranke, *Collected Works*, p. 227.

250 **"Not again will I so easily find":** Leopold von Ranke, *Collected Works*, p. 258.

250 **"with humble tenderness":** Theodore von Laue, *Leopold Ranke: The Formative Years* (Princeton: Princeton University Press, 1950), p. 115.

250 **"heroic study of records":** Lord Acton, "Study of History," p. 18.

251 **great science is always impersonal:** Richard Crossman, "When Lightning Struck the Ivory Tower," *The Charm of Politics: And Other Essays in Political Criticism* (New York: Harper and Northumberland Press, 1958).

252 **"That was no lecture":** Georg G. Iggers and Konrad von Moltke, introduction to Leopold von Ranke, *The Theory and Practice of History* (Indianapolis: Bobbs-Merrill, 1973), p. xxxi.

253 **"If you saw him":** Wilhelm von Giesebrecht, *Gedächtnisrede auf Leopold von Ranke* (Munich, 1887), p. 14.

253 **"achieved a peculiar sainthood":** Theodore von Laue, *Leopold Ranke*, p. 52.

255 **"The common understanding":** Robinson, *Islamic Historiography*, pp. 5–6.

255 **"By judicious selection":** Macaulay, "History," *Critical and Historical Essays*.

255 **"I felt unable":** Barker, *Superhistorians*, pp. 150–51.

CHAPTER 10. ONCE UPON A TIME

256 **"Historian: an unsuccessful novelist":** H. L. Mencken, *A Mencken Chrestomathy* (New York: Knopf, 1949).

256 **"If we write novels so":** Henry James, reviewing George Eliot, *Middlemarch*. See Sally Beauman, "Encounters with George Eliot," *The New Yorker*, 18 April 1994, p. 92.

259 **Mark Twain even claimed:** Barker, *Superhistorians*, p. 118.

259 **"When it came to his estates":** A. N. Wilson, *The Laird of Abbotsford: A View of Sir Walter Scott* (Oxford: Oxford University Press, 1980), p. 59

261 **"glorious national past shrouded in the mists of time":** Colin Wells, *A Brief History of History*, p. 223.

262 **"All other possible Scotlands"**: Hilary Mantel, "The Iron Maiden," Second Reith Lecture, 2017.

263 **"fiction was what historians wrote"**: Jill Lepore, "Just the Facts, Ma'am," *The New Yorker,* 24 March 2008.

263 **"the lessons of history"**: György Lukács, *The Historical Novel* (London: Merlin Press, 1962), p. 20.

264 **"that group of brilliant"**: Edith Wharton, *The Writing of Fiction* (New York: Scribner, 1997), p. 11.

265 **"[He] was such a great novelist"**: Isaiah Berlin, *Karl Marx* (London: Oxford University Press, 1959), p. 205.

265 **"Yes, that's it!"**: Jacques Bonnet, *Phantoms of the Bookshelves* (London: Macclehose Press, 2010), pp. 82–83.

265 **"What was new in both Balzac and Stendhal"**: Wharton, *Writing of Fiction,* p. 9.

265 **"Fiction is history"**: Joseph Conrad, "Henry James, An Appreciation," *Notes on Life and Letters* (CreateSpace Independent Publishing, 2016).

266 **"The fact-by-fact decision-making"**: Thomas Mallon, "Never Happened," *The New Yorker,* 21 November 2011, p. 117.

266 **"They do now"**: Doctorow's editor, Gerald Howard, recalled the exchange in an email to the author, 2016. Gore Vidal took a similar view over an encounter between Theodore Roosevelt and William Randolph Hearst at the White House around 1906, as depicted in *Empire,* the fifth in his historical series Narratives of Empire. "No one knows what they actually said," wrote Vidal. "I like to think my dialogue captures, if nothing else, what each felt about the other."

266 **"none of this really matters"**: Emmanuel Le Roy Ladurie, "Balzac's Country Doctor: Simple Technology and Rural Folklore," *The Mind and Method of a Historian,* trans. Sian and Ben Reynolds (Chicago: University of Chicago Press, 1981), p. 123. Other quotations are all from this essay.

269 **"Fidelity to historical reality"**: Milan Kundera, *The Art of the Novel,* trans. Linda Asher (New York: Grove, 1988), p. 44. In the same book Kundera makes two good points. First (p. 36), he recalls that in the years following the 1968 Russian invasion of Czechoslovakia "the reign of terror against the public was preceded by officially organized massacres of dogs. An episode totally forgotten and without importance for a historian, for a political scientist, but of the utmost anthropological importance!" Second (p. 38), he gives an example from his novel, *The Unbearable Lightness of Being,* where Alexander Dubček, after being arrested by the Russian army, kidnapped, jailed, and forced to negotiate with Brezhnev, returns to Prague: "He speaks over the radio, but he cannot speak, he gasps for breath, in mid-sentence he makes long, awful pauses." This episode would have been completely forgotten, since radio technicians were instructed to cut out the painful pauses, had Kundera not re-created the episode.

269 **"the magical ventriloquism"**: "Up Front: Brenda Wineapple," *The New York Times Book Review,* 9 July 2010.

269 **"facts and artifacts"**: Geoffrey Woolf, "A Nineteenth-Century Turn," *The New York Times Book Review,* 11 March 2007, p. 1.

270 **"recent historians like"**: A. S. Byatt, *On Histories and Stories* (Cambridge, Mass.: Harvard University Press, 2002).

270 **"Where does one draw"**: Robinson, *Islamic Historiography,* pp. 154–55.

270 **"We're all having our stab at truth"**: Michael Howard, in conversation with the author, October 2017.

271 **"History is like a deaf man"**: Isaiah Berlin, *Russian Thinkers* (London: Penguin, 1994), p. 242.

272 **"and won't permit skipping"**: Maxwell Perkins, *Editor to Author: The Letters of Maxwell E. Perkins* (New York: Scribner, 1991), p. 64. Percy Lubbock, in his classic study *The Craft of Fiction* (New York: Viking, 1957), p. 35, also objected to "these maddening interruptions": "Wherever 'the historians' are mentioned he [the reader] knows that several pages can be turned at once."

272 **"In historic events"**: Leo Tolstoy, *War and Peace,* trans. Aylmer Maude (1812), book 9, ch. 1.

272 **"tubby, dumpy"**: William Golding, *The Hot Gates and Other Occasional Pieces* (New York: Harcourt, Brace, 1966), p. 123.

272 **"It was not Napoleon"**: Leo Tolstoy, *War and Peace,* trans. Andrew Bromfield (New York: Ecco, 2007), pp. 399, 751.

273 **"As soon as Napoleon"**: Janet Malcolm, *Reading Chekhov: A Critical Journey* (New York: Random House, 2002), p. 121.

273 **"What could this possibly"**: *Golos,* no. 93, 3 April 1865.

273 **"the work is not a novel"**: See Count Nikolai Tolstoy, introduction to *War and Peace,* trans. Andrew Bromfield (New York: Ecco Press, 2007), p. viii.

274 **"Moscow meanwhile was empty"**: *War and Peace,* trans. Andrew Bromfield, book 3, part 3, ch. 20.

275 **"better works insofar"**: Alan Edwin Day, *History: A Reference Handbook* (London: Clive Bingley, 1977), p. 178.

276 **"not only György Lukács"**: Perry Anderson, "From Progress to Catastrophe," *London Review of Books,* 28 July 2011.

278 **"That's shallow"**: Nick Ripatzrone, *Longing for an Absent God* (New York: Fortress Press, 2020).

279 **"I was inspired by the silence"**: Hilton Als, "Ghosts in the House," *The New Yorker,* 27 October 2003, reprinted 27 July 2020, p. 35.

280 **"emotional memory"**: Alexis Okeowo, "Secret Histories," *The New Yorker,* 26 October 2020, p. 44.

280 **"Anyone who doesn't know"**: Toni Morrison, "A Knowing So Deep," *Essence,* 15th Anniversary Issue, April 1985; reprinted in *What Moves at the Margin: Selected Nonfiction,* ed. Carolyn Denard (Jackson: University Press of Mississippi, 2008).

281 **"She saw it as her task"**: Alexander Lee, "Portrait of the Author as a Historian: Toni Morrison," *History Today,* vol. 67, issue 2, 2 February 2017. Cf. also "Anyone who doesn't know": Toni Morrison, "A Knowledge So Deep," *Essence,* 15th Anniversary Issue, April 1985; reprinted in *What Moves at the Margin: Selected Nonfiction* (Jackson: University Press of Mississippi, 2008).

281 **"Morrison is relighting the angles"**: Als, "Ghosts in the House," p. 32.

282 **His alter ego, Ivan Denisovich Shukhov**: Michael Scammell, "Solzhenitsyn the Stylist," *The New York Times Book Review,* 31 August 2008, p. 23.

282 **"Once you give up survival"**: Gary Saul Morson, "Solzhenitsyn's Cathedrals," *The New Criterion,* 20 October 2017.

282 **"Oh my god, socialist realism"**: Michael Scammell, "Solzhenitsyn the Stylist," *The New York Times Book Review,* 31 August 2008, p. 23.

284 **has come to signify**: Michael Scammell, "Circles of Hell," *The New York Review of Books,* 28 April 2011, p. 46; and Anne Applebaum, *Gulag: A History* (New York: Doubleday, 2003).

285 **"Well, yes, he is an expert"**: David Remnick, *Reporting* (New York: Knopf, 2006), p. 197. The original essay, "Deep in the Woods," was published in *The New Yorker* in 2001.

285 **"I have to dismantle each stone"**: Interview, "Solzhenitsyn in Zurich," *Encounter* 46, no. 4 (April 1976): 12.

285 **"History and polemic"**: Scammell, "Solzhenitsyn the Stylist," p. 23.

287 **"Can anybody be so naïve"**: Vladimir Nabokov, "Good Readers and Good Writers," *Lectures on Literature* (New York: Mariner Books, 2002), p. 1. These lectures were first given at Cornell and elsewhere in 1946.

287 **"Historians and novelists are kin"**: Jill Lepore, "Just the Facts, Ma'am," *The New Yorker,* 24 March 2008, p. 79.

287 **"history is not the past"**: Quotations from the Reith Lectures are on the BBC website.

289 **"As it is, the book announces"**: Hilary Mantel, email to the author, 19 April 2018.

290 **"Once you play around"**: Larissa MacFarquhar, "The Dead Are Real," *The New Yorker,* 15 October 2012, p. 55.

CHAPTER 11. AMERICA AGAINST ITSELF

292 **"All wars are fought twice"**: Viet Thanh Nguyen, *Nothing Ever Dies: Vietnam and the Memory of War* (Cambridge: Harvard University Press, 2016), p. 4.

292 **128,000 books about Hitler**: The figure comes from Volker Ullrich, *Hitler: Ascent, 1889–1939* (New York: Knopf, 2016). See also Alex Ross, "The Hitler Vortex," *The New Yorker*, 30 April 2018, p. 66.

292 **"for the American imagination"**: Robert Penn Warren, *The Legacy of the Civil War: Meditations on the Centennial* (New York: Random House, 1961), p. 3.

293 **a total of 1,094,453 casualties**: See C. Vann Woodward, "The Great American Butchery," *The New York Review of Books*, 6 March 1975.

293 **"One section of our country"**: David Von Drehle, "150 Years After Fort Sumter: Why We're Still Fighting the Civil War," *Time*, 7 April 2011.

295 **"a disorganized, murderous fist-fight"**: Shelby Foote, quoted in Eugene G. Stevens, *Sunset at Shiloh* (New York: Barnes and Noble, 2014), p. 5.

295 **"an all-out war"**: Bruce Catton, *Prefaces to History* (New York: Doubleday, 1970), p. 36.

295 **it was possible to walk**: Drew Gilpin Faust, *This Republic of Suffering: Death and the American Civil War* (New York: Knopf, 2008), p. 58.

297 **"Whatever we do"**: *Walt Whitman Speaks: His Final Thoughts on Life, Writing, Spirituality, and the Promise of America* (New York: Library of America, 2019).

297 **the result of Northern aggressors**: Von Drehle, "150 Years After Fort Sumter."

297 **"slavery haunted every step"**: Jill Lepore, *These Truths: A History of the United States* (New York: Norton, 2018), p. 221.

297 **"the tremendous n----- question"**: Lieutenant Charles Francis Adams, Jr., quoted in episode 3 of Ken Burns's TV series on the war. Just possibly, Adams was referring to a controversial essay by Thomas Carlyle, "Occasional Discourse on the Nigger Question," issued as a pamphlet in 1853.

298 **In the harsh winter**: Robert Conquest, "Robert E. Lee," *Encounter*, June 1975, p. 50.

298 **"We have now infused"**: Eddie S. Glaude, Jr., *Begin Again: James Baldwin's America and Its Urgent Lessons for Our Own* (New York: Crown, 2020), p. 73.

298 **Textbook publishers caved in**: Margaret MacMillan, *Dangerous Games: The Uses and Abuses of History* (New York: Random House, 2008), p. 56.

299 **"great and vile movie"**: Adam Gopnik, "Memorials," *The New Yorker*, 9 May 2011, p. 21.

299 **"Elderly men wearing"**: Ari Kelman, "An Impertinent Discourse," *The Times Literary Supplement*, 24 February 2012, p. 7.

300 **"Not surprisingly"**: MacMillan, *Dangerous Games*, p. 56.

301 **"honor was inseparable"**: William Yardley, obituary of Bertram Wyatt-Brown, *The New York Times*, 14 November 2012.

301 **"Helped freeze the white South"**: Foner, *Who Owns History?* p. 17.

301 **"The sudden freeing of the Negroes"**: Mary C. Simms Oliphant, *The New Simms History of South Carolina, Centennial Edition 1840–1940* (Columbia, S.C.: The State Company, 1940), p. 265.

302 **the North had generally accepted**: David Blight, *Race and Reunion: The Civil War in American Memory* (Cambridge, Mass.: Belknap Press, 2001).

302 *The Burden of Southern History*: Joe Klein, "Trump, the Astute Salesman, Has Captured and Targeted America's Prevailing Mood: Nostalgic," *Time*, 19 May 2016, p. 29.

304 **"First a long, deep rumble"**: Bruce Catton, *A Stillness at Appomattox* (New York: Random House, 1953), pp. 242–43.

305 **In a sensitive account**: For a full review of Blight's handling of Catton's career, see Andrew Delbanco, "The Central Event of Our Past: Still Murky," *The New York Review of Books*, 9 February 2012.

305 **"Americans tend not to have"**: David Blight, in conversation with Ken Burns and Adam Goodheart, *Times Talks*, 4 April 2011, Times Center, New York, New York.

306 **"denied that sectional differences"**: James M. McPherson, "What Drove the Terrible War?" *The New York Review of Books*, 14 July 2011, p. 34.

306 **"Energized by the Depression"**: CivilWarTalk.com.

308 **"was part of a bulk purchase"**: Colson Whitehead, *The Underground Railroad* (New York: Doubleday, 2016), p. 3.

308 **imposed disciplines**: Eric Foner, "A Brutal Process," *The New York Times Book Review*, 5 October 2014, p. 21.

308 **"There is no reason in the world"**: Adam Gopnik, "Better Angel," *The New Yorker*, 28 September 2020, p. 66.

309 **"segregation began in the North"**: Louis Menand, "In the Eye of the Law," *The New Yorker*, 4 February 2019.

309 **"How is it"**: Samuel Johnson, "Taxation No Tyranny," 1775.

309 **"He was concerned—with good reason"**: James McPherson, "A Bombshell on the American Public," *The New York Review of Books*, 22 November 2012.

Thucydides Smith, having resolved to write the story of the great Rebellion, is astounded at seeing a few of the books he has to read before commencing his great work. Thinks he had better give it up.

310 **"The long-headed man"**: W.E.B. Du Bois, *The Soul of Black Folk* (1903; repr. Chicago: A. C. McClurg, 1953), p. 15. The 1903 first printing was 1,000 copies, and the total royalties paid to the author came to $150. Du Bois made seven substantive changes for the 1953 edition, mainly to eliminate possible anti-Semitic connotations.

310 **"You and we are different races"**: "Address on Colonization to a Deputation of Negroes," 14 August 1862, *Collected Works of Abraham Lincoln*, vol. 5 (New Brunswick, N.J.: Rutgers University Press, 1953–1955). According to *The New Yorker*, more than fifteen thousand books about Lincoln are in print, and in February 2020 the magazine devoted a four-page article by Adam Gopnik to yet another study, *Congress at War: How Republican Reformers Fought the Civil War, Defied Lincoln, Ended Slavery, and Remade America* (New York: Knopf, 2020), by the radical historian Fergus M. Bordewich, who characterized Lincoln as a weak and dithering temporizer, "a photogenic free rider in a tall hat." The book, Gopnik concludes, "thoroughly reflects the larger revisionism of our day."

310 **"set the South on fire"**: Lepore, *These Truths*, p. 297.

311 **adding emancipation**: Joan Waugh, *U. S. Grant: American Hero, American Myth* (Chapel Hill: University of North Carolina Press, 2009), p. 145.

311 **"A regiment from Lincoln's home state"**: Quoted in Ken Burns's *Civil War* series. See also Stephen Galloway, *The Hollywood Reporter*, 22 March 2015.

311 **"When I entered"**: James McPherson, "America's Greatest Movement," *The New York Review of Books*, 27 October 2016, p. 63.

312 **"The decline of Civil War studies"**: Eric Foner, *Politics and Ideology in the Age of the Civil War* (New York: Oxford University Press, 1980), p. 4.

313 **"The Confederacy didn't die"**: Henry Louis Gates, Jr., "The 'Lost Cause' Built Jim Crow," *The New York Times*, 10 November 2019.

313 **"the wait was sometimes hours long"**: Robert Wilson, *Mathew Brady: Portraits of a Nation* (New York: Bloomsbury, 2013), p. 82.

314 **no photographs of cannons firing**: Sanford Schwartz, "The Art of Our Terrible War," *The New York Review of Books*, 25 April 2013, p. 10.

314 **The early war photographers**: N. H. Mallett, "How Early Photographers Captured History's First Images of War," *Military History Now*, 12 June 2012.

316 **"Only when some yellow-bleached photograph"**: William James, *Essays in Morality and Religion*, vol. 9 (Boston: Harvard University Press, 1982), p. 72.

316 **"After the Second World War"**: Peter Tonguette, "With the Civil War, Ken Burns Reinvented the Television History Documentary," *Humanities*, vol. 36, no. 5 September/October 2015.

318 **"I want to teach"**: *The Correspondence of Shelby Foote and Walker Percy*, ed. Jay Tolson (Durham, N.C.: DoubleTake, 1997), pp. 65, 82.

318 **"It is possible to argue"**: *Dictionary of Literary Biography*, vol. 17, p. 155.

319 **"That was how it looked"**: Shelby Foote, *The Civil War: A Narrative: Fredericksburg to Meridian* (New York: Random House, 1963), p. 855.

319 **"the historian's standards without his paraphernalia"**: Shelby Foote, *The Civil War: A Narrative: Fort Sumter to Perryville* (1958; repr. New York: Vintage, 1986), p. 815.

320 **"I understood after a while"**: Ken Burns, interview with the author, 6 May 2011.

321 **"the alpha anecdotalist"**: Ian Parker, "Mr. America," *The New Yorker*, 4 September 2017, p. 53.

321 **speaking through his soft beard**: The phrase is Adam Gopnik's. See "American Prophet," *The New Yorker*, 15 October 2018, p. 80.

321 **"essentially to put our arms"**: Ken Burns, interview with the author, 6 May 2011.

322 **"to an unmatched degree"**: Von Drehle, "150 Years After Fort Sumter."

323 **"America is an idea"**: David Blight, in conversation with Ken Burns and Adam Goodheart, *Times Talks*, 4 April 2011.

323 **"Americans have always had"**: Foner, *Who Owns History?* p. 150.

323 **Foner also contributed an essay**: *Ken Burns's "The Civil War": Historians Respond*, ed. Robert B. Toplin (New York: Oxford University Press, 1996).

CHAPTER 12. OF SHOES AND SHIPS AND SEALING WAX

325 **"The good historian"**: Marc Bloch, *Apologie pour l'Histoire ou le métier d'historien*, critical edition, ed. Étienne Bloch (Paris: Armand Colin, 1993), p. 83.

326 **"variable" measurements and wide boundaries**: Carole Fink, *Marc Bloch: A Life in History* (Cambridge, U.K.: Cambridge University Press, 1989), pp. 32–33.

327 **"not joyfully but resolutely"**: Fink, *Marc Bloch*, p. 55.

328 **"There were, of course, significant"**: Fink, *Marc Bloch*, p. 98.

329 **"in which nothing would be"**: Evans, *Eric Hobsbawm*, p. 130.

330 **"Friedrich Nietzsche had distinguished"**: Friedrich Nietzsche, "The Use and Abuse of History for Life," one of four "untimely meditations," 1874, reprinted Scotts Valley, South Carolina: CreateSpace Independent Publishing Platform, 2018. A more accurate translation of the title is "On the Uses and Disadvantages of History for Life."

330 **"leftists with a socialist sensibility"**: André Burguière, *The Annales School: An Intellectual History*, trans. Jane Marie Todd (Ithaca, N.Y.: Cornell University Press, 2009), p. 19.

331 **"the totality of the mental universe"**: Burguière, *Annales School*, p. ix.

331 **"There were forty of us"**: Lucien Lebvre, "Combats pour l'histoire," *Annales*, 1953, pp. 329–37.

331 **"That is the anthem of the *Annales*"**: Burguière, *Annales School*, p. 24.

331 **"deep and profoundly turbulent"**: Burguière, *Annales School*, p. 39.

331 **more impulsive**: Burguière, *Annales School*, p. 26.

331 **"like an old married couple"**: Burguière, *Annales School*, p. 43.

332 **"the spatial representation"**: Robert D. Kaplan, *The Revenge of Geography: What the Map Tells Us About Coming Conflicts and the Battle Against Fate* (New York: Random House, 2012).

333 **"The essential thing"**: Burguière, *Annales School*, p. 89.

333 **"At fifty, he was"**: Fink, *Marc Bloch*, p. 190.

334 **"his nationality, his ideas, and his name"**: Marc Bloch to Erna Patzelt, 13 April 1938.

335 **"Long ago we fought together"**: "A Lucien Febvre; en manière de dédicace," *Fougères*, 10 May 1941, sent to Febvre in Bloch's letter of 17 October 1942.

336 **"I didn't know it was so difficult"**: Burguière, *Annales School*, p. 47.

336 **"a gentleman of fifty"**: Georges Altman, foreword to Marc Bloch, *Strange Defeat: A Statement of Evidence Written in 1940*, trans. Gerard Hopkins (1968; repr. New York: Norton, 1999), p. xv.

338 **"A latent Darwinism"**: Burguière, *Annales School*, pp. 147, 151, 159.

338 **"in the manner of a novelist"**: Alexander Lee, "Portrait of the Author as a Historian: Fernand Braudel," *History Today*, vol. 66, issue 8, August 2016.

338 **"He experienced his new environment"**: Lee, *History Today*.

339–40 **"surprise and distance"**: Richard Mayne, preface to Fernand Braudel, *A History of Civilizations* (London: Penguin, 1995).

340 **"*The Mediterranean* does not date"**: Fernand Braudel, *The Mediterranean and the Mediterranean World in the Age of Philip II*, trans. Siân Reynolds (London: William Collins, second edition 1966), p. 15.

340 **"interminable imprisonment"**: Fernand Braudel, *On History* (Chicago: University of Chicago Press, 1980), p. vii.

341 **"Bowled over by his daring sweep"**: Lee, *History Today*.

341 **"perfect historical work"**: Jack H. Hexter, *On Historians: Reappraisals of Some of the Masters of Modern History* (Cambridge: Harvard University Press, 1986), p. 111.

341 **"one gets the feeling"**: Wells, *Brief History of History*, p. 292.

341 **"historians are never on holiday"**: "Panel Discussion: Conversations with Eric Hobsbawm," *India International Centre Quarterly* 31, no. 4 (Spring 2005): 101–25 (corrected).

341 **"the distinction between the three levels"**: Alan Macfarlane, "Fernand Braudel and Global History," talk given on 1 February 1996 at the Institute of Historical Research.

342 **"All these occurrences"**: Fernand Braudel, *On History*, trans. Sarah Matthews (Chicago: University of Chicago Press, 1982).

343 **"There is also"**: Wickham, *Framing the Early Middle Ages*, p. 42.

343 **"History—perhaps the least structured"**: Braudel, *On History*.

344 **Ibn Khaldūn's complaint**: Malise Ruthven, "Will Geography Decide Our Destiny?" *The New York Review of Books*, 21 February 2013, p. 44.

345 **a man of great creative energy**: Macfarlane, "Fernand Braudel and Global History," p. 1.

345 **"he would take on"**: André Burguière, interview with the author, Paris, 22 September 2017.

347 **"France is full"**: Harriet Swain, "Paratrooping Truffler," *Times Higher Education*, 9 October 1998. Swain's article on Ladurie is the best I have read on the historian, and pp. 347-48 are largely based on her work.

347 **His devoutly Catholic family**: Swain, "Paratrooping Truffler."

348 **"If we are subjected to violence"**: Swain, "Paratrooping Truffler."

348 **"In this study of southern French peasantry"**: Marnie Huges-Warrington, *Fifty Key Thinkers on History* (London: Routledge, 2000), p. 194.

349 **The history he liked**: Swain, "Paratrooping Truffler."

349 **"When you are not young"**: Swain, "Paratrooping Truffler." The summary about historians is also hers.

350 **"the unity of an intellectual movement"**: Jacques Revel, "Histoire et sciences sociales: les paradigmes des Annales," *Annales,* 1979, 34–36, pp. 1360–1376.

CHAPTER 13. THE RED HISTORIANS

351 **"Under Marxism the future is well-known"**: Sir Lewis Namier also came up with "Historians imagine the past and remember the future." See *Conflicts: Studies in Contemporary History* (London, 1942), p. 70.

351 **"Dear Herr Doctor"**: Kenneth Atchity, *A Writer's Time: Making the Time to Write* (New York: Norton, 1986), p. 135.

351 **"He gave to our subject"**: Hugh Trevor-Roper, "Marxism Without Regrets," *Sunday Telegraph,* 15 June 1997, review section, p. 13.

353 **"inseparable"**: Eric Hobsbawm, *How to Change the World: Tales of Marx and Marxism* (New York: Little, Brown, 2011), p. vii.

353 **"passionately irreconcilable"**: Jonathan Sperber, *Karl Marx: A Nineteenth-Century Life* (New York: Norton, 2013), ch. 14.

354 **"The Dogberry Club"**: Edward Royle, *Victorian Infidels: The Origins of the British Secularist Movement, 1791–1866* (Manchester, U.K.: Manchester University Press, 1974).

354 **"scribbling furiously through the night"**: Francis Wheen, *Karl Marx: A Life* (New York: Norton, 2000), p. 119.

355 **"the thing *Manifesto*"**: Sperber, *Karl Marx,* p. 203.

355 **A force that would dissolve**: Thomas Friedman, *The World Is Flat: A Brief History of the Twenty-first Century* (New York: Farrar, Straus and Giroux, 2005).

355 **"a hodgepodge"**: Timothy Shenk, "Find the Method," *London Review of Books,* 29 June 2017, p. 17.

355 **no settled conception**: Isaiah Berlin, *Karl Marx: His Life and Environment,* 4th ed. (Oxford, U.K.: Oxford University Press, 1996).

356 **"If anything is certain"**: Quoted by Engels in a letter to Eduard Bernstein, 2–3 November 1882, *Marx/Engels Collected Works,* vol. 46, p. 353, first published in Marx Engels Archives, Moscow, 1924.

356 **"defeat our intelligence"**: John Gray, "The Real Karl Marx," *The New York Review of Books,* 9 May 2013, p. 38.

357 **"What is extraordinary"**: Gareth Stedman Jones, "In Retrospect: Das Kapital," *Nature,* 547, 27 July 2017, pp. 401–2.

358 **"Such was my first political test"**: James D. Young, *Socialism Since 1889: A Biographical History* (Totowa, N.J.: Barnes and Noble, 1988), p. 182.

359 **"Some said Trotsky"**: Louis Fischer, *The Life of Stalin* (New York: Harper, 1964), p. 181.

360 **"Lenin's methods lead to this"**: Leon Trotsky, "Our Political Tasks," first published in 1904 as "Nashi Politicheskiya Zadachi."

361 **a vodka-soaked peasant**: Irving Howe, *Leon Trotsky* (New York: Viking, 1978), p. 22.

362 **"For intellectuals throughout the world"**: Howe, *Leon Trotsky,* p. 64.

362 **"He was, whatever his personal magnetism"**: Robert Conquest, *The Great Terror: A Reassessment,* 3rd ed. (London: Hutchinson, 1990), p. 412.

363 **At one gathering of the Politburo**: Stephen Kotkin, *Stalin: Waiting for Hitler, 1929–1941* (London: Penguin, 2017).

365 **He had a particular view**: Neil Davidson, "Leon Trotsky, the Historian," *Jacobin,* reprinted *Socialist Worker,* 24 January 2018.

365 **"It's not on any side, stupid"**: Tom Stoppard, *Night and Day* (New York: Grove, 2018).

365 **"endured the flood"**: Leon Trotsky, *History of the Russian Revolution*, trans. Max Eastman (1932; repr. Chicago: Haymarket Books, 2008), p. 215.

365 **"Indignation, anger, revulsion?"**: Tariq Ali, *Street-Fighting Years: An Autobiography of the Sixties* (London: Verso, 2018), p. 324.

369 **"The chief demerit"**: Martin Amis, "The Deadliest Idealism," *The New York Times Book Review*, 22 October 2017, p. 11.

370 **"where we really became historians"**: Hobsbawm, *Interesting Times*, p. 191.

370 **In late 1952 an anonymous article**: Henry St. L. B. Moss, "A Marxist View of Byzantium," *Times Literary Supplement*, 12 December 1952.

371 **"both idealism and the false god of objectivity"**: Mark Mazower, "Clear, Inclusive, and Lasting," *New York Review of Books*, 23 July 2020, p. 43.

371 **"Brash and confident"**: Gil Shohat, "The Historians' Group of the Communist Party—Ten Years That Reshaped History," *Imperial Global Forum*, 8 March 2016.

371 **"The Communist Party never"**: Stephen Kotkin, "Left Behind," *The New Yorker*, 29 September 2003.

371 **"the reddest and most radical generation"**: Frances Stonor Saunders, "Stuck on the Flypaper," *London Review of Books*, 28 March and 9 April 2015.

373 **"lacked the ability to express himself"**: Evans, *Eric Hobsbawm*, p. 462.

373 **"the most widely read"**: Tim Rogan, *The Moral Economists: R. H. Tawney, Karl Polanyi, E. P. Thompson, and the Critique of Captalism* (Princeton: Princeton University Press, 2018).

373 **"uncovered details about workshop customs"**: Emma Griffin, "E. P. Thompson: The Unconventional Historian," *The Guardian*, 6 March 2013.

373 **"History was not words"**: Christopher Hill, preface to *Democracy and the Labour Movement: Essays in Honour of Dona Torr* (London: Lawrence & Wishart, 1954).

373 **"The Marxist narrative"**: Kotkin, "Left Behind."

375 **"the best-known and most widely read"**: Evans, *Eric Hobsbawm*, p. vii.

375 **"lean, fair-haired, Jewish-looking"**: Karl Miller, "Eric Hobsbawm," *London Review of Books*, 25 October 2012, p. 12.

375 **"shy, ironic, whispering person"**: Modern Records Centre, Warwick University, 1215/23; diary ("Tagebuch"), 22 January 1943.

376 **"psychologically an unsystematic"**: Modern Records Centre, Warwick University, 937/7/8/1; "Rathaus/history," January 2008.

376 **"As a lecturer I know"**: Modern Records Centre, Warwick University, 937/7/8/1; "Paperback Writer" typescript 2003, pp. 4–5.

376 **"No historian now writing"**: Neal Ascherson, "Profile: The Age of Hobsbawm," *Independent on Sunday*, 2 October 1994.

376 **"arguably our greatest living historian"**: David Caute, *The Spectator*, 19 October 2002.

377 **"Hobsbawm doesn't just know"**: Tony Judt, "The Last Romantic," *The New York Review of Books*, 20 November 2000.

377 **when it came to historical**: Susan Pedersen, "I Want to Love It," *London Review of Books*, 18 April 2019, p. 16.

377 **"In a period in which"**: "Michael Ignatieff Interviews Eric Hobsbawm," *The Late Show*, BBC, 24 October 1994.

378 **"Of course I had ideas"**: Eric Hobsbawm, email to the author, 29 April 2011.

378 **"Whatever assumptions are made"**: Eric Hobsbawm, *The Age of Extremes: A History of the World, 1914–1991* (London: Weidenfeld, 1994), p. 393.

379 **"I did not come into Communism"**: Eric Hobsbawm, *How to Change the World: Reflections on Marx and Marxism* (London: Michael Joseph, 2011), p. 268.

379 **"of someone who became politicized"**: Paul Barker, "Waking from History's Great Dream," *Independent on Sunday*, 4 February 1990.

380 **"a devastating blow"**: Evans, *Eric Hobsbawm*, p. 23.

380 **"lived without intimacy"**: Hobsbawm, *Interesting Times*, p. 42. See also Richard J. Evans, *Biographical Memoirs of Fellows of the British Academy*, vol. 14, pp. 207–260.

380 **"a light, dry feeling"**: Saunders, "Stuck on the Flypaper." The article was originally the second of 2015's LRB Winter Lectures at the British Museum.

381 **"The first thing to understand"**: Interview with Ivan T. Berend, Center for European and Eurasian Studies, 2 May 2004.

381 **"a tribal matter"**: Evans, *Eric Hobsbawm*, p. 614.

381 **"I could prove myself"**: Perry Anderson, "The Age of EJH," *London Review of Books*, 3 October 2002.

381 **"became conscious of being a historian"**: Hobsbawm, *Interesting Times*, p. viii.

382 **perhaps the first King's man:** Saunders, "Stuck on the Flypaper."

382 **"an ideal wish-fulfillment"**: Modern Records Centre, Warwick University, 1215/21; diary ("Tagebuch") 8 March 1940.

382 **"a challenge to the profession"**: George Lichtheim, "Hobsbawm's Choice," *Encounter*, March 1965, p. 70.

383 **"Intellectuals are the chorus"**: Modern Records Centre, Warwick University, 1215/17, diary ("Tagebuch") 4 June 1935.

383 **"a sort of quasi-underground"**: Hobsbawm, *Interesting Times*, p. 81.

384 **"the sort of conditions"**: Kotkin, "Left Behind."

384 **"If you are on a ship"**: Evans, *Eric Hobsbawm*, p. 488.

384 **Early on, he had ridden:** Tony Judt, *Reappraisals: Reflections on the Forgotten Twentieth Century* (London: Penguin Books, 2009).

385 **"I have abandoned, nay, rejected it"**: Hobsbawm, *Interesting Times*, p. 56.

385 **"throughout his career"**: Evans, *Eric Hobsbawm*, p. 543.

385 **"historical understanding . . . not agreement"**: Hobsbawm, *Interesting Times*, p. xii.

385 **"like one loves a woman"**: Mark Mazower, "Clear, Inclusive, and Lasting," p. 42.

385 **"Eric wanted to have his cake and eat it"**: Evans, *Eric Hobsbawm*, p. 352.

386 **"For over sixty years"**: Saunders, "Stuck on the Flypaper."

387 **"Reed's account of the events"**: George Frost Kennan, *Russia Leaves the War: Soviet-American Relations, 1917–1920* (Princeton: Princeton University Press, 1956), pp. 68–69.

387 **Liberal anti-Communists became:** John Earl Haynes and Harvey Klehr, *In Denial: Historians, Communism, and Espionage* (San Francisco: Encounter Books, 2003), p. 33.

388 **"Far too much academic writing"**: Haynes and Klehr, *In Denial*, p. 231.

389 **Well over 20 percent:** Terry Eagleton, "Indomitable," *London Review of Books*, 3 March 2011, p. 14.

389 **"shows an angel looking"**: Walter Benjamin, *Ninth Thesis on the Philosophy of History*; see also Raymond Barglow, "The Angel of History: Walter Benjamin's Vision of Hope and Despair," *Tikkun*, November 1998.

CHAPTER 14. HISTORY FROM THE INSIDE

390 **"The man who plays a part"**: Leo Tolstoy, *War and Peace*.

390 **"History is written by the winners"**: Hilary Mantel, letter to the author, 2010.

390 **"Until lions have their historians"**: This is attributed to the Nigerian novelist Chinua Achebe (1930–2013), but I suspect it has had a long history, certainly in Kenya and Zimbabwe.

390 **"the losers make the best historians"**: Evans, *Eric Hobsbawm*, p. 569.

391 **"The basic thing about history"**: Evans, *Eric Hobsbawm*, pp. 564–65.

394 **seven letters at once:** Pliny, *Natural History*, 7.91.

395 **Caesar's writing was little:** Josephine Quinn, "Caesar Bloody Caesar," *The New York Review of Books*, 22 March 2018, p. 26.

395 **a book of his favorite jokes:** James Davidson, "Laugh as Long as You Can," *London Review of Books*, 16 July 2015, p. 35.

395 **"There is nothing better in the writing"**: Cicero, *Brutus*, 62.

397 **He avoids interpreting motives:** T. A. Dorey, "Caesar: The Gallic War," in *Latin Historians*, ed. T. A. Dorey (London: Routledge, 1966), pp. 65–84.

397 **he mentions an elk:** Julius Caesar, *De Bello Gallico*, 6, 27.

398 **he once threw his baker:** Stacy Schiff, *Cleopatra: A Life* (New York: Little, Brown, 2010), p. 65

399 **His civil war history:** Julius Caesar, *De Bello Gallico,* 1. 32–33.

399 **In a further instance:** Adrian Goldsworthy, *Caesar: Life of a Colossus* (London: Weidenfeld, 2006).

400 **"The proconsul's tone":** Goldsworthy, *Caesar,* p. 407.

402 **Cicero at first refused:** Barry Strauss, *The Death of Caesar* (New York: Simon & Schuster, 2015), p. 32.

404 **a messy and almost bungled murder:** Mary Beard, *SPQR: A History of Ancient Rome* (New York: Norton, 2015), p. 337. As the twentieth century opened, two of the world's greatest powers were still led by a kaiser and a czar, each name a rendering of the word *Caesar.*

405 **a volume of aphorisms:** Napoleon Bonaparte, *Aphorisms and Thoughts* (1838; repr. London: Oneworld, 2008). *The Military Maxims of Napoleon* was originally translated in 1831, assumed to be from a French edition compiled by one of his officers, a General Burnod, with a revised edition in 1901. Most of the maxims seem to have been Napoleon's.

405 **"My history is made up of events":** Napoleon Bonaparte, *Aphorisms and Thoughts,* aphorism no. 484.

405 **"Classic works are composed by rhetoricians":** Bonaparte, *Aphorisms and Thoughts,* no. 257.

405 **"He even refashioned his historic remarks":** Jacques Bainville, *Napoleon* (Boston: Little, Brown, 1933), p. 392.

406 **"The vague historical":** Anthony Burgess, *Napoleon Symphony* (New York: Knopf, 1974), p. 365.

406 **"Among the bloody skins":** Adam Gopnik, "Shot of Courage," *The New Yorker,* 2 October 2017, p. 64.

407 **"A Mr. Ralston":** Ulysses S. Grant, *Personal Memoirs of U. S. Grant* (New York: Charles L. Webster & Company, 1885–86), vol. 1, ch. 1.

408 **the most daring in the academy:** Lloyd Lewis, *Captain Sam Grant* (Boston: Little, Brown, 1950), p. 82.

408 **"furnished the only element":** John Keegan, *The Mask of Command* (New York: Viking, 1987), p. 204.

409 **"People talked":** William S. McFeely, *Grant: A Biography* (New York: Norton, 1981), p. 66.

409 **"slid him back into uniform":** T. J. Stiles, "A Man of Moral Courage," *The New York Times Book Review,* 23 October 2016, p. 12.

409 **"when he fought, he rose":** Stiles, "A Man of Moral Courage."

409 **"The art of war is simple enough":** *Personal Memoirs of John H. Brinton, Major and Surgeon, U.S.V., 1861–1865* (New York: Neale Publishing Co., 1914), p. 239.

409 **the most popular man:** James Ford Rhodes, *History of the Civil War* (New York: Macmillan, 1917), p. 304.

409 **"Grant is certainly":** Edmund Wilson, *Patriotic Gore: Studies in the Literature of the American Civil War* (New York: Oxford University Press, 1966), p. 160.

410 **"His memory was astounding":** Elizabeth F. Diggs, letter to the author, 4 April 2016.

410 **"A quiet man":** Herman Melville, *Battle-Pieces and Aspects of the War: Civil War Poems* (New York: Harper, 1866).

411 **dumb, inarticulate man of genius:** John Lothrop Motley to his wife, 14 August 1867, *The Correspondence of John Lothrop Motley,* ed. George William Curtis, vol. 2 (New York, 1900), p. 283.

411 **It was the evolution of weaponry:** Keegan, *Mask of Command,* p. 232. See also Henry M. W. Russell, "The Memoirs of Ulysses S. Grant: The Rhetoric of Judgment," *Virginia Quarterly Review* 66, no. 2 (Spring 1990): 189–209.

411 **Nor do the memoirs mention:** *Personal Memoirs of U. S. Grant,* vol. 2, pp. 175–76.

412 **and was never hit:** *Personal Memoirs of U. S. Grant,* vol. 1, p. 34.

412 **"seemed to take in the situation":** *Personal Memoirs of U. S. Grant,* vol. 1, pp. 278–79.

See also Shelby Foote, *The Civil War: A Narrative* (New York: Random House, 1958–74), vol. 1, pp. 149–52.

412   **he would not eat beef:** Horace Porter, *Campaigning with Grant* (1897; Rockville, Md.: Wildside Press, 2010).

414   **"the incurable sucker":** Wilson, *Patriotic Gore,* p. 167.

414   **he wouldn't listen:** Wilson, *Patriotic Gore,* p. 131.

415   **"It had never been my intention":** *Autobiography of Mark Twain,* ed. Benjamin Griffin and Harriet Elinor Smith, vol. 2 (Berkeley: University of California Press, 2013), p. 60.

416   **"For the last twenty-four years":** Joan Waugh, *The Memory of the Civil War in American Culture* (Durham: University of North Carolina Press, 2004), pp. 175–76.

417   **"Grant's *Memoirs* are a unique":** Wilson, *Patriotic Gore,* pp. 133, 143–44.

417   **"He was venturing":** *Autobiography of Mark Twain,* vol. 2, p. 71.

417   **"If you could imagine":** Waugh, *Memory of the Civil War,* p. 180.

417   **"It is one of the great pictures":** "Eric," user on Goodreads.com, review published 29 January 2010.

419   **"It seems that man's destiny":** Letter of 8 July 1885. See Wilson, *Patriotic Gore,* pp. 138–39.

CHAPTER 15. THE SPINNING OF HISTORY

421   **the family business:** Peter Clarke, *Mr. Churchill's Profession: Statesman, Orator, Writer* (London: Bloomsbury, 2012), p. 5.

421   **"The only thing that worries me":** Reginald Pound, *The Strand Magazine, 1891–1950* (London: Heinemann, 1966), p. 3.

422   **at the top of the tree:** Adam Gopnik, "Finest Hours," *The New Yorker,* 30 August 2010, p. 76.

423   **"imaginary pictures":** Sullivan, *Macaulay,* p. 314.

423   **Churchill's direct experience:** A point made by Andrew Roberts, in conversation with Robert Tombs, *Spectator* event held in Westminster, 9 October 2018.

423   **"It is useless to preach":** *Companion Volumes to the Official Biography,* vol. 1, part 1, p. 676, quoted in Andrew Roberts, *Churchill,* p. 38.

424   **"thundering liar":** *Time,* 21 March 1960.

425   **"from mouth to hand":** Winston Churchill, *The Second World War,* vol. 1 (London: Cassell, 1948), p. 62 (p. 79 in U.S. edition).

425   **"Successive cigarettes":** Winston Churchill, *Savrola: A Tale of Revolution in Laurania* (London: 2013), p. 18.

425   **Thereafter he came:** Robert Rhodes James, *Churchill: A Study in Failure, 1900–39* (London: Weidenfeld, 1970), p. 24.

425   **was heard all day booming away:** A. G. Gardiner, *Prophets, Priests, and Kings* (1917; repr. London: Forgotten Books, 2017), p. 228.

427   **"the author resorts":** Clarke, *Mr. Churchill's Profession,* p. 75.

427   **"truths, half truths":** Christopher M. Bell, *Churchill and the Dardanelles* (Oxford, U.K.: Oxford University Press, 2017), p. 369.

429   **"First I lay the track":** David Reynolds, *In Command of History: Churchill Fighting and Writing the Second World War* (New York: Basic Books, 2005), p. 69.

430   **"*Marlborough* alone":** Churchill in a letter to Clementine Churchill, 7 January 1937.

430   **"Every word of it":** Clarke, *Mr. Churchill's Profession,* p. 160.

430   **"The scholarly activity":** Clarke, *Mr. Churchill's Profession,* pp. 161–62.

431   **"The Almighty in His infinite wisdom":** Churchill, *Second World War,* vol. 4, p. 640.

431   **"cutting off your fingernails":** *Speaking for Themselves: The Personal Letters of Winston and Clementine Churchill,* ed. Mary Soames (New York: Doubleday, 1998), p. 433.

432   **"as he might one day":** Churchill Papers, CHAR 1/398B/107; see also Allen Packwood, "Churchill and Napoleon," private paper, September 2011.

432   **"the greatest man of action":** Churchill, *Second World War,* vol. 3, *The Age of Revolution,* Book 9.

433 **"It's one more"**: Andrew Roberts, *The Holy Fox: A Life of Lord Halifax* (London: Weidenfeld, 1991), pp. 204–6.

433 **"Of course I realize"**: *The Neville Chamberlain Diary Letters,* vol. 4, *The Downing Street Years, 1934–1940,* ed. Robert Self (London: Ashgate, 2005), p. 448.

433 **"For Churchill, writing history"**: Roberts, *Churchill,* p. 373.

433 **"Whatever Churchill said"**: Johnson, *Churchill Factor,* p. 66.

434 **"How difficult it will be"**: John Colville, *The Fringes of Power* (London: Hodder, 1985), p. 553.

434 **"What for shorthand"**: Reynolds, *In Command of History,* p. 75 and ff.

434 **"I do not describe it"**: Churchill, *Second World War,* vol. 1, p. iv.

434 **"I'm not writing a book"**: A. H. Booth, *The True Story of Winston Churchill* (Chicago, 1958), pp. 135–36.

434 **"Did you cook the whole banquet"**: Denis Kelly, TS memoirs (1985), ch. 3, p. 3; see also Reynolds, *In Command of History,* pp. 502, 437.

435 **"was like watching"**: Roy Jenkins, *Churchill: A Biography* (London: Macmillan, 2005) p. 822.

435 **"Churchill the historian"**: A.J.P. Taylor, *Churchill: Four Faces and the Man* (London: Allen Lane, 1969), p. 149.

435 **"It is said that journalism"**: Roberts, *Churchill,* p. 357.

435 **"I have followed"**: Churchill, *Second World War,* vol. 1, p. iii.

435 **key documents were frequently cut out**: Reynolds, *In Command of History,* pp. 78, 173.

436 **the word *memoirs* was off-putting**: Reynolds, *In Command of History,* p. 81.

436 **"One wonders whether"**: Lord Moran, *Winston Churchill: The Struggle for Survival, 1940–1965* (London: Constable, 1966), pp. 830–31.

436 **"immensely"**: See, for instance, Max Hastings, "Big Man to Uncle Joe," *London Review of Books,* 22 November 2018, p. 35.

436 **"The longer you can look back"**: Roberts, *Churchill,* p. 688.

437 **he received the news**: Anthony Montague Browne, *Long Sunset* (London: Podkin Press, 2009), p. 133.

437 **Churchill's deepest objective**: Reynolds, *In Command of History,* pp. 507, 440–42, 467.

437 **"the foul baboonery of Bolshevism"**: *Winston S. Churchill: His Complete Speeches, 1897–1963,* ed. Robert Rhodes James, 8 vols. (New York: Chelsea House, 1974), vol. 3, p. 2761.

438 **"The statesman who turns chronicler"**: *New Statesman and Nation,* 4 August 1951.

438 **"I hate Indians"**: Johann Hari, "The Two Churchills," *The New York Times Book Review,* 15 August 2010, p. 11.

439 **"We had no idea"**: Churchill, *Second World War,* vol. 3, p. 605. The scene famously ends: "Being saturated and satiated with emotion and sensation, I went to bed and slept the sleep of the saved and thankful."

439 **"a spectacular piece of bad news editing"**: Roberts, *Churchill,* p. 692.

440 **"A participant's account"**: Henry Kissinger, *White House Years* (Boston: Little, Brown, 1979), pp. xxii–xxiii.

440 **"It is not history"**: Roy Jenkins, *Churchill: A Biography* (London: Macmillan, 2005), p. 824.

CHAPTER 16. MIGHTY OPPOSITES

441 **"The natural state of affairs"**: Clive James, *Cultural Amnesia: Necessary Memories from History and the Arts* (New York: Norton, 2007), p. 836.

441 **"Going for the largest game"**: Mehta, "The Flight of Crook-Taloned Birds," *The New Yorker,* 8 December 1962, pp. 59–147 and 15 December 1962, pp. 47–129; see also Mehta, *The Fly and the Fly-Bottle: Encounters with British Intellectuals* (London: Weidenfeld, 1963).

442 **I tried to track down the details**: Charles Moore, email to the author, 14 August 2017: "I think it highly unlikely re Taylor and HTR, because in those days (until the mid-1980s) the *Telegraph* had rather second-rate obits, almost all done in-house." So it is un-

likely, but not necessarily untrue. On 21 June 1991, Trevor-Roper wrote a long and revealing letter to Adam Sisman, Taylor's biographer and soon to be appointed Trevor-Roper's, which ended with his comments on a review he had written in *The Daily Telegraph* of Éva Haraszti's book about her late husband. The article, he regretted, had made an important omission. Trevor-Roper had written, "He should be judged, as all writers should be judged, not by the perishable froth, of which no doubt he generated too much, but by his best work." "The printed version," lamented its author, "omitted the word 'best,' making the sentence meaningless."

443 **"terrible, almost physical difficulty"**: Hugh Trevor-Roper, *100 Letters from Hugh Trevor-Roper,* ed. Richard Davenport-Hines and Adam Sisman (London: Oxford University Press, 2014), p. 48.

443 **"a sort of P. G. Wodehouse character"**: Dwight Garner, "A Reputation Staked, and Shattered, on the Forged Diaries of Hitler," *The New York Times,* 6 December 2011.

443 **his neatly parted hair**: Adam Sisman, *Hugh Trevor-Roper: The Biography* (London: Weidenfeld, 2010), p. 20.

444 **broke the code**: Sisman, *Hugh Trevor-Roper,* p. 81.

444 **"To doubt the theories of one's predecessors"**: Eric Hobsbawm, "Fabianism and the Fabians 1884–1914," PhD dissertation, University of Cambridge, 1950, preface, p. 2.

444 **Russians were spreading rumors**: Ron Rosenbaum, *Explaining Hitler* (New York: Random House, 1998), p. 64.

444 **had been spotted in Dublin**: See Adam Sisman, "The Hunt for Hitler," *Slightly Foxed,* no. 61, Spring 2019, p. 54.

445 **"He might—perhaps he should"**: Obituary of Baron Dacre, *Daily Telegraph,* 27 January 2003.

445 **"tears of envy"**: A.J.P. Taylor, review of *History and Imagination: Essays in Honour of H. R. Trevor-Roper,* edited by Hugh Lloyd-Jones, Valerie Pearl, and Blair Worden, *London Review of Books,* 5 November 1981.

447 **"farting exhibitionist"**: Sisman, *Hugh Trevor-Roper,* p. 88.

447 **"The amount of man-hours"**: *The* (London) *Times,* 7 June 1957.

447 **not only in scholarly journals**: Brendan Simms, "Hugh Trevor-Roper: The Biography, by Adam Sisman," *The Independent,* 16 July 2010.

448 **"Arnold Toynbee's Bible"**: Hugh Trevor-Roper, "Arnold Toynbee's Millennium," *Encounter,* 8, no. 6, 1957.

448 **"one of the most savage and cruel"**: Martin Seymour-Smith, *Birmingham Post,* 7 January 1964.

448 **"I don't think I have ever laughed"**: Richard Cobb, *My Dear Hugh: Letters from Richard Cobb to Hugh Trevor-Roper and Others,* ed. Tim Heald (London: Frances Lincoln, 2011), p. 27.

449 **"a cauldron of discord"**: Neal Ascherson, "Liquidator: Hugh Trevor-Roper," *London Review of Books,* 19 August 2010, pp. 10–12.

449 **"To look at him"**: Ron Rosenbaum, *Explaining Hitler* (New York: Random House, 1998), p. 66.

450 **"I hate your tedious trouncings"**: Neville Masterman, *Encounter,* VIII, no. 6, 1957.

451 **"like a sea-urchin"**: Trevor-Roper, *100 Letters,* p. 49.

451 **"the English Great Rebellion"**: Stefan Collini, "Hugh Trevor-Roper: The Biography," *The Guardian,* 16 July 2010.

452 **"probably the greatest letter-writer"**: Sir David Cannadine, from a review in 2014, quoted in publisher's publicity.

452 **"Part of the explanation"**: Simms, "Hugh Trevor-Roper."

453 **"notorious outbursts of eccentricity"**: D. C. Watt, comments made at the Conference on International History, the London School of Economics, June 1993; see also Kathleen Burk, *Troublemaker: The Life and History of A.J.P. Taylor* (New Haven: Yale University Press, 2000), p. 206.

454 **"A Galician priest"**: A.J.P. Taylor, "Accident Prone, or What Happened Next," *From Napoleon to the Second International: Essays on the 19th Century* (London: Viking, 1994), p. 1. Why Galician? Possibly because that was where Namier was brought up.

454 **"the chance-minded historian"**: David Marquand, *The New Statesman,* 21 April 1961.

455 **"To a quite remarkable degree"**: Linda Colley, *Lewis Namier* (London: Weidenfeld, 1989), p. 100.

455 **"primal urge"**: Burk, *Troublemaker.*

455 **"Most of his writing"**: Collini, "Man Who Made History."

456 **"Though his collected works"**: Mehta, "The Flight of Crook-Taloned Birds." Namier's star pupil and later co-author for the parliamentary studies, John Brooke, told Mehta: "If Sir Lewis were now living, his presence would be enough to prevent Trevor-Roper from laying into Taylor. His very existence deterred people from writing bad reviews and bad books."

456 **"good at interesting people"**: Stephan Collini, "The Man Who Made History," *The Guardian,* August 26, 2000.

456 **"No use writing history"**: Paul Johnson, "A.J.P. Taylor: A Saturnine Star Who Had Intellectuals Rolling in the Aisles," *The Spectator,* 11 March 2006. See also A.J.P. Taylor, *A Personal History* (New York: Atheneum, 1983), p. 124.

457 **"I am not a philosophic historian"**: A.J.P. Taylor, *Englishmen and Others* (London: Hamish Hamilton, 1956), preface.

457 **"It's a characteristically Taylorian"**: Collini, "The Man Who Made History."

458 **"It . . . could have been written"**: Denis Mack Smith, first written 6 November 1954, reprinted in *The Cambridge Mind: Ninety Years of the Cambridge Review, 1879–1969;* ed. Eric Homberger, William Janeway, and Simon Schama (London: Cape, 1970), p. 91.

458 **"How refreshing it is"**: Michael Howard, "The Iron Chancellor," *The New Statesman and Nation,* vol. 50, no. 1270, 9 July 1955, pp. 47–48.

458 **"The eyes which have coldly assigned"**: A bon mot by Philip Guedalla (1889–1944), a Spanish lawyer and poet who attended Balliol, famous for his epigrams.

459 **"I would rather be mentioned"**: Trevor-Roper, *100 Letters,* p. 353.

459 **What if he operated within**: R. J. Stove, "A.J.P. Taylor Is History," *The American Conservative,* 12 September 2013.

460 **"After one has said the worst"**: Mehta, "The Flight of Crook-Taloned Birds," Part 1.

461 **"the real determinants"**: Hugh Trevor-Roper, "A.J.P. Taylor, Hitler, and the War," *Encounter,* July 1961.

461 **"a gangster solely intent on power"**: Trevor-Roper, *100 Letters,* p. 286.

461 **"In spite of his statements"**: Trevor-Roper, "A.J.P. Taylor, Hitler, and the War," p. 95.

463 **"Odious though Hitler was"**: Colin Wilson, "Prophets in Reverse," *Daily Telegraph* color magazine, 1970, p. 23.

463 **"For me, Taylor's book"**: Mehta, "The Flight of Crook-Taloned Birds," p. 82.

463 **"He writes as if public applause"**: Trevor-Roper, *100 Letters.*

463   "[Taylor] *ought* to have been made": Trevor-Roper, *100 Letters*, p. 391.

464   "*genus irritabile*": Trevor-Roper, *100 Letters*, p. 373.

465   "The smallness of English intellectual society": Mehta, "The Flight of Crook-Taloned Birds," Part 1.

465   "a gaggle of muddle-headed muffaroos": Trevor-Roper, *100 Letters*, p. 276.

465   "They live in their comfortable little mouse-holes": Trevor-Roper, *100 Letters*, p. 363.

467   "Eva says I have bad breath": Sally McGrane, "Diary of the Hitler Diary Hoax," *The New Yorker*, 25 April 2013.

467   "a sort of innocence": Ascherson, "Liquidator."

467   "Hugh Very-Ropey": *Private Eye*, 6 May 1983, pp. 13–14.

467   "a scholar who played with fire": G. W. Bowersock, "The Audacious Historian," *The New York Review of Books*, 2 December 2011, p. 48.

468   "The idea of Hitler keeping a diary": Paul Johnson, "Misfortune Made the Man," *Standpoint*, March 2014.

CHAPTER 17. THE WOUNDED HISTORIAN

470   "Every man thinks meanly of himself": James Boswell, *Life of Samuel Johnson* (1791), entry for 10 April 1778.

470   A number of writers have produced: Manguel, *History of Reading*, p. 291.

470   sometimes giving a half whistle: Christopher Hibbert, *The Personal History of Samuel Johnson* (New York: Harper & Row, 1971).

470   David Hume, like Gibbon: See Roy Porter, *Flesh in the Age of Reason* (London: Allen Lane, 2003).

472   "'Tony, you are so lucky'": Ed Pilkington, *The Guardian*, 8 January 2010.

473   "secret world": John Keegan, *Six Armies in Normandy* (London: Cape, 1982), p. 2.

473   "I had my first sight": Keegan, *Six Armies*, p. 14.

474   "The noise!": Elizabeth Grice, "War Memories: John Keegan's Life and Times," *The Daily Telegraph*, 17 September 2009.

474   "in an open-air ward with snow": Grice, "War Memories."

474   "At first, confined to bed": Matthew Keegan, draft of a proposed biography of his father, *The Crooked Gate of History: In the Footsteps of John Keegan*, shared with the author May 2017.

476   "Despite having little money": Mary Keen, interview with the author, 19 June 2017.

476   "shrunken boy-man": Matthew Keegan, in a letter to Anthony Sheil, p. 12.

477   "the doctors laughed": John Keegan, *Desert Island Discs*, BBC Radio 4, 6 December 1998.

479   "Nobody describes a battle": Niall Ferguson, *The Sunday Times* (London), 27 September 1998.

479   How exactly did an outnumbered: "Bryan," on goodreads.com, 8 December 2014.

480   "I'm very rebellious": Daniel Snowman, *Historians* (Basingstoke, U.K.: Palgrave, 2007), p. 89.

481   The rejection rankled: Sir Michael Howard, email to the author, 6 July 2017.

483   "Catholic widow needed the evidence": John Keegan, *The Price of Admiralty: War at Sea from Man of War to Submarine* (London: Hutchinson, 1988).

483   "the military historian": John Keegan, "The View from Across No-Man's Land," in *The Face of Battle: A Study of Agincourt, Waterloo and the Somme* (London: Jonathan Cape, 1983).

484   his books verged on potboilers: Based on Antony Beevor, 20 June 2017, Max Hastings, 23 June 2017, interviews with the author; and emails to the author from Michael Howard, 5 and 6 July 2017.

484   "All his books are worth reading": Michael Howard, email to the author, 5 July 2017.

484   "an admiration for warriors": Brian Bond, *Times Higher Education Supplement*, 24 September 1993.

484   "unabashed English Romantic": Ian McIntyre, "A Special Relationship with the Past," *The Times* (London), 13 July 1995.

485   "an extraordinary feat": Anthony Sheil, interview with the author, March 2016.

CHAPTER 18. HERSTORY

488 **"I, the unworthy writer"**: Nancy Lee Swann, *Pan Chao: Foremost Woman Scholar of China* (Michigan classics in Chinese studies, no. 5) (Ann Arbor: Center for Chinese Studies, University of Michigan, 2001), p. 236.

490 **"My material"**: Leonora Neville, *Anna Komnene: The Life and Work of a Medieval Historian* (New York: Oxford University Press, 2016), p. 78.

490 **One reason for the scarcity**: Tessa Hadley, "I Scribble, You Write," *London Review of Books,* 26 September 2016, p. 31.

491 **"have figures in erotic postures"**: St. Clement of Alexandria, *Paedagogus,* 2.11.116.

491 **"is an imperfect animal"**: Thomas Jackson, *Babbling of Green Fields, A Confession,* privately printed 2019, p. 226.

491 **between 1580 and 1640:** Joan Acocella, "Turning the Page," *The New Yorker,* 15 October 2012, pp. 88–93.

492 **signing is mechanical:** Jill Lepore, "The Prodigal Daughter," *The New Yorker,* 8 and 15 July 2015, p. 35.

492 **"until the eighteenth century"**: Joan Acocella, *The New Yorker,* October 15, 2012.

493 **"Experts declared"**: Charlotte Gordon, introduction, *Frankenstein* (New York: Penguin, 2018), p. viii.

493 **"If you happen"**: John Gregory, *A Father's Legacy to His Daughters* (London, 1774), quoted in Mary Wollstonecraft, *A Vindication of the Rights of Women and The Wrongs of Women,* p. 124.

493 **"A man is in general"**: Samuel Johnson, quoted in "Apophthegms, Sentiments, Opinions and Occasional Reflections of Sir John Hawkins (1787–1789)," in *Johnsonian Miscellanies* (1897), ed. George Birkbeck Hill, vol. 2, p. 11.

494 **"the husbands in England"**: Lady Mary Wortley Montagu, *Selected Letters,* ed. Isobel Grundy (London: Penguin, 1997).

494 **"trite observations"**: Montagu, *Selected Letters.*

495 **the most neglected:** Tom Furniss, "Mary Wollstonecraft's French Revolution," *The Cambridge Companion to Mary Wollstonecraft,* ed. Claudia L. Johnson (Cambridge, U.K.: Cambridge University Press, 2002), pp. 59–81.

497 **"Mary's story in France astonished me"**: Richard Holmes, *Footsteps: Adventures of a Romantic Biographer* (London: Hodder, 1985), p. 130.

499 **Talleyrand observed tartly:** Lucy Moore, *Liberty: The Lives and Times of Six Women in Revolutionary France* (New York: Harper, 2007), p. 350).

499 **"In her own house she was amiable"**: Lord Byron, *The Complete Miscellaneous Prose,* ed. Andrew Nicholson (Oxford: Clarendon Press, 1991), p. 222.

499 **"her family had literary tendencies"**: Geri Walton, "Lucy Aikin (Mary Godolphin): The English Author," geriwalton.com/english-author-lucy-aikin-mary-godolphin/.

500 **"Miss Strickland"**: Elizabeth Lee, *The Dictionary of National Biography, 1885–1900,* vol. 55.

500 **"she founded a whole new school"**: Antonia Fraser, introduction to Agnes Strickland, *Lives of the Queens of England* (London: Continuum, 2011).

502 **she then poured:** Elizabeth Longford, *Oxford Dictionary of National Biography,* 2004.

502 **"Cecil was a frail woman"**: Alan Bennett, "Baffled at a Bookcase," *London Review of Books,* 28 July 2011, p. 7.

503 **"not only a mastery"**: A. L. Rowse, Veronica Wedgwood obituary, *The Independent,* 11 March 1997.

503 **"Miracles do happen"**: Francis Hackett, "Books of the Times," *The New York Times,* 30 November 1944.

504 **"I enjoy the unexacting company"**: "C. V. Wedgwood," *The Economist.*

504 **She would walk around battlefields:** "C. V. Wedgwood," *The Economist,* 10 March 1997.

504 **"elegant, surprisingly astringent mind"**: Schama, *Scribble Scribble Scribble,* p. 135.

504 **She had intended:** Rowse, Wedgwood obituary.

504 **"The whole value of the study of history"**: Kelly Boyd, *Encyclopedia of Historians and Historical Writing,* vol. 2 (Chicago: Fitzroy Dearborn, 1999), p. 1288.

505 **"Veronica was short and dark"**: Elias Canetti, *Party in the Blitz: The English Years,* trans. Michael Hofmann (New York: New Directions, 2003), pp. 109–10. In an interview in *The New York Times,* the author Larry Kramer asserted: "Most historians taken seriously are always straight. They wouldn't know a gay person if they took him to lunch. A good example is Ron Chernow's biography of Hamilton, which doesn't include the fact that he was both gay and in love with George Washington." "Larry Kramer Wishes More People Wrote About Gay History," The *New York Times,* January 16, 2020.

506 **by 1913, Feminism:** Nancy F. Cott, *The Grounding of Modern Feminism* (New Haven: Yale University Press, 1987), p. 13.

507 **"If we take feminism"**: Susan Pedersen, "The Future of Feminist History," *Perspectives on History* (magazine of the American Historical Association), October 2000.

507 **A pioneering study:** Sheila Rowbotham, *Hidden from History: 300 Years of Women's Oppression and the Fight Against It* (London: Pluto Press, 1973, 1992).

507 **"Often, if you want"**: Hilary Mantel, "Royal Bodies," *London Review of Books,* 21 February 2013.

507 **"We are the custodians"**: Carolyn Kizer, *Pro Femina* (Kansas City: BkMk Press, 2000).

508 **which spawned women-centered presses:** Christina Hoff Sommers, *Who Stole Feminism? How Women Have Betrayed Women* (London: Touchstone, 1995).

508 **"Any medieval woman whose life"**: Barbara Tuchman, *A Distant Mirror: The Calamitous Fourteenth Century* (New York: Ballantine, 1978), p. xvi.

509 **"I am too old"**: Robert K. Massie, foreword to Barbara Tuchman, *The Guns of August* (New York: Ballantine, 1994), p. viii.

509 **"one of the finest"**: John Simpson, *We Chose to Speak of War and Strife: The World of the Foreign Correspondent* (London: Bloomsbury, 2016), pp. 36–50.

510 **"not a historian's historian"**: Oliver B. Pollak, *Jewish Women in America: An Historical Encyclopedia,* ed. Paula E. Hyman and Deborah Dash Moore (New York: Routledge, 1997), p. 1415.

510 **"Academics—most academic medievalists"**: TV interview with Richard D. Heffner, "Open Mind," 1979.

511 **a 1999 book of essays:** Eileen Boris and Nupur Chaudhuri, eds., *Voices of Women Historians: The Personal, the Political, the Professional* (Bloomington: Indiana University Press, 1999).

512 **"I thought for sure"**: Dartmouth College Commencement Address, 1998.

513 **"Restlessly descending to the street"**: Doris Kearns Goodwin, *Team of Rivals: The Political Genius of Abraham Lincoln* (New York: Simon & Schuster, 2005), p. 5.

514 **"a story"**: Kearns Goodwin, *Team of Rivals,* p. xvii.

514 **"possessed what was then considered"**: Kearns Goodwin, *Team of Rivals,* p. xviii.

514 **"I think it made me want to tell stories"**: Philip Gilanes, "Table for Three," Style Section, *The New York Times,* 30 October 2016, p. 12.

516 **"Bright kids at that age"**: Rebecca Mead, "The Troll Slayer," *The New Yorker,* 1 September 2014.

516 **"Playing around with other people's husbands"**: Robert McCrum, "Up Pompeii with the Roguish Don," *The Observer,* 23 August 2008.

518 **"To all intents"**: Mary Beard, "Diary," *London Review of Books,* 24 August 2000, p. 34.

518 **"There are very few people"**: Mary Beard, *London Review of Books,* 4 October 2001.

519 **"When I started"**: Mead, "The Troll Slayer." See also Andrew Billen, "Mary Beard: Consent Is a Complicated Issue," *The Times* (London), 12 February 2018. I have run together some of Beard's remarks taken from Mead, McCrum, Higgins, and Billen, but never, I hope, changing her meaning or intent.

520 **"In one of the Roman world's most quoted jibes"**: Mary Beard, *SPQR: A History of Ancient Rome* (New York: Norton, 2015), p. 228.

520 **"amiable indignation"**: Mead, "Troll Slayer."

521 **"You've complained there are loads"**: Charlotte Higgins, "The Cult of Mary Beard," *The Guardian,* 30 January 2018.

521 **What happens to our vision:** Karen Offen, "Going Against the Grain," *Voices of Women Historians,* ed. Boris and Chaudhuri, p. 98.

522 **"When I grow up I want to be"**: Megan Beech, *When I Grow Up I Want to Be Mary Beard* (London: Burning Eye Books, 2013).

523 **Judith's life abounds in tragedy**: Litcharts, online study source, 2020.

CHAPTER 19. WHO TELLS OUR STORY?

524 **"It is the responsibility"**: James Baldwin, symposium at Howard University in 1963, quoted in Glaude, *Begin Again*, p. 4.

524 **"I'm a student of history, sir"**: Ralph Ellison, *Invisible Man* (1952; repr. New York: Random House, 1994), p. 62.

524 **even before Southern authors**: See Colin McConarty, "George Washington Williams: A Historian Ahead of His Time," *We're History*, 26 February 2016, available at werehistory.org/williams/.

528 **"may be identified"**: Wilson Jeremiah Moses, *The Golden Age of Black Nationalism, 1850–1925* (New York: Shoe String Press, 1978), p. 28.

528 **"as if Negroes required"**: Moses, *Golden Age of Black Nationalism,* p. 97.

528 **"It is at the bottom of life"**: Booker T. Washington, "Atlanta Compromise Speech," 1895, available at historymatters.gmu.edu/d/39/.

528 **"Let me heartily congratulate you"**: David Levering Lewis, *W.E.B. Du Bois: Biography of a Race, 1868–1919* (New York: Holt, 1993), p. 175.

528 **"The time is come"**: Du Bois, *The Souls of Black Folk* (New York: Dover Thrift, 2016, first published 1903), p. 44.

528 **"a compromiser"**: Du Bois, *The Souls of Black Folk,* p. 49.

528 **"An American, a Negro"**: Du Bois, *The Souls of Black Folk,* p. 3.

529 **"frequently championed"**: Wilson Jeremiah Moses, *Afrotopia: The Roots of African American Popular History* (Cambridge, U.K.: Cambridge University Press, 1998), p. 136.

529 **"careful of that man Du Bois"**: *The Autobiography of W.E.B. DuBois* (New York: Diasporic Africa Press, 2013), p. 263. Du Bois would have taken the warning as a compliment. As he wrote in *The Souls of Black Folk,* "The South believed an educated Negro to be a dangerous Negro," p. 32.

529 **"perhaps the most beloved"**: Moses, *Afrotopia,* p. 86.

530 **"the world [would] see the Negro"**: Darlene Clark Hine, "Carter G. Woodson, White Philanthropy and Negro Historiography," *The History Teacher,* vol. 19, no. 3, May 1986.

531 **"I have made every sacrifice"**: Hine, "Carter G. Woodson."

532 **"We should emphasize not Negro history"**: Carter Godwin Woodson, "The Celebration of Negro History Week, 1927," *Journal of Negro History,* April 1927.

534 **"an accomplished ironist"**: Moses, *Afrotopia,* p. 43.

535 **I first learned of him**: John Henrik Clarke, "Who Is J. A. Rogers?" *Black History,* 9 June 2013. See also W. Burghardt Turner, "J. A. Rogers: Portrait of an Afro-American Historian," *The Black Scholar,* vol. 6, no. 5, 1975; and Lawrence Watson, "Joel Augustus Rogers: Popularizer of Black History," doctoral thesis, Cornell University, January 1978.

535 **"I grew up with a lot of lap time"**: This and other quotations in this section come from "John Henrik Clarke—A Great and Mighty Walk," a 94-minute talk he delivered, aged eighty and blind, now on YouTube.

535 **"It's no disgrace to be right"**: "Dr. John Henrik Clarke," *Race and History,* available at raceandhistory.com/Historians/henrik_clarke.htm.

537 **"Africa and its people"**: John Henrik Clarke, *The Black Collegian,* 1997, available at hunter.cuny.edu/afprl/clarke/why-africana-history-by-dr.-john-henrik-clarke.

537 **"I was right there"**: Robert D. G. Kelley, "The Lives They Lived: John Henrik Clarke; Self-Made Angry Man," *The New York Times,* 3 January 1999.

539 **"I tried to think of better things"**: Walter Mosley, *Black Betty* (New York: Norton, 1994), p. 11.

540 **"Thackeray, not Marx"**: C.L.R. James, *Beyond a Boundary* (1963, repr. New York: Pantheon, 1983), p. 47.

540 **"the best book on sports ever written"**: Frank Rosengarten, "C.L.R. James's Engage-

ment with Marxism," *Urbane Revolutionary: C.L.R. James and the Struggle for a New Society* (Jackson: University Press of Mississippi, 2008), p. 134.

540 **"the social passions"**: James, *Beyond a Boundary*, p. 60.

540 **"within a frame of reference"**: James, *Beyond a Boundary*, p. 17.

540 **"Social explosions take place"**: James, *Beyond a Boundary*, p. 221.

541 **"To establish his own identity"**: James, *Beyond a Boundary*, p. 9.

541 **"his great study"**: Adam Shatz, "Where Life Is Seized," *London Review of Books*, 19 January 2017.

542 **"It is a question"**: Frantz Omar Fanon, *The Wretched of the Earth,* trans. Constance Farrington (New York: Grove Weidenfeld, 1963).

Relevance

543 **"The colored woman of to-day"**: Anna Julia Cooper, "The Status of Women in America," *Words of Fire: An Anthology of African American Feminist Thought,* ed. Beverly Guy-Sheftal (New York: The New Press, 1995).

545 **"Historical knowledge"**: Quoted in Leith Mullings, "Neoliberal Racism and the Movement for Black Lives in the United States," *Black and Indigenous Resistance in the Americas: From Multiculturalism to Racist Backlash,* ed. Juliet Hooker (New York: Lexington Books, 2020), p. 265.

546 **"paradox of integration"**: Mullings, "Neoliberal Racism," p. 256.

547 **"not just as a murder"**: Gary Younge, "What Black America Means to Europe," *New York Review of Books,* 23 July 2020, p. 9.

547 **Such a moment makes special demands:** Patrick Vernon, "Where Are All the Black Historians?" Mediadiversified.org, 30 March 2016. Vernon took issue with a BBC Radio 4 "Making History" program on the plight of Black historians.

548 **"a long-overdue racial reckoning"**: Jennifer Schuessler, "Clash of Historians over Andrew Jackson," *New York Times,* 27 July 2020.

548 **"a broader struggle"**: Schuessler, "Clash of Historians."

548   **"to generate new scholarship"**: Schuessler, "Clash of Historians."

548   **"to reframe our country's history"**: David Covucci, "Conservatives Are Livid the New York Times Is Writing Articles About Slavery," *The Daily Dot,* 19 August 2019.

548   **"The United States is a nation"**: "The 1619 Project Examines the Legacy of Slavery in America," *The New York Times Magazine,* 14 August 2019.

550   **"These were not minor points"**: Bret Stephens, "The 1619 Chronicles," *The New York Times,* 9 October 2020.

550   **"I was concerned that critics"**: Leslie M. Harris, "I Helped Fact-Check the 1619 Project. The *Times* Ignored Me," *Politico,* 6 March 2020.

551   **"I know when I talk to people"**: Adam Serwer, "The Fight over the 1619 Project Is Not About the Facts," *The Atlantic,* 23 December 2019.

551   **In May 2020:** Jeff Barrus, "Nikole Hannah-Jones Wins Pulitzer Prize for 1619 Project," Pulitzer Center, 4 May 2020.

551   **"I just told them to bring me"**: Vinson Cunningham, "How Chris Jackson Is Building a Black Literary Movement," *The New York Times Magazine,* 2 February 2016.

552   **"the fundamental facts"**: Ken Burns and Isobel Wilkerson, University of Michigan Penny Stamps Speaker Series, 2 October 2020.

553   **The memory still haunts:** Z. Z. Packer, "Preacher of the New Antiracist Gospel," *GQ Magazine,* 20 August 2020. Kendi's book title, *Stamped from the Beginning,* comes from a speech Jefferson Davis made in the Senate on 12 April 1860 in which he declared that the "inequality of the white and black races" was "stamped from the beginning."

555   **the practice of mortgage lenders:** The definition of redlining is taken from a dictionary, but the formal source is federalreserve.gov/boarddocs/supmanual/cch/fair_lend_fhact.pdf.

555   **"They point out that"**: https://blackdemographics.com/households/middle-class.

555   **"in a time of plague"**: Michael Powell, "A Marxist's Views on Race and Class Expose a Rift Among Socialists," *The New York Times,* 15 August 2020, p. A13.

556   **"American Negroes do not propose"**: W.E.B. Du Bois, "The Negro and Communism," *Crisis* 38, September 1931, pp. 313–15. See also Gerald Horne, "The Apocalypse of Settler Colonialism," *Monthly Review,* vol. 68, no. 11, 2018: "The roots of the M4BL can be found in the Three Horsemen of the Apocalypse: Slavery, White Supremacy and Capitalism."

556   **"Afrocentrism . . . is a gallant"**: Cornel West, *Race Matters* (Boston: Beacon Press, 1993), p. 4.

556   **"My entire life"**: Bob Herbert, in conversation with the author, 22 July 2020.

558   **"Of course you can take"**: Eric Foner, in conversation with the author, 26 August 2020.

558   **"My dad was a postman"**: Eddie S. Glaude, Jr., in conversation with the author, 18 September 2020.

558   **"Colleges and universities are the places"**: Jamie Saxon, "What I Think: Eddie Glaude Jr." Princeton University, 4 January 2016, available at princeton.edu/news/2016/01/04/what-i-think-eddie-glaude-jr.

558   **"fundamentally good and innocent"**: Eddie S. Glaude, "A Celebration of James Baldwin with Eddie S. Glaude Jr. and Jon Meacham," Zoom conversation produced by Politics and Prose Bookshop, Washington, D.C., 2 August 2020.

559   **"something as radical"**: Glaude, "Celebration of James Baldwin."

559   **"Our history suggests"**: Glaude, "Celebration of James Baldwin."

559   **"profound disillusionment"**: Glaude, *Begin Again,* p. xvii.

559   **"At the core of this"**: Glaude, *Begin Again,* p. xx.

559   **"a blues-soaked hope"**: Glaude, in conversation with the author, 18 September 2020.

560   **"In the twenty-first century"**: John Henrik Clarke, "Why Africana History?" *The Black Collegian,* 1997.

560   **"In all the repression and racism"**: Elizabeth Hinton, in conversation with the author, 30 July 2020.

561   **"You can't kidnap a civilization"**: Aaron Sorkin, "Six Meetings Before Lunch," *The*

West Wing, season 1, episode 18. Sorkin, the Jewish New Yorker who wrote eighty-seven screenplays for the series, must have been aware that a Robert Jefferson "Jeff" Breckinridge (1800–1871) was in real life a Kentucky politician, a white Presbyterian minister who both owned slaves and yet vociferously opposed slavery—a pleasing irony for those in on the joke. The episode also recalls Barack Obama's fight to get the Black American abolitionist Harriet Tubman on a U.S. banknote, well aware that who is represented on notes plays a major part in how a nation understands its history.

CHAPTER 20. BAD HISTORY

562 **"'I suppose history never lies, does it?'"**: Charles Dickens, *The Personal History, Adventures, Experience and Observation of David Copperfield the Younger of Blunderstone Rookery (Which He Never Meant to Publish on Any Account)* (1850; repr. London: Collins, 1910), ch. 17, pp. 291–92.

562 **There, in a downtown park**: Rob Sharp, "How to Subvert a Strongman," *Prospect,* February 2017, p. 12.

563 **"American Division Kills Hundreds"**: Sheryl Gay Stolberg, "Paying Respects, Pentagon Revives Vietnam, and War over Truth," *The New York Times,* 10 October 2014, pp. A1, A3.

563 **"vital information is being deleted"**: Matthew Connelly, "Closing the Court of History," *The New York Times,* 5 February 2020.

563 **"It's almost as though we are"**: Brian Naylor, "Off the Record: Trump Administration Criticized for How It Keeps Documents," NPR, 24 February 2020.

566 **"one of the greatest historical frauds"**: W. Bramsen, *Japanese Chronology and Calendars, T.A.S.J.,* vol. 37, Tokyo, 1910, quoted in *Historians of China and Japan,* ed. W. G. Beasley and E. G. Pulleyblank (New York: Oxford University Press, 1961), p. 221.

566 **"that had no basis"**: Ku Chien-Kang, *The Autobiography of a Chinese Historian,* trans. Arthur W. Hummel (1926; first English edition Leyden: E. J. Brill, 1931), p. xxvi.

566 **"The more remote from a given event"**: Ku Chien-Kang, *Autobiography,* p. xxvii.

566 **"The commonly accepted chronology"**: Ku Chien-Kang, *Autobiography,* p. 77.

566 **"the muddled account-book"**: Ku Chien-Kang, *Autobiography,* p. xxx.

570 **"History always emphasizes"**: Antony Beevor, *The Fall of Berlin, 1945* (New York: Viking, 2002), p. xxxiii.

571 **is more likely**: Ian Buruma, "From Tenderness to Savagery in Seconds," *The New York Review of Books,* 13 October 2011, p. 27.

571 **possibly one hundred thousand Asians**: Ian Buruma, "The Worst Railroad Job," *The New York Review of Books,* 20 November 2014, p. 19.

572 **"On weekdays, I had to take"**: Choe Sang-Hun, obituary of Kim Bok-dong, *The New York Times,* 30 January 2019, p. A20.

572 **"durability or perishability"**: Mindy Kotler, "The Comfort Women and Japan's War on Truth," *The New York Times,* 16 November 2014, p. 4.

572 **"victim consciousness"**: John Dower, *Embracing Defeat: Japan in the Wake of World War II* (New York: Norton, 199), p. 27ff.

573 **"History is not just something"**: Nobukatsu Fujioka, *Reforming Modern History Education: Overcoming Good Guy, Bad Guy History* (Tokyo: Meiji Tosho, 1996), p. 21.

573 **"spring-break party"**: Robert Marquand, "Koizumi's Visits Boost Controversial Version of History," *Christian Science Monitor,* 21 October 2005.

574 **One might argue**: Adam Hochschild, "A Brutal Peace," *The New York Times Book Review,* 29 September 2013, p. 18.

576 **forcing them to commit**: Martin Fackler, "In Textbook Fight, Japan Leaders Seek to Recast History," *The New York Times,* 29 December 2013, A6; and Bronwen Maddox, "Conquerors with Crew Cuts, Go Home!" *The Times* (London), 11 March 2010, p. 34.

576 **where Chinese prisoners**: Jonathan Fenby, "The Terror That Is Not Forgiven or Forgotten," *The* (London) *Times,* 1 July 2013, p. 20.

576 **"Despite the efforts of some"**: Eri Hotta, *Japan 1941: Countdown to Infamy* (New York: Knopf, 2014), quoted in Rana Miter, "The Smooth Path to Pearl Harbor," *The New York Review of Books*, 22 May 2014, p. 21.

576 **"There's nothing wrong with fostering"**: Ingyu Oh and Douglas Ishizawa-Grbić, "Forgiving the Culprits: Japanese Historical Revisionism in a Post-Cold War Context," *International Journal of Peace Studies*, 1999.

576 **"It is not the business"**: Official Minutes of the Budget Meeting, 18 February 2006.

577 **"It can be dangerous"**: MacMillan, *Dangerous Games*, p. 49.

577 **"It is true"**: John Lukacs, *Historical Consciousness, or the Remembered Past* (New York: Harper, 1968), p. 344.

577 **"I know it is the fashion"**: George Orwell, "Looking Back on the Spanish War," *New Road*, 1943, reprinted in *The Collected Essays, Journalism, and Letters of George Orwell*, ed. Sonia Orwell and Ian Angus (London: Penguin, 1968).

577 **"Already there are countless people"**: George Orwell, "The Prevention of Literature," *Polemic*, no. 2, 1946, reprinted in *The Collected Essays*.

578 **"peculiarly powerful combination"**: Anne Applebaum, *Iron Curtain: The Crushing of Eastern Europe 1945–56* (London: Allen Lane, 2012).

579 **The completeness of the state:** David Remnick, *Lenin's Tomb* (New York: Random House, 1993), p. 37.

579 **"half gramophones, half gangsters"**: See T. R. Fyvel, *George Orwell: A Personal Memoir* (London: Weidenfeld, 1962), p. 66.

580 **"Dictators, perhaps because"**: MacMillan, *Dangerous Games*, pp. 22–23.

581 **Practitioners were admonished:** Samuel H. Baron and Nancy W. Heer, "The Soviet Union: Historiography Since Stalin," *International Handbook of Historical Studies: Contemporary Research and Theory* (Westport, Conn.: Greenwood, 1979), p. 282.

581 **"You still had to toe a Marxist line"**: Dominic Lieven, email to the author, 22 May 2015.

581 **Academics were allowed room:** Masha Gessen, *The Future Is History: How Totalitarianism Reclaimed Russia* (New York: Riverhead, 2017).

582 **The distinguished poet Anna Akhmatova:** Martin Puchner, *The Written World: The Power of Stories to Shape People, History, and Civilization* (New York: Random House, 2017).

582 **"Something had changed"**: Remnick, *Lenin's Tomb*, p. 4.

583 **"calculating man"**: Remnick, *Lenin's Tomb*, p. 115.

583 **The old textbooks became:** In 1987 I commissioned Tariq Ali to write a book about the Soviet Union. His chapter "The Chimes of History" charts the evolution of history writing from Stalin's day on. It begins: "History has always played a vital part inside the Soviet Communist Party. It has always been seen as a weapon." Tariq Ali, *Revolution from Above: Where Is the Soviet Union Going?* (London: Hutchinson, 1988), p. 89.

583 **books had appeared in Russian schools:** David Remnick, "Patriot Games," *The New Yorker*, 3 March 2014, p. 34.

584 **"dictatorship of one man"**: Dmitri Volkogonov, *Stalin: Triumph and Tragedy* (New York: Grove, 1991), p. 313.

584 **"The system worked"**: Orlando Figes, "Putin vs. the Truth," *The New York Review of Books*, 30 April 2009.

585 **Another visitor:** Jonathan Brent, *Inside the Stalin Archives: Discovering the New Russia* (New York: Atlas, 2009). See also Evans, *Eric Hobsbawm*, pp. 456–57.

586 **"Whom you photograph"**: Joshua Rothman, "Afterimage," *The New Yorker*, 12 November 2018, pp. 34–44.

590 **his government studiously ignored it:** Neil MacFarquhar, "'Revolution? What Revolution?' Kremlin Asks 100 Years Later," *The New York Times*, 11 March 2017, pp. A1, A7.

590 **"With each year that passes"**: Karl Ove Knausgaard, "A Literary Road Trip into the Heart of Russia," trans. Barbara J. Haveland, *The New York Times Magazine*, 18 February 2018, p. 51.

591 **"every museum, indeed every country"**: Masha Gessen, *Never Remember: Searching for Russia's Gulags in Putin's Russia* (New York: Columbia Global Reports, 2018).

591 **"mafia state ruling over a totalitarian society"**: Robert Cottrell, "Russia's Gay Demons," *The New York Review of Books,* 7 December 2017, p. 37.

591 **"Conference participant"**: Figes, "Putin vs. the Truth."

592 **a chapter was added**: Mikhail Shishkin, "How Russians Lost the War," *The New York Times,* 9 May 2015, p. A19.

593 **"What we are seeing"**: Luke Harding, "Russian Historian Arrested in Clampdown on Stalin Era," *The Guardian,* 15 October 2009.

593 **"There is freedom of expression"**: David Remnick, "The Civil Archipelago," *The New Yorker,* 19 and 26 December 2011, p. 107.

594 **"Sometimes . . . history serves mainly"**: Eric Foner, *Who Owns History?* p. 87.

594 **"With Germany again united"**: Annalisa Quinn, "Solving a Sinister Puzzle with 40 Million Clues," *New York Times,* August 12, 2021.

595 **"Sometimes you're lucky"**: Angelika Tannhof, "The Stasi Puzzle with 600 Million Pieces," *Deutsche Welle,* 22 August 2013, dw.com/en/the-stasi-puzzle-with-600-million -pieces/a-17039143; see also Helen Pidd, "Germans Piece Together Millions of Lives Spied on by Stasi," *The Guardian,* 13 March 2011; Chris Bowlby, "Stasi Files: The World's Biggest Jigsaw Puzzle," BBC Radio 4, 14 September 2012.

595 **truth is the daughter**: Francis Bacon, *Novum Organum Scientiarum* (1620; repr. New York: CreateSpace, 2017). The quotation in full: "With regard to authority, it is the greatest weakness to attribute infinite credit to particular authors, and to refuse his own prerogative to time, the author of all authors, and, therefore, of all authority. For, truth is rightly named the daughter of time, not of authority."

CHAPTER 21. THE FIRST DRAFT

596 **"Histories . . . are a kind of distilled newspapers"**: Thomas Carlyle, *Heroes, Hero Worship, and the Heroic in History* (1841; repr. London: CreateSpace, 2017).

596 **"I suppose, in the end"**: Robert Fisk, *The Great War for Civilisation: The Conquest of the Middle East* (London: Fourth Estate, 2005), p. xxv.

596 **feared he was going blind**: See *The Historian as Detective: Essays on Evidence,* ed. Robert W. Wink (London: HarperCollins, 1978).

596 **September 2, 1666: Lords day**: Samuel Pepys, "The Fire of London," in *Eyewitness to History,* ed. John Carey (Cambridge: Harvard University Press, 1988), p. 188.

597 **"So near to the fire"**: Pepys, "Fire of London," p. 191.

598 **"an unequalled record"**: Claire Tomalin, *Samuel Pepys: The Unequalled Self* (London: Penguin, 2003), p. 279.

599 **even a foreign invasion**: Clare Jackson, "Still Open for Business," *Times Literary Supplement,* 16 September 2016, p. 20.

600 **The public's longing**: David Carr, "Start the Presses," *The New York Times Book Review,* 8 June 2014, p. 26.

600 **Britain's first daily**: Simpson, *We Chose to Speak of War and Strife* (London: Bloomsbury, 2016), pp. 25–31.

601 **a printer called John Twyn**: Dr. Matthew Green, "The History of Fleet Street," theater program, *Ink,* play by James Graham, Duke of York's Theatre, London, October 2017.

601 **"mostly old, foreign, and unreliable"**: Jill Lepore, "Back Issues," *The New Yorker,* 26 January 2009, p. 68.

602 **"the swish and crackle of paper"**: Lewis Mumford, *The Culture of Cities* (Fort Washington, Penn.: Harvest Books, 1970), ch. 4, section 9.

602 **"They were passing through the Strand"**: William Makepeace Thackeray, *The History of Pendennis: His Fortunes and Misfortunes, His Friends and His Greatest Enemy* (London: 1856), p. 260.

602 **"the daily historian of the time"**: John Pendleton, *Newspaper Reporting in Olden Time and To-day* (London: Elliot Stock, 1890), p. vii.

603 **During its early years**: Varsity Tutors Internet entry for "America's First Newspaper."

603   **four times as fast:** Jill Lepore, "The Party Crashers," *The New Yorker,* 22 February 2016, p. 24.

603   **"In the early nineteenth century":** Nicholas Lemann, "Can Journalism Be Saved?" *The New York Review of Books,* 27 February 2020, p. 40.

605   **"he seems to have been":** Max Hastings, introduction, *William Russell: Special Correspondent of The Times,* ed. Roger Hudson (London: The Folio Society, 1995), p. xi.

607   **he was telling his readers a story:** Max Hastings, *William Russell,* p. xvi.

608   **"brought home to the War Office":** Edwin Godkin, quoted in Max Hastings, *William Russell,* p. xv.

609   **"overeating and excessive drinking":** Amanda Foreman, *A World on Fire: Britain's Crucial Role in the American Civil War* (New York: Random House, 2011).

610   **"a vain, middle-aged man":** Christopher Dickey, *Our Man in Charleston* (New York: Crown, 2015), p. 229.

610   **"Journalists are sometimes":** Patrick Cockburn, "The First Draft of History: How War Reporters Get It Wrong, and What They Can Do to Get It Right," *The Independent,* 17 April 2016.

611   **"If to this business of getting out":** John Maxwell Hamilton, "In the Foothills of Change," *Columbia Journalism Review,* 20 March 2009.

611   **"Good evening. Today is Good Friday":** Ian Jack, "Time for Several Whiskies," *London Review of Books,* 30 August 2018, p. 3.

612   **"to protect against bullets":** Ted Conover, *Immersion: A Writer's Guide to Going Deep* (Chicago: University of Chicago Press, 2016), p. 22.

612   **"Of course he shot":** Quoted in John Sutherland, *Orwell's Nose: A Pathological Biography* (London: Reaktion Books, 2016), p. 47.

612   **Poverty was to become Blair's consuming subject:** Peter Stansky and William Miller Abrahams, *The Unknown Orwell* (New York: Knopf, 1972).

612   **"He was awfully likely":** Sylvia Topp, *Eileen: The Making of George Orwell* (London: Unbound, 2020).

612   **"like . . . watching":** Stephen Wadhams, *Remembering Orwell* (London: Penguin, 1984), p. 106.

613   **"Practically everyone":** D. J. Taylor, *Orwell: The Life* (New York: Holt, 2003).

613   **"a good round English name":** Dominic Cavendish, "George Orwell: From Animal Farm to Zog, an A–Z of Orwell," *The Telegraph,* 20 March 2018.

615   **"No one who was in Barcelona":** George Orwell, *Homage to Catalonia* (New York: Harcourt Brace Jovanovich, 1952), p. 21.

615   **Even the original seed:** See *The Week* (U.K. edition), 15 June 2019, reviewing Dorian Lynskey's *The Ministry of Truth* (Picador).

616   **"Of course, there may be a certain":** Patrick Cockburn, *Chaos and Caliphate: Jihadis and the West in the Struggle for the Middle East* (New York: OR Books, 2016).

616   **"meaning, not speed":** Joseph E. Persico, *Edward R. Murrow: An American Original* (New York: McGraw-Hill, 1988), p. 163.

616   **"This is London":** A. M. Sperber, *Murrow: His Life and Times* (New York: Fordham University Press, 1998).

616   **"The fires up the river":** Persico, *Edward R. Murrow,* p. 170.

617   **"the specific gravity of journalism":** See Ian Parker, "Mr. America," *The New Yorker,* 4 September 2017, p. 61.

617   **Even so, Murrow:** Stanley Cloud and Lynne Olson, *The Murrow Boys: Pioneers on the Front Lines of Broadcast Journalism* (New York: Mariner, 1996).

617   **"The bigger and richer":** David Halberstam, *The Powers That Be* (New York: Knopf, 1979), p. 712.

618   **"I have witnessed":** Martha Gellhorn, "Suffer the Little Children," *Ladies Home Journal,* January 1967.

618   **"It is a difficult business":** John Simpson, *Despatches from the Barricades* (London: Hutchinson, 1990), p. 6. In the view of John Darnton, a foreign correspondent for *The New York Times* who won a Pulitzer Prize for his reporting in Poland in the 1970s, four

journalists turned the American public against the war in Vietnam: Morley Safer (showing villages being burned); Walter Cronkite (declaring on his return from Vietnam that the war was being lost); Sy Hersh (revealing the My Lai massacre); and Neil Sheehan (writing "The Making of a Dove" in *The New York Times Magazine*). Letter to the author, 19 May 2018.

618 **the tools and access available:** William Hammond, *Reporting Vietnam: Media and Military at War,* vol. 1 (Lawrence: University Press of Kansas, 1998).

620 **It coincided with:** "Journalist Stanley Karnow Dies," Associated Press, 27 January 2013.

620 **"He was known for his precision":** *Los Angeles Times,* January 27, 2013.

620 **"The compliments I have valued most":** Interview with Sir Max Hastings, Historynet, undated.

620 **"There is no such thing":** Hunter S. Thompson, *Fear and Loathing: On the Campaign Trail '72* (New York: Grand Central, 1985), p. 48.

622 **the main influence:** Belarusian Telegraph Agency, 8 October 2015.

622 **"because there is great catharsis":** Rachel Donadio, "The Laureate of Russian Misery," *The New York Times,* 21 May 2016, C1.

622 **"some tales were blood-curdling":** "The War for Memory," *The Economist,* 20 July 2017.

622 **"Who will go to fight":** Ibid.

622 **"I sought out people":** Orlando Figes, "Alexievich's New Kind of History," *The New York Review of Books,* 13 October 2016, p. 18.

623 **"a spoken literature":** Figes, "Alexievich's New Kind of History," p. 19.

623 **"a diminutive woman":** Rachel Donadio, "Svetlana Alexievich, Nobel Laureate of Russian Misery, Has an English-Language Milestone," *The New York Times,* 20 May, 2016.

624 **"an outpouring of vitriol":** Masha Gessen, "The Memory Keeper," *The New Yorker,* 26 October 2015, p. 38.

624 **"Alexievich is a master":** Sana Krasikov, "Child's-Eye View," *The New York Times Book Review,* 18 August 2019, p. 13.

624 **"At the morgue":** Svetlana Alexievich, *Chernobyl: The Oral History of a Nuclear Disaster,* trans. and preface by Keith Gessen (New York: Picador, 2006).

CHAPTER 22. ON TELEVISION

626 **"Modern history's another":** Aaron Sorkin, "The Women of Kumar," *The West Wing,* season 3, episode 9.

627 **"He's a great historian":** "Reputations: A.J.P. Taylor," narrated by Russel Tarr, ATV, 1995.

627 **"team seemed not only":** C. J. Wrigley, *A.J.P. Taylor: Radical Historian of Europe* (London: Harvester Press, 1980), p. 25.

628 **"this cocky, lizard-like little figure":** Maurice Richardson, *The Observer,* 1980.

628 **many of them half-wanting:** Burk, *Troublemaker,* pp. 383, 389.

629 **"Don't like Bohemians":** Paul Johnson, "A.J.P. Taylor: A Saturnine Star Who Had Intellectuals Rolling in the Aisles," *The Spectator,* 11 March 2006.

629 **the personification of the engaged:** Simon Schama, "History Beyond the Page," Jerusalem History Lecture, 5 December 2017.

629 **there would be no historian:** Richard J. Evans, "Is History History?" *The Guardian,* 28 May 2012, p. 26.

630 **"Herky-jerky, sped-up newsreels":** Rosenbaum, *Explaining Hitler,* p. 71.

630 **"TV is seldom":** Charles McGrath, "Bomb," *The New York Times Magazine,* 13 April 2003, p. 16.

630 **"The first and greatest sin":** Peter Morgan, *Frost/Nixon,* 2008.

631 **Donald Trump, when interviewed:** See James Poniewozik, "Trump's Tweets Pivot, Loudly, to Video," *The New York Times,* 15 September 2018, C6.

631 **"When an action is captured":** Hilary Mantel, Reith Lectures, Talk 5: Adaptation.

631   **"events *flow* in time"**: David Denby, Diary, *The Atlantic,* 25 August 2016.

631   **Footage showed:** "The Battle of Orgreave," *The Week,* 12 November 2016, p. 13.

632   **Egypt's so-called January 25 Revolution:** Christopher Walker and Robert W. Orttung, "Lies and Videotape," *The New York Times,* 22 April 2011.

632   **"an indestructible and terrifying giant"**: Dave Itzkoff, "Notes of a Screenwriter, Mad as Hell," *The New York Times,* 22 May 2011.

632   **"It was feared"**: *The Week,* 1 December 2019, p. 47.

633   **"I always tell my younger producers"**: Interview with the author, March 2019.

633   **"with a will"**: John Preston, "David Starkey: A Man with a Past," *Daily Telegraph,* 16 December 2007.

633   **"There was a huge pall"**: Nikki Spencer, "David Starkey: My Family Values," *The Guardian,* 18 May 2012.

634   **"I actually remember thinking"**: "David Starkey: The History Man," *The Independent,* 9 December 2006.

634   **"There were two really dominant figures"**: Preston, "David Starkey."

634   **"It's a kind of Goldilocks period"**: Preston, "David Starkey."

634   **"Oh, that magic moment"**: "David Starkey: The History Man."

635   **"a relatively impecunious historian"**: Michael Buerk, *The Road Taken* (London: Hutchinson, 2004), quoted in theguardian.com/books/2004/oct/10/history.academicexperts.

636   **"I suppose in those days"**: "David Starkey: The History Man."

636   **"I do have this very powerful"**: Preston, "David Starkey."

636   **"'Oh my God'"**: "David Starkey: The History Man."

636   **"rich as a Tudor monarch"**: MacMillan, *Dangerous Games,* p. 4.

636   **"If you want to ask"**: Preston, "David Starkey."

637   **"riddled with corruption"**: Preston, "David Starkey."

637   **"The repeated claim of BLM"**: David Starkey, "A Perversion of Puritanism," *The Critic,* 22 June 2020.

638   **"Salem-style puritanism"**: Camilla Tominey, "At Home with 'the Rudest Man in Britain,'" *Daily Telegraph,* 12 September 2020.

638   **"Simon Schama and I were lucky"**: Interview with the author, 26 September 2017.

639   **a relative who broke:** Simon Schama with Tom Brokaw, 92nd Street Y, New York City, 26 April 2011.

639   **made him want to be a historian:** Elizabeth Jensen, "The Historical Becomes Personal," *The New York Times,* 23 March 2014, p. 22.

640   **"the master storyteller"**: Mark Mazower, "Fizz and Crackle," *The New York Review of Books,* 22 March 2018, p. 32.

641   **"recklessness undeservedly"**: Charlotte Philby, *The Independent,* 27 June 2009.

642   **"slightly noisy"**: Phone interview with the author, 23 March 2019.

642   **"a behavioral history"**: Phone conversation with the author, 4 January 2021.

642   **"There were many hundreds of years"**: Simon Schama, "Roughing Up the Surface," *Civilization,* February/March 1998, p. 88.

644   **"Mary Beard: Julius Caesar Revealed"**: Craig Brown's Diary, *Private Eye,* 20 February 2018.

645   **"It's when historians"**: Evans, "Is History History?"

645   **"the rise of a counterfeit"**: Tony Judt, *The Memory Chalet* (New York: Penguin, 2010), p. 152.

645   **"There is a thin line"**: Nicholas Hytner, *The Guardian Review,* 16 September 2006, p. 14.

645   **"the wrong end of the stick"**: Alan Bennett, *The History Boys* (London: Faber, 2004), p. 35.

646   **"Meretricious, of course"**: Bennett, *History Boys,* p. 60.

648   **"about as networked as they come"**: Josh Clancy, *The Sunday Times Magazine,* 24 September 2017, p. 39.

648   **"enfant terrible of the Oxbridge historical establishment"**: Michael Hirsh, "Follow the Money," *The New York Times Book Review,* 28 December 2008, p. 9.

648 **"authorial overstretch"**: John Lewis Gaddis, "The Last Empire, for Now," *The New York Times Book Review,* 25 July 2004, p. 11.

648 **"sometimes shaky taste"**: Adam Gopnik, "Decline, Fall, Rinse, Repeat," *The New Yorker,* 12 September 2011, p. 43. The *New Yorker* profile, "Thinking the Unthinkable," was written by Robert Boynton and appeared on 12 April 1999.

649 **"The scientific credentials of network theory"**: John Gray, "Circling the Square," *The New York Review of Books,* 22 March 2018, p. 29.

649 **"Anyone who has been"**: R. W. Johnson, *London Review of Books,* 18 February 1999.

649 **"It has always struck me"**: Bennett, *History Boys,* p. xxiii.

649 **"The doyen of TV historians"**: Bennett, *History Boys,* p. xxiv.

650 **Bennett objects to:** "The Villainous Teacher of *The History Boys,*" *Slate,* 22 November 2006.

651 **"There's never been anything"**: John Leonard, *New York* magazine, 24 September 1990.

651 **"more Americans get their history"**: Parker, "Mr. America," p. 59.

652 **"You see a 19th century photograph"**: George F. Will, *The Washington Post,* 20 September 1990.

653 **Burns describes his films:** Parker, "Mr. America," p. 58.

653 **"We just happen to work in history"**: Ian Parker, "Mr. America," *The New Yorker,* 4 September 2017, p. 53.

653 **"Considered as the presentation"**: Burrow, *History of Histories,* p. 484.

653 **"The day we buried"**: Sunny Jane Morton, "Five Questions with Henry Louis Gates Jr," *Family Tree Magazine,* July/August 2012.

654 **"the biggest mistake"**: Henry Louis Gates, Jr., Paula Kerger, and Eric Deggans, "Reconstruction: America After the Civil War," SXSW EDU, 6 March 2019, available at sxswedu.com/news/2019/watch-henry-louis-gates-jr-paula-kerger-on-reconstruction-america-after-the-civil-war-video/.

655 **"I love storytelling"**: Gates, Kerger, and Deggans, "Reconstrution."

655 **"I see myself as a student"**: Gates, Kerger, and Deggans, "Reconstruction."

655 **"The guy has charisma"**: Sean O'Hagan, "The Biggest Brother," *The Observer,* 20 July 2003.

655 **"Since the day"**: O'Hagan, "Biggest Brother."

657 **"Alex never had"**: "Russell Wilson with Dr. Henry Louis Gates, Jr. at The Richmond Forum," YouTube, 18 April 2016, available at youtube.com/watch?v=4aZCBlL8P6U.

657 **"Now, God help me!"**: *Finding Your Roots,* PBS, Season 2, Episode 3, 7 October 2014.

657 **"I've tried in all my work"**: "American Fault Line: Race and the American Ideal": Henry Louis Gates, Jr. and Ken Burns in discussion with Michael Martin, Brooklyn Academy of Music, 18 March 2016, available at bam.org/talks/2016/american-fault-line.

AFTERWORD

658 **"Professionals do well"**: C. Vann Woodward, "The Great American Butchery," *New York Review of Books,* 10 March 1975.

658 **"But what are your criteria"**: Simon Schama, in conversation with the author, 4 January 2021.

659 **the growth in cheap computing power**: Laura Spinney, "History as a Giant Data Set: How Analyzing the Past Could Help Save the Future," *The Guardian,* 12 November 2019.

659 **television can be guilty**: David Greenberg, "Class Warfare," *Slate,* 24 July 2006. Some of the comments that follow are inspired by Greenberg's essay.

660 **"must be strictly impartial"**: William Hickling Prescott, *Biographical and Critical Miscellanies* (New York: Fred De Fau, 1912), p. 64.

INDEX

RICHARD COHEN is the author of *Chasing the Sun, By the Sword,* and *How to Write Like Tolstoy.* The former publishing director of two leading London publishing houses, Cohen has edited books that have won the Pulitzer, Booker, and Whitbread/Costa prizes, while twenty-one have been #1 bestsellers. Among the authors he has worked with are Madeleine Albright, David Boies, John Keegan, Richard Holmes, Hilary Spurling, Vanessa Redgrave, Harold Evans, Studs Terkel, John le Carré, Anthony Burgess, Jeffrey Archer, Jean Auel, Kingsley Amis, and Sebastian Faulks.

For more than thirty-five years, Cohen has lectured on numerous subjects around the globe, most recently for New York Times Journeys, from the Galápagos Islands to the First World War battlefields of France and Belgium. He was program director of the Cheltenham Festival of Literature for two years, and during his tenure it became the largest book festival in the world. For seven years he was a visiting professor in creative writing at the University of Kingston-upon-Thames in London, and for a semester a visiting scholar at Magdalene College, Cambridge. He is a fellow of the Royal Society of Literature.

Five times U.K. national saber champion, Cohen was selected for the British Olympic fencing team in 1972, 1976, 1980, and 1984 and has been four times world veteran saber champion. He has written for most British quality newspapers and, since moving to New York in 1999, *The New York Times, The Wall Street Journal,* and *The New York Times Book Review.*

ABOUT THE TYPE

This book was set in Bembo, a typeface based on an old-style Roman face that was used for Cardinal) Pietro Bembo's tract *De Aetna* in 1495. Bembo was cut by Francesco Griffo (1450–1518) in the early sixteenth century for Italian Renaissance printer and publisher Aldus Manutius (1449–1515). The Lanston Monotype Company of Philadelphia brought the well-proportioned letterforms of Bembo to the United States in the 1930s.